CCNP Self-Study

CCNP BCMSN Exam Certification Guide

David Hucaby, CCIE No. 4594

Cisco Press

Cisco Press
800 East 96th Street, 3rd Floor
Indianapolis, IN 46240 USA

CCNP BCMSN Exam Certification Guide

David Hucaby

Copyright © 2004 Cisco Systems, Inc.

Published by:
Cisco Press
800 East 96th Street, 3rd Floor
Indianapolis, IN 46240 USA

Printed in the United States of America 1 2 3 4 5 6 7 8 9 0

First Printing September 2003

Library of Congress Cataloging-in-Publication Number: 2002115604

ISBN: 1-58720-077-5

Warning and Disclaimer

This book is designed to provide information about selected topics for the Building Cisco Multilayer Switched Networks (BCMSN) exam for the CCNP certification. Every effort has been made to make this book as complete and as accurate as possible, but no warranty or fitness is implied.

The information is provided on an "as is" basis. The authors, Cisco Press, and Cisco Systems, Inc., shall have neither liability nor responsibility to any person or entity with respect to any loss or damages arising from the information contained in this book or from the use of the discs or programs that may accompany it.

The opinions expressed in this book belong to the author and are not necessarily those of Cisco Systems, Inc.

Feedback Information

At Cisco Press, our goal is to create in-depth technical books of the highest quality and value. Each book is crafted with care and precision, undergoing rigorous development that involves the unique expertise of members from the professional technical community.

Readers' feedback is a natural continuation of this process. If you have any comments regarding how we could improve the quality of this book or otherwise alter it to better suit your needs, you can contact us through e-mail at feedback@ciscopress.com. Please make sure to include the book title and ISBN in your message.

We greatly appreciate your assistance.

Trademark Acknowledgments

All terms mentioned in this book that are known to be trademarks or service marks have been appropriately capitalized. Cisco Press or Cisco Systems, Inc., cannot attest to the accuracy of this information. Use of a term in this book should not be regarded as affecting the validity of any trademark or service mark.

Publisher: John Wait

Editor-In-Chief: John Kane

Executive Editor: Brett Bartow

Cisco Representative: Anthony Wolfenden

Cisco Press Program Manager: Sonia Torres Chavez

Manager, Marketing Communications, Cisco Systems: Scott Miller

Cisco Marketing Program Manager: Edie Quiroz

Production Manager: Patrick Kanouse

Development Editor: Christopher Cleveland

Project Editor: San Dee Phillips

Copy Editor: Marcia Ellett

Technical Editors: Stephen Daleo, Steve McQuerry, Geoff Tagg

Team Coordinator: Tammi Ross

Book Designer: Gina Rexrode

Cover Designer: Louisa Adair

Indexer: Tim Wright

Composition: Octal Publishing, Inc.

CISCO SYSTEMS

Corporate Headquarters
Cisco Systems, Inc.
170 West Tasman Drive
San Jose, CA 95134-1706
USA
www.cisco.com
Tel: 408 526-4000
    800 553-NETS (6387)
Fax: 408 526-4100

European Headquarters
Cisco Systems International BV
Haarlerbergpark
Haarlerbergweg 13-19
1101 CH Amsterdam
The Netherlands
www-europe.cisco.com
Tel: 31 0 20 357 1000
Fax: 31 0 20 357 1100

Americas Headquarters
Cisco Systems, Inc.
170 West Tasman Drive
San Jose, CA 95134 1706
USA
www.cisco.com
Tel: 408 526-7660
Fax: 408 527-0883

Asia Pacific Headquarters
Cisco Systems, Inc.
Capital Tower
168 Robinson Road
#22-01 to #29-01
Singapore 068912
www.cisco.com
Tel: +65 6317 7777
Fax: +65 6317 7799

Cisco Systems has more than 200 offices in the following countries and regions. Addresses, phone numbers, and fax numbers are listed on the
Cisco.com Web site at www.cisco.com/go/offices.

Argentina • Australia • Austria • Belgium • Brazil • Bulgaria • Canada • Chile • China PRC • Colombia • Costa Rica • Croatia • Czech Republic
Denmark • Dubai, UAE • Finland • France • Germany • Greece • Hong Kong SAR • Hungary • India • Indonesia • Ireland • Israel • Italy
Japan • Korea • Luxembourg • Malaysia • Mexico • The Netherlands • New Zealand • Norway • Peru • Philippines • Poland • Portugal
Puerto Rico • Romania • Russia • Saudi Arabia • Scotland • Singapore • Slovakia • Slovenia • South Africa • Spain • Sweden
Switzerland • Taiwan • Thailand • Turkey • Ukraine • United Kingdom • United States • Venezuela • Vietnam • Zimbabwe

About the Author

David Hucaby, CCIE No. 4594, is a lead network engineer for a large medical environment, using Cisco multilayer switching and security products. He is also an independent networking consultant, focusing on Cisco-based solutions for healthcare and banking clients. David lives in Kentucky with his wife, Marci, and two daughters.

About the Technical Reviewers

Stephen Daleo, president of Golden Networking Consultants, Inc. is a network consultant whose clients include the University of South Florida – St. Petersburg, FL and North Broward Hospital District (Fort Lauderdale, FL). Steve was one of the course developers for Cisco Internet Learning Solutions Group – BCMSN 2.0 class. Steve is a frequent contributor to the technical content of Cisco Press books and is an active certified Cisco Systems instructor (97025) teaching the BCMSN, BCRAN, CIPT, CIT, BSCI, and ICND Cisco courses.

Steve McQuerry, CCIE No. 6108, is an instructor, technical writer, and internetworking consultant with over 10 years of networking industry experience. He is a certified Cisco Systems instructor teaching routing and switching concepts to internetworking professionals throughout the world. Steve is also a founding partner in Intrellix, an internetworking consulting company specializing in post-sales consulting services.

Geoff Tagg runs a networking consultancy in the UK, where he has over 20 years experience in working with companies ranging from small local businesses to large multinationals. Prior to that, he was a systems programmer for a number of years. Geoff's main specialty is IP network design and implementation. Geoff lives in Oxford, England with his wife, Christine, and family, and is a visiting professor at nearby Oxford Brookes University.

Dedications

As always, this book is dedicated to the most important people in my life—my wife, Marci, and my two little daughters, Lauren and Kara. Their love, encouragement, and support carry me along. I'm so grateful to God, who gives endurance and encouragement (Romans 15:5) and has allowed me to work on projects like this.

I would also like to dedicate this book to the memory of two teachers who have made an impact on me:

Mabel "Stoney" Stonecipher, my college technical writing teacher and family friend, who made writing about technical things fun and educational.

Ron Sabel, my high school biology and physics teacher, who taught me an important lesson: "The 'A' student doesn't have all the answers—the 'A' student knows where to find all the answers!"

Acknowledgments

It has been my great pleasure to work on another Cisco Press project. I enjoy the networking field very much, and technical writing even more. And more than that, I'm thankful for the joy and inner peace that Jesus Christ gives, making everything more abundant.

Technical writing may be hard work, but I'm finding that it's also quite fun because I'm working with very good friends. I can't say enough good things about Chris Cleveland. Somehow, Chris is able to handle many book projects all at once, while giving each one an incredible amount of attention and improvement. Brett Bartow is a constant source of organization, project management, and encouragement. I'm glad he agreed to have me back for another project!

Now a few words about another group of good friends—the technical reviewers that made this a much, much better book. I am very grateful for the insight, suggestions, and helpful comments that Steve Daleo, Steve McQuerry, and Geoff Tagg contributed. Each one offered a different perspective, which helped make this a more well-rounded book and me a more educated author. Christopher Paggen also provided some early help with new Catalyst features and development.

Lastly, for the very first time, I am able to announce that no laptop computers were harmed in the writing of this book.

Contents at a Glance

Foreword   xxiii

Introduction: Overview of Certification and How to Succeed   xxiv

PART I   **Overview and Design of a Campus Network   2**

Chapter 1   Campus Network Overview   5

Chapter 2   Modular Network Design   33

PART II   **Building a Campus Network   54**

Chapter 3   Switch Operation   57

Chapter 4   Switch Configuration   83

Chapter 5   Switch Port Configuration   107

Chapter 6   VLANs and Trunks   137

Chapter 7   VLAN Trunking Protocol (VTP)   167

Chapter 8   Aggregating Switch Links   189

Chapter 9   Traditional Spanning Tree Protocol   209

Chapter 10   Spannning Tree Configuration   239

Chapter 11   Protecting the Spanning Tree Protocol Topology   263

Chapter 12   Advanced Spanning Tree Protocol   279

PART III   **Layer 3 Switching   302**

Chapter 13   Multilayer Switching   305

Chapter 14   Router Redundancy and Load Balancing   327

Chapter 15   Multicast   353

PART IV   **Campus Network Services   374**

Chapter 16   Quality of Service Overview   377

Chapter 17   DiffServ QoS Configuration   401

Chapter 18   IP Telephony   431

Chapter 19   Securing Switch Access   451

Chapter 20   Securing with VLANs   469

PART V   **Scenarios for Final Preparation   494**

Chapter 21   Scenarios for Final Preparation   497

PART VI   **Appendix   514**

Appendix A   Answers to Chapter "Do I Know This Already?" Quizzes and Q&A
Sections   517

Index   582

Contents

Foreword   xxiii

Introduction: Overview of Certification and How to Succeed   xxiv

Part I   Overview and Design of a Campus Network   2

Chapter 1   Campus Network Overview   5

"Do I Know This Already?" Quiz   5

Foundation Topics   9

Switching Functionality   9

Layer 2 Switching   10

Layer 3 Routing   10

Layer 3 Switching   11

Layer 4 Switching   12

Multilayer Switching (MLS)   12

Campus Network Models   12

Shared Network Model   13

LAN Segmentation Model   14

Network Traffic Models   17

Predictable Network Model   19

Hierarchical Network Design   19

Access Layer   20

Distribution Layer   21

Core Layer   21

Cisco Products in the Hierarchical Design   21

Access Layer Switches   22

Distribution Layer Switches   23

Core Layer Switches   24

Product Summary   25

Foundation Summary   27

Q&A   30

Chapter 2   Modular Network Design   33

"Do I Know This Already?" Quiz   33

Foundation Topics   37

Modular Network Design   37

The Switch Block   38

Sizing a Switch Block   39

The Core Block   41

Collapsed Core   42

Dual Core   43

Core Size in a Campus Network   45

Other Building Blocks   45

    Server Farm Block   46

    Network Management Block   46

    Enterprise Edge Block   47

    Service Provider Edge Block   47

Can I Use Layer 2 Distribution Switches?   48

Foundation Summary   50

Q&A   52

Part II   Building a Campus Network   54

Chapter 3   Switch Operation   57

"Do I Know This Already?" Quiz   57

Foundation Topics   61

Layer 2 Switch Operation   61

    Transparent Bridging   61

    Follow That Frame!   63

Multilayer Switch Operation   66

    Types of Multilayer Switching   66

    Follow That Packet!   67

    Multilayer Switching Exceptions   69

Tables Used in Switching   69

    Content Addressable Memory (CAM)   70

    Ternary Content Addressable Memory (TCAM)   71

        TCAM Structure   71

        TCAM Example   72

        Port Operations in TCAM   74

Troubleshooting Switching Tables   75

    CAM Table Operation   75

    TCAM Operation   76

Foundation Summary   77

Q&A   79

Chapter 4   Switch Configuration   83

"Do I Know This Already?" Quiz   83

Foundation Topics   87

Switch Management   87

    Operating Systems   87

    Identifying the Switch   88

    Passwords and User Access   89

        Password Recovery   90

    Remote Access   90

    Inter-Switch Communication—Cisco Discovery Protocol   91

Switch File Management   91

    OS Image Files   92

        Filename Conventions   93

    Configuration Files   93

    Other Catalyst Switch Files   94

    Moving Catalyst Switch Files Around   94

Troubleshooting from the Operating System   96

    Show Configuration and File Contents   96

    Debugging Output   97

    View CDP Information   98

Foundation Summary   100

Q&A   103

Chapter 5   **Switch Port Configuration   107**

"Do I Know This Already?" Quiz   107

Foundation Topics   112

Ethernet Concepts   112

    Ethernet (10 Mbps)   112

    Long Reach Ethernet (LRE)   113

    Fast Ethernet   114

        Full-Duplex Fast Ethernet   115

    Gigabit Ethernet   117

    10Gigabit Ethernet   118

    Metro Ethernet   119

Connecting Switch Block Devices   120

    Console Port Cables/Connectors   120

    Ethernet Port Cables and Connectors   121

    Gigabit Ethernet Port Cables and Connectors   121

Switch Port Configuration   123

    Selecting Ports to Configure   123

    Identifying Ports   124

    Port Speed   124

    Port Mode   125

    Managing Error Conditions on a Switch Port   125

        Detecting Error Conditions   125

        Automatically Recover from Error Conditions   126

    Enable and Use the Switch Port   126

    Troubleshooting Port Connectivity   126

        Looking for the Port State   127

        Looking for Speed and/or Duplex Mismatches   127

Foundation Summary   129

Q&A   133

Chapter 6   VLANs and Trunks   137

"Do I Know This Already?" Quiz   137

Foundation Topics   141

Virtual LANs   141

   VLAN Membership   142

      Static VLANs   142

      Configuring Static VLANs   143

      Dynamic VLANs   144

   Deploying VLANs   144

      End-to-End VLANs   145

      Local VLANs   145

VLAN Trunks   146

   VLAN Frame Identification   146

      Inter-Switch Link Protocol   148

      IEEE 802.1Q Protocol   148

   Dynamic Trunking Protocol   150

VLAN Trunk Configuration   150

   VLAN Trunk Configuration   150

Service Provider Tunneling   153

   IEEE 802.1Q Tunnels   153

   Configuring a 802.1Q Tunnel   155

   Layer 2 Protocol Tunnels   155

   Configuring Layer 2 Protocol Tunneling   156

   Ethernet over MPLS Tunneling   157

   Troubleshooting VLANs and Trunks   159

Foundation Summary   162

Q&A   164

Chapter 7   VLAN Trunking Protocol (VTP)   167

"Do I Know This Already?" Quiz   167

Foundation Topics   171

VLAN Trunking Protocol   171

   VTP Domains   171

   VTP Modes   171

   VTP Advertisements   172

VTP Configuration   175

   Configuring a VTP Management Domain   175

   Configuring the VTP Mode   176

   Configuring the VTP Version   177

   VTP Status   178

VTP Pruning   179

   Enabling VTP Pruning   181

Troubleshooting VTP   182

Foundation Summary   184

Q&A   186

Chapter 8   Aggregating Switch Links   189

    "Do I Know This Already?" Quiz   189

    Foundation Topics   193

    Switch Port Aggregation with EtherChannel   193

        Bundling Ports with EtherChannel   194

        Distributing Traffic in EtherChannel   194

        Configuring EtherChannel Load Balancing   195

    EtherChannel Negotiation Protocols   197

        Port Aggregation Protocol (PAgP)   197

        Link Aggregation Control Protocol (LACP)   198

    EtherChannel Configuration   198

        Configuring a PAgP EtherChannel   199

        Configuring a LACP EtherChannel   199

    Troubleshooting an EtherChannel   200

    Foundation Summary   204

    Q&A   206

Chapter 9   Traditional Spanning Tree Protocol   209

    "Do I Know This Already?" Quiz   209

    Foundation Topics   213

    IEEE 802.1D Overview   213

        Bridging Loops   213

        Preventing Loops with Spanning Tree Protocol   217

        Spanning Tree Communication: Bridge Protocol Data Units   217

        Electing a Root Bridge   218

        Electing Root Ports   220

        Electing Designated Ports   223

        STP States   225

        STP Timers   227

        Topology Changes   228

    Types of STP   229

        Common Spanning Tree (CST)   229

        Per-VLAN Spanning Tree (PVST)   229

        Per-VLAN Spanning Tree Plus (PVST+)   230

    Foundation Summary   231

    Q&A   234

Chapter 10   Spannning Tree Configuration   239

    "Do I Know This Already?" Quiz   239

    Foundation Topics   243

    STP Root Bridge   243

        Root Bridge Placement   243

        Root Bridge Configuration   246

Spanning Tree Customization 248
Tuning the Root Path Cost 248
Tuning the Port ID 249
Tuning Spanning Tree Convergence 250
Modifying STP Timers 250
Redundant Link Convergence 252
PortFast: Access Layer Nodes 252
UplinkFast: Access Layer Uplinks 253
BackboneFast: Redundant Backbone Paths 254
Troubleshooting STP 255
Foundation Summary 257
Q&A 258

Chapter 11 Protecting the Spanning Tree Protocol Topology 263

"Do I Know This Already?" Quiz 263
Foundation Topics 267
Protecting Against Unexpected BPDUs 267
Root Guard 267
BPDU Guard 268
Protecting Against Sudden Loss of BPDUs 269
BPDU Skew Detection 270
Loop Guard 270
UDLD 271
Troubleshooting STP Protection 273
Foundation Summary 274
Q&A 276

Chapter 12 Advanced Spanning Tree Protocol 279

"Do I Know This Already?" Quiz 279
Foundation Topics 283
Rapid Spanning Tree Protocol (RSTP) 283
RSTP Port Behavior 283
BPDUs in RSTP 284
RSTP Convergence 285
Port Types 286
Synchronization 287
Topology Changes and RSTP 288
RSTP Configuration 290
Multiple Spanning Tree (MST) Protocol 290
MST Overview 292
MST Regions 292

        Spanning Tree Instances Within MST *293*

           IST Instances 293

           MST Instances 294

        MST Configuration *295*

      Foundation Summary 298

      Q&A 300

Part III Layer 3 Switching 302

Chapter 13 Multilayer Switching 305

      "Do I Know This Already?" Quiz 305

      Foundation Topics 309

      InterVLAN Routing 309

        Types of Interfaces *310*

        Configuring InterVLAN Routing *310*

           Layer 2 Port Configuration 310

           Layer 3 Port Configuration 311

           SVI Port Configuration 312

      Multilayer Switching with CEF 312

        Traditional MLS Overview *312*

        CEF Overview *313*

        Forwarding Information Base (FIB) *314*

        Adjacency Table *315*

        Packet Rewrite *316*

        Configuring CEF *316*

        Fallback Bridging *317*

      Verifying Multilayer Switching 318

        InterVLAN Routing *318*

        CEF *319*

        Fallback Bridging *321*

      Foundation Summary 322

      Q&A 324

Chapter 14 Router Redundancy and Load Balancing 327

      "Do I Know This Already?" Quiz 327

      Foundation Topics 331

      Router Redundancy in Multilayer Switching 331

        Packet Forwarding Review *331*

        Hot Standby Router Protocol (HSRP) *332*

           HSRP Router Election 332

           Conceding the Election 333

           HSRP Gateway Addressing 334

           Load Balancing with HSRP 335

        Virtual Router Redundancy Protocol (VRRP) *336*

Gateway Load Balancing Protocol (GLBP) 337

Active Virtual Gateway 338

Active Virtual Forwarder 339

GLBP Load Balancing 340

Enabling GLBP 340

Server Load Balancing (SLB) 343

SLB Configuration 344

Server Farms 344

Virtual Servers 345

Verifying Redundancy and Load Balancing 346

Foundation Summary 347

Q&A 350

Chapter 15 Multicast 353

"Do I Know This Already?" Quiz 353

Foundation Topics 357

Multicast Overview 357

Multicast Addressing 358

Routing Multicast Traffic 359

Multicast Trees 359

Reverse Path Forwarding 360

IGMP 360

IGMPv1 360

IGMPv2 361

PIM 361

PIM Dense Mode 362

PIM Sparse Mode 363

PIM Sparse-Dense Mode 365

PIM Version 1 365

PIM Version 2 366

Switching Multicast Traffic 367

IGMP Snooping 367

CGMP 368

Verifying Multicast Routing and Switching 369

Multicast Routing with PIM 369

Multicast Switching 369

What Would Happen Without a Multicast Router? 370

Foundation Summary 371

Q&A 373

Part IV Campus Network Services 374

Chapter 16 Quality of Service Overview 377

"Do I Know This Already?" Quiz 377

Foundation Topics 381

The Need for Quality of Service   381

    Types of QoS   382

        Best Effort Delivery   382

        Integrated Services Model   382

        Differentiated Services Model   383

DiffServ QoS   383

    Layer 2 QoS Classification   384

    Layer 3 QoS Classification with DSCP   384

        Class Selector   386

        Drop Precedence   386

QoS Building Blocks   387

    Ingress Queueing   388

    Classification, Trust, and Marking   388

    Policers   389

    Scheduling   390

    Congestion Avoidance   391

        Tail Drop   391

        Weighted Random Early Detection   392

Switch Port Queues   393

Foundation Summary   396

Q&A   398

Chapter 17   DiffServ QoS Configuration   401

"Do I Know This Already?" Quiz   401

Foundation Topics   405

Applying QoS Trust   406

    Trust QoS on an Interface   406

    Do Not Trust any QoS Information   407

    Mapping Inbound QoS Information   407

Defining a QoS Policy   409

    Defining a QoS Class to Classify Traffic   409

        Classifying Traffic with an Access List   410

        Classifying Traffic with NBAR   410

        What Happens When NBAR Is Enabled?   411

    Defining a QoS Policy   411

        Identifying the QoS Class Maps   411

        Marking QoS Information   412

        Trusting QoS Information   412

        Policing Classified Traffic   412

    Apply a QoS Policy to an Interface   413

Tuning Egress Scheduling   414

Using Congestion Avoidance   414

    Mapping Internal DSCP Values to CoS Values for Queueing   414

    Mapping Packets into Egress Queues   415

Avoiding Congestion by Using Tail Drop   416

Avoiding Congestion by Using WRED   416

Setting WRED Thresholds   416

A QoS Configuration Example   417

Configuring QoS Trust   418

Configuring a QoS Class to Classify Traffic   419

Configuring a QoS Policy to Act on Classified Traffic   420

Egress Queue Tuning   421

Verifying and Troubleshooting QoS   422

Foundation Summary   425

Q&A   428

Chapter 18   IP Telephony   431

"Do I Know This Already?" Quiz   431

Foundation Topics   435

IP Telephony Overview   435

Inline Power   435

How Inline Power Works   436

Configuring Inline Power   437

Voice VLANs   437

Voice VLAN Configuration   438

Voice QoS   440

QoS Trust   440

Voice Packet Classification   441

Queuing for Voice Traffic   442

Verifying Inline Power, Voice VLANs, and Voice QoS   442

Verifying Inline Power   443

Verifying Voice VLANs   443

Verifying Voice QoS   444

Foundation Summary   448

Q&A   449

Chapter 19   Securing Switch Access   451

"Do I Know This Already?" Quiz   451

Foundation Topics   455

Switch AAA   455

Authentication   455

Authorization   457

Accounting   459

Port Security   460

Port-Based Authentication   461

802.1x Configuration   462

Foundation Summary   464

Q&A   466

Chapter 20   Securing with VLANs   469

    "Do I Know This Already?" Quiz   469

    Foundation Topics   473

    VLAN Access Lists   473

       VACL Configuration   *473*

    Private VLANs   474

       Private VLAN Configuration   *477*

          Configure the Private VLANs   477

          Associate Ports with Private VLANs   477

          Associate Secondary VLANs to a Primary VLAN SVI   479

    Switch Port Monitoring   480

       Local SPAN and VSPAN   *481*

          Local SPAN and VSPAN Configuration   482

       Remote SPAN   *484*

          Remote SPAN Configuration   485

    Foundation Summary   488

    Q&A   491

Part V   Scenarios for Final Preparation   494

Chapter 21   Scenarios for Final Preparation   497

    Scenario 1: Trunking and DTP   497

    Scenario 2: VLANs, Trunking, and VTP   499

    Scenario 3: Traditional STP   500

    Scenario 4: Advanced STP   500

    Scenario 5: Router Redundancy with HSRP and GLBP   501

    Scenario 6: Multicast   503

    Scenario 7: QoS in a Switched Network   504

    Scenario 8: Securing Access and Managing Traffic in a Switched Network   505

    Scenario Answers   506

    Scenario 1 Answers   506

    Scenario 2 Answers   506

    Scenario 3 Answers   507

    Scenario 4 Answers   508

    Scenario 5 Answers   509

    Scenario 6 Answers   510

    Scenario 7 Answers   510

    Scenario 8 Answers   512

Part VI   Appendix   514

Appendix A   Answers to Chapter "Do I Know This Already?" Quizzes and Q&A
    Sections   517

Index   582

Icons Used in This Book

 Router

 Bridge

 Hub

 DSU/CSU

 Catalyst Switch

Multilayer Switch

 Modem

 ATM Switch

 ISDN/Frame Relay Switch

 Communication Server

 Gateway

 Access Server

 PC

 PC with Software

 Sun Workstation

 Macintosh

 Terminal

 Cisco Works Workstation

 Web Server

 File Server

 Laptop

Printer

 IBM Mainframe

 Front End Processor

 Cluster Controller

Line: Ethernet

Line: Serial

Line: Switched Serial

Token Ring

FDDI

Network Cloud

Command Syntax Conventions

The conventions used to present command syntax in this book are the same conventions used in the Cisco IOS Command Reference. The Command Reference describes these conventions as follows:

- Vertical bars (|) separate alternative, mutually exclusive elements.

- Square brackets [ ] indicate optional elements.

- Braces { } indicate a required choice.

- Braces within brackets [{ }] indicate a required choice within an optional element.

- Boldface indicates commands and keywords that are entered literally as shown. In actual configuration examples and output (not general command syntax), boldface indicates commands that are manually input by the user (such as a show command).

- Italics indicate arguments for which you supply actual values.

Foreword

CCNP BCMSN Exam Certification Guide is a complete study tool for the CCNP BCMSN exam, allowing you to assess your knowledge, identify areas in which to concentrate your study, and master key concepts to help you succeed on the exams and in your daily job. The book is filled with features that help you master the skills to implement appropriate technologies to build scalable, multilayer switched networks. This book was developed in cooperation with the Cisco Internet Learning Solutions Group. Cisco Press books are the only self-study books authorized by Cisco for CCNP exam preparation.

Cisco and Cisco Press present this material in text-based format to provide another learning vehicle for our customers and the broader user community in general. Although a publication does not duplicate the instructor-led or e-learning environment, we acknowledge that not everyone responds in the same way to the same delivery mechanism. It is our intent that presenting this material via a Cisco Press publication will enhance the transfer of knowledge to a broad audience of networking professionals.

Cisco Press will present study guides on existing and future exams through these Exam Certification Guides to help achieve Cisco Internet Learning Solutions Group's principal objectives: to educate the Cisco community of networking professionals and to enable that community to build and maintain reliable, scalable networks. The Cisco Career Certifications and classes that support these certifications are directed at meeting these objectives through a disciplined approach to progressive learning. To succeed on the Cisco Career Certifications exams, as well as in your daily job as a Cisco certified professional, we recommend a blended learning solution that combines instructor-led, e-learning, and self-study training with hands-on experience. Cisco Systems has created an authorized Cisco Learning Partner program to provide you with the most highly qualified instruction and invaluable hands-on experience in lab and simulation environments. To learn more about Cisco Learning Partner programs available in your area, please go to www.cisco.com/go/authorizedtraining.

The books Cisco Press creates in partnership with Cisco Systems will meet the same standards for content quality demanded of our courses and certifications. It is our intent that you will find this and subsequent Cisco Press certification and training publications of value as you build your networking knowledge base.

Thomas M. Kelly
Vice-President, Internet Learning Solutions Group
Cisco Systems, Inc.
August 2003

Introduction: Overview of Certification and How to Succeed

Professional certifications have been an important part of the computing industry for many years and will continue to become more important. Many reasons exist for these certifications, but the most popularly cited reason is that of credibility. All other considerations held equal, the certified employee/consultant/job candidate is considered more valuable than one who is not.

Objectives and Methods

The most important and somewhat obvious objective of this book is to help you pass the Cisco BCMSN exam (642-811) In fact, if the primary objective of this book were different, the book's title would be misleading; however, the methods used in this book to help you pass the BCMSN exam are designed to also make you much more knowledgeable about how to do your job. While this book and the accompanying CD-ROM have many example test questions, the method in which they are used is not to simply make you memorize as many questions and answers as you possibly can.

One key methodology used in this book helps you discover the exam topics about which you need more review, to help you fully understand and remember those details, and to help you prove to yourself that you have retained your knowledge of those topics. So, this book does not try to help you pass by memorization, but by helping you truly learn and understand the topics. The BCMSN exam is just one of the foundation topics in the CCNP and CCDP certifications, and the knowledge contained within is vitally important to consider yourself a truly skilled routing and switching engineer or specialist. This book would do you a disservice if it did not attempt to help you learn the material. To that end, the book can help you pass the BCMSN exam by using the following methods:

- Helping you discover which test topics you have not mastered

- Providing explanations and information to fill in your knowledge gaps

- Supplying exercises and scenarios that enhance your ability to recall and deduce the answers to test questions

- Providing practice exercises on the topics and the testing process through test questions on the CD-ROM

Who Should Read This Book?

This book is not designed to be a general networking topics book; although, it can be used for that purpose. This book is intended to tremendously increase your chances of passing the Cisco BCMSN exam. Although other objectives can be achieved from using this book, the book is written with one goal in mind: to help you pass the exam.

The BCMSN exam is primarily based on the content of the Building Cisco Multilayer Switched Networks (BCMSN) 2.0 CCNP course. You should have either taken the course, read through the BCMSN coursebook or this book, or have a couple of years of LAN switching experience.

Exam Overview

Cisco offers three levels of certification, each with an increasing level of proficiency: Associate, Professional, and Expert. These are commonly known by their acronyms CCNA/CCDA (Cisco Certified Network/Design Associate), CCNP/CCDP (Cisco Certified Network/Design Professional), and CCIE (Cisco Certified Internetworking Expert). There are others as well, but this book focuses on the certifications for enterprise networks.

For the CCNP certification, you must pass a series of four core exams or pass a longer foundations exam plus one support exam. The BCMSN exam or its content is included and required for either path. For most exams, Cisco does not publish the scores needed for passing. You need to take the exam to find that out for yourself.

To see the most current requirements for the CCNP or CCDP certifications, go to www.cisco.com; then, click Learning and Events, followed by Career Certifications and Paths.

The BCMSN exam itself is composed of 60 to 70 questions, presented in a variety of formats. You can expect to find multiple-choice single answer, multiple-choice multiple answer, drag-and-drop, fill-in-the-blank, and simulations. To find more specific information about the topics that can be covered on the BCMSN exam, go to www.cisco.com; then, click Learning and Events, followed by Exam Information and then Certification Exams. The exam lasts 90 minutes and is offered through either Pearson VUE or Prometric testing centers only. See www.cisco.com/en/US/learning/le3/le11/learning_about_registering_for_exams.html for the most current information about registering for the exam.

Strategies for Exam Preparation

The strategy you use to prepare for the BCMSN exam might be slightly different than strategies used by other readers, mainly based on the skills, knowledge, and experience you already have obtained. For instance, if you have attended the BCMSN course, you might take a different approach than someone who learned switching through on-the-job training.

Regardless of the strategy you use or the background you have, this book is designed to help you get to the point where you can pass the exam with the least amount of time required. For instance, there is no need for you to practice or read about IP addressing and subnetting if you fully understand it already. However, many people like to make sure that they truly know a topic and read over material that they already know. Several book features help you gain the confidence that you know some material already and also help you know what topics you need to study more.

How This Book Is Organized

Although this book can be read cover-to-cover, it is designed to be flexible and allow you to easily move between chapters and sections of chapters to cover only the material that you need more work with. Chapters 1 through 20 are the core chapters and can be covered in any order, though some chapters are related and build upon each other. If you do intend to read them all, the order in the book is an excellent sequence to use.

When you finish with the core chapters, you have several options on how to finish your exam preparation. Chapter 21, "Scenarios for Final Preparation," provides many scenarios to help you review and refine your knowledge, without giving you a false sense of preparedness that you would get with simply reviewing a set of multiple-choice questions. You can review the questions at the end of each chapter, and you can use the CD-ROM testing software to practice the exam.

Each core chapter covers a subset of the topics on the BCMSN exam. The core chapters are organized into parts. The core chapters cover the following topics:

PART I: Overview and Design of a Campus Network

- Chapter 1, "Campus Network Overview"—This chapter covers the use of switches in the OSI model's various layers, the different campus network models, hierarchical network design, and how Cisco's switching products fit into a hierarchical network design.

- Chapter 2 "Modular Network Design"—This chapter covers how to design, size, and scale a campus network using a modular approach

PART II: Building a Campus Network

- Chapter 3, "Switch Operation"—This chapter covers Layer 2 and multilayer switch operation, how various CAM and TCAM tables are used to make switching decisions, and how to monitor these tables to aid in troubleshooting.

- Chapter 4, "Switch Configuration"—This chapter covers the operating system software available on Cisco Catalyst switches, basic switch configuration and administration, switch file management, and how to verify that a switch is functioning properly to aid in troubleshooting.

- Chapter 5, "Switch Port Configuration"—This chapter covers basic Ethernet concepts, using scalable Ethernet, connecting switch block devices, and verifying switch port operation to aid in troubleshooting.

- Chapter 6, "VLANs and Trunks"—This chapter covers basic VLAN concepts, transporting multiple VLANs over single links, configuring VLAN trunks, Layer 2 and Ethernet over MPLS tunnels, and verifying VLAN and trunk operation.

- Chapter 7, "VLAN Trunking Protocol (VTP)"—This chapter covers VLAN management using VTP, configuring VTP, managing traffic through VTP pruning, and verifying VTP operation.

- Chapter 8, "Aggregating Switch Links"—This chapter covers switch port aggregation with EtherChannel, EtherChannel negotiation protocols, configuring EtherChannel, and verifying EtherChannel operation.

- Chapter 9, "Traditional Spanning Tree Protocol"—This chapter covers IEEE 802.1D Spanning Tree Protocol (STP), as well as an overview of the other STP types that might be running on a switch.

- Chapter 10, "Spanning Tree Configuration"—This chapter covers the STP Root Bridge, customizing the STP topology, tuning STP convergence, redundant link convergence, and verifying STP operation.

- Chapter 11, "Protecting the Spanning Tree Protocol Topology"—This chapter covers protecting the STP topology using Root Guard, BPDU Guard, and Loop Guard, as well as how to detect delayed BPDU reception using BPDU Skew Detection, and verifying that these STP protection mechanisms are functioning properly.

- Chapter 12, "Advanced Spanning Tree Protocol"—This chapter covers Rapid Spanning Tree Protocol (RSTP) and Multiple Spanning Tree (MST) Protocol.

PART III: Layer 3 Switching

- Chapter 13, "Multilayer Switching"—This chapter covers interVLAN routing, multilayer switching with CEF, and verifying that multilayer switching is functioning properly.

- Chapter 14, "Router Redundancy and Load Balancing"—This chapter covers providing redundant router or gateway addresses on Catalyst switches, server load balancing, and verifying that redundancy and load balancing are functioning properly.

- Chapter 15, "Multicast"—This chapter covers general multicast concepts, routing and switching multicast traffic, and verifying that multicast routing and switching are functioning properly.

PART IV: Campus Network Services

- Chapter 16, "Quality of Service Overview"—This chapter covers the Differentiated Services QoS model, the building blocks of the DiffServ QoS model, and switch port queues.

- Chapter 17, "Diffserv QoS Configuration"—This chapter covers applying QoS trust, defining a DiffServ QoS policy, tuning egress scheduling, configuring congestion avoidance, and verifying that QoS operation is functioning properly.

- Chapter 18, "IP Telephony"—This chapter covers how a Catalyst switch can provide power to operate a Cisco IP Phone, how voice traffic can be carried over the links between an IP Phone and a Catalyst switch, QoS for voice traffic, and verifying that IP Telephony features are functioning properly.

- Chapter 19, "Securing Switch Access"—This chapter covers Switch Authentication, Authorization, and Accounting (AAA), port security using MAC addresses, and port-based security using IEEE 802.1x.

- Chapter 20, "Securing with VLANs"—This chapter covers how to control traffic within a VLAN using access lists, implementing private VLANs, and monitoring traffic on switch ports for security reasons.

Each chapter in the book uses several features to help you make the best use of your time in that chapter. The features are as follows:

- Assessment—Each chapter begins with a "Do I Know This Already?" quiz that helps you determine the amount of time you need to spend studying that chapter. If you intend to read the entire chapter, you can save the quiz for later use. Questions are all multiple-choice, single-answer, to give a quick assessment of your knowledge.

- Foundation Topics—This is the core section of each chapter that explains the protocols, concepts, and configuration for the topics in the chapter.

- Foundation Summary—At the end of each chapter, a Foundation Summary collects key concepts, facts, and commands into an easy-to-review format. A more lengthy "Q&A" section follows, where many review questions are presented. Questions are mainly open-ended, rather than multiple choice, as found on the exams. This is done to focus more on understanding the subject matter than on memorizing details.

- Scenarios—Scenarios are collected in the final chapter to allow a much more in-depth examination of a network implementation. Rather than posing a simple question asking for a single fact, the scenarios let you design, configure, and troubleshoot networks (at least on paper) without the clues inherent in a multiple-choice quiz format.

- CD-based practice exam—The companion CD-ROM contains two separate test banks—one composed of the questions from the book and an entirely new test bank of questions to reinforce your understanding of the book's concepts. In addition to the multiple choice questions, you also encounter some configuration simulation questions where you actually perform configurations. This is the best tool for helping you prepare for the actual test-taking process.

How to Use This Book for Study

Retention and recall are the two features of human memory most closely related to performance on tests. This exam preparation guide focuses on increasing both retention and recall of the topics on the exam. The other human characteristic involved in successfully passing the exam is intelligence; this book does not address that issue!

Adult retention is typically less than that of children. For example, it is common for 4-year-olds to pick up basic language skills in a new country faster than their parents. Children retain facts as an end unto itself; adults typically either need a stronger reason to remember a fact, or must have a reason to think about that fact several times to retain it in memory. For these reasons, a student who attends a typical Cisco course and retains 50 percent of the material is actually quite an amazing student.

Memory recall is based on connectors to the information that needs to be recalled—the greater the number of connectors to a piece of information, the better chance and better speed of recall. For example, if the exam asks what VTP stands for, you automatically add information to the question. You know the topic is switching because of the nature of the test. You might recall the term "VTP domain," which implies that this is a type of switch domain. You might also remember that it is talking about VLANs. Having read one of the multiple-choice answers "VLAN Trunk Protocol," you might even have the infamous "aha" experience, in which you are then sure that your answer is correct—and possibly a brightly lit bulb is hovering over your head. All these added facts and assumptions are the connectors that eventually lead your brain to the fact that needs to be recalled. Of course, recall and retention work together. If you do not retain the knowledge, recalling it will be difficult.

This book is designed with features to help you increase retention and recall. It does this in the following ways:

- By providing succinct and complete methods of helping you decide what you recall easily and what you do not recall at all.

- By giving references to the exact passages in the book that review those concepts you did not recall, so you can quickly be reminded about a fact or concept. Repeating information that connects to another concept helps retention, and describing the same concept in several ways throughout a chapter increases the number of connectors to the same pieces of information.

- By including exercise questions that supply fewer connectors than multiple-choice questions. This helps you exercise recall and avoids giving you a false sense of confidence, as an exercise with only multiple-choice questions might do. For example, fill-in-the-blank questions require you to have better and more complete recall than multiple-choice questions.

- By pulling the entire breadth of subject matter together. A separate chapter (Chapter 21) contains scenarios and several related questions that cover every topic on the exam and gives you the chance to prove that you have gained mastery over the subject matter. This reduces the connectors implied by questions residing in a particular chapter and requires you to exercise other connectors to remember the details.

- Finally, accompanying this book is a CD-ROM that has exam-like questions in a variety of formats. These are useful for you to practice taking the exam and to get accustomed to the time restrictions imposed during the exam.

In taking the "Do I Know This Already?" assessment quizzes in each chapter, make sure you treat yourself and your knowledge fairly. If you come across a question that makes you guess at an answer, mark it wrong immediately. This forces you to read through the part of the chapter that relates to that question and forces you to learn it more thoroughly.

If you find that you do well on the assessment quizzes, it still might be wise to quickly skim through each chapter to find sections or topics that do not readily come to mind. Sometimes, even reading through the detailed table of contents will reveal topics that are unfamiliar or unclear. If that happens to you, mark those chapters or topics and spend time working through those parts of the book.

Strategies for the Exam

Try to schedule the exam far enough in advance so that you have ample time for study. Consider the time of day and even the day of the week so that you choose a timeframe that suits your daily routine. Because the exam lasts 90 minutes, you should make sure the exam time does not coincide with your regular lunchtime or some other part of the day when you are usually tired or trying to wake up. As for the day of the week, your work schedule might prevent you from studying a few days before the exam.

Hopefully, you can find a testing center located nearby. In any event, be sure to familiarize yourself with the driving and parking directions well ahead of time. You do not want to be frantically searching for streets or buildings a few minutes before the exam is scheduled to start. You will need at least one form of picture ID to present at the testing center.

Think about common-sense things, such as eating a nutritious meal before you leave for the exam. You need to be as comfortable as possible for the entire 90-minute exam, so it pays not to be hungry. Limiting the amount of liquids you consume right before test time might also be wise. After the exam begins, the clock does not stop for a restroom break. Also, think about taking a lightweight jacket along, in case the exam room feels cold.

During the exam, try to pace yourself by knowing that there are at most 70 questions in a 90-minute period. That does not mean that every question should be answered in a little over a minute; it means only that you should try to move along at a regular pace. Be aware that if you are unsure about an answer, you are not allowed to mark the question and return to it later. That was allowed in exams of years past, not anymore. This might force you into a guessing position on a question, just so you can move along to the others before the time runs out.

At the end of the exam, you receive your final score and news of your passing or failing. If you pass, congratulate yourself and breathe a sigh of relief at not having to study more!

If you fail, remind yourself that you are not a failure. It is never a disgraceful thing to fail a Cisco test, as long as you decide to try it again. Anybody that has ever taken a Cisco exam knows that to be true; just ask the people who have attempted the CCIE lab exam. As soon as you can, schedule to take the same exam again. Allow a few days so that you can study the topics that gave you trouble. The exam score should also break down the entire exam into major topics, each with its respective score. Do not be discouraged about starting over with your studies—the majority is already behind you. Just spend time brushing up on the "low spots" where you lack knowledge or confidence.

CCNP Exam Topics

Carefully consider the exam topics Cisco has posted on its website as you study, particularly for clues as to how deeply you should know each topic. Beyond that, you cannot go wrong by developing a broader knowledge of the subject matter. You can do that by reading and studying the topics presented in this book. Remember that it is in your best interest to become proficient in each of the CCNP subjects. When it is time to use what you have learned, being well-rounded counts more than being well-tested.

Table I-1 shows the official exam topics for the BCMSN exam, as posted on Cisco.com. Note that Cisco has historically changed exam topics without changing the exam number, so do not be alarmed if small changes in the exam topics occur over time. When in doubt, go to www.cisco.com, click Learning and Events, and select Career Certifications and Paths.

Table I-1 *BCMSN Exam Topics*

Exam Topic	Part of This Book Where Exam Topic Is Covered
Technology	
Describe the Enterprise Composite Model used for designing networks and explain how it addresses enterprise network needs for performance, scalability and availability.	Part I
Describe the physical, data-link, and network layer technologies used in a switched network, and identify when to use each.	Part II
Explain the role of switches in the various modules of the Enterprise Composite Model (Campus Infrastructure, Server Farm, Enterprise Edge, Network Management).	Part I
Explain the function of the Switching Database Manager (specifically, Content Addressable Memory [CAM] and Ternary Content Addressable Memory [TCAM]) within a Catalyst switch.	Part II
Describe the features and operation of VLANs on a switched network.	Part II
Describe the features of the VLAN trunking protocols, including 802.1Q, ISL (emphasis on 802.1Q), and dynamic trunking protocol.	Part II
Describe the features and operation of 802.1Q Tunneling (802.1QinQ) within a service provider network.	Part II
Describe the operation and purpose of managed VLAN services.	Part II

continues

Table I-1 *BCMSN Exam Topics (Continued)*

Exam Topic	Part of This Book Where Exam Topic Is Covered
Technology *(Continued)*	
Describe how VTP versions 1 and 2 operate, including domains, modes, advertisements, and pruning.	Part II
Explain the function of the Switching Database Manager (specifically Content Addressable Memory [CAM] and Ternary Content Addressable Memory [TCAM]) within a Catalyst switch.	Part II
Explain the operation and purpose of the Spanning Tree Protocol (STP) on a switched network.	Part II
Identify the specific types of Cisco route switch processors, and provide implementation details.	Part III
List and describe the operation of the key components required to implement interVLAN routing.	Part III
Explain the types of redundancy in a multilayer switched network, including hardware and software redundancy.	Part III
Explain how IP multicast operates on a multilayer switched network, including PIM, CGMP, and IGMP.	Part III
Describe the quality issues with voice traffic on a switched data network, including jitter and delay.	Part IV
Describe the QoS solutions that address voice-quality issues.	Part IV
Describe the features and operation of network analysis modules on Catalyst switches to improve network traffic management.	Part IV
Implementation and Operation	
Describe Transparent LAN Services and how they are implemented in a service provider network.	Part II
Configure access ports for static and multi-VLAN membership.	Part II
Configure and verify 802.1Q trunks.	Part II
Configure and verify ISL trunks.	Part II
Configure VTP domains in server, client, and transparent modes.	Part II

Table I-1 *BCMSN Exam Topics (Continued)*

Exam Topic	Part of This Book Where Exam Topic Is Covered
Implementation and Operation *(Continued)*	
Enable Spanning Tree on ports and VLANs.	Part II
Configure Spanning Tree parameters including: port priority, VLAN priority, Root Bridge, BPDU guard, PortFast, and UplinkFast.	Part II
Implement IP technology on a switched network with auxiliary VLANs.	Part IV
Configure and verify router redundancy using HSRP, VRRP, GLBP, SRM, and SLB.	Part III
Configure QoS features on multilayer switched networks to provide optimal quality and bandwidth utilization for applications and data.	Part IV
Configure Fast EtherChannel and Gigabit EtherChannel to increase bandwidth for interswitch connections.	Part II
Planning and Design	
Compare end-to-end and local VLANs, and determine when to use each.	Part I
Design a VLAN configuration with VTP to work for a given specific scenario.	Part II
Select multilayer switching architectures, given specific multilayer switching needs.	Part II
Describe the general design models when implementing IP telephony in a switched network environment.	Part IV
Plan QoS implementation within a multilayer switched network.	Part IV

For More Information

If you have any comments about the book, you can submit those via the www.ciscopress.com web site. Just go to the web site, select Contact Us, and type in your message.

Cisco might make changes that affect the CCNP certification from time to time. You should always check www.cisco.com for the latest details. Also, you can look to www.ciscopress.com/1587200775, where we will publish any information pertinent to how you might use this book differently in light of Cisco's future changes. For instance, if Cisco decided to remove a major topic from the exam, it might post that on its website; Cisco Press would make an effort to list that information, as well.

PART I: Overview and Design of a Campus Network

Chapter 1   Campus Network Overview

Chapter 2   Modular Network Design

This part of the book covers the following BCMSN exam topics:

- Describe the Enterprise Composite Model used for designing networks and explain how it addresses enterprise network needs for performance, scalability, and availability.

- Explain the role of switches in the various modules of the Enterprise Composite Model (Campus Infrastructure, Server Farm, Enterprise Edge, Network Management).

- Compare end-to-end and local VLANs; determine when to use each.

This chapter covers the following topics that you need to master for the CCNP BCMSN exam:

- **Switching Functionality**—This section covers the use of switches in the OSI model layers. You learn about the functions and application of routing and switching in Layers 2, 3, and 4, along with the concept of multilayer switching.

- **Campus Network Models**—This section presents the concept of a campus network, and describes the traditional campus model and models based on traffic patterns. This section also describes the factors that affect a campus network's design.

- **Hierarchical Network Design**—This section details a three-layer, hierarchical structure of campus network designs.

- **Cisco Products in the Hierarchical Design**—This section describes how Cisco switching products fit into the network hierarchy and presents guidelines for selecting the product based on the design requirements.

CHAPTER 1

Campus Network Overview

As campus networks have grown and technologies have matured, network engineers and architects have many more options to consider than the hubs, Ethernet switches, and routers traditionally put in place. You can use switches to improve network performance in many ways. However, simply replacing existing shared networks with switched networks is not enough. The switching function alone alleviates congestion and increases bandwidth (in addition to more complex capabilities) if properly placed and designed. Switches themselves have also improved over time. The type of switch, its capabilities, and its location within a network can greatly enhance network performance.

This chapter presents a logical design process that you can use to build a new campus network or to modify and improve an existing network.

"Do I Know This Already?" Quiz

The purpose of the "Do I Know This Already?" quiz is to help you decide if you need to read the entire chapter. If you already intend to read the entire chapter, you do not necessarily need to answer these questions now.

The 12-question quiz, derived from the major sections in the "Foundation Topics" portion of the chapter, helps you determine how to spend your limited study time.

Table 1-1 outlines the major topics discussed in this chapter and the "Do I Know This Already?" quiz questions that correspond to those topics.

Table 1-1 *"Do I Know This Already?" Foundation Topics Section-to-Question Mapping*

Foundation Topics Section	Questions Covered in This Section
Switching Functionality	1-3
Campus Networks, Traffic Pattern Models	4-7
Hierarchical Design Model	8-10
Cisco Products in the Hierarchical Design	11-12

> **CAUTION** The goal of self-assessment is to gauge your mastery of the topics in this chapter. If you do not know the answer to a question or are only partially sure of the answer, you should mark this question wrong. Giving yourself credit for an answer you correctly guess skews your self-assessment results and might provide you with a false sense of security.

1. Layer 2 switching uses which of the following values to forward data?

   a. IP address

   b. IPX address

   c. MAC address

   d. RIP address

   e. UDP port

2. Multilayer switching (MLS) forwards packets based on what OSI layers:

   a. Layer 1

   b. Layer 2

   c. Layer 3

   d. Layer 4

   e. b, c, d

   f. a, b, c, d

3. Which of the following does a multilayer switch perform?

   a. Forwarding according to MAC address

   b. Forwarding according to IP address

   c. Forwarding according to UDP/TCP port numbers

   d. All of the above

4. What does the 20/80 rule of networking state? (Pick one.)

   a. Only 20 out of 80 packets arrive at the destination.

   b. Twenty percent of the network is used 80 percent of the time.

   c. Twenty percent of the traffic on a network segment travels across the network, while 80 percent of it stays local.

   d. Twenty percent of the traffic on a network segment stays local, while 80 percent of it travels across the network.

5. Where does a collision domain exist in a switched network?

   a. On a single switch port

   b. Across all switch ports

   c. On a single VLAN

   d. Across all VLANs

6. Where does a broadcast domain exist in a switched network?

   a. On a single switch port

   b. Across all switch ports

   c. On a single VLAN

   d. Across all VLANs

7. What is a VLAN primarily used for?

   a. To segment a collision domain

   b. To segment a broadcast domain

   c. To segment an autonomous system

   d. To segment a spanning-tree domain

8. In which OSI layer should devices in the distribution layer typically operate?

   a. Layer 1

   b. Layer 2

   c. Layer 3

   d. Layer 4

9. How many layers are recommended in the hierarchical campus network design model?

   a. 1

   b. 2

   c. 3

   d. 4

   e. 7

10. A hierarchical network's distribution layer aggregates which of the following?

    a. Core switches

    b. Broadcast domains

    c. Routing updates

    d. Access layer switches

11. Which Cisco switch products should not be used in a campus network distribution layer?

    a. Catalyst 2950

    b. Catalyst 3550

    c. Catalyst 4000/4500

    d. Catalyst 6500

12. Which of these attributes might make a Catalyst 2950 a good choice for use in a wiring closet?

    a. High density of low cost 10/100 ports

    b. Advanced quality of service features

    c. High density of 1000BASE-X ports

    d. Large modular chassis

You can find the answers to the quiz in Appendix A, "Answers to Chapter 'Do I Know This Already?' Quizzes and Q&A Sections." The suggested choices for your next step are as follows:

- **6 or less overall score**—Read the entire chapter. This includes the "Foundation Topics," "Foundation Summary," and "Q&A" sections.

- **7–9 overall score**—Begin with the "Foundation Summary" section and then follow up with the "Q&A" section at the end of the chapter.

- **10 or more overall score**—If you want more review on these topics, skip to the "Foundation Summary" section and then go to the "Q&A" section at the end of the chapter. Otherwise, move on to Chapter 2, "Modular Network Design."

Foundation Topics

Switching Functionality

To understand how switches and routers should be chosen and placed in a network design, you should first understand how to take advantage of data communication at different layers.

The OSI reference model separates data communication into seven layers, as shown in Table 1-2. Each layer has a specific function and a specific protocol so that two devices can exchange data on the same layer. A *protocol data unit (PDU)* is the generic name for a block of data that a layer on one device exchanges with the same layer on a peer device. A PDU is encapsulated in a layer's protocol before it is made available to a lower-level layer, or unencapsulated before being handed to a higher-level layer.

Table 1-2 *Layers of Data Communications*

OSI Layer	Protocol Data Unit	Mechanism to Process PDU
7 (application)		
6 (presentation)		
5 (session)		
4 (transport)	TCP segment	TCP port
3 (network)	Packet	Router
2 (data link)	Frame	Switch/bridge
1 (physical)		

In Table 1-2, Layers 2, 3, and 4 are represented by the data link, network, and transport layers, respectively, with PDUs' *frame*, *packet*, and *TCP segment*. When a TCP segment (Layer 4) needs to be transmitted to another station, the TCP segment is encapsulated as a packet (Layer 3), and further encapsulated as a frame (Layer 2). The receiving station unencapsulates Layers 2 and 3 before processing the original TCP segment.

The layered protocols also apply to networking devices. For example, a Layer 2 device transfers data by looking at Layer 2's PDU header information. Upper-layer protocols are not looked at or even understood. Layer-specific devices are discussed in detail in the sections that follow.

Layer 2 Switching

Devices that forward frames at Layer 2 involve the following functions:

- MAC addresses are learned from the incoming frames' source addresses.

- A table of MAC addresses and their associated bridge and switch ports is built and maintained.

- Broadcast and multicast frames are flooded out to all ports (except the one that received the frame).

- Frames destined to unknown locations are flooded out to all ports (except the one that received the frame).

- Bridges and switches communicate with each other using the Spanning Tree Protocol to eliminate bridging loops.

A Layer 2 switch performs essentially the same function as a transparent bridge. However, a switch can have many ports and can perform *hardware-based bridging.* Frames are forwarded using specialized hardware, called *application-specific integrated circuits (ASICs).* This hardware gives switching great scalability, with wire-speed performance, low latency, low cost, and high-port density.

As long as Layer 2 frames are being switched between two Layer 1 interfaces of the same media type, such as two Ethernet connections or an Ethernet connection and a Fast Ethernet connection, the frames do not have to be modified. However, if the two interfaces are different media, such as Ethernet and Token Ring or Ethernet and Fiber Distributed Data Interface (FDDI), the Layer 2 switch must translate the frame contents before sending out the Layer 1 interface.

Layer 2 switching is used primarily for workgroup connectivity and network segmentation. You can contain traffic between users and servers in a workgroup within the switch. In addition, the number of stations on a network segment can be reduced with a switch, minimizing the collision domain size.

One drawback to Layer 2 switching is that it cannot be scaled effectively. Switches must forward broadcast frames to all ports, causing large switched networks to become large broadcast domains. In addition, Spanning Tree Protocol (STP) can have a slow convergence time when the switch topology changes. STP can also block certain switch ports, preventing data transfer. (Chapters 9 through 12 discuss STP and its variations in further detail.) Layer 2 switching alone cannot provide an effective, scalable network design.

Layer 3 Routing

Devices involved in Layer 3 routing perform the following functions:

- Packets are forwarded between networks based on Layer 3 addresses.

- An optimal path is determined for a packet to take through a network to the next router.

- Packet forwarding involves a table lookup of the destination network, next-hop router address, and the router's own outbound interface.

- An optimal path can be chosen from among many possibilities.

- Routers communicate with each other using *routing protocols*.

By nature, routers do not forward broadcast packets and only forward multicast packets to segments with multicast clients. This action provides control over broadcast propagation and offers network *segmentation* into areas of common Layer 3 addressing.

Logical addressing is possible on a network with routers because the Layer 3 (network layer) address uniquely identifies a device only at the network layer of the OSI reference model. Actual frame forwarding occurs using the Layer 2, or data link, address of devices. Therefore, some method must exist to associate a device's data link layer (MAC) address with its network layer (IP) address. A router must also have addresses from both layers assigned to each of its interfaces connected to a network. This assignment gives the router the functionality to support the logical network layer addresses assigned to the physical networks.

In addition, a router must examine each packet's Layer 3 header before making a routing decision. Layer 3 security and control can be implemented on any router interface using the source and destination addresses, protocol, or other Layer 3 attribute to make decisions on whether to limit or forward the packets.

Layer 3 routing is generally performed by microprocessor-based engines, which require CPU cycles to examine each packet's network layer header. The routing table of optimal paths to Layer 3 networks can also be a large table of dynamic values, requiring a finite lookup delay. Although you can place a router anywhere in a network, the router can become a bottleneck due to a latency of packet examination and processing.

Layer 3 Switching

Devices involved in Layer 3 switching perform the following functions:

- Packets are forwarded at Layer 3, just as a router would do.

- Packets are switched using specialized hardware, application-specific integrated circuits (ASICs) for high-speed and low latency.

- Packets can be forwarded with security control and quality of service (QoS) using Layer 3 address information.

Layer 3 switches are designed to examine and forward packets in high-speed LAN environments. Whereas, a router might impose a bottleneck to forwarding throughput, a Layer 3 switch can be placed anywhere in the network with little or no performance penalty.

Layer 4 Switching

Devices involved in Layer 4 switching perform the following functions:

- Packets are forwarded using hardware switching, based on both Layer 3 addressing and Layer 4 application information. (Layer 2 addressing is also inherently used.)
- Layer 4 protocol types (UDP or TCP, for example) in packet headers are examined.
- Layer 4 segment headers are examined to determine application port numbers.

Switching at Layer 4 allows finer control over the movement of information. For example, traffic can be prioritized according to the source and destination port numbers, and QoS can be defined for end users. Therefore, video or voice data can be switched at a higher level of service with more bandwidth availability than file transfer or HTTP traffic. Layer 4 port numbers for source and destination can also perform traffic accounting.

A Layer 4 switch must also allocate a large amount of memory to its forwarding tables. Layer 2 and Layer 3 devices have forwarding tables based on MAC and network addresses, making those tables only as large as the number of network devices. Layer 4 devices, however, must keep track of application protocols and conversations occurring in the network. Their forwarding tables become proportional to the number of network devices multiplied by the number of applications.

Multilayer Switching (MLS)

Devices involved in MLS perform the following functions:

- Packets are forwarded in hardware that combines Layer 2, Layer 3, and Layer 4 switching.
- Packets are forwarded at wire speed.
- The traditional Layer 3 routing function is provided using Cisco Express Forwarding (CEF), where a database of routes to every destination network is maintained and distributed to switching ASICs for very high forwarding performance.

Cisco switches perform multilayer switching at Layer 3 and Layer 4. At Layer 3, the Catalyst family of switches caches traffic flows based on IP addresses. At Layer 4, traffic flows are cached based on source and destination addresses, in addition to source and destination ports. All switching is performed in hardware, providing equal performance at both Layer 3 and Layer 4 switching.

Campus Network Models

A *campus network* is an enterprise network consisting of many LANs in one or more buildings, all connected and all usually in the same geographic area. A company typically owns the entire campus network, as well as the physical wiring. Campus networks commonly consist of Ethernet, 802.11

wireless LANs, higher-speed Fast Ethernet, Fast EtherChannel, and Gigabit Ethernet LANs. Some campus networks also consist of legacy Token Ring and FDDI.

An understanding of traffic flow is a vital part of the campus network design. While you can leverage high-speed LAN technologies to improve any traffic movement, the emphasis should be on providing an overall design tuned to known, studied, or predicted traffic flows. The network traffic can then be effectively moved and managed, and you can scale the campus network to support future needs.

The next sections present various network models that you can use to classify and to design campus networks. Beginning with traditional shared networks, the models build on each other to leverage traffic movement and provide predictable behavior.

Shared Network Model

In the early 1990s, campus networks were traditionally constructed of a single LAN for all users to connect to and use. All devices on the LAN were forced to share the available bandwidth. LAN media such as Ethernet and Token Ring both had distance limitations, as well as limitations on the number of devices that could be connected to a single LAN.

Network availability and performance declined as the number of connected devices increased. For example, an Ethernet LAN required all devices to share the available 10-Mbps half duplex bandwidth. Ethernet also used the carrier sense multiple access collision detect (CSMA/CD) scheme to determine when a device could transmit data on the shared LAN. If two or more devices tried to transmit at the same time, network collisions occurred, and all devices had to become silent and wait to retransmit their data. This type of LAN is a *collision domain* because all devices are susceptible to collisions. Token Ring LANs are not susceptible to collisions because they are deterministic and allow stations to transmit only when they receive a "token" that passes around the ring.

One solution used to relieve network congestion was to segment, or divide, a LAN into discrete collision domains. This solution used transparent bridges, which only forwarded Layer 2 data frames to the network segment where the destination address was located. Bridges enabled the number of devices on a segment to be reduced, lessened the probability of collisions on segments, and increased the physical distance limitations by acting as a repeater.

Bridges normally forward frames to the LAN segment where the destination address is located. However, frames containing the broadcast MAC address (ff:ff:ff:ff:ff:ff) must be flooded out to all connected segments. Broadcast frames are usually associated with requests for information or services, including network service announcements. IP uses broadcasts for Address Resolution Protocol (ARP) requests to ask what MAC address is associated with a particular IP address. Other broadcast frame examples include Dynamic Host Control Protocol (DHCP) requests, IPX Get Nearest Server (GNS) requests, Service Advertising Protocol (SAP) announcements, Routing

Information Protocol (RIP—both IP and IPX) advertisements, and NetBIOS name requests. A *broadcast domain* is a group of network segments where a broadcast is flooded.

Multicast traffic is traffic destined for a specific set or group of users, regardless of their location on the campus network. Multicast frames must be flooded to all segments because they are a form of broadcast. Although end users must join a multicast group to enable their applications to process and receive the multicast data, a bridge must flood the traffic to all segments because it doesn't know which stations are members of the multicast group. Multicast frames will use shared bandwidth on a segment, but will not force the use of CPU resources on every connected device. Only CPUs that are registered as multicast group members will actually process those frames. Some multicast traffic is sporadic, as in the case of various routing protocol advertisements, while other traffic, such as Cisco IP/TV multicast video, can consume most or all network resources with a steady stream of real-time data.

Broadcast traffic presents a two-fold performance problem on a bridged LAN because all broadcast frames flood all bridged network segments. First, as a network grows, the broadcast traffic can grow in proportion and monopolize the available bandwidth. Second, all end-user stations must listen to, decode, and process every broadcast frame. This function is performed by the CPU, which must look further into the frame to see with which upper-layer protocol the broadcast is associated. While today's CPUs are robust and might not show a noticeable degradation from processing broadcasts, forcing unnecessary broadcast loads on every end user is not wise.

> **NOTE**   For a discussion of analysis performed by Cisco on the effects of various protocol broadcasts on CPU performance, refer to *Broadcasts in Switched LAN Internetworks* at www.cisco.com/univercd/cc/td/doc/cisintwk/idg4/nd20e.htm.

LAN Segmentation Model

Referred to as *network segmentation*, localizing the traffic and effectively reducing the number of stations on a segment is necessary to prevent collisions and broadcasts from reducing a network segment's performance. By reducing the number of stations, the probability of a collision decreases because fewer stations can be transmitting at a given time. For broadcast containment, the idea is to provide a barrier at the edge of a LAN segment so that broadcasts cannot pass outward or be forwarded on. The network designer can provide segmentation by using either a router or a switch.

You can use routers to connect the smaller subnetworks and either route Layer 3 packets or bridge Layer 2 packets. You can improve the effect of collisions by placing fewer stations on each segment. A router cannot propagate a collision condition from one segment to another, and broadcasts are not forwarded to other subnets by default, unless bridging (or some other specialized feature) is enabled on the router. Figure 1-1 shows an example of how a router can physically segment a campus network. Although broadcasts are contained, the router becomes a potential bottleneck because it must process and route every packet leaving each subnet.

Figure 1-1 *Network Segmentation with a Router*

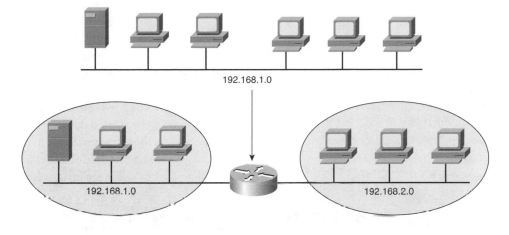

Another option is to replace shared LAN segments with switches. Switches offer greater performance with dedicated bandwidth on each port. Think of a switch as a fast multiport bridge. Each switch port becomes a separate collision domain and will not propagate collisions to any other port. However, broadcast and multicast frames are flooded out all switch ports unless more advanced switch features are invoked. Multicast switch features are covered in Chapter 15.

To contain broadcasts and segment a broadcast domain, you can implement virtual LANs (VLANs) within the switched network. A switch can logically divide its ports into isolated segments (broadcast domains). A VLAN is a group of switch ports (and the end devices to which they are connected) that communicate as if attached to a single shared-media LAN segment. By definition, a VLAN becomes a single broadcast domain. VLAN devices don't have to be physically located on the same switch or in the same building, as long as the VLAN itself is somehow connected between switches end-to-end. Figure 1-2 shows how you can segment a network into three broadcast and collision domains using three VLANs on a switch. Note that stations on a VLAN cannot communicate with stations on another VLAN in the figure—the VLANs are truly isolated.

By default, all ports on a switch are assigned to a single VLAN. With additional configuration, a switch can assign its ports to many specific VLANs. Each VLAN, although present on the same switch, is effectively separated from other VLANs. Frames will not be forwarded from one VLAN to another. To communicate between VLANs, a router (or Layer 3 device) is required, as illustrated by Figure 1-3.

Figure 1-2 *Segmentation Using VLANs*

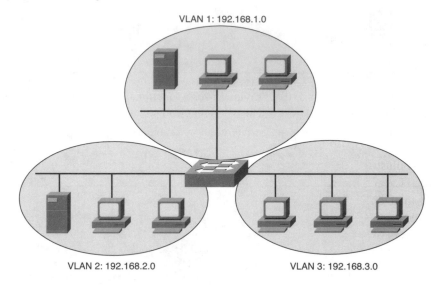

Figure 1-3 *Routing Traffic with VLANs*

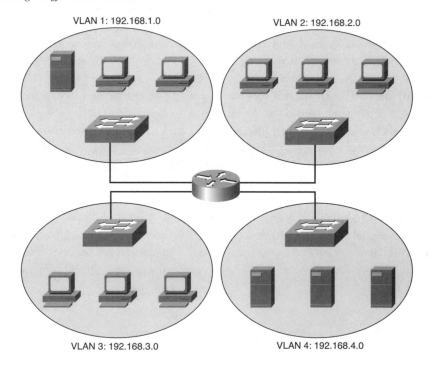

Ports on each switch have been grouped and assigned to one VLAN. A port from each VLAN then connects to the router. The router then forwards packets between VLANs through these ports.

To gain the most benefit from routed approaches and VLAN approaches, most campus networks are now built with a combination of Layer 2 switches and routers, or with multilayer switches. Again, the Layer 2 switches are generally placed where the small broadcast domains are located, linked by routers (or multilayer switches) that provide Layer 3 functionality. In this manner, broadcast traffic can be controlled or limited. Users can also be organized and given access to common workgroups, and traffic between workgroups can be interconnected and secured.

Figure 1-4 illustrates the structure of a typical routed and switched campus network. Here, the concept of Layer 2 switches and routers has been extended a bit. Each switch in the buildings supports three different VLANs for its users. A single switch port from each connects back to a router. Any switch port can normally carry only one VLAN, so something special must be occurring. These ports have been configured as *trunk links*, carrying multiple VLANs. (Trunking is discussed in Chapter 6, "VLANs and Trunks.")

Figure 1-4 *Typical Campus Network Structure*

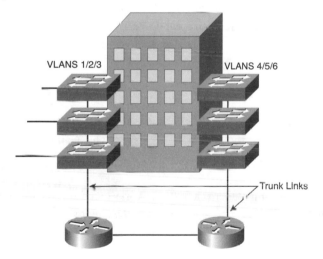

Network Traffic Models

To design and build a successful campus network, you must gain a thorough understanding of the traffic generated by applications in use, plus the traffic flow to and from the user communities. All devices on the network will produce data to be transported across the network. Each device can involve many applications that generate data with differing patterns and loads.

Applications, such as e-mail, word processing, printing, file transfer, and most web browsers, bring about data traffic patterns that are predictable from source to destination. However, newer applications, such as videoconferencing, TV or video broadcasts, and IP telephony, have a more dynamic user base, which makes traffic patterns difficult to predict or model.

Traditionally, users with similar applications or needs have been placed in common workgroups, along with the servers they access most often. Whether these workgroups are logical (VLAN) or physical networks, the idea is to keep the majority of traffic between clients and servers limited to the local network segment. In the case of the switched LANs connected by routers mentioned earlier, both clients and servers would be connected to a Layer 2 switch in the workgroup's proximity. This connection provides good performance while minimizing the traffic load on the routed network backbone.

This concept of network traffic patterns is known as the *80/20 rule*. In a properly designed campus network, 80 percent of the traffic on a given network segment is local (switched). No more than 20 percent of the traffic is expected to move across the network backbone (routed).

If the backbone becomes congested, the network administrator will realize that the 80/20 rule is no longer being met. What recourses are available to improve network performance again? Because of expense and complexity, upgrading the campus backbone is not a desirable option. The idea behind the 80/20 rule is to keep traffic off the backbone. Instead, the administrator can implement the following solutions:

- Reassign existing resources to bring the users and servers closer together.
- Move applications and files to a different server to stay within a workgroup.
- Move users logically (assigned to new VLANs) or physically to stay near their workgroups.
- Add more servers, which can bring resources closer to the respective workgroups.

Needless to say, conforming modern campus networks to the 80/20 rule has become difficult for the network administrator. Newer applications still use the client/server model, but server portions have been centralized in most enterprises. For example, databases, Internet and intranet technologies, and e-mail are all available from centralized servers. Not only do these applications involve larger amounts of data, but they also require a greater percentage of traffic to cross a network backbone to reach common destinations—quite a departure from the 80/20 rule.

This new model of campus traffic has become known as the *20/80 rule*. Now, only 20 percent of the traffic is local to the workgroup, while at least 80 percent of the traffic is expected to travel off the local network and across the backbone.

This shift in traffic patterns puts a greater burden on the campus backbone's Layer 3 technology. Now, because traffic from anywhere on the network can be destined for any other part of the network, the Layer 3 performance ideally should match the Layer 2 performance. Generally, Layer 3 forwarding involves more processing resources because the data packets must be examined in greater depth. This added computation load can create bottlenecks in the campus network, unless carefully designed.

Likewise, a campus network with many VLANs can become difficult to manage. In the past, VLANs were used to logically contain common workgroups and common traffic. With the 20/80 rule, end devices need to communicate with many other VLANs. Measuring traffic patterns and redesigning the campus network become too cumbersome just to keep up with the 20/80 rule model.

Predictable Network Model

Ideally, you should design a network with a predictable behavior in mind to offer low maintenance and high availability. For example, a campus network needs to recover from failures and topology changes quickly and in a predetermined manner. You should scale the network to easily support future expansions and upgrades. With a wide variety of multiprotocol and multicast traffic, the network should be able to support the 20/80 rule from a traffic standpoint. In other words, design the network around *traffic flows* instead of a particular type of traffic.

Traffic flows in a campus network can be classified as three types, based on where the network service is located in relation to the end user. Table 1-3 lists these types, along with the extent of the campus network that is crossed.

Table 1-3 *Types of Network Services*

Service Type	Location of Service	Extent of Traffic Flow
Local	Same segment/VLAN as user	Access layer only
Remote	Different segment/VLAN as user	Access to distribution layers
Enterprise	Central to all campus users	Access to distribution to core layers

The terms *access layer*, *distribution layer*, and *core layer* are each distinct components of the hierarchical network design model. The network is divided into logical levels, or layers, according to function. These terms and the hierarchical network design are discussed in the next section.

Hierarchical Network Design

You can structure the campus network so that each of the three types of traffic flows or services outlined in Table 1-3 are best supported. Cisco has refined a hierarchical approach to network design that enables network designers to logically create a network by defining and using layers of devices. The resulting network is efficient, intelligent, scalable, and easily managed.

The hierarchical model breaks a campus network down into three distinct layers, as illustrated in Figure 1-5.

Figure 1-5 *Hierarchical Network Design*

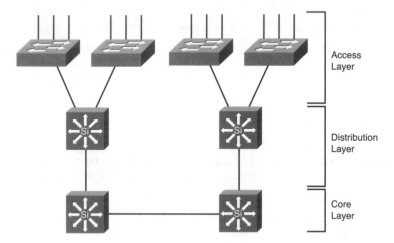

These layers are the *access layer*, *distribution layer*, and *core layer*. Each layer has attributes that provide both physical and logical network functions at the appropriate point in the campus network. Understanding each layer and its functions or limitations is important to properly apply the layer in the design process.

Access Layer

The access layer is present where the end users are connected to the network. Devices in this layer, sometimes called *building access switches*, should have the following capabilities:

- Low cost per switch port
- High port density
- Scalable uplinks to higher layers
- User access functions such as VLAN membership, traffic and protocol filtering, and QoS
- Resiliency through multiple uplinks

Distribution Layer

The distribution layer provides interconnection between the campus network's access and core layers. Devices in this layer, sometimes called *building distribution switches*, should have the following capabilities:

- High Layer 3 throughput for packet handling
- Security and *policy-based connectivity* functions through access lists or packet filters
- QoS features
- Scalable and resilient high-speed links to the core and access layers

Core Layer

A campus network's core layer provides connectivity of all distribution layer devices. The core, sometimes referred to as the *backbone*, must be capable of switching traffic as efficiently as possible. Core devices, sometimes called *campus backbone switches*, should have the following attributes:

- Very high throughput at Layer 2 or Layer 3
- No costly or unnecessary packet manipulations (access lists, packet filtering)
- Redundancy and resilience for high availability
- Advanced QoS functions

Cisco Products in the Hierarchical Design

Before delving into the design practices needed to build a hierarchical campus network, you should have some idea of the actual devices that you can place at each layer. Cisco has switching products tailored for layer functionality, as well as the size of the campus network.

For the purposes of this discussion, a large campus can be considered to span across several or many buildings in a single location. A medium campus might make use of one or several buildings, whereas a small campus might have only a single building.

Choose your Cisco products based on the functionality that is expected at each layer of a small, medium, or large campus. The products available at press time are described in the sections that follow and are summarized in table form for comparison. Don't get lost in the details of the tables. Rather, try to understand which switch fits into which layer for a given network size.

> **NOTE** Although Cisco offers a wide range of LAN switching products, several different operating systems and user interfaces are supported on different switch models. For the purposes of this book and the CCNP BCMSN exam, you should only be concerned with switches that run the Cisco IOS Software. Only these switches are listed in the tables that follow.

Although campus network design is presented as a three-layer approach (access, distribution, and core layers), the hierarchy can be collapsed or simplified in certain cases. For example, small or medium-sized campus networks might not have the size, multilayer switching, or volume requirements that would require the functions of all three layers. Here, you could combine the distribution and core layers for simplicity and cost savings. In this case, choose switch products based on the distribution layer features and access layer aggregation port densities needed.

Access Layer Switches

Recall that access layer devices should have these features:

- High port density to connect to end users
- Low cost
- Multiple uplinks to higher layers of the campus network
- Layer 2 services (traffic filtering, VLAN membership, and basic QoS)

Small or medium campus networks can use the Catalyst 2950 or 3550 (standard multilayer software image, SMI) series switches as access layer devices. These switches are useful to provide access to groups of less than 50 users and servers. Both switch families offer high-performance backplanes for efficient switching, and Fast or Gigabit Ethernet uplinks to distribution layer switches. These switches are also stackable, using Gigabit Ethernet links as a shared bus or as daisy-chained links to add port density in an access layer wiring closet. These switch families also offer a rich feature set, including QoS and switch clustering for improved performance and management.

For large campuses, the Catalyst 4000/4500 series switches provide advanced enterprise access layer functions. These switches can connect groups of less than 250 users and servers (10/100/1000BASE-T), or up to 92 dedicated Gigabit Ethernet devices. Greater Layer 2 functionality is provided as security, multicast support, and advanced QoS. The Catalyst 6500 can also be used for even higher user or server port densities in a large campus environment. For example, the Catalyst 6513 can support up to 576 FastEthernet ports.

> **NOTE**   On the Catalyst 4000/4500, only Supervisor III and IV support Cisco IOS Software. Be aware that other Supervisor modules run the Catalyst OS (also known as XDI, CatOS, or COS), but those are not dealt with here or in the exam.

Table 1-4 lists each Catalyst switch family suitable for the access layer, along with the maximum port densities and backplane speeds.

Table 1-4 *Catalyst Switches for the Access Layer*

Catalyst Model	Max Port Density	Uplinks	Max Backplane	Other Features
2950	12, 24, or 48 10/100	2 100FX or 1000BASE-X	13.6 Gbps	QoS, security
3550 (SMI)	24 or 48 10/100 or 12 10/100/1000BASE-T	2 1000BASE-X	24 Gbps (12-port), 13.6 Gbps (48-port), or 8.8 Gbps (24-port)	Advanced QoS, security, redundant power, inline power (24-port only)
4000/4500 (Sup III or IV)	240 10/100 or 10/100/1000BASE-T	100 or 1000BASE-X	64 Gbps	Advanced QoS, security, redundant power, inline power

Distribution Layer Switches

Switches used in the distribution layer should offer these features:

- Aggregation of access layer devices
- High Layer 3 multilayer switching throughput
- QoS support
- Port density of high-speed links to both the core and access layer switches
- Efficient support for redundant links and resiliency

In the distribution layer, uplinks from all access layer devices are aggregated, or come together. The distribution layer switches must be capable of processing the total volume of traffic from all the connected devices. These switches should have a port density of high-speed links to support the collection of access layer switches.

VLANs and broadcast domains converge at the distribution layer, requiring routing, filtering, and security. The switches at this layer must be capable of performing multilayer switching with high throughput. Only certain Catalyst switch models can provide multilayer switching; be sure to understand which ones can do this. (Chapter 13, "Multilayer Switching," covers this topic in greater detail.)

The Catalyst 3550-12G or 3550-12T can serve as a distribution layer switch for up to 10 1000BASE-X and 2 10/100/1000BASE-T or 2 1000BASE -X and 10 10/100/1000BASE-T access layer uplinks, respectively, as might be found in small to mid-sized networks. (The Catalyst 3550 must run the Enhanced Multilayer switching software image (EMI) to support Layer 3 routing protocols.

Based on port density and certain functionality, you can use many Catalyst switches in more than one layer of a campus network. For example, because the Catalyst 3550 can offer a fixed 24 or 48-port 10/100BASE-T configuration with two Gigabit Ethernet uplinks, you might want to use it in wiring closets or the access layer to connect workgroups or hubs. The Gigabit Ethernet uplinks would then be links to distribution layer switches. In some cases, multiple access layer 2950 or 3550 switches can uplink into another 3550 at the distribution layer.

For larger campus networks, the Catalyst 4000/4500 and 6500 families offer high densities of Fast and Gigabit Ethernet for the distribution layer. A fully populated Catalyst 4006, for example, can support up to 30 Gigabit Ethernet ports or 240 10/100/1000BASE-T Ethernet ports. The Supervisor III or IV module provides both Cisco IOS Software and high-performance multilayer switching.

The Catalyst 6500 family offers much higher performance and port density that larger distribution layers can use. For example, the Catalyst 6513 can support up to 194 Gigabit Ethernet ports or 576 10/100 Ethernet ports. Multilayer switching is performed using an integrated Multilayer Switch Feature Card (MSFC), providing a throughput of up to 210 million packets per second.

Table 1-5 in the section "Product Summary" provides information on Cisco distribution layer switch products based on campus size.

Core Layer Switches

Recall the features required in core layer switches:

- Very high multilayer switching throughput
- No unnecessary packet manipulations (access lists and packet filtering), unless performed at wire speed
- Redundancy and resiliency for high availability
- Advanced QoS functionality

Devices in a campus network's core layer or backbone should be optimized for high-performance Layer 2 or Layer 3 switching. Because the core layer must handle large amounts of campus-wide data (due to the new 20/80 rule of traffic flow), the core layer should be designed with simplicity and efficiency in mind.

Small campus networks can use the Catalyst 3550 or 4000 family in the core layer. These switches provide reasonable port densities of Fast and Gigabit Ethernet to aggregate access layer uplinks. If the distribution and core layers are combined, both of these switch families can support multilayer switching in hardware.

Medium-sized and large campus networks can use the Catalyst 6500 family. Again, high port densities of Gigabit Ethernet are possible. This family of switches has high-performance, scalable switching from 32 Gbps to 256 Gbps. With the new Supervisor Engine 720, the performance is even greater at 720 Gbps! Layer 3 security, powerful QoS, and complete routing protocol support are available with the combination of Supervisor and MSFC modules, as well as the native Cisco IOS Software.

Table 1-5 in the section, "Product Summary," provides information on Cisco core layer switch products based on campus size.

Product Summary

As a quick review, see Table 1-5 for a summary of the various Catalyst switch families used for various applications. The table is broken down by campus network size and by campus network layer. The application of a particular switch in a network layer is a matter of choice and is not required. For example, if an access layer wiring closet in a small campus network has 200 users attached, choosing a single Catalyst 4000 might make more sense than several Catalyst 3550s. In this case, the size of the access layer workgroup dictates the choice of switch and port density more than the overall campus network size.

Table 1-5 *Summary of Catalyst Switch Products and Typical Layer Applications*

Campus Size	Layer	Catalyst Switch	Key Features
Any	Access	2950	< 50 users 10/100BASE T; 100BaseFX or 1000BASE-X uplinks
		3550	< 50 users 10/100BASE-T; 1000BASE-X uplinks
		4000/4500; (Sup III or IV)	< 250 users 10/100/1000BASE-T; 1000BASE-X uplinks
		6500	> 250 users 10/100/1000Base-T; 1000Base-X uplinks

continues

Table 1-5 *Summary of Catalyst Switch Products and Typical Layer Applications (Continued)*

Campus Size	Layer	Catalyst Switch	Key Features
Small Campus	Distribution	3550-12T (EMI)	up to 10 10/100/1000BASE-T access devices; 2 1000BASE-X uplinks; MLS
		3550-12G (EMI)	up to 10 1000BASE-X access devices; 2 10/100/1000BASE-T uplinks; MLS
		4006/4500 (Sup III or IV)	up to 30 1000BASE-X or 240 10/100/ 1000BASE-T access or core devices; MLS
		6500	High 100 and 1000BASE-X densities; high performance; MLS; scalable for future growth
	Core	Usually combined with distribution	
Medium Campus	Distribution	4006/4500 (Sup III or IV)	up to 30 1000BASE-X or 240 10/100/ 1000BASE-T access or core devices; MLS
		6500	High 100 and 1000BASE-X densities; high performance; MLS; scalable for future growth
	Core	6500	High 100 and 1000BASE-X densities; high performance; MLS; scalable for future growth
Large Campus	Distribution	6500	High 100 and 1000BASE-X densities; high performance; MLS; scalable for future growth
	Core	6500	High 100 and 1000BASE-X densities; high performance; MLS; scalable for future growth

Foundation Summary

The Foundation Summary is a collection of tables and figures that provides a convenient review of many key concepts in this chapter. If you are already comfortable with the topics in this chapter, this summary might help you recall a few details. If you just read this chapter, this review should help solidify some key facts. If you are doing your final preparation before the exam, the following tables and figures are a convenient way to review the day before the exam.

Table 1-6 *Layers of Data Communications*

OSI Layer	Protocol Data Unit	Mechanism to Process PDU
7 (application)		
6 (presentation)		
5 (session)		
4 (transport)	TCP segment	TCP port
3 (network)	Packet	Router
2 (data link)	Frame	Switch/bridge
1 (physical)		

Table 1-7 *Types of Network Services*

Service Type	Location of Service	Extent of Traffic Flow
Local	Same segment/VLAN as user	Access layer only
Remote	Different segment/VLAN as user	Access to distribution layers
Enterprise	Central to all campus users	Access to distribution to core layers

Table 1-8 *Comparison of Hierarchical Layers*

Layer	Attributes
Access	High port density to connect to end users, low cost, uplinks to higher layers of the campus network, and Layer 2 services (traffic filtering, VLAN membership, and basic QoS)
Distribution	Aggregation of access layer devices, high Layer 3 throughput, QoS features, security and policy-based functions, and scalable and resilient high-speed links into the core and access layers
Core	Fast data transport, no "expensive" Layer 3 processing, redundancy and resiliency for high availability, and advanced QoS

Table 1-9 *Catalyst Switches for the Access Layer*

Catalyst Model	Max Port Density	Uplinks	Max Backplane	Other Features
2950	12, 24, or 48 10/100	2 100FX or 1000BASE-X	13.6 Gbps	QoS, security
3550 (SMI)	24 or 48 10/100 or 12 10/100/1000BASE-T	2 1000BASE-X	24 Gbps (12-port), 13.6 Gbps (48-port), or 8.8 Gbps (24-port)	Advanced QoS, security, redundant power, inline power (24-port only)
4000/4500 (Sup III or IV)	240 10/100 or 10/100/ 1000BASE-T	100 or 1000BASE-X	64 Gbps	Advanced QoS, security, redundant power, inline power

Table 1-10 *Summary of Catalyst Switch Products and Typical Layer Applications*

Campus Size	Layer	Catalyst Switch	Key Features
Any	Access	2950	< 50 users 10/100BASE-T; 100BaseFX or 1000BASE-X uplinks
		3550	< 50 users 10/100BASE-T; 1000BASE-X uplinks
		4000/4500; (Sup III or IV)	< 250 users 10/100/1000BASE-T; 1000BASE-X uplinks
		6500	> 250 users 10/100/1000Base-T; 1000Base-X uplinks
Small Campus	Distribution	3550-12T (EMI)	up to 10 10/100/1000BASE-T access devices; 2 1000BASE-X uplinks; MLS
		3550-12G (EMI)	up to 10 1000BASE-X access devices; 2 10/100/1000BASE-T uplinks; MLS
		4006/4500 (Sup III or IV)	up to 30 1000BASE-X or 240 10/100/ 1000BASE-T access or core devices; MLS
		6500	High 100 and 1000BASE-X densities; high performance; MLS; scalable for future growth
	Core	Usually combined with distribution	

Table 1-10 *Summary of Catalyst Switch Products and Typical Layer Applications (Continued)*

Campus Size	Layer	Catalyst Switch	Key Features
Medium Campus	Distribution	4006/4500 (Sup III or IV)	up to 30 1000BASE-X or 240 10/100/ 1000BASE-T access or core devices; MLS
		6500	High 100 and 1000BASE-X densities; high performance; MLS; scalable for future growth
	Core	6500	High 100 and 1000BASE-X densities; high performance; MLS; scalable for future growth
Large Campus	Distribution	6500	High 100 and 1000BASE-X densities; high performance; MLS; scalable for future growth
	Core	6500	High 100 and 1000BASE-X densities; high performance; MLS; scalable for future growth

Q&A

The questions and scenarios in this book are more difficult than what you should experience on the actual exam. The questions do not attempt to cover more breadth or depth than the exam; however, they are designed to make sure that you know the answer. Rather than allowing you to derive the answers from clues hidden inside the questions themselves, the questions challenge your understanding and recall of the subject. Hopefully, these questions will help limit the number of exam questions on which you narrow your choices to two options and then guess.

You can find the answers to these questions in Appendix A.

1. For each layer of the OSI model, match the forwarding criteria used by a switch:

____ Layer 1	A. IP address
____ Layer 2	B. UDP/TCP port
____ Layer 3	C. None
____ Layer 4	D. MAC address

2. What is multilayer switching (MLS)?

3. Fill in the blanks in the following statement:

   In the 20/80 rule of networking, 20 percent of the traffic on a segment usually stays _____ while 80 percent travels _____.

4. What is a collision domain, and where does it exist in a switched LAN?

5. What is a broadcast domain, and where does it exist in a switched LAN?

6. What is a VLAN, and why is it used?

7. At what OSI Layer(s) do devices in the distribution layer usually operate?

8. What is network segmentation? When is it necessary, and how is it done in a campus network design?

9. Is it possible to use Layer 2 switches in the distribution layer, rather than Layer 3 switches? If so, what are the limitations?

10. Which of the following Cisco switch products should be used in a campus network's distribution layer? (Check all that apply.)

   a. Catalyst 2950

   b. Catalyst 3550 (SMI)

   c. Catalyst 3550 (EMI)

   d. Catalyst 4000/4500

   e. Catalyst 6500

11. When might you select a Catalyst 4000 to use in a wiring closet? What attributes make it a good choice?

12. Which Cisco switch family has the most scalable performance?

This chapter covers the following topics that you need to master for the CCNP BCMSN exam:

- **Modular Network Design**—This section covers the process of designing a campus network, based on breaking it into functional modules.

- **Sizing the Modules in a Network**—You also learn how to size and scale the modules in a design.

CHAPTER 2

Modular Network Design

This chapter presents a set of building blocks that can organize and streamline even a large, complex campus network. These building blocks can then be placed using several campus design models to provide maximum efficiency, functionality, and scalability.

"Do I Know This Already?" Quiz

The "Do I Know This Already?" quiz's purpose is to help you decide if you need to read the entire chapter. If you already intend to read the entire chapter, you do not necessarily need to answer these questions now.

The 12-question quiz, derived from the major sections in the "Foundation Topics" portion of the chapter, helps you determine how to spend your limited study time.

Table 2-1 outlines the major topics discussed in this chapter and the "Do I Know This Already?" quiz questions that correspond to those topics.

Table 2-1 *"Do I Know This Already?" Foundation Topics Section-to-Question Mapping*

Foundation Topics Section	Questions Covered in This Section
Modular Network Design	1–12

CAUTION The goal of self-assessment is to gauge your mastery of the topics in this chapter. If you do not know the answer to a question or are only partially sure of the answer, you should mark this question wrong. Giving yourself credit for an answer you correctly guess skews your self-assessment results and might provide you with a false sense of security.

1. What is the purpose of breaking a campus network down into a hierarchical design?

   a. To facilitate documentation

   b. To follow political or organizational policies

   c. To make the network predictable and scalable

   d. To make the network more redundant and secure

2. Which of the following are building blocks or modules used to build a scalable campus network? (Check all that apply.)

   a. Access block

   b. Distribution block

   c. Core block

   d. Server farm block

   e. Switch block

3. What are the components of a typical switch block?

   a. Access layer switches

   b. Distribution layer switches

   c. Core layer switches

   d. E-commerce servers

   e. Service provider switches

4. What are two types of core, or backbone, designs?

   a. Collapsed core

   b. Loop-free core

   c. Dual core

   d. Layered core

5. In a properly designed hierarchical network, a broadcast from one PC will be confined to what?

   a. One access layer switch port

   b. One access layer switch

   c. One switch block

   d. The entire campus network

6. What is the maximum number of access layer switches that can connect into a single distribution layer switch?

   a. 1

   b. 2

   c. Limited only by the number of ports on the access layer switch

   d. Limited only by the number of ports on the distribution switch

   e. Unlimited

7. A switch block should be sized according to what?

   a. The number of access layer users

   b. A maximum of 250 access layer users

   c. A study of the traffic patterns and flows

   d. The amount of rack space available

   e. The number of servers accessed by users

8. What evidence can be seen when a switch block is too large? (Choose all that apply.)

   a. IP address space is exhausted.

   b. You run out of access layer switch ports.

   c. Broadcast traffic becomes excessive.

   d. Traffic is throttled at the distribution layer switches.

   e. Network congestion occurs.

9. How many distribution switches should be built into each switch block?

   a. 1

   b. 2

   c. 4

   d. 8

10. What are the most important aspects to consider when designing the core layer in a large network? (Choose all that apply.)

    a. Low cost

    b. Switches that can efficiently forward traffic, even when every uplink is at 100 percent capacity

    c. High port density of high-speed ports

    d. A low number of Layer 3 routing peers

11. Which services are typically located at the enterprise edge block? (Choose all that apply.)

    a. Network management

    b. Intranet server farms

    c. VPN and remote access

    d. E-commerce servers

    e. End users

12. In a server farm block, where should redundancy be provided? (Choose all that apply.)

    a. Dual connections from each distribution switch to the core

    b. Dual connections from each access switch to the distribution switches

    c. Dual connections from each server to the access switches

    d. No redundancy is necessary

You can find the answers to the quiz in Appendix A, "Answers to Chapter 'Do I Know This Already?' Quizzes and Q&A Sections." The suggested choices for your next step are as follows:

- **6 or less overall score**—Read the entire chapter. This includes the "Foundation Topics," "Foundation Summary," and "Q&A" sections.

- **7–9 overall score**—Begin with the "Foundation Summary" section and then follow up with the "Q&A" section at the end of the chapter.

- **10 or more overall score**—If you want more review on these topics, skip to the "Foundation Summary" section and then go to the "Q&A" section at the end of the chapter. Otherwise, move on to Chapter 3, "Switch Operation."

Foundation Topics

Modular Network Design

Recall from Chapter 1 that a network is best constructed and maintained using a three-tiered hierarchical approach. Taking a given network and making it conform to a layered architecture might seem a little confusing.

You can design a campus network in a logical manner, using a modular approach. In this approach, each layer of the hierarchical network model can be broken down into basic functional units. These units, or modules, can then be sized appropriately and connected together, while allowing for future scalability and expansion.

You can divide enterprise campus networks into the following basic elements:

- **Switch block** — A group of access layer switches together with their distribution switches
- **Core block** — The campus network's backbone

Other related elements can exist. Although these elements don't contribute to the campus network's overall function, they can be designed separately and added to the network design. These elements are as follows:

- **Server Farm block** — A group of enterprise servers along with their access and distribution (layer) switches
- **Management block** — A group of network management resources along with their access and distribution switches.
- **Enterprise Edge block** — A collection of services related to external network access, along with their access and distribution switches.
- **Service Provider Edge block** — The external network services contracted or used by the enterprise network; these are the services with which the enterprise edge block interfaces.

The collection of all these elements is also known as the *enterprise composite network model*. Figure 2-1 shows a modular campus design's basic structure. Notice how each of the building-block elements can be confined to a certain area or function. Also notice how each is connected into the core block.

Figure 2-1 *Modular Approach to Campus Network Design*

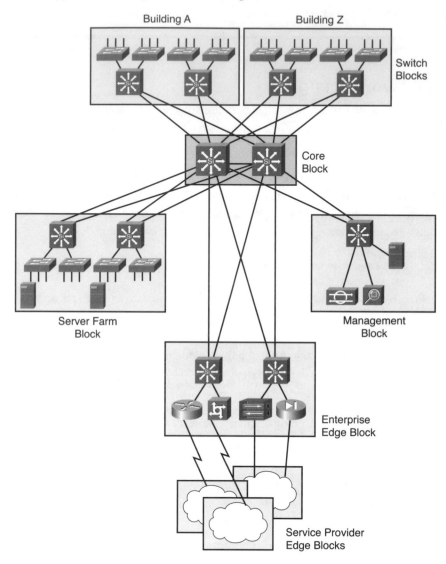

The Switch Block

Recall how a campus network is divided into access, distribution, and core layers. The switch block contains switching devices from the access and distribution layers. All switch blocks then connect into the core block, providing end-to-end connectivity across the campus.

Switch blocks contain a balanced mix of Layer 2 and Layer 3 functionality, as might be present in the access and distribution layers. Layer 2 switches located in wiring closets (access layer) connect end users to the campus network. With one end user per switch port, each user receives dedicated bandwidth access.

Upstream, each access layer switch connects to devices in the distribution layer. Here, Layer 2 functionality transports data between all connected access switches at a central connection point. Layer 3 functionality can also be provided in the form of routing and other networking services (security, quality of service (QoS), and so on). Therefore, a distribution layer device should be a multilayer switch. Layer 3 functionality is discussed in more detail in Chapter 13, "Multilayer Switching."

The distribution layer also shields the switch block from certain failures or conditions in other parts of the network. For example, broadcasts will not be propagated from the switch block into the core and other switch blocks. Therefore, the Spanning Tree Protocol (STP) will be confined to each switch block, where a virtual LAN (VLAN) is bounded, keeping the spanning tree domain well defined and controlled.

Access layer switches can support VLANs by assigning individual ports to specific VLAN numbers. In this way, stations connected to the ports configured for the same VLAN can also share the same Layer 3 subnet. However, be aware that a single VLAN can support multiple subnets. Because the switch ports are configured for a VLAN number only (and not a network address), any station connected to a port can present any subnet address range. The VLAN functions as traditional network media and allows any network address to connect.

In this network design model, you should not extend VLANs beyond distribution switches. The distribution layer should always be the boundary of VLANs, subnets, and broadcasts. Although Layer 2 switches can extend VLANs to other switches and other layers of the hierarchy, this activity is discouraged. VLAN traffic should not traverse the network core. (*Trunking*, or the capability to carry many VLANs over a single connection, is discussed in Chapter 6, "VLANs and Trunks.")

Sizing a Switch Block

Containing access and distribution layer devices, the switch block is simple in concept. You should consider several factors, however, to determine an appropriate size for the switch block. The range of available switch devices makes the switch block size very flexible. At the access layer, switch selection is usually based on port density or the number of connected users.

The distribution layer must be sized according to the number of access layer switches that are collapsed or brought into a distribution device. Consider the following factors:

- Traffic types and patterns
- Amount of Layer 3 switching capacity at the distribution layer
- Number of users connected to the access layer switches
- Geographical boundaries of subnets or VLANs
- Size of Spanning Tree domains

Designing a switch block based solely on the number of users or stations that are contained within the block is usually inaccurate. Usually, no more than 2000 users should be placed within a single switch block. Though useful for initially estimating a switch block's size, this idea doesn't take into account the many dynamic processes that occur on a functioning network.

Instead, switch block size should be primarily based on the following:

- Traffic types and behavior
- Size and number of common workgroups

Due to the dynamic nature of networks, you can size a switch block too large to handle the load that is placed upon it. Also, the number of users and applications on a network tends to grow over time. A provision to break up or downsize a switch block is necessary. Again, base these decisions on the actual traffic flows and patterns present in the switch block. You can estimate, model, or measure these parameters with network analysis applications and tools.

> **NOTE** The actual network analysis process is beyond the scope of this book. Traffic estimation, modeling, and measurement are complex procedures, each requiring its own dedicated analysis tool.

Generally, a switch block is too large if the following conditions are observed:

- The routers (multilayer switches) at the distribution layer become traffic bottlenecks. This congestion could be due to the volume of interVLAN traffic, intensive CPU processing, or switching times required by policy or security functions (access lists, queuing, and so on).
- Broadcast or multicast traffic slows down the switches in the switch block. Broadcast and multicast traffic must be replicated and forwarded out many ports. This process requires some overhead in the multilayer switch, which can become too great if significant traffic volumes are present.

Access switches can have one or more redundant link to distribution layer devices. This situation provides a fault-tolerant environment, where access layer connectivity is preserved on a secondary link if the primary link fails. In fact, because Layer 3 devices are used in the distribution layer, traffic can be load balanced across both redundant links using redundant gateways.

Generally, you should provide two distribution switches in each switch block for redundancy, with each access layer switch connecting to the two distribution switches. Then, each Layer 3 distribution switch can load balance traffic over its redundant links into the core layer (also Layer 3 switches) using routing protocols.

Figure 2-2 shows a typical switch block design. At Layer 3, the two distribution switches can use one of several redundant gateway protocols to provide an active IP gateway and a standby gateway at all times. These protocols are discussed in Chapter 14, "Router Redundancy and Load Balancing."

Figure 2-2 *Typical Switch Block Design*

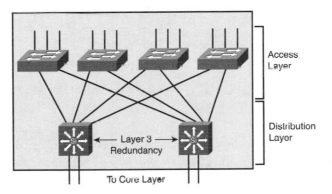

The Core Block

A core block is required to connect two or more switch blocks in a campus network. Because all traffic passing to and from all switch blocks, server farm blocks, and the enterprise edge block must cross the core block, the core must be as efficient and resilient as possible. The core is the campus network's basic foundation and carries much more traffic than any other block.

A network core can use any technology (frame, cell, or packet) to transport campus data. Many campus networks use Gigabit and 10 Gigabit Ethernet as a core technology. Ethernet core blocks are reviewed at length here.

Recall that both the distribution and core layers provide Layer 3 functionality. Individual IP subnets connect all distribution and core switches. At least two subnets should be used to provide resiliency and load balancing into the core; although, you can use a single VLAN. As VLANs end at the distribution layer, they are routed into the core.

The core block might consist of a single multilayer switch, taking in the two redundant links from the distribution layer switches. Due to the importance of the core block in a campus network, you should implement two or more identical switches in the core to provide redundancy.

The links between layers should also be designed to carry at least the amount of traffic load handled by the distribution switches. The links between core switches in the same core subnet should be of sufficient size to carry the aggregate amount of traffic coming into the core switch. Consider the average link utilization, but allow for future growth. An Ethernet core allows simple and scalable upgrades of magnitude; consider the progression from Ethernet to Fast Ethernet to Fast EtherChannel to Gigabit Ethernet to Gigabit EtherChannel, and so on.

Two basic core block designs are presented in the following sections, each designed around a campus network's size:

- Collapsed core
- Dual core

Collapsed Core

A collapsed core block is one where the hierarchy's core layer is collapsed into the distribution layer. Here, both distribution and core functions are provided within the same switch devices. This situation is usually found in smaller campus networks, where a separate core layer (and additional cost or performance) is not warranted.

Figure 2-3 shows the basic collapsed core design. Although the distribution and core layer functions are performed in the same device, keeping these functions distinct and properly designed is important. Note also that the collapsed core is not an independent building block but is integrated into the distribution layer of the individual standalone switch blocks.

In the collapsed core design, each access layer switch has a redundant link to each distribution and core layer switch. All Layer 3 subnets present in the access layer terminate at the distribution switches' Layer 3 ports, as in the basic switch block design. The distribution and core switches connect to each other by one or more link, completing a path to use during a redundancy failover.

Figure 2-3 *Collapsed Core Block Design*

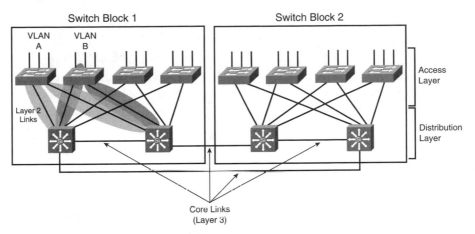

Connectivity between the distribution and core switches is accomplished using Layer 3 links (Layer 3 switch interfaces, with no inherent VLANs). The Layer 3 switches route traffic to and from each other directly. Figure 2-3 shows the extent of two VLANs. Notice that VLAN A and VLAN B each extend only from the access layer switches where their respective users are located down to the distribution layer over the Layer 2 uplinks. The VLANs terminate there because the distribution layer uses Layer 3 switching. This is good because it limits the broadcast domains, removes the possibility of Layer 2 bridging loops, and provides fast failover if one uplink fails.

At Layer 3, redundancy is provided through a redundant gateway protocol for IP (covered in Chapter 14). In some of the protocols, the two distribution switches provide a common default gateway address to the access layer switches, but only one is active at any time. In other protocols, the two switches can both be active, load balancing traffic. In the event of a distribution and core switch failure, connectivity to the core is maintained because the redundant Layer 3 switch is always available.

Dual Core

A dual core connects two or more switch blocks in a redundant fashion. Although the collapsed core can connect two switch blocks with some redundancy, the core is not scalable when more switch blocks are added. Figure 2-4 illustrates the dual core. Notice that this core appears as an independent module and is not merged into any other block or layer.

Figure 2-4 *Dual Network Core Design*

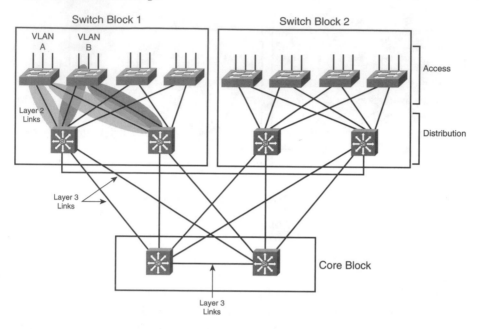

In the past, the dual core was usually built with Layer 2 switches to provide the simplest and most efficient throughput. Layer 3 switching was provided in the distribution layer. Multilayer switches have now become cost effective and offer high switching performance. Building a dual core with multilayer switches is both possible and recommended. The dual core uses two identical switches to provide redundancy. Redundant links connect each switch block's distribution layer portion to each of the dual core switches. The two core switches connect by a common link. In a Layer 2 core, the switches cannot be linked to avoid any bridging loops. A Layer 3 core uses routing rather than bridging, so bridging loops are not an issue.

In the dual core, each distribution switch has two equal-cost paths to the core, allowing the available bandwidth of both paths to be used simultaneously. Both paths remain active because the distribution and core layers use Layer 3 devices that can manage equal-cost paths in routing tables. The routing protocol in use determines the availability or loss of a neighboring Layer 3 device. If one switch fails, the routing protocol reroutes traffic using an alternate path through the remaining redundant switch.

Notice again in Figure 2-4 the extent of the access VLANs. Although Layer 3 devices have been added into a separate core layer, VLANs A and B still extend only from the Layer 2 access layer switches down to the distribution layer. Although the distribution layer switches use Layer 3 switch interfaces to provide Layer 3 functionality to the access layer, these links actually pass traffic only at Layer 2.

Core Size in a Campus Network

The dual core is made up of redundant switches, and is bounded and isolated by Layer 3 devices. Routing protocols determine paths and maintain the core's operation. As with any network, you must pay some attention to the overall design of the routers and routing protocols in the network. Because routing protocols propagate updates throughout the network, network topologies might be undergoing change. The network's size (the number of routers) then affects routing protocol performance as updates are exchanged and network convergence takes place.

Although the network shown previously in Figure 2-4 might look small with only two switch blocks of two Layer 3 switches (route processors within the distribution layer switches) each, large campus networks can have many switch blocks connected into the core block. If you think of each multilayer switch as a router, you will recall that each route processor must communicate with and keep information about each of its directly connected peers. Most routing protocols have practical limits on the number of peer routers that can be directly connected on a point-to-point or multiaccess link. In a network with a large number of switch blocks, the number of connected routers can grow quite large. Should you be concerned about a core switch peering with too many distribution switches?

No, because the actual number of directly connected peers is quite small, regardless of the campus network size. Access layer VLANs terminate at the distribution layer switches. The only peering routers at that boundary are pairs of distribution switches, each providing routing redundancy for each of the access layer VLAN subnets. At the distribution and core boundary, each distribution switch connects to only two core switches over Layer 3 switch interfaces. Therefore, only pairs of router peers are formed.

When multilayer switches are used in the distribution and core layers, the routing protocols running in both layers regard each pair of redundant links between layers as equal-cost paths. Traffic is routed across both links in a load-sharing fashion, utilizing the bandwidth of both.

One final core layer design point is to scale the core switches to match the incoming load. At a minimum, each core switch must handle switching each of its incoming distribution links at 100 percent capacity.

Other Building Blocks

Other resources in the campus network can be identified and pulled into the building block model. For example, a server farm can be made up of servers running applications that are accessed by users from all across the enterprise. Most likely, those servers need to be scalable for future expansion, need to be need to be highly accessible, and need to benefit from traffic and security policy control.

To meet these needs, you can group the resources into building blocks that are structured and placed just like regular switch block modules. These blocks should have a distribution layer of switches and redundant uplinks directly into the core layer, and should contain enterprise resources.

A list of the most common examples follows. Refer back to Figure 2-1 to see how each of these are grouped and connected into the campus network. Most of these building blocks are present in medium and large campus networks. Be familiar with the concept of pulling an enterprise function into its own switch block, as well as the structure of that block.

Server Farm Block

Any server or application accessed by most of the enterprise users usually already belongs to a server farm. The entire server farm can be identified as its own switch block and given a layer of access switches uplinked to dual distribution switches (multilayer). Connect these distribution switches into the core layer with redundant high-speed links.

Individual servers can have single network connections to one of the distribution switches. However, this presents a single point of failure. If a redundant server is used, it should connect to the alternate distribution switch. Another more resilient approach is to give each server dual network connections, one going to each distribution switch. This is known as *dual-homing* the servers.

Examples of enterprise servers include corporate e-mail, intranet services, Enterprise Resource Planning (ERP) applications, and mainframe systems. Notice that each of these is an internal resource that would normally be located inside a firewall or secured perimeter.

Network Management Block

Often, campus networks must be monitored through the use of network management tools so that performance and fault conditions can be measured and detected. You can group the entire suite of network management applications into a single network management switch block. This is the reverse of a server farm block because the network management tools are not enterprise resources accessed by most of the users. Rather, these tools go out to access other network devices, application servers, and user activity in all other areas of the campus network.

The network management switch block usually has a distribution layer that connects into the core switches. Because these tools are used to detect equipment and connectivity failures, availability is important. Redundant links and redundant switches should be used.

Examples of network management resources in this switch block include the following:

- Network monitoring applications
- System logging (syslog) servers
- Authentication, authorization, and accounting (AAA) servers
- Policy management applications
- System administration and remote control services
- Intrusion detection management applications

> **NOTE** You can easily gather network management resources into a single switch block to centralize these functions. Each switch and router in the network must have an IP address assigned for management purposes. In the past, it was easy to "centralize" all these management addresses and traffic into a single "management" VLAN, which extended from one end of the campus to the other.
>
> The end-to-end VLAN concept is now considered a poor practice. VLANs should be isolated, as described in Chapter 1. Therefore, assigning management addresses to as many VLANs or subnets as is practical and appropriate for a campus network is now acceptable.

Enterprise Edge Block

At some point, most campus networks must connect to service providers for access to external resources. This is usually known as the *edge* of the enterprise or campus network. These resources are available to the entire campus and should be centrally accessible as an independent switch block connected to the network core.

Edge services are usually divided into these categories:

- **Internet access**—Supports outbound traffic to the Internet, as well as inbound traffic to public services, such as e-mail and extranet web servers. This connectivity is provided by one or more Internet service provider (ISP). Network security devices are generally placed here.

- **Remote access and VPN**—Supports inbound dialup access for external or roaming users through the Public Switched Telephone Network (PSTN). If voice traffic is supported over the campus network, Voice over IP (VoIP) gateways connect to the PSTN here. In addition, virtual private network (VPN) devices connected to the Internet support secure tunneled connections to remote locations.

- **E-commerce**—Supports all related web, application, and database servers and applications, as well as firewalls and security devices. This switch block connects to one or more ISPs.

- **WAN access**—Supports all traditional WAN connections to remote sites. This can include Frame Relay, ATM, leased line, ISDN, and so on.

Service Provider Edge Block

Each service provider that connects to an enterprise network must also have a hierarchical network design of its own. A service provider network meets an enterprise at the service provider edge, connecting to the enterprise edge block.

Studying a service provider network's structure isn't necessary because it should follow the same design principles presented here. In other words, a service provider is just another enterprise or campus network itself. Just be familiar with the fact that a campus network has an edge block, where it connects to the edge of each service provider's network.

Can I Use Layer 2 Distribution Switches?

This chapter covered the best practice design that places Layer 3 switches at both the core and distribution layers. What would happen if you could not afford Layer 3 switches at the distribution layer?

Figure 2-5 shows the dual-core campus network with Layer 2 distribution switches. Notice how each access VLAN extends not only throughout the switch block but also into the core. This is because the VLAN terminates at a Layer 3 boundary present only in the core. As an example, VLAN A's propagation is shaded in the figure.

Figure 2-5 *Design Using Layer 2 Distribution Switches*

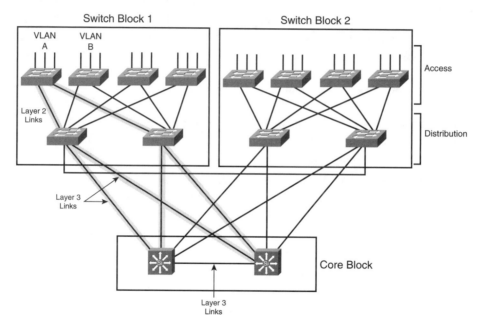

Here are some implications with this design:

■ Redundant Layer 3 gateways can still be used in the core.

■ Each VLAN propagates across the redundant trunk links from the access to the core layers. Because of this, Layer 2 bridging loops form.

- The STP must run in all layers to prevent Layer 2 loops. This causes traffic on some links to be blocked. As a result, only one of every two access layer switch uplinks can be used at any time.

- When Layer 2 uplinks go down, the STP can take several seconds to unblock redundant links, causing downtime.

- Access VLANs can propagate from one end of the campus to the other, if necessary.

- Broadcast traffic on any access layer VLAN also reaches into the core layer. Bandwidth on uplinks and within the core can be unnecessarily wasted.

Foundation Summary

The Foundation Summary is a collection of tables, figures, lists, and other information that provides a convenient review of many key concepts in this chapter. If you are already comfortable with the topics in this chapter, this summary might help you recall a few details. If you just read this chapter, this review should help solidify some key facts. If you are doing your final preparation before the exam, the following information is a convenient way to review the day before the exam.

A campus network can be logically divided into these building blocks:

- **Switch block**—A group of access layer switches together with their distribution switches.
- **Core block**—The campus network's backbone.
- **Server Farm block**—A group of enterprise servers along with their access and distribution layer switches.
- **Management block**—A group of network management resources along with their access and distribution switches.
- **Enterprise Edge block**—A collection of services related to external network access, along with their access and distribution switches.
- **Service Provider Edge block**—The external network services contracted or used by the enterprise network; these are the services with which the enterprise edge block interfaces.

Other than the core block, each switch block should have the following characteristics:

- Switches that form an access layer
- Dual distribution switches
- Redundant connections into the access and core layers

The most important factors to consider when choosing a switch block's size are as follows:

- The number of users connected to the access layer switches
- The extent of the access VLAN or subnet
- Multilayer switching capacity of the distribution switches in the switch block
- The types, patterns, and volume of traffic passing through the switch block

The core layer in a campus network can be designed as follows:

■ **Collapsed core**—The distribution and core layer switches are combined. This is usually acceptable in a small to medium-sized network.

■ **Dual core**—The distribution and core layers are separate; the core layer consists of dual or redundant multilayer switches.

Q&A

The questions and scenarios in this book are more difficult than what you should experience on the actual exam. The questions do not attempt to cover more breadth or depth than the exam; however, they are designed to make sure that you know the answer. Rather than allowing you to derive the answers from clues hidden inside the questions themselves, the questions challenge your understanding and recall of the subject. Hopefully, these questions will help limit the number of exam questions on which you narrow your choices to two options and then guess.

You can find the answers to these questions in Appendix A.

1. Where is the most appropriate place to connect a block of enterprise (internal) servers? Why?

2. How can you provide redundancy at the switch and core block layers? (Consider physical means, as well as functional methods using protocols, algorithms, and so on.)

3. What factors should you consider when sizing a switch block?

4. What are the signs of an oversized switch block?

5. What are the attributes and issues of having a collapsed core block?

6. How many switches are sufficient in a core block design?

7. What building blocks are used to build a scalable campus network?

8. What are two types of core, or backbone, designs?

9. Why should links and services provided to remote sites be grouped in a distinct building block?

10. Why should network management applications and servers be placed in a distinct building block?

PART II: Building a Campus Network

Chapter 3   Switch Operation

Chapter 4   Switch Configuration

Chapter 5   Switch Port Configuration

Chapter 6   VLANs and Trunks

Chapter 7   VLAN Trunking Protocol (VTP)

Chapter 8   Aggregating Switch Links

Chapter 9   Traditional Spanning Tree Protocol

Chapter 10   Spanning Tree Configuration

Chapter 11   Protecting the Spanning Tree Protocol Topology

Chapter 12   Advanced Spanning Tree Protocol

This part of the book covers the following BCMSN exam topics:

- Describe the physical, data-link, and network layer technologies used in a switched network, and identify when to use each.

- Explain the function of the Switching Database Manager within a Catalyst switch.

- Describe the features and operation of VLANs on a switched network.

- Describe the features of the VLAN trunking protocols, including 802.1Q, ISL, and dynamic trunking protocol.
- Describe the features and operation of 802.1Q Tunneling (802.1QinQ) within a service provider network.
- Describe the operation and purpose of managed VLAN services.
- Describe how VTP versions 1 and 2 operate, including domains, modes, advertisements, and pruning.
- Explain the function of the Switching Database Manager (CAM and TCAM) within a Catalyst switch
- Explain the operation and purpose of the Spanning Tree Protocol (STP) on a switched network.
- Describe Transparent LAN Services in a service provider network.
- Configure access ports for static and multi-VLAN membership.
- Configure and verify 802.1Q trunks.
- Configure and verify ISL trunks.
- Configure VTP domains in server, client, and transparent modes.
- Enable Spanning Tree on ports and VLANs.
- Configure Spanning Tree parameters including port priority, VLAN priority, Root Bridge, BPDU Guard, PortFast, and UplinkFast.
- Configure Fast and Gigabit EtherChannel to increase bandwidth for interswitch connections.
- Design a VLAN configuration with VTP to work for a given specific scenario.
- Select multilayer switching architectures, given specific multilayer switching needs.

This chapter covers the following topics that you need to master for the CCNP BCMSN exam:

- **Layer 2 Switch Operation**—This section describes the functionality of a switch that forwards Ethernet frames.

- **Multilayer Switch Operation**—This section describes the mechanisms that forward packets at OSI Layers 3 and 4.

- **Tables Used in Switching**—This section explains how tables of information and computation are used to make switching decisions. Coverage focuses on the Content Addressable Memory table, involved in Layer 2 forwarding, and the Ternary Content Addressable Memory, used in Layers 2 through 4 packet-handling decisions.

- **Troubleshooting Switching Tables**—This section reviews the Catalyst commands that you can use to monitor the switching tables and memory. These commands can be useful when troubleshooting or tracing the sources of data or problems in a switched network.

CHAPTER 3

Switch Operation

To have a good understanding of the many features that you can configure on a Catalyst switch, you should first understand the fundamentals of the switching function itself.

This chapter serves as a primer, describing how an Ethernet switch works. It presents Layer 2 forwarding, along with the hardware functions that make forwarding possible. Multilayer switching is also explained. A considerable portion of the chapter deals with the memory architecture that performs switching at Layers 3 and 4 both flexibly and efficiently. This chapter also provides a brief overview of useful switching table management commands.

"Do I Know This Already?" Quiz

The purpose of the "Do I Know This Already?" quiz is to help you decide if you need to read the entire chapter. If you already intend to read the entire chapter, you do not necessarily need to answer these questions now.

The 12-question quiz, derived from the major sections in the "Foundation Topics" portion of the chapter, helps you determine how to spend your limited study time.

Table 3-1 outlines the major topics discussed in this chapter and the "Do I Know This Already?" quiz questions that correspond to those topics.

Table 3-1 *"Do I Know This Already?" Foundation Topics Section-to-Question Mapping*

Foundation Topics Section	Questions Covered in This Section
Layer 2 Switch Operation	1–5
Multilayer Switch Operation	6–9
Switching Tables	10–11
Troubleshooting Switching Tables	12

> **CAUTION** The goal of self-assessment is to gauge your mastery of the topics in this chapter. If you do not know the answer to a question or are only partially sure of the answer, you should mark this question wrong. Giving yourself credit for an answer you correctly guess skews your self-assessment results and might provide you with a false sense of security.

1. Which of these performs transparent bridging?

    a. Ethernet hub

    b. Layer 2 switch

    c. Layer 3 switch

    d. Router

2. When a PC is connected to a Layer 2 switch port, how far does the collision domain spread?

    a. No collision domain exists.

    b. One switch port.

    c. One VLAN.

    d. All ports on the switch.

3. What information is used to forward frames in a Layer 2 switch?

    a. Source MAC address

    b. Destination MAC address

    c. Source switch port

    d. IP addresses

4. What does a switch do if a MAC address can't be found in the CAM table?

    a. The frame is forwarded to the default port.

    b. The switch generates an ARP request for the address.

    c. The switch floods the frame out all ports (except the receiving port).

    d. The switch drops the frame.

5. In the Catalyst 6500, frames can be filtered with access lists for security and QoS purposes. This filtering occurs according to which of the following?

   a. Before a CAM table lookup

   b. After a CAM table lookup

   c. Simultaneously with a CAM table lookup

   d. According to how the access lists are configured

6. Access list contents can be merged into which of the following?

   a. A CAM table

   b. A TCAM table

   c. A FIB table

   d. An ARP table

7. Multilayer switches using CEF are based on which of these techniques?

   a. Route caching

   b. Netflow switching

   c. Topology-based switching

   d. Demand-based switching

8. Which answer describes multilayer switching with CEF?

   a. The first packet is routed, and then the flow is cached.

   b. The switch supervisor CPU forwards each packet.

   c. The switching hardware learns station addresses and builds a routing database.

   d. A single database of routing information is built for the switching hardware.

9. In a switch, frames are placed in which buffer after forwarding decisions are made?

   a. Ingress queues

   b. Egress queues

   c. CAM table

   d. TCAM

10. What size are the mask and pattern fields in a TCAM entry?

    a. 64 bits

    b. 128 bits

    c. 134 bits

    d. 168 bits

11. Access list rules are compiled as TCAM entries. When a packet is matched against an access list, in what order are the TCAM entries evaluated?

    a. Sequentially in the order of the original access list.

    b. Numerically by the access list number.

    c. Alphabetically by the access list name.

    d. All entries are evaluated in parallel.

12. Which Catalyst 3550 command can you use to display the addresses in the CAM table?

    a. show cam

    b. show mac address-table

    c. show mac

    d. show cam address-table

You can find the answers to the quiz in Appendix A, "Answers to Chapter 'Do I Know This Already?' Quizzes and Q & A Sections." The suggested choices for your next step are as follows:

- **7 or less overall score**—Read the entire chapter. This includes the "Foundation Topics," "Foundation Summary," and the "Q&A" section.

- **8–10 overall score**—Begin with the "Foundation Summary" section and then follow up with the "Q&A" section at the end of the chapter.

- **11 or more overall score**—If you want more review on these topics, skip to the "Foundation Summary" section and then go to the "Q&A" section at the end of the chapter. Otherwise, move on to Chapter 4, "Switch Configuration."

Foundation Topics

Layer 2 Switch Operation

Recall that with shared Ethernet networks using hubs, many hosts are connected to a single broadcast and collision domain. In other words, shared Ethernet media operates at OSI Layer 1.

Each host must share the available bandwidth with every other connected host. When more than one host tries to talk at one time, a collision occurs, and everyone must back off and wait to talk again. This forces every host to operate in half-duplex mode, by either talking *or* listening at any given time. In addition, when one host sends a frame, all connected hosts hear it. When one host generates a frame with errors, everyone hears that, too.

At its most basic level, an Ethernet switch provides isolation from other connected hosts in several ways:

- The collision domain's scope is severely limited. On each switch port, the collision domain consists of the switch port itself and the devices directly connected to that port—either a single host or if a shared-media hub is connected, the set of hosts connected to the hub.

- Host connections can operate in full-duplex mode because there is no contention on the media. Hosts can talk *and* listen at the same time.

- Bandwidth is no longer shared. Instead, each switch port offers dedicated bandwidth across a switching fabric to another switch port. (These connections change dynamically.)

- Errors in frames are not propagated. Each frame received on a switch port is checked for errors. Good frames are regenerated when they are forwarded or transmitted. This is known as *store-and-forward* switching technology, where packets are received, stored for inspection, and then forwarded.

- You can limit broadcast traffic to a volume threshold.

- Other types of intelligent filtering or forwarding become possible.

Transparent Bridging

A switch is basically a multiport transparent bridge, where each switch port is its own Ethernet LAN segment, isolated from the others. Frame forwarding is based completely on the MAC addresses contained in each frame, such that the switch won't forward a frame unless it knows the destination's location. (In cases where the switch doesn't know where the destination is, it makes some safe assumptions.) Figure 3-1 shows the progression from a two-port to a multiport transparent bridge, and then to a switch.

Figure 3-1 *A Comparison of Transparent Bridges and Switches*

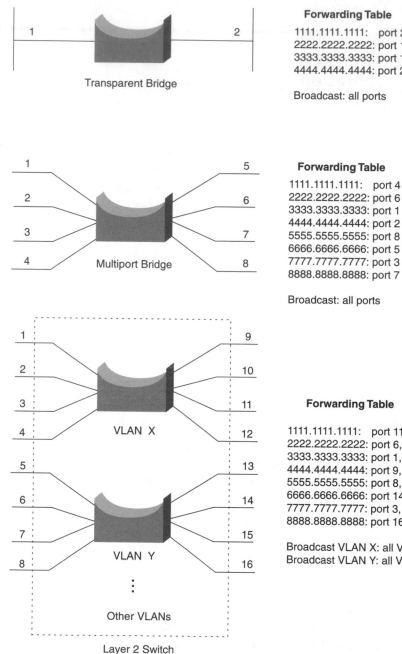

Forwarding Table

1111.1111.1111:   port 2
2222.2222.2222: port 1
3333.3333.3333: port 1
4444.4444.4444: port 2

Broadcast: all ports

Transparent Bridge

Forwarding Table

1111.1111.1111:   port 4
2222.2222.2222: port 6
3333.3333.3333: port 1
4444.4444.4444: port 2
5555.5555.5555: port 8
6666.6666.6666: port 5
7777.7777.7777: port 3
8888.8888.8888: port 7

Broadcast: all ports

Multiport Bridge

VLAN X

Forwarding Table

1111.1111.1111:   port 11, vlan X
2222.2222.2222: port 6, vlan Y
3333.3333.3333: port 1, vlan X
4444.4444.4444: port 9, vlan X
5555.5555.5555: port 8, vlan Y
6666.6666.6666: port 14, vlan Y
7777.7777.7777: port 3, vlan X
8888.8888.8888: port 16, vlan Y

Broadcast VLAN X: all VLAN X ports
Broadcast VLAN Y: all VLAN Y ports

VLAN Y

Other VLANs

Layer 2 Switch

The entire process of forwarding Ethernet frames then becomes figuring out what MAC addresses connect to which switch ports. A switch must either be told explicitly where hosts are located, or it must learn this information for itself. You can configure MAC address locations through a switch's command-line interface, but this quickly gets out of control when there are many stations on the network or when stations move around.

To dynamically learn about station locations, a switch listens to incoming frames and keeps a table of address information. As a frame is received on a switch port, the switch inspects the source MAC address. If that address is not in the address table already, the MAC address, switch port, and Virtual LAN (VLAN) on which it arrived are recorded in the table. Learning the address locations of the incoming packets is easy and straightforward.

Incoming frames also include the destination MAC address. Again, the switch looks this address up in the address table, hoping to find the switch port and VLAN where the address is attached. If it is found, the frame can be forwarded on out that switch port. If the address is not found in the table, the switch must take more drastic action—the frame is forwarded in a "best effort" fashion by *flooding* it out all switch ports assigned to the source VLAN. This is known as *unknown unicast flooding*, where the unicast destination location is unknown. Figure 3-2 illustrates this process, using only a single VLAN for simplification.

A switch constantly listens to incoming frames on each of its ports, learning source MAC addresses. However, be aware that the learning process is allowed only when the Spanning Tree Protocol (STP) algorithm has decided a port is stable for normal use. STP is concerned only with maintaining a loop-free network, where frames will not be recursively forwarded. If a loop were to form, a flooded frame could follow the looped path, where it would be flooded again and again.

In a similar manner, frames containing a broadcast or multicast destination address are also flooded. These destination addresses are not unknown—the switch knows them well. They are destined for multiple locations, so they must be flooded by definition. In the case of multicast addresses, flooding is performed by default. Other more elegant means of determining the destination locations are available and are discussed in Chapter 15, "Multicast."

Follow That Frame!

You should have a basic understanding of the operations that a frame undergoes as it passes through a Layer 2 switch. This helps you get a firm grasp on how to configure the switch for complex functions. Figure 3-3 shows a typical Layer 2 Catalyst switch and the decision processes that take place to forward each frame.

Figure 3-2 *Unknown Unicast Flooding*

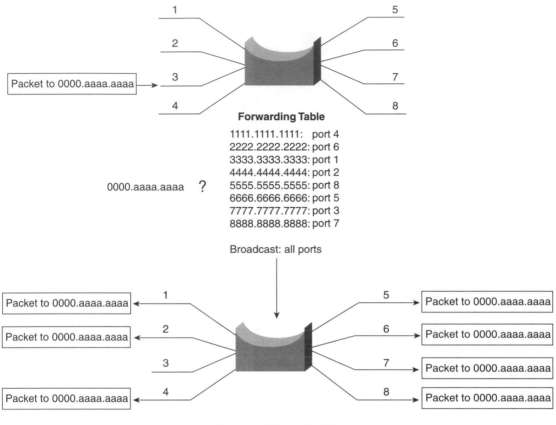

Unknown Unicast Flooding

When a frame arrives at a switch port, it is placed into one of the port's ingress queues. The queues can each contain frames to be forwarded, each queue having a different priority or service level. The switch port can then be fine-tuned so that important frames get processed and forwarded before less-important frames. This can prevent time-critical data from being "lost in the shuffle" during a flurry of incoming traffic.

Figure 3-3   *Operations Within a Layer 2 Catalyst Switch*

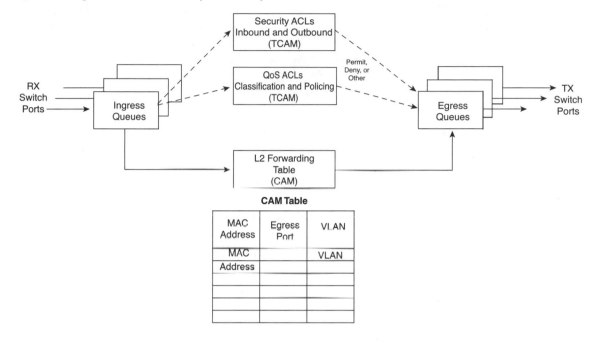

As the ingress queues are serviced and a frame is pulled off, the switch must figure out not only *where* to forward the frame but also *if* it should be forwarded and *how.* There are three fundamental decisions to be made—one concerned with finding the egress switch port, and two concerned with forwarding policies. All of these decisions are made *simultaneously* by independent portions of switching hardware and can be described as follows:

- **L2 Forwarding Table**   The frame's destination MAC address is used as an index, or key, into the Content Addressable Memory (CAM) or address table. If the address is found, the egress switch port and the appropriate VLAN ID are read from the table. (If the address is not found, the frame is marked for flooding so that it is forwarded out every switch port in the VLAN.)

- **Security ACLs**—Access control lists (ACLs) can be used to identify frames according to their MAC addresses, protocol types (for non-IP frames), IP addresses, protocols, and Layer 4 port numbers. The Ternary Content Addressable Memory (TCAM) contains ACLs in a compiled form, such that a decision can be made on whether to forward a frame in a single table lookup.

- **QoS ACLs**—Other ACLs can classify incoming frames according to quality of service (QoS) parameters, to police or control the rate of traffic flows, and to mark QoS parameters in outbound frames. The TCAM is also used to make these decisions in a single table lookup.

The CAM and TCAM tables are discussed in greater detail in the "CAM" and "TCAM" sections later in this chapter. After the CAM and TCAM table lookups have occurred, the frame is placed into the appropriate egress queue on the appropriate outbound switch port. The egress queue is determined by QoS values either contained in the frame or passed along with the frame. Like the ingress queues, the egress queues are serviced according to importance or time criticality; frames are sent out without being delayed by other outbound traffic.

Multilayer Switch Operation

Catalyst switches, such as the 3550 (with the appropriate Cisco IOS Software image), 4500, and 6500, can also forward frames based on Layer 3 and 4 information contained in packets. This is known as *multilayer switching (MLS)*. Naturally, Layer 2 switching is performed at the same time, because even the higher layer encapsulations are still contained in Ethernet frames.

Types of Multilayer Switching

Catalyst switches have supported two basic generations or types of MLS—route caching (first generation MLS) and topology-based (second generation MLS). This section presents an overview of both, although only the second generation is supported in the Cisco IOS Software-based Catalyst 3550, 4500, and 6500 switch families. You should understand the two types, as well as the differences between them:

- **Route caching**—The first generation of MLS, requiring a route processor (RP) and a switch engine (SE). The RP must process a traffic flow's first packet to determine the destination. The SE listens to the first packet and to the resulting destination, and sets up a "shortcut" entry in its MLS cache. The SE forwards subsequent packets in the same traffic flow based on shortcut entries in its cache.

  This type of MLS is also known by the names *Netflow LAN switching, flow-based* or *demand-based switching*, and "*route once, switch many.*" Even if this isn't used to forward packets in IOS-based Catalyst switches, the technique still generates traffic flow information and statistics.

- **Topology-based**—The second generation of MLS, utilizing specialized hardware. Layer 3 routing information builds and prepopulates a single database of the entire network topology. This database, an efficient table lookup in hardware, is consulted so that packets can be forwarded at high rates. The longest match found in the database is used as the correct Layer 3 destination. As the routing topology changes over time, the database contained in the hardware can be updated dynamically with no performance penalty.

This type of MLS is known as *Cisco Express Forwarding (CEF)*, where a routing process running on the switch downloads the current routing table database into the *Forwarding Information Base (FIB)* area of hardware. CEF is discussed in greater detail in Chapter 13, "Multilayer Switching."

Follow That Packet!

The path that a Layer 3 packet follows through a multilayer switch is similar to that of a Layer 2 switch. Obviously, some means of making a Layer 3 forwarding decision must be added. Beyond that, several sometimes-unexpected things can happen to packets as they are forwarded.

Figure 3-4 shows a typical multilayer switch and the decision processes that must occur. Packets arriving on a switch port are placed in the appropriate ingress queue, just as in a Layer 2 switch.

Each packet is pulled off an ingress queue and inspected for both Layer 2 and Layer 3 destination addresses. Now, the decision *where* to forward the packet is based on two address tables, whereas the decision *how* to forward the packet is still based on access list results. Like Layer 2 switching, all these multilayer decisions are performed simultaneously in hardware:

- **L2 Forwarding Table**—The destination MAC address is used as an index to the CAM table. If the frame contains a Layer 3 packet to be forwarded, the destination MAC address is that of a Layer 3 port on the switch. In this case, the CAM table results are used only to decide that the frame should be processed at Layer 3.

- **L3 Forwarding Table**—The FIB table is consulted, using the destination IP address as an index. The longest match in the table is found (both address and mask), and the resulting next-hop Layer 3 address is obtained. The FIB also contains each next-hop entry's Layer 2 MAC address and the egress switch port (and VLAN ID), so that further table lookups are not necessary.

- **Security ACLs**—Inbound and outbound access lists are compiled into TCAM entries so that decisions whether to forward a packet can be determined as a single table lookup.

- **QoS ACLs**—Packet classification, policing, and marking can all be performed as single table lookups in the QoS TCAM.

Figure 3-4   *Operations Within a MultiLayer Catalyst Switch*

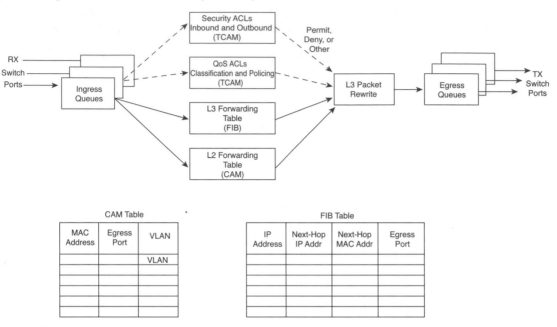

As with Layer 2 switching, the packet must be finally placed in the appropriate egress queue on the appropriate egress switch port.

However, recall that during the multilayer switching process, the next-hop destination was obtained from the FIB table—just as a router would do. The Layer 3 address identified the next hop and found its Layer 2 address. Only the Layer 2 address would be used so that the Layer 2 frames could be sent on.

The next-hop Layer 2 address must be put into the frame in place of the original destination address (the multilayer switch). The frame's Layer 2 source address must also become that of the multilayer switch before it is sent on to the next hop. As any good router must do, the Time-To-Live (TTL) value in the Layer 3 packet must be decremented by one.

Because the contents of the Layer 3 packet (the TTL value) have changed, the Layer 3 header checksum must be recalculated. And because both Layer 2 and 3 contents have changed, the Layer 2 checksum must be recalculated. In other words, the entire Ethernet frame must be rewritten before it goes into the egress queue. This is also accomplished efficiently in hardware.

Multilayer Switching Exceptions

To forward packets using the simultaneous decision processes described in the preceding section, the packet must be "MLS-ready" and require no additional decisions. For example, CEF can directly forward most IP packets between hosts. This occurs when the source and destination addresses (both MAC and IP) are already known, and no other IP parameters must be manipulated.

Other packets cannot be directly forwarded by CEF and must be handled in more detail. This is done by a quick inspection during the forwarding decisions. If a packet meets criteria such as the following, it is flagged for further processing and sent to the switch CPU for *process switching*:

- ARP requests and replies
- IP packets requiring a response from a router (TTL has expired, MTU is exceeded, fragmentation is needed, and so on)
- IP broadcasts that will be relayed as unicast (DHCP requests, IP helper-address functions)
- Routing protocol updates
- Cisco Discovery Protocol packets
- IPX routing protocol and service advertisements
- Packets needing encryption
- Packets triggering Network Address Translation (NAT)
- Other non-IP and non-IPX protocol packets (AppleTalk, DECnet, and so on)

NOTE   On the Catalyst 6500, both IP and IPX packets are CEF switched in hardware. All other protocols are handled by process switching on the MSFC module (the routing CPU). On the Catalyst 4500, only IP packets are CEF switched. All other routable protocols, including IPX, are flagged for process switching by the switch CPU.

With the Catalyst 3550, only IP is CEF switched in hardware. Other non-IP protocols are not routed at all. Instead, they are flagged for *fallback bridging*, where they are treated as transparently bridged (Layer 2 switched) packets. An external router or multilayer switch must handle any routing that is still needed during fallback bridging.

Tables Used in Switching

Catalyst switches maintain several types of tables to be used in the switching process. The tables are tailored for Layer 2 switching or MLS, and are kept in very fast memory so that many fields within a frame or packet can be compared in parallel.

Content Addressable Memory (CAM)

All Catalyst switch models use a Content Addressable Memory (CAM) table for Layer 2 switching. As frames arrive on switch ports, the source MAC addresses are learned and recorded in the CAM table. The port of arrival and the VLAN are both recorded in the table, along with a timestamp. If a MAC address learned on one switch port has moved to a different port, the MAC address and timestamp are recorded for the most recent arrival port. Then, the previous entry is deleted. If a MAC address is found already present in the table for the correct arrival port, only its timestamp is updated.

Switches generally have large CAM tables so that many addresses can be looked up for frame forwarding. However, there is not enough table space to hold every possible address on large networks. To manage the CAM table space, *stale entries* (addresses that have not been heard from for a period of time) are aged out. By default, idle CAM table entries are kept for 300 seconds before they are deleted. You can change the default setting using the following configuration command:

```
Switch(config)# mac address-table aging-time seconds
```

By default, MAC addresses are learned dynamically from incoming frames. You can also configure static CAM table entries that contain MAC addresses that might not otherwise be learned. To do this, use the following configuration command:

```
Switch(config)# mac address-table static mac-address vlan vlan-id interface type mod/num
```

Here, the MAC address (in dotted triplet hex format) is identified with the switch port and VLAN where it appears.

> **NOTE**   Until Catalyst IOS version 12.1(11)EA1, the syntax for CAM table commands used the keywords **mac-address-table**. In more recent IOS versions, the syntax has changed to use the keywords **mac address-table** (first hyphen omitted).

What happens when a host's MAC address is learned on one switch port, and then the host moves so that it appears on a different switch port? Ordinarily, the host's original CAM table entry would have to age out after 300 seconds, while its address was learned on the new port. To avoid having duplicate CAM table entries, a switch purges any existing entries for a MAC address that has just been learned on a different switch port. This is a safe assumption because MAC addresses are unique, and a single host should never be seen on more than one switch port unless problems exist in the network. If a switch notices that a MAC address is being learned on alternating switch ports, it generates an error message that flags the MAC address as "flapping" between interfaces.

Ternary Content Addressable Memory (TCAM)

In traditional routing, ACLs can match, filter, or control specific traffic. Access lists are made up of one or more access control entities (ACEs) or matching statements that are evaluated in sequential order. Evaluating an access list can take up additional time, adding to the latency of forwarding packets.

In multilayer switches, however, all of the matching process that ACLs provide is implemented in hardware. TCAM allows a packet to be evaluated against an entire access list in a single table lookup. Most switches have multiple TCAMs so that both inbound and outbound security and QoS ACLs can be evaluated simultaneously, or entirely in parallel with a Layer 2 or Layer 3 forwarding decision.

The Catalyst IOS Software has two components that are part of the TCAM operation:

■ **Feature Manager (FM)**—After an access list has been created or configured, the Feature Manager software compiles, or merges, the ACEs into entries in the TCAM table. The TCAM can then be consulted at full frame forwarding speed.

■ **Switching Database Manager (SDM)**—You can partition the TCAM on Catalyst switches into areas for different functions. The SDM software configures or tunes the TCAM partitions, if needed.

TCAM Structure

The TCAM is an extension of the CAM table concept. Recall that a CAM table takes in an index or key value (usually a MAC address) and looks up the resulting value (usually a switch port or VLAN ID). Table lookup is fast and always based on an exact key match consisting of two input values: 0 and 1 bits.

TCAM also uses a table lookup operation but is greatly enhanced to allow a more abstract operation. For example, binary values (0s and 1s) make up a key into the table, but a mask value is also used to decide which bits of the key are actually relevant. This effectively makes a key consisting of three input values: 0, 1, and X (don't care) bit values—a three-fold or *ternary* combination.

TCAM entries are composed of Value, Mask, and Result (VMR) combinations. Fields from frame or packet headers are fed into the TCAM, where they are matched against the value and mask pairs to yield a result. As a quick reference, these can be described as follows:

■ **Values** are always 134-bit quantities, consisting of source and destination addresses and other relevant protocol information—all patterns to be matched. The information concatenated to form the value is dependent upon the type of access list, as shown in Table 3-2. Values in the TCAM come directly from any address, port, or other protocol information given in an ACE.

- **Masks** are also 134-bit quantities, in exactly the same format, or bit order, as the values. Masks select only the value bits of interest; a mask bit is set to exactly match a value bit, or not set for value bits that don't matter. The masks used in the TCAM stem from address or bit masks in ACEs.

- **Results** are numerical values that represent what action to take after the TCAM lookup occurrs. Where traditional access lists offer only a *permit* or *deny* result, TCAM lookups offer a number of possible results or actions. For example, the result can be a permit or deny decision, an index value to a QoS policer, a pointer to a next-hop routing table, and so on.

Table 3-2 *TCAM Value Pattern Components*

Access List Type	Value and Mask Components, 134 Bits Wide (Number of Bits)
Ethernet	Source MAC (48), destination MAC (48), Ethertype (16)
ICMP	Source IP (32), destination IP (32), protocol (16), ICMP code (8), ICMP type (4), IP type of service (ToS) (8)
Extended IP using TCP/UDP	Source IP (32), destination IP (32), protocol (16), IP ToS (8), source port (16), source operator (4), destination port (16), destination operator (4)
Other IP	Source IP (32), destination IP (32), protocol (16), IP ToS (8)
IGMP	Source IP (32), destination IP (32), protocol (16), IP ToS (8), IGMP message type (8)
IPX	Source IPX network (32), destination IPX network (32), destination node (48), IPX packet type (16)

The TCAM is always organized by masks, where each unique mask has eight value patterns associated with it. For example, the Catalyst 6500 TCAM (one for security ACLs and one for QoS ACLs) holds up to 4096 masks and 32,768 value patterns. The trick is that each of the mask-value pairs is evaluated *simultaneously,* or in parallel, revealing the best or longest match in a single table lookup.

TCAM Example

Figure 3-5 shows how the TCAM is built and used. This is a simple example, and might or might not be identical to the results that the Feature Manager produces. This is because the ACEs might need to be optimized or rewritten to achieve certain TCAM algorithm requirements.

Figure 3-5 *How an Access List Is Merged into TCAM*

access-list 100 permit tcp host 192.168.199.14 10.41.0.0 0.0.255.255 eq telnet
access-list 100 permit ip any 192.168.100.0 0.0.0.255
access-list 100 deny udp any 192.168.5.0 0.0.0.255 gt 1024
access-list 100 deny udp any 192.168.199.0 0.0.0.255 range 1024 2047

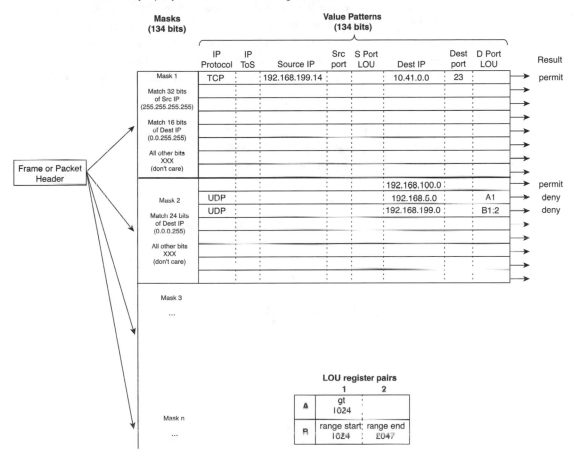

The example access list 100 (extended IP) is configured and merged into TCAM entries. First, the mask values must be identified in the access list. When an address value and a corresponding address mask are specified in an ACE, those mask bits must be set for matching. All other mask bits can remain in the "don't care" state. The access list contains only three unique masks: one that matches all 32 bits of the source IP address (found with an address mask of 255.255.255.255 or the keyword **host**), one that matches 16 bits of the destination address (found with an address mask of

0.0.255.255), and one that matches only 24 bits of the destination address (found with an address mask of 0.0.0.255). The keyword **any** in the ACEs means match anything or "don't care."

The unique masks are placed into the TCAM. Then, for each mask, all possible value patterns are identified. For example, a 32-bit source IP mask (Mask 1) can be found only in ACEs with a source IP address of 192.168.199.14 and a destination of 10.41.0.0. (The rest of Mask 1 is the destination address mask 0.0.255.255.) Those address values are placed into the first value pattern slot associated with Mask 1. Mask 2 has three value patterns: destination addresses 192.168.100.0, 192.168.5.0, and 192.168.199.0. Each of these is placed in the three pattern positions of Mask 2. This process continues until all ACEs have been merged.

When a mask's eighth pattern position has been filled, the next pattern with the same mask must be placed under a new mask. A bit of a balancing act occurs to try and fit all ACEs into the available mask and pattern entries without an overflow.

Port Operations in TCAM

You might have noticed that matching strictly based on values and masks only covers ACE statements that involve exact matches (either the **eq** port operation keyword or no Layer 4 port operations). For example, ACEs like the following involve specific address values, address masks, and port numbers:

```
access-list test permit ip 192.168.254.0 0.0.0.255 any
access-list test permit tcp any host 192.168.199.10 eq www
```

What about ACEs that use port operators, where a comparison must be made? Consider the following:

```
access-list test permit udp any host 192.168.199.50 gt 1024
access-list test permit tcp any any range 2000 2002
```

A simple logical operation between a mask and a pattern cannot generate the desired result. The TCAM also provides a mechanism for performing a Layer 4 operation or comparison, also done during the single table lookup. If an ACE has a port operator, such as **gt**, **lt**, **neq**, or **range**, the Feature Manager software compiles the TCAM entry to include the use of the operator and the operand in a Logical Operation Unit (LOU) register. Only a limited number of LOUs are available in the TCAM. If there are more ACEs with comparison operators than there are LOUs, the Feature Manager must break the ACEs up into multiple ACEs with only regular matching (using the **eq** operator).

In Figure 3-5, two ACEs require a Layer 4 operation:

- One that checks for UDP destination ports greater than 1024
- One that looks for the UDP destination port range 1024 to 2047

The Feature Manager checks all ACEs for Layer 4 operation, and places these into Logical Operation Unit (LOU) register pairs. These can be loaded with operations, independent of any other ACE parameters. The LOU contents can be reused if other ACEs need the same comparisons and values. After the LOUs are loaded, they are referenced in the TCAM entries that need them. This is shown by LOUs "A1" and the "B1:2" pair. A finite number (actually a rather small number) of LOUs are available in the TCAM, so the Feature Manager software must use them carefully.

Troubleshooting Switching Tables

If you see strange behavior in a Catalyst switch, it might be useful to examine the contents of the various switching tables. In any event, you might, at times, need to find out on which switch port a specific MAC address has been learned.

CAM Table Operation

To view the contents of the CAM table, you can use the following EXEC command:

```
Switch# show mac address-table dynamic [address mac-address | interface type mod/num |
vlan vlan-id]
```

The entries that have been dynamically learned will be shown. You can add the **address** keyword to specify a single MAC address, or the **interface** or **vlan** keywords to see addresses that have been learned on a specific interface or VLAN.

For example, assume you need to find the learned location of the host with MAC address 0050.8b11.54da. The **show mac address-table dynamic address 0050.8b11.54da** command might produce the output in Example 3-1.

Example 3-1 *Determining Host Location by MAC Address*

```
Switch# show mac address-table dynamic address 0050.8b11.54da
          Mac Address Table
-------------------------------------------

Vlan    Mac Address       Type        Ports
----    -----------       ----        -----
  54    0050.8b11.54da    DYNAMIC     Fa0/1
Total Mac Addresses for this criterion: 1
Switch#
```

From this, you can see that the host is somehow connected to interface FastEthernet 0/1, on VLAN 54.

Suppose this same command produced no output for the interface and VLAN. What might that mean? Either the host has not sent a frame that the switch can use for learning its location, or something odd is going on. Perhaps, the host is using two network interface cards (NICs) to load balance traffic—one NIC is only receiving traffic while the other is only sending. Therefore, the switch never hears and learns the receiving-only NIC address.

To see the CAM table's size, use the **show mac address-table count** command. MAC address totals are shown for each active VLAN on the switch. This can give you a good idea about the size of the CAM table and how many hosts are using the network. Be aware that many MAC addresses can be learned on a switch's uplink ports.

CAM table entries can be manually cleared, if needed, by using the following EXEC command:

```
Switch# clear mac address-table dynamic [address mac-address | interface type mod/num |
vlan vlan-id]
```

Frequently, you will need to know where a user with a certain MAC address is connected. In a large network, discerning at which switch and switch port a MAC address can be found might be difficult. Start out at the network's center, or core, and display the CAM table entry for the MAC address. Look at the switch port shown in the entry and move to the neighboring switch connected to that port. Then, repeat the CAM table process. Keep moving from switch to switch until you reach the edge of the network where the MAC address connects.

TCAM Operation

The TCAM in a switch is more or less self-sufficient. Access lists are automatically compiled or merged into the TCAM, so there is nothing to configure. The only concept you need to be aware of is how the TCAM resources are being used.

TCAMs have a limited number of usable mask, value pattern, and LOU entries. If access lists grow to be large, or many Layer 4 operations are needed, the TCAM tables and registers can overflow. To see the current TCAM resource usage, use the **show tcam counts** EXEC command. To see the current TCAM partitioning, you can use the **show sdm prefer** EXEC command. You can repartition the TCAM with some configuration commands, but that is beyond the scope of this book.

Foundation Summary

The Foundation Summary is a collection of tables, lists, and other information that provides a convenient review of many key concepts in this chapter. If you are already comfortable with the topics in this chapter, this summary might help you recall a few details. If you just read this chapter, this review should help solidify some key facts. If you are doing your final prep before the exam, the following information is a convenient way to review the day before the exam:

■ Layer 2 switches learn incoming MAC addresses and record their locations based on the inbound switch ports.

■ Layer 2 switching information is stored in the Content Addressable Memory (CAM) table. The CAM is consulted to find the outbound switch port when forwarding frames.

■ Multilayer switching looks at the Layer 2 addresses, along with Layer 3 and 4 address and port information, to forward packets.

■ Multilayer switching is performed in hardware using the Cisco Express Forwarding (CEF) method.

■ CEF builds Layer 3 destination information from routing tables and Layer 2 data. This information is stored in hardware as a Forwarding Information Base (FIB) table.

■ Multilayer switches can make many policy decisions in parallel, using the Ternary Content Addressable Memory (TCAM) contents.

■ TCAM combines a 134-bit Value, or pattern (made up of addresses, port numbers, or other appropriate fields) with a 134-bit Mask to yield a Result value. The Result instructs the switch hardware how to finish forwarding the packet.

■ Access lists for security (traditional router ACLs and VLAN ACLs) and QoS ACLs are compiled or merged into TCAM entries. These access lists can then be processed on each packet that passes through the switch, as a single table lookup.

■ As a packet exits a multilayer switch, it must be rewritten so that its header and checksum values are valid. The fields in the original packet that the switch updates are as follows:

— Source MAC address becomes the Layer 3 switch MAC address.

— Destination MAC address becomes the next-hop MAC address.

— IP TTL value is decremented by one.

— IP checksum is recomputed.

— Ethernet frame checksum is recomputed.

Table 3-3 *Switching Table Commands*

Task	Command Syntax
Set the CAM table aging time.	**mac address-table aging-time** *seconds*
Configure a static CAM entry.	**mac address-table static** *mac-address* **vlan** *vlan-id* **interface** *type mod/num*
Clear a CAM table entry.	**clear mac address-table dynamic** [**address** *mac-address* | **interface** *type mod/num* | **vlan** *vlan-id*]
Set privileged level password.	**enable password level 15** *password*
View the CAM table.	**show mac address-table dynamic** [**address** *mac-address* | **interface** *type mod/num* | **vlan** *vlan-id*]
View the CAM table size.	**show mac address-table count**
View TCAM resource information.	**show tcam counts**

Q&A

The questions and scenarios in this book are more difficult than what you should experience on the actual exam. The questions do not attempt to cover more breadth or depth than the exam; however, they are designed to make sure that you know the answer. Rather than allowing you to derive the answers from clues hidden inside the questions themselves, the questions challenge your understanding and recall of the subject. Hopefully, these questions will help limit the number of exam questions on which you narrow your choices to two options and then guess.

You can find the answers to these questions in Appendix A.

1. By default, how long are CAM table entries kept before they are aged out?

2. A TCAM lookup involves which values?

3. How many table lookups are required to find a MAC address in the CAM table?

4. How many table lookups are required to match a packet against an access list that has been compiled into 10 TCAM entries?

5. How many value patterns can a TCAM store for each mask?

6. Can all packets be switched in hardware by a multilayer switch?

7. Multilayer switches must rewrite which portions of an Ethernet frame?

8. If a station only receives Ethernet frames and doesn't transmit anything, how will a switch learn of its location?

9. What is a TCAM's main purpose?

10. Why do the TCAM mask and pattern fields consist of so many bits?

11. In a multilayer switch with a TCAM, a longer access list (more ACEs or statements) takes longer to process for each frame. True or false?

12. A multilayer switch receives a packet with a certain destination IP address. Suppose the switch has that IP address in its Layer 3 forwarding table, but no corresponding Layer 2 address. What happens to the packet next?

13. If a multilayer switch can't support a protocol with CEF, it relies on *fallback bridging*. Can the switch still route that traffic?

14. To configure a static CAM table entry, the **mac address-table static** *mac-address* command is used. Which two other parameters must also be given?

15. As a network administrator, what aspects of a switch TCAM should you be concerned with?

16. What portion of the TCAM is used to evaluate port number comparisons in an access list?

17. Someone has asked you where the host with MAC address 00-10-20-30-40-50 is located. Assuming you already know the switch it is connected to, what command can you use to find it?

18. Complete this command to display the size of the CAM table: **show mac** _____.

19. What protocol is used to advertise CAM table entries among neighboring switches?

20. Suppose a host uses one MAC address to send frames and another to receive them. In other words, one address will always be the source address sent in frames, and the other is only used as a destination address in incoming frames. Is it possible for that host to communicate with others through a Layer 2 switch? If so, how?

This chapter covers the following topics that you need to master for the CCNP BCMSN exam:

- **Switch Management**—This section describes the software operating systems that are available on Cisco Catalyst switches, along with the command-line interface (CLI) that is used for configuration and troubleshooting. In addition, this section covers the basic Catalyst switch configuration and administration commands and techniques for interswitch communication.

- **Switch File Management**—This section explains the various files and file systems used in a Catalyst switch, along with the commands necessary to manage them.

- **Troubleshooting from the Operating System**—This section presents a brief overview of the commands that you can use to verify or troubleshoot basic switch operation.

CHAPTER 4

Switch Configuration

Chapter 3 covered the topic of switch operation from the ground up. This chapter adds to that by reviewing the Catalyst operating systems—the mechanisms by which you can connect to a switch to configure and monitor how it works. Catalyst file systems are explained, along with the files needed to make a switch functional.

This chapter also covers the configuration steps for switch management. Management functions include the methods used to connect to a switch, and configuring switch identification, user authentication, inter-switch communication, and file management. A brief overview of useful troubleshooting commands is also given.

"Do I Know This Already?" Quiz

The purpose of the "Do I Know This Already?" quiz is to help you decide if you need to read the entire chapter. If you already intend to read the entire chapter, you do not necessarily need to answer these questions now.

The 12-question quiz, derived from the major sections in the "Foundation Topics" portion of the chapter, helps you determine how to spend your limited study time.

Table 4-1 outlines the major topics discussed in this chapter and the "Do I Know This Already?" quiz questions that correspond to those topics.

Table 4-1 *"Do I Know This Already?" Foundation Topics Section-to-Question Mapping*

Foundation Topics Section	Questions Covered in This Section
Switch Management	1-7
Switch File Management	8-10
Troubleshooting from the Operating System	11-12

> **CAUTION** The goal of self-assessment is to gauge your mastery of the topics in this chapter. If you do not know the answer to a question or are only partially sure of the answer, you should mark this question wrong. Giving yourself credit for an answer you correctly guess skews your self-assessment results and might provide you with a false sense of security.

1. Which of the following is an operating system available on Cisco Catalyst 3550, 4500, and 6500 family switches?

   a. Catalyst OS

   b. IOS

   c. SNMP

   d. QoS

2. Which of the following is *not* a valid way to connect to a Catalyst switch?

   a. Telnet

   b. rsh

   c. async serial

   d. rlogin

3. Which user interface mode allows the greatest authority for making configuration changes?

   a. User EXEC mode

   b. Privileged EXEC (enable) mode

   c. Telnet mode

   d. Root mode

4. To configure a password for Telnet access to a switch, which one of the following must the password be applied to?

   a. **interface vlan 1**

   b. **line con 0**

   c. **line vty 0 15**

   d. **hostname**

5. Which of the following is not required to set up Telnet access to a switch?

   a. Password on vty

   b. IP address

   c. Default gateway or route

   d. Enable password

6. Which protocol is used to exchange information between connected Cisco neighbors?

   a. SNMP

   b. VTP

   c. CDP

   d. STP

7. Cisco Discovery Protocol is sent over which OSI layer?

   a. Layer 1

   b. Layer 2

   c. Layer 3

   d. Layer 4

8. Which Catalyst file system contains the running IOS software image?

   a. Running-config

   b. RAM

   c. Flash

   d. NVRAM

9. Which command saves newly made configuration changes so they will be automatically used after the next switch reload?

   a. save all

   b. copy running-config flash:

   c. copy startup-config running-config

   d. copy running-config startup-config

10. If the **erase flash:** command is given, what is the next logical step?

   a. **copy tftp: flash:**

   b. **copy running-config startup-config**

   c. **erase startup-config**

   d. **copy startup-config flash:**

11. What command can you use to examine the Gigabit Ethernet 3/1 interface's current configuration?

   a. **show interface gigabitethernet 3/1**

   b. **show gigabit ethernet 3/1**

   c. **show startup-config interface gig 3/1**

   d. **show running-config int gig 3/1**

12. What command can you use to view information received from a neighboring Cisco switch, including its version of IOS?

   a. **show neighbors**

   b. **show cdp neighbors all**

   c. **show all neighbors**

   d. **show cdp neighbors detail**

You can find the answers to the quiz in Appendix A, "Answers to Chapter 'Do I Know This Already?' Quizzes, and Q&A Sections." The suggested choices for your next step are as follows:

■ **7 or less overall score**—Read the entire chapter. This section includes the "Foundation Topics," "Foundation Summary," and "Q&A" sections.

■ **8–10 overall score**—Begin with the "Foundation Summary" section and then go to the "Q&A" section at the end of the chapter.

■ **11 or more overall score**—If you want more review on these topics, skip to the "Foundation Summary" section and then go to the "Q&A" section at the end of the chapter. Otherwise, move to Chapter 5, "Switch Port Configuration."

Foundation Topics

Switch Management

Managing a Catalyst switch can be broken up into several topics. A switch runs an operating system, which provides a user interface and controls all processes that are used to forward packets. The following sections address all these topics.

Operating Systems

You can configure Cisco Catalyst switch devices to support many different requirements and features. When a PC is connected to the serial console port, configuration is generally done with a terminal emulator application on the PC. You can perform further configurations through a Telnet session across the LAN or through a web-based interface. These topics are covered in later sections.

Catalyst switches support one of two operating systems, each having a different type of user interface for configuration:

- **Cisco IOS Software**—The user interface is identical to that of Cisco routers, having an EXEC mode for session and monitoring commands, and a hierarchical configuration mode for switch configuration commands.

  Cisco IOS Software is supported on the Catalyst 2950, 3550, 4500 (with Supervisors III and IV), and 6500 (with Supervisor II and MSFC "Supervisor IOS," and Supervisor 720). This operating system can support Layer 2-only switching or Layer 3, depending on the software license.

- **Catalyst OS (CatOS or COS, also called XDI)**—This user interface allows session and monitoring commands to be intermingled with set-based (using the **set** and **clear** commands) configuration commands.

CatOS is supported on switch families such as the Catalyst 4000 (Supervisor I or II), Catalyst 5000, and Catalyst 6500 (any Supervisor module). This operating system can support only Layer 2 switching.

> **NOTE**   The Catalyst OS is mentioned here only for comparison. It is not covered in detail in the BCMSN 2.0 course; therefore, it is not covered in this text. For more information about Catalyst OS comparisons and side-by-side configuration commands, refer to these sources:
>
> *Cisco Field Manual: Catalyst Switch Configuration* by David Hucaby and Steve McQuerry, Cisco Press, ISBN 1-58705-043-9
>
> Comparison of the Cisco Catalyst and Cisco IOS Operating Systems for the Cisco Catalyst 6500 Series Switch at www.cisco.com/en/US/customer/products/hw/switches/ps708/products_white_paper09186a00800c8441.shtml

Generally speaking, you are provided with an interface where you can issue commands, such as **show**, to display many different types of information about the switch, its configuration, and dynamic operation. This is called the *User EXEC* mode. Users are given access to various commands according to their privilege level, ranging from Level 1 through 15. By default, a user is given Level 1. To make any configuration changes, a user must enter a higher level, such as Level 15, through the **enable** command.

When in the *privileged EXEC* or *enable* mode, you can make configuration changes using the **config** command. Configuration is performed in layers, starting with the *global configuration*. Each time you select a specific item to configure in global configuration mode, you are moved into that respective configuration mode.

The switch prompt changes to give you a clue about your current mode. For example, *normal* or user EXEC mode is generally shown with the name of the switch followed by a greater than (**>**) character. Privileged EXEC (enable) mode replaces the **>** with a hash or pound sign (**#**). Global configuration is shown as the switch name followed by **(config)**. If you select an interface to configure, you enter *interface configuration* mode, signified by **(config-if)**.

Basically, if you are familiar with router EXEC and configuration commands and the IOS user interface, you will be right at home working with the Catalyst IOS Software.

Identifying the Switch

All switches come from the factory with a default configuration and a default system name or prompt. You can change this name so that each switch in a campus network has a unique identity. This option is useful when you are using Telnet to move from switch to switch in a network.

To change the host or system name, enter the following command in configuration mode:

```
Switch(config)# hostname hostname
```

The host name is a string of 1 to 255 alphanumeric characters. As soon as this command is executed, the system prompt changes to reflect the new host name.

> **NOTE** Configuration changes made on IOS-based switches apply only to the active *running configuration*, stored in RAM. To make the changes permanent, in effect even after a power cycle, remember to copy the switch configuration into the *startup configuration*, stored in NVRAM. This is discussed in the "Switch File Management" section of this chapter.

Passwords and User Access

Normally, a network device should be configured to secure it from unauthorized access. Catalyst switches offer a simple form of security by setting passwords to restrict who can log in to the user interface. Two levels of user access are available: regular login, or *user EXEC mode*, and enable login, or *privileged EXEC mode*. User EXEC mode is the first level of access, which gives access to the basic user interface through any line or the console port. The privileged EXEC mode requires a second password and gives access to set or change switch operating parameters or configurations.

Cisco offers various methods for providing device security and user authentication. Many of these methods are more secure and robust than using the login passwords. Chapter 19, "Securing Switch Access," describes these features in greater detail.

To set the login passwords for user EXEC mode, enter the following commands in global configuration mode:

```
Switch(config)# line con 0
Switch(config-line)# password password
Switch(config-line)# login
Switch(config)# line vty 0 15
Switch(config-line)# password password
Switch(config-line)# login
Switch(config)# enable secret enable-password
```

Here, the user EXEC mode password is set on the console (**line con 0**) and on all the virtual terminal (**line vty 0 15**) lines used for Telnet access. The enable mode password (**enable secret**), which is automatically encrypted when set, is a global value for all users. The user EXEC password is a string of 1 to 80 alphanumeric characters. The enable secret password is a string of 1 to 25 alphanumeric characters. All passwords are case-sensitive.

You can change the passwords by reconfiguring the passwords with different strings. To completely remove a password, use the **no password** or **no enable secret** command in the appropriate line configuration mode.

Password Recovery

After the EXEC and enable passwords are configured, there is always a chance that you could forget them. You might also inherit a switch that has its passwords set to unknown values. In this case, you must take the switch through a password recovery procedure. The procedure varies among the different Catalyst switch families. Refer to the following documents:

- Catalyst 2950 and 3550—www.cisco.com/warp/public/474/pswdrec_2900xl.html

- Catalyst 4000 and 4500 (Supervisor III and IV)—www.cisco.com/warp/public/474/pswdrec_cat4000_supiii_21229.html

- Catalyst 6500 (Supervisor IOS)—www.cisco.com/warp/public/474/pswdrec_6000IOS.html

For a complete list of password recovery procedures for any model of Cisco equipment, refer to the handy *Password Recovery Procedures* technical tip at www.cisco.com/warp/public/474/.

> **TIP** Although password recovery is not explicitly covered in the BCMSN course (nor likely in the CCNP BCMSN exam), you should be aware of the concepts needed to regain access to a switch.

Remote Access

By default, the switch allows user access only via the console port. To use Telnet to access a switch from within the campus network, to use ping to test a switch's reachability, or to monitor a switch by SNMP, you must configure for remote access.

Even if a switch operates at Layer 2, the switch supervisor processor must maintain an IP stack at Layer 3 for administrative purposes. An IP address and subnet mask can then be assigned to the switch so that remote communications with the switch supervisor are possible.

By default, all ports on a switch are assigned to the same virtual LAN (VLAN) or broadcast domain. The switch supervisor and its IP stack must be assigned to a VLAN before remote Telnet and ping sessions will be supported. VLANs are discussed further in Chapter 6, "VLANs and Trunks."

You can assign an IP address to the management VLAN (default is VLAN 1) with the following commands in global configuration mode:

```
Switch(config)# interface vlan vlan-id
Switch(config-if)# ip address ip-address netmask
Switch(config-if)# ip default-gateway ip-address
Switch(config-if)# no shutdown
```

As demonstrated by the preceding command syntax, an IP address and subnet mask are assigned to the VLAN "interface," which is really the switch supervisor's IP stack listening on VLAN number *vlan-id*. Any VLAN number can be used, as long as the VLAN has been defined and is active (in use on a physical switch interface).

To send packets off that local VLAN subnet, a default gateway IP address must also be assigned. This default gateway has nothing to do with processing packets that are passed through the switch; rather, the default gateway is used only to forward traffic between a user and the switch supervisor for management purposes. (This concept can be greatly expanded on a Layer 3 switch, which can perform its own "routing" functions and can use dynamic routing protocols.)

Inter-Switch Communication—Cisco Discovery Protocol

Because switch devices are usually interconnected, management is usually simplified if the switches can communicate on some level to become aware of each other. Cisco has implemented protocols on its devices so that neighboring Cisco equipment can be found and identified.

Cisco uses a proprietary protocol on both switches and routers to discover neighboring devices. You can enable the Cisco Discovery Protocol (CDP) on interfaces to periodically advertise the existence of a device and exchange basic information with directly connected neighbors. The information exchanged in CDP messages includes the device type, software version, links between devices, and the number of ports within each device.

By default, CDP runs on each port of a Catalyst switch, and CDP advertisements occur every 60 seconds. CDP communication occurs at the data link layer so that it is independent of any network layer protocol that might be running on a network segment. This means that CDP can be sent and received using only Layer 2 functionality. CDP frames are sent as multicasts, using a destination MAC address of 01:00:0c:cc:cc:cc.

Cisco Catalyst switches regard the CDP address as a special address designating a multicast frame that should *not* be forwarded. Instead, CDP multicast frames are redirected to the switch's management port and are processed by the switch supervisor alone. Cisco switches become aware only of other directly connected Cisco devices.

CDP is enabled by default on all switch interfaces. To manually enable or disable CDP on an interface, use the following interface configuration command:

```
Switch(config-if)# [no] cdp enable
```

If a switch port connects to a non-Cisco device or to a network outside your administrative control, consider disabling CDP on that port. Add the **no** keyword to disable CDP.

Switch File Management

A Catalyst switch uses several types of files while it is operating. To manage a switch, you should understand what type of file is used for what purpose, how to move these files around, and how to upgrade them.

The following files are typically used in a Catalyst switch:

- **IOS image files**—The software or code that the switch CPU executes. Image files are compiled and tailored for specific switch hardware models.

- **Configuration files**—Text files containing all configuration commands needed to operate a switch in a network.

All Catalyst files can be stored in various file systems so they can be accessed and used by the switch hardware. Files can also be stored in file systems external to the switch, either as backup copies or as downloadable upgrades.

The typical file systems available to a Catalyst switch are as follows:

- **Flash memory**—Nonvolatile memory present in the switch; files stored here remain intact even after a power cycle.

- **Network servers**—Systems apart from the switch that are connected to the network and provide TFTP, FTP, or remote copy program (rcp) file transfer services.

- **NVRAM**—Nonvolatile memory that contains the switch configuration used during bootup. On many switches, the NVRAM file system is actually emulated in Flash memory.

- **RAM**—Volatile memory available to the switch for a variety of purposes. The switch configuration used during runtime and altered by configuration commands is stored here.

OS Image Files

The Catalyst IOS Software is packaged as an IOS image file, just as it is for routers. IOS image files are stored in the Flash memory on a switch. Only one image file can be executed while the switch is running, but more than one image file can be stored on the switch.

Switches such as the Catalyst 2950 and 3550 have one Flash area where images are stored. This is always named *flash:*. Larger, more modular switches can have several Flash file systems. For example, a Catalyst 4500 has one named *cat4000_flash:* that contains the VLAN database file and another called *bootflash:* that contains the IOS image and bootstrap image files. Flash memory can also be present in the form of a PCMCIA card, so stored files can be swapped out by replacing the Flash card. These cards are named *slot0:*, *slot1:*, and so on.

You can copy IOS image files from one file system to another or to an external location. This allows an image file to be backed up in case of a switch failure. Image files can also be copied into the switch Flash file system so that the software version can be upgraded.

Filename Conventions

IOS image files are named according to a predefined format. The filenames follow this basic template:

mmmmm-fffff-mm.vvvv.bin

- *mmmmm* represents the Catalyst switch model (for example, *c3550* corresponds to Catalyst 3550, *cat4000* to Catalyst 4000, and *c6sup22* to Catalyst 6500 Supervisor II).

- *fffff* represents the feature sets included in the image; generally, *i* followed by anything denotes an IP feature set, *s* is the IP "Plus," *k* denotes a cryptographic feature set (Data Encryption Standard [DES] or 3DES), *j* is the enterprise set, *p* is for service providers, and *d* is the desktop (IP, IPX, AppleTalk, DECnet) feature set.

- *mm* denotes the file format: The first letter is *m* if the image runs in RAM, and the second letter is *z* if the image is Zip compressed.

- *vvvv* represents the IOS version, in the format *vvv-mmm.bbb*; the major release (*vvv*) is given first and followed by a dash; then, the maintenance release (*mmm*) is given and followed by a period. The build level (*bbb*) is given using one or more letters and a number. The first letter denotes the type of build: *E* means an early deployment of features. The next letter is the interim build level, where *A* means the first build, and so on. The number following denotes the number of times the interim build has been incrementally released.

  Therefore, *121-12c.EA1* means version 12.1(12c)EA1, or early deployment build A1 (the first "A" build) of the 12.1(12c) code.

- *.bin* flags the image file as a binary executable (not readable text).

Configuration Files

The switch configuration is a file containing all the commands needed to configure each switch feature and function. Here are three of the most common configuration files:

- **startup-config**—When a switch first boots up, the startup-config file is read, parsed, and executed. The startup-config is stored in NVRAM (actually the *nvram:* file system) so it survives power failures.

- **running-config**—While a switch is running, this contains a copy of the current state of every command in use. This file is dynamic, such that it is updated with each configuration command entered.

  The running-config's contents are volatile, causing all commands in it to be lost during a power failure or a switch reload. (To preserve the running-config, it must be copied into the startup-config prior to the next switch reload.)

- **vlan.dat**—As VLANs are defined or changed, their configurations are entered into the VLAN database file, *vlan.dat*. This file is updated as you make configuration changes to the VLAN database on a switch and as any VLAN Trunking Protocol (VTP) updates occur.

  The VLAN database (*vlan.dat*) is stored in Flash memory and is normally configured through the **vlan database** or **vlan** configuration commands. Its contents are preserved across a power failure or reload.

Other Catalyst Switch Files

You can also find several other files stored in the file systems on a Catalyst switch. Most of the time, you will not need to do anything with them. They are mentioned here for your understanding and if you need to access the information they contain. These files can include the following:

- **system_env_vars**—A text file containing system variables such as the MAC address, model number, serial number, and various module information. This file is consulted to get the system information displayed by the **show version** command.
- **crashinfo**—A file or directory containing text output from previous switch crashes. This is normally stored and accessed as *flash:crashinfo* (a file) or *crashinfo:* (a directory).

Moving Catalyst Switch Files Around

A switch can copy files to and from various locations, including those in Table 4-2.

Table 4-2 *Locations of Catalyst Switch Files*

File System Name	Function
flash:	Flash memory, usually containing bootable IOS image files (some models emulate nvram: here)
bootflash:	Flash memory, usually containing bootable IOS image files
slot0:	Optional removable Flash card memory; can store any type of files
nvram:	NVRAM area, usually containing the startup-config file
system:	RAM area; contains the running-config file, as well as a directory of all dynamic switch memory areas
tftp:	An external TFTP server where any type of switch file can be stored or retrieved; no user authentication needed
ftp:	An external FTP server where any type of switch file can be stored or retrieved; user authentication required
rcp:	An external rcp server where any type of switch file can be stored or retrieved; user authentication required

Cisco IOS Software allows you to navigate and manipulate the Flash file system in much the same way other operating systems, such as UNIX and DOS, do. In Flash memory, you can find plain text files, binary executable files, and directories. You are free to "move" up and down into directories. You can also copy, rename, or delete files.

In the EXEC mode, you are always positioned in the "root" directory, *flash:*, by default. To perform a function in the Flash file system, use one of the following commands:

- **dir** [**flash:**[*directory*]]—Show a list of all files in the current Flash directory or the *directory* given.
- **cd flash:***directory*—Change directory to the *directory* given.
- **cd ..**—Change directory one level up.
- **cd**—Change directory to the home or root Flash directory.
- **copy flash:**[*filename*] **tftp:**   Copy the file *filename* from Flash to a TFTP server. The server address and destination filename are prompted.
- **copy tftp: flash:**[*filename*]—Copy a file from the TFTP server into Flash memory. The TFTP server address and any unresolved filenames are prompted.
- **delete flash:***filename*—The file *filename* is deleted from Flash memory.
- **erase flash:**   All files in Flash memory are erased in one command.
- **format flash:**—The Flash file system is reformatted, destroying all existing files. Formatting is appropriate when the Flash memory has been corrupted.

You can also manipulate the switch configuration files from privileged EXEC (enable) mode. Remember that two configuration files exist at all times—the *running-config* and *startup-config*. Any configuration changes you make to a switch are applied immediately to the running-config file. The only way to update the startup-config is by manually copying another file to it.

Cisco IOS Software allows the following commands to manipulate the configuration files:

- **copy running-config startup-config**—The contents of the running-config are copied into the startup-config, replacing any similar commands there. After this is done, any dynamic configuration changes are saved and are preserved across power failures or switch reloads. (This command should be used regularly to save any new configuration changes. Use it prudently, if you need to back out a large number of changes.)
- **copy startup-config running-config**—The permanent contents of the startup-config file are copied into the running-config, replacing any similar commands there. The entire running-config isn't simply overwritten; rather, the **startup-config** commands are copied over while any other existing **running-config** commands are kept active. This operation is performed as a switch boots up. (This command can quickly restore a misconfigured switch to a known state.)

- **copy running-config tftp:**—A switch's current running configuration is copied to a TFTP server. The server address and destination filename are prompted. Use this command to store a backup snapshot copy of the switch configuration.

- **copy tftp: startup-config**—When a switch configuration is lost or needs to be restored to a known state, a backup copy of the configuration is copied from a TFTP server to the startup-config file. The new changes won't take effect until the switch is reloaded, or until the startup-config is copied to the running-config. (You could also use **copy tftp: running-config**, but this would make immediate configuration changes as commands from the TFTP file are copied over. Use caution so that your configuration changes occur under controlled circumstances.)

- **erase startup-config**—The entire contents of the startup-config file are erased. Use this command when a switch has been retired from one function and needs to be relocated or completely reconfigured.

Troubleshooting from the Operating System

The Cisco Catalyst IOS Software provides many commands that can verify or troubleshoot a switch in its current environment. Sometimes, you might wonder what software image or configuration commands are being used by a switch. A switch can also produce real-time debugging information about a feature or condition to aid in troubleshooting. Information is also available to help identify other neighboring Cisco devices in a network. This section explains each of these tasks and how to accomplish them using the relevant commands.

Show Configuration and File Contents

Cisco IOS Software offers many commands that you can use from the EXEC mode command line to display the contents of files, current configuration states, and values for troubleshooting. You can use the following commands to view and troubleshoot switch files and file systems:

- **show version**—Displays the current version of IOS running in a switch, along with many details about available hardware, RAM and Flash memory, switch uptime, current running IOS image file, reason for the last reload, and the configuration register's contents.

- **show running-config** [**interface** *type mod/num* | **vlan** *vlan-id* | **module** *mod*]—Displays the contents of the running-config configuration file. You can jump to the relevant configuration of a specific interface, VLAN, or switch module, if desired.

- **show startup-config**—Displays the startup-config configuration file's contents.

- **show tech-support**—Provides information to Cisco TAC support personnel; almost every known bit of information about the switch is displayed. Be sure to configure your terminal emulator to capture text to a file before issuing this command.

- **verify flash:***filename*—Verifies the checksum of the Flash file *filename*. This can ensure that an IOS image is not corrupted after it has been copied into Flash memory. (During the actual copy process, the checksum is automatically verified. You can use the **verify** command to make sure the file has not become corrupted since it was originally copied.)

- **more** *filesystem:filename*—Displays the contents of a plain text file from the command line. This can be useful when you need to read configuration files that have been stored in a Flash file system. You can also view text files that are stored on a remote TFTP server—from the IOS command line.

> **NOTE**   You can filter the output of any **show** command so that you see only lines containing specific keywords. Append the "pipe" symbol (|) to the command line, followed by one of these keywords: **begin** *text* (start the output with the line containing *text*), **include** *text* (only display lines that contain *text*), or **exclude** *text* (only display lines that don't contain *text*).
>
> When a large amount of output is displayed, the switch usually shows a page at a time, pausing with a "-More-" prompt. You can either press the SPACE key to display the next page, the RETURN (**Enter**) key to display the next line, or /*text* to search forward and begin the page of output at the line containing *text*. Using the slash key allows a quick search within the context of the entire output.

Debugging Output

For more focused and real-time information about a certain switch feature, you can use the **debug** EXEC command. Debug output is not normally used, unless you suspect a problem with a feature or an interaction with other switches in the network.

You can use many options with the **debug** command—each pertaining to a switch feature or a specific activity. Type the **debug** command followed by **?** to get context-based help on all the supported debugging commands and keywords.

After you enable a **debug** command, you can see the debug output listed as events can occur on the switch.

> **CAUTION**   Use the **debug** commands cautiously because they can generate a tremendous amount of output. Not only can this display slowly on a serial console connection, but also the debug process itself can bog the switch CPU down to the point that it severely impacts traffic forwarding.

Always be sure to turn off any debugging commands when you finish with them. Do so by using the **no debug** *options* command, where the *options* keywords match the ones you used to enable debugging. To quickly disable *all* active debugging commands, use the **no debug all** or **undebug all** commands.

View CDP Information

To view information learned from CDP advertisements of neighboring Cisco devices, use one of the following commands:

```
Switch# show cdp interface [type mod/num]
Switch# show cdp neighbors [type mod/num | vlan vlan-id] [detail]
```

The first command displays CDP information pertaining to a specific interface. If the type, module, and port information is omitted, CDP information from all interfaces is listed. The second command displays CDP information about neighboring Cisco devices. A specific interface or VLAN can be given to display only neighbors connected to it. Using the **detail** keyword results in the display of all possible CDP information about each neighbor.

Recall that CDP messages are sent out every 60 seconds, and all entries received are placed in a cache. The cache is updated with new entries, and stale entries are aged out after a hold time of 180 seconds. If you suspect a problem with a neighboring switch, you might want to clear the CDP cache of all potentially state information to see what new information is being received from neighbors. Do this with the **clear cdp table** command.

As demonstrated in Example 4-1, the **show cdp neighbors** and the **show cdp neighbors detail** command can be useful when you are connected to a switch and need to know more about what other switches are nearby in a network. Particularly useful are the IP address entries, allowing Telnet access to previously unknown switches. To see a brief listing of only the neighbor switch names and their management IP addresses, use the **show cdp entry * protocol** command.

Example 4-1 *Displaying CDP Information for Neighboring Devices*

```
Switch# show cdp neighbors
Capability Codes: R - Router, T - Trans Bridge, B - Source Route Bridge
                  S - Switch, H - Host, I - IGMP, r - Repeater

Device ID        Local Intrfce    Holdtme    Capability  Platform  Port ID
BuildingA-1      Gig 2/1           158         S I        WS-C3550-4Gig 0/1
CoreSwitch-1     Gig 1/1           158         T S        WS-C6509  4/16
Switch# show cdp neighbors gig 1/1 detail
-----------------------
Device ID: CoreSwitch-1
Entry address(es):
  IP address: 192.168.199.9
```

Example 4-1 *Displaying CDP Information for Neighboring Devices (Continued)*

```
Platform: WS-C6509,  Capabilities: Trans-Bridge Switch
Interface: GigabitEthernet1/1,  Port ID (outgoing port): 4/16
Holdtime : 130 sec

Version :
WS-C6509 Software, Version McpSW: 7.2(2) NmpSW: 7.2(2)
Copyright (c) 1995-2002 by Cisco Systems


advertisement version: 2
VTP Management Domain: 'Core'
Switch# show cdp entry * protocol
Protocol information for BuildingA-1 :
  IP address: 192.168.199.107
Protocol information for CoreSwitch-1 :
  IP address: 192.168.199.9
Switch#
```

Foundation Summary

The Foundation Summary is a collection of tables that provides a convenient review of many key concepts in this chapter. If you are already comfortable with the topics in this chapter, this summary can help you recall a few details. If you just read this chapter, this review should help solidify some key facts. If you are doing your final preparation before the exam, the following tables are a convenient way to review the day before the exam.

Table 4-3   *Switch Management Configuration Commands*

Task	Command Syntax
Identify switch	**hostname** *hostname*
Set EXEC level password	**line** *type number* **password** *password*
Set privileged level password	**enable secret** *password*
Set IP address	**interface vlan** *vlan-id* **ip address** *ip-address netmask* **ip default-gateway** *ip-address*
CDP (default is enabled on every switch port)	**cdp enable**

Table 4-4   *File Management Commands*

Task	Command Syntax
Directory of Flash	**dir** [**flash**:[*directory*]]
Change directory	**cd flash**:*directory*
Copy a file between Flash and a TFTP server	**copy flash:**[*filename*] **tftp:** -OR- **copy tftp: flash:**[*filename*]
Delete a file in Flash	**delete flash:***filename*

Table 4-4 *File Management Commands (Continued)*

Task	Command Syntax
Clear Flash contents	**erase flash:** -OR- **format flash:**
Save the running configuration	**copy running-config startup-config** -OR- **copy running-config tftp:**
Overwrite the running configuration	**copy startup-config running-config**
Overwrite the permanent configuration	**copy tftp: startup-config** -OR- **erase startup-config**

Table 4-5 *Troubleshooting Commands*

Task	Command Syntax
Display the current running environment and IOS version	**show version**
Display the running configuration	**show running-config** [**interface** *type mod/num* | **vlan** *vlan id* | **module** *mod*]
Display the permanent configuration	**show startup-config** -OR- **show config**
Display all technical support information	**show tech-support**
Verify an image checksum	**verify flash:***filename*

continues

Table 4-5   *Troubleshooting Commands (Continued)*

Task	Command Syntax
Enable or disable debugging	**debug** *keywords* **no debug** *keywords* -OR- **no debug all** -OR- **undebug all**
Display CDP information	**show cdp interface** [*type mod/num*] -OR- **show cdp neighbors** [*type mod/num* | **vlan** *vlan-id*] [**detail**] -OR- **show cdp entry * protocol**

Q&A

The questions and scenarios in this book are more difficult than what you should experience on the actual exam. The questions do not attempt to cover more breadth or depth than the exam; however, they are designed to make sure that you know the answer. Rather than allowing you to derive the answer from clues hidden inside the questions themselves, the questions challenge your understanding and recall of the subject. Hopefully, these questions will help limit the number of exam questions on which you narrow your choices to two options and then guess.

You can find the answers to these questions in Appendix A.

1. When Cisco IOS Software is used on a Catalyst switch, the switch must perform routing. True or false?

2. What is the major difference between the IOS and CatOS command sets?

3. What switch command will enter privileged EXEC or "enable" mode on a Catalyst 4500?

4. Match these default command line prompts with their respective modes:

    a. Switch#   ____ Normal user EXEC mode

    b. Switch(config)   ____ Privileged EXEC or enable

    c. Switch(config-if)#   ____ Global configuration

    d. Switch>   ____ Interface configuration

5. With the command line prompt **testlab#**, what command has been used to customize the prompt?

6. The following commands have just been entered, assuming interface VLAN 10 did not previously exist:

```
interface vlan 10
ip address 192.168.199.10 255.255.255.0
no shutdown
```

Suddenly, the power cord is pulled out of the switch. What will happen when the power is restored?

7. Can you configure an enable secret password (**enable secret** *password*) for the switch console and a different enable secret for Telnet access?

8. When you configure an IP address and subnet mask on a Layer 2 switch for management purposes, which VLAN are you required to use?

   a. VLAN 1

   b. VLAN 0

   c. VLAN 1001

   d. Any VLAN that is appropriate

   e. You can't assign an IP address to a VLAN.

9. What commands will allow Telnet and ping access to a switch management interface at 192.168.200.10, subnet mask 255.255.255.0, on VLAN 5? A router is available at address 192.168.200.1.

10. CDP advertisements occur every _____ seconds.

11. When a Cisco Catalyst switch receives a CDP multicast frame, it relays it to neighboring switches. True or false?

12. Eight access layer switches connect to a central distribution layer switch using Gigabit Ethernet connections. Each connection is assigned to VLAN 1 so that no link is in trunking mode. On one of the access switches, how many neighboring switches will be shown by the **show cdp neighbor gigabit 0/1**?

13. Which IOS image file is more recent: c3550-i5q3l2-mz.121-12c.EA1.bin or c3550-i9q3l2-mz.121-11c.EA1.bin?

14. A new switch has just been configured with 100 command lines from the console. You realize the need to save the new configuration and type **copy start run**. Where will your configuration be stored?

15. What command can you use to see what Cisco IOS Software version is currently running on a switch?

16. Complete this command so that the output is displayed starting with the configuration for interface VLAN 100:

show run _____

17. The **debug spanning-tree all** command has been given from the EXEC mode command line. What commands can you use to stop or disable the debugging output?

18. What command can you use to verify CDP configuration on switch port GigabitEthernet 3/1?

This chapter covers the following topics that you need to master for the CCNP BCMSN exam:

- **Ethernet Concepts**—This section discusses the concepts and technology behind various forms of Ethernet media. Ethernet solutions for service providers, such as Long Reach Ethernet (LRE) and Metro Ethernet, are also covered.

- **Connectivity with Scalable Ethernet**—This section covers the configuration steps and commands needed to use Catalyst Ethernet, Fast Ethernet, and Gigabit and 10Gigabit Ethernet switch ports in a network.

- **Connecting Switch Block Devices**—This section discusses the physical cabling and connectivity used with Catalyst switches, including console and Ethernet interfaces.

- **Troubleshooting Port Connectivity**—This section covers some of the symptoms, methods, and switch commands that you can use to diagnose problems with Ethernet switch connections.

CHAPTER **5**

Switch Port Configuration

Chapters 1 and 2 dealt with the logical processes that you can use to design a campus network. Connections between switch blocks were discussed, such that traffic could be efficiently trans ported across the campus. Single connections, load balancing, and redundant paths connected switches in modular blocks for complete connectivity. However, these paths were only functional paths—no specifics were presented about how much traffic the network could handle, or what physical capabilities were supported. These topics become important when you begin to size traffic loads and actually connect Cisco switch devices.

This chapter presents the various Ethernet network technologies used to establish switched connections within the campus network. The chapter also details the switch commands required for configuring and troubleshooting Ethernet LAN ports.

"Do I Know This Already?" Quiz

The purpose of the "Do I Know This Already?" quiz is to help you decide if you need to read the entire chapter. If you already intend to read the entire chapter, you do not necessarily need to answer these questions now.

The 13-question quiz, derived from the major sections in the "Foundation Topics" portion of the chapter, helps you determine how to spend your limited study time.

Table 5-1 outlines the major topics discussed in this chapter and the "Do I Know This Already?" quiz questions that correspond to those topics.

Table 5-1   *"Do I Know This Already?" Foundation Topics Section-to-Question Mapping*

Foundation Topics Section	Questions Covered in This Section
Ethernet Concepts	1-8
Connecting Switch Block Devices	9-10
Switch Port Configuration	11
Troubleshooting Port Connectivity	12-13

CAUTION   The goal of self-assessment is to gauge your mastery of the topics in this chapter. If you do not know the answer to a question or are only partially sure of the answer, you should mark this question wrong. Giving yourself credit for an answer you correctly guess skews your self-assessment results and might provide you with a false sense of security.

1.   What does the IEEE 802.3 standard define?

   a.   Spanning Tree Protocol

   b.   Token Ring

   c.   Ethernet

   d.   Switched Ethernet

2.   At what layer are traditional 10 Mbps Ethernet, Fast Ethernet, and Gigabit Ethernet the same?

   a.   Layer 1

   b.   Layer 2

   c.   Layer 3

   d.   Layer 4

3.   At what layer are traditional 10 Mbps Ethernet, Fast Ethernet, and Gigabit Ethernet different?

   a.   Layer 1

   b.   Layer 2

   c.   Layer 3

   d.   Layer 4

4. What is the maximum cable distance for a Category 5 100BASE-TX connection?

   a. 100 feet

   b. 100 meters

   c. 328 meters

   d. 500 meters

5. Where is Cisco Long Reach Ethernet typically used?

   a. In a campus access layer (to the desktop users)

   b. In a campus core layer

   c. Between campus buildings

   d. In a multitenant building

6. What is the maximum length of a Cisco LRE connection?

   a. 100 feet

   b. 100 meters

   c. 500 feet

   d. 5000 feet

7. Ethernet autonegotiation determines which of the following?

   a. Spanning Tree mode

   b. Duplex mode

   c. Quality of service mode

   d. Error threshold

8. Which of the following cannot be determined if the far end of a connection doesn't support autonegotiation?

   a. Link speed

   b. Link duplex mode

   c. Link media type

   d. MAC address

9. Which of these is not a standard type of Gigabit Interface Converter (GBIC)?

    a. 1000BASE-LX/LH

    b. 1000BASE-T

    c. 1000BASE-FX

    d. 1000BASE-ZX

10. What type of cable should you use to connect two switches back-to-back using their FastEthernet 10/100 ports?

    a. Rollover cable

    b. Transfer cable

    c. Crossover cable

    d. Straight-through cable

11. Assume you have just entered the **configure terminal** command. To configure the speed of the first FastEthernet interface on a Catalyst 3550 to 100 Mbps, which of these commands should you enter first?

    a. **speed 100 mbps**

    b. **speed 100**

    c. **interface fastethernet 0/1**

    d. **interface fast ethernet 0/1**

12. If a switch port is in the "errdisable" state, what is the first thing you should do?

    a. Reload the switch.

    b. Use the **clear errdisable port** command.

    c. Use the **shut** and **no shut** interface configuration commands.

    d. Determine the cause of the problem.

13. Which of the following **show interface** outputs can you use to diagnose a switch port problem?

    a. Port state

    b. Port speed

    c. Input errors

    d. Collisions

    e. All of the above

You can find the answers to the quiz in Appendix A, "Answers to Chapter 'Do I Know This Already?' Quizzes and Q&A Sections." The suggested choices for your next step are as follows:

- **7 or less overall score**—Read the entire chapter. This includes the "Foundation Topics," "Foundation Summary," and "Q&A" sections.

- **8–10 overall score**—Begin with the "Foundation Summary" section and follow up with the "Q&A" section at the end of the chapter.

- **11 or more overall score**—If you want more review on these topics, skip to the "Foundation Summary" section and then go to the "Q&A" section at the end of the chapter. Otherwise, move to the Chapter 6, "VLANs and Trunks."

Foundation Topics

Ethernet Concepts

This section reviews the varieties of Ethernet and their application in a campus network. Recall how the bandwidth requirements for each network segment are determined by the types of applications in use, the traffic flows within the network, and the size of the user community served. Ethernet scales to support increasing bandwidths and should be chosen to match the need at each point in the campus network. As network bandwidth requirements grow, you can scale the links between access, distribution, and core layers to match the load.

Other network media technologies available include Fiber Distribution Data Interface (FDDI), Copper Distribution Data Interface (CDDI), Token Ring, and Asynchronous Transfer Mode (ATM). Although some networks still use these media, Ethernet has emerged as the most popular choice in installed networks. Ethernet is chosen because of its low cost, market availability, and scalability to higher bandwidths.

Ethernet (10 Mbps)

Ethernet is a LAN technology based on the Institute of Electrical and Electronics Engineers (IEEE) 802.3 standard. Ethernet (in contrast to Fast Ethernet and later versions) offers a bandwidth of 10 Mbps between end users. In its most basic form, Ethernet is a shared media that becomes both a collision and a broadcast domain. As the number of users on the shared media increases, so does the probability that a user is trying to transmit data at any given time. Ethernet is based on the carrier sense multiple access collision detect (CSMA/CD) technology, which requires that transmitting stations back off for a random period of time when a collision occurs. The more crowded an Ethernet segment becomes, the less efficient it is.

Ethernet switching addresses this problem by dynamically allocating a dedicated 10-Mbps bandwidth to each of its ports. The resulting increased network performance occurs by reducing the number of users connected to an Ethernet segment.

Although switched Ethernet's job is to offer fully dedicated bandwidth to each connected device, assuming that network performance will improve across the board when switching is introduced is a common mistake. For example, consider a workgroup of users connected by a shared media Ethernet hub. These users regularly access an enterprise server located elsewhere in the campus network. To improve performance, the decision is made to replace the hub with an Ethernet switch so that all users get dedicated 10-Mbps connections. Because the switch offers dedicated bandwidth for connections between the end user devices connected to its ports, any user-to-user traffic would probably see improved performance. However, the enterprise server is still located elsewhere in the network, and all the switched users must still share available bandwidth across the campus to reach it. As discussed in Chapter 1, "Campus Network Overview," rather than throwing raw bandwidth at a problem, a design based on careful observation of traffic patterns and flows offers a better solution.

Because switched Ethernet can remove the possibility of collisions, stations do not have to listen to each other to take a turn transmitting on the wire. Instead, stations can operate in full-duplex mode—transmitting and receiving simultaneously. Full-duplex mode further increases network performance, with a net throughput of 10 Mbps in each direction, or 20 Mbps total throughput on each port.

Another consideration when dealing with 10-Mbps Ethernet is the physical cabling. Ethernet cabling involves the use of unshielded twisted-pair (UTP) wiring (10BASE-T Ethernet), usually restricted to an end-to-end distance of 100 meters (328 feet) between active devices. Keeping cable lengths as short as possible in the wiring closet also reduces noise and crosstalk when many cables are bundled together.

In a campus network environment, Ethernet is usually used in the access layer, between end user devices and the access layer switch. Many networks still use Ethernet to connect end users to shared media hubs, which then connect to access layer switches. Ethernet is not typically used at either the distribution or core layer.

> **NOTE**   Ethernet applications (10BASE2, 10BASE5, 10BASE-F, and so on) use other cabling technologies, though they are not discussed here. For the most part, 10BASE-T with UTP wiring is the most commonly used. A useful website for further reading about Ethernet technology is Charles Spurgeon's Ethernet Web Site, at www.ethermanage.com/ethernet/.

Long Reach Ethernet (LRE)

In cases where buildings do not have Category 5 UTP wiring, standard 10-Mbps Ethernet might not be possible. Cisco has implemented a different form of Ethernet that can be transported long distances over Category 1, 2, or 3 wiring. This is called Cisco *Long Reach Ethernet (LRE)*.

Cisco LRE is available in the Catalyst 2900 LRE XL Switch Series. Multiple LRE ports are used to connect into existing building wiring (often used for telephone connections) to provide Ethernet capability to a building's tenants. LRE can provide 5 Mbps full-duplex bandwidth over connections up to 5000 feet, 10 Mbps up to 4000 feet, or 15 Mbps up to 3000 feet. LRE can co-exist on the same physical building wiring pairs with POTS and ISDN, and in the same building (different wiring pairs) with Asymmetric Digital Subscriber Line (ADSL).

The following equipment is needed to complete an LRE connection:

- **Cisco Catalyst 2900 LRE XL switch**—Aggregates 12 or 24 LRE connections at the building head-end

- **Cisco 575 or 585 LRE CPE**—Terminates the LRE connection in the tenant room

- **Cisco LRE 48 POTS Splitter**—Separates POTS and LRE on 48 ports when existing phone wiring is used in a building

Figure 5-1 shows how LRE might be used in two typical multitenant buildings. The building on the left uses existing but spare building wiring pairs to provide the LRE connection between a central Catalyst 2900 LRE XL switch and a Cisco 575 LRE CPE unit in each tenant office. The building on the right has an existing PBX that provides telephone services to the tenants. LRE is provided over the same telephone wiring through a central LRE 48-port POTS splitter. Then, a Catalyst 2900 LRE XL connects to multiple Cisco 575 units over the existing cabling.

Figure 5-1 *Typical LRE Installation*

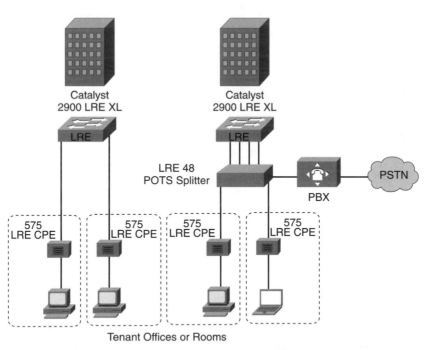

Fast Ethernet

Rather than require campuses to invest in a completely new technology to gain increased bandwidth, the networking industry developed a higher-speed Ethernet based on existing Ethernet standards.

Fast Ethernet operates at 100 Mbps and is defined in the IEEE 802.3u standard. The Ethernet cabling schemes, CSMA/CD operation, and all upper-layer protocol operations are maintained with Fast Ethernet. The net result is the same data link Media Access Control (MAC) layer merged with a new physical layer.

The campus network can use Fast Ethernet to link access and distribution layer switches, if no higher-speed links are available. These links can support the aggregate traffic from multiple Ethernet segments in the access layer. Fast Ethernet is generally used to connect end user workstations to the access layer switch and to provide improved connectivity to enterprise servers.

Cabling for Fast Ethernet can involve either UTP or fiber. Table 5-2 lists the specifications for Fast Ethernet that define the media types and distances.

Table 5-2 *Cabling Specifications for Fast Ethernet*

Technology	Wiring Type	Pairs	Cable Length
100BASE-TX	EIA/TIA Category 5 UTP	2	100 m
100BASE-T2	EIA/TIA Category 3,4,5 UTP	2	100 m
100BASE-T4	EIA/TIA Category 3,4,5 UTP	4	100 m
100BASE-FX	Multimode fiber (MMF); 62.5 micron core, 125 micron outer cladding (62.5/125)	1	400 m half duplex or 2000 m full duplex
	Single-mode fiber (SMF)	1	10 km

Full-Duplex Fast Ethernet

As with traditional Ethernet, the natural progression to improve performance is to use full-duplex operation. Fast Ethernet can provide 100 Mbps in each direction on a switched connection, for 200 Mbps total throughput. This throughput is possible only when a workstation, server, or a router directly connects to a switch port, or when two switches directly connect to each other. In any case, the operating system or firmware on each end of the connection must support full-duplex operation.

The Fast Ethernet specification also offers backward-compatibility to support traditional 10-Mbps Ethernet. In the case of 100BASE-TX, switch ports are often called "10/100" ports, to denote the dual speed. To provide this support, the two devices at each end of a network connection can automatically negotiate link capabilities so that they can both operate at a maximum common level. This negotiation involves detecting and selecting the highest physical layer technology (available bandwidth) and half-duplex or full-duplex operation. To properly negotiate a connection, both ends should be configured for autonegotiation.

116   Chapter 5: Switch Port Configuration

The link speed is determined by electrical signaling, so that either end of a link can determine what the other end is trying to use. If both ends of the link are configured to autonegotiate, they will use the highest speed that is common to them.

A link's duplex mode, however, is negotiated through an exchange of information. This means that for one end to successfully autonegotiate the duplex mode, the other end must also be set to auto-negotiate. Otherwise, one end will never see any duplex information from the other end and won't determine the correct common mode. If duplex autonegotiation fails, a switch port falls back to its default setting—half-duplex. Beware of a duplex mismatch when both ends of a link are not set for autonegotiation.

Autonegotiation uses the priorities shown in Table 5-3 for each mode of Ethernet to determine which technology to agree upon. If both devices can support more than one technology, the technology with the highest priority is used. For example, if two devices can support both 10BASE-T and 100BASE-TX, both devices will use the higher priority 100BASE-TX mode.

Table 5-3 *Autonegotiation Selection Priorities*

Priority	Ethernet Mode
7	100BASE-T2 (full duplex)
6	100BASE-TX (full duplex)
5	100BASE-T2 (half duplex)
4	100BASE-T4
3	100BASE-TX
2	10BASE-T (full duplex)
1	10BASE-T

To assure proper configuration at both ends of a link, Cisco recommends that the appropriate values for transmission speed and duplex mode be manually configured on switch ports. This precludes any possibility that one end of the link will change its settings, resulting in an unusable connection.

Cisco provides one additional capability to Fast Ethernet, which allows several Fast Ethernet links to be bundled together for increased throughput. *Fast EtherChannel (FEC)* allows two to eight full-duplex Fast Ethernet links to act as a single physical link, for 400- to 1600-Mbps duplex bandwidth. This technology is described in greater detail in Chapter 8, "Aggregating Switch Links."

For further reading about Fast Ethernet technology, refer to the article, "Fast Ethernet 100-Mbps Solutions," at Cisco's website: www.cisco.com/warp/public/cc/so/neso/lnso/lnmnso/feth_tc.htm.

Gigabit Ethernet

You can scale Fast Ethernet by an additional order of magnitude with Gigabit Ethernet (which supports 1000 Mbps or 1 Gbps), using the same IEEE 802.3 Ethernet frame format as before. This scalability allows network designers and managers to leverage existing knowledge and technologies to install, migrate, manage, and maintain Gigabit Ethernet networks.

However, the physical layer has been modified to increase data transmission speeds. Two technologies were merged together to gain the benefits of each: the IEEE 802.3 Ethernet standard and the American National Standards Institute (ANSI) X3T11 FibreChannel. IEEE 802.3 provided the foundation of frame format, CSMA/CD, full duplex, and other Ethernet characteristics. FibreChannel provided a base of high-speed ASICs, optical components, and encoding/decoding and serialization mechanisms. The resulting protocol is termed IEEE 802.3z Gigabit Ethernet.

Gigabit Ethernet supports several cabling types, referred to as *1000BASE-X*. Table 5-4 lists the cabling specifications for each type.

In a campus network, you can use Gigabit Ethernet in the switch block, core block, and server block. In the switch block, it connects access layer switches to distribution layer switches. In the core, it connects the distribution layer to the core switches and interconnects the core devices. In a server block, a Gigabit Ethernet switch can provide high-speed connections to individual servers

Table 5-4   *Gigabit Ethernet Cabling and Distance Limitations*

GE Type	Wiring Type	Pairs	Cable Length
1000BASE-CX	Shielded twisted-pair (STP)	1	25 m
1000BASE-T	EIA/TIA Category 5 UTP	4	100 m
1000BASE-SX	Multimode fiber (MMF) with 62.5 micron core; 850 nm laser	1	275 m
	MMF with 50 micron core; 850 nm laser	1	550 m
1000BASE-LX/LH	MMF with 62.5 micron core; 1300 nm laser	1	550 m
	Single-mode fiber (SMF) with 50 micron core; 1300 nm laser	1	550 m
	SMF with 9 micron core; 1300 nm laser	1	10 km
1000BASE-ZX	SMF with 9 micron core; 1550 nm laser	1	70 km
	SMF with 8 micron core; 1550 nm laser	1	100 km

The "Gigabit over copper" solution that the 1000BASE-T media provides is based on the IEEE 802.3ab standard. Most Gigabit Ethernet switch ports used between switches are fixed at 1000 Mbps. However, other switch ports can support a fallback to Fast or Legacy Ethernet speeds. Here, speed can be autonegotiated between end nodes to the highest common speed — 10 Mbps, 100 Mbps, or 1000 Mbps. These ports are often called "10/100/1000" ports to denote the triple speed. Here, the autonegotiation supports the same priority scheme as Fast Ethernet, although 1000BASE-T full duplex becomes the highest priority, followed by 1000BASE-T half duplex. Gigabit Ethernet's port duplex mode is always set to full duplex on Cisco switches, so duplex autonegotiation is not possible.

Finally, Cisco has extended the concept of Fast EtherChannel to bundle several Gigabit Ethernet links to act as a single physical connection. With *Gigabit EtherChannel (GEC)*, two to eight full-duplex Gigabit Ethernet connections can be aggregated, for a single logical link of up to 16-Gbps throughput. Port aggregation and the EtherChannel technology are described further in Chapter 8.

> **NOTE** The Gigabit Ethernet Alliance offers further reading about Gigabit Ethernet and its operation, migration, and standards. Refer to the web site at www.10gea.org.

10Gigabit Ethernet

Ethernet scales by orders of magnitude, beginning with 10 Mbps, progressing to 100, and then to 1000 Mbps. To meet the demand for aggregating many Gigabit Ethernet links over a single connection, 10Gigabit Ethernet was developed. Again, the Layer 2 characteristics of Ethernet have been preserved; the familiar 802.3 frame format and size, as well as the MAC protocol, remain unchanged.

10Gigabit Ethernet, also known as *10GbE,* and the IEEE 802.3ae standard, differs from its predecessors only at the physical layer (PHY). Basically, 10Gigabit Ethernet operates only over fiber-optic media, and only at full duplex. The standard defines several different transceivers that can be used as Physical Media Dependent (PMD) fiber-optic interfaces. These are classified into the following:

- **LAN PHY** — Interconnects switches in a campus network, predominantly in the core layer
- **WAN PHY** — Interfaces with existing synchronous optical network (SONET) or synchronous digital hierarchy (SDH) networks typically found in metropolitan-area networks (MANs)

The PMD interfaces also have a common labeling scheme, much as Gigabit Ethernet does. Where Gigabit Ethernet uses 1000BASE-X to indicate the media or Gigabit Interface Converter (GBIC) type, 10Gigabit Ethernet uses 10GBASE-X. Table 5-5 lists the different PMDs defined in the standard, along with the type of fiber and distance limitations. At press time, Cisco Catalyst switches supported only two PMDs; these are also shown in the table. All of the PMDs can be used as either a LAN or WAN PHY, except for the 10GBASE-LX4, which is only a LAN PHY.

Table 5-5 *10Gigabit Ethernet PMD Types and Characteristics*

PMD type[1]	Fiber Media	Maximum Distance	Catalyst Switch
10GBASE-SR/SW (850 nm serial)	MMF: 50 micron	66 m	N/A
	MMF: 50 micron (2GHz * km modal bandwidth)	300 m	
	MMF: 62.5 micron	33 m	
10GBASE-LR/LW (1310 nm serial)	SMF: 9 micron	10 km	Catalyst 6500
10GBASE-ER/EW (1550 nm serial)	SMF: 9 micron	40 km	Catalyst 6500
10GBASE-LX4/LW4 (1310 nm WWDM)	MMF: 50 micron	300 m	N/A
	MMF: 62.5 micron	300 m	
	SMF: 9 micron	10 km	

[1] Transceiver types are denoted by a two-letter suffix. The first letter specifies the wavelength used: S=short, L=long, E=extra long wavelength. The second letter specifies the PHY type: R=LAN PHY, W=WAN PHY. In the case of LX4 and LW4, L refers to a long wavelength, X and W refer to the coding used, and 4 refers to the number of wavelengths transmitted. "WWDM" is wide wavelength division multiplexing.

Metro Ethernet

If an enterprise exists in several geographic locations, high-speed WAN connections are often desired between the locations. To accomplish this, Ethernet frames can also be transported over several different types of connections. Service providers can offer this type of transport, called *Metro Ethernet*, to many customers over an existing WAN or MAN infrastructure.

Metro Ethernet can offer these types of connectivity to an end customer:

- **Transparent LAN Service (TLS)**—*All* of a customer's connected sites appear as a single common VLAN (broadcast domain). Implementation is very simple, although the service provider is limited to 4096 customer VLANs total.

- **Directed VLAN Service (DVS)**—A customer's VLANs can be connected wherever they exist, rather than everywhere. This allows one VLAN to be connected between two sites while another VLAN connects to two other sites, and so on. A customer is allowed to have multiple VLANs transported by the service provider network. The VLAN ID is used in the service provider (SP) core to switch frames to the destination. Implementation is more complicated, requiring knowledge of the customer's VLAN topology and the existence of the Per-VLAN Spanning Tree Protocol (PVST+) to prevent bridging loops.

The following service provider infrastructures can transport Ethernet frames:

- **Metro Ethernet over SONET**—SONET is widely used in ring topologies between cities or within cities. SONET has inherent fault tolerance and rich management and alarm capabilities. Customers receive fixed bandwidth access to the ring in large increments.

- **Metro Ethernet over Dense Wave Division Multiplexing (DWDM)**—A single fiber connection transports many different Gigabit Ethernet datastreams by placing each within a different wavelength (represented by the Greek letter *lambda* λ) of light. Each lambda is completely independent, and each has complete dedicated bandwidth.

- **Metro Ethernet over Coarse Wave Division Multiplexing (CWDM)**—Similar to DWDM, with fewer lambdas (8) supported on a fiber connection over a shorter distance. CWDM is available directly on Catalyst switch GBIC modules.

Connecting Switch Block Devices

Switch deployment in a network involves two steps: physical connectivity and switch configuration. This section describes the connections and cabling requirements for devices in a switch block. Cable connections must be made to a switch's console port to make initial configurations. Physical connectivity between switches and end users involves cabling for the various types of LAN ports.

Console Port Cables/Connectors

A terminal emulation program on a PC is usually required to interface with the console port on a switch. Various types of console cables and console connectors are associated with each Cisco switch family.

All Catalyst switch families use an RJ-45-to-RJ-45 *rollover cable* to make the console connection between a PC (or terminal or modem) and the console port. A rollover cable is made so that pin 1 on one RJ-45 connector goes to pin 8 on the other RJ-45 connector, pin 2 goes to pin 7, and so forth. In other words, the cable remains flat while the two RJ-45 connectors point in opposite directions.

To connect the PC end, the rollover cable plugs into an RJ-45 to DB-9 or DB-25 "terminal" adapter (or a DB-25 "modem" adapter for a modem connection). At the switch end, the rollover cable plugs directly into the console port's RJ-45 jack.

After the console port is cabled to the PC, terminal, or modem, a terminal emulation program can be started or a user connection can be made. The console ports on all switch families require an asynchronous serial connection at 9600 baud, 8 data bits, no parity, 1 stop bit, and no flow control.

Ethernet Port Cables and Connectors

Catalyst switches support a variety of network connections, including all forms of Ethernet. In addition, Catalyst switches support several types of cabling, including UTP and optical fiber.

Fast Ethernet (100BASE-FX) ports use two-strand multimode fiber (MMF) with MT-RJ or SC connectors to provide connectivity. The MT-RJ connectors are small and modular, each containing a pair of fiber-optic strands. The connector snaps into position, but you must press a tab to remove it. The SC connectors on the fiber cables are square in shape. These connectors snap in and out of the switch port connector as the connector is pushed in or pulled out. One fiber strand is used as a transmit path and the other as a receive path. The transmit fiber on one switch device should connect to the receive fiber on the other end.

All Catalyst switch families support 10/100 autosensing (using Fast Ethernet autonegotiation) and Gigabit Ethernet. Switched 10/100 ports use RJ-45 connectors on Category 5 UTP cabling to complete the connections. These ports can connect to other 10BASE-T, 100BASE-TX, or 10/100 autosensing devices. UTP cabling is arranged so that RJ-45 pins 1,2 and 3,6 form two twisted pairs. These pairs connect straight through to the far end.

To connect two 10/100 switch ports back-to-back, as in an access layer to distribution layer link, you must use a Category 5 UTP crossover cable. In this case, RJ-45 pins 1,2 and 3,6 are still twisted pairs, but 1,2 on one end connects to 3,6 on the other end, and 3,6 on one end connects to 1,2 on the other end.

> **NOTE** Because UTP Ethernet connections use only pairs 1,2 and 3,6, some cable plant installers connect only these pairs and leave the remaining two pair positions empty. Although this move provides Ethernet connectivity, it is not good practice for future needs. Instead, all four RJ-45 connector pairs should be connected end-to-end. For example, a full four-pair UTP cable plant can be used for either Ethernet or Token Ring connectivity, without rewiring. (Token Ring UTP connections use pairs 3,6 and 4,5.) Also, to be compatible with the new IEEE 802.3ab standard for Gigabit Ethernet over copper (1000BASE-T), all four pairs must be used end-to-end.

Gigabit Ethernet Port Cables and Connectors

Gigabit Ethernet connections take a different approach by providing modular connectivity options. Catalyst switches with Gigabit Ethernet ports have standardized rectangular openings that accept GBICs. The GBIC modules provide the media personality for the port so that various cable media can connect. In this way, the switch chassis is completely modular and requires no major change to accept a new media type. Instead, the appropriate GBIC module is hot-swappable and is plugged into the switch to support the new media. GBICs are available for the following Gigabit Ethernet media:

- **1000BASE-SX GBIC**—Short wavelength connectivity using SC fiber connectors and MMF for distances up to 550 meters (1804 feet).

- **1000BASE-LX/LH GBIC**—Long wavelength/long haul connectivity using SC fiber connectors and either MMF or single-mode fiber (SMF); MMF can be used for distances up to 550 meters (1804 feet), and SMF can be used for distances up to 10 km (32,810 feet). MMF requires a special mode-conditioning cable for fiber distances less than 100 m (328 feet) or greater than 300 m (984 feet). This keeps the GBIC from overdriving the far-end receiver on a short cable and lessens the effect of differential mode delay on a long cable.

- **1000BASE-ZX GBIC**—Extended distance connectivity using SC fiber connectors and SMF; works for distances up to 70 km, and even to 100 km when used with premium grade SMF.

- **GigaStack GBIC**—Uses a proprietary connector with a high-data-rate copper cable with enhanced signal integrity and electromagnetic interference (EMI) performance; provides a GBIC-to-GBIC connection between stacking Catalyst switches or between any two Gigabit switch ports over a short distance. The connection is full duplex if only one of the two stacking connectors is used; if both connectors are used, they each become half duplex over a shared bus.

- **1000BASE-T GBIC**—Sports an RJ-45 connector for 4-pair UTP cabling; works for distances up to 100 m (328 feet).

> **NOTE** You must use a four-pair Category 5 UTP crossover cable to connect two 1000BASE-T switch ports back-to-back. In this case, RJ-45 pins 1,2, 3,6, 4,5 and 7,8 are still twisted pairs on one end, connecting to pins 3,6, 1,2, 7,8, and 4,5 respectively on the other end.

> **CAUTION** The fiber-based GBICs always have the receive fiber on the left SC connector and the transmit fiber on the right SC connector, as you face the connectors. These GBICs could produce invisible laser radiation from the transmit SC connector. Therefore, always keep unused SC connectors covered with the rubber plugs, and don't ever look directly into the SC connectors.

Figure 5-2 illustrates three GBIC modules.

Figure 5-2 *Gigabit Interface Converters*

1000BASE-SX
1000BASE-LX/LH
1000BASE-ZX   GigaStack   1000BASE-T

Switch Port Configuration

You can configure the individual ports on a switch with various information and settings, as detailed in the following sections.

Selecting Ports to Configure

Before you can modify port settings, you must select one or more switch ports. Catalyst switches running the Catalyst operating system (CatOS) refer to these as *ports*, whereas switches running the Cisco IOS Software refer to them as *interfaces*. The BCMSN exam is based on IOS-based switches only.

To select a single switch port, enter the following command in global configuration mode:

```
Switch(config)# interface module/number
```

The port is identified by the physical module or "blade" where it is located, along with the port number within the module. Some switches, such as the Catalyst 2950 and 3550, don't have multiple modules. For those models, ports have a module number of 0 (zero).

To select multiple ports for a common configuration setting, enter them as a list separated by commas with spaces. You must also identify the type of switch port (that is, **fastethernet**, **gigabitethernet**, **tengigabitethernet**, or **vlan**). Use this command in global configuration mode:

```
Switch(config)# interface range type module/number [, type module/number ...]
```

You can also select a range of ports, from a beginning interface to an ending interface. Enter the interface type and module, followed by the beginning and ending port number separated by a dash with spaces. Use this command in global configuration mode:

```
Switch(config)# interface range type module/first-number - last-number
```

Lastly, you might sometimes need to make configuration changes to several groups or ranges of ports. You can define a macro that contains a list of interfaces or ranges of interfaces. Then, you can invoke the interface range macro just prior to configuring the port settings. This applies the port settings to each interface that is identified by the macro. Define the macro to contain a list or range of ports (extend these commands with as many ports or ranges of ports as needed):

```
Switch(config)# define interface-range macro-name type module/number [, type module/
number ...]
-OR-
Switch(config)# define interface-range macro-name type module/first-number - last-
number
```

Then, invoke the macro called *macro-name* just as you would with a regular interface:

```
Switch(config)# interface range macro macro-name
```

Identifying Ports

You can add a text description to a switch port's configuration to help identify it. This description is meant as a comment field only, as a record of port use or other unique information. The port description is included when displaying the switch configuration.

To assign a comment or description to a port, enter the following command in interface configuration mode:

```
Switch(config-if)# description description-string
```

The description string can have embedded spaces between words, if needed. To remove a description, use the **no description** interface configuration command.

Port Speed

You can assign a specific speed to switch ports through switch configuration commands. Fast Ethernet 10/100 ports can be set to speeds of *10*, *100*, and *Auto* (the default) for autonegotiate mode. Gigabit Ethernet GBIC ports are always set to a speed of *1000*, while 1000BASE-T ports can be set to speeds of *10*, *100*, *1000*, and *Auto* (the default).

> **NOTE**   If a 10/100 or a 10/100/1000 port is assigned a speed of **auto**, both its speed and duplex mode will be negotiated.

To specify the port speed on a particular Ethernet port, use the following interface configuration command:

```
Switch(config-if)# speed {10 | 100 | 1000 | auto}
```

Port Mode

You can also assign a specific link mode to Ethernet-based switch ports. Therefore, the port operates in half-duplex, full-duplex, or autonegotiated mode. Autonegotiation is allowed only on UTP Fast Ethernet and Gigabit Ethernet ports. In this mode, the port will *participate* in a negotiation by attempting full-duplex operation first, and then half-duplex if full duplex is not successful. The autonegotiation process repeats whenever the link status changes. Be sure to set both ends of a link to the same speed and duplex settings to eliminate any chance that the two ends will be mismatched.

NOTE   A 10-Mbps Ethernet link (fixed speed) defaults to half duplex, whereas a 100-Mbps Fast Ethernet (dual speed 10/100) link defaults to full duplex. Multispeed links default to autonegotiate the duplex mode.

To set the link mode on a switch port, enter the following command in interface configuration mode:

```
Switch(config-if)# duplex {auto | full | half}
```

Managing Error Conditions on a Switch Port

Traditionally, a network management application was used to detect a serious error condition on a switch port. A switch would be periodically polled and switch port error counters would be examined to see if an error condition had occurred. If so, an alert was issued so that someone could take action to correct the problem.

Catalyst switches can now detect error conditions without any further help. If a serious error occurs on a switch port, that port can be automatically shut down until someone manually enables the port again, or until a predetermined time has elapsed.

Detecting Error Conditions

By default, a Catalyst switch detects an error condition on every switch port for every possible cause. If an error condition is detected, the switch port is put into the *errdisable* state and disabled. You can tune this behavior so that only certain causes trigger a port being disabled. Use the following command in global configuration mode:

```
Switch(config)# errdisable detect cause [all | cause-name]
```

One of the following causes triggers the errdisable state (note that the command can be repeated to give more than one cause):

■ **all**—Detects every possible cause

■ **bpduguard**—Detects when a Spanning Tree bridge protocol data unit (BPDU) is received on a port configured for STP portfast

- **dtp-flap**—Detects when trunking encapsulation is changing from one type to another
- **link-flap**—Detects when the port link state is "flapping" between the up and down states
- **pagp-flap**—Detects when an EtherChannel bundle's ports no longer have consistent configurations
- **rootguard**—Detects when an STP BPDU is received from the root bridge on an unexpected port
- **udld**—Detects when a link is seen to be unidirectional (data passing in only one direction)

Automatically Recover from Error Conditions

By default, ports put into the errdisable state must be manually re-enabled. This is done by issuing the **shutdown** command in interface configuration mode, followed by the **no shutdown** command.

You can decide to have a switch automatically re-enable an errdisabled port if it is more important to keep the link up until the problem can be resolved. To automatically re-enable an errdisabled port, you must first specify the errdisable causes that can be re-enabled. Use this command in global configuration mode, with a *cause-name* from the preceding list:

```
Switch(config)# errdisable recovery cause [all | cause-name]
```

If any errdisable causes are configured for automatic recovery, the errdisabled port stays down for 300 seconds, by default. To change the recovery timer, use the following command in global configuration mode:

```
Switch(config)# errdisable recovery interval seconds
```

You can set the interval from 30 to 86,400 seconds (24 hours).

Enable and Use the Switch Port

If the port is not automatically enabled or activated, use the **no shutdown** interface configuration command. To view a port's current speed and duplex state, use the **show interface** command.

Troubleshooting Port Connectivity

Suppose you are experiencing problems with a switch port. How would you troubleshoot it? The following sections cover a few common troubleshooting techniques.

Looking for the Port State

Use the **show interface** EXEC command to see complete information about the switch port. The port's current state is given in the first line of output, as in Example 5-1.

Example 5-1 *Determining Port State Information*

```
sbrn-437-c1# show interface fastethernet 0/1
FastEthernet0/1 is up, line protocol is up
  Hardware is Fast Ethernet, address is 0009.b7ee.9801 (bia 0009.b7ee.9801)
  MTU 1500 bytes, BW 100000 Kbit, DLY 100 usec,
     reliability 255/255, txload 1/255, rxload 1/255
```

The first **up** tells the state of the port's physical or data link layer. If this is shown as **down**, the link is physically disconnected, or a link cannot be detected. The second state, given as **line protocol is up**, shows the Layer 2 status. If the state is given as **errdisable**, the switch has detected a serious error condition and automatically disabled the port.

To quickly see a list of states for all switch ports, use the **show interface status** EXEC command. Likewise, you can see a list of all ports in the errdisable state (as well as the cause) by using the **show interface status err-disabled** EXEC command.

Looking for Speed and/or Duplex Mismatches

If a user notices slow response time or low throughput on a 10/100 or 10/100/1000 switch port, the problem could be due to a mismatch of the port speed or duplex mode between the switch and the host. This is particularly common when one end of the link is set to autonegotiate the link settings, and the other end is not.

Use the **show interface** command for a specific interface and look for any error counts that are greater than 0. For example, in the following output in Example 5-2, the switch port is set to autonegotiate the speed and duplex mode. It has decided on 100 Mbps at half duplex. Notice that there are a large number of *runts* (packets that were truncated before they were fully received) and input errors. These are symptoms that a setting mismatch exists between the two ends of the link.

Because this port is autonegotiating the link speed, it must have detected an electrical signal that indicated 100 Mbps in common with the host. However, the host was most likely configured for 100 Mbps at full duplex (not autonegotiating). The switch was unable to exchange duplex information, so it fell back to its default of half duplex. Again, always make sure both ends of a connection are set to the same speed and duplex.

Example 5-2 *Determining Link Speed and Duplex Mode*

```
switch# show interface fastethernet 0/13
FastEthernet0/13 is up, line protocol is up
  Hardware is Fast Ethernet, address is 00d0.589c.3e8d (bia 00d0.589c.3e8d)
  MTU 1500 bytes, BW 10000 Kbit, DLY 1000 usec,
     reliability 255/255, txload 2/255, rxload 1/255
  Encapsulation ARPA, loopback not set
  Keepalive not set
Auto-duplex (Half), Auto Speed (100), 100BASETX/FX  ARP type: ARPA, ARP
    Timeout 04:00:00
Last input never, output 00:00:01, output hang never
  Last clearing of "show interface" counters never
  Queueing strategy: fifo
  Output queue 0/40, 0 drops; input queue 0/75, 0 drops
  5 minute input rate 0 bits/sec, 0 packets/sec
  5 minute output rate 81000 bits/sec, 49 packets/sec
     500867 packets input, 89215950 bytes
     Received 12912 broadcasts, 374879 runts, 0 giants, 0 throttles
     374879 input errors, 0 CRC, 0 frame, 0 overrun, 0 ignored
     0 watchdog, 0 multicast
     0 input packets with dribble condition detected
     89672388 packets output, 2205443729 bytes, 0 underruns
     0 output errors, 0 collisions, 3 interface resets
     0 babbles, 0 late collision, 0 deferred
     0 lost carrier, 0 no carrier
     0 output buffer failures, 0 output buffers swapped out
```

Foundation Summary

The Foundation Summary is a collection of tables that provides a convenient review of many key concepts in this chapter. If you are already comfortable with the topics in this chapter, this summary might help you recall a few details. If you just read this chapter, this review should help solidify some key facts. If you are doing your final prep before the exam, the following tables are a convenient way to review the day before the exam.

Table 5-6 *Ethernet Standards*

Ethernet Type	Media Name	Standard Name
10 Mbps Ethernet	10BASE-X	IEEE 802.3
Cisco Long Reach Ethernet	n/a	n/a (Cisco proprietary)
Fast Ethernet	100BASE-X	IEEE 802.3u
Gigabit Ethernet	1000BASE-X	IEEE 802.3z (fiber) IEEE 802.3ab (UTP)
10Gigabit Ethernet	10GBASE-X	IEEE 802.3ae

Table 5-7 *Ethernet Cabling Specifications*

Technology	Wiring Type	Pairs	Cable Length
10BASE-T	EIA/TIA Category 5 UTP	2	100 m
LRE	Category 1, 2, 3 UTP	1	5000 feet (5 Mbps), 4000 feet (10 Mbps), 3000 feet (15 Mbps)
100BASE-TX	EIA/TIA Category 5 UTP	2	100 m
100BASE-T2	EIA/TIA Category 3,4,5 UTP	2	100 m
100BASE-T4	EIA/TIA Category 3,4,5 UTP	4	100 m
100BASE-FX	Multimode fiber (MMF); 62.5 micron core, 125 micron outer cladding (62.5/125)	1	400 m half duplex or 2000 m full duplex
	Single-mode fiber (SMF)	1	10 km

continues

Table 5-7 *Ethernet Cabling Specifications (Continued)*

Technology	Wiring Type	Pairs	Cable Length
1000BASE-CX	Shielded twisted-pair (STP)	1	25 m
1000BASE-T	EIA/TIA Category 5 UTP	4	100 m
1000BASE-SX	MMF with 62.5 micron core; 850 nm laser	1	275 m
	MMF with 50 micron core; 850 nm laser	1	550 m
1000BASE-LX/LH	MMF with 62.5 micron core; 1300 nm laser	1	550 m
	SMF with 50 micron core; 1300 nm laser	1	550 m
	SMF with 9 micron core; 1300 nm laser	1	10 km
1000BASE-ZX	SMF with 9 micron core; 1550 nm laser	1	70 km
	SMF with 8 micron core; 1550 nm laser	1	100 km
10GBASE-SR/SW (850 nm serial)	MMF: 50 micron MMF: 62.5 micron	1 1	66 m 33 m
10GBASE-LR/LW (1310 nm serial)	SMF: 9 micron	1	10 km
10GBASE-ER/EW (1550 nm serial)	SMF: 9 micron	1	40 km
10GBASE-LX4 (1310 nm WWDM)	MMF: 50 micron MMF: 62.5 micron SMF: 9 micron	1 1 1	300 m 300 m 10 km

Table 5-8 *Metro Ethernet Review*

	Name	Attributes
Metro Services	Transparent LAN Service (TLS)	Each customer connected by one VLAN
	Directed VLAN Service (DVS)	Each customer can have multiple VLANs; switching by VLAN ID
Metro Transport	Metro Ethernet over SONET	Widely deployed ring topologies; fault tolerant
	Metro Ethernet over DWDM	Many Gigabit Ethernet datastreams transported over many lambdas
	Metro Ethernet over CWDM	Only eight lambdas supported over a short distance

Table 5-9 *Switch Port Configuration Commands*

Task	Command Syntax
Select a port	**interface** *module/number*
Select multiple ports	**interface range** *type module/number* [, *type module/number* ...] -OR- **interface range** *type module/first-number – last-number*
Define an interface macro	**define interface-range** *macro-name type module/number* [, *type module/number* ...] -OR- **define interface-range** *macro-name type module/first-number – last-number* **interface range macro** *macro-name*
Identify port	**description** *description-string*
Set port speed	**speed** {**10** | **100** | **1000** | **auto**}
Set port mode	**duplex** {**auto** | **full** | **half**}

Table 5-9 *Switch Port Configuration Commands (Continued)*

Task	Command Syntax
Detect port error conditions	**errdisable detect cause** [**all** | *cause-name*]
Automatically recover from errdisable	**errdisable recovery cause** [**all** | *cause-name*] **errdisable recovery interval** *seconds*
Manually recover from errdisable	**shutdown** **no shutdown**

Q&A

The questions and scenarios in this book are more difficult than what you should experience on the actual exam. The questions do not attempt to cover more breadth or depth than the exam; however, they are designed to make sure that you know the answer. Rather than allowing you to derive the answers from clues hidden inside the question themselves, the questions challenge your understanding and recall of the subject. Hopefully, these questions will help limit the number of exam questions on which you narrow your choices to two options and then guess.

You can find the answers to these questions in Appendix A.

1. Put the following Ethernet standards in order of increasing bandwidth:

    a. 802.3z

    b. 802.3ae

    c. 802.3

    d. 802.3u

2. What benefits does switched Ethernet have over shared Ethernet?

3. When a 10/100 Ethernet link is autonegotiating, which will be chosen if both stations can support the same capabilities—10BASE-T full duplex, 100BASE-TX half duplex, or 100BASE-TX full duplex?

4. How many pairs of copper wires does a 1000BASE-T connection need?

5. A switch port is being configured as shown here. What command is needed next to set the port to full-duplex mode?

    ```
    Switch(config)# interface fastethernet 0/13
    Switch(config-if)#
    ```

6. If a full-duplex Gigabit Ethernet connection offers 2 Gbps throughput, can a single host send data at 2 Gbps?

7. Which GBIC would you use for a connection over multimode fiber (MMF)?

8. When might Long Reach Ethernet be a good candidate for a connection?

9. A Category 5 cable having only pins 1,2 and 3,6 has been installed and used for a Fast Ethernet link. Can this same cable be used for a migration to Gigabit Ethernet using 1000BASE-T GBICs, assuming the length is less than 100 meters?

10. A Catalyst 3550 switch port has been configured for 100 Mbps full-duplex mode, but a link cannot be established. What are some commands that you could use to investigate and correct the problem?

11. 10Gigabit Ethernet is backward-compatible with other forms of Ethernet at Layer _____ but not at Layer _____.

12. What type(s) of Ethernet are commonly used to connect geographically separate locations?

13. What form of Metro Ethernet allows several enterprise VLANs to be transported between locations—TLS or DVS?

14. What one switch command will select Fast Ethernet interfaces 4/1 through 48 for a common configuration?

15. What is a GBIC's purpose?

16. Suppose you need to apply several different common configurations to Fast Ethernet interfaces 3/1 through 12, 3/34, 3/48, and 5/14 through 48. What commands are needed to create an interface macro to accomplish this, and what command would apply the macro?

17. If a switch port is configured with the **speed 100** and **duplex full** commands, what will happen if the PC connected to it is set for autonegotiated speed and duplex? Now reverse the roles (the switch will autonegotiate, but the PC won't). What will happen?

18. By default, what will a switch do if one of its ports has a serious error condition, and how can you tell when this has happened?

19. What port speeds can you assign to a UTP Gigabit Ethernet switch port? Consider both 1000BASE-T GBIC and native RJ-45 copper switch module ports.

20. What command can you use to make sure that no switch ports are automatically shut down in an errdisable state for any reason?

21. Suppose you commonly find that switch ports are being shut down in errdisable due to users making their connections go up and down too often. Thinking this might be due to odd PC behavior, you would like to visit each user to troubleshoot the problem. However, this is a minor error and you don't want to inconvenience the end users too much. What command(s) can you use to have the switch automatically re-enable the ports after 10 minutes? Make sure a flapping link will be automatically recovered in this time frame.

22. Look at the following **show interface** output. Does the high number of collisions indicate a problem? Why or why not?

```
FastEthernet0/6 is up, line protocol is up
  Hardware is Fast Ethernet, address is 000a.f4d2.5506 (bia 000a.f4d2.5506)
  Description: kelly-107-1d1,pc
  MTU 1500 bytes, BW 10000 Kbit, DLY 1000 usec,
     reliability 255/255, txload 1/255, rxload 1/255
  Encapsulation ARPA, loopback not set
  Keepalive set (10 sec)
  Half-duplex, 10Mb/s
  input flow-control is off, output flow-control is off
  ARP type: ARPA, ARP Timeout 04:00:00
  Last input never, output 00:00:00, output hang never
  Last clearing of "show interface" counters never
  Input queue: 0/75/0/0 (size/max/drops/flushes); Total output drops: 0
  Queueing strategy: fifo
  Output queue :0/40 (size/max)
  5 minute input rate 0 bits/sec, 0 packets/sec
  5 minute output rate 0 bits/sec, 0 packets/sec
     1321140 packets input, 227738894 bytes, 0 no buffer
     Received 13786 broadcasts, 0 runts, 0 giants, 0 throttles
     1 input errors, 1 CRC, 0 frame, 0 overrun, 0 ignored
     0 watchdog, 42 multicast, 0 pause input
     0 input packets with dribble condition detected
     87798820 packets output, 2662785561 bytes, 1316 underruns
     6 output errors, 400070 collisions, 3 interface resets
     0 babbles, 0 late collision, 19458 deferred
     0 lost carrier, 0 no carrier, 0 PAUSE output
     1316 output buffer failures, 0 output buffers swapped out
```

This chapter covers the following topics that you need to master for the CCNP BCMSN exam:

- **Virtual LANs**—This section reviews VLANs, VLAN membership, and VLAN configuration on a Catalyst switch.

- **VLAN Trunks**—This section covers transporting multiple VLANs over single links and VLAN trunking with Ethernet.

- **VLAN Trunk Configuration**—This section outlines the Catalyst switch commands that configure VLAN trunks.

- **Service Provider Tunneling**—This section covers IEEE 802.1Q (Q-in-Q) and Layer 2 Protocol tunnels for transporting customer trunks across a service provider network.

- **Ethernet over MPLS Tunneling**—This section discusses tunneling Ethernet frames across an MPLS core network

- **Troubleshooting VLANs and Trunks**—This section provides commands to use when a VLAN or trunk is not operating properly.

CHAPTER 6

VLANs and Trunks

Switched campus networks can be broken up into distinct broadcast domains or virtual LANs (VLANs). A flat network topology, or a network with a single broadcast domain, can be simple to implement and manage. However, flat network topology is not scalable. Instead, the campus can be divided into segments using VLANs, while Layer 3 routing protocols manage interVLAN communication.

This chapter details the process of defining common workgroups within a group of switches. It covers switch configuration for VLANs, along with the method of identifying and transporting VLANs on various types of links.

"Do I Know This Already?" Quiz

The purpose of the "Do I Know This Already?" quiz is to help you decide if you need to read the entire chapter. If you already intend to read the entire chapter, you do not necessarily need to answer these questions now.

The 12-question quiz, derived from the major sections in the "Foundation Topics" portion of the chapter, helps you determine how to spend your limited study time.

Table 6-1 outlines the major topics discussed in this chapter and the "Do I Know This Already?" quiz questions that correspond to those topics.

Table 6-1 *"Do I Know This Already?" Foundation Topics Section-to-Question Mapping*

Foundation Topics Section	Questions Covered in This Section
Virtual LANs	1–4
VLAN Trunks VLAN Trunk Configuration	5-10
Q-in-Q Tunneling	11-12

> **CAUTION** The goal of self-assessment is to gauge your mastery of the topics in this chapter. If you do not know the answer to a question or are only partially sure of the answer, you should mark this question wrong. Giving yourself credit for an answer you correctly guess skews your self-assessment results and might give you a false sense of security.

1. A VLAN is which of the following?

   a. Collision domain

   b. Spanning Tree domain

   c. Broadcast domain

   d. VTP domain

2. Switches provide VLAN connectivity at which layer of the OSI model?

   a. Layer 1

   b. Layer 2

   c. Layer 3

   d. Layer 4

3. Which one of the following is needed to pass data between two PCs, each connected to a different VLAN?

   a. A Layer 2 switch

   b. A Layer 3 switch

   c. A trunk

   d. A tunnel

4. Which switch command is used to assign a port to a VLAN?

   a. **access vlan** *vlan-id*

   b. **switchport access vlan** *vlan-id*

   c. **vlan** *vlan-id*

   d. **set port vlan** *vlan-id*

5. Which of the following is a standardized method of trunk encapsulation?

   a. 802.1d

   b. 802.1Q

   c. 802.3z

   d. 802.1a

6. What is the Cisco proprietary method for trunk encapsulation?

   a. CDP

   b. EIGRP

   c. ISL

   d. DSL

7. Which of these protocols dynamically negotiates trunking parameters?

   a. PAgP

   b. STP

   c. CDP

   d. DTP

8. How many different VLANs can an 802.1Q trunk support?

   a. 256

   b. 1024

   c. 4096

   d. 32,768

   e. 65,536

9. Which of the following incorrectly describes a native VLAN?

   a. Frames are untagged on an 802.1Q trunk.

   b. Frames are untagged on an ISL trunk.

   c. Frames can be interpreted by a nontrunking host.

   d. The native VLAN can be configured for each trunking port.

10. If two switches each support all types of trunk encapsulation on a link between them, which one will be negotiated?

    a. ISL

    b. 802.1Q

    c. DTP

    d. VTP

11. Which answer gives the purpose of an 802.1Q tunnel?

    a. Encrypting the data on an 802.1Q trunk

    b. Passing an ISL trunk across an 802.1Q domain

    c. Transporting an 802.1Q trunk across a service provider network

    d. Transporting an 802.1Q trunk across an ISL domain

12. What types of protocols *cannot* be tunneled by a Layer 2 Protocol Tunnel?

    a. TCP

    b. CDP

    c. STP

    d. VTP

The answers to the quiz are found in Appendix A, "Answers to Chapter 'Do I Know This Already?' Quizzes and Q&A Sections." The suggested choices for your next step are as follows:

- **6 or less overall score**—Read the entire chapter. This includes the "Foundation Topics," "Foundation Summary," and "Q&A" sections.

- **7–9 overall score**—Begin with the "Foundation Summary" section and then follow with the "Q&A" section at the end of the chapter.

- **10 or more overall score**—If you want more review on these topics, skip to the "Foundation Summary" section and then go to the "Q&A" section at the end of the chapter. Otherwise, move on to Chapter 7, "VLAN Trunking Protocol (VTP)."

Foundation Topics

Virtual LANs

Consider a network design that consists of Layer 2 devices only. For example, this design could be a single Ethernet segment, an Ethernet switch with many ports, or a network with several interconnected Ethernet switches. A full Layer 2-only switched network is referred to as a *flat network topology*. A flat network is a single broadcast domain, such that every connected device sees every broadcast packet that is transmitted. As the number of stations on the network increases, so does the number of broadcasts.

Due to the Layer 2 foundation, flat networks cannot contain redundant paths for load-balancing or fault tolerance. The reason for this is explained in Chapters 9 through 12. To gain any advantage from additional paths to a destination, Layer 3 routing functions must be introduced.

A switched environment offers the technology to overcome flat network limitations. Switched networks can be subdivided into VLANs. By definition, a VLAN is a single broadcast domain. All devices connected to the VLAN receive broadcasts from other VLAN members. However, devices connected to a different VLAN will not receive those same broadcasts. (Naturally, VLAN members also receive unicast packets directed toward them from other VLAN members.)

A VLAN consists of defined members communicating as a logical network segment. In contrast, a physical segment consists of devices that must be connected to a physical cable segment. A VLAN can have connected members located anywhere in the campus network, as long as VLAN connectivity is provided between all members. Layer 2 switches are configured with a VLAN mapping and provide the logical connectivity between the VLAN members.

Figure 6-1 shows how a VLAN can provide logical connectivity between switch ports. Two workstations on the left Catalyst switch are assigned to VLAN 1, while a third workstation is assigned to VLAN 100. In this example, no communication can occur between VLAN 1 and VLAN 100. Both ends of the link between the Catalysts are assigned to VLAN 1. One workstation on the right Catalyst is also assigned to VLAN 1. Because there is end-to-end connectivity of VLAN 1, any of the workstations on VLAN 1 can communicate as if they were connected to a physical network segment.

Figure 6-1 *VLAN Functionality*

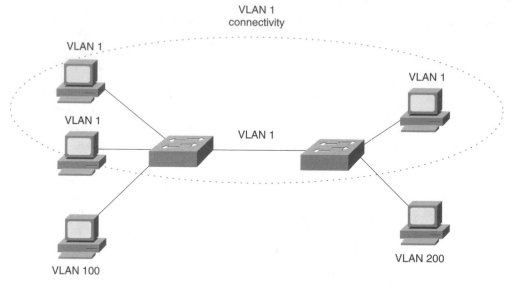

VLAN Membership

When a VLAN is provided at an access layer switch, an end user must have some means to gain membership to it. Two membership methods exist on Cisco Catalyst switches:

- Static VLAN Configuration
- Dynamic VLAN Assignment

Static VLANs

Static VLANs offer *port-based* membership, where switch ports are assigned to specific VLANs. End user devices become members in a VLAN based on the physical switch port to which they are connected. No handshaking or unique VLAN membership protocol is needed for the end devices; they automatically assume VLAN connectivity when they connect to a port. Normally, the end device is not even aware that the VLAN exists. The switch port and its VLAN are simply viewed and used as any other network segment, with other "locally attached" members on the wire.

Switch ports are assigned to VLANs by the manual intervention of the network administrator, hence the static nature. Each port receives a Port VLAN ID (PVID) that associates it with a VLAN number. The ports on a single switch can be assigned and grouped into many VLANs. Even though two devices are connected to the same switch, traffic will not pass between them if they are connected to ports on different VLANs. To perform this function, you could use either a Layer 3 device to route packets or an external Layer 2 device to bridge packets between the two VLANs.

The static port-to-VLAN membership is normally handled in hardware with application-specific integrated circuits (ASICs) in the switch. This membership provides good performance because all port mappings are done at the hardware level with no complex table lookups needed.

Configuring Static VLANs

This section describes the switch commands needed to configure static VLANs. By default, all switch ports are assigned to VLAN 1, are set to be a VLAN type of Ethernet, and have a maximum transmission unit (MTU) size of 1500 bytes.

First, the VLAN must be created on the switch, if it does not already exist. Then, the VLAN must be assigned to specific switch ports.

To configure static VLANs, you can first define the VLAN with the following command in global configuration mode:

```
Switch(config)# vlan vlan-num
Switch(config-vlan)# name vlan-name
```

The VLAN is created and stored in a database, along with its number and a descriptive name. The VLAN database is automatically stored in a special *vlan.dat* file in Flash memory, separate from the switch configuration.

Next, you should assign one or more switch ports to the VLAN. Use the following configuration commands:

```
Switch(config)# interface type module/number
Switch(config-if)# switchport mode access
Switch(config-if)# switchport access vlan vlan-num
```

The **switchport access vlan** command configures the port for static VLAN membership, according to the VLAN number given by *vlan-num* (1 to 1005). The range of VLAN numbers can be 1 to 4094 if the switch is configured in VTP transparent mode. To verify VLAN configuration, use the **show vlan** command to output a list of all VLANs defined in the switch, in addition to the ports assigned to each VLAN. Example 6-1 shows some sample output from the **show vlan** command.

Example 6-1 *Verifying VLAN Configuration with* **show vlan** *Command*

```
Switch# show vlan
VLAN Name                             Status    Ports
---- -------------------------------- --------- -------------------------------
1    default                          active    Gi1/1, Gi1/2, Gi3/20, Gi4/20
2    Engineering                      active    Gi4/2, Gi4/3, Gi4/4, Gi4/5
                                                Gi4/6, Gi4/7, Gi4/8, Gi4/9
                                                Gi4/10, Gi4/11, Gi4/12
```

continues

Example 6-1   *Verifying VLAN Configuration with* **show vlan** *Command (Continued)*

```
101  Marketing                       active    Gi2/5, Gi2/6, Gi2/7, Gi2/8
                                                Gi2/9, Gi2/10, Gi2/11, Gi2/12
                                                Gi2/13, Gi2/14, Gi2/15, Gi2/16
                                                Gi2/17, Gi2/18
```

Dynamic VLANs

Dynamic VLANs provide membership based on the MAC address of an end user device. When a device is connected to a switch port, the switch must, in effect, query a database to establish VLAN membership. A network administrator must assign the user's MAC address to a VLAN in the database of a VLAN Membership Policy Server (VMPS).

With Cisco switches, dynamic VLANs are created and managed using network management tools such as CiscoWorks 2000. Dynamic VLANs allow a great deal of flexibility and mobility for end users but require more administrative overhead.

> **NOTE**   Dynamic VLANs are not covered in this text or in the BCMSN course or exam (at press time). For more information, refer to "Configuring VMPS" at www.cisco.com/univercd/cc/td/doc/product/lan/c3550/12112cea/3550scg/swvlan.htm#xtocid35.

Deploying VLANs

To implement VLANs, you must consider the number of VLANs you need and how best to place them. As usual, the number of VLANs will be dependent on traffic patterns, application types, segmenting common workgroups, and network management requirements.

An important factor to consider is the relationship between VLANs and the IP addressing schemes used. Cisco recommends a one-to-one correspondence between VLANs and IP subnets. This recommendation means that if a subnet with a 24-bit mask is used for a VLAN, no more than 254 devices should be in the VLAN. In addition, VLANs not extending beyond the Layer 2 domain of the distribution switch is recommended. In other words, the VLAN should not reach across a network's core and into another switch block. The idea again is to keep broadcasts and unnecessary traffic movement out of the core block.

VLANs can be scaled in the switch block by using two basic methods:

- End-to-end VLANs
- Local VLANs

End-to-End VLANs

End-to-end VLANs, also called *campus-wide VLANs*, span the entire switch fabric of a network. They are positioned to support maximum flexibility and mobility of end devices. Users are assigned to VLANs regardless of physical location. As a user moves around the campus, that user's VLAN membership stays the same. This means that each VLAN must be made available at the access layer in every switch block.

End-to-end VLANs should group users according to common requirements. All users in a VLAN should have roughly the same traffic flow patterns, following the 80/20 rule. Recall that this rule estimates that 80 percent of user traffic stays within the local workgroup, while 20 percent is destined for a remote resource in the campus network. Although only 20 percent of the traffic in a VLAN is expected to cross the network core, end-to-end VLANs make it possible for all traffic within a single VLAN to cross the core.

Because all VLANs must be available at each access layer switch, VLAN trunking must be used to carry all VLANs between the access and distribution layer switches.

> **NOTE** End-to-end VLANs are not recommended in an enterprise network, unless there is a good reason. Broadcast traffic must be carried over a VLAN from one end of the network to the other. For this reason, a broadcast storm or Layer 2 bridging loop can also spread across the extent of a VLAN, exhausting the bandwidth of distribution and core layer links, as well as switch CPU resources. When such a problem occurs, troubleshooting becomes more difficult. In other words, the risks of end-to-end VLANs outweigh the convenience and benefits.

Local VLANs

Because most enterprise networks have moved toward the 20/80 rule (where server and intranet/Internet resources are centralized), end-to-end VLANs have become cumbersome and difficult to maintain. The 20/80 rule reverses the traffic pattern of the end-to-end VLAN—only 20 percent of traffic is local, while 80 percent is destined to a remote resource across the core layer. End users require access to central resources outside their VLAN. Users must cross into the network core more frequently. In this type of network, VLANs are designed to contain user communities based on geographic boundaries, with little regard to the amount of traffic leaving the VLAN.

Local or geographic VLANs range in size from a single switch in a wiring closet to an entire building. Arranging VLANs in this fashion enables the Layer 3 function in the campus network to intelligently handle the interVLAN traffic loads. This scenario provides maximum availability by using multiple paths to destinations, maximum scalability by keeping the VLAN within a switch block, and maximum manageability.

VLAN Trunks

At the access layer, end user devices connect to switch ports that provide simple connectivity to a single VLAN each. The attached devices are unaware of any VLAN structure, and simply attach to what appears to be a normal physical network segment. Remember, sending information from an access link on one VLAN to another VLAN is not possible without the intervention of an additional device—either a Layer 3 router or an external Layer 2 bridge.

Note that a single switch port can support more than one IP subnet for the devices attached to it. For example, consider a shared Ethernet hub that is connected to a single Ethernet switch port. One user device on the hub might be configured for 192.168.1.1 255.255.255.0, while another is assigned 192.168.17.1 255.255.255.0. Although these subnets are discontiguous, unique, and are both communicating on one switch port, they cannot be considered separate VLANs. The switch port supports one VLAN, but multiple subnets can exist on that single VLAN.

A *trunk link*, however, can transport more than one VLAN through a single switch port. Trunk links are most beneficial when switches are connected to other switches or switches are connected to routers. A trunk link is not assigned to a specific VLAN. Instead, one, many, or all active VLANs can be transported between switches using a single physical trunk link.

Connecting two switches with separate physical links for each VLAN is possible. The top half of Figure 6-2 shows how two switches might be connected in this fashion.

As VLANs are added to a network, the number of links can quickly grow. A more efficient use of physical interfaces and cabling involves the use of trunking. The bottom half of the figure shows how one trunk link can replace many individual VLAN links.

Cisco supports trunking on both Fast Ethernet and Gigabit Ethernet switch links, as well as aggregated Fast and Gigabit EtherChannel links. To distinguish between traffic belonging to different VLANs on a trunk link, the switch must have a method of identifying each frame with the appropriate VLAN. Several available identification methods are discussed in the next section.

VLAN Frame Identification

Because a trunk link can transport many VLANs, a switch must identify frames with their VLANs as they are sent and received over a trunk link. Frame identification, or *tagging*, assigns a unique user-defined ID to each frame transported on a trunk link. Think of this ID as the VLAN number or VLAN "color," as if each VLAN was drawn on a network diagram in a unique color.

VLAN frame identification was developed for switched networks. As each frame is transmitted over a trunk link, a unique identifier is placed in the frame header. As each switch along the way receives these frames, the identifier is examined to determine to which VLAN the frames belong, and then removed.

Figure 6-2 *Passing VLAN Traffic Using Single Links Versus Trunk Links*

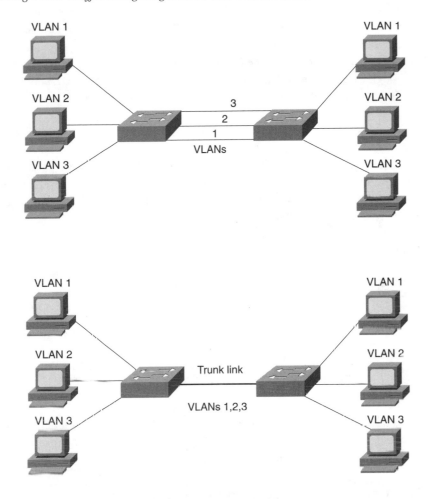

If frames must be transported out another trunk link, the VLAN identifier is added back into the frame header. Otherwise, if frames are destined out an access (nontrunk) link, the switch removes the VLAN identifier before transmitting the frames to the end station. Therefore, all traces of VLAN association are hidden from the end station.

VLAN identification can be performed using two methods, each using a different frame identifier mechanism:

- Inter-Switch Link (ISL) protocol
- IEEE 802.1Q protocol

These methods are described in the sections that follow.

Inter-Switch Link Protocol

The Inter-Switch Link (ISL) protocol is a Cisco proprietary method for preserving the source VLAN identification of frames passing over a trunk link. ISL performs frame identification in Layer 2 by encapsulating each frame between a header and trailer. Any Cisco switch or router device configured for ISL can process and understand the ISL VLAN information. ISL is primarily used for Ethernet media, although Cisco has included provisions to carry Token Ring, FDDI, and ATM frames over Ethernet ISL. (A Frame-Type field in the ISL header indicates the source frame type.)

When a frame is destined out a trunk link to another switch or router, ISL adds a 26-byte header and a 4-byte trailer to the frame. The source VLAN is identified with a 10-bit VLAN ID field in the header. The trailer contains a cyclic redundancy check (CRC) value to ensure the data integrity of the new encapsulated frame. Figure 6-3 shows how Ethernet frames are encapsulated and forwarded out a trunk link. Because tagging information is added at the beginning and end of each frame, ISL is sometimes referred to as *double tagging*.

Figure 6-3 *ISL Frame Identification*

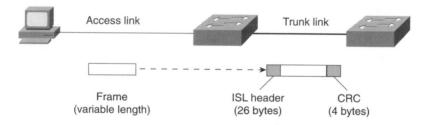

If a frame is destined for an access link, the ISL encapsulation (both header and trailer) is not rewritten into the frame before transmission. This removal preserves ISL information only for trunk links and devices that can understand the protocol.

> **TIP** The ISL method of VLAN identification or trunking encapsulation is no longer supported across all Cisco Catalyst switch platforms. Even so, you should still be familiar with it and know how it compares to the standards-based IEEE 802.1Q method.

IEEE 802.1Q Protocol

The IEEE 802.1Q protocol can also carry VLAN associations over trunk links. However, this frame identification method is standardized, allowing VLAN trunks to exist and operate between equipment from multiple vendors.

In particular, the IEEE 802.1Q standard defines an architecture for VLAN use, services provided with VLANs, and protocols and algorithms used to provide VLAN services. You can find further information about the 802.1Q standard at grouper.ieee.org/groups/802/1/pages/802.1Q.html.

Like Cisco ISL, IEEE 802.1Q can be used for VLAN identification with Ethernet trunks. Instead of encapsulating each frame with a VLAN ID header and trailer, 802.1Q embeds its tagging information within the Layer 2 frame. This method is referred to as *single-tagging* or *internal tagging*.

802.1Q also introduces the concept of a *native VLAN* on a trunk. Frames belonging to this VLAN are *not* encapsulated with any tagging information. In the event that an end station is connected to an 802.1Q trunk link, the end station can receive and understand only the native VLAN frames. This provides a simple way to offer full trunk encapsulation to the devices that can understand it, while giving normal access stations some inherent connectivity over the trunk.

In an Ethernet frame, 802.1Q adds a four-byte tag just after the source address field, as shown in Figure 6-4.

Figure 6-4 *IEEE 802.1Q Frame Tagging Standard*

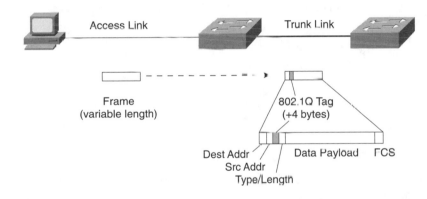

The first two bytes are used as a Tag Protocol Identifier (TPID) and always have a value of 0x8100 to signify an 802.1Q tag. The remaining two bytes are used as a Tag Control Information (TCI) field. The TCI information contains a three-bit Priority field, which is used to implement class-of-service (CoS) functions in the accompanying 802.1Q/802.1p prioritization standard. One bit of the TCI is a Canonical Format Indicator (CFI), flagging whether the MAC addresses are in Ethernet or Token Ring format. (This is also known as *canonical format*, as well as little-endian or big-endian format.) The last 12 bits are used as a VLAN Identifier (VID) to indicate the source VLAN for the frame. The VID can have values from 0 to 4095, but VLANs 0, 1, and 4095 are reserved.

Note that both ISL and 802.1Q tagging methods have one implication: they add to the length of an Ethernet frame. ISL adds a total of 30 bytes to each frame, whereas 802.1Q adds 4 bytes. Because Ethernet frames cannot exceed 1518 bytes, the additional VLAN tagging information can cause the frame to be too large. Frames that barely exceed the MTU size are called *baby giant frames*. Switches usually report these frames as Ethernet errors or oversize frames.

> **NOTE**   Baby giant, or oversized, frames can exceed the frame size set in various standards. To properly handle and forward them anyway, Catalyst switches use proprietary hardware with the ISL encapsulation method. In the case of 802.1Q encapsulation, switches can comply with the IEEE 802.3ac standard, which extends the maximum frame length to 1522 bytes.

Dynamic Trunking Protocol

You can manually configure trunk links on Catalyst switches for either ISL or 802.1Q mode. In addition, Cisco has implemented a proprietary, point-to-point protocol called *Dynamic Trunking Protocol (DTP)* that negotiates a common trunking mode between two switches. The negotiation covers the encapsulation (ISL or 802.1Q) as well as whether the link becomes a trunk at all. This allows trunk links to be used without a great deal of manual configuration or administration. The use of DTP is explained in the next section.

> **NOTE**   DTP negotiation should be disabled if a switch has a trunk link connected to a router because the router cannot participate in the DTP negotiation protocol. A trunk link can be negotiated between two switches only if both switches belong to the same VLAN Trunking Protocol (VTP) management domain, or if one or both switches have not defined their VTP domain (that is, the *NULL* domain). VTP is discussed in Chapter 7. If the two switches are in different VTP domains and trunking is desired between them, you must set the trunk links to "on" mode or "nonegotiate" mode. This setting will force the trunk to be established. These options are explained in the next section.

VLAN Trunk Configuration

By default, all switch ports are non-trunking and operate as access links until some intervention changes the mode. Specifically, ports actively try to become trunks if the far end agrees. In that case, a common encapsulation is chosen, favoring ISL if both support it. The sections that follow demonstrate the commands necessary to configure VLAN trunks.

VLAN Trunk Configuration

Use the following commands to create a VLAN trunk link:

```
Switch(config)# interface type mod/port
Switch(config-if)# switchport trunk encapsulation {isl | dot1q | negotiate}
Switch(config-if)# switchport trunk native vlan vlan-id
Switch(config-if)# switchport trunk allowed vlan {vlan-list | all |
  {add | except | remove} vlan-list}
Switch(config-if)# switchport mode {trunk | dynamic {desirable | auto}}
```

You can configure the trunk encapsulation with the **switchport trunk encapsulation** command, as one of the following:

- **isl**—VLANs are tagged by encapsulating each frame using the Cisco ISL protocol.

- **dot1q**—VLANs are tagged in each frame using the IEEE 802.1Q standard protocol. The only exception is the native VLAN, which is sent normally and not tagged at all.

- **negotiate** (the default)—The encapsulation is negotiated to select either ISL or IEEE 802.1Q, whichever is supported by both ends of the trunk. If both ends support both types, ISL is favored. (The Catalyst 2950 switch does not support ISL encapsulation.)

In the case of an IEEE 802.1Q trunk, you should configure the native VLAN with the **switchport trunk native vlan** command, identifying the untagged or native VLAN number as *vlan-id* (1 to 4094). In the case of an ISL trunk, using this command has no effect because ISL doesn't support an untagged VLAN.

The last command, **switchport trunk allowed vlan**, defines which VLANs can be trunked over the link. By default, a switch transports all active VLANs (1 to 4094) over a trunk link. There might be times when the trunk link should not carry all VLANs. For example, broadcasts are forwarded to every switch port on a VLAN—including the trunk link because it, too, is a member of the VLAN. If the VLAN does not extend past the far end of the trunk link, propagating broadcasts across the trunk makes no sense.

You can tailor the list of allowed VLANs on the trunk by using the **switchport trunk allowed vlan** command with one of the following:

- *vlan-list*—An explicit list of VLAN numbers, separated by commas or dashes.

- **all**—All active VLANs (1 to 4094) will be allowed.

- **add** *vlan-list*—A list of VLAN numbers will be added to the already configured list; this is a shortcut to keep from typing out a long list of numbers.

- **except** *vlan-list*—All VLANs (1 to 4094) will be allowed, except for the VLAN numbers listed; this is a shortcut to keep from typing out a long list of numbers.

- **remove** *vlan-list*—A list of VLAN numbers will be removed from the already configured list; this is a shortcut to keep from typing out a long list of numbers.

NOTE   You can never remove VLANs 1 or 1002 through 1005 from a trunk. These are reserved for special uses: VLAN 1 is the Cisco default, which carries control protocols such as CDP, VTP, and STP. VLANs 1002 through 1005 have historically been reserved for FDDI and Token Ring.

In the **switchport mode** command, you can set the trunking mode to any of the following:

- **trunk**—This setting places the port in permanent trunking mode. The corresponding switch port at the other end of the trunk should be similarly configured because negotiation is not allowed. You should also manually configure the encapsulation mode.

- **dynamic desirable** (the default)—The port actively attempts to convert the link into trunking mode. If the far-end switch port is configured to **trunk**, **dynamic desirable**, or **dynamic auto** mode, trunking is successfully negotiated.

- **dynamic auto**—The port converts the link into trunking mode. If the far-end switch port is configured to **trunk** or **dynamic desirable**, trunking is negotiated. Because of the passive negotiation behavior, the link never becomes a trunk if both ends of the link are left to the **dynamic auto** default.

> **NOTE** In all these modes, DTP frames are sent out every 30 seconds to keep neighboring switch ports informed of the link's mode. On critical trunk links in a network, manually configuring the trunking mode on both ends is best so that the link can never be negotiated to any other state.
>
> If you decide to configure *both ends* of a trunk link as a fixed trunk (**switchport mode trunk**), you can disable DTP completely so that these frames are not exchanged. To do this, add the **switchport nonegotiate** command to the interface configuration. Be aware that after DTP frames are disabled, no future negotiation is possible until the configuration is reversed.

To view the trunking status on a switch port, use the **show interface** *type mod/port* **trunk** command, as demonstrated in Example 6-2.

Example 6-2 *Determining Switch Port Trunking Status*

```
Switch# show interface gig 2/1 trunk
Port      Mode          Encapsulation  Status       Native vlan
Gi2/1     on            802.1q         trunking     1

Port      Vlans allowed on trunk
Gi2/1     1-4094

Port      Vlans allowed and active in management domain
Gi2/1     1-2,526,539,998,1002-1005

Port      Vlans in spanning tree forwarding state and not pruned
Gi2/1     1-2,526,539,998,1002-1005
```

Service Provider Tunneling

An IEEE 802.1Q trunk is a method that you can use to carry one or more VLANs across a single physical link. Trunks are commonly deployed in campus networks, where the trunk links are easily implemented and managed in-house. Now, consider a campus network that is geographically separated; the same Layer 2 connectivity must be obtained from a service provider.

If the service provider can offer a high-speed, seamless VLAN between several locations with Metro Ethernet, for example, the campus customer can directly connect an existing switch to the provider's VLAN link. If several customer VLANs need to be transported, connecting a single trunk link to the service provider's network, rather than several single-VLAN links, is much more efficient.

The IEEE 802.1Q trunk concept has been extended to allow a straightforward transport of an entire trunk across a third-party network. In fact, trunks from many different customers can be carried or tunneled independently across a service provider's core network using normal Layer 2 switching equipment.

Tunneling can also be accomplished across a service provider's core network without 802.1Q trunks. In this case, a Multiprotocol Label Switching (MPLS) core is required, where traffic traveling between a specific customer's sites receives a unique MPLS tag. This technique is known as Ethernet over MPLS (EoMPLS).

These two tunneling methods are described in the sections that follow.

IEEE 802.1Q Tunnels

At the edge of a campus network, an IEEE 802.1Q *trunk port* connects to a service provider's IEEE 802.1Q *tunnel port*. Every VLAN that is active on the trunk tunnels into and across the provider's core network, to terminate at the customer's remote location.

802.1Q tunneling is accomplished by adding a second layer of VLAN tagging to every frame on a trunk. Recall that an 802.1Q trunk takes every frame and adds a 4-byte tag, containing the EtherType value 0x8100, CoS flags, and the VLAN ID (1 to 4094) of the source VLAN. An 802.1Q tunnel takes this a step further by encapsulating the entire trunk into a new trunk, where a second "outer" 4-byte tag is added to every frame.

The net effect is that the contents of a customer's trunk link (all VLANs) are tagged with an overall VLAN ID that corresponds to that customer's identity. The double-tagged tunnel, also known as a *nested IEEE 802.1Q trunk* or a *Q-in-Q tunnel*, can be switched within the service provider's network as normal Layer 2 frames. The customer VLAN ID switches the tunneled frames to the appropriate remote tunnel endpoint.

The Layer 3 source and destination addresses in the original frames become inaccessible in the tunnel because of the double-layer encapsulation. The Layer 3 addresses are buried within the 802.1Q encapsulations and cannot be examined after frames are tunneled. Keep this in mind when other features that need Layer 3 information are in use. Examples of this include access lists, Layer 3 QoS, and EtherChannels, which can distribute frames according to Layer 3 source and destination addresses.

Figure 6-5 shows the basic connections between two locations of a campus customer and the service provider's network. Each customer site edge must present an 802.1Q trunk to the service provider. These trunks contain every VLAN that must be transported between sites. The provider mates an 802.1Q *tunnel* port to each trunk so that the entire trunk can be tunneled from end to end.

Figure 6-5 *IEEE 802.1Q Tunnel Concept*

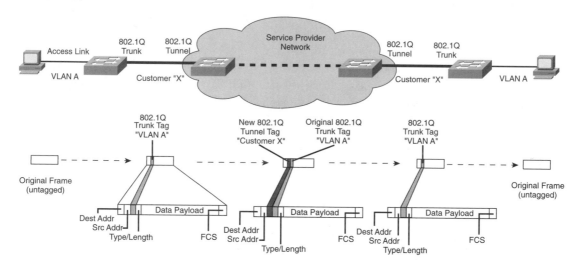

The lower portion of Figure 6-5 shows how a frame is modified as it moves along from one customer site to another, across the service provider network. A PC on the left transmits the frame with no tagging at all. The customer edge switch carries the frame over an 802.1Q trunk, where the frame has been tagged with its original source VLAN, VLAN A. At the service provider edge, the 802.1Q tunnel port encapsulates all the customer's trunked VLANs into a new 802.1Q trunk. This time, all frames receive a second tag that indicates a VLAN ID representing "Customer X."

Within the service provider core network, every customer has its frames uniquely identified by the respective tunnels. Now that individual customers are known by unique VLAN numbers, all tunneled data can be transported across the core over regular 802.1Q trunk links. The customer VLAN number unencapsulates the tunnel at the remote end, where the second layer of tagging information is removed. At the remote customer site, the tunnel port connects to an 802.1Q trunk port, where only the original VLAN ID tags remain.

> **NOTE** Because an 802.1Q tunnel increases the size of each frame by 4 bytes, you should consider the MTU across the length of the tunnel path. By default, Ethernet frames have an MTU of 1500 bytes. You can increase the MTU to 2000 bytes (Gigabit Ethernet) or 1546 bytes (Fast Ethernet) by using the **system mtu** global configuration command.

Configuring a 802.1Q Tunnel

Use the following commands on the service provider edge switches that touch a customer's networks to configure an 802.1Q tunnel:

```
Switch(config)# interface type mod/num
Switch(config-if)# switchport access vlan vlan-id
Switch(config-if)# switchport mode dot1qtunnel
Switch(config-if)# exit
Switch(config)# vlan dot1q tag native
```

The **switchport access vlan** command must first identify the VLAN ID for the customer connected to the physical interface. Because the interface will become an 802.1Q tunnel (built around a trunk), it might seem like the access VLAN has no purpose. However, this command works in conjunction with the 802.1Q tunnel mode so that the customer ID is picked up from the access VLAN definition.

The **switchport mode dot1qtunnel** command then puts the switch port into the tunnel mode. It is important to keep all tunneled traffic uniform with two layers of 802.1Q tags. When an 802.1Q trunk native VLAN (no tags) enters a tunnel, those frames receive only one tag layer—that of the tunnel itself. This way, the native VLAN can be sent to a nontunnel port within the service provider network because it looks like a normal 802.1Q trunk with one layer of tagging.

Use the **vlan dot1q tag native** global configuration command to force the provider's edge switch to require tags on all native VLAN frames on 802.1Q trunks. Untagged ingress frames on customer trunks will be dropped, but native VLAN frames initiated inside the service provider network will be automatically tagged. This command must be used on *all* service provider switches so that the native VLAN is interpreted consistently.

Layer 2 Protocol Tunnels

User data frames sent over the VLANs in an 802.1Q trunk can be directly encapsulated in an 802.1Q tunnel. However, frames that contain switch-related data cannot be correctly handled in a tunnel. For example, switches use several protocols to communicate with each other for management or control purposes, including the Spanning Tree Protocol (STP), VLAN Trunking Protocol (VTP), and Cisco Discovery Protocol (CDP). These frames are known as Layer 2 *control protocol data units (PDUs)*.

If an edge switch receives such a frame on its 802.1Q tunnel port, should it blindly encapsulate the frame into the tunnel, or should it try to process the frame itself as an important control message from another neighboring switch?

Control protocol PDUs (STP, VTP, CDP) are normally sent over VLAN 1 on a trunk. When these protocols are received at a service provider's 802.1Q tunnel port, they are interpreted by the edge switch rather than being tunneled. STP and VTP are dropped (not accepted) because they don't directly apply to the service provider's internal network. The CDP frames, however, are interpreted because the edge switch thinks it should learn of its connected neighbors.

The net result is that none of these protocols are forwarded on across the tunnel, as the customer expects. To remedy this, a *Layer 2 Protocol Tunnel* can be used at the service provider edge that performs Generic Bridge PDU Tunneling (GBPT). Here, the edge switch receives these frames from the customer's 802.1Q trunk and rewrites them to have a GBPT destination MAC address of 0100.0ccd.cdd0 (a Cisco proprietary multicast address). The encapsulated frames are then sent into the 802.1Q tunnel, as if they came from the native VLAN on the customer's trunk.

Other switches in the provider's network recognize the GBPT destination address and unencapsulate the control PDUs. GBPT can be performed on the control protocols selectively, so only the desirable protocols are tunneled.

Configuring Layer 2 Protocol Tunneling

To configure Layer 2 Protocol tunneling, use the following commands:

```
Switch(config)# interface type mod/port
Switch(config-if)# l2protocol-tunnel [cdp | stp | vtp]
Switch(config-if)# l2protocol-tunnel drop-threshold pps [cdp | stp | vtp]
Switch(config-if)# l2protocol-tunnel shutdown-threshold pps [cdp | stp | vtp]
```

This feature must be configured on *every* service provider edge switch so that the control protocols can be encapsulated and unencapsulated correctly.

In the first **l2protocol-tunnel** command, all control protocols can be tunneled if no arguments are given. Otherwise, you can select which of the CDP, STP, and VTP protocols will be tunneled.

As an option, you can set thresholds to control the rate of control protocol frames that are tunneled. With the **drop-threshold** keyword, only *pps* (1 to 4096) frames are tunneled in any 1-second interval. After the threshold is reached, additional control frames are dropped until that second has elapsed. As a more drastic action, the **shutdown-threshold** keyword causes the tunnel port to shut down in the errdisable state if more than *pps* (1 to 4096) control frames are received in a 1-second interval.

Ethernet over MPLS Tunneling

A service provider can tunnel customer traffic using EoMPLS if it already has an MPLS core network.

You can use the MPLS method to forward packets across a large network efficiently. Basically, routers at the edge of a service provider's core network function as *edge label switch routers (LERs or edge LSRs)*. Packets that match some criteria for a particular customer or a particular flow are recognized at the network edge and are assigned a unique MPLS label or tag.

Routers within the MPLS cloud, known as *label switch routers (LSRs)*, examine only the MPLS labels to make forwarding decisions. Therefore, they do not need to examine IP addresses—the MPLS label has sufficient information. LSRs must also exchange information so that they all understand the labels that are in use, as well as how to route packets with a given label. This is done through the Cisco Tag Distribution Protocol (TDP) or the Label Distribution Protocol (LDP).

The original Layer 2 frame is then encapsulated as an MPLS frame so that any MPLS router in the network forwards it appropriately. The frame receives a new Layer 2 source and destination address, corresponding to the current and next-hop routers, respectively, as would normally be done by a router.

An MPLS label is placed into the new frame, right after the MAC addresses. In fact, as an MPLS label is added to a frame, any existing labels are simply "pushed" down so that the new one is always found early in the frame. The labels form a stack so that MPLS routers can "pop" a label out of a frame to reveal the next label.

Why would a frame need more than one MPLS label? This label stacking mechanism makes MPLS very flexible. For example, after frames have received a label, they can be tunneled within the MPLS network simply by adding another MPLS label to the stack. MPLS routers examine only the first or topmost label to make a forwarding decision.

Finally, after the last or bottommost label, the original Layer 3 packet is placed into the frame. After the packet is forwarded across the MPLS network, the far-end edge router pops the final label off the frame, recognizes that there are no more layers of labels, and sends the unencapsulated packet on.

> **TIP** The BCMSN course and exam cover only the theory behind EoMPLS tunnels and do not present any configuration commands. Therefore, be sure you understand how EoMPLS works and how it contrasts with 802.1Q or Q-in-Q tunnels for a service provider.

MPLS by itself encapsulates Layer 3 packets in a Layer 2 frame, along with one or more MPLS labels. The Layer 3 packet is always retained within the encapsulation. It is then more of a Layer 3 tunneling mechanism. To accomplish Layer 2 tunneling across an MPLS network, EoMPLS tunneling must be used.

EoMPLS takes advantage of the MPLS label stack to identify both the customer and the customer's VLAN uniquely. Frames from one site of a customer's network must be delivered to the remote customer site at the far end of the tunnel. If the customer presents an 802.1Q trunk to the provider, each VLAN on the trunk is considered a virtual circuit (VC) that must be preserved at the far end.

EoMPLS also extends beyond MPLS by retaining the entire original *Layer 2* frame, including the original source and destination MAC addresses. This allows EoMPLS to tunnel frames between sites transparently at Layer 2, as if the two customer endpoints were directly connected.

Figure 6-6 shows the end-to-end EoMPLS procedure. When a frame arrives at the edge of a customer's network, an EoMPLS router encapsulates the frame. The VLAN or VC number is first added as an MPLS label. Then, the customer ID or tunnel label is pushed onto the label stack so that the customer can be identified across the MPLS core network. After the frame is delivered to the edge of the network at the customer's remote site, the tunnel label is popped off, and the VC label is examined to see which VLAN should receive the frame.

Figure 6-6 *EoMPLS Tunnel Concept*

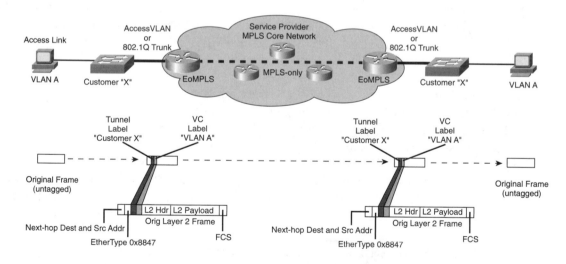

Notice that two things are required for an EoMPLS tunnel:

- There must be a seamless MPLS network within the service provider core network.

- EoMPLS must be configured *only* on the edge routers that interface with the customer networks.

Troubleshooting VLANs and Trunks

Remember that a VLAN is nothing more than a logical network segment that can be spread across many switches. If a PC in one location cannot communicate with a PC in another location, where both are assigned to the same IP subnet, make sure that both of their switch ports are configured for the same VLAN. If they are, examine the path between the two. Is the VLAN carried continuously along the path? If there are trunks along the way, is the VLAN being carried across the trunks?

To verify a VLAN's configuration on a switch, use the **show vlan id** *vlan-id* EXEC command, as demonstrated in Example 6-3. Make sure the VLAN is shown to have an "active" status and that it has been assigned to the correct switch ports.

Example 6-3 *Verifying Switch VLAN Configuration*

```
Switch# show vlan id 2

VLAN Name                             Status    Ports
---- --------------------------       -----     -------------------------------
2    Engineering                      active    Gi2/1, Gi2/2, Gi2/3, Gi2/4
                                                Gi4/2, Gi4/3, Gi4/4, Gi4/5
                                                Gi4/6, Gi4/7, Gi4/8, Gi4/9
                                                Gi4/10, Gi4/11, Gi4/12


VLAN Type  SAID       MTU   Parent RingNo BridgeNo Stp  BrdgMode Trans1 Trans2
---- ----- ---------- ----- ------ ------ -------- ---- -------- ------ ------
2    enet  100002     1500  -      -      -        -    -        0      0

Primary Secondary Type               Ports
------- --------- ----------------   -------------------------------------------

Switch#
```

For a trunk, these parameters must be agreeable on both ends before the trunk operates correctly:

- Trunking mode (unconditional trunking, negotiated, or nonnegotiated).

- Trunk encapsulation (ISL, IEEE 802.1Q, or negotiated through DTP).

- Native VLAN (802.1Q only) in which you can bring up a trunk with different native VLANs on each end; however, both switches will log error messages about the mismatch, and the potential exists that traffic will not pass correctly between the two native VLANs.

- Allowed VLANs. By default, a trunk will allow all VLANs to be transported across it. If one end of the trunk is configured to disallow a VLAN, that VLAN will not be contiguous across the trunk.

To verify a switch port's active trunking parameters, use the **show interface** *type mod/num* **trunk** command. The trunk mode, encapsulation type, status, native VLAN, and allowed VLANs can all be examined.

To see a comparison between how a switch port is configured for trunking versus its active state, use the **show interface** *type mod/num* **switchport** command, as demonstrated in Example 6-4. Look for the "administrative" versus "operational" values, respectively, to see if the trunk is working the way you configured it.

Notice that the port has been configured to negotiate a trunk through DTP ("dynamic auto"), but that the port is operating in the "static access" (nontrunking) mode. This should tell you that both ends of the link are probably configured for the auto mode, such that neither will actively request a trunk.

Example 6-4 *Comparing Switch Port Trunking Configuration and Active State*

```
Switch# show interface fast 0/2 switchport
Name: Fa0/2
Switchport: Enabled
Administrative Mode: dynamic auto
Operational Mode: static access
Administrative Trunking Encapsulation: dot1q
Operational Trunking Encapsulation: native
Negotiation of Trunking: On
Access Mode VLAN: 1 (default)
Trunking Native Mode VLAN: 1 (default)
Administrative private-vlan host-association: none
Administrative private-vlan mapping: none
Operational private-vlan: none
Trunking VLANs Enabled: ALL
Pruning VLANs Enabled: 2-1001

Protected: false
Unknown unicast blocked: disabled
Unknown multicast blocked: disabled

Voice VLAN: none (Inactive)
Appliance trust: none
Switch#
```

For more concise information about a trunking port, you can use the **show interface** [*type mod/num*] **trunk** command, as demonstrated in Example 6-5.

Example 6-5   *Viewing Concise Information About a Trunking Port*

```
Switch# show interface fast 0/2 trunk

Port       Mode            Encapsulation  Status          Native vlan
Fa0/2      auto            802.1q         not-trunking    1

Port       Vlans allowed on trunk
Fa0/2      1

Port       Vlans allowed and active in management domain
Fa0/2      1

Port       Vlans in spanning tree forwarding state and not pruned
Fa0/2      1
Switch#
```

To see if and how DTP is being used on a switch, use the **show dtp** [**interface** *type mod/num*] command. Specifying an interface shows the DTP activity in greater detail.

Foundation Summary

The Foundation Summary is a collection of tables that provides a convenient review of many key concepts in this chapter. If you are already comfortable with the topics in this chapter, this summary could help you recall a few details. If you just read this chapter, this review should help solidify some key facts. If you are doing your final preparation before the exam, these tables and figures are a convenient way to review the day before the exam.

Table 6-2 *VLAN Trunk Encapsulations*

Encapsulation	Tagging Characteristics
ISL	Adds a 26-byte header, a 4-byte trailer to each frame, and includes a 10-bit VLAN ID
IEEE 802.1Q	Adds a 4-byte tag; includes a 12-bit VLAN ID

Table 6-3 *VLAN and Trunking Configuration Commands*

Task	Command Syntax
Create VLAN	`vlan vlan-num` `name vlan-name`

Assign port to VLAN	`interface type module/number`
	`switchport mode access`
	`switchport access vlan vlan-num`

Configure trunk	`interface type mod/port` `switchport trunk encapsulation {isl	dot1q	negotiate}` `switchport trunk native vlan vlan-id` `switchport trunk allowed vlan {vlan-list	all	{add	except	remove} vlan-list}` `switchport mode {trunk	dynamic {desirable	auto}}`

Configure 802.1Q tunnel	`interface type mod/num`
	`switchport access vlan vlan-id`
	`switchport mode dot1qtunnel`
	`exit`
	`vlan dot1q tag native`

Configure Layer 2 protocol tunnel	`interface type mod/port` `l2protocol-tunnel [cdp	stp	vtp]` `l2protocol-tunnel drop-threshold pps [cdp	stp	vtp]` `l2protocol-tunnel shutdown-threshold pps [cdp	stp	vtp]`

Table 6-4 *VLAN and Trunking Troubleshooting Commands*

Task	Command Syntax
Verify VLAN configuration	`show vlan id` *vlan-id*
Verify active trunk parameters	`show interface` *type mod/num* `trunk`
Compare trunk configuration and active parameters	`show interface` *type mod/num* `switchport`
Verify DTP operation	`show dtp [interface` *type mod/num*`]`

Q&A

The questions and scenarios in this book are more difficult than what you should experience on the actual exam. The questions do not attempt to cover more breadth or depth than the exam; however, they are designed to make sure that you know the answers. Rather than allowing you to derive the answers from clues hidden inside the questions themselves, the questions challenge your understanding and recall of the subject. Hopefully, these questions will help limit the number of exam questions on which you narrow your choices to two options and then guess.

The answers to these questions can be found in Appendix A.

1. What is a VLAN? When is it used?

2. When a VLAN is configured on a Catalyst switch port, in how much of the campus network will the VLAN number be unique and significant?

3. Name two types of VLANs in terms of spanning areas of the campus network.

4. What switch commands configure Fast Ethernet port 4/11 for VLAN 2?

5. Generally speaking, what must be configured (both switch and end user device) for a port-based VLAN?

6. What is the default VLAN on all ports of a Catalyst switch?

7. What is a trunk link?

8. What methods of Ethernet VLAN frame identification can be used on a Catalyst switch trunk?

9. What is the difference between the two trunking methods? How many bytes are added to trunked frames for VLAN identification in each method?

10. What is the purpose of Dynamic Trunking Protocol (DTP)?

11. What commands are needed to configure a Catalyst switch trunk port Gigabit 3/1 to transport only VLANs 100, 200 through 205, and 300 using IEEE 802.1Q? (Assume that trunking is enabled and active on the port already. Also, assume the **interface gigabit 3/1** command has already been entered.)

12. Two neighboring switch trunk ports are set to the *auto* mode with *ISL* trunking encapsulation mode. What will the resulting trunk mode become?

13. Complete this command to configure the switch port to use DTP to actively ask the other end to become a trunk:

    switchport mode _____

14. Which command can set the native VLAN of a trunk port to VLAN 100 after the interface has been selected?

15. What command can configure a trunk port to stop sending and receiving DTP packets completely?

16. What command can be used on a Catalyst switch to verify exactly what VLANs will be transported over trunk link gigabitethernet 4/4?

17. Suppose a switch port is configured with the following commands. A PC with a nontrunking NIC card is then connected to that port. What, if any, traffic will the PC successfully send and receive?

    ```
    interface fastethernet 0/12
    switchport trunk encapsulation dot1q
    switchport trunk native vlan 10
    switchport trunk allowed vlan 1-1005
    switchport mode trunk
    ```

18. What type of switch port must a customer present to a service provider if an IEEE 802.1Q tunnel is desired?

19. What type of switch port must a service provider present to a customer if an IEEE 802.1Q tunnel is desired?

20. What command is needed to form a Layer 2 protocol tunnel for CDP traffic?

This chapter covers the following topics that you need to master for the CCNP BCMSN exam:

- **VLAN Trunking Protocol**—This section presents Cisco VLAN Trunking Protocol (VTP) for VLAN management in a campus network.

- **VTP Configuration**—This section covers the Catalyst switch commands used to configure VTP.

- **VTP Pruning**—This section details traffic management by pruning within VTP domains, along with the commands needed for configuration.

- **Troubleshooting VTP**—This section gives a brief summary of things to consider and commands to use when VTP is not operating properly.

CHAPTER 7

VLAN Trunking Protocol (VTP)

When VLANs are defined and used on switches throughout an enterprise or campus network, the administrative overhead can easily increase. Using the VLAN Trunking Protocol (VTP) makes VLAN administration more organized and manageable. This chapter covers VTP and its configuration.

A similar standards-based VLAN management protocol for IEEE 802.1q trunks is called GARP VLAN Registration Protocol (GVRP). The GARP and GVRP protocols are defined in the IEEE 802.1D and 802.1q (clause 11) standards, respectively. At press time, GVRP was not supported in any of the Cisco IOS Software-based Catalyst switches. Therefore, it is not covered in this text or in the BCMSN course.

"Do I Know This Already?" Quiz

The purpose of the "Do I Know This Already?" quiz is to help you decide if you need to read the entire chapter. If you already intend to read the entire chapter, you do not necessarily need to answer these questions now.

The 12-question quiz, derived from the major sections in the "Foundation Topics" portion of the chapter, helps you determine how to spend your limited study time.

Table 7-1 outlines the major topics discussed in this chapter and the "Do I Know This Already?" quiz questions that correspond to those topics.

Table 7-1 *"Do I Know This Already?" Foundation Topics Section-to-Question Mapping*

Foundation Topics Section	Questions Covered in This Section
VTP VTP Configuration	1–8
VTP Pruning	9–10
Troubleshooting VTP	11–12

> **CAUTION** The goal of self-assessment is to gauge your mastery of the topics in this chapter. If you do not know the answer to a question or are only partially sure of the answer, you should mark this question wrong. Giving yourself credit for an answer you correctly guess skews your self-assessment results and might give you a false sense of security.

1. Which of the following is not a Catalyst switch VTP mode?

    a. Server

    b. Client

    c. Designated

    d. Transparent

2. A switch in VTP transparent mode can do which one of the following?

    a. Create a new VLAN

    b. Only listen to VTP advertisements

    c. Send its own VTP advertisements

    d. Cannot make VLAN configuration changes

3. Which one of the following is a valid VTP advertisement?

    a. Triggered update

    b. VLAN database

    c. Subset

    d. Domain

4. Which one of the following is needed for VTP communication?

    a. A management VLAN

    b. Trunk link

    c. An access VLAN

    d. An IP address

5. Which one of the following VTP modes does not allow any manual VLAN configuration changes?

   a. Server

   b. Client

   c. Designated

   d. Transparent

6. Select all the parameters that decide whether to accept new VTP information:

   a. VTP priority

   b. VTP domain name

   c. Configuration revision number

   d. VTP server name

7. How many VTP management domains can a Catalyst switch participate in?

   a. 1

   b. 2

   c. Unlimited

   d. 4096

8. Which command configures a Catalyst 3550 for VTP client mode?

   a. **set vtp mode client**

   b. **vtp client**

   c. **vtp mode client**

   d. **vtp client mode**

9. What is the purpose of VTP pruning?

   a. Limit the number of VLANs in a domain

   b. Stop unnecessary VTP advertisements

   c. Limit the extent of broadcast traffic

   d. Limit the size of the virtual tree

10. Which VLAN number is never eligible for VTP pruning?

    a. 0

    b. 1

    c. 1000

    d. 1001

11. Which of the following might present a VTP problem?

    a. Two or more VTP servers in a domain

    b. Two servers with the same configuration revision number

    c. A server in two domains

    d. A new server with a higher configuration revision number

12. If a VTP server is configured for VTP version 2, what else must happen for successful VTP communication in a domain?

    a. A VTP version 2 password must be set.

    b. All other switches in the domain must be version 2 capable.

    c. All other switches must be configured for VTP version 2.

    d. The VTP configuration revision number must be reset.

The answers to the quiz are found in Appendix A, "Answers to the Chapter 'Do I Know This Already?' Quizzes and Q&A Sections." The suggested choices for your next step are as follows:

- **6 or less overall score**—Read the entire chapter, including the "Foundation Topics," "Foundation Summary," and the "Q&A" sections.

- **7–9 overall score**—Begin with the "Foundation Summary" section and then follow with the "Q&A" section at the end of the chapter.

- **10 or more overall score**—If you want more review on these topics, skip to the "Foundation Summary" section and then go to the "Q&A" section at the end of the chapter. Otherwise, move on to Chapter 8, "Aggregating Switch Links."

Foundation Topics

VLAN Trunking Protocol

As the previous chapter demonstrated, VLAN configuration and trunking on a switch or a small group of switches is fairly intuitive. Campus network environments, however, usually consist of many interconnected switches. Configuring and managing a large number of switches, VLANs, and VLAN trunks can quickly get out of control.

Cisco has developed a method to manage VLANs across the campus network. The VLAN Trunking Protocol (VTP) uses Layer 2 trunk frames to communicate VLAN information among a group of switches. VTP manages the addition, deletion, and renaming of VLANs across the network from a central point of control. Any switch participating in a VTP exchange is aware of and can use any VLAN that VTP manages.

VTP Domains

VTP is organized into *management domains,* or areas with common VLAN requirements. A switch can belong to only one VTP domain, in addition to sharing VLAN information with other switches in the domain. Switches in different VTP domains, however, do not share VTP information.

Switches in a VTP domain advertise several attributes to their domain neighbors. Each advertisement contains information about the VTP management domain, VTP revision number, known VLANs, and specific VLAN parameters. When a VLAN is added to a switch in a management domain, other switches are notified of the new VLAN through *VTP advertisements.* In this way, all switches in a domain can prepare to receive traffic on their trunk ports using the new VLAN.

VTP Modes

To participate in a VTP management domain, each switch must be configured to operate in one of several modes. The VTP mode determines how the switch processes and advertises VTP information. You can use the following modes:

- **Server mode**—VTP servers have full control over VLAN creation and modification for their domains. All VTP information is advertised to other switches in the domain, while all received VTP information is synchronized with the other switches. By default, a switch is in VTP server mode. Note that each VTP domain must have at least one server so that VLANs can be created, modified, or deleted, and VLAN information can be propagated.

■ **Client mode**—VTP clients do not allow the administrator to create, change, or delete any VLANs. Instead, they listen to VTP advertisements from other switches and modify their VLAN configurations accordingly. In effect, this is a passive listening mode. Received VTP information is forwarded out trunk links to neighboring switches in the domain, so the switch also acts as a VTP relay.

■ **Transparent mode**—VTP transparent switches do not participate in VTP. While in transparent mode, a switch does not advertise its own VLAN configuration, and a switch does not synchronize its VLAN database with received advertisements. In VTP version 1, a transparent-mode switch does not even relay VTP information it receives to other switches, unless its VTP domain names and VTP version numbers match those of the other switches. In VTP version 2, transparent switches do forward received VTP advertisements out of their trunk ports, acting as VTP relays. This occurs regardless of the VTP domain name setting.

> **NOTE** While a switch is in VTP transparent mode, it can create and delete VLANs that are local only to itself. These VLAN changes, however, will *not* be propagated to any other switch.

VTP Advertisements

Each Cisco switch participating in VTP advertises VLANs (only VLANs 1 to 1005), revision numbers, and VLAN parameters on its trunk ports to notify other switches in the management domain. VTP advertisements are sent as multicast frames. The switch intercepts frames sent to the VTP multicast address and processes them with its supervisory processor. VTP frames are forwarded out trunk links as a special case.

Because all switches in a management domain learn of new VLAN configuration changes, a VLAN must be created and configured only on one VTP server switch in the domain.

By default, management domains are set to use nonsecure advertisements without a password. You can add a password to set the domain to secure mode. The same password must be configured on every switch in the domain so that all switches exchanging VTP information use identical encryption methods.

The VTP advertisement process starts with configuration revision number *0 (zero)*. When subsequent changes are made, the revision number is incremented before advertisements are sent out. When listening switches receive an advertisement with a greater revision number than is locally stored, the advertisement overwrites any stored VLAN information. Because of this, forcing any newly added network switches to have revision number 0 is important. The VTP revision number is stored in NVRAM and is not altered by a power cycle of the switch. Therefore, the revision number can be initialized only to 0 using one of the following methods:

- Change the switch's VTP mode to *transparent,* and then change the mode back to *server.*
- Change the switch's VTP domain to a bogus name (a nonexistent VTP domain), and then change the VTP domain back to the original name.

If the VTP revision number is not reset to 0, a new server switch might advertise VLANs as nonexistent or deleted. If the advertised revision number happens to be greater than previous legitimate advertisements, listening switches overwrite good VLAN database entries with null or deleted VLAN status information. This is referred to as a *VTP synchronization problem.*

Advertisements can originate as requests from client-mode switches that want to learn about the VTP database at boot-up time. Advertisements can also originate from server-mode switches as VLAN configuration changes occur.

VTP advertisements can occur in three forms:

- **Summary advertisements**—VTP domain servers send summary advertisements every 300 seconds and every time a VLAN database change occurs. The summary advertisement lists information about the management domain, including VTP version, domain name, configuration revision number, timestamp, MD5 encryption hash code, and the number of subset advertisements to follow. For VLAN configuration changes, summary advertisements are followed by one or more subset advertisements with more specific VLAN configuration data. Figure 7-1 shows the summary advertisement format.

Figure 7-1 *VTP Summary Advertisement Format*

Version (1 byte)	Type (Summary Adv) (1 byte)	Number of subset advertisements to follow (1 byte)	Domain name length (1 byte)
Management Domain Name (zero-padded to 32 bytes)			
Configuration Revision Number (4 bytes)			
Updater Identity (orginating IP address: 4 bytes)			
Update Timestamp (12 bytes)			
MD5 Digest hash code (16 bytes)			

- **Subset advertisements**—VTP domain servers send subset advertisements after a VLAN configuration change occurs. These advertisements list the specific changes that have been performed, such as creating or deleting a VLAN, suspending or activating a VLAN, changing the name of a VLAN, and changing a VLAN's (Maximum Transmission Unit (MTU). Subset advertisements can list the following VLAN parameters: status of the VLAN, VLAN type (such as Ethernet or Token Ring), MTU, length of the VLAN name, VLAN number, Security Association Identifier (SAID) value, and the VLAN name. VLANs are listed individually in sequential subset advertisements. Figure 7-2 shows the VTP subset advertisement format.

Figure 7-2 *VTP Subset Advertisement and VLAN Info Field Formats*

VTP Subset Advertisement

0	1	2	3
Version (1 byte)	Type (Subset Adv) (1 byte)	Subset sequence number (1 byte)	Domain name length (1 byte)
Management Domain Name (zero-padded to 32 bytes)			
Configuration Revision Number (4 bytes)			
VLAN Info Field 1 (see below)			
VLAN Info Field ...			
VLAN Info Field N			

VTP VLAN Info Field

0	1	2	3
Info Length	VLAN Status	VLAN Type	VLAN Name Length
VLAN ID		MTU Size	
802.10 SAID			
VLAN Name (padded with zeros to multiple of 4 bytes)			

- **Advertisement requests from clients**—A VTP client can request any lacking VLAN information. For example, a client switch might be reset and have its VLAN database cleared, and its VTP domain membership might be changed, or it might hear a VTP summary advertisement with a higher revision number than it currently has. After a client advertisement request, the VTP domain servers respond with summary and subset advertisements. Figure 7-3 shows the advertisement request format.

Figure 7-3 *VTP Advertisement Request Format*

0	1	2	3
Version (1 byte)	Type (Adv request) (1 byte)	Reserved (1 byte)	Domain name length (1 byte)
Management Domain Name (zero-padded to 32 bytes)			
Starting advertisement to request			

Catalyst switches in server mode store VTP information separately from the switch configuration in NVRAM. VLAN and VTP data are saved in the *vlan.dat* file on the switch's Flash memory file system. All VTP information, including the VTP configuration revision number, is retained even when the switch power is off. In this manner, a switch can recover the last known VLAN configuration from its VTP database after it reboots.

VTP Configuration

By default, every switch operates in VTP server mode for the management domain NULL (a blank string), with no password or secure mode. If the switch hears a VTP summary advertisement on a trunk port from any other switch, it automatically learns the VTP domain name, VLANs, and the configuration revision number it hears. This makes it easy to bring up a new switch in an existing VTP domain. However, be aware that the new switch stays in VTP server mode—something that might not be desirable.

The following sections discuss the commands and considerations that you should use to configure a switch for VTP operation.

Configuring a VTP Management Domain

Before a switch is added into a network, the VTP management domain should be identified. If this switch is the first one on the network, the management domain must be created. Otherwise, the switch might have to join an existing management domain with other existing switches.

You can use the following global configuration command to assign a switch to a management domain, where the *domain-name* is a text string up to 32 characters long:

```
Switch(config)# vtp domain domain-name
```

Configuring the VTP Mode

Next, you need to choose the VTP mode for the new switch. The three VTP modes of operation and their guidelines for use are as follows:

- **Server mode**—Server mode can be used on any switch in a management domain, even if other server and client switches are in use. This mode provides some redundancy in the event of a server failure in the domain. However, each VTP management domain should have at least one server. The first server defined in a network also defines the management domain that will be used by future VTP servers and clients. Server mode is the default VTP mode and allows VLANs to be created and deleted.

> **NOTE** Multiple VTP servers can coexist in a domain. This is usually recommended for redundancy. The servers do not elect a primary or secondary server—they all simply function as servers. If one server is configured with a new VLAN or VTP parameter, it advertises the changes to the rest of the domain. All other servers synchronize their VTP databases to this advertisement, just as any VTP client would.

- **Client mode**—If other switches are in the management domain, a new switch should be configured for client mode operation. In this way, the switch learns any existing VTP information from a server.

  If this switch is used as a redundant server, it should start out in client mode to learn all VTP information from reliable sources. If the switch was initially configured for server mode instead, it might propagate incorrect information to the other domain switches. After the switch has learned the current VTP information, it can be reconfigured for server mode.

- **Transparent mode**—This mode is used if a switch is not going to share VLAN information with any other switch in the network. VLANs can still be created, deleted, and modified on the transparent switch. However, they are not advertised to other neighboring switches. VTP advertisements received by a transparent switch, however, are forwarded to other switches on trunk links.

  Keeping switches in transparent mode can eliminate the chance for duplicate, overlapping VLANs in a large network with many network administrators. For example, two administrators might configure VLANs on switches in their respective areas but use the same VLAN identification or VLAN number. Even though the two VLANs have different meanings and purposes, they could overlap if both administrators advertised them using VTP servers.

You can configure the VTP mode with the following sequence of global configuration commands:

```
Switch(config)# vtp mode {server | client | transparent}
Switch(config)# vtp password password
```

If the domain is operating in secure mode, a password can also be defined. The password can be configured only on VTP servers and clients. It builds an MD5 digest that is sent in VTP advertisements (servers) and validates received advertisements (clients). The password is a string of 1 to 32 characters (case-sensitive).

If secure VTP is implemented using passwords, begin by configuring a password on the VTP servers. The client switches retain the last known VTP information but are unable to process received advertisements until the same password is configured on them, too.

Configuring the VTP Version

Two versions of VTP are available for use in a management domain. Catalyst switches are capable of running either VTP version 1 or VTP version 2. Within a management domain, the two versions are not interoperable. Therefore, the same VTP version must be configured on every switch in a domain. VTP version 1 is the default protocol on a switch.

If a switch is capable of running VTP version 2, however, a switch can coexist with other version 1 switches, as long as its VTP version 2 is not enabled. This situation becomes important if you want to use version 2 in a domain. Then, only one server mode switch needs to have VTP version 2 enabled. The new version number is propagated to all other version 2-capable switches in the domain, causing them all to automatically enable version 2 for use.

The two versions of VTP differ in the features they support. VTP version 2 offers the following additional features over version 1:

- **Version-dependent transparent mode**—In transparent mode, VTP version 1 matches the VTP version and domain name before forwarding the information to other switches using VTP. VTP version 2 in transparent mode forwards the VTP messages without checking the version number. Because only one domain is supported in a switch, the domain name doesn't have to be checked.

- **Consistency checks**—VTP version 2 performs consistency checks on the VTP and VLAN parameters entered from the command line interface (CLI) or by Simple Network Management Protocol (SNMP). This checking helps prevent errors in such things as VLAN names and numbers from being propagated to other switches in the domain. However, no consistency checks are performed on VTP messages that are received on trunk links or on configuration and database data that is read from NVRAM.

- **Token Ring support**—VTP version 2 supports the use of Token Ring switching and Token Ring VLANs. (If Token Ring switching is being used, VTP version 2 must be enabled.)

■ **Unrecognized Type-Length-Value (TLV) support**— VTP version 2 switches propagate received configuration change messages out other trunk links, even if the switch supervisor cannot parse or understand the message. For example, a VTP advertisement contains a *Type* field to denote what type of VTP message is being sent. VTP message type 1 is a summary advertisement, and message type 2 is a subset advertisement. An extension to VTP that utilizes other message types and other message length values could be in use. Instead of dropping the unrecognized VTP message, version 2 still propagates the information and keeps a copy in NVRAM.

The VTP version number is configured using the following global configuration command:

```
Switch(config)# vtp version {1 | 2}
```

By default, a switch uses VTP version 1.

VTP Status

The current VTP parameters for a management domain can be displayed using the **show vtp status** command. Example 7-1 demonstrates some sample output of this command.

Example 7-1 **show vtp status** *Reveals VTP Parameters for a Management Domain*

```
Switch# show vtp status
VTP Version                    : 2
Configuration Revision         : 89
Maximum VLANs supported locally : 1005
Number of existing VLANs       : 74
VTP Operating Mode             : Client
VTP Domain Name                : CampusDomain
VTP Pruning Mode               : Enabled
VTP V2 Mode                    : Disabled
VTP Traps Generation           : Disabled
MD5 digest                     : 0x4B 0x07 0x75 0xEC 0xB1 0x3D 0x6F 0x1F
Configuration last modified by 192.168.199.1 at 11-19-02 09:29:56
Switch#
```

VTP message and error counters can also be displayed with the **show vtp counters** command. You can use this command for basic VTP troubleshooting to see if the switch is interacting with other VTP nodes in the domain. Example 7-2 demonstrates some sample output from the **show vtp counters** command.

Example 7-2 **show vtp counters** *Reveals VTP Message and Error Counters*

```
Switch# show vtp counters
VTP statistics:
Summary advertisements received    : 1
Subset advertisements received     : 2
Request advertisements received    : 1
Summary advertisements transmitted : 1630
Subset advertisements transmitted  : 0
Request advertisements transmitted : 4
Number of config revision errors   : 0
Number of config digest errors     : 0
Number of V1 summary errors        : 0


VTP pruning statistics:

Trunk            Join Transmitted Join Received   Summary advts received from
                                                  non-pruning-capable device
---------------- ---------------- --------------- ---------------------------
Gi0/1            82352            82931           0
Switch#
```

VTP Pruning

Recall that by definition, a switch must forward broadcast frames out all available ports in the broadcast domain because broadcasts are destined everywhere there is a listener. Multicast frames, unless forwarded by more intelligent means, follow the same pattern.

In addition, frames destined for an address that the switch has not yet learned or has forgotten (the MAC address has aged out of the address table) must be forwarded out all ports in an attempt to find the destination. These frames are referred to as *unknown unicast*.

When forwarding frames out all ports in a broadcast domain or VLAN, trunk ports are included if they transport that VLAN. By default, a trunk link transports traffic from all VLANs, unless specific VLANs are removed from the trunk. Generally, in a network with several switches, trunk links are enabled between switches, and VTP is used to manage the propagation of VLAN information. This scenario causes the trunk links between switches to carry traffic from *all* VLANs—not just from the specific VLANs created.

Consider the network shown in Figure 7-4. When end user HostPC in VLAN 3 sends a broadcast, Catalyst switch C forwards the frame out all VLAN 3 ports, including the trunk link to Catalyst A. Catalyst A, in turn, forwards the broadcast on to Catalysts B and D over those trunk links. Catalysts B and D forward the broadcast out only their access links that have been configured for VLAN 3. If Catalysts B and D do not have any active users in VLAN 3, forwarding that broadcast frame to them would consume bandwidth on the trunk links and processor resources in both switches, only to have switches B and D discard the frames.

Figure 7-4   *Flooding in a Catalyst Switch Network*

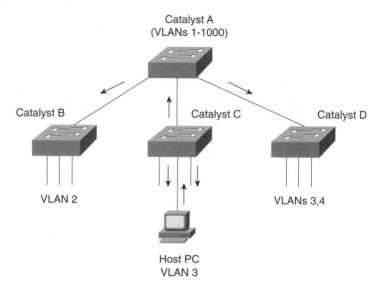

VTP pruning makes more efficient use of trunk bandwidth by reducing unnecessary flooded traffic. Broadcast and unknown unicast frames on a VLAN are forwarded over a trunk link only if the switch on the receiving end of the trunk has ports in that VLAN. VTP pruning occurs as an extension to VTP version 1, using an additional VTP message type. When a Catalyst switch has a port associated with a VLAN, the switch sends an advertisement to its neighbor switches that it has active ports on that VLAN. The neighbors keep this information, enabling them to decide if flooded traffic from a VLAN should use a trunk port or not.

Figure 7-5 shows the network from Figure 7-4 with VTP pruning enabled. Because Catalyst B has not advertised its use of VLAN 3, Catalyst A will prune VLAN 3 from the trunk to B and will choose not to flood VLAN 3 traffic to B over the trunk link. Catalyst D has advertised the need for VLAN 3, so traffic will be flooded to it.

Figure 7-5 *Flooding in a Catalyst Switch Network Using VTP Pruning*

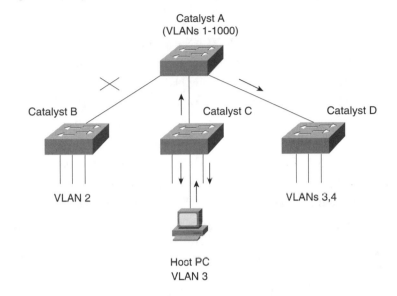

> **NOTE** Even when VTP pruning has determined that a VLAN is not needed on a trunk, an instance of the Spanning Tree Protocol (STP) will run for *every* VLAN that is allowed on the trunk link. To reduce the number of STP instances, you should manually "prune" unneeded VLANs from the trunk and allow only the needed ones. Use the **switchport trunk allowed vlan** command to identify the VLANs that should be added or removed from a trunk.

Enabling VTP Pruning

By default, VTP pruning is disabled on IOS-based switches. To enable pruning, use the following global configuration command:

```
Switch(config)# vtp pruning
```

If this command is used on a VTP server, pruning is enabled for the entire management domain. When pruning is enabled, all general-purpose VLANs become eligible for pruning on all trunk links, if needed. However, you can modify the default list of pruning eligibility with the following interface configuration command:

```
Switch(config)# interface type mod/num
Switch(config-if)# switchport trunk pruning vlan {add | except | none | remove} vlan-list
```

By default, VLANs 2 through 1001 are eligible, or "enabled," for potential pruning on every trunk. Use the following keywords with the command to tailor the list:

- *vlan-list*—An explicit list of eligible VLAN numbers (anything from 2 to 1001), separated by commas or by dashes.

- **all**—All active VLANs (1 to 4094) are eligible.

- **add** *vlan-list*—A list of VLAN numbers (anything from 2 to 1001) are added to the already configured list; this is a shortcut to keep from typing out a long list of numbers.

- **except** *vlan-list*—All VLANs (1 to 4094) are eligible except for the VLAN numbers listed (anything from 2 to 1001); this is a shortcut to keep from typing out a long list of numbers.

- **remove** *vlan-list*—A list of VLAN numbers (anything from 2 to 1001) are removed from the already configured list; this is a shortcut to keep from typing out a long list of numbers.

> **NOTE** Be aware that VTP pruning has no effect on switches in the VTP transparent mode. Instead, those switches must be configured manually to "prune" VLANs from trunk links. In this case, pruning is always configured on the upstream side of a trunk.
>
> By default, VLANs 2 to 1001 are eligible for pruning. VLAN 1 has a special meaning because it is normally used for control traffic and is never eligible for pruning. In addition, VLANs 1002 through 1005 are reserved for Token Ring and FDDI VLANs and are never eligible for pruning.

Troubleshooting VTP

If a switch does not seem to be receiving updated information from a VTP server, consider these possible causes:

- The switch is configured for VTP transparent mode. In this mode, incoming VTP advertisements are not processed; they are relayed only to other switches in the domain.

- If the switch is configured as a VTP client, there might not be another switch functioning as a VTP server. In this case, configure the local switch to become a VTP server itself.

- The link toward the VTP server is not in trunking mode. VTP advertisements are sent only over trunks. Use the **show interface** *type mod/num* **switchport** to verify the operational mode as a trunk.

- Make sure the VTP domain name is correctly configured to match that of the VTP server.

- Make sure the VTP version is compatible with other switches in the VTP domain.

■ Make sure the VTP password matches others in the VTP domain. If the server doesn't use a password, make sure the password is disabled or cleared on the local switch.

NOTE Above all else, verify a switch's VTP configuration *BEFORE* connecting it to a production network. If the switch has been previously configured or used elsewhere, it might already be in VTP server mode with a VTP configuration revision number that is higher than other switches in the production VTP domain. In that case, other switches will listen and learn from the new switch because it has a higher revision number and must know more recent information. This could cause the new switch to introduce bogus VLANs into the domain or, worse yet, to cause *all* other switches in the domain to delete all their active VLANs.

To prevent this from happening, reset the configuration revision number of every new switch that is added to a production network.

Table 7-2 lists and describes the commands that are useful for verifying or troubleshooting VTP configuration.

Table 7-2 *VTP Configuration Troubleshooting Commands*

Function	Command syntax
Display current VTP parameters, including the last advertising server	`show vtp status`
Display VTP advertisement and pruning statistics	`show vtp counters`
Display defined VLANs	`show vlan brief`
Display trunk status, including pruning eligibility	`show interface` *type mod/num* `switchport`
Display VTP pruning state	`show interface` *type mod/num* `pruning`

Foundation Summary

The Foundation Summary is a collection of information that provides a convenient review of many key concepts in this chapter. If you are already comfortable with the topics in this chapter, this summary can help you recall a few details. If you just read this chapter, this review should help solidify some key facts. If you are doing your final preparation before the exam, this information is a convenient way to review the day before the exam.

Table 7-3 *Catalyst VTP Modes*

VTP Mode	Characteristics
Server	All VLAN and VTP configuration changes occur here. The server advertises settings and changes to all other servers and clients in a VTP domain. (This is the default mode for Catalyst switches.)
Client	Listens to all VTP advertisements from servers in a VTP domain. Advertisements are relayed out other trunk links. No VLAN or VTP configuration changes can be made on a client.
Transparent	VLAN configuration changes are made locally, independent of any VTP domain. VTP advertisements are not received but merely relayed out other trunk links, if possible.

Table 7-4 *Types of VTP Advertisements*

Advertisement Type	Function
Summary	Sent by server every 300 seconds and after a topology change. Contains a complete dump of all VTP domain information.
Subset	Sent by server only after a VLAN configuration change. Contains only information about the specific VLAN change.
Advertisement request	Sent by client when additional VTP information is needed. Servers sent summary or subset advertisements in response.
Pruning request	Sent by clients and servers to announce VLANs that are in active use on local switch ports. (These messages are destined for nearest-neighbor switches and are not relayed throughout the domain.)

Table 7-5   *VTP Configuration Commands*

Task	Command Syntax
Define the VTP domain	**vtp domain** *domain-name*
Set the VTP mode	**vtp mode {server	client	transparent}**
Define an optional VTP password	**vtp password** *password*
Configure VTP version	**vtp version {1	2}**
Enable VTP pruning	**vtp pruning**
Select VLANs eligible for pruning on a trunk interface	**interface** *type mod/num* **switchport trunk pruning vlan {add	except	none	remove}** *vlan-list*

Q&A

The questions and scenarios in this book are more difficult than what you should experience on the actual exam. The questions do not attempt to cover more breadth or depth than the exam; however, they are designed to make sure that you know the answers. Rather than allowing you to derive the answers from clues hidden inside the questions themselves, the questions challenge your understanding and recall of the subject. Hopefully, these questions will help limit the number of exam questions on which you narrow your choices to two options and then guess.

The answers to these questions can be found in Appendix A.

1. True or false: You can use VTP domains to separate broadcast domains.

2. What VTP modes can a Catalyst switch be configured for? Can VLANs be created in each of the modes?

3. How many VTP management domains can a Catalyst switch participate in? How many VTP servers can a management domain have?

4. What conditions must exist for two Catalyst switches to be in the same VTP management domain?

5. On a VTP server switch, identify what you can do to reset the VTP configuration revision number to 0.

6. How can you clear the configuration revision number on a VTP client?

7. Complete this command to make all VLANs other than 30 and 100 eligible for pruning on the trunk interface:

   switchport trunk pruning vlan _____

8. Which VLAN numbers are never eligible for VTP pruning? Why?

9. What does the acronym VTP stand for?

10. What VTP domain name is defined on a new switch with no configuration?

11. In a network of switches, VTP domain Engineering has been configured with VLANs 1, 10 through 30, and 100. The VTP configuration revision number is currently at 23. Suppose a new switch is connected to the network, and it has the following configuration: VTP domain Engineering, VTP server mode, only VLANs 1 and 2 are defined, and the configuration revision number is 30.

12. What happens when the switch is connected to the network?

13. A VTP client switch has VLANs 1, 2, 3, 10, and 30 configured as part of a VTP domain; however, the switch has users connected only to access switch ports defined on VLANs 3 and 30. If VTP pruning is enabled and all VLANs are eligible, which VLANs will be pruned on the upstream switch?

14. The VTP domain Area3 consists of one server and several clients. The server's VTP configuration revision number is at 11. A new switch is added to the network. It has VTP domain name Area5 and a configuration revision number of 10. What happens when the new switch is added to the network? What happens when the VTP domain name is changed to Area3 on the new switch?

15. What command shows information about the VTP configuration on a Catalyst 3550?

This chapter covers the following topics that you need to master for the CCNP BCMSN exam:

- **Switch Port Aggregation with Ether-Channel**—This section discusses the concept of aggregating, or "bundling," physical ports into a single logical link. Methods for load-balancing traffic across the physical links are also covered.

- **EtherChannel Negotiation Protocols**—This section discusses two protocols that dynamically negotiate and control Ether-Channels: Port Aggregation Protocol (PAgP), a Cisco proprietary protocol, and Link Aggregation Control Protocol (LACP), a standards-based protocol.

- **EtherChannel Configuration**—This section discusses the Catalyst switch commands needed to configure EtherChannel.

- **Troubleshooting an EtherChannel**—This section gives a brief summary of things to consider and commands to use when an aggregated link is not operating properly.

CHAPTER 8

Aggregating Switch Links

In previous chapters, you learned about campus network design and connecting and organizing switches into blocks and common workgroups. Using these principles, end users can be given effective access to resources both on and off the campus network. However, today's mission-critical applications and services demand networks that provide high availability and reliability.

This chapter presents technologies that you can use in a campus network to provide higher bandwidth and reliability between switches.

"Do I Know This Already?" Quiz

The purpose of the "Do I Know This Already?" quiz is to help you decide if you need to read the entire chapter. If you already intend to read the entire chapter, you do not necessarily need to answer these questions now.

The 13-question quiz, derived from the major sections in the "Foundation Topics" portion of the chapter, helps you determine how to spend your limited study time.

Table 8-1 outlines the major topics discussed in this chapter and the "Do I Know This Already?" quiz questions that correspond to those topics.

Table 8-1 *"Do I Know This Already?" Foundation Topics Section-to-Question Mapping*

Foundation Topics Section	Questions Covered in This Section
Switch Port Aggregation with EtherChannel	1–7
EtherChannel Negotiation	8–11
EtherChannel Configuration	11–12
Troubleshooting an EtherChannel	13

> **CAUTION** The goal of self-assessment is to gauge your mastery of the topics in this chapter. If you do not know the answer to a question or are only partially sure of the answer, you should mark this question wrong. Giving yourself credit for an answer you correctly guess skews your self-assessment results and might give you a false sense of security.

1. If Fast Ethernet ports are bundled into an EtherChannel, what is the maximum throughput supported on a Catalyst switch?

   a. 100 Mbps

   b. 200 Mbps

   c. 400 Mbps

   d. 800 Mbps

   e. 1600 Mbps

2. Which of these distributes traffic over an EtherChannel?

   a. Round robin

   b. Least-used link

   c. A function of address

   d. A function of packet size

3. What type of interface represents an EtherChannel as a whole?

   a. Channel

   b. Port

   c. Port-channel

   d. Channel-port

4. Which of the following is not a valid method for EtherChannel load balancing?

   a. Source MAC address

   b. Source and destination MAC addresses

   c. Source IP address

   d. IP precedence

   e. UDP/TCP port

5. The EtherChannel load-balancing method can be set _____.

   a. Per switch port

   b. Per EtherChannel

   c. Globally per switch

   d. Can't be configured

6. What logical operation is performed to calculate EtherChannel load balancing as a function of two addresses?

   a. OR

   b. AND

   c. XOR

   d. NOR

7. Which one of the following is a valid combination of ports for an EtherChannel?

   a. Two access links (one VLAN 5, one VLAN 5)

   b. Two access links (one VLAN 1, one VLAN 10)

   c. Two trunk links (one VLANs 1-10, one VLANs 1, 11-20)

   d. Two Fast Ethernet links (both full-duplex, one 10 Mbps)

8. Which of these is a method for negotiating an EtherChannel?

   a. PAP

   b. CHAP

   c. LAPD

   d. LACP

9. Which of the following is a valid EtherChannel negotiation mode combination between two switches?

   a. PAgP auto, PAgP auto

   b. PAgP auto, PAgP desirable

   c. on, PAgP auto

   d. LACP passive, LACP passive

10. When would PagP's "desirable silent" mode be useful?

   a. When the switch should not send PAgP frames

   b. When the switch should not form an EtherChannel

   c. When the switch should not expect to receive PAgP frames

   d. When the switch is using LACP mode

11. Which of the following EtherChannel modes does not send or receive any negotiation frames?

    a. **channel-group 1 mode passive**

    b. **channel-group 1 mode active**

    c. **channel-group 1 mode on**

    d. **channel-group 1 mode desirable**

    e. **channel-group 1 mode auto**

12. Two computers are the only hosts sending IP data across an EtherChannel between two switches. Several different applications are being used between them. Which of these load-balancing methods would be more likely to use the most links in the EtherChannel?

    a. Source and destination MAC addresses

    b. Source and destination IP addresses

    c. Source and destination TCP/UDP ports

    d. None of the above

13. Which command can be used to see the status of an EtherChannel's links?

    a. **show channel link**

    b. **show etherchannel status**

    c. **show etherchannel summary**

    d. **show ether channel status**

The answers to the quiz are found in Appendix A, "Answers to Chapter 'Do I Know This Already?' Quizzes and Q&A Sections." The suggested choices for your next step are as follows:

- **8 or less overall score**—Read the entire chapter. This includes the "Foundation Topics," "Foundation Summary," and "Q&A" sections.

- **9–11 overall score**—Begin with the "Foundation Summary" section and then follow up with the "Q&A" section at the end of the chapter.

- **12 or more overall score**—If you want more review on these topics, skip to the "Foundation Summary" section and then go to the "Q&A" section at the end of the chapter. Otherwise, move to Chapter 9, "Traditional Spanning Tree Protocol."

Foundation Topics

Switch Port Aggregation with EtherChannel

As discussed in Chapter 5, "Switch Port Configuration," switches can use Ethernet, Fast Ethernet, or Gigabit Ethernet ports to scale link speeds by a factor of ten. Cisco offers another method of scaling link bandwidth by aggregating, or bundling, parallel links, termed the *EtherChannel* technology. Two to eight links of either Fast Ethernet (FE) or Gigabit Ethernet (GE) are bundled as one logical link of *Fast EtherChannel (FEC)* or *Gigabit EtherChannel (GEC)*, respectively. This bundle provides a full-duplex bandwidth of up to 1600 Mbps (8 links of Fast Ethernet) or 16 Gbps (8 links of Gigabit Ethernet).

This also provides an easy means to "grow," or expand, a link's capacity between two switches, without having to continually purchase hardware for the next magnitude of throughput. For example, a single FastEthernet link (200-Mbps throughput) can be incrementally expanded up to eight FastEthernet links (1600 Mbps) as a single Fast EtherChannel. If the traffic load grows beyond that, the growth process can begin again with a single Gigabit Ethernet link (2-Gbps throughput). Up to seven additional Gigabit Ethernet links can be added to that Gigabit EtherChannel (16 Gbps). The process repeats again by moving to a single 10Gigabit Ethernet link, and so on.

Ordinarily, having multiple or parallel links between switches creates the possibility of bridging loops—an undesirable condition. EtherChannel avoids this situation by bundling parallel links into a single, logical link, which can act as either an access or a trunk link. Switches or devices on each end of the EtherChannel link must understand and use the EtherChannel technology for proper operation.

Although an EtherChannel link is seen as a single logical link, the link does not have an inherent total bandwidth equal to the sum of its component physical links. For example, suppose an FEC link is made up of four full-duplex, 100-Mbps Fast Ethernet links. Although it is possible for the FEC link to carry a throughput of 800 Mbps, the single resulting FEC link does not operate at this speed. Instead, traffic is balanced across the individual links within the EtherChannel. Each of these links operates at its inherent speed (200 Mbps full-duplex for FE) but carries only the frames placed on it by the EtherChannel hardware. The load-balancing process is explained further in the next section.

EtherChannel also provides redundancy with several bundled physical links. If one of the links in the bundle fails, traffic sent through that link moves to an adjacent link. Failover occurs in less than a few milliseconds and is transparent to the end user. As more links fail, more traffic moves to further adjacent links. Likewise, as links are restored, the load redistributes among the active links.

Bundling Ports with EtherChannel

EtherChannel bundles can consist of up to eight physical ports of the same Ethernet media type and speed. Some configuration restrictions exist to ensure that only similarly configured links are bundled.

Generally, all bundled ports must first belong to the same VLAN. If used as a trunk, bundled ports must all be in trunking mode, have the same native VLAN, and pass the same set of VLANs. Each of the ports should also have the same speed and duplex settings before they are bundled. Bundled ports must also be configured with identical Spanning Tree settings.

Distributing Traffic in EtherChannel

Traffic in an EtherChannel is distributed across the individual bundled links in a deterministic fashion. However, the load is not necessarily balanced equally across all the links. Instead, frames are forwarded on a specific link as a result of a hashing algorithm. The algorithm can use source IP address, destination IP address, or a combination of source and destination IP addresses, source and destination MAC addresses, or TCP/UDP port numbers. The hash algorithm computes a binary pattern that selects a link number in the bundle for each frame.

If only one address or port number is hashed, a switch forwards each frame by using one or more low-order bits of the hash value as an index into the bundled links. If two addresses or port numbers are hashed, a switch performs an exclusive-OR (XOR) operation on one or more low-order bits of the addresses or TCP/UDP port numbers as an index into the bundled links.

For example, an EtherChannel consisting of two links bundled together requires a one-bit index. Either the lowest order address bit or the XOR of the last bit of the addresses in the frame is used. A four-link bundle uses a hash of the last two bits. Likewise, an eight-link bundle uses a hash of the last three bits. The hashing operation's outcome selects the EtherChannel's outbound link. Table 8-2 shows the results of an XOR on a two-link bundle, using the source and destination addresses.

The XOR operation is performed independently on each bit position in the address value. If the two address values have the same bit value, the XOR result is 0. If the two address bits differ, the XOR result is 1. In this way, frames can be statistically distributed among the links with the assumption that MAC or IP addresses are statistically distributed throughout the network. In a four-link EtherChannel, the XOR is performed on the lower two bits of the address values resulting in a 2-bit XOR value (each bit is computed separately) or a link number from 0 to 3.

Table 8-2 *Frame Distribution on a Two-Link EtherChannel*

Binary Addresses	Two-Link EtherChannel XOR and Link Number
Addr1: ... xxxxxxx0 Addr2: ... xxxxxxx0	... xxxxxxx0: Use link 0
Addr1: ... xxxxxxx0 Addr2: ... xxxxxxx1	... xxxxxxx1: Use link 1
Addr1: ... xxxxxxx1 Addr2: ... xxxxxxx0	... xxxxxxx1: Use link 1
Addr1: ... xxxxxxx1 Addr2: ... xxxxxxx1	... xxxxxxx0: Use link 0

As an example, consider a packet being sent from IP address 192.168.1.1 to 172.31.67.46. Because EtherChannels can be built from two to eight individual links, only the rightmost (least significant) three bits are needed as a link index. These bits are 001 (1) and 110 (6), respectively. For a two-link EtherChannel, a one-bit XOR is performed on the rightmost address bit: 1 XOR 0 = 1, causing Link 1 in the bundle to be used. A four-link EtherChannel produces a two-bit XOR: 01 XOR 10 = 11, causing Link 3 in the bundle to be used. Finally, an eight-link EtherChannel requires a three-bit XOR: 001 XOR 110 = 111, where Link 7 in the bundle is selected.

A conversation between two devices is always sent through the same EtherChannel link because the two endpoint addresses stay the same. However, when a device talks to several other devices, chances are that the destination addresses are equally distributed with 0s and 1s in the last bit (even and odd address values). This causes the frames to be distributed across the EtherChannel links. Note that a conversation between two end devices to create a load imbalance is possible using one of the links in a bundle because all traffic between a pair of stations will use the same link.

Configuring EtherChannel Load Balancing

The hashing operation can be performed on either MAC or IP addresses, and can be based solely on source or destination addresses, or both. Use the following command to configure frame distribution for all EtherChannel switch links:

```
Switch(config)# port-channel load-balance method
```

Table 8-3 lists the possible values for the *method* variable, along with the hashing operation and supporting switch models.

Table 8-3   *Types of EtherChannel Load-Balancing Methods*

method Value	Hash input	Hash operation	Switch Model
src-ip	Source IP address	bits	6500/4500
dst-ip	Destination IP address	bits	6500/4500
src-dst-ip	Source and destination IP address	XOR	6500/4500/3550
src-mac	Source MAC address	bits	6500/4500/3550
dst-mac	Destination MAC address	bits	6500/4500/3550
src-dst-mac	Source and destination MAC	XOR	6500/4500
src-port	Source port number	bits	6500/4500
dst-port	Destination port number	bits	6500/4500
src-dst-port	Source and destination port	XOR	6500/4500

The default configuration is to use source XOR destination IP addresses. (The default for the Catalyst 3550 is **src-mac**, which uses the source MAC address for Layer 2 and source XOR destination IP addresses for Layer 3 switching.)

Normally, the default action should result in a statistical distribution of frames. However, you should determine if the EtherChannel is imbalanced according to the traffic patterns present. For example, if a single server is receiving most of the traffic on an EtherChannel, the server's address (the destination IP address) will always remain constant in the many conversations. This can cause one link to be overused if the destination IP address is used as a component of a load-balancing method. In the case of a four-link EtherChannel, perhaps two of the four links are overused. Configuring the use of MAC addresses, or only the source IP addresses, might cause the distribution to be more balanced across all the bundled links.

> **NOTE**   To verify how effective a configured load-balancing method is performing, you can use the **show etherchannel port-channel** command. Each link in the channel will be displayed, along with a "Load" value.

In some applications, EtherChannel traffic might consist of protocols other than IP. For example, IPX or SNA frames might be switched along with IP. Non-IP protocols need to be distributed according to MAC addresses because IP addresses are not applicable. Here, the switch should be configured to use MAC addresses instead of the IP default.

> **NOTE**   A special case results when a router is connected to an EtherChannel. Recall that a router always uses its burned-in MAC address in Ethernet frames, even though it is forwarding packets to and from many different IP addresses. In other words, many end stations send frames to their local router address with the router's MAC address as the destination. This means that the destination MAC address is the same for all frames destined through the router.
>
> Usually, this will not present a problem because the source MAC addresses are all different. When two routers are forwarding frames to each other, however, both source and destination MAC addresses will remain constant, and only one link of the EtherChannel will be used. If the MAC addresses are remaining constant, choose IP addresses instead. Beyond that, if most of the traffic is between the same two IP addresses, as in the case of two servers talking, choose IP port numbers to disperse the frames across different links.

You should choose the load-balancing method that provides the greatest distribution or variety when the channel links are indexed. Also, consider the type of addressing that is being used on the network. If most of the traffic is IP, it might make sense to load balance according to IP addresses or TCP/UDP port numbers. But, if IP load balancing is being used, what happens to non-IP frames? If a frame can't meet the load-balancing criteria, the switch automatically falls back to the "next lowest" method. With Ethernet, MAC addresses must always be present, so the switch distributes those frames according to their MAC addresses.

A switch also provides some inherent protection against bridging loops with EtherChannels. When ports are bundled into an EtherChannel, no inbound (received) broadcasts and multicasts sent back out over any of the remaining ports in the channel. Outbound broadcast and multicast frames are load balanced like any other—the broadcast or multicast address becomes part of the hashing calculation to choose an outbound channel link.

EtherChannel Negotiation Protocols

EtherChannels can be negotiated between two switches to provide some dynamic link configuration. Two protocols are available to negotiate bundled links in Catalyst switches. The Port Aggregation Protocol (PAgP) is a Cisco-proprietary solution, and the Link Aggregation Control Protocol (LACP) is standards-based.

Port Aggregation Protocol (PAgP)

To provide automatic EtherChannel configuration and negotiation between switches, Cisco developed the *Port Aggregation Protocol (PAgP)*. PAgP packets are exchanged between switches over EtherChannel-capable ports. The identification of neighbors and port group capabilities are learned and compared with local switch capabilities. Ports that have the same neighbor device ID and port group capability are bundled together as a bidirectional, point-to-point EtherChannel link.

PAgP forms an EtherChannel only on ports that are configured for either identical static VLANs or trunking. PAgP also dynamically modifies parameters of the EtherChannel if one of the bundled ports is modified. For example, if the VLAN, speed, or duplex mode of a port in an established bundle is changed, PAgP changes that parameter for all ports in the bundle.

PAgP can be configured in active mode ("desirable"), where a switch actively asks a far-end switch to negotiate an EtherChannel, or in passive mode ("auto," the default), where a switch negotiates an EtherChannel only if the far-end initiates it.

Link Aggregation Control Protocol (LACP)

LACP is a standards-based alternative to PAgP, defined in IEEE 802.3ad (also known as IEEE 802.3 Clause 43, "Link Aggregation"). LACP packets are exchanged between switches over EtherChannel-capable ports. Like PAgP, the identification of neighbors and port group capabilities is learned and compared with local switch capabilities. However, LACP also assigns roles to the EtherChannel's endpoints.

The switch with the lowest *system priority* (a 2-byte priority value followed by a 6-byte switch MAC address) is allowed to make decisions about what ports are actively participating in the EtherChannel at a given time.

Ports are selected and become active according to their *port priority* value (a 2-byte priority followed by a 2-byte port number), where a low value indicates a higher priority. A set of up to 16 potential links can be defined for each EtherChannel. Through LACP, a switch selects up to eight of these having the lowest port priorities as active EtherChannel links at any given time. The other links are placed in a standby state and will be enabled in the EtherChannel if one of the active links goes down.

Like PAgP, LACP can be configured in active mode ("active"), where a switch actively asks a far-end switch to negotiate an EtherChannel, or in passive mode ("passive"), where a switch negotiates an EtherChannel only if the far-end initiates it.

EtherChannel Configuration

For each EtherChannel on a switch, you must choose the EtherChannel negotiation protocol and assign individual switch ports to the EtherChannel. Both PAgP and LACP negotiated EtherChannels are described in the following sections. You can also configure an EtherChannel to use the **on** mode, which unconditionally bundles the links. In this case, neither PAgP nor LACP packets will be sent or received.

As ports are configured to be members of an EtherChannel, the switch automatically creates a logical port channel interface. This interface represents the channel as a whole.

Configuring a PAgP EtherChannel

To configure switch ports for PAgP negotiation (the default), use the following commands:

```
Switch(config)# interface type mod/num
Switch(config-if)# channel-protocol pagp
Switch(config-if)# channel-group number mode {on | auto | desirable}
```

On all IOS-based Catalyst models (3550, 4500, and 6500), you can select between PAgP and LACP as a channel negotiation protocol. The Catalyst 2950, however, offers only PAgP, so the **channel-protocol** command is not available. Each interface that will be included in a single EtherChannel bundle must be assigned to the same unique channel group *number* (1 to 64). Channel negotiation must be set to **on** (unconditionally channel; no PAgP negotiation), **auto** (passively listen and wait to be asked), or **desirable** (actively ask).

By default, PAgP operates in "silent" mode with the **desirable** and **auto** modes, and allows ports to be added to an EtherChannel even if the other end of the link is silent and never transmits PAgP packets. This might seem to go against the idea of PAgP, where two endpoints negotiate a channel. However, this allows a switch to form an EtherChannel with a device, such as a file server or a network analyzer, that doesn't participate in PAgP. Then, what's the point of running PAgP? Because links should be added to the EtherChannel bundle as PAgP would normally do. In the case of a network analyzer connected to the far end, you might also want to see the PAgP packets generated by the switch, as if you were using a normal PAgP EtherChannel.

If you expect a PAgP-capable switch to be on the far end, you should add the **non-silent** keyword to the **desirable** or **auto** mode. This requires each port to receive PAgP packets before adding them to a channel. If PAgP isn't heard on an active port, the port remains in the "up" state, but PAgP reports to the Spanning Tree Protocol (STP) that the port is down.

Configuring a LACP EtherChannel

To configure switch ports for LACP negotiation, use the following commands:

```
Switch(config)# lacp system-priority priority
Switch(config)# interface type mod/num
Switch(config-if)# channel-protocol lacp
Switch(config-if)# channel-group number mode {on | passive | active}
Switch(config-if)# lacp port-priority priority
```

First, the switch should have its LACP system priority defined (1 to 65,535, default 32,768). If desired, one switch should be assigned a lower system priority than the other so that it can make decisions about the EtherChannel's makeup. Otherwise, both switches will have the same system priority (32,768), and the one with the lower MAC address will become the decision-maker.

Each interface included in a single EtherChannel bundle must be assigned to the same unique channel group *number* (1 to 64). Channel negotiation must be set to **on** (unconditionally channel; no LACP negotiation), **passive** (passively listen and wait to be asked), or **active** (actively ask).

You can configure more interfaces in the channel group *number* than are allowed to be active in the channel. This prepares extra standby interfaces to replace failed active ones. Configure a lower port priority (1 to 65,535, default 32,768) for any interfaces that must be active, and a higher priority to ones that might be held in the standby state. Otherwise, just use the default scenario, where all ports default to 32,768, and the lower port numbers are used to select the active ports.

Troubleshooting an EtherChannel

If you find that an EtherChannel is having problems, remember that the whole concept is based around consistent configurations on both ends of the channel. Here are some reminders about EtherChannel operation and interaction:

- EtherChannel **on** mode does not send or receive PAgP or LACP packets. Therefore, both ends should be set to the **on** mode.

- EtherChannel **desirable** (PAgP) or **active** (LACP) mode attempts to ask the far end to bring up a channel. Therefore, the other end must be set to either **desirable** or **auto** mode.

- EtherChannel **auto** (PAgP) or **passive** (LACP) mode participates in the channel protocol, but only if the far end asks for participation. Two switches in the **auto** or **passive** mode will not form an EtherChannel.

- PAgP **desirable** and **auto** modes default to the **silent** submode, where no PAgP packets are expected from the far end. If ports are set to **non-silent** submode, PAgP packets must be received before a channel will form.

First, verify the EtherChannel state with the **show etherchannel summary** command. Each port in the channel will be shown, along with flags indicating the port's state, as shown in Example 8-1.

Example 8-1   show etherchannel summary *Command Output*

```
Switch# show etherchannel summary
Flags:  D - down        P - in port-channel
        I - stand-alone s - suspended
        H - Hot-standby (LACP only)
        R - Layer3      S - Layer2
        u - unsuitable for bundling
        U - in use      f - failed to allocate aggregator

        d - default port
Number of channel-groups in use: 1
```

Example 8-1 **show etherchannel summary** *Command Output (Continued)*

```
Number of aggregators:          1

Group  Port-channel Protocol   Ports
------+------------+----------+-------------------------------------------------
1      Po1(SU)       PAgP      Fa0/41(P)  Fa0/42(P)  Fa0/43(D)  Fa0/44(P)
                               Fa0/45(P)  Fa0/46(P)  Fa0/47(P)  Fa0/48(P)
```

The status of the port-channel shows the EtherChannel logical interface as a whole. This should show "SU" (Layer 2 channel, in use) if the channel is operational. You can also examine the status of each port within the channel. Notice that most of the channel ports have flags "(P)," indicating that they are active in the port-channel. One port shows "(D)" because it is physically not connected or down. If a port is connected but not bundled in the channel, it will have an independent, or "(I)," flag.

You can verify the channel negotiation mode with the **show etherchannel port** command, as shown in Example 8-2. The local switch is shown using desirable mode with PAgP. Notice that you can also see the far end's negotiation mode under the **Partner Flags** heading, as **A**, or auto mode.

Example 8-2 **show etherchannel port** *Command Output*

```
Switch# show etherchannel port
                 Channel-group listing:
                 ----------------------


Group: 1
----------
                 Ports in the group:
                 -------------------
Port: Fa0/41
-----------


Port state     = Up Mstr In-Bndl
Channel group = 1              Mode = Desirable-Sl    Gcchange = 0
Port-channel  = Po1            GC   = 0x00010001          Pseudo port-channel = Po1
Port index     = 0             Load = 0x00         Protocol =    PAgP


Flags:   S - Device is sending Slow hello.  C - Device is in Consistent state.
         A - Device is in Auto mode.        P - Device learns on physical port.
         d - PAgP is down.
Timers:  H - Hello timer is running.        Q - Quit timer is running.
         S - Switching timer is running.    I - Interface timer is running.

Local information:
                                  Hello    Partner  PAgP     Learning  Group
```

continues

Example 8-2 **show etherchannel port** *Command Output (Continued)*

```
Port      Flags State   Timers  Interval Count   Priority  Method  Ifindex
Fa0/41    SC    U6/S7   H       30s      1       128       Any     55

Partner's information:

          Partner               Partner               Partner           Partner Group
Port      Name                  Device ID             Port      Age Flags Cap.
Fa0/41    FarEnd                00d0.5849.4100        3/1       19s SAC   11

Age of the port in the current state: 00d:08h:05m:28s
```

Within a switch, an EtherChannel cannot form unless each of the component or member ports is consistently configured. Each must have the same mode (access or trunk), native VLAN, trunked VLANs, port speed, port duplex mode, and so on.

You can display a port's configuration by looking at the **show running-config interface** *type mod/num* output. Also, the **show interface** *type mod/num* **etherchannel** shows all active EtherChannel parameters for a single port. If you configure a port inconsistently with others for an EtherChannel, you see error messages from the switch.

Some messages from the switch might look like errors but are part of the normal EtherChannel process. For example, as a new port is configured as a member of an existing EtherChannel, this message might be seen:

```
4d00h: %EC-5-L3DONTBNDL2: FastEthernet0/2 suspended: incompatible partner port with
FastEthernet0/1
```

When the port is first added to the EtherChannel, it is incompatible because the STP runs on the channel and the new port. After STP takes the new port through its progression of states, the port is automatically added into the EtherChannel.

Other messages do indicate a port compatibility error. In these cases, the cause of the error is shown. For example, the following message tells that FastEthernet0/3 has a different duplex mode than the other ports in the EtherChannel:

```
4d00h: %EC-5-CANNOT_BUNDLE2: FastEthernet0/3 is not compatible with FastEthernet0/1 and
will be suspended (duplex of Fa0/3 is full, Fa0/1 is half)
```

Finally, you can verify the EtherChannel load-balancing or hashing algorithm with the **show etherchannel load-balance** command. Remember that the switches on either end of an EtherChannel can have different load-balancing methods. The only drawback to this is that the load balancing will be asymmetric in the two directions across the channel.

Table 8-4 lists the commands useful for verifying or troubleshooting EtherChannel operation.

Table 8-4 *EtherChannel Troubleshooting Commands*

Display Function	Command Syntax
Current EtherChannel status of each member port	**show etherchannel summary** **show etherchannel port**
Timestamps of EtherChannel changes	**show etherchannel port-channel**
Detailed status about each EtherChannel component	**show etherchannel detail**
Load balancing hashing algorithm	**show etherchannel load-balance**
Load balancing port index used by hashing algorithm	**show etherchannel port-channel**
EtherChannel Neighbors on each port	**show {pagp	lacp} neighbor**
LACP System ID	**show lacp sys-id**

Foundation Summary

The Foundation Summary is a collection of information that provides a convenient review of many key concepts in this chapter. If you are already comfortable with the topics in this chapter, this summary can help you recall a few details. If you just read this chapter, this review should help solidify some key facts. If you are doing your final preparation before the exam, this information is a convenient way to review the day before the exam.

Table 8-5 *Frame Distribution on an EtherChannel*

Channel size	A1: ... xxxxx000 A2: ... xxxxx000 (address bits the same)	A1: ... xxxxx000 A2: ... xxxxx111 (address bits differ)
2-port	Link index: 0 (0) (lowest)	Link index: 1 (1) (highest)
4-port	Link index: 00 (0) (lowest)	Link index: 11 (3) (highest)
8-port	Link index 000 (0) (lowest)	Link index: 111 (7) (highest)

Example address bits are shown. The XOR operation produces a 0 bit if the two input bits are the same (0,0 or 1,1) and a 1 bit if the two input bits are different (0,1 or 1,0).

Table 8-6 *EtherChannel Load-Balancing Methods*

method Value	Hash Input	Hash Operation	Switch Model
src-ip	Source IP address	bits	6500/4500
dst-ip	Destination IP address	bits	6500/4500
src-dst-ip	Source and destination IP address	XOR	6500/4500
src-mac	Source MAC address	bits	6500/4500/3550
dst-mac	Destination MAC address	bits	6500/4500/3550
src-dst-mac	Source and destination MAC	XOR	6500/4500
src-port	Source port number	bits	6500/4500
dst-port	Destination port number	bits	6500/4500
src-dst-port	Source and destination port	XOR	6500/4500

Table 8-7 *EtherChannel Negotiation Protocols*

Negotiation Mode		Negotiation Packets Sent?	Characteristics
PAgP	LACP		
on	on	No	All ports channeling
auto	passive	Yes	Waits to channel until asked
desirable	active	Yes	Actively asks to form a channel

Table 8-8 *EtherChannel Configuration Commands*

Task	Command Syntax
Select a load-balancing method for the switch.	`port-channel load-balance` *method*

Use a PAgP mode on an interface.	`channel-protocol pagp`
	`channel-group` *number* `mode {on ǀ auto [non-silent] ǀ`
	`desirable [non-silent]}`

Assign the LACP system priority.	`lacp system-priority` *priority*

Use an LACP mode on an interface.	`channel-protocol lacp`
	`channel-group` *number* `mode {on ǀ passive ǀ active}`
	`lacp port-priority` *priority*

Q&A

The questions in this book are more difficult than what you should experience on the actual exam. The questions do not attempt to cover more breadth or depth than the exam; however, they are designed to make sure that you know the answers. Rather than allowing you to derive the answers from clues hidden inside the questions themsselves, the questions challenge your understanding and recall of the subject. Hopefully, these questions will help limit the number of exam questions on which you narrow your choices to two options and then guess.

The answers to these questions can be found in Appendix A.

1. What are some benefits of an EtherChannel?

2. How many links can be aggregated into an EtherChannel?

3. Traffic between two hosts will be distributed across all links in an EtherChannel. True or false?

4. Which methods can you use to distribute traffic in an EtherChannel?

5. How does an EtherChannel distribute broadcasts and multicasts?

6. When load balancing, what hashing functions choose a link for a frame?

7. What protocols can negotiate an EtherChannel between two switches?

8. Suppose a switch at one end of an EtherChannel is configured to use source MAC addresses for load balancing. The switch on the other end is configured to use both source and destination IP addresses. What happens?

9. Two switches have a 4-port EtherChannel between them. Both switches are load balancing using source and destination IP addresses. If a packet has the source address 192.168.15.10 and destination address 192.168.100.31, what is the EtherChannel link index?

10. What does the acronym PAgP stand for?

11. Two switches should be configured to negotiate an EtherChannel. If one switch is using PAgP "auto" mode, what should the other switch use?

12. What is the LACP system priority value used for?

13. Complete the following command to put an interface into EtherChannel group 3, and to use PAgP to ask the far-end switch to participate in the EtherChannel. This switch port should also require PAgP packets back from the far-end switch.

    Switch(config-if)# **channel-group** _____

14. What interface configuration command is needed to select LACP as the EtherChannel negotiation protocol?

15. What command could you use to see the status of every port in an EtherChannel?

16. What command could you use to verify the hashing algorithm used for EtherChannel load balancing?

17. Suppose a switch is used in a small data center where one server offers an IP-based application to many clients throughout the campus. An EtherChannel connects the data center switch to a Layer 3 core switch, which routes traffic to all clients. What EtherChannel load-balancing method might be most appropriate at the data center switch?

    a. Source MAC address

    b. Source IP address

    c. Destination MAC address

    d. Destination IP address

    e. Source and destination MAC address

    f. Source and destination IP address

18. Suppose a mainframe is connected to a switch that has an EtherChannel uplink to a campus network. The EtherChannel has been configured with the **port-channel load-balance src-dst-ip** command. Most of the mainframe traffic is SNA (non-IP). What will happen to the SNA frames when they are switched? Would it be better to reconfigure the channel with **port-channel load-balance src-dst-mac**?

19. What attributes of a set of switch ports must match to form an EtherChannel?

20. What happens if one port of an EtherChannel is unplugged or goes dead? What happens when that port is reconnected?

This chapter covers the following topics that you need to master for the CCNP BCMSN exam:

- **IEEE 802.1D Overview**—This section discusses the original, or more traditional, Spanning Tree Protocol (STP). This protocol is the foundation for the default Catalyst STP, as well as for all of the enhancements that are described in Chapters 10 through 12.

- **Types of STP**—This section discusses other types of STP that might be running on a Catalyst switch specifically, the Common Spanning Tree, Per-VLAN Spanning Tree (PVST), and PVST+.

CHAPTER 9

Traditional Spanning Tree Protocol

Previous chapters covered robust network designs where redundant links are used between switches. While this increases the network availability, it also opens up the possibility for conditions that would impair the network. In a Layer 2 switched network, preventing bridging loops from forming over redundant paths is important. Spanning Tree Protocol was designed to monitor and control the Layer 2 network so that a loop-free topology is maintained.

This chapter discusses the theory and operation of the Spanning Tree Protocol (STP). More specifically, the original, or traditional, STP is covered, as defined in IEEE 802.1D. Several chapters explain STP topics in this book. Here is a brief roadmap, so you can chart a course:

Chapter 9, "Traditional Spanning Tree Protocol"—Covers the theory of IEEE 802.1D

Chapter 10, "Spanning Tree Configuration"—Covers the configuration commands needed for IEEE 802.1D

Chapter 11, "Protecting the Spanning Tree Protocol Topology"—Covers the features and commands to filter and protect a converged STP topology from conditions that could destabilize it

Chapter 12, "Advanced Spanning Tree Protocol"—Covers the newer 802.1w and 802.1s enhancements to STP, allowing more scalability and faster convergence

"Do I Know This Already?" Quiz

The purpose of the "Do I Know This Already?" quiz is to help you decide if you need to read the entire chapter. If you already intend to read the entire chapter, you do not necessarily need to answer these questions now.

The 12-question quiz, derived from the major sections in the "Foundation Topics" portion of the chapter, helps you determine how to spend your limited study time.

Table 9-1 outlines the major topics discussed in this chapter and the "Do I Know This Already?" quiz questions that correspond to those topics.

Table 9-1 *"Do I Know This Already?" Foundation Topics Section-to-Question Mapping*

Foundation Topics Section	Questions Covered in This Section
IEEE 802.1D	1–10
Types of STP	11–12

CAUTION The goal of self-assessment is to gauge your mastery of the topics in this chapter. If you do not know the answer to a question or are only partially sure of the answer, you should mark this question wrong. Giving yourself credit for an answer you correctly guess skews your self-assessment results and might give you a false sense of security.

1. How is a bridging loop best described?

   a. A loop formed between switches for redundancy

   b. A loop formed by the Spanning Tree Protocol

   c. A loop formed between switches where frames circulate endlessly

   d. The round-trip path a frame takes from source to destination

2. Which of these is one of the parameters used to elect a Root Bridge?

   a. Root Path Cost

   b. Path Cost

   c. Bridge Priority

   d. BPDU revision number

3. If all switches in a network are left at their default STP values, which one of the following is not true?

   a. The Root Bridge will be the switch with the lowest MAC address.

   b. The Root Bridge will be the switch with the highest MAC address.

   c. One or more switches will have a Bridge Priority of 32,768.

   d. A secondary Root Bridge will be present on the network.

4. Configuration BPDUs are originated by which of the following?

   a. All switches in the STP domain

   b. Only the Root Bridge switch

   c. Only the switch that detects a topology change

   d. Only the secondary Root Bridge when it takes over

5. Which of these is the single most important design decision to be made in a network running STP?

   a. Removing any redundant links

   b. Making sure all switches run the same version of IEEE 802.1D

   c. Root Bridge placement

   d. Making sure all switches have redundant links

6. What happens to a port that is neither a Root Port nor a Designated Port?

   a. It is available for normal use.

   b. It can be used for load balancing.

   c. It is put into the Blocking state.

   d. It is disabled.

7. What is the maximum number of Root Ports that a Catalyst switch can have?

   a. 1

   b. 2

   c. Unlimited

   d. None

8. What mechanism is used to set STP timer values for all switches in a network?

   a. Configuring the timers on every switch in the network.

   b. Configuring the timers on the Root Bridge switch.

   c. Configuring the timers on both primary and secondary Root Bridge switches.

   d. The timers can't be adjusted.

9. If a switch port is in this STP state, MAC addresses can be placed into the CAM table, but no data can be sent or received:

    a. Blocking

    b. Forwarding

    c. Listening

    d. Learning

10. What is the default "hello" time for IEEE 802.1D?

    a. 1 second

    b. 2 seconds

    c. 30 seconds

    d. 60 seconds

11. Which of the following is the Spanning Tree Protocol defined in the IEEE 802.1Q standard?

    a. PVST

    b. CST

    c. EST

    d. MST

12. If a switch has 10 VLANs defined and active, how many instances of STP will run using PVST+ versus CST?

    a. 1 for PVST+, 1 for CST

    b. 1 for PVST+, 10 for CST

    c. 10 for PVST+, 1 for CST

    d. 10 for PVST+, 10 for CST

You can find the answers to the quiz in Appendix A, "Answers to Chapter 'Do I Know This Already?' Quizzes and Q&A Sections." The suggested choices for your next step are as follows:

■ **7 or less overall score**—Read the entire chapter. This includes the "Foundation Topics," "Foundation Summary," and "Q&A" sections.

■ **8–10 overall score**—Begin with the "Foundation Summary" section and then follow up with the "Q&A" section at the end of the chapter.

■ **11 or more overall score**—If you want more review on these topics, skip to the "Foundation Summary" section and then go to the "Q&A" section at the end of the chapter. Otherwise, move to Chapter 10, "Spanning Tree Configuration."

Foundation Topics

IEEE 802.1D Overview

A robust network design not only includes efficient transfer of packets or frames but also considers how to recover quickly from faults in the network. In a Layer 3 environment, the routing protocols in use keeps track of redundant paths to a destination network so that a secondary path can be quickly utilized if the primary path fails. Layer 3 routing allows many paths to a destination to remain up and active, and allows load sharing across multiple paths.

In a Layer 2 environment (switching or bridging), however, no routing protocols are used, and active redundant paths are not allowed. Instead, some form of bridging provides data transport between networks or switch ports. The Spanning Tree Protocol (STP) provides network link redundancy so that a Layer 2 switched network can recover from failures without intervention in a timely manner. The STP is defined in the IEEE 802.1D standard.

STP is discussed in relation to the problems it solves in the sections that follow.

Bridging Loops

Recall that a Layer 2 switch mimics the function of a transparent bridge. A transparent bridge must offer segmentation between two networks, while remaining transparent to all the end devices connected to it. For the purpose of this discussion, consider a two-port Ethernet switch and its similarities to a two-port transparent bridge.

A transparent bridge (and the Ethernet switch) must operate as follows:

- The bridge has no initial knowledge of any end device's location; therefore, the bridge must "listen" to frames coming into each of its ports to figure out on which network a device resides. The source address in an incoming frame is the clue to a device's whereabouts—the bridge assumes the source device is located behind the port that the frame arrived on. As the listening process continues, the bridge builds a table containing source MAC addresses and the Bridge Port numbers associated with them.

  The bridge can constantly update its bridging table upon detecting the presence of a new MAC address or upon detecting a MAC address that has changed location from one Bridge Port to another. The bridge can then forward frames by looking at the destination address, looking up the address in the bridge table, and sending the frame out the port where the destination device is located.

■ If a frame arrives with the broadcast address as the destination address, the bridge must forward, or flood, the frame out all available ports. However, the frame is not forwarded out the port that initially received the frame. In this way, broadcasts can reach all available networks. A bridge only segments collision domains—it does not segment broadcast domains.

■ If a frame arrives with a destination address that is not found in the bridge table, the bridge is unable to determine which port to forward the frame to for transmission. This type of frame is known as an *unknown unicast*. In this case, the bridge treats the frame as if it were a broadcast and forwards it out all remaining ports. After a reply to that frame is overheard, the bridge learns the location of the unknown station and adds it to the bridge table for future use.

■ Frames forwarded across the bridge cannot be modified by the bridge itself. Therefore, the bridging process is effectively *transparent*.

Bridging or switching in this fashion works well. Any frame forwarded, whether to a known or unknown destination, will be forwarded out the appropriate port or ports so that it is likely to be received successfully at the end device. Figure 9-1 shows a simple two-port switch functioning as a bridge, forwarding frames between two end devices. However, this network design offers no additional links or paths for redundancy, should the switch or one of its links fail.

Figure 9-1 *Transparent Bridging with a Switch*

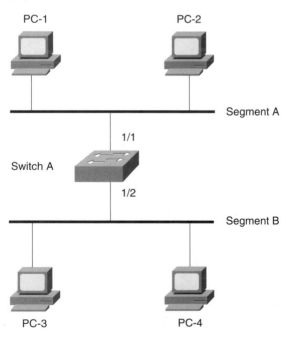

To add some redundancy, you can add a second switch between the two original network segments, as shown in Figure 9-2. Now, two switches offer the transparent bridging function in parallel.

Figure 9-2 *Redundant Bridging with Two Switches*

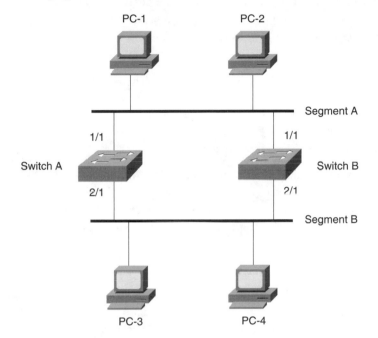

Consider what happens when PC-1 sends a frame to PC-4. For now, assume that both PC-1 and PC-4 are known to the switches and are in their address tables. PC-1 sends the frame out onto network Segment A. Switch A and Switch B both receive the frame on their 1/1 ports. Because PC-4 is already known to the switches, the frame is forwarded out ports 2/1 on each switch onto Segment B. The end result is that PC-4 receives two copies of the frame from PC-1. This is not ideal but is not disastrous either.

Now, consider the same process of sending a frame from PC-1 to PC-4. This time, however, neither switch knows anything about PC-1 or PC-4. PC-1 sends the frame to PC-4 by placing it on Segment A. The sequence of events is as follows:

Step 1   Both Switch A and Switch B receive the frame on their 1/1 ports. Because PC-1's MAC address has not yet been seen or recorded, each switch records PC-1's MAC address in its address table along with the receiving port number, 1/1. From this information, both switches infer that PC-1 must reside on Segment A.

Step 2   Because PC-4's location is unknown, both switches forward the frame out all available ports (their 2/1 ports) and onto Segment B.

Step 3   Each switch places a new frame on its 2/1 port on Segment B. PC-4, located on Segment B, receives the two frames destined for it. However, Switch A hears the new frame forwarded by Switch B, and Switch B hears the new frame forwarded by Switch A.

Step 4   Switch A sees that the "new" frame is from PC-1 to PC-4. From the address table, the switch had learned that PC-1 was on port 1/1, or Segment A. However, PC-1's source address has just been heard on port 2/1 on Segment B. By definition, the switch must relearn PC-1's location, which is now incorrectly assumed to be Segment B. (Switch B follows the same procedure, based on the "new" frame from Switch A.)

Step 5   At this point, neither Switch A nor Switch B has learned PC-4's location because no frames have been received with PC-4 as the source address. Therefore, the frame must be forwarded out all available ports in an attempt to find PC-4. This frame is then sent out Switch A's 1/1 port and onto Segment A.

Step 6   Now, both switches relearn PC-1's location as Segment A and forward the "new" frames back onto Segment B; then the entire process repeats.

This process of forwarding a single frame around and around between two switches is known as a *bridging loop*. Neither switch is aware of the other, so each happily forwards the same frame back and forth between its segments. Also note that because two switches are involved in the loop, the original frame has been duplicated and now is sent around in two counter-rotating loops. What stops the frame from being forwarded in this fashion forever? Nothing. PC-4 begins receiving frames addressed to it as fast as the switches can forward them.

Notice how the PCs' learned location keeps changing as frames get looped. Even a unicast frame has caused a bridging loop to form, and each switch's bridge table is repeatedly corrupted with incorrect data.

What would happen if PC-1 sent a broadcast frame instead? The bridging loops (remember that two of them are produced by the two parallel switches) form exactly as before. The broadcast frames continue to circulate forever. Now, however, every end-user device located on both Segments A and B receives and processes each and every broadcast frame. This type of broadcast storm can easily saturate the network segments and bring every host on the segments to a halt.

The only way to end the bridging loop is to physically break the loop by disconnecting switch ports or shutting a switch down. Obviously, preventing bridging loops rather than be faced with breaking them after they form would be better.

Preventing Loops with Spanning Tree Protocol

Bridging loops form because parallel switches (or bridges) are unaware of each other. STP was developed to overcome the possibility of bridging loops so that redundant switches and switch paths could be used for their benefits. Basically, the protocol enables switches to become aware of each other so they can negotiate a loop-free path through the network.

> **NOTE**   Because STP is involved in loop detection, many people refer to the catastrophic loops as "Spanning Tree loops." This is technically incorrect, as the Spanning Tree Protocol's entire function is to *prevent* bridging loops. The correct terminology for this condition is a *bridging loop*.

Loops are discovered before they are made available for use, and redundant links are shut down to prevent the loops from forming. In the case of redundant links, switches can be made aware that a link shut down for loop prevention should be quickly brought up in case of a link failure. This is discussed in later sections of this chapter.

STP is communicated between all connected switches on a network. Each switch executes the Spanning Tree Algorithm based on information received from other neighboring switches. The algorithm chooses a reference point in the network and calculates all the redundant paths to that reference point. When redundant paths are found, the Spanning Tree Algorithm picks one path by which to forward frames and disables, or blocks, forwarding on the other redundant paths.

As its name implies, STP computes a tree structure that spans all switches in a subnet or network. Redundant paths are placed in a Blocking or Standby state to prevent frame forwarding. The switched network is then in a loop-free condition. However, if a forwarding port fails or becomes disconnected, the Spanning Tree Algorithm recomputes the Spanning Tree topology so that blocked links can be reactivated.

Spanning Tree Communication: Bridge Protocol Data Units

STP operates as switches communicate with one another. Data messages are exchanged in the form of *Bridge Protocol Data Units (BPDUs)*. A switch sends a BPDU frame out a port, using the unique MAC address of the port itself as a source address. The switch is unaware of the other switches around it. Therefore, the BPDU frame has a destination address of the well-known STP multicast address 01-80-c2-00-00-00 to reach all listening switches.

Two types of BPDU exist:

- *Configuration BPDU*, used for Spanning Tree computation
- *Topology Change Notification (TCN) BPDU*, used to announce changes in the network topology

The Configuration BPDU message contains the fields shown in Table 9-2. The TCN BPDU is discussed in the "Topology Changes" section later in this chapter.

Table 9-2 *Configuration BPDU Message Content*

Field Description	Number of Bytes
Protocol ID (always 0)	2
Version (always 0)	1
Message Type (Configuration or TCN BPDU)	1
Flags	1
Root Bridge ID	8
Root Path Cost	4
Sender Bridge ID	8
Port ID	2
Message Age (in 256^{ths} of a second)	2
Maximum Age (in 256^{ths} of a second)	2
Hello Time (in 256^{ths} of a second)	2
Forward Delay (in 256^{ths} of a second)	2

The exchange of BPDU messages works toward the goal of electing reference points as a foundation for a stable Spanning Tree topology. Loops can also be identified and removed by placing specific redundant ports in a Blocking or Standby state. Notice that several key fields in the BPDU are related to bridge (or switch) identification, path costs, and timer values. These all work together so that the network of switches can converge upon a common Spanning Tree topology and select the same reference points within the network. These reference points are defined in the sections that follow.

BPDUs are sent out all switch ports every two seconds so that current topology information is exchanged and loops are identified quickly.

Electing a Root Bridge

For all switches in a network to agree on a loop-free topology, a common frame of reference must exist to use as a guide. This reference point is called the *Root Bridge.* (The term "bridge" continues to be used even in a switched environment because STP was developed for use in bridges. Therefore, when you see "bridge," think "switch.")

An election process among all connected switches chooses the Root Bridge. Each switch has a unique *Bridge ID* that identifies it to other switches. The Bridge ID is an 8-byte value consisting of the following fields:

- **Bridge Priority (2 bytes)**—The priority or weight of a switch in relation to all other switches. The priority field can have a value of 0 to 65,535 and defaults to 32,768 (or 0x8000) on every Catalyst switch.

- **MAC Address (6 bytes)**—The MAC address used by a switch can come from the Supervisor module, the backplane, or a pool of 1024 addresses that are assigned to every Supervisor or backplane depending on the switch model. In any event, this address is hardcoded and unique, and the user cannot change it.

When a switch first powers up, it has a narrow view of its surroundings and assumes that it is the Root Bridge itself. This notion will probably change as other switches check in and enter the election process. The election process then proceeds as follows: Every switch begins by sending out BPDUs with a Root Bridge ID equal to its own Bridge ID and a Sender Bridge ID of its own Bridge ID. The Sender Bridge ID simply tells other switches who is the actual sender of the BPDU message. (After a Root Bridge is decided upon, configuration BPDUs are only sent by the Root Bridge. All other bridges must forward or relay the BPDUs, adding their own Sender Bridge IDs to the message.)

Received BPDU messages are analyzed to see if a "better" Root Bridge is being announced. A Root Bridge is considered better if the Root Bridge ID value is *lower* than another. Again, think of the Root Bridge ID as being broken up into Bridge Priority and MAC address fields. If two Bridge Priority values are equal, the lower MAC address makes the Bridge ID better. When a switch hears of a better Root Bridge, it replaces its own Root Bridge ID with the Root Bridge ID announced in the BPDU. The switch is then required to recommend or advertise the new Root Bridge ID in its own BPDU messages; although, it will still identify itself as the Sender Bridge ID.

Sooner or later, the election converges and all switches agree on the notion that one of them is the Root Bridge. As might be expected, if a new switch with a lower Bridge Priority powers up, it begins advertising itself as the Root Bridge. Because the new switch does indeed have a lower Bridge ID, all the switches will soon reconsider and record it as the new Root Bridge. This can also happen if the new switch has a Bridge Priority equal to the existing Root Bridge but a lower MAC address. Root Bridge election is an ongoing process, triggered by Root Bridge ID changes in the BPDUs every two seconds.

As an example, consider the small network shown in Figure 9-3. For simplicity, assume that each Catalyst switch has a MAC address of all 0s with the last hex digit equal to the switch label.

Figure 9-3 *Example of Root Bridge Election*

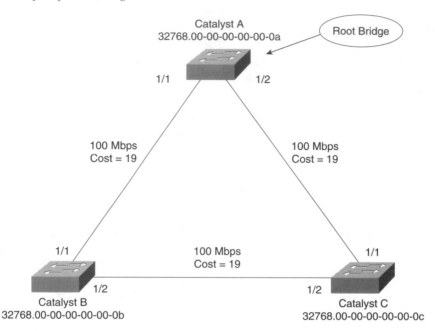

In this network, each switch has the default Bridge Priority of 32,768. The switches are interconnected with FastEthernet links, having a default path cost of 19. All three switches try to elect themselves as the Root, but all of them have equal Bridge Priority values. The election is determined by the lowest MAC address—that of Catalyst A.

Electing Root Ports

Now that a reference point has been nominated and elected for the entire switched network, each nonroot switch must figure out where it is in relation to the Root Bridge. This action can be performed by selecting only one *Root Port* on each nonroot switch.

STP uses the concept of cost to determine many things. Selecting a Root Port involves evaluating the *Root Path Cost*. This value is the cumulative cost of all the links leading to the Root Bridge. A particular switch link has a cost associated with it, too, called the *Path Cost*. To understand the difference between these values, remember that only the Root Path Cost is carried inside the BPDU. (See Table 9-2 again.) As the Root Path Cost travels along, other switches can modify its value to make it cumulative. The Path Cost, however, is not contained in the BPDU. It is known only to the local switch where the port (or "path" to a neighboring switch) resides.

Path Costs are defined as a 1-byte value, with the default values shown in Table 9-3. Generally, the higher the bandwidth of a link, the lower the cost of transporting data across it. The original IEEE 802.1D standard defined Path Cost as 1000 Mbps divided by the link bandwidth in Mbps. These values are shown in the center column of the table. Modern networks commonly use GigabitEthernet and OC-48 ATM, which are both either too close to or greater than the maximum scale of 1000 Mbps. The IEEE now uses a nonlinear scale for Path Cost, as shown in the right column of the table.

> **TIP**   Be aware that there are two STP path cost scales—one that is little used with a linear scale and one commonly used that is nonlinear. If you decide to memorize some common Path Cost values, learn only the ones in the "new" righthand column of the table.

Table 9-3   *STP Path Cost*

Link Bandwidth	Old STP Cost	New STP Cost
4 Mbps	250	250
10 Mbps	100	100
16 Mbps	63	62
45 Mbps	22	39
100 Mbps	10	19
155 Mbps	6	14
622 Mbps	2	6
1 Gbps	1	4
10 Gbps	0	2

The Root Path Cost value is determined in the following manner:

1.   The Root Bridge sends out a BPDU with a Root Path Cost value of 0 because its ports sit directly on the Root Bridge.

2.   When the next-closest neighbor receives the BPDU, it adds the Path Cost of its own port where the BPDU arrived. (This is done as the BPDU is *received*.)

3.   The neighbor sends out BPDUs with this new cumulative value as the Root Path Cost.

4.   This value is added to by subsequent switch port Path Costs as each switch receives the BPDU on down the line.

> **NOTE** Notice the emphasis on incrementing the Root Path Cost as BPDUs are *received*. When computing the Spanning Tree Algorithm manually, remember to compute a new Root Path Cost as BPDUs *come in* to a switch port—not as they go out.

After incrementing the Root Path Cost, a switch also records the value in its memory. When a BPDU is received on another port and the new Root Path Cost is lower than the previously recorded value, this lower value becomes the new Root Path Cost. In addition, the lower cost tells the switch that the path to the Root Bridge must be better using this port than it was on other ports. The switch has now determined which of its ports has the best path to the Root—the *Root Port*.

Figure 9-4 shows the same network from Figure 9-3 in the process of Root Port selection.

Figure 9-4 *Example of Root Port Selection*

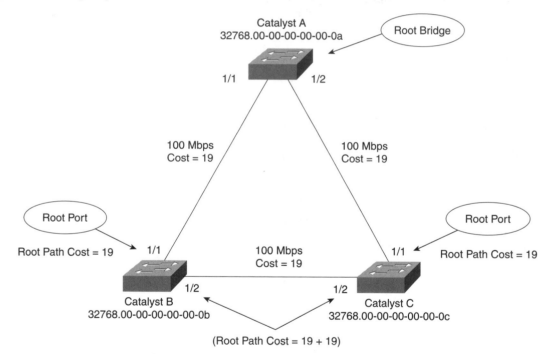

The Root Bridge, Catalyst A, has already been elected. Therefore, every other switch in the network must choose one port that has the best path to the Root Bridge. Catalyst B selects its port 1/1, with a Root Path Cost of 0 plus 19. Port 1/2 is not chosen because its Root Path Cost is 0 (BPDU from Catalyst A) plus 19 (Path Cost of A-C link) plus 19 (Path Cost of C-B link), or a total of 38. Catalyst C makes a similar choice of port 1/1.

Electing Designated Ports

By now, you should begin to see the process unfolding: a starting or reference point has been identified, and each switch "connects" itself toward the reference point with the single link that has the best path. A tree structure is beginning to emerge, but links have been identified only at this point. All links are still connected and could be active, leaving bridging loops.

To remove the possibility of bridging loops, STP makes a final computation to identify one Designated Port on each network segment. Suppose that two or more switches have ports connected to a single common network segment. If a frame appears on that segment, all the bridges attempt to forward it to its destination. Recall that this behavior was the basis of a bridging loop and should be avoided.

Instead, only one of the links on a segment should forward traffic to and from that segment. This location is the Designated Port. Switches choose a Designated Port based on the lowest cumulative Root Path Cost to the Root Bridge. For example, a switch always has an idea of its own Root Path Cost, which it announces in its own BPDUs. If a neighboring switch on a shared LAN segment sends a BPDU announcing a lower Root Path Cost, the neighbor must have the Designated Port. If a switch learns only of higher Root Path Costs from other BPDUs received on a port, however, it then correctly assumes that its own receiving port is the Designated Port for the segment.

Notice that the entire STP determination process has served only to identify bridges and ports. All ports are still active, and bridging loops might still lurk in the network. STP has a set of progressive states that each port must go through, regardless of the type or identification. These states actively prevent loops from forming and are described in the next section.

> **NOTE** In each determination process discussed so far, two or more links having identical Root Path Costs is possible. This results in a tie condition, unless other factors are considered. All STP decisions are based on the following sequence of four conditions:
>
> **1.** Lowest Root Bridge ID
>
> **2.** Lowest Root Path Cost to Root Bridge
>
> **3.** Lowest Sender Bridge ID
>
> **4.** Lowest Sender Port ID

Figure 9-5 demonstrates an example of Designated Port selection. This figure is identical to Figure 9-3 and Figure 9-4, with further Spanning Tree development. The only changes shown are the choices of Designated Ports, although seeing all STP decisions shown in one network diagram is handy.

Figure 9-5 *Example of Designated Port Selection*

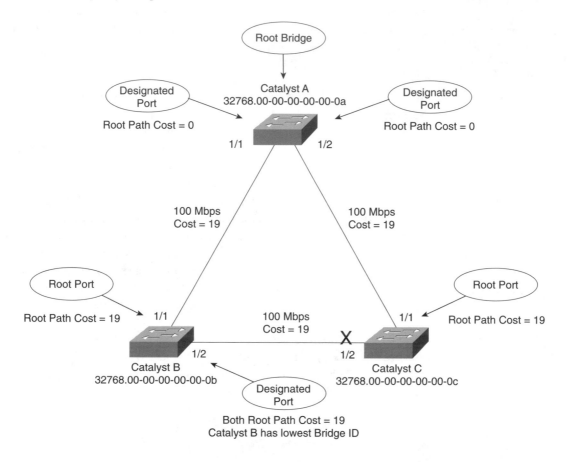

The three switches have chosen their Designated Ports (DP) for the following reasons:

- **Catalyst A**—Because this switch is the Root Bridge, all its active ports are Designated Ports by definition. At the Root Bridge, the Root Path Cost of each port is 0.

- **Catalyst B**—Catalyst A port 1/1 is the DP for the Segment A-B because it has the lowest Root Path Cost (0). Catalyst B port 1/2 is the DP for segment B-C. The Root Path Cost for each end of this segment is 19, determined from the incoming BPDU on port 1/1. Because the Root Path Cost is equal on both ports of the segment, the DP must be chosen by the next criteria—the lowest Sender Bridge ID. When Catalyst B sends a BPDU to Catalyst C, it has the lowest MAC address in the Bridge ID. Catalyst C also sends a BPDU to Catalyst B, but its Sender Bridge ID is higher. Therefore, Catalyst B port 1/2 is selected as the segment's DP.

- **Catalyst C**—Catalyst A port 1/2 is the DP for Segment A-C because it has the lowest Root Path Cost (0). Catalyst B port 1/2 is the DP for Segment B-C. Therefore, Catalyst C port 1/2 will be neither a Root Port nor a Designated Port. As discussed in the next section, any port that is not elected to either position enters the Blocking state. Where blocking occurs, bridging loops are broken.

STP States

To participate in STP, each port of a switch must progress through several states. A port begins its life in a Disabled state, moving through several passive states and, finally, into an active state if allowed to forward traffic. The STP port states are as follows:

- **Disabled**—Ports that are administratively shut down by the network administrator, or by the system due to a fault condition, are in the Disabled state. This state is special and is not part of the normal STP progression for a port.

- **Blocking**—After a port initializes, it begins in the Blocking state so that no bridging loops can form. In the Blocking state, a port cannot receive or transmit data and cannot add MAC addresses to its address table. Instead, a port is allowed to receive only BPDUs so that the switch can hear from other neighboring switches. In addition, ports that are put into standby mode to remove a bridging loop enter the Blocking state.

- **Listening**—The port will be moved from Blocking to Listening if the switch thinks that the port can be selected as a Root Port or Designated Port. In other words, the port is on its way to begin forwarding traffic. In the Listening state, the port still cannot send or receive data frames. However, the port is allowed to receive and send BPDUs so that it can actively participate in the Spanning Tree topology process. Here, the port is finally allowed to become a Root Port or Designated Port because the switch can advertise the port by sending BPDUs to other switches. Should the port lose its Root Port or Designated Port status, it returns to the Blocking state.

- **Learning**—After a period of time called the Forward Delay in the Listening state, the port is allowed to move into the Learning state. The port still sends and receives BPDUs as before. In addition, the switch can now learn new MAC addresses to add to its address table. This gives the port an extra period of silent participation and allows the switch to assemble at least some address table information.

- **Forwarding**—After another Forward Delay period of time in the Learning state, the port is allowed to move into the Forwarding state. The port can now send and receive data frames, collect MAC addresses in its address table, and send and receive BPDUs. The port is now a fully functioning switch port within the Spanning Tree topology.

NOTE Remember that a switch port is allowed into the Forwarding state only if no redundant links (or loops) are detected and if the port has the best path to the Root Bridge as the Root Port or Designated Port.

Example 9-1 shows the output from a switch as one of its ports progresses through the STP port states.

Example 9-1 *Port Progressing Through the STP Port States*

```
*Mar 16 14:31:00 UTC: STP SW: Fa0/1 new disabled req for 1 vlans
Switch(config)# interface fast 0/1
Switch(config-if)#no shut
Switch(config-if)#^-Z
*Mar 16 14:31:00 UTC: STP SW: Fa0/1 new blocking req for 1 vlans

Switch#show spanning interface fast 0/1

Vlan            Port ID                     Designated          Port ID
Name            Prio.Nbr    Cost Sts        Cost Bridge ID      Prio.Nbr
--------------- --------- --------- --- --------- -------------------- --------
VLAN0001        128.1           19 LIS          0 32769 000a.f40a.2980 128.1

*Mar 16 14:31:15 UTC: STP SW: Fa0/1 new learning req for 1 vlans

Switch#show spanning interface fast 0/1
Vlan            Port ID                     Designated          Port ID
Name            Prio.Nbr    Cost Sts        Cost Bridge ID      Prio.Nbr
--------------- --------- --------- --- --------- -------------------- --------
VLAN0001        128.1           19 LRN          0 32768 00d0.5849.4100  32.129

*Mar 16 14:31:30 UTC: STP SW: Fa0/1 new forwarding req for 1 vlans

Switch#show spanning interface fast 0/1

Vlan            Port ID                     Designated          Port ID
Name            Prio.Nbr    Cost Sts        Cost Bridge ID      Prio.Nbr
--------------- --------- --------- --- --------- -------------------- --------
VLAN0001        128.1           19 FWD          0 32768 00d0.5849.4100  32.129
```

The example begins as the port is administratively disabled from the command line. When the port is enabled, successive **show spanning-tree interface** *type mod/port* commands display the port state as Listening, Learning, and then Forwarding. These are shown in the shaded text of the example. Notice, also, the timestamps and port states provided by the **debug spanning-tree switch state** command, which give a sense of the timing between port states. Because this port was eligible as a Root Port, the **show** command was never able to execute fast enough to show the port in the Blocking state.

STP Timers

STP operates as switches send BPDUs to each other in an effort to form a loop-free topology. The BPDUs take a finite amount of time to travel from switch to switch. In addition, news of a topology change (such as a link or Root Bridge failure) can suffer from propagation delays as the announcement travels from one side of a network to the other. Because of the possibility of these delays, keeping the Spanning Tree topology from settling out or converging until all switches have had time to receive accurate information is important.

STP uses three timers to make sure that a network converges properly before a bridging loop can form. The timers and their default values are as follows:

- **Hello Time**—The time interval between Configuration BPDUs sent by the Root Bridge. The Hello Time value configured in the Root Bridge switch determines the Hello Time for all nonroot switches because they just relay the Configuration BPDUs as they are received from the root. However, all switches have a locally configured Hello Time that is used to time TCN BPDUs when they are retransmitted. The IEEE 802.1D standard specifies a default Hello Time value of 2 seconds.

- **Forward Delay**—The time interval that a switch port spends in both the Listening and Learning states. The default value is 15 seconds.

- **Max (maximum) Age**—The time interval that a switch stores a BPDU before discarding it. While executing the STP, each switch port keeps a copy of the "best" BPDU that it has heard. If the BPDU's source loses contact with the switch port, the switch notices that a topology change occurred after the Max Age time elapses and the BPDU is aged out. The default Max Age value is 20 seconds.

The STP timers can be configured or adjusted from the switch command line. However, the timer values should never be changed from the defaults without careful consideration. Then, the values should be changed only on the Root Bridge switch. Recall that the timer values are advertised in fields within the BPDU. The Root Bridge ensures that the timer values propagate to all other switches.

> **NOTE** The default STP timer values are based on some assumptions about the size of the network and the length of the Hello Time. A reference model of a network having a diameter of seven switches derives these values. The diameter is measured from the Root Bridge switch outward, including the Root Bridge. In other words, if you drew the STP topology, the diameter would be the number of switches connected in series from the Root Bridge out to the end of any branch in the tree. The Hello Time is based on the time it takes for a BPDU to travel from the Root Bridge to a point seven switches away. A Hello Time of 2 seconds is used in this computation.

The network diameter can be configured on the Root Bridge switch to more accurately reflect the true size of the physical network. Making that value more accurate reduces the total STP convergence time during a topology change. Cisco also recommends that if changes need to be made, only the network diameter value should be modified on the Root Bridge switch. When the diameter is changed, the switch calculates new values for all three timers. This option is discussed in the "Selecting the Root Bridge" section in Chapter 10.

Topology Changes

To announce a change in the active network topology, switches send a TCN BPDU. Table 9-4 shows the format of these messages.

Table 9-4 *Topology Change Notification BPDU Message Content*

Field Description	# of Bytes
Protocol ID (always 0)	2
Version (always 0)	1
Message Type (Configuration or TCN BPDU)	1

A topology change occurs when a switch either moves a port into the Forwarding state or moves a port from Forwarding or Learning into the Blocking state. In other words, a port on an active switch comes up or goes down. The switch sends a TCN BPDU out its Root Port so that, ultimately, the Root Bridge receives news of the topology change. Notice that the TCN BPDU carries no data about the change, but informs recipients only that a change has occurred. Also notice that the switch will not send TCN BPDUs if the port has been configured with PortFast enabled.

The switch continues sending TCN BPDUs every Hello Time interval until it gets an acknowledgment from an upstream neighbor. As the upstream neighbors receive the TCN BPDU, they propagate it on toward the Root Bridge. When the Root Bridge receives the BPDU, the Root Bridge also sends out an acknowledgment. However, it also sends out the Topology Change flag in a Configuration BPDU so that all other bridges shorten their bridge table aging times from the default (300 seconds) to only the Forward Delay value (default 15 seconds).

This condition causes the learned locations of MAC addresses to be flushed out much sooner than they normally would, easing the bridge table corruption that might occur because of the change in topology. However, any stations that are actively communicating during this time are kept in the bridge table. This condition lasts for the sum of the Forward Delay and the Max Age (default 15 + 20 seconds).

Types of STP

So far, this chapter has discussed STP in terms of its operation to prevent loops and to recover from topology changes in a timely manner. STP was originally developed to operate in a bridged environment, basically supporting a single LAN (or one VLAN). Implementing STP into a switched environment has required additional consideration and modification to support multiple VLANs. Because of this, the IEEE and Cisco have approached STP differently. This section reviews the three traditional types of STP that are encountered in switched networks and how they relate to one another. No specific configuration commands are associated with the various types of STP. Rather, you need a basic understanding of how they interoperate in a network.

NOTE   The IEEE has produced additional standards for Spanning Tree enhancements that greatly improve on its scalability and convergence aspects. These are covered in Chapter 12, "Advanced Spanning Tree Protocol." After you have a firm understanding of the more traditional forms of STP presented in this chapter, you can grasp the enhanced versions much easier.

Common Spanning Tree (CST)

The IEEE 802.1Q standard specifies how VLANs are to be trunked between switches. It also specifies only a single instance of STP for all VLANs. This instance is referred to as the *Common Spanning Tree (CST)*. All CST BPDUs are transmitted over the native VLAN as untagged frames.

Having a single STP for many VLANs simplifies switch configuration and reduces switch CPU load during STP calculations. However, having only one STP instance can cause limitations, too. Redundant links between switches will be blocked with no capability for load balancing. Conditions can also occur that would cause forwarding on a link that does not support all VLANs, while other links would be blocked.

Per-VLAN Spanning Tree (PVST)

Cisco has a proprietary version of STP that offers more flexibility than the CST version. *Per-VLAN Spanning Tree (PVST)* operates a separate instance of STP for each individual VLAN. This allows the STP on each VLAN to be configured independently, offering better performance and tuning for specific conditions. Multiple Spanning Trees also make load balancing possible over redundant links when the links are assigned to different VLANs.

Due to its proprietary nature, PVST requires the use of Cisco Inter-Switch Link (ISL) trunking encapsulation between switches. In networks where PVST and CST coexist, interoperability problems occur. Each requires a different trunking method, so BPDUs will never be exchanged between STP types.

Per-VLAN Spanning Tree Plus (PVST+)

Cisco has a second proprietary version of STP that allows devices to interoperate with both PVST and CST. *Per-VLAN Spanning Tree Plus (PVST+)* effectively supports three groups of STP operating in the same campus network:

- Catalyst switches running PVST
- Catalyst switches running PVST+
- Switches running CST over 802.1Q

To do this, PVST+ acts as a translator between groups of CST switches and groups of PVST switches. PVST+ can communicate directly with PVST by using ISL trunks. To communicate with CST, however, PVST+ exchanges BPDUs with CST as untagged frames over the native VLAN. BPDUs from other instances of STP (other VLANs) are propagated across the CST portions of the network by tunneling. PVST+ sends these BPDUs by using a unique multicast address so that the CST switches forward them on to downstream neighbors without interpreting them first. Eventually, the tunneled BPDUs reach other PVST+ switches where they are understood.

Foundation Summary

The Foundation Summary is a collection of information that provides a convenient review of many key concepts in this chapter. If you are already comfortable with the topics in this chapter, this summary can help you recall a few details. If you just read this chapter, this review should help solidify some key facts. If you are doing your final preparation before the exam, this information is a convenient way to review the day before the exam.

STP has a progression of states that each port moves through. Each state allows a port to do only certain functions, as shown in Table 9-5.

Table 9-5 *STP states and Port Activity*

STP State	The port can...	The port cannot...	Duration
Disabled		Send or receive data	N/A
Blocking	Receive BPDUs	Send or receive data or learn MAC addresses	Indefinite if loop has been detected
Listening	Send and receive BPDUs	Send or receive data or learn MAC addresses	Forward Delay timer (15 seconds)
Learning	Send and receive BPDUs and learn MAC addresses	Send or receive data	Forward Delay timer (15 seconds)
Forwarding	Send and receive BPDUs, learn MAC addresses, and send and receive data		Indefinite as long as port is up and loop is not detected

Table 9-6 *Basic Spanning Tree Operation*

Task	Procedure
1. Elect Root Bridge.	Lowest Bridge ID
2. Select Root Port (one per switch).	Lowest Root Path Cost; if equal, use tie-breakers
3. Select Designated Port (one per segment).	Lowest Root Path Cost; if equal, use tie-breakers
4. Block ports with loops.	Block ports that are non-Root and non-Designated Ports

To manually work out a Spanning Tree topology using a network diagram, follow the basic steps in Table 9-7.

Table 9-7 *Manual STP Computation*

Task	Description
1. Identify Path Costs on links.	For each link between switches, write the Path Cost that each switch uses for the link.
2. Identify Root Bridge.	Find the switch with the lowest Bridge ID; mark it on the drawing.
3. Select Root Ports (one per switch).	For each switch, find the one port that has the best path to the Root Bridge. This is the one with the lowest Root Path Cost. Mark the port with an "RP" label.
4. Select Designated Ports (one per segment).	For each link between switches, identify which end of the link will be the Designated Port. This is the one with the lowest Root Path Cost; if equal on both ends, use STP tie-breakers. Mark the port with a "DP" label.
5. Identify the blocking ports.	Every switch port that is neither a Root nor Designated Port will be put into the Blocking state. Mark these with an "X."

Table 9-8 *Spanning Tree Tie Breaker Criteria*

Sequence	Criteria
1	Lowest Root Bridge ID
2	Lowest Root Path Cost
3	Lowest Sender Bridge ID
4	Lowest Sender Port ID

Table 9-9 *STP Path Cost*

Link Bandwidth	STP Cost (Nonlinear Scale)
4 Mbps	250
10 Mbps	100
16 Mbps	62
45 Mbps	39

Table 9-9   *STP Path Cost (Continued)*

Link Bandwidth	STP Cost (Nonlinear Scale)
100 Mbps	19
155 Mbps	14
622 Mbps	6
1 Gbps	4
10 Gbps	2

Table 9-10   *STP Timers*

Timer	Function	Default Value
Hello	Interval between Configuration BPDUs.	2 seconds
Forward Delay	Time spent in Listening and Learning states before transitioning toward Forwarding state.	15 seconds
Max Age	Maximum length of time a BPDU can be stored without receiving an update; timer expiration signals an indirect failure with Designated or Root Bridge.	20 seconds

Table 9-11   *Types of STP*

Type of STP	Function
CST	One instance of STP, over the native VLAN; 802.1Q-based
PVST	One instance of STP per VLAN; Cisco ISL-based
PVST+	Provides interoperability between CST and PVST; operates over both 802.1Q and ISL

Q&A

The questions and scenarios in this book are more difficult than what you should experience on the actual exam. The questions do not attempt to cover more breadth or depth than the exam; however, they are designed to make sure that you know the answers. Rather than allowing you to derive the answers from clues hidden inside the questions themselves, the questions challenge your understanding and recall of the subject. Hopefully, these questions will help limit the number of exam questions on which you narrow your choices to two options and then guess.

You can find the answers to these questions in Appendix A.

1. What is a bridging loop? Why is it bad?

2. Put the following STP port states in chronological order:

    a. Learning

    b. Forwarding

    c. Listening

    d. Blocking

3. Choose two types of STP messages used to communicate between bridges:

    a. Advertisement BPDU

    b. Configuration BPDU

    c. ACK BPDU

    d. TCN BPDU

4. What criteria are used to select the following?

    a. Root Bridge

    b. Root Port

    c. Designated Port

    d. Redundant (or secondary) Root Bridges

5. Which of the following switches become the Root Bridge, given the information in the following table? Which switch becomes the secondary Root Bridge if the Root Bridge fails?

Switch Name	Bridge Priority	MAC Address	Port Costs
Catalyst A	32,768	00-d0-10-34-26-a0	All are 19
Catalyst B	32,768	00-d0-10-34-24-a0	All are 4
Catalyst C	32,767	00-d0-10-34-27-a0	All are 19
Catalyst D	32,769	00-d0-10-34-24-a1	All are 19

6. What conditions cause an STP topology change? What effect does this have on STP and the network?

7. A Root Bridge has been elected in a switched network. Suppose a new switch is installed with a lower Bridge ID than the existing Root Bridge. What will happen?

8. Suppose a switch receives Configuration BPDUs on two of its ports. Both ports are assigned to the same VLAN. Each of the BPDUs announces Catalyst A as the Root Bridge. Can the switch use both of these ports as Root Ports? Why?

9. How is the Root Path Cost calculated for a switch port?

10. What conditions can cause ports on a network's Root Bridge to move into the Blocking state? (Assume that all switch connections are to other switches. No crossover cables are used to connect two ports together on the same switch.)

11. What parameters can be tuned to influence the selection of a port as a Root or Designated Port?

12. After a bridging loop forms, how can you stop the endless flow of traffic?

13. In a BPDU, when can the Root Bridge ID have the same value as the Sender Bridge ID?

14. Which of these is true about the Root Path Cost?

    a. It is a value sent by the Root Bridge that cannot be changed along the way.

    b. It is incremented as a switch receives a BPDU.

    c. It is incremented as a switch sends a BPDU.

    d. It is incremented by the Path Cost of a port.

15. Suppose two switches are connected by a common link. Each must decide which one will have the Designated Port on the link. Which switch takes on this role, if these STP advertisements occur?

    - The link is on switch A's port number 12 and on switch B's port number 5.
    - Switch A has a Bridge ID of 32,768:0000.1111.2222, and switch B has 8192:0000.5555.6666.
    - Switch A advertises a Root Path Cost of 8, while B advertises 12.

16. Using the default STP timers, how long does it take for a port to move from the Blocking state to the Forwarding state?

17. If the Root Bridge sets the Topology Change flag in the BPDU, what must the other switches in the network do?

18. Over what VLAN(s) does the CST form of STP run?

    a. VLAN 1

    b. All active VLANs

    c. All VLANs (active or inactive)

    d. The native VLAN

19. What is the major difference between PVST and PVST+?

20. Two switches are connected by a common active link. When might neither switch have a Designated Port on the link?

    a. When neither has a better Root Path Cost.

    b. When the switches are actually the primary and secondary Root Bridges.

    c. When one switch has its port in the Blocking state.

    d. Never; this can't happen.

This chapter covers the following topics that you need to master for the CCNP BCMSN exam:

- **STP Root Bridge**—This section discusses the importance of identifying a Root Bridge, as well as suggestions for its placement in the network. This section also presents the Root Bridge configuration commands.

- **Spanning Tree Customization**—This section covers the configuration commands that allow you to alter the spanning tree's topology.

- **Tuning Spanning Tree Convergence**—This section discusses how to alter, or tune, the STP timers to achieve optimum convergence times in a network.

- **Redundant Link Convergence**—This section describes the methods that cause a network to converge more quickly after a topology change.

- **Troubleshooting STP**—This section offers a brief summary of the commands you can use to verify that an STP instance is working properly.

CHAPTER 10

Spannning Tree Configuration

This chapter presents the design and configuration considerations necessary to implement the IEEE 802.1D Spanning Tree Protocol (STP) in a campus network. This chapter also provides a refresher on the commands needed to configure the STP features, as previously described in Chapter 9, "Traditional Spanning Tree Protocol."

You can also tune STP or make it converge more efficiently in a given network. This chapter presents the theory and commands needed to accomplish this.

"Do I Know This Already?" Quiz

The purpose of the "Do I Know This Already?" quiz is to help you decide what parts of this chapter to use. If you already intend to read the entire chapter, you do not necessarily need to answer these questions now.

The quiz, derived from the major sections in the "Foundation Topics" portion of the chapter, helps you determine how to spend your limited study time.

Table 10-1 outlines the major topics discussed in this chapter and the "Do I Know This Already?" quiz questions that correspond to those topics.

Table 10-1   *"Do I Know This Already?" Foundation Topics Section-to-Question Mapping*

Foundation Topics Section	Questions Covered in This Section
STP Root Bridge	1–5
Spanning Tree Customization	6–7
Tuning Spanning Tree Convergence	8–9
Redundant Link Convergence	10–12

CAUTION   The goal of self-assessment is to gauge your mastery of the topics in this chapter. If you do not know the answer to a question or are only partially sure of the answer, you should mark this question wrong. Giving yourself credit for an answer you correctly guess skews your self-assessment results and might give you a false sense of security.

1. Where should the Root Bridge be placed on a network?

   a. On the fastest switch

   b. Closest to the most users

   c. Closest to the center of the network

   d. On the least-used switch

2. Which of the following is a result of a poorly placed Root Bridge in a network?

   a. Bridging loops form.

   b. STP topology can't be resolved.

   c. STP topology can take unexpected paths.

   d. Root Bridge election flapping.

3. Which of these parameters should you change to make a switch become a Root Bridge?

   a. Switch MAC address

   b. Path Cost

   c. Port Priority

   d. Bridge Priority

4. What is the default STP Bridge Priority on a Catalyst switch?

   a. 0

   b. 1

   c. 32,768

   d. 65,535

5. Which of the following commands can make a switch become the Root Bridge for VLAN 5, assuming that all switches have the default STP parameters?

   a. **spanning-tree root**

   b. **spanning-tree root vlan 5**

   c. **spanning-tree vlan 5 priority 100**

   d. **spanning-tree vlan 5 root**

6. What is the default Path Cost of a Gigabit Ethernet switch port?

    a. 1

    b. 2

    c. 4

    d. 19

    e. 1000

7. What command can change the Path Cost of interface Gigabit Ethernet 3/1 to a value of 8?

    a. spanning-trcc path-cost 8

    b. spanning-tree cost 8

    c. spanning-trcc port-cost 8

    d. spanning-tree gig 3/1 cost 8

8. What happens if the Root Bridge switch and another switch are configured with different STP hello timer values?

    a. Nothing; each sends hellos at different times.

    b. A bridging loop could form because the two switches are out of sync.

    c. The switch with the lower hello timer becomes the Root Bridge.

    d. The other switch changes its hello timer to match the Root Bridge.

9. What network diameter value is the basis for the default STP timer calculations?

    a. 1

    b. 3

    c. 7

    d. 9

    e. 15

10. Where should the STP PortFast feature be used?

    a. An access layer switch port connected to a PC

    b. An access layer switch port connected to a hub

    c. A distribution layer switch port connected to an access layer switch

    d. A core layer switch port

11. Where should the STP UplinkFast feature be enabled?

   a. An access layer switch

   b. A distribution layer switch

   c. A core layer switch

   d. All of the above

12. If used, the STP BackboneFast feature should be enabled on which of these?

   a. All backbone or core layer switches

   b. All backbone and distribution layer switches

   c. All access layer switches

   d. All switches in the network

The answers to the "Do I Know This Already?" quiz are found in Appendix A, "Answers to Chapter 'Do I Know This Already?' Quizzes and Q&A Sections." The suggested choices for your next step are as follows:

- **10 or less overall score**—Read the entire chapter. This includes the "Foundation Topics," "Foundation Summary," and "Q&A" sections.

- **11 or 12 overall score**—If you want more review on these topics, skip to the "Foundation Summary" section and then go to the "Q&A" section at the end of the chapter. Otherwise, move to Chapter 11, "Protecting the Spanning Tree Protocol Topology."

Foundation Topics

STP Root Bridge

STP and its computations are predictable; however, other factors exist that might subtly influence STP decisions, making the resulting tree structure neither expected nor ideal.

The network administrator can make adjustments to the Spanning Tree operation to control its behavior. The location of the Root Bridge should be determined as part of the design process. You can also use redundant links for load balancing in parallel, if configured correctly. You can also configure Spanning Tree Protocol (STP) to converge quickly and predictably in the event of a major topology change.

> **NOTE** By default, STP is enabled on all ports of a switch. STP should remain enabled in a network to prevent bridging loops from forming. However, if STP has been disabled, you can re-enabled it with the following global configuration command:
>
> ```
> Switch (config)# spanning tree vlan vlan-id
> ```

Root Bridge Placement

While STP is wonderfully automatic with its default values and election processes, the resulting tree structure might perform quite differently than expected. The Root Bridge election is based on the idea that one switch is chosen as a common reference point, and all other switches choose ports that have the best cost path to the Root. The Root Bridge election is also based on the idea that the Root Bridge can become a central hub that interconnects other legs of the network. Therefore, the Root Bridge can be faced with heavy switching loads in its central location.

If the Root Bridge election is left to its default state, several things can occur to make a poor choice. For example, the *slowest* switch (or bridge) can be elected as the Root Bridge. If heavy traffic loads are expected to pass through the Root Bridge, the slowest switch is not the ideal candidate. Recall that the only criteria for Root Bridge election is the lowest Bridge ID (Bridge Priority and MAC address)—not necessarily the best choice to ensure optimal performance. If the slowest switch has the same Bridge Priority as the others and has the lowest MAC address, the slowest switch will be chosen as the Root.

A second factor to consider relates to redundancy. If all switches are left to their default states, only one Root Bridge is elected with no clear choice for a "backup." What happens if that switch fails? Another Root Bridge election occurs, but again, the choice might not be the ideal switch or the ideal location.

The final consideration is the location of the Root Bridge switch. As before, an election with default switch values could place the Root Bridge in an unexpected location in the network. More importantly, an inefficient Spanning Tree structure could result, causing traffic from a large portion of the network to take a long and winding path just to pass through the Root Bridge.

Figure 10-1 shows a portion of a real-world hierarchical campus network.

Figure 10-1   *Campus Network with an Inefficient Root Bridge Election*

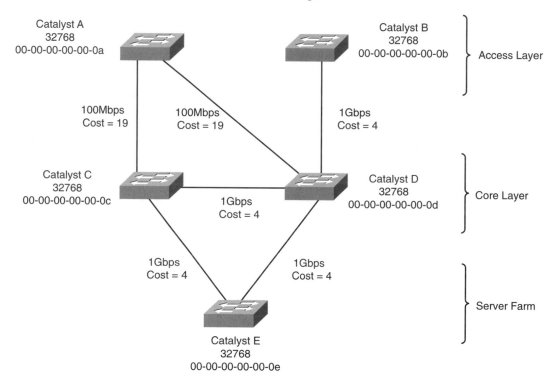

Catalyst switches A and B are two access layer devices; Catalysts C and D form the core layer and Catalyst E connects a server farm into the network core. Notice that most of the switches use redundant links to other layers of the hierarchy, as suggested in Chapter 2, "Modular Network Design." At the time of this example, however, many switches like Catalyst B still have only a single connection into the core. These switches are slated for an "upgrade," where a redundant link will be added to the other half of the core.

As you will see, Catalyst A will become the Root Bridge because of its low MAC address. All switches have been left to their default STP states—the Bridge Priority of each is 32,768.

Figure 10-2 shows the converged state of STP. For the purposes of this discussion, the Root Ports and Designated Ports are simply shown on the network diagram. As an exercise, you should work out the Spanning Tree based on the information shown in the figure. The more examples you can work out by hand, the better you will understand the entire Spanning Tree process.

Figure 10-2 *Campus Network with STP Converged*

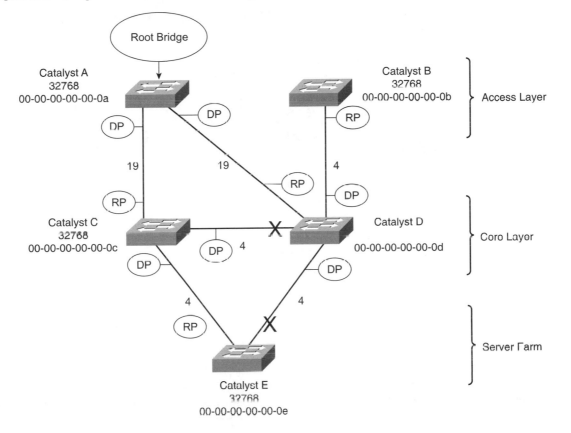

Notice that Catalyst A, one of the access layer switches, has been elected the Root Bridge. Unfortunately, Catalyst A cannot take advantage of the 1-Gbps links, unlike the other switches. Also note the location of the X symbols over the ports that are neither Root Ports nor Designated Ports. These ports will enter the Blocking state.

Finally, Figure 10-3 shows the same network with the Blocking links removed. Now, you can see the true structure of the final Spanning Tree.

Figure 10-3   *Final Spanning Tree Structure for the Campus Network*

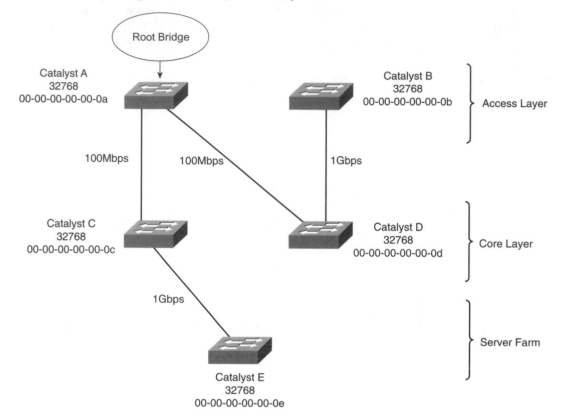

Catalyst A, an access layer switch, is the Root Bridge. Workstations on Catalyst A can reach servers on Catalyst E by crossing through the core layer (Catalyst C), as expected. However, notice what has happened to the other access layer switch, Catalyst B. Workstations on this switch must cross into the core layer (Catalyst D), back into the access layer (Catalyst A), back through the core (Catalyst C), and finally to the server farm (Catalyst E). This action is obviously inefficient. For one, Catalyst A is probably not a high-end switch because it is used in the access layer. However, the biggest issue is that other access layer areas are forced to thread through the relatively slow uplinks on Catalyst A. This winding path will become a major bottleneck to the users.

Root Bridge Configuration

To prevent the surprises outlined in the previous section, you should *always* do two things:

- Configure one switch as a Root Bridge in a determined fashion.

- Configure another switch as a secondary Root Bridge in case of primary Root Bridge failure.

As the common reference point, the Root Bridge (and the secondary) should be placed near the center of the Layer 2 network. For example, a switch in the distribution layer would make a better Root Bridge choice than one in the access layer because more traffic is expected to pass through the distribution layer devices. In a flat switched network (no Layer 3 devices), a switch near a server farm would be a more efficient Root Bridge than switches elsewhere. Most traffic will be destined to and from the server farm and will benefit from a predetermined, direct path.

To configure a Catalyst switch to become the Root Bridge, use one of the following methods:

- Directly modify the Bridge Priority value so that a switch can be given a lower-than-default Bridge ID value to win a Root Bridge election:

  ```
  Switch (config)# spanning-tree vlan vlan-id priority bridge-priority
  ```

  The *bridge-priority* value defaults to 32,768, but you can also assign a value of 0 to 65,535. Remember that Catalyst switches run one instance of STP for each VLAN (PVST+), so the VLAN ID must always be given. You should designate an appropriate Root Bridge for each VLAN.

- Let the switch become the Root by automatically choosing a Bridge Priority value:

  ```
  Switch(config)# spanning-tree vlan vlan-id root {primary | secondary}
  [diameter diameter]
  ```

  This command is actually a macro on the Catalyst that executes several other commands. The result is a more direct and automatic way to force one switch to become the Root Bridge. Actual Bridge Priorities are not given in the command. Rather, the switch modifies STP values according to the current values in use within the active network. *These values are modified only once, when the macro command is issued.*

  Use the **primary** keyword to make the switch attempt to become the primary Root Bridge. This command modifies the switch's Bridge Priority value to become less than the Bridge Priority of the current Root Bridge. If the current Root Priority is more than 24,576, the local switch sets its priority to 24,576. If the current Root Priority is less than that, the local switch sets its priority to 4096 less than the current Root.

  For the **secondary** Root Bridge, the Root Priority is set to 28,672. There is no way to query or listen to the network to find another potential secondary Root, so this priority is used under the assumption that it is less than the default priorities (32,768) that might be used elsewhere.

  You can also modify the network diameter with this command, if needed. This modification is discussed further in the "Tuning Spanning Tree Convergence" section later in the chapter.

> **NOTE**   The **spanning-tree vlan** *vlan-id* **root** command will not be shown in a Catalyst switch configuration because the command is actually a macro executing other switch commands. The actual commands and values produced by the macro will be shown, however. For example, the macro can potentially adjust the four STP values as follows:
>
> ```
> Switch(config)#spanning-tree vlan 1 root primary
>   vlan 1 bridge priority set to 24576
>   vlan 1 bridge max aging time unchanged at 20
>   vlan 1 bridge hello time unchanged at 2
>   vlan 1 bridge forward delay unchanged at 15
> ```
>
> Be aware that this macro doesn't guarantee that the switch will become the Root and maintain that status. It is entirely possible for the Bridge Priority to be configured to a lower value on another switch in the network, displacing the switch that ran the macro.
>
> On the Root, it is usually good practice to directly modify the Bridge Priority to an artificially low value (even priority 1 or 0!) with the **spanning-tree vlan** *vlan-id* **priority** *bridge-priority* command. This will make it more difficult for another switch in the network to win the Root Bridge election.

Spanning Tree Customization

The most important decision you can make when designing your Spanning Tree topology is the placement of the Root Bridge. Other decisions, such as the exact loop-free path structure, will occur automatically as a result of the Spanning Tree Algorithm (STA). Occasionally, the path might need additional tuning, but only under special circumstances and after careful consideration.

Recall the sequence of four criteria that STP uses to choose a path:

1.   Lowest Bridge ID

2.   Lowest Root Path Cost

3.   Lowest Sender Bridge ID

4.   Lowest Sender Port ID

The previous section discussed how to tune a switch's Bridge ID to place the Root Bridge in a network. You can use this technique to force a switch to have the lowest Bridge ID and also to influence the sending Bridge ID of other switches (lowest Bridge ID and lowest Sender Bridge ID). However, only the automatic STP computation has been discussed, using the default switch port costs to make specific path decisions.

Tuning the Root Path Cost

The Root Path Cost for each active port of a switch is determined by the cumulative cost as a BPDU travels along. As a switch *receives* a BPDU, the port cost of the receiving port is added to the Root

Path Cost in the BPDU. The port or path cost is inversely proportional to the port's bandwidth. If desired, a port's cost can be modified from the default value.

> **NOTE**   Before modifying a switch port's path cost, you should always calculate the Root Path costs of other alternate paths through the network. Changing one port's cost might influence STP to choose that port as a Root Port, but other paths could still be preferred. You should also calculate a port's existing path cost to determine what the new cost value should be. Careful calculation will ensure that the desired path will indeed be chosen.

Use the following interface configuration command to set a switch port's path cost:

```
Switch (config-if)# spanning-tree [vlan vlan-id] cost cost
```

If the **vlan** parameter is given, the port cost is modified only for the specified VLAN. Otherwise, the cost is modified for the port as a whole (all active VLANs). Table 10-2 lists the cost value ranges from 1 to 65,535, according to the standard IEEE values.

Table 10-2   *STP Path Cost*

Link Bandwidth	STP Cost
4 Mbps	250
10 Mbps	100
16 Mbps	62
45 Mbps	39
100 Mbps	19
155 Mbps	14
622 Mbps	6
1 Gbps	4
10 Gbps	2

Tuning the Port ID

The fourth criteria of an STP decision is the Port ID. The Port ID value that a switch uses is actually a 16-bit quantity—8 bits for the Port Priority and 8 bits for the Port Number. Port Priority is a value from 0 to 255 and defaults to 128 for all ports. The Port Number can range from 0 to 255 and represents the port's actual physical mapping. Port Numbers begin with 1 at port 0/1 and increment across each module. (The numbers might not be consecutive because each module is assigned a particular range of numbers.)

Obviously, switch port's Port Number is fixed because it is based on hardware location. The Port ID, however, can be modified to influence an STP decision by using the Port Priority. You can configure the Port Priority with this interface configuration command:

```
Switch(config-if)# spanning-tree [vlan vlan-list] port-priority port-priority
```

You can modify the Port Priority for a specific VLAN by using the **vlan** parameter. Otherwise, the Port Priority is set for the port as a whole (all active VLANs). The value of *port-priority* can range from 0 to 255 and defaults to 128.

Tuning Spanning Tree Convergence

STP uses several timers, a sequence of states that ports must move through, and specific topology change conditions to prevent bridging loops from forming in a complex network. Each of these parameters or requirements is based on certain default values for a typical network size and function. For the majority of cases, the default STP operation is sufficient to keep the network loop free and enable users to communicate.

However, in certain situations, the default STP can cause network access to be delayed while timers expire and while preventing loops on links where loops are not possible. For example, when a single PC is connected to a switch port, a bridging loop is simply not possible. Another situation relates to the size of a Layer 2 switched network—the default STP timers are based on a benchmark network size. In a network that is smaller, waiting until the default timer values expire might not make sense when they could be safely set to shorter values. In situations like this, you can safely make adjustments to the STP convergence process for more efficiency.

Modifying STP Timers

Recall that STP uses three timers to keep track of various port operation states and communication between bridges. The three STP timers can be adjusted by using the commands documented in the sections that follow. Remember that the timers need only be modified on the Root Bridge because the Root Bridge propagates all three timer values throughout the network as fields in the Configuration BPDU.

Use one or more of the following global configuration commands to modify STP timers:

```
Switch(config)# spanning-tree [vlan vlan-id] hello-time seconds
Switch(config)# spanning-tree [vlan vlan-id] forward-time seconds
Switch(config)# spanning-tree [vlan vlan-id] max-age seconds
```

The *Hello Timer* triggers periodic "hello" (actually the Configuration BPDU) messages that are sent from the Root to other bridges in the network. This timer also sets the interval in which a bridge expects to hear a hello relayed from its neighboring bridges. Configuration BPDUs are sent every 2 seconds, by default. You can modify the Hello Timer per VLAN with the **hello-time** keyword, along with a value of 1 to 10 seconds.

The *Forward Delay Timer* determines the amount of time a port stays in the Listening state before moving into the Learning state and how long it stays in the Learning state before moving to the Forwarding state. You can modify the Forward Delay Timer per VLAN with the **forward-time** keyword. The default value is 15 seconds but can be set to a value of 4 to 30 seconds. This timer should be modified only under careful consideration because the value is dependent upon the diameter of the network and the propagation of BPDUs across all switches. A value too low allows loops to form and cripples a network.

The *MaxAge Timer* specifies a stored BPDU's lifetime that has been received from a neighboring switch with a Designated Port. Suppose BPDUs are being received on a non-Designated switch port every 2 seconds, as expected. Then an *indirect failure*, or one that doesn't involve a physical link going down, occurs that prevents BPDUs from being sent. The receiving switch waits until the Max Age Timer expires to listen for further BPDUs. If none are received, the non-Designated Port moves into the Listening state, and the receiving switch generates Configuration BPDUs. This port then becomes the Designated Port to restore connectivity on the segment.

To modify the Max Age Timer on a per-VLAN basis, use the **max-age** keyword. The timer value defaults to 20 seconds but can be set from 6 to 40 seconds.

NOTE Modifying STP timers can be tricky given the conservative nature of the default values and the calculations needed to derive proper STP operation. Timer values are basically dependent on the Hello Time and the switched network's diameter, in terms of switch hops. Catalyst switches offer a single command that can change the timer values in a more controlled fashion. Although described earlier, the **spanning-tree vlan** *vlan-id* **root** macro command is a better tool to use than setting the timers with the individual commands. This global configuration command has the following syntax:

```
Switch(config)# spanning-tree vlan vlan-id root {primary | secondary} [diameter
    diameter [hello hello-time]]
```

Here, STP timers will be adjusted according to the formulas specified in the 802.1D standard by giving only the Hello Time and the network's diameter (the maximum number of switches that traffic will traverse across a Layer 2 network). Again, this command can be used on a per-VLAN basis to modify the timers for a particular VLAN's spanning tree. The network diameter can be a value from one to seven switch hops. Because this command makes a switch become the Root Bridge, all the modified timer values resulting from this command will be propagated to other switches through the Configuration BPDU.

Redundant Link Convergence

Some additional methods that exist to allow faster STP convergence in the event of a link failure include the following:

■ **PortFast**—Enables fast connectivity to be established on access layer switch ports to workstations that are booting up

■ **UplinkFast**—Enables fast uplink failover on an access layer switch when dual uplinks are connected into the distribution layer

■ **BackboneFast**—Enables fast convergence in the network backbone (core) after a Spanning Tree topology change occurs

Rather than modifying timer values, these methods work by controlling convergence on specifically located ports within the network hierarchy.

> **NOTE**   The Spanning Tree Protocol has been enhanced to allow almost instantaneous topology changes, rather than rely on these Cisco-proprietary extensions. This enhancement is known as the Rapid Spanning Tree Protocol, or IEEE 802.1w, and is covered in Chapter 12, "Advanced Spanning Tree Protocol." You should become familiar with the topics in this chapter first because they provide the basis for the concepts in Chapter 12.

PortFast: Access Layer Nodes

An end-user workstation is usually connected to a switch port in the access layer. If the workstation is powered off and then turned on, the switch port will not be in a usable state until STP cycles from the Blocking state to the Forwarding state. With the default STP timers, this transition takes at least 30 seconds (15 seconds Listening to Learning and 15 seconds Learning to Fowarding). Therefore, the workstation is unable to transmit or receive any useful data until the Forwarding state is reached on the port.

> **NOTE**   Port initialization delays of up to 50 seconds can be observed. As discussed, 30 of these seconds are due to the STP state transitions. If a switch port is running Port Aggregation Protocol (PAgP) to negotiate EtherChannel configuration, an additional 20-second delay can occur.

On switch ports that connect only to single workstations or specific devices, bridging loops should never be possible. Catalyst switches offer the PortFast feature that shortens the Listening and Learning states to a negligible amount of time. When a workstation link comes up, the switch immediately moves the PortFast port into the Forwarding state. Spanning tree loop detection is still in operation, however, and the port moves into the Blocking state if a loop is ever detected on the port.

To enable or disable the PortFast feature on a switch port, use the following interface configuration command:

```
Switch(config-if)# spanning-tree portfast
```

Obviously, you should not enable PortFast on a switch port that is connected to a hub or another switch because bridging loops could possibly form. One other benefit of PortFast is that topology change notification (TCN) BPDUs are not sent when a switch port in PortFast mode goes up or down. This simplifies the TCN transmission on a large network when end-user workstations are coming up or shutting down.

UplinkFast: Access Layer Uplinks

Consider an access layer switch that has redundant uplink connections to two distribution layer switches. Normally, one uplink would be in the Forwarding state and the other in the Blocking state. If the primary uplink went down, up to 50 seconds could elapse before the redundant uplink could be used.

The *UplinkFast* feature on Catalyst switches enables leaf-node switches or switches at the ends of the spanning tree branches to have a functioning Root Port while keeping *one or more* redundant or potential Root Ports in Blocking mode. When the primary Root Port uplink fails, another blocked uplink can be immediately brought up for use.

> **NOTE**   Many Catalyst switches have two built-in, high-speed uplink ports (Gigabit Ethernet, for example). You might get the idea that UplinkFast can only toggle between two leaf-node uplink ports. This is entirely untrue—UplinkFast keeps a record of *all* parallel paths to the Root Bridge. All uplink ports but one are kept in the Blocking state. If the Root Port fails, the uplink with the next-lowest Root Path Cost is unblocked and used.

To enable the UplinkFast feature, use the following global configuration command.

```
Switch(config)# spanning-tree uplinkfast [max-update-rate pkts-per-second]
```

When UplinkFast is enabled, it is enabled for the entire switch and all VLANs. UplinkFast works by keeping track of possible paths to the Root Bridge. Therefore, the command *is not allowed on the Root Bridge switch*. UplinkFast also makes some modifications to the local switch to ensure that it does not become the Root Bridge, and that the switch is not used as a transit switch to get to the Root Bridge. First, the switch's Bridge Priority is raised to 49,152, making it unlikely that the switch will be elected to Root Bridge status. The Port Cost of all local switch ports is incremented by 3000, making the ports undesirable as paths to the Root for any downstream switches.

The command also includes a **max-update-rate** parameter. When an uplink on a switch goes down, UplinkFast makes it easy for the local switch to update its bridging table of MAC addresses to point to the new uplink. However, UplinkFast also provides a mechanism for the local switch to notify other upstream switches that stations downstream (or on toward the access layer) can be reached over the newly activated uplink.

This action is accomplished by sending dummy multicast frames to destination 0100.0ccd.cdcd that contain the MAC addresses of the stations in the Content-Addressable Memory (CAM) table. These multicast frames are sent out at a rate specified by the **max-update-rate** parameter in packets per second. The default is 150 packets per second (pps), but the rate can range from 0 to 65,535 pps. If the value is 0, no dummy multicasts are sent.

BackboneFast: Redundant Backbone Paths

In the network backbone, or core layer, a different method is used to shorten STP convergence. *BackboneFast* works by having a switch actively determine if alternate paths exist to the Root Bridge in the event that the switch detects an *indirect link failure*. Indirect link failures occur when a link not directly connected to a switch fails. A switch detects an indirect link failure when it receives inferior BPDUs from its Designated Bridge on either its Root Port or a Blocked Port. (Inferior BPDUs are sent from a Designated Bridge that has lost its connection to the Root Bridge, making it announce itself as the new Root.)

Normally, a switch must wait for the Max Age timer to expire before responding to the inferior BPDUs. However, BackboneFast begins to determine if other alternate paths to the Root Bridge exist according to the type of port that received the inferior BPDU. If the inferior BPDU arrives on a port in the Blocking state, the switch considers the Root Port and all other blocked ports to be alternate paths to the Root Bridge. If the inferior BPDU arrives on the Root Port itself, the switch considers all blocked ports to be alternate paths to the Root Bridge. If the inferior BPDU arrives on the Root Port and no ports are blocked, however, the switch assumes it has lost connectivity with the Root Bridge. In this case, the switch assumes that it has become the Root Bridge and, BackboneFast allows it to do so before the Max Age timer expires.

Detecting alternate paths to the Root Bridge also involves an interactive process with other bridges. If the local switch has blocked ports, BackboneFast begins to use the *Root Link Query (RLQ)* protocol to see if upstream switches have stable connections to the Root Bridge. RLQ Requests are sent out. If a switch receives an RLQ Request and is either the Root Bridge or has lost connection to the

Root, it sends an RLQ Reply. Otherwise, the RLQ Request is propagated on to other switches until an RLQ Reply can be generated. On the local switch, if an RLQ Reply is received on its current Root Port, the path to the Root Bridge is intact and stable. If it is received on a non-Root Port, an alternate Root Path must be chosen. The Max Age Timer is immediately expired so that a new Root Port can be found.

BackboneFast is simple to configure and operates by short-circuiting the Max Age Timer when needed. Although this function shortens the time a switch waits to detect a Root Path failure, ports still must go through full-length Forward Delay Timer intervals during the Listening and Learning states. Where PortFast and UplinkFast enable immediate transitions, BackboneFast can only reduce the maximum convergence delay from 50 to 30 seconds.

To configure BackboneFast, use the following global configuration command:

```
Switch(config)# spanning-tree backbonefast
```

When used, BackboneFast should be enabled on *all* switches in the network because BackboneFast requires the use of the RLQ Request and Reply mechanism to inform switches of Root Path stability. The RLQ protocol is active only when BackboneFast is enabled on a switch. By default, BackboneFast is disabled.

Troubleshooting STP

Because the STP running in a network uses several timers, costs, and dynamic calculations, predicting the current state in your head is difficult. You can take a network diagram and work out the STP topology by hand, but any change on the network could produce an entirely different outcome. Then figure in something like PVST+, where you have one instance of STP running for each VLAN present. Obviously, simply viewing the STP status on the active network devices would be better.

You can display information about many aspects of the STP from a Catalyst switch command-line interface (CLI). Specifically, you need to find out the current Root Bridge and its location in the network. You might also want to see the Bridge ID of the switch where you are connected, to see how it participates in STP. Use the information in Table 10-2 to determine what command is useful for what situation.

Table 10-3   *Commands for Displaying Spanning Tree Information*

Task	Command Syntax
View all possible STP parameters for all VLANs and ports.	**show spanning-tree**
Find the Root Bridge ID, the Root Port, and the Root Path Cost.	**show spanning-tree [vlan** *vlan-id*] **root**
Find the Designated Ports and Designated Bridge IDs on each port.	**show spanning-tree [vlan** *vlan-id*] **brief**
Show the total number of switch ports in each STP state.	**show spanning-tree [vlan** *vlan-id*] **summary**
Show the STP PortFast status of each switch port.[1]	**show spanning-tree	include (port | portfast)**
Show the STP UplinkFast status.	**show spanning-tree uplinkfast**
Show the STP BackboneFast status.	**show spanning-tree backbonefast**

[1]   The PortFast state is not readily accessible but is included in the large amount of information from the **show spanning-tree** command. You can add output filters to include only the lines that reference the Port and the portfast status.

Foundation Summary

The Foundation Summary is a collection of information that provides a convenient review of many key concepts in this chapter. If you are already comfortable with the topics in this chapter, this summary can help you recall a few details. If you just read this chapter, this review should help solidify some key facts. If you are doing your final preparation before the exam, these tables and figures are a convenient way to review the day before the exam.

Table 10-4 *STP Configuration Commands*

Task	Command Syntax
Enable STP.	**spanning-tree** *vlan-id*
Set Bridge Priority.	**spanning-tree vlan** *vlan-id* **priority** *bridge-priority*
Set Root Bridge (macro).	**spanning-tree vlan** *vlan-id* **root** {**primary** | **secondary**} [**diameter** *diameter*]
Set Port Cost.	**spanning-tree** [**vlan** *vlan-id*] **cost** *cost*
Set Port Priority.	**spanning-tree** [**vlan** *vlan-id*] **port-priority** *port-priority*
Set STP Timers.	**spanning-tree** [**vlan** *vlan-id*] **hello-time** *seconds*
	spanning-tree [**vlan** *vlan-id*] **forward-time** *seconds*
	spanning-tree [**vlan** *vlan-id*] **max-age** *seconds*
Set PortFast on an interface.	**spanning-tree portfast**
Set UplinkFast on a switch.	**spanning-tree uplinkfast** [**max-update-rate** *pkts-per-second*]
Set BackboneFast on a switch.	**spanning-tree backbonefast**

Q&A

The questions and scenarios in this book are more difficult than what you should experience on the actual exam. The questions do not attempt to cover more breadth or depth than the exam; however, they are designed to make sure that you know the answers. Rather than allowing you to derive the answers from clues hidden inside the questions themselves, the questions challenge your understanding and recall of the subject. Hopefully, these questions will help limit the number of exam questions on which you narrow your choices to two options and then guess.

You can find the answers to these questions in Appendix A.

1. What commands can configure a Catalyst 4500 switch as the Root Bridge on VLAN 10, assuming that the other switches are using the default STP values?

2. Using your Root Bridge answer from Question 1, what commands can configure a Catalyst 3550 switch as a secondary or backup Root Bridge on VLAN 10?

3. Which of the following switches will become the Root Bridge, given the information in the following table? Which switch will become the secondary Root Bridge if the Root Bridge fails?

Switch Name	Bridge Priority	MAC Address	Port Costs
Catalyst A	32,768	00-d0-10-34-26-a0	All are 19
Catalyst B	32,768	00-d0-10-34-24-a0	All are 4
Catalyst C	32,767	00-d0-10-34-27-a0	All are 19
Catalyst D	32,769	00-d0-10-34-24-a1	All are 19

Questions 4 through 7 are based on a network that contains two switches, Catalyst A and B. Their Bridge Priorities and MAC addresses are 32,768:0000.aaaa.aaaa and 32,768:0000.bbbb.bbbb, respectively.

4. Which switch will become the Root Bridge?

5. If switch B's Bridge Priority is changed to 10,000, which one will be Root?

6. If switch B's Bridge Priority is changed to 32,769, which one will be Root?

7. If switch C is introduced with 40000:0000.0000.cccc, which will be the secondary Root?

8. Suppose a switch is configured with the **spanning-tree vlan 10 root primary** command. Then another switch is connected to the network. The new switch has a Bridge Priority of 8192. Which one of the following happens?

   a. When the new switch advertises itself, the original Root Bridge detects it and lower its Bridge Priority to 4096 less than the new switch.

   b. The new switch becomes and stays the Root Bridge (Bridge Priority 8192).

   c. No change; both switches keep their current Bridge Priorities.

   d. The new switch detects that a Root Bridge already exists and raises its own Bridge Priority to 32,768.

9. Three switches in a network have the following Bridge Priorities: 32,768, 16,384, and 8192. If a fourth switch is configured with **spanning-tree vlan 1 root secondary**, what is the Bridge Priority of the switches that becomes the primary and secondary Root Bridge?

10. What STP timer values can be automatically modified by setting the network diameter?

11. Which STP timer determines how long a port stays in the Listening state? What is its default value?

12. What is the purpose of the Max Age timer?

13. Three switches are connected to each other, forming a triangle shape. STP prevents a loop from forming. What is the most accurate value that could be used for the network diameter?

14. Which of the following will not benefit from STP UplinkFast?

   a. An access layer switch with one uplink port

   b. An access layer switch with two uplink ports

   c. An access layer switch with three uplink ports

   d. An access layer switch with four uplink ports

15. What command can enable the STP PortFast feature on a switch? What configuration mode must you enter first?

16. What happens if the STP Hello Time is decreased to 1 second in an effort to speed up STP convergence? What happens if the Hello Time is increased to 10 seconds?

17. What switch command can safely adjust the STP timers on the Root Bridge in VLAN 7? Assume that the network consists of Catalyst A, B, and C, all connected to each other in a triangle fashion.

For questions 18 and 19, refer to the following output:

```
Switch# show spanning-tree vlan 50 brief
VLAN50
  Spanning tree enabled protocol ieee
  Root ID    Priority    8000
             Address     00d0.0457.3831
             Cost        12
             Port        49 (GigabitEthernet0/1)
             Hello Time   2 sec  Max Age 20 sec  Forward Delay 15 sec

  Bridge ID  Priority    32818  (priority 32768 sys-id-ext 50)
             Address     0009.b7ee.9800
             Hello Time   2 sec  Max Age 20 sec  Forward Delay 15 sec
             Aging Time 300

Interface                                   Designated
Name             Port ID Prio  Cost Sts     Cost Bridge ID           Port ID
---------------- ------- ---  ------ ---    ---- -------------------- -------
FastEthernet0/1    128.1  128     19 FWD      12 32818 0009.b7ee.9800 128.1
FastEthernet0/2    128.2  128     19 FWD      12 32818 0009.b7ee.9800 128.2
FastEthernet0/4    128.4  128    100 FWD      12 32818 0009.b7ee.9800 128.4
FastEthernet0/7    128.7  128     19 FWD      12 32818 0009.b7ee.9800 128.7
FastEthernet0/8    128.8  128     19 FWD      12 32818 0009.b7ee.9800 128.8
FastEthernet0/9    128.9  128     19 FWD      12 32818 0009.b7ee.9800 128.9
FastEthernet0/10  128.10  128     19 FWD      12 32818 0009.b7ee.9800 128.10
FastEthernet0/11  128.11  128     19 FWD      12 32818 0009.b7ee.9800 128.11
FastEthernet0/12  128.12  128     19 FWD      12 32818 0009.b7ee.9800 128.12
FastEthernet0/17  128.13  128     19 FWD      12 32818 0009.b7ee.9800 128.13
FastEthernet0/20  128.16  128     19 FWD      12 32818 0009.b7ee.9800 128.16
FastEthernet0/21  128.17  128     19 FWD      12 32818 0009.b7ee.9800 128.17
FastEthernet0/23  128.19  128     19 FWD      12 32818 0009.b7ee.9800 128.19
FastEthernet0/24  128.20  128     19 FWD      12 32818 0009.b7ee.9800 128.20
```

18. What is the Bridge ID for the current Root Bridge? Is the switch that produced this output the actual Root Bridge?

19. What is the Path Cost of interface FastEthernet 0/4, and why is it different from the others?

20. Why does the column marked "Designated Bridge ID" have the same value for every switch port?

21. Suppose you need to troubleshoot your Spanning Tree topology and operation. What commands and information can you use on a switch to find information about the current STP topology in VLAN 39?

This chapter covers the following topics that you need to master for the CCNP BCMSN exam:

- **Root Guard**—This section discusses how to protect the STP topology against unexpected switches advertising to become the Root Bridge.

- **BPDU Guard**—This section covers unexpected STP advertisements on switch ports configured for PortFast, where single hosts connect.

- **BPDU Skew Detection**—This section shows how to detect delayed BPDU reception.

- **Loop Guard**—This section discusses how to protect the STP topology against the loss of BPDUs from the Root Bridge on a switch port.

- **UDLD**—This section presents a feature to detect and protect against unidirectional, switch-to-switch links.

- **Troubleshooting STP Protection**—This section summarizes the commands that diagnose or verify actions that take to protect the topology.

CHAPTER 11

Protecting the Spanning Tree Protocol Topology

Achieving and maintaining a loop-free Spanning Tree Protocol (STP) topology revolves around the simple process of sending and receiving bridge protocol data units (BPDUs). Under normal conditions where all switches are playing fairly and according to the rules, a loop-free topology is dynamically determined.

This chapter discusses two basic conditions that can occur to disrupt the loop-free topology (even while STP is running):

- On a port that has not been receiving BPDUs, BPDUs are not expected. When BPDUs suddenly appear for some reason, the STP topology can reconverge to give unexpected results.
- On a port that normally receives BPDUs, BPDUs are always expected. When BPDUs suddenly disappear for some reason, a switch can make incorrect assumptions about the topology and unintentionally create loops.

"Do I Know This Already?" Quiz

The purpose of the "Do I Know This Already?" quiz is to help you decide what parts of this chapter to use. If you intend to read the entire chapter, you do not necessarily need to answer these questions now.

The quiz, derived from the major sections in the "Foundation Topics" portion of the chapter, helps you determine how to spend your limited study time.

Table 11-1 outlines the major topics discussed in this chapter and the "Do I Know This Already?" quiz questions that correspond to those topics.

Table 11-1 *"Do I Know This Already?" Foundation Topics Section-to-Question Mapping*

Foundation Topics Section	Questions Covered in This Section
Root Guard	1–4
BPDU Guard	5
BPDU Skew Detection	6
Loop Guard	7–9
UDLD	10–12

CAUTION   The goal of self-assessment is to gauge your mastery of the topics in this chapter. If you do not know the answer to a question or are only partially sure of the answer, you should mark this question wrong. Giving yourself credit for an answer you correctly guess skews your self-assessment results and might give you a false sense of security.

1.   Why is it important to protect the placement of the Root Bridge?

   a. To keep two Root Bridges from becoming active

   b. To keep the STP topology stable

   c. So all hosts have the correct gateway

   d. So the Root Bridge can have complete knowledge of the STP topology

2.   Which of the following features protects a switch port from accepting superior BPDUs?

   a. STP loop guard

   b. STP BPDU guard

   c. STP root guard

   d. UDLD

3.   Which of the following commands can you use to enable STP root guard on a switch port?

   a. **spanning-tree root guard**

   b. **spanning-tree root-guard**

   c. **spanning-tree guard root**

   d. **spanning-tree rootguard enable**

4. Where should the STP root guard feature be enabled on a switch?

   a. All ports

   b. Only ports where the Root Bridge should never appear

   c. Only ports where the Root Bridge should be located

   d. Only ports with PortFast enabled

5. Which of the following features protects a switch port from accepting BPDUs when PortFast is enabled?

   a. STP loop guard

   b. STP BPDU guard

   c. STP root guard

   d. UDLD

6. Which of the following features can you use to identify when BPDUs are delayed as they pass through the topology?

   a. UDLD

   b. BPDU guard

   c. BPDU authentication

   d. BPDU skew detection

7. To maintain a loop-free STP topology, which one of the following should a switch uplink be protected against?

   a. A sudden loss of BPDUs

   b. Too many BPDUs

   c. The wrong version of BPDUs

   d. BPDUs relayed from the Root Bridge

8. Which of the following commands can enable STP loop guard on a switch port?

   a. **spanning-tree loop guard**

   b. **spanning-tree guard loop**

   c. **spanning-tree loop-guard**

   d. **spanning-tree loopguard enable**

9. STP loop guard detects which of the following conditions?

    a. The sudden appearance of superior BPDUs

    b. The sudden lack of BPDUs

    c. The appearance of duplicate BPDUs

    d. The appearance of two Root Bridges

10. Which of the following features can actively test for the loss of the receive side of a link between switches?

    a. POST

    b. BPDU

    c. UDLD

    d. STP

11. UDLD must detect a unidirectional link before which of the following?

    a. The Max Age Timer

    b. STP moves the link to the blocking state

    c. STP moves the link to the forwarding state

    d. STP moves the link to the listening state

12. What must a switch do when it receives a UDLD message on a link?

    a. Relay the message on to other switches.

    b. Send a UDLD acknowledgment.

    c. Echo the message back across the link.

    d. Drop the message.

You can find the answers to the "Do I Know This Already?" quiz in Appendix A, "Answers to Chapter 'Do I Know This Already?' Quizzes and Q&A Sections." The suggested choices for your next step are as follows:

- **10 or less overall score**—Read the entire chapter. This includes the "Foundation Topics," "Foundation Summary," and "Q&A" sections.

- **11 or 12 overall score**—If you want more review on these topics, skip to the "Foundation Summary" section, and then go to the "Q&A" section at the end of the chapter. Otherwise, move to Chapter 12, "Advanced Spanning Tree Protocol."

Foundation Topics

Protecting Against Unexpected BPDUs

A network running STP uses BPDUs to communicate between switches (bridges). Switches become aware of each other and of the topology that interconnects them. After a Root Bridge is elected, BPDUs are generated by the Root and are relayed down through the spanning-tree topology. Eventually, all switches in the STP domain receive the Root's BPDUs such that the network converges and a stable loop-free topology forms.

To maintain an efficient topology, the placement of the Root Bridge must be predictable. Hopefully, you configured one switch to become the Root Bridge and a second one to be the secondary Root. What happens when a "foreign" or rogue switch is connected to the network, and that switch is suddenly able to become the Root Bridge? Cisco added two STP features that help prevent the unexpected: root guard and BPDU guard.

Root Guard

After an STP topology has converged and becomes loop-free, switch ports are assigned the following roles:

- **Root Port**—The one port on a switch that is closest (lowest Root Path Cost) to the Root Bridge.

- **Designated Port**—The port on a LAN segment that is closest to the Root; this port relays, or transmits, BPDUs on down the tree.

- **Blocking**—Ports that are neither Root nor Designated Ports

- **Alternate Ports**—Ports that are candidate Root Ports (they are also close to the Root Bridge) but are in the blocking state; these ports are identified for quick use by the STP UplinkFast feature.

- **Forwarding**—Ports where no other STP activity is detected or expected; these are ports with normal end user connections.

The Root Bridge is always expected to be seen on the Root Port and the Alternate Ports because these are "closest" (have the best cost path) to it.

Suppose that another switch is introduced into the network with a Bridge Priority that is more desirable (lower) than the current Root Bridge. The new switch would then become the Root Bridge, and the STP topology might reconverge to a new shape. This is entirely permissible by the STP, as the switch with the lowest Bridge ID always wins the Root election.

However, this is not always desirable to you, the network administrator, because the new STP topology might be something totally unacceptable. In addition, while the topology is reconverging, your production network might become unavailable.

The *root guard* feature was developed as a means to control where candidate Root Bridges can be connected and found on a network. Basically, a switch learns the cureent Root Bridge's Bridge ID. If another switch advertises a *superior BPDU*, or one with a better Bridge ID, on a port where root guard is enabled, the local switch will not allow the new switch to become the Root. As long as the superior BPDUs are being received on the port, the port will be kept in the *root-inconsistent* STP state. No data can be sent or received in that state, but the switch can listen to BPDUs received on the port.

In essence, root guard designates that a port can only relay BPDUs and not receive them. The port can never become a Root Port that would normally only receive BPDUs.

Root guard is enabled on a per-port basis. By default, it is disabled on all switch ports. To enable it, use the following interface configuration command:

```
Switch(config-if)# spanning-tree guard root
```

When the superior BPDUs are no longer received, the port is cycled through the normal STP states to return to normal use.

Use root guard on switch ports where you never expect to find the Root Bridge for a VLAN. In fact, root guard affects the entire port so that a Root Bridge can never be allowed on *any* VLAN on the port. When a superior BPDU is heard on the port, the entire port, in effect, becomes blocked.

BPDU Guard

Recall that the traditional STP offers the PortFast feature, where switch ports are allowed to imme-diately enter the Forwarding state as soon as the link comes up. Normally, PortFast provides quick network access to end-user devices, where bridging loops are never expected to form. Even while PortFast is enabled on a port, STP is still running and can detect a bridging loop. However, a loop can be detected only in a finite amount of time—the length of time required to move the port through the normal STP states.

> **NOTE** Remember that enabling PortFast on a port is not the same as disabling the Spanning Tree Protocol on it.

By definition, if you enable PortFast, you are never expecting to find anything that can cause a bridging loop—especially another switch or device that produces BPDUs. Suppose that a switch is connected by mistake to a port where PortFast is enabled. Now, there is a potential for a bridging loop to form. An even greater consequence is that the potential now exists for a new device to advertise itself and become the new Root Bridge.

The BPDU guard feature was developed to further protect the integrity of switch ports that have PortFast enabled. If any BPDU (whether superior to the current Root or not) is received on a port where BPDU guard is enabled, that port is immediately put into the *errdisable* state. The port is shut down in an error condition and must either be manually re-enabled or automatically recovered through the errdisable timeout function.

BPDU guard is configured on a per-port basis. By default, it is disabled on all switch ports. To enable it, use the following interface configuration command:

```
Switch(config-if)# spanning-tree bpduguard enable
```

When the BPDUs are no longer received, the port still remains in the errdisable state. See Chapter 5, "Switch Port Configuration," for more information about recovering from the errdisable state.

Use BPDU guard on all switch ports where STP PortFast is enabled. This prevents any possibility of a switch being added to the port, either intentionally or by mistake. An obvious application for BPDU guard is on access layer switch ports where users and end devices connect. BPDUs would not normally be expected there and would be detected if a switch or hub was inadvertently connected. Naturally, BPDU guard does not prevent a bridging loop from forming if a hub is connected to the PortFast port.

Protecting Against Sudden Loss of BPDUs

STP BPDUs are used as probes to learn about a network topology. When the switches participating in STP converge on a common and consistent loop-free topology, BPDUs must still be sent by the Root Bridge and relayed by every other switch in the STP domain. The STP topology's integrity then depends on a continuous and regular flow of BPDUs from the Root.

What happens if a switch doesn't receive BPDUs in a timely manner, or when it doesn't receive any at all? The switch can view that condition as acceptable—the topology must have changed, so blocked ports can be unblocked again. If the absence of BPDUs is actually a mistake, bridging loops can easily form. Cisco has added three STP features that help detect or prevent the unexpected:

- BPDU skew detection
- Loop guard
- Unidirectional Link Detection (UDLD)

BPDU Skew Detection

Recall that the Root Bridge is the one central source of BPDUs in an STP domain. All other switches merely receive copies of BPDUs that were relayed down the tree from the Root. The Root also sets the interval (hello time) that BPDUs are regularly sent out. This defaults to every two seconds.

After downstream switches learn the hello time interval from the Root, they expect to receive BPDUs at that interval. Under some conditions, a downstream switch might receive a BPDU but cannot relay it for a period of time. For example, the switch CPU might be busy performing other tasks before the BPDU can be processed and propagated; or an input queue on a switch might be so full that an incoming BPDU is simply lost.

In any event, BPDUs that arrive late or are lost can affect the STP topology's stability. How can you know if BPDUs have gone missing or are straggling? The BPDU skew detection feature allows the switch to monitor incoming BPDUs and report any skewing of their arrival times.

BPDU skew detection measures the amount of time that elapses from the time a BPDU is expected to when it actually arrives. This time difference is called the *skew time*. The switch also keeps track of the duration of the skewing condition, to give you an idea of how long BPDUs were arriving skewed. BPDU skew detection is just that—it detects only the condition and reports it via syslog messages. The switch cannot do anything else about the condition.

BPDU skew detection messages are rate-limited to protect the switch CPU resources. Only one syslog message can be generated per minute, unless the skew delay rises to over half of the Max Age timer (default 20 seconds). In that case, the skewing is severe and could affect the topology. At that time, the syslog messages are generated as they happen.

> **TIP** The BPDU skew detection feature is not yet available in Cisco IOS Software for Catalyst switches. However, its theory is covered in the BCMSN course, possibly on the exam, and is available in the Catalyst OS code (using **set** commands). Therefore, you would be wise to understand how the feature works.

Loop Guard

Suppose a switch port is receiving BPDUs, and the switch port is in the blocking state. The port makes up a redundant path; it is blocking because it is neither a Root Port nor a Designated Port. If, for some reason, the flow of BPDUs stops, the last known BPDU is kept until the Max Age timer expires. Then, that BPDU is flushed, and the switch thinks there is no longer a need to block the port. The port moves through the STP states until it begins to forward traffic—and form a bridging loop. In its final state, the port becomes a Designated Port.

To prevent this situation, you can use the loop guard STP feature. When enabled, loop guard keeps track of the BPDU activity on nondesignated ports. While BPDUs are received, the port is allowed to behave normally. When BPDUs go missing, loop guard moves the port into the *loop-inconsistent* state. The port is effectively blocking at this point to prevent a loop from forming and to keep it in the nondesignated role.

After BPDUs are received on the port again, loop guard allows the port to move through the normal STP states and become active. In this fashion, loop guard automatically governs ports without the need for manual intervention.

Loop guard is configured on a per-port basis, but its corrective blocking action is taken on a per-VLAN basis. (The entire port is not blocked; only the offending VLANs.) By default, loop guard is disabled on all switch ports. To enable it, use the following interface configuration command:

```
Switch(config-if)# spanning-tree guard loop
```

You can enable loop guard on all switch ports. It figures out which ports are nondesignated and monitors the BPDU activity to keep them nondesignated. Nondesignated ports are generally the Root Port, alternate Root Ports, and ports that are normally blocking.

UDLD

In a campus network, switches connect together by bidirectional (traffic can flow in two directions, as in full-duplex) links. Clearly, if a link has a physical layer problem, the two switches it connects detects a problem and the link is shown as not connected. What would happen if just one side (receive or transmit) of the link had an odd failure, such as malfunctioning transmit circuitry in a gigabit interface converter (GBIC)? In some cases, the two switches would still see a functional link. However, traffic could be delivered only in one direction and neither switch would notice.

A unidirectional link poses a potential danger to STP topologies because BPDUs will not be received on one end of the link. If that end of the link should be in the blocking state, it will not be for long. That switch thinks the absence of BPDUs means that the port can be moved through the STP states so that traffic can be forwarded on it. When that happens, a bridging loop forms and the switch never realizes the mistake.

To prevent this situation, you can use the unidirectional link detection (UDLD) STP feature. When enabled, UDLD interactively monitors a port to see if the link is truly bidirectional. The switch sends special Layer 2 UDLD frames identifying the switch port at regular intervals. UDLD expects the far-end switch to echo those frames back across the same link, with the far-end switch port's identification added. If a UDLD frame is received in return, and both neighboring ports are identified in the frame, the link must be bidirectional. However, if the echoed frames are not seen, the link is unidirectional.

Naturally, an echo process like this means that *both ends* of the link must be configured for UDLD. Otherwise, one end of the link will not echo the frames back.

You can configure the message interval used by UDLD (the default is 15 seconds). The objective behind UDLD is to detect a unidirectional link condition before STP has time to move a Blocked port into the Forwarding state. The target time would then be the Max Age timer plus two intervals of the Forward Delay timer, or 50 seconds. UDLD can detect a unidirectional link after about three times the UDLD message interval (45 seconds, using the default).

UDLD has two modes of operation:

- **Normal mode**—After a unidirectional link condition is detected, the port is allowed to continue its operation. UDLD merely marks the port as having an *undetermined* state and generates a syslog message.

- **Aggressive mode**—After a unidirectional link condition is detected, the switch takes action to re-establish the link. UDLD messages are sent out once a second for 8 seconds. If none of those messages are echoed back, the port is placed in the *errdisable* state so that it cannot be used.

UDLD is configured on a per-port basis, although it can be globally enabled for all fiber optic switch ports (either native fiber or fiber-based GBICs). By default, UDLD is disabled on all switch ports. To enable it globally, use the following global configuration command:

```
Switch(config)# udld {aggressive | enable | message time seconds}
```

For normal mode, use the **enable** keyword; for aggressive mode, use the **aggressive** keyword. You can set the message time interval to *seconds*, ranging from 7 to 90 seconds. (The Catalyst 3550 default is 7 seconds, the Catalyst 4500 and 6500 default is 15 seconds.)

You can also enable or disable UDLD on individual switch ports, if needed, using the following interface configuration command:

```
Switch(config-if)# udld {aggressive | disable | enable}
```

Here, you can configure the **disable** keyword to completely disable UDLD on a fiber-optic interface.

NOTE   The default UDLD message interval times differ among Catalyst switch platforms. Although two neighbors might have mismatched message time values, UDLD still works correctly. The two neighbors echo only each other's UDLD messages back (while silently extracting neighbor information), so no other interaction occurs between them as messages are sent back and forth.

If you decide to change the default message time, make sure that UDLD can still detect a fault *before* STP decides to move a link to the forwarding state.

You can enable UDLD on all switch ports. The switch globally enables UDLD only on ports that use fiber-optic media. Twisted pair or copper media does not suffer from the physical layer conditions that allow a unidirectional link to form. However, you can enable UDLD on non-fiber links individually, if you want.

At this point, you might be wondering how UDLD can be enabled gracefully on the two end switches. Recall that in aggressive mode, UDLD disables the link if the neighbor does not reflect the messages back within a certain time period. If you are enabling UDLD on a production network, is there a chance that UDLD will disable working links before you can get the far end configured?

The answer is no—UDLD makes some intelligent assumptions when it is enabled on a link for the first time. First, UDLD has no record of any neighbor on the link. It starts sending out messages, hoping that a neighboring switch will hear and echo them. Obviously, the device at the far end must also support UDLD so that the messages will be echoed back. If the neighboring switch does not yet have UDLD enabled, UDLD will keep trying and will not disable the link. After the neighbor has UDLD configured too, both switches become aware of each other and the bidirectional state of the link. From then on, if messages are not received, the normal UDLD procedures are followed.

Finally, be aware that if UDLD detects a unidirectional condition on a link, it takes action on only that link. This becomes important in an EtherChannel—if one link within the channel becomes unidirectional, UDLD only flags or disables the offending link and not the entire EtherChannel. UDLD sends and echoes its messages on each link within a channel independently.

Troubleshooting STP Protection

With several different types of STP protection features available, you might need to know which (if any) has been configured on a switch port. Table 11-2 lists and describes the EXEC commands useful for verifying the features presented in this chapter.

Table 11-2 *Commands for Verifying and Troubleshooting STP Protection Features*

Display Function	Command Syntax
List the ports that have been labeled in an inconsistent state	**show spanning-tree inconsistentports**
Look for detailed reasons for inconsistencies	**show spanning-tree interface** *type mod/num* [**detail**]
Display the Global BPDU guard state	**show spanning-tree summary**
Display the UDLD status on one or all ports	**show udld** [*type mod/num*]
Re-enable ports that UDLD aggressive mode has errdisabled	**udld reset**

Foundation Summary

The Foundation Summary is a collection information that provides a convenient review of many key concepts in this chapter. If you are already comfortable with the topics in this chapter, this summary could help you recall a few details. If you just read this chapter, this review can help solidify some key facts. If you are doing your final preparation before the exam, these tables and figures are a convenient way to review the day before the exam.

With so many similar and mutually exclusive STP protection features available, you might have a hard time remembering which ones to use where. Use Figure 11-1 as a quick reference.

The figure shows two backbone switches (Catalyst A and B), along with an access layer switch (Catalyst C) having redundant uplinks. Users are connected to the access switch, where PortFast is in use. An additional access switch (Catalyst D) has an uplink to access layer switch C. All switch-to-switch links are fiber-based Gigabit Ethernet. Obviously, a Root Bridge should never appear out of Catalyst D.

Table 11-3 *STP Protection Configuration Commands*

Task	Command Syntax
Enable root guard on an interface.	**spanning-tree guard root**
Enable BPDU guard on an interface.	**spanning-tree bpduguard enable**
Enable loop guard on an interface.	**spanning-tree guard loop**
Globally enable UDLD.	**udld {aggressive l enable l message time** *seconds*}
Alter UDLD on a single interface.	**udld {aggressive l disable l enable}**

Table 11-4 *STP Protection Activity Commands*

Task	Command Syntax
Look for ports that have been put in an inconsistent state.	**show spanning-tree inconsistentports**
Show UDLD status.	**show udld** [*type mod/num*]
Re-enable all ports that UDLD has errdisabled.	**udld reset**

Figure 11-1 *Guidelines for Applying STP Protection Features in a Network*

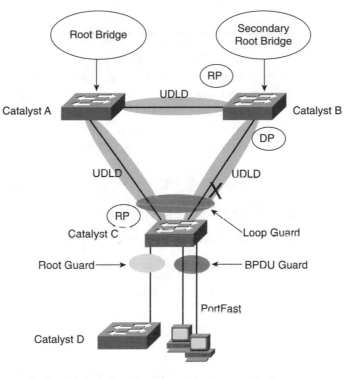

Root guard: Apply to ports where root is never expected.

BPDU guard: Apply to all user ports where PortFast is enabled.

Loop guard: Apply to nondesignated ports; but okay to apply to all ports.

UDLD: Apply to all fiber optic links between switches (must be enabled on both ends).

Permissible Combinations on a Switch port:
     Loop guard and UDLD
     Root guard and UDLD

Not permissible on a switch port:

     Root guard and Loop guard
     Root guard and BPDU guard

Q&A

The questions and scenarios in this book are more difficult than what you should experience on the actual exam. The questions do not attempt to cover more breadth or depth than the exam; however, they are designed to make sure that you know the answers. Rather than allowing you to derive the answers from clues hidden inside the questions themselves, the questions challenge your understanding and recall of the subject. Hopefully, these questions will help limit the number of exam questions on which you narrow your choices to two options and then guess.

The answers to these questions can be found in Appendix A.

1. Why would a unidirectional link be bad?

2. What condition must be met to keep a switch port in the blocking state?

3. If a switch port is shown to be in the root-inconsistent state, what has happened on it?

4. When root guard has been triggered on a switch port, what must be done to enable the port for use again?

5. When BPDU guard is enabled on a switch port, what state will the port be put in if a BPDU is received on it?

6. When BPDU guard has been triggered on a switch port, what must be done to enable the port for use again?

7. What can happen if BPDUs are delayed or "skewed" as they pass along from switch to switch?

8. What action does BPDU skew detection take when late BPDUs are detected?

9. When loop guard is enabled on a switch port and what state will the port be put in if BPDUs are noted to be missing?

10. Can STP loop guard be enabled on all switch ports?

11. When UDLD is enabled on a switch port, what else must be done to detect a unidirectional link on the port?

12. What is the difference between the UDLD normal and aggressive modes?

13. What command enables UDLD aggressive mode on a switch interface?

14. If two switches enable UDLD on the ports that have a common link, do their UDLD message times have to agree?

15. UDLD should be used on switch ports with what type of media?

16. Can UDLD be used on all switch ports without causing problems?

17. Complete the following command to display all ports that are disabled due to STP protection features:

show spanning-tree _____

This chapter covers the following topics that you need to master for the CCNP BCMSN exam:

- **Rapid Spanning Tree Protocol (RSTP)** — This section discusses the enhancements that allow switches to run STP efficiently, offering fast convergence.

- **Multiple Spanning Tree (MST) Protocol** — This section discusses the latest IEEE standard that supports a reduced number of STP instances for a campus network, while using RSTP for efficient operation.

CHAPTER 12

Advanced Spanning Tree Protocol

Familiarity with the IEEE 802.1D STP standard is essential because that protocol is used universally to maintain loop free bridged and switched networks. However, it is now considered a legacy protocol, offering topology change and convergence times that are not as acceptable as they once were.

This chapter discusses the many STP enhancements that are available in new standards. The Rapid STP (RSTP) is presented first because it provides the foundation for efficient STP activity. The Multiple STP (MST or MSTP) is also discussed here. MST allows VLANs to be individually mapped into STP instances, while RSTP operates in the background. These two protocols allow a Layer 2 campus network to undergo change quickly and efficiently, with little downtime for today's applications.

"Do I Know This Already?" Quiz

The purpose of the "Do I Know This Already?" quiz is to help you decide if you need to read the entire chapter. If you already intend to read the entire chapter, you do not necessarily need to answer these questions now.

The quiz, derived from the major sections in the "Foundation Topics" portion of the chapter, helps you determine how to spend your limited study time.

Table 12-1 outlines the major topics discussed in this chapter and the "Do I Know This Already?" quiz questions that correspond to those topics.

Table 12-1   *"Do I Know This Already?" Foundation Topics Section-to-Question Mapping*

Foundation Topics Section	Questions Covered in This Section
Rapid STP	1–8
Multiple STP (MST)	9–12

> **CAUTION** The goal of self-assessment is to gauge your mastery of the topics in this chapter. If you do not know the answer to a question or are only partially sure of the answer, you should mark this question wrong. Giving yourself credit for an answer you correctly guess skews your self-assessment results and might give you a false sense of security.

1. Which one of the following enables the use of RSTP?

   a. PVST+

   b. 802.1D

   c. CST

   d. MST

2. Upon which standard is RSTP based?

   a. 802.1Q

   b. 802.1D

   c. 802.1w

   d. 802.1s

3. Which of the following is not a port state in RSTP?

   a. Listening

   b. Learning

   c. Discarding

   d. Forwarding

4. When a switch running RSTP receives an 802.1D BPDU, what happens?

   a. The BPDU is discarded or dropped.

   b. An ICMP message is returned.

   c. The switch begins to use 802.1D rules on that port.

   d. The switch disables RSTP.

5. When does an RSTP switch consider a neighbor to be down?

   a. After three BPDUs are missed

   b. After six BPDUs are missed

   c. After the Max Age timer expires

   d. After the Forward Timer expires

6. Which process is used during RSTP convergence?

   a. BPDU propagation

   b. Synchronization

   c. Forward Timer expiration

   d. BPDU acknowledgments

7. What causes RSTP to view a port as a point-to-point port?

   a. Port speed

   b. Port media

   c. Port duplex

   d. Port priority

8. Which of the following events triggers a topology change with RSTP on a nonedge port?

   a. A port comes up or goes down.

   b. A port comes up.

   c. A port goes down.

   d. A port moves to the forwarding state.

9. Which of the following is not a characteristic of MST?

   a. A reduced number of STP instances

   b. Fast STP convergence

   c. Eliminates the need for CST

   d. Interoperability with PVST+

10. Which of the following standards defines the MST protocol?

    a. 802.1Q

    b. 802.1D

    c. 802.1w

    d. 802.1s

11. How many instances of STP are supported in the Cisco implementation of MST?

    a. 1

    b. 16

    c. 256

    d. 4096

12. What switch command can be used to change from PVST+ to MST?

    a. spanning-tree mst enable

    b. no spanning-tree pvst+

    c. spanning-tree mode mst

    d. spanning-tree mst

You can find the answers to the "Do I Know This Already?" quiz in Appendix A, "Answers to Chapter 'Do I Know This Already?' Quizzes and Q&A Sections." The suggested choices for your next step are as follows:

■ **10 or less overall score**—Read the entire chapter. This includes the "Foundation Topics," "Foundation Summary," and "Q&A" sections.

■ **11 or 12 overall score**—If you want more review on these topics, skip to the "Foundation Summary" section and then go to the "Q&A" section at the end of the chapter. Otherwise, move to Chapter 13, "Multilayer Switching."

Foundation Topics

Rapid Spanning Tree Protocol (RSTP)

The IEEE 802.1D Spanning Tree Protocol was designed to keep a switched or bridged network loop free, with adjustments made to the network topology dynamically. A topology change typically takes 30 seconds, where a port moves from the Blocking state to the Forwarding state after two intervals of the Forward Delay timer. As technology has improved, 30 seconds has become an unbearable length of time to wait for a production network to failover or "heal" itself during a problem.

The IEEE 802.1w standard was developed to take 802.1D's principle concepts and make the resulting convergence much faster. This is also known as the Rapid Spanning Tree Protocol (RSTP). RSTP defines how switches must interact with each other to keep the network topology loop free, in a very efficient manner. Like 802.1D, RSTP's basic functionality can be applied as a single or multiple instances. This can be done as the IEEE 802.1s Multiple Spanning Tree (MST), covered in this chapter, and also as the Cisco-proprietary, Rapid Per-VLAN Spanning Tree Protocol (RPVST+). RSTP operates consistently in each, but replicating RSTP as multiple instances requires different approaches.

RSTP Port Behavior

In 802.1D, each switch port is assigned a role and a state at any given time. Depending on the port's proximity to the Root Bridge, it takes on one of the following roles:

- Root Port
- Designated Port
- Blocking Port (neither Root nor Designated).

The Cisco-proprietary UplinkFast feature also reserved a hidden Alternate Port role for ports that offered parallel paths to the Root but were in the Blocking state.

Recall that each switch port is also assigned one of five possible states:

- Disabled
- Blocking
- Listening
- Learning
- Forwarding

Only the Forwarding state allows data to be sent and received. A port's state is somewhat tied to its role. For example, a Blocking Port cannot be a Root Port or a Designated Port.

RSTP achieves its rapid nature by letting each switch interact with its neighbors through each port. This interaction is performed based on a port's role, not strictly on the BPDUs that are relayed from the Root Bridge. After the role is determined, each port can be given a state that determines what it does with incoming data.

The Root Bridge in a network using RSTP is elected just as with 802.1D—by the lowest Bridge ID. After all switches agree on the identity of the Root, the following port roles are determined:

- **Root Port**—The one switch port on each switch that has the best root path cost to the Root. This is identical to 802.1D. (By definition, the Root Bridge has no Root Ports.)

- **Designated Port**—The switch port on a network segment that has the best root path cost to the Root.

- **Alternate Port**—A port that has an alternate path to the Root, different than the path the Root Port takes. This path is less desirable than that of the Root Port. (An example of this is an access layer switch with two uplink ports; one becomes the Root Port, the other is an Alternate Port.)

- **Backup Port**—A port that provides a redundant (but less desirable) connection to a segment where another switch port already connects. If that common segment is lost, the switch might or might not have a path back to the Root.

RSTP defines port states only according to what the port does with incoming frames. (Naturally, if incoming frames are ignored or dropped, so are outgoing frames.) Any port role can have any of these port states:

- **Discarding**—Incoming frames are simply dropped; no MAC addresses are learned. (This state combines the 802.1D Disabled, Blocking, and Listening states, as all three did not effectively forward anything. The Listening state is not needed, because RSTP can quickly negotiate a state change without listening for BPDUs first.)

- **Learning**—Incoming frames are dropped, but MAC addresses are learned.

- **Forwarding**—Incoming frames are forwarded according to MAC addresses that have been (and are being) learned.

BPDUs in RSTP

In 802.1D, BPDUs basically originate from the Root Bridge and are relayed by all switches down through the tree. It is because of this propagation of BPDUs that 802.1D convergence must wait for steady-state conditions before proceeding.

RSTP uses the 802.1D BPDU format for backward-compatibility. However, some previously unused bits in the Message Type field are used. The sending switch port identifies itself by its RSTP role and state. The BPDU version is also set to 2, to distinguish RSTP BPDUs from 802.1D BPDUs. Also, RSTP uses an interactive process so that two neighboring switches can negotiate state changes. Some BPDU bits are used to flag messages during this negotiation.

BPDUs are sent out every switch port at Hello Time intervals, regardless of whether BPDUs are received from the Root. In this way, any switch anywhere in the network can play an active role in maintaining the topology. Switches can also expect to receive regular BPDUs from their neighbors. When three BPDUs are missed in a row, that neighbor is presumed to be down, and all information related to the port leading to the neighbor is immediately aged out. This means that a switch can detect a neighbor failure in three Hello intervals (default 6 seconds), versus the Max Age Timer interval (default 20 seconds) for 802.1D.

Because RSTP distinguishes its BPDUs from 802.1D BPDUs, it can coexist with switches still using 802.1D. Each port attempts to operate according to the STP BPDU that is received. For example, when an 802.1D BPDU (version 0) is received on a port, that port begins to operate according to the 802.1D rules. However, each port has a measure that locks the protocol in use for the duration of the migration delay timer. This keeps the protocol type from flapping or toggling during a protocol migration. After the timer expires, the port is free to change protocols if needed.

RSTP Convergence

The convergence of STP in a network is the process that takes all switches from a state of independence (each thinks it must be the STP Root) to one of uniformity, where each switch has a place in a loop-free tree topology. You can think of convergence as a two-stage process:

1. One common Root Bridge must be "elected," and all switches must know about it.

2. The state of every switch port in the STP domain must be brought from a Blocking state to the appropriate state to prevent loops.

Convergence generally takes time, as messages are propagated from switch to switch. The traditional 802.1D STP also requires the expiration of several timers before switch ports can be safely allowed to forward data.

RSTP takes a different approach when a switch needs to decide how to participate in the tree topology. When a switch first joins the topology (perhaps it was just powered up) or has detected a failure in the existing topology, RSTP requires it to base its forwarding decisions on the type of port.

Port Types

Every switch port can be considered one of the following types:

- **Edge Port**—A port at the "edge" of the network, where only a single host connects. Traditionally, this has been identified by enabling the STP PortFast feature. RSTP keeps the PortFast concept for familiarity. By definition, the port cannot form a loop as it connects to one host, so it can be immediately placed in the Forwarding state. However, if a BPDU is ever received on an edge port, the port immediately loses its edge port status.

- **Root Port**—The port that has the best cost to the root of the STP instance. Only one Root Port can be selected and active at any time, although alternate paths to the root can exist through other ports. If alternate paths are detected, those ports are identified as Alternate Root Ports and can be immediately placed in the Forwarding state when the existing Root Port fails.

- **Point-to-Point Port**—Any port that connects to another switch and becomes a Designated Port. A quick handshake with the neighboring switch, rather than a timer expiration, decides the port state. BPDUs are exchanged back and forth in the form of a proposal and an agreement. One switch proposes that its port becomes a Designated Port; if the other switch agrees, it replies with an agreement message.

  Point-to-point ports are automatically determined by the duplex mode in use. Full-duplex ports are considered point-to-point because only two switches can be present on the link. STP convergence can quickly occur over a point-to-point link through RSTP handshake messages.

  Half-duplex ports, on the other hand, are considered to be on a shared media with possibly more than two switches present. They are not point-to-point ports. STP convergence on a half-duplex port must occur between several directly connected switches. Therefore, the traditional 802.1D style convergence must be used. This results in a slower response because the shared-media ports must go through the fixed listening and learning state time periods.

It's easy to see how two switches can quickly converge to a common idea of which one is the Root and which one will have the Designated Port after just a single exchange of BPDUs. What about a larger network, where 802.1D BPDUs would normally have to be relayed from switch to switch?

RSTP handles the complete STP convergence of the network as a propagation of handshakes over point-to-point links. When a switch needs to make an STP decision, a handshake is made with the nearest neighbor. After that is successful, the handshake sequence is moved to the next switch and the next, as an ever-expanding wave moving toward the network's edges.

During each handshake sequence, a switch must take measures to be completely sure it will not introduce a bridging loop before moving the handshake out. This is done through a synchronization process.

Synchronization

To participate in RSTP convergence, a switch must decide the state of each of its ports. Nonedge ports begin in the Discarding state. After BPDUs are exchanged between the switch and its neighbor, the Root Bridge can be identified. If a port receives a superior BPDU from a neighbor, that port becomes the Root Port.

For each nonedge port, the switch exchanges a proposal-agreement handshake to decide the state of each end of the link. Each switch assumes that its port should become the Designated Port for the segment, and a proposal message (a Configuration BPDU) is sent to the neighbor suggesting this.

When a switch receives a proposal message on a port, the following sequence of events occurs (Figure 12-1 shows the sequence, based around the center Catalyst switch):

1. If the proposal's sender has a superior BPDU, the local switch realizes that the sender should be the Designated Switch (having the Designated Port), and that its own port must become the new Root Port.

2. Before the switch agrees to anything, it must first synchronize itself with the topology.

3. All nonedge ports are immediately moved into the Discarding (blocking) state so that no bridging loops can form.

4. An agreement message (a Configuration BPDU) is sent back to the sender, indicating that the switch is in agreement with the new Designated Port choice. This also tells the sender that the switch is in the process of synchronizing itself.

5. The Root Port is immediately moved to the Forwarding state. The sender's port can also immediately begin forwarding.

6. For each nonedge port that is currently in the Discarding state, a proposal message is sent to the respective neighbor.

7. An agreement message is expected and received from a neighbor on a nonedge port.

8. The nonedge port is immediately moved to the Forwarding state.

Notice how the RSTP convergence begins with a switch sending a proposal message. The recipient of the proposal must synchronize itself by effectively isolating itself from the rest of the topology. All nonedge ports are blocked until a proposal message can be sent, causing the nearest neighbors to synchronize themselves. This creates a moving "wave" of synchronizing switches, which can quickly decide to start forwarding on their links only if their neighbors agree. Figure 12-2 shows how the synchronization wave travels through a network at three successive time intervals. Isolating the switches along the traveling wave inherently prevents bridging loops.

Figure 12-1   *Sequence of Events During RSTP Convergence*

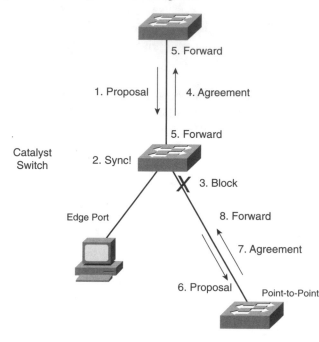

The entire convergence process happens quickly, at the speed of BPDU transmission, without the use of any timers. A Designated Port that sends a proposal message might not receive an agreement message reply. Suppose the neighboring switch does not understand RSTP or has a problem replying. The sending switch must then become overly cautious and begin playing by the 802.1D rules—the port must be moved through the legacy Listening and Learning states (using the Forward Delay timer) before moving to the Forwarding state.

Topology Changes and RSTP

Recall that when an 802.1D switch detects a port state change (either up or down), it signals the Root Bridge by sending topology change notification (TCN) BPDUs. The Root Bridge must then signal a topology change by sending out a TCN message that is relayed to all switches in the STP domain.

RSTP detects a topology change only when a nonedge port transitions to the Forwarding state. This might seem odd because a link failure is not used as a trigger. RSTP uses all of its rapid convergence mechanisms to prevent bridging loops from forming. Therefore, topology changes are detected only so that bridging tables can be updated and corrected as hosts appear first on a failed port and then on a different functioning port.

Figure 12-2 *RSTP Synchronization Traveling Through a Network*

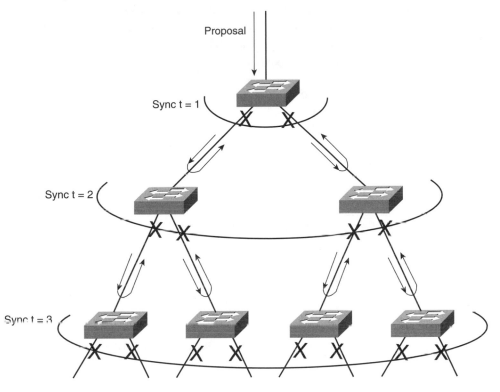

When a topology change is detected, a switch must propagate news of the change to other switches in the network so they can correct their bridging tables, too. This process is similar to the convergence and synchronization mechanism—topology change (TC) messages propagate through the network in an ever-expanding wave.

BPDUs, with their TC bit set, are sent out all of the nonedge designated ports. This is done until the "TC While" timer expires, after two times the Hello time. This notifies neighboring switches of the new link and the topology change. In addition, all MAC addresses associated with the nonedge Designated Ports are flushed from the content-addressable memory (CAM) table. This forces the addresses to be relearned after the change, in case hosts now appear on a different link.

All neighboring switches that receive the TC messages must also flush the MAC addresses learned on all ports except the one that received the TC message. Those switches must then send TC messages out their nonedge Designated Ports, and so on.

RSTP Configuration

By default, a switch operates in the Per VLAN Spanning Tree Plus (PVST+) mode using traditional 802.1D STP. Therefore, RSTP cannot be used until a different Spanning Tree mode (MST or RPVST+) is enabled. Remember that RSTP is just the underlying mechanism that a Spanning Tree mode can use to detect topology changes and converge a network into a loop-free topology.

The only configuration changes related to RSTP affect the port or link type. The link type is used to determine how a switch negotiates topology information with its neighbors.

To configure a port as an RSTP edge port, use the following interface configuration command:

```
Switch(config-if)# spanning-tree portfast
```

You should already be familiar with this command from the 802.1D STP configuration. After PortFast is enabled, the port is considered to have only one host and is positioned at the edge of the network.

By default, RSTP automatically decides that a port is a point-to-point link if it is operating in full-duplex mode. Ports connecting to other switches are usually full-duplex because there are only two switches on the link. However, you can override the automatic determination if needed. For example, a port connecting to one other switch might be operating at half-duplex for some reason. To force the port to act as a point-to-point link, use the following interface configuration command:

```
Switch(config-if)# spanning-tree link-type point-to-point
```

Multiple Spanning Tree (MST) Protocol

Chapter 9 covered two "flavors" of Spanning Tree implementations—IEEE 802.1Q and PVST+—both based on the 802.1D STP. These also represent the two extremes of Spanning Tree Protocol operation in a network:

- **802.1Q**—Only a single instance of STP is used for all VLANs. If there are 500 VLANs, only one instance of STP will be running. This is called the Common Spanning Tree (CST) and operates over the trunk's native VLAN.

- **PVST+**—One instance of STP is used for each active VLAN in the network. If there are 500 VLANs, 500 independent instances of STP will be running.

In most networks, each switch has a redundant path to another switch. For example, an access layer switch usually has two uplinks, each connecting to a different distribution or core layer switch. If 802.1Q's CST is used, only one STP instance will run. That means there is only one loop-free topology at any given time, and that only one of the two uplinks in the access layer switch will be forwarding. The other uplink will always be blocking.

Obviously, arranging the network so that both uplinks can be used simultaneously would be best. One uplink should carry one set of VLANs, while the other carries a different set, as a type of load balancing.

PVST+ seems more attractive to meet that goal because it allows different VLANs to have different topologies, so that each uplink can be forwarding. But, think of the consequences—as the number of VLANs increases, so does the number of independent STP instances. Each instance uses some amount of the switch CPU and memory resources. The more instances in use, the less CPU resources available for switching.

Beyond that, what is the real benefit of having 500 STP topologies for 500 VLANs, when only a small number of possible topologies exist for a switch with two uplinks? Figure 12-3 shows a typical network with an access layer switch connecting to a pair of core switches. Two VLANs are in use, with the Root Bridges configured to support load balancing across the two uplinks. The right portion of the figure shows every possible topology for VLANs A and B. Notice that because the access layer switch has only two uplinks, only two topologies actually matter—one where the left uplink forwards, and one where the right uplink forwards.

Figure 12-3 *The Possible STP Topologies for Two VLANs*

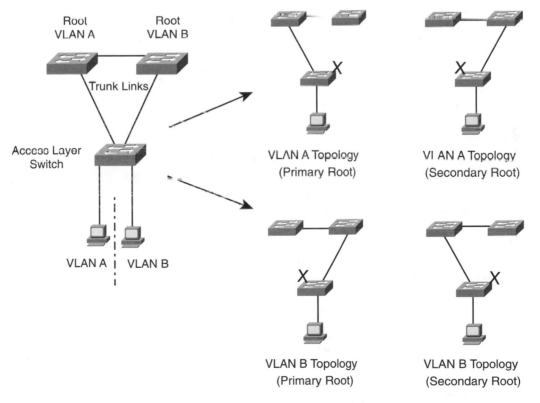

Notice also that the number of useful topologies is independent of the number of VLANs. If 10 or 100 VLANs were used in the figure, there would still be only two possible outcomes at the access layer switch. Therefore, running 10 or 100 instances of STP when only a couple would suffice is rather wasteful.

The Multiple Spanning Tree Protocol (MST or MSTP) was developed to address the lack of and surplus of STP instances. As a result, the network administrator can configure exactly the number of STP instances that make sense for the enterprise network—no matter how many VLANs are in use. MST is defined in the IEEE 802.1s standard.

MST Overview

MST is built on the concept of mapping one or more VLANs to a single STP instance. Multiple instances of STP can be used (hence the name MST), with each instance supporting a different group of VLANs.

For the network shown in Figure 12-3, only two MST instances would be needed. Each could be tuned to result in a different topology, so that Instance 1 would forward on the left uplink, while Instance 2 would forward on the right uplink. Therefore, VLAN A would be mapped to Instance 1, and VLAN B to Instance 2.

To implement MST in a network, you need to determine the following:

- The number of STP instances needed to support the desired topologies.
- Whether to map a set of VLANs to each instance.

MST Regions

MST is different than 802.1Q and PVST+, although it can interoperate with them. If a switch is configured to use MST, it must somehow figure out which of its neighbors are using which type of STP. This is done by configuring switches into common MST regions, where every switch in a region runs MST with compatible parameters.

In most networks, a single MST region is sufficient, although you can configure more than one region. Within the region, all switches must run the instance of MST that is defined by the following attributes:

- MST configuration name (32 characters)
- MST configuration revision number (0 to 65535)
- MST instance-to-VLAN mapping table (4096 entries)

If two switches have the same set of attributes, they belong to the same MST region. If not, they belong to two independent regions.

MST BPDUs contain configuration attributes so that switches receiving BPDUs can compare them against their local MST configurations. If the attributes match, the STP instances within MST can be shared as part of the same region. If not, a switch is seen to be at the MST region boundary, where one region meets another or one region meets traditional 802.1D STP.

> **NOTE** The entire MST instance-to-VLAN mapping table is not sent along in the BPDUs because the instance mappings must be configured on each switch. Instead, a digest, or a code computed from the table contents, is sent. As the contents of the table change, the digest value will be different. Therefore, a switch can quickly compare a received digest to its own to see if the advertised table is the same or different.

Spanning Tree Instances Within MST

MST was designed to interoperate with all other forms of STP. Therefore, it must also support STP instances from each. This is where MST can get confusing. Think of the entire enterprise network having a single CST topology, such that one instance of STP represents any and all VLANs and MST regions present. The CST serves to maintain a common loop-free topology, while integrating all forms of STP that might be in use.

To do this, CST must regard each MST region as a single "black box" bridge because it has no idea what is inside the region, nor does it care. CST only maintains a loop-free topology with the links that connect the regions to each other and to standalone switches running 802.1Q CST.

IST Instances

Something other than CST must work out a loop-free topology inside each MST region. Within a single MST region, an Internal Spanning Tree (IST) instance runs to work out a loop-free topology between the links where CST meets the region boundary and all switches inside the region. Think of the IST instance as a locally significant CST, bounded by the edges of the region.

The IST presents the entire region as a single virtual bridge to the CST outside. BPDUs are exchanged at the region boundary only over the native VLAN of trunks, as if a single CST were in operation. And, indeed, it is.

Figure 12-4 shows the basic concept behind the IST instance. The network at the left has an MST region, where several switches are running compatible MST configurations. Another switch is outside the region because it is running only the CST from 802.1Q.

The same network is shown at the right, where the IST has produced a loop-free topology for the network inside the region. The IST makes the internal network look like a single bridge (the "big switch" in the cloud) that can interface with the CST running outside the region.

Figure 12-4 *Concepts Behind the IST Instance*

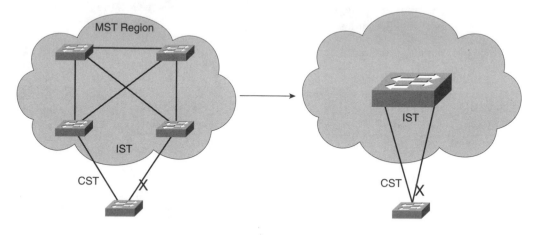

MST Instances

Recall that the whole idea behind MST is the capability to map multiple VLANs to a smaller number of STP instances. Inside a region, the actual MST instances (MSTIs) exist alongside the IST. Cisco supports a maximum of 16 MSTIs in each region. IST always exists as MSTI number 0, leaving MSTI 1 through 15 available for use.

Figure 12-5 shows how different MSTIs can exist within a single MST region. The left portion of the figure is identical to that of Figure 12-4. In this network, two MST instances, MSTI 1 and MSTI 2, are configured with different VLANs mapped to each. Their topologies follow the same structure as the network on the left side of the figure, but each has converged differently. Notice that within the MST cloud, we now have three independent STP instances coexisting—MSTI1, MSTI 2, and the IST.

Only the IST (MSTI 0) is allowed to send and receive MST BPDUs. Information about each of the other MSTIs is appended to the MST BPDU as an M-record. Therefore, even if a region has all 16 instances active, only one BPDU is needed to convey STP information about them all.

Each of the MSTIs are significant only within a region, even if an adjacent region has the same MSTIs in use. In other words, the MSTIs combine with the IST only at the region boundary to form a subtree of the CST. That means only IST BPDUs are sent into and out of a region.

Figure 12-5 *Concepts Behind MST Instances*

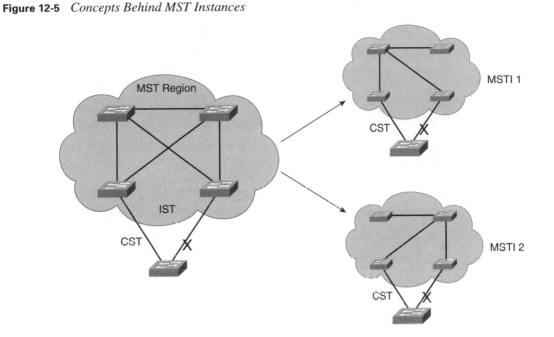

What if an MST region connects with a switch running PVST+? MST can detect this situation by listening to the received BPDUs. If BPDUs are heard from more than one VLAN (the CST), PVST+ must be in use. When the MST region sends a BPDU toward the PVST+ switch, the IST BPDUs are replicated into all of the VLANs on the PVST+ switch trunk.

> **NOTE**   Keep in mind that the IST instance is active on *every* port on a switch. Even if a port does not carry VLANs that have been mapped to the IST, IST must still be running on the port.
>
> Also, by default, all VLANs are mapped to the IST instance. You must explicitly map them to other instances if needed.

MST Configuration

You must manually configure the MST configuration attributes on each switch in a region. There is currently no method to propagate this information from one switch to another, as is done with a protocol like VLAN Trunking Protocol (VTP). To define the MST region, use the followig configuration commands in order:

Step 1   Enable MST on the switch:

```
Switch(config)# spanning-tree mode mst
```

Step 2   Enter the MST configuration mode:

Switch(config)# **spanning-tree mst configuration**

Step 3   Assign a region configuration name (up to 32 characters):

Switch(config-mst)# **name** *name*

Step 4   Assign a region configuration revision number (0 to 65,535):

Switch(config-mst)# **revision** *version*

The configuration revision number gives you a means to track changes to the MST region configuration. Each time you make changes to the configuration, you should increase the number by one. Remember that the region configuration (including the revision number) must match on all switches in the region. Therefore, you also need to update the revision numbers on the other switches to match.

Step 5   Map VLANs to an MST instance:

Switch(config-mst)# **instance** *instance-id* **vlan** *vlan-list*

The *instance-id* (0 to 15) carries topology information for the VLANs listed in *vlan-list*. The list can contain one or more VLANs separated by commas. You can also add a range of VLANs to the list by separating numbers with a hyphen. VLAN numbers can range from 1 to 4094. (Remember that by default, all VLANs are mapped to instance 0, the IST.)

Step 6   Show the pending changes you have made:

Switch(config-mst)# **show pending**

Step 7   Exit the MST configuration mode; commit the changes to the active MST region configuration:

Switch(config-mst)# **exit**

After MST is enabled and configured, PVST+ operation stops and the switch changes to RSTP operation. A switch cannot run both MST and PVST+ at the same time.

You can also tune the parameters that MST uses when it interacts with CST or traditional 802.1D. The parameters and timers are identical to those discussed in Chapter 10, "Spanning Tree Configuration." In fact, the commands are very similar except for the addition of the **mst** keyword and the *instance-id*. Rather than tuning STP for a VLAN instance, you use an MST instance.

Table 12-2 summarizes the commands as a quick reference. Notice that the timer configurations are applied to MST as a whole, and not to a specific MST instance. This is because all instance timers are defined through the IST instance and BPDUs.

Table 12-2 *MST Configuration Commands*

Task	Command Syntax
Set Root Bridge (macro)	**spanning-tree mst** *instance-id* **root {primary | secondary}** [**diameter** *diameter*]
Set Bridge Priority	**spanning-tree mst** *instance-id* **priority** *bridge-priority*
Set Port Cost	**spanning-tree mst** *instance-id* **cost** *cost*
Set Port Priority	**spanning-tree mst** *instance-id* **port-priority** *port-priority*
Set STP Timers	**spanning-tree mst hello-time** *seconds* **spanning-tree mst forward-time** *seconds* **spanning-tree mst max-age** *seconds*

Foundation Summary

The Foundation Summary is a collection of information that provides a convenient review of many key concepts in this chapter. If you are already comfortable with the topics in this chapter, this summary can help you recall a few details. If you just read this chapter, this review should help solidify some key facts. If you are doing your final preparation before the exam, this information is a convenient way to review the day before the exam.

RSTP port roles:

- Root Port
- Designated Port
- Alternate Port
- Backup Port

RSTP port states:

- Discarding
- Learning
- Forwarding

Table 12-3 *RSTP Configuration Commands*

Task	Command Syntax
Define an edge port	**spanning-tree portfast**
Override a port type	**spanning-tree link-type point-to-point**

STP instances involved with MST:

- **Common Spanning Tree (CST)**—Used to maintain a single loop-free topology for the entire network
- **Internal Spanning Tree (IST)**—Used like CST to maintain a single, loop-free topology *inside* an MST region
- **MST Instances (MSTIs)**—Used inside an MST region to maintain loop-free topologies for sets of mapped VLANs

Table 12-4 *MST Region Configuration Commands*

Task	Command Syntax
Enable MST on a switch	**spanning-tree mode mst**
Enter MST configuration mode	**spanning-tree mst configuration**
Name the MST region	**name** *name*
Set the configuration revision number	**revision** *version*
Map VLANs to an MST instance	**instance** *instance-id* **vlan** *vlan-list*
Confirm new MST configuration changes	**show pending**
Commit new MST changes	**exit**

Table 12-5 *MST Tuning Configuration Commands*

Task	Command Syntax
Set the Root Bridge	**spanning-tree mode mst** *instance-id* **root** {**primary** | **secondary**} [**diameter** *diameter*]
Set Bridge Priority	**spanning-tree mst** *instance-id* **priority** *bridge-priority*
Set Port Cost	**spanning-tree mst** *instance-id* **cost** *cost*
Set Port Priority	**spanning-tree mst** *instance-id* **port-priority** *port-priority*
Set STP Timers	**spanning-tree mst hello-time** *seconds* **spanning-tree mst forward-time** *seconds* **spanning-tree mst max-age** *seconds*

Q&A

The questions and scenarios in this book are more difficult than what you should experience on the actual exam. The questions do not attempt to cover more breadth or depth than the exam; however, they are designed to make sure that you know the answers. Rather than allowing you to derive the answers from clues hidden inside the questions themselves, the questions challenge your understanding and recall of the subject. Hopefully, these questions will help limit the number of exam questions on which you narrow your choices to two options and then guess.

You can find the answers to these questions in Appendix A.

1. What is synchronization in RSTP?

2. What is an Alternate Port?

3. What is the difference between an Alternate Port and a Backup Port?

4. Can a switch port be a Designated Port and be in the Discarding state?

5. Which of the following ports can participate in RSTP synchronization?

    a. Root Port

    b. Designated Port

    c. Edge Port

    d. Nonedge Port

    e. Point-to-point Port

6. What two messages must be exchanged during RSTP synchronization?

7. After an agreement message is received from a neighboring switch, how much time elapses before the port can begin forwarding? (Consider any timers that must expire or other conditions that must be met.)

8. After a switch receives news of a topology change, how long does it wait to flush entries out of its CAM table?

9. What command configures a port as an RSTP edge port?

10. Suppose interface FastEthernet 0/1 is in half-duplex mode, but you want it to be considered a point-to-point link for RSTP. What command can accomplish this?

11. Put the following in order of the number of supported STP instances, from lowest to highest:

   a. MST

   b. PVST+

   c. CST

   d. 802.1D

12. What three parameters must be configured to uniquely define an MST region?

13. What parameter does a switch examine to see if its neighbors have the same VLAN to MST instance mappings? How is that information passed among switches?

14. Which MST instance in a region corresponds to the CST of 802.1Q?

15. Which MST instance is the IST?

16. When an MST region meets a PVST+ domain, how is each MST instance propagated into PVST+?

17. Is it wise to assign VLANs to MST Instance 0? Why or why not?

18. The commands have just been entered to define an MST region on a switch. You are still at the MST configuration prompt. What command must you enter to commit the MST changes on the switch?

19. Which of the following methods can you use to assign or propagate MST configuration information to other switches?

   a. Manual configuration

   b. CDP

   c. VTP

   d. MSTP

20. A switch can interact with both 802.1D and RSTP. Can it run both PVST+ and MST simultaneously?

PART III: Layer 3 Switching

Chapter 13 Multilayer Switching

Chapter 14 Router Redundancy and Load Balancing

Chapter 15 Multicast

This part of the book covers the following BCMSN exam topics:

- Identify the specific types of Cisco route switch processors and provide implementation details.

- List and describe the operation of the key components required to implement interVLAN routing.

- Explain the types of redundancy in a multilayer switched network, including hardware and software redundancy.

- Explain how IP multicast operates on a multilayer switched network, including PIM, CGMP, and IGMP.

- Configure and verify router redundancy using HSRP, VRRP, GLBP, SRM, and SLB.

This chapter covers the following topics that you need to master for the CCNP BCMSN exam:

- **InterVLAN Routing**—This section discusses how you can use a routing function with a switch to forward packets between VLANs.

- **Multilayer Switching with CEF**—This section discusses Cisco Express Forwarding (CEF) and how it is implemented on Catalyst switches. CEF forwards or routes packets in hardware at a high throughput.

- **Troubleshooting Multilayer Switching**—This section provides a brief summary of the commands that can verify the configuration and operation of InterVLAN routing, CEF, and fallback bridging.

CHAPTER 13

Multilayer Switching

Chapter 3 presented a functional overview of how multilayer switching (MLS) is performed at Layers 3 and 4. The actual MLS process can take two forms—InterVLAN routing and Cisco Express Forwarding (CEF). This chapter expands on multilayer switch operation by discussing both of these topics in greater detail.

"Do I Know This Already?" Quiz

The purpose of the "Do I Know This Already?" quiz is to help you decide what parts of this chapter to use. If you already intend to read the entire chapter, you do not necessarily need to answer these questions now.

The quiz, derived from the major sections in the "Foundation Topics" portion of the chapter, helps you determine how to spend your limited study time.

Table 13-1 outlines the major topics discussed in this chapter and the "Do I Know This Already?" quiz questions that correspond to those topics.

Table 13-1 *"Do I Know This Already?" Foundation Topics Section-to-Question Mapping*

Foundation Topics Section	Questions Covered In This Section
InterVLAN Routing	1–5
Multilayer Switching with CEF	6–11
Troubleshooting Multilayer Switching	12

CAUTION The goal of self-assessment is to gauge your mastery of the topics in this chapter. If you do not know the answer to a question or are only partially sure of the answer, you should mark this question wrong. Giving yourself credit for an answer you correctly guess skews your self-assessment results and might give you a false sense of security.

1. Which of the following arrangements can be considered InterVLAN routing?

    a. One switch, two VLANs, one connection to a router

    b. One switch, two VLANs, two connections to a router

    c. Two switches, two VLANs, two connections to a router

    d. All of the above

2. How many interfaces are needed in a "router on a stick" implementation for InterVLAN routing among four VLANs?

    a. 1

    b. 2

    c. 4

    d. Cannot be determined

3. Which of the following commands configures a switch port for Layer 2 operation?

    a. **switchport**

    b. **no switchport**

    c. **ip address 192.168.199.1 255.255.255.0**

    d. **no ip address**

4. Which of the following commands configures a switch port for Layer 3 operation?

    a. **switchport**

    b. **no switchport**

    c. **ip address 192.168.199.1 255.255.255.0**

    d. **no ip address**

5. Which one of the following interfaces is an SVI?

    a. **interface fastethernet 0/1**

    b. **interface gigabit 0/1**

    c. **interface vlan 1**

    d. **interface svi 1**

6. What information must be learned before CEF can forward packets?

   a. The source and destination of the first packet in a traffic flow

   b. The MAC addresses of both the source and destination

   c. The contents of the routing table

   d. The outbound port of the first packet in a flow

7. Which of the following best defines an adjacency?

   a. Two switches connected by a common link

   b. Two contiguous routes in the FIB

   c. Two multilayer switches connected by a common link

   d. The MAC address of a host is known

8. Assume CEF is active on a switch. What happens to a packet that arrives needing fragmentation?

   a. The packet is switched by CEF and kept intact.

   b. The packet is fragmented by CEF.

   c. The packet is dropped.

   d. The packet is sent to the Layer 3 engine.

9. Suppose a host sends a packet to a destination IP address, and the CEF-based switch does not yet have a valid MAC address for the destination. How is the ARP entry (MAC address) of the next-hop destination in the FIB obtained?

   a. The sending host must send an ARP request for it.

   b. The Layer 3 forwarding engine (CEF hardware) must send an ARP request for it.

   c. CEF must wait until the Layer 3 engine sends an ARP request for it.

   d. All packets to the destination are dropped.

10. During a packet rewrite, what happens to the source MAC address?

   a. There is no change.

   b. It is changed to the destination MAC address.

   c. It is changed to the MAC address of the outbound Layer 3 switch interface.

   d. It is changed to the MAC address of the next-hop destination.

11. What Spanning Tree Protocol is used for fallback bridging?

    a. 802.1D

    b. IBM STP

    c. PVST+

    d. VLAN-bridge

12. What command can you use to view the CEF FIB table contents?

    a. **show fib**

    b. **show ip cef fib**

    c. **show ip cef**

    d. **show fib-table**

You can find the answers to the "Do I Know This Already?" quiz in Appendix A, "Answers to Chapter 'Do I Know This Already?' Quizzes and Q&A Sections." The suggested choices for your next step are as follows:

- **10 or less overall score**—Read the entire chapter. This includes the "Foundation Topics," "Foundation Summary," and "Q&A" sections.

- **11 or 12 overall score**—If you want more review on these topics, skip to the "Foundation Summary" section and then go to the "Q&A" section at the end of the chapter. Otherwise, move to Chapter 14, "Router Redundancy and Load Balancing."

Foundation Topics

InterVLAN Routing

Recall that a Layer 2 network is defined as a broadcast domain. A Layer 2 network can also exist as a VLAN inside one or more switches. VLANs are essentially isolated from each other so that packets in one VLAN cannot cross into another VLAN.

To transport packets between VLANs, you must use a Layer 3 device. Traditionally, this has been a router's function. The router must have a physical or logical connection to each VLAN so that it can forward packets between them. This is known as *interVLAN routing*.

InterVLAN routing can be performed by an external router that connects to each of the VLANs on a switch. Separate physical connections can be used, or the router can access each of the VLANs through a single trunk link. Part A of Figure 13-1 illustrates this concept. The external router can also connect to the switch through a single trunk link, carrying all the necessary VLANs, as illustrated in Part B of Figure 13-1. Part B illustrates what is commonly referred to as a "router on a stick" or a "one-armed router" because the router needs only a single interface to do its job.

Finally, Part C of Figure 13-1 shows how the routing and switching functions can be combined into one device—a multilayer switch. No external router is needed.

Figure 13-1   *Examples of InterVLAN Routing Connections*

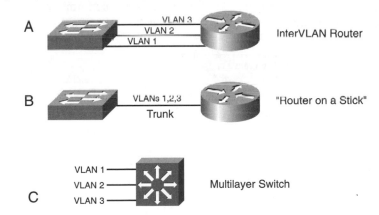

Types of Interfaces

Multilayer switches can perform both Layer 2 switching and interVLAN routing, as appropriate. Layer 2 switching occurs between interfaces that are assigned to Layer 2 VLANs or Layer 2 trunks. Layer 3 switching can occur between any type of interface, as long as the interface can have a Layer 3 address assigned to it.

Like a router, a multilayer switch can assign a Layer 3 address to a physical interface. It can also assign a Layer 3 address to a logical interface that represents an entire VLAN. This is known as a *Switched Virtual Interface*.

Configuring InterVLAN Routing

InterVLAN routing first requires that routing be enabled for the Layer 3 protocol. In addition, you must configure static routes or a dynamic routing protocol. These topics are fully covered in the BSCI course.

Because a multilayer switch supports many different types of interfaces for Layer 2 or Layer 3 switching, you must define each interface on a switch that will be used. By default, every switch port on a Catalyst 2950, 3550, or 4500 is a Layer 2 interface, whereas every switch port on a Catalyst 6500 (Native IOS) is a Layer 3 interface. If another type or mode is needed, you must explicitly configure it. A port is either in the Layer 2 or Layer 3 mode, depending on the use of the **switchport** configuraton command. Figure 13-2 shows how the different types of interface modes can be used within a single switch.

Layer 2 Port Configuration

By default, all switch ports on Catalyst 2950, 3550, and 4500 platforms operate in the Layer 2 mode. If you need to reconfigure a port for Layer 2 functionality, use the following command sequence:

```
Switch(config)# interface type mod/num
Switch(config-if)# switchport
```

The **switchport** command puts the port in Layer 2 mode. Then, you can use other **switchport** command keywords to configure trunking, access VLANs, and so on. Figure 13-2 shows several Layer 2 ports, each assigned to a specific VLAN. A Layer 2 port can also act as a trunk, transporting multiple VLANs.

Figure 13-2 *Catalyst Switch with Various Types of Ports*

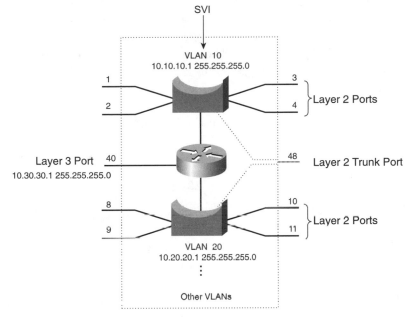

Layer 3 Port Configuration

Physical switch ports can also operate as Layer 3 interfaces, where a Layer 3 network address is assigned and routing can occur. Figure 13-2 shows an example of this. By default, all switch ports on the Catalyst 6500 (native IOS) platform operate in the Layer 3 mode. For Layer 3 functionality, you must explicitly configure switch ports with the following command sequence.

```
Switch(config)# interface type mod/num
Switch(config-if)# no switchport
Switch(config-if)# ip address ip address mask [secondary]
```

The **no switchport** command takes the port out of Layer 2 operation. You can then assign a network address to the port, as you would to a router interface.

> **NOTE**   Keep in mind that a Layer 3 port assigns a network address to one specific physical interface. If using EtherChannel, it too can become a Layer 3 port. In that case, the network address is assigned to the **port-channel** interface and not to the individual links within the channel.

SVI Port Configuration

On a multilayer switch, you can also enable Layer 3 functionality for an entire VLAN on the switch. This allows a network address to be assigned to a logical interface—that of the VLAN itself. This is useful when the switch has many ports assigned to a common VLAN, and routing is needed in and out of that VLAN. Figure 13-2 shows how an IP address is applied to the Switched Virtual Interface (SVI) called VLAN 10. Notice that the SVI itself has no physical connection to the outside world; to reach the outside, VLAN 10 must extend through a Layer 2 port or trunk.

The logical Layer 3 interface is known as an *SVI*. However, when it is configured, it uses the much more intuitive interface name **vlan** *vlan-id*, as if the VLAN itself is a physical interface. First, define or identify the VLAN interface, and then assign any Layer 3 functionality to it with the following configuration commands:

```
Switch(config)# interface vlan vlan-id
Switch(config-if)# ip address ip-address mask [secondary]
```

The VLAN must be defined and active on the switch before the SVI can be used. Make sure the new VLAN interface is also enabled with the **no shutdown** interface configuration command.

> **NOTE**   The VLAN and the SVI are configured separately, even though they interoperate. Creating or configuring the SVI doesn't create or configure the VLAN. You must still define each one independently.

Multilayer Switching with CEF

Catalyst switches can use several methods to forward packets based on Layer 3 and 4 information. The current generation of Catalyst multilayer switches uses the efficient Cisco Express Forwarding (CEF) method. This section describes the progression of multilayer switching and discusses CEF in detail. Although CEF is easy to configure and use, the underlying switching mechanisms are more involved and should be understood.

Traditional MLS Overview

Multilayer switching began as a dual effort between a route processor (RP) and a switching engine (SE). The basic idea is to "route once, and switch many." The RP receives the first packet of a new traffic flow between two hosts, as usual. A routing decision is made, and the packet is forwarded on toward the destination.

To participate, the SE must know the identity of each RP. The SE can then listen in to the first packet going to the router and then going away from the router. If the SE can switch the packet in both directions, it can learn a "shortcut path" so that subsequent packets of the same flow can be switched directly to the destination port without passing through the RP.

This technique is also known as *NetFlow switching* or *route cache switching*. Traditionally, NetFlow switching was performed on Cisco hardware, such as the Catalyst 6000 Supervisor 1/1a and Multilayer Switch Feature Card (MSFC), Catalyst 5500 with a Route Switch Module (RSM), Route Switch Feature Card (RSFC), or external router, and so on. Basically, the hardware consisted of an independent RP component and a NetFlow-capable SE component.

CEF Overview

NetFlow switching has given way to a more efficient form of multilayer switching—Cisco Express Forwarding (CEF). Cisco developed CEF for its line of routers, offering high-performance packet forwarding through the use of dynamic lookup tables.

CEF has also been carried over to the Catalyst switching platforms. The Catalyst 6500 Supervisor 720 (with an integrated MSFC3), Catalyst 6500 Supervisor 2/MSFC2 combination, Catalyst 4500 Supervisor III and IV, and the Catalyst 3550 families all perform CEF in hardware. CEF runs by default, taking advantage of the specialized hardware.

A CEF-based multilayer switch consists of two basic functional blocks, as shown in Figure 13-3: The *Layer 3 Engine* is involved in building routing information that the *Layer 3 Forwarding Engine* can use to switch packets in hardware.

Figure 13-3   *Packet Flow Through a CEF-Based Multilayer Switch*

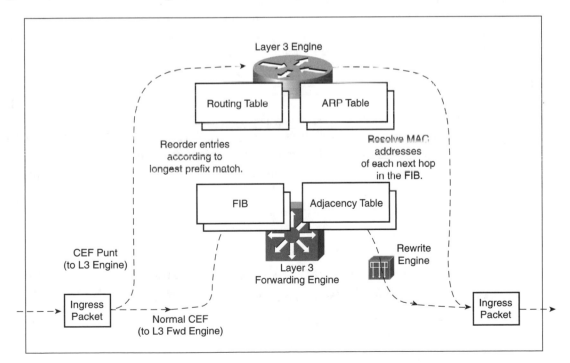

Forwarding Information Base (FIB)

The Layer 3 engine (essentially a router) maintains routing information, whether from static routes or dynamic routing protocols. Basically, the routing table is reformatted into an ordered list with the most specific route first, for each IP destination subnet in the table. The new format is called a Forwarding Information Base (FIB) and contains routing or forwarding information that the network prefix can reference.

In other words, a route to 10.1.0.0/16 might be contained in the FIB, along with routes to 10.1.1.0/24 and 10.1.1.128/25, if those exist. Notice that these examples are increasingly more specific subnets. In the FIB, these would be ordered with the most specific, or *longest match,* first, followed by less specific subnets. When the switch receives a packet, it can easily examine the destination address and find the longest match entry in the FIB.

The FIB also contains the next-hop address for each entry. When a longest match entry is found in the FIB, the Layer 3 next-hop address is found, too.

You might be surprised to know that the FIB also contains host route (subnet mask 255.255.255.255) entries. These are not normally found in the routing table unless they are advertised or manually configured. Host routes are maintained in the FIB for the most efficient routing lookup to directly connected or *adjacent* hosts.

Like a routing table, the FIB is dynamic in nature. When the Layer 3 engine sees a change in the routing topology, it sends an update to the FIB. Any time the routing table receives a change to a route prefix or the next-hop address, the FIB receives the same change. Also, if a next-hop address is changed or aged out of the Address Resolution Protocol (ARP) table, the FIB must reflect the same change.

After the FIB is built, packets can be forwarded along the bottom dashed path in Figure 13-3. This follows the hardware switching process, where no "expensive" or time-consuming operations are needed. At times, a packet cannot be switched in hardware, according to the FIB. Packets are then marked as "CEF punt" and are immediately sent to the Layer 3 engine for further processing, as shown in the top dashed path in Figure 13-3. Some of the conditions that cause this are as follows:

- An entry cannot be located in the FIB.
- The FIB table is full.
- The IP Time To Live (TTL) has expired.
- The maximum transmission unit (MTU) is exceeded, and the packet must be fragmented.
- An Internet Control Message Protocol (ICMP) redirect is involved.
- The encapsulation type is not supported.

- Tunneled packets, where a compression or encryption operation is needed.

- An access list with the **log** option is triggered.

- A Network Address Translation (NAT) operation must be performed (except on the Catalyst 6500 Supervisor 720, which can handle NAT in hardware).

CEF operations can be handled on a single hardware platform, as with the Catalyst 3550 switch. The FIB is generated and contained centrally in the switch. CEF can also be optimized through the use of specialized forwarding hardware, using the following techniques:

- **Accelerated CEF (aCEF)**—CEF is distributed across multiple Layer 3 forwarding engines, typically located on Catalyst 6500 line cards. These engines do not have the capability to store and use the entire FIB, so only a portion of the FIB is downloaded to them at any time. This functions as a FIB "cache," containing entries that are likely to be used again. If FIB entries are not found in the cache, requests are sent to the Layer 3 engine for more FIB information. The net result is that CEF is accelerated on the line cards, but not necessarily at a sustained wirespeed rate.

- **Distributed CEF (dCEF)**—CEF can be completely distributed among multiple Layer 3 forwarding engines for even greater performance. Because the FIB is self-contained for complete Layer 3 forwarding, it can be replicated across any number of independent Layer 3 forwarding engines. The Catalyst 6500 has line cards that support dCEF, each with its own FIB table and forwarding engine. A central Layer 3 engine (the MSFC2, for example) maintains the routing table and generates the FIB, which is then dynamically downloaded in full to each of the line cards.

Adjacency Table

A router normally maintains a routing table containing Layer 3 network and next hop information, and an ARP table containing Layer 3 to Layer 2 address mapping. These tables are kept independently.

Recall that the FIB keeps the Layer 3 next-hop address for each entry. To streamline packet forwarding even more, the FIB has corresponding Layer 2 information for every next-hop entry. This portion of the FIB is called the *adjacency table*, consisting of the MAC addresses of nodes that can be reached in a single Layer 2 hop.

The adjacency table information is built from the ARP table. As a next-hop address receives a valid ARP entry, the adjacency table is updated. If an ARP entry does not exist, the FIB entry is marked as "CEF glean." This means that the Layer 3 forwarding engine can't forward the packet in hardware, due to the missing Layer 2 next-hop address. The packet is sent to the Layer 3 engine so that it can generate an ARP request and receive an ARP reply. This is known as the "CEF glean" state, where the Layer 3 engine must glean the next-hop destination's MAC address.

During the time that a FIB entry is in the CEF glean state waiting for the ARP resolution, subsequent packets to that host are immediately dropped so that the input queues do not fill and the Layer 3 engine does not become too busy worrying about the need for duplicate ARP requests. This is called *ARP throttling* or *throttling adjacency*. If an ARP reply is not received in two seconds, the throttling is released so that another ARP request can be triggered. Otherwise, after an ARP reply is received, the throttling is released, the FIB entry can be completed, and packets can be forwarded completely in hardware.

Packet Rewrite

After a multilayer switch finds valid entries in the FIB and adjacency tables, a packet is almost ready to be forwarded. One step remains—the packet header information must be rewritten. Keep in mind that multilayer switching occurs as quick table lookups, to find the next-hop address and the outbound switch port. The packet is untouched, still having the original destination MAC address of the switch itself. The IP header must also be adjusted, as if a traditional router had done the forwarding.

The switch has an additional functional block that performs a packet rewrite in real time. The packet rewrite engine (as shown in Figure 13-3) makes the following changes to the packet just prior to forwarding:

- **Layer 2 destination address**—Changed to the next-hop device's MAC address
- **Layer 2 source address**—Changed to the outbound Layer 3 switch interface's MAC address
- **Layer 3 IP Time To Live (TTL)**—Decremented by one, as one router hop has just occurred
- **Layer 3 IP checksum**—Recalculated to include changes to the IP header
- **Layer 2 frame checksum**—Recalculated to include changes to the Layer 2 and Layer 3 headers

A traditional router would normally make the same changes to each packet. The multilayer switch must act as if a traditional router were being used, making identical changes. However, the multilayer switch can do this very efficiently with dedicated packet rewrite hardware and address information obtained from table lookups.

Configuring CEF

CEF is enabled on all CEF-capable Catalyst switches by default. In fact, the Catalyst 3550, 4500, and 6500 (with a Supervisor 720 and its integrated MSFC3 or a Supervisor 2 and MSFC2 combination) all run CEF inherently, so CEF can never be disabled.

Fallback Bridging

For protocols that can't be routed or switched by CEF, a technique known as *fallback bridging* is used. Example protocols are IPX and AppleTalk, which are routable but not supported by CEF, as well as SNA and LAT, which are not routable at all. To summarize, each SVI associated with a VLAN where nonroutable protocols are being used is assigned to a bridge group. Packets that cannot be routed from one VLAN to another are transparently bridged instead, as long as the two VLANs belong to the same bridge group.

> **NOTE**   Only the Catalyst 3550 offers fallback bridging, as it can CEF switch IP packets but no others. The Catalyst 4500 and 6500 (all Supervisor models running Cisco IOS Software) can also CEF switch IP but can handle other routable protocols more slowly with their Layer 3 engines. Those two platforms have no need for fallback bridging.

Bridge groups used in fallback bridging do not interact with normal Layer 2 switching (also using bridging). They do use a special Spanning Tree Protocol to maintain loop-free fallback bridging, but these bridge protocol data units (BPDUs) are not exchanged with other 802.1D, Rapid Spanning Tree Protocol (RSTP), or Multiple Spanning Tree (MST) BPDUs on VLANs. Instead, the *VLAN-bridge* STP is used, with one instance per fallback bridge group.

To configure fallback bridging, first decide which VLANs have traffic that CEF cannot route. Begin by enabling a fallback bridge group and its instance of the VLAN bridge STP:

```
Switch(config)# bridge-group bridge-group protocol vlan-bridge
```

Next, for each VLAN SVI where nonroutable traffic will be bridged, assign it to the appropriate bridge group:

```
Switch(config)# interface vlan vlan-id
Switch(config-if)# bridge-group bridge-group
```

You can configure up to 31 different fallback bridge groups on a switch. Although the VLAN bridge STP instance running on each bridge group does not interact with normal 802.1D STP, it does behave similarly. For example, you can configure the bridge priority, port priority and cost, Hello timer, Forward Delay timer, and Max Age timer. These parameters should all look familiar, as they are used in the 802.1D STP. Rather than using the **spanning-tree** command to adjust the parameter values, you must adjust them according to the bridge group number with the **bridge-group** *bridge-group* command keywords.

Verifying Multilayer Switching

The multilayer switching topics presented in this chapter are not difficult to configure. However, you might have a need to verify how a switch is forwarding packets. In particular, the following sections discuss the commands that you can use to verify the operation of InterVLAN routing, CEF, and fallback bridging.

InterVLAN Routing

To verify the configuration of a Layer 2 port, you can use the following EXEC command:

```
Switch# show interface type mod/num switchport
```

The output from this command displays the access VLAN or the trunking mode and native VLAN. The *administrative* modes reflect what has been configured for the port, while the *operational* modes show the port's active status.

You can use this same command to verify the configuration of a Layer 3 or routed port. In this case, you should see the switchport (Layer 2) mode disabled, as in Example 13-1.

Example 13-1 *Verifying Configuration of a Layer 3 Switch Port*

```
Switch# show interface fastethernet 0/16 switchport
Name: Fa0/16
Switchport: Disabled
```

To see the physical interface's status, use the command without the **switchport** keyword. To see a summary listing of all interfaces, you can use the **show interface status** command.

To verify the configuration of an SVI, you can use the following EXEC command:

```
Switch# show interface vlan vlan-id
```

The VLAN interface should be up with the line protocol also up. If this is not true, either the interface is disabled with the **shutdown** command, or the VLAN itself has not been defined on the switch. Use the **show vlan** command to see a list of configured VLANs.

Example 13-2 shows the output produced from the **show vlan** command. Notice that each defined VLAN is shown, along with the switch ports that are assigned to it.

Example 13-2 *Displaying a List of Configured VLANs*

```
Switch# show vlan

VLAN Name                             Status    Ports
---- -------------------------------- --------- -------------------------------
1    default                          active    Fa0/5, Fa0/6, Fa0/7, Fa0/8
                                                Fa0/9, Fa0/10, Fa0/11, Fa0/12
                                                Fa0/13, Fa0/14, Fa0/15, Fa0/17
                                                Fa0/18, Fa0/19, Fa0/20, Fa0/21
                                                Fa0/22, Fa0/23, Fa0/24, Fa0/25
                                                Fa0/26, Fa0/27, Fa0/28, Fa0/29
                                                Fa0/30, Fa0/32, Fa0/33, Fa0/34
                                                Fa0/36, Fa0/37, Fa0/38, Fa0/39
                                                Fa0/41, Fa0/42, Fa0/43, Fa0/44
                                                Fa0/45, Fa0/46, Fa0/47, Gi0/1
                                                Gi0/2
2    VLAN0002                         active    Fa0/40
5    VLAN0005                         active
10   VLAN0010                         active
11   VLAN0011                         active    Fa0/31
12   VLAN0012                         active
99   VLAN0099                         active    Fa0/35
```

CEF

CEF operation depends on the correct routing information being generated and downloaded to the Layer 3 forwarding engine hardware. This information is contained in the FIB and is dynamically maintained. To view the entire FIB, use the following EXEC command:

```
Switch# show ip cef
```

Example 13-3 shows sample output from this command.

Example 13-3 *Displaying the FIB Contents for a Switch*

```
Switch# show ip cef
Prefix               Next Hop          Interface
0.0.0.0/32           receive
192.168.199.0/24     attached          Vlan1
192.168.199.0/32     receive
192.168.199.1/32     receive
192.168.199.2/32     192.168.199.2     Vlan1
192.168.199.255/32   receive
```

On this switch, only VLAN 1 has been configured with the IP address 192.168.199.1 255.255.255.0. Notice several things about the FIB for such a small configuration:

■ **0.0.0.0/32**—A FIB entry has been reserved for the default route. No next hop is defined, so the entry is marked "receive" so that packets will be sent to the Layer 3 engine for further processing.

■ **192.168.199.0/24**—The subnet assigned to the VLAN 1 interface is given its own entry. This is marked "attached" because it is directly connected to an SVI, VLAN 1.

■ **192.168.199.0/32**—A FIB entry has been reserved for the exact network address. This is used to contain an adjacency for packets sent to the network address, if the network is not directly connected. In this case, there is no adjacency, and the entry is marked "receive."

■ **192.168.199.1/32**—An entry has been reserved for the VLAN 1 SVI's IP address. Notice that this is a host route (/32). Packets destined for the VLAN 1 interface must be dealt with internally, so the entry is marked "receive."

■ **192.168.199.2/32**—This is an entry for a neighboring multilayer switch, found on the VLAN 1 interface. The next-hop field has been filled in with the same IP address, denoting that an adjacency is available.

■ **192.168.199.255/32**—A FIB entry has been reserved for the 192.168.199.0 subnet's broadcast address. The route processor (Layer 3 engine) handles all directed broadcasts, so the entry is marked "receive."

To see complete FIB and adjacency table information for a specific interface, use the following EXEC command:

```
Switch# show ip cef type mod/num [detail]
```

To get an idea of the number of packets being referred to the Layer 3 engine (not hardware CEF switched), use the following EXEC command:

```
Switch# show cef not-cef-switched
```

Counters are shown for these CEF punt reasons:

■ **No_adj**—No adjacency entry is available for the next hop.

■ **No_encap**—A frame needs further processing for ARP resolution.

■ **Unsupp'ted**—The frame type is unsupported.

■ **Redirect**—An ICMP redirect is involved.

- **Receive**—Packets are received and sent directly to the L3 engine.

- **Options**—The IP options are being used.

- **Access**—An access list needs further processing.

- **Frag**—Fragmentation is needed.

Fallback Bridging

To verify the operation of fallback bridging, you can use the following EXEC commands:

```
Switch# show bridge group
Switch# show bridge bridge-group [verbose]
```

The first command shows a summary of all active fallback bridge groups, along with their STP states. The second command displays the bridging table contents for a specific fallback bridge group.

Foundation Summary

The Foundation Summary is a collection of information that provides a convenient review of many key concepts in this chapter. If you are already comfortable with the topics in this chapter, this summary can help you recall a few details. If you just read this chapter, this review should help solidify some key facts. If you are doing your final preparation before the exam, this information is a convenient way to review the day before the exam.

Table 13-2 *InterVLAN Routing Configuration Commands*

Task	Command Syntax
Put a port into Layer 2 mode.	**switchport**
Put a port into Layer 3 mode.	**no switchport**
Define an SVI.	**interface vlan** *vlan-id*

Components of CEF:

- **Forwarding Information Base (FIB)**—Contains routing and next-hop information; lookups are performed according to longest match IP prefix.

- **Adjacency table**—Contains Layer 2 address information for next-hop FIB entries that are one hop away.

- **Packet rewrite**—Hardware dedicated to rewriting the Layer 2 and Layer 3 header information of outbound packets after the forwarding decisions have been made.

Table 13-3 *Fallback Bridging Configuration Commands*

Task	Command Syntax
Define a fallback bridge group.	**bridge-group** *bridge-group* **protocol vlan-bridge**
Assign an interface to a bridge group.	**bridge-group** *bridge-group*

Table 13-4 *Multilayer Switching Verification Commands*

Task	Command Syntax
Show a Layer 2 port status.	**show interface** *type mod/num* **switchport**
Show a Layer 3 port status.	**show interface** *type mod/num*
Show an SVI status.	**show interface vlan** *vlan-id*
View the FIB contents.	**show ip cef**
View FIB and adjacency information for an interface.	**show ip cef** *type mod/num* [**detail**]
View counters for packets not switched by CEF.	**show cef not-cef-switched**
Show fallback bridge group status.	**show bridge group**
Show fallback bridging table contents.	**show bridge** *bridge-group*

Q&A

The questions and scenarios in this book are more difficult than what you should experience on the actual exam. The questions do not attempt to cover more breadth or depth than the exam; however, they are designed to make sure that you know the answers. Rather than allowing you to derive the answers from clues hidden inside the questions themselves, the questions challenge your understanding and recall of the subject. Hopefully, these questions will help limit the number of exam questions on which you narrow your choices to two options and then guess.

You can find the answers to these questions in Appendix A.

1. What might you need to implement interVLAN routing?

2. Can interVLAN routing be performed over a single trunk link?

3. To configure an SVI, what commands are needed?

4. What command can verify the VLAN assignments on a Layer 2 port?

5. A switch has the following interface configurations in its running configuration:

    ```
    interface fastethernet 0/1
    switchport access vlan 5
    interface vlan 5
    ip address 192.168.10.1 255.255.255.0
    no shutdown
    ```

    What is necessary for packets to get from the FastEthernet interface to the VLAN 5 SVI?

6. What is the source of FIB information?

7. How often is the FIB updated?

8. What is meant by the term "CEF punt?"

9. What happens to the FIB when distributed CEF (dCEF) is used?

10. What happens during a "CEF glean" process?

11. What does a multilayer switch do to the IP TTL value just before a packet is forwarded?

12. What is fallback bridging?

13. Is it possible for an SVI to go down? If so, what are the reasons?

This chapter covers the following topics that you need to master for the CCNP BCMSN exam:

- **Router Redundancy**—This section discusses three protocols that are available on Catalyst switches to provide redundant router or gateway addresses. The protocols include HSRP, VRRP, and GLBP.

- **Server Load Balancing**—This section covers a technique that provides a virtual server address as a front end to an entire logical server farm. The server farm is composed of one or more real or physical servers. Client connections to the virtual server address are load balanced to the real servers.

- **Verifying Redundancy and Load Balancing**—This section provides a brief summary of the commands that verify the configuration and operation of HSRP, VRRP, GLBP, and SLB.

CHAPTER 14

Router Redundancy and Load Balancing

A multilayer switch can provide routing functions for devices on a network, as described in Chapter 13, "Multilayer Switching." If that switch happens to fail, clients have no way to have their traffic forwarded; their gateway has gone away.

Other multilayer switches can be added into the network to provide redundancy in the form of redundant router or gateway addresses. This chapter describes the protocols that can be used for redundant router addresses, load balancing across multiple routers, and load balancing into a server farm.

"Do I Know This Already?" Quiz

The purpose of the "Do I Know This Already?" quiz is to help you decide what parts of this chapter to use. If you already intend to read the entire chapter, you do not necessarily need to answer these questions now.

The quiz, derived from the major sections in the "Foundation Topics" portion of the chapter, helps you determine how to spend your limited study time.

Table 14-1 outlines the major topics discussed in this chapter and the "Do I Know This Already?" quiz questions that correspond to those topics.

Table 14-1 *"Do I Know This Already?" Foundation Topics Section-to-Question Mapping*

Foundation Topics Section	Questions Covered in This Section
Router Redundancy: HSRP	1–5
Router Redundancy: VRRP	6–7
Router Redundancy: GLBP	8–10
Server Load Balancing	11–12

CAUTION The goal of self-assessment is to gauge your mastery of the topics in this chapter. If you do not know the answer to a question or are only partially sure of the answer, you should mark this question wrong. Giving yourself credit for an answer you correctly guess skews your self-assessment results and might give you a false sense of security.

1. Which one of the following do multilayer switches share when running HSRP?

    a. Routing tables

    b. ARP cache

    c. CAM table

    d. IP address

2. What HSRP group uses the MAC address 0000.0c07.ac11?

    a. Group 0

    b. Group 7

    c. Group 11

    d. Group 17

3. Two routers are configured for an HSRP group. One router uses the default HSRP priority. What priority should be assigned to the other router to make it more likely to be the active router?

    a. 1

    b. 100

    c. 200

    d. 500

4. How many routers are in the Standby state in an HSRP group?

    a. 0

    b. 1

    c. 2

    d. All but the active router

5. A multilayer switch is configured as follows:

```
interface fastethernet 1/1
no switchport
ip address 192.168.199.3 255.255.255.0
standby 1 ip 192.168.199.2
```

Which IP address should a client PC use as its default gateway?

a. 192.168.199.1

b. 192.168.199.2

c. 192.168.199.3

d. Any of the above

6. Which one of the following is based on an IETF RFC standard?

a. HSRP

b. VRRP

c. GLBP

d. STP

7. What VRRP group uses the virtual MAC address 0000.5e00.01ff?

a. Group 0

b. Group 1

c. Group 255

d. Group 94

8. Which one of the following protocols is the best choice for load balancing redundant gateways?

a. HSRP

b. VRRP

c. GLBP

d. GVRP

9. Which one of the following GLBP functions answers ARP requests?

a. AVF

b. VARP

c. AVG

d. MVR

10. By default, which of the following virtual MAC address will be sent to the next client that looks for the virtual gateway?

    a. The GLBP interface's MAC address

    b. The next virtual MAC address in the sequence

    c. The virtual MAC address of the least-used router

    d. 0000.0c07.ac00

11. In SLB, with what must a virtual server be linked?

    a. A virtual address pool

    b. A server farm

    c. A real server

    d. A list of clients

12. In SLB, what command specifies the IP address of a server in a server farm?

    a. server-address 192.168.199.1

    b. ip slb server 192.168.199.1

    c. real 192.168.199.1

    d. server-farm 192.168.199.1

The answers to the "Do I Know This Already?" quiz are found in Appendix A, "Answers to Chapter 'Do I Know This Already?' Quizzes and Q&A Sections." The suggested choices for your next step are as follows:

■ **10 or less overall score**—Read the entire chapter. This includes the "Foundation Topics," "Foundation Summary," and "Q&A" sections.

■ **11 or 12 overall score**—If you want more review on these topics, skip to the "Foundation Summary" section, and then go to the "Q&A" section at the end of the chapter. Otherwise, move to Chapter 15, "Multicast."

Foundation Topics

Router Redundancy in Multilayer Switching

Multilayer switches can act as IP gateways for connected hosts by providing gateway addresses at VLAN SVIs and Layer 3 physical interfaces. These switches can also participate in routing protocols, just as traditional routers do.

For high availability, multilayer switches should offer a means to prevent one switch (gateway) failure from isolating an entire VLAN. This chapter discusses several approaches to providing router redundancy including the following:

- Hot Standby Router Protocol (HSRP)
- Virtual Router Redundancy Protocol (VRRP)
- Gateway Load Balancing Protocol (GLBP)

Packet Forwarding Review

When a host must communicate with a device on its local subnet, it can generate an Address Resolution Protocol (ARP) request, wait for the ARP reply, and exchange packets directly. However, if the far end is located on a different subnet, the host must rely on an intermediate system (a router, for example) to relay packets to and from that subnet.

A host identifies its nearest router, also known as the default gateway or next hop, by its IP address. If the host understands something about routing, it recognizes that all packets destined off-net must be sent to the gateway's MAC address, rather than the far end's MAC address. Therefore, the host first sends an ARP request to find the gateway's IP address. Then, packets can be relayed to the gateway directly without having to look for ARP entries for individual destinations.

If the host is not so savvy about routing, it might still generate ARP requests for every off-net destination, hoping that someone will answer. Obviously, the off-net destinations cannot answer because they never receive the ARP requests; these requests are not forwarded across subnets. Rather, you can configure the gateway to provide a proxy ARP function so that it will reply to ARP requests with its own MAC address, as if the destination itself had responded.

Now the issue of gateway availability becomes important. If the gateway router for a subnet or VLAN goes down, packets have no way to be forwarded off the local subnet. Several protocols are available that allow multiple routing devices to share a common gateway address so that if one goes down, another can pick up the active gateway role. The sections that follow describe these protocols.

Hot Standby Router Protocol (HSRP)

HSRP is a Cisco-proprietary protocol developed to allow several routers (or multilayer switches) to appear as a single gateway address. RFC 2281 describes this protocol in more detail.

Basically, each of the routers that provides redundancy for a given gateway address is assigned to a common HSRP group. One router is elected as the primary, or *active,* HSRP router, another is elected as the *standby* HSRP router, and all the others remain in the *listen* HSRP state. The routers exchange HSRP hello messages at regular intervals, so they can remain aware of each other's existence, as well as that of the active router.

> **NOTE**   HSRP sends its hello messages to the multicast destination 224.0.0.2 ("all routers") using UDP port 1985.

An HSRP group can be assigned an arbitrary group number, from 0 to 255. If you configure HSRP groups on several VLAN interfaces, it can be handy to make the group number the same as the VLAN number. However, most Catalyst switches support only up to 16 unique HSRP group numbers. If you have more than 16 VLANs, you will quickly run out of group numbers. An alternative is to make the group number the same (that is, 1) for every VLAN interface. This is perfectly valid because the HSRP groups are only locally significant on an interface. HSRP Group 1 on interface VLAN 10 is unique from HSRP Group 1 on interface VLAN 11.

HSRP Router Election

HSRP election is based on a priority value (0 to 255) that is configured on each router in the group. By default, the priority is 100. The router with the highest priority value (255 is highest) becomes the active router for the group. If all router priorities are equal or set to the default value, the router with the highest IP address on the HSRP interface becomes the active router. To set the priority, use the following interface configuration command:

```
Switch(config-if)# standby group priority priority
```

When HSRP is configured on an interface, the router progresses through a series of states before becoming active. This forces a router to listen for others in a group and see where it fits into the pecking order. The HSRP state sequence is Disabled, Init, Listen, Speak, Standby, and, finally, Active.

Only the standby (second highest priority) router monitors the hello messages from the active router. By default, hellos are sent every 3 seconds. If hellos are missed for the duration of the *holdtime* timer (default 10 seconds, or 3 times the hello timer), the active router is presumed down. The standby router is then clear to assume the active role. If other routers are sitting in the Listen state, the next-highest priority router is allowed to become the new standby router. If you need to change the timer values, use the following interface configuration command:

```
Switch(config-if)# standby group timers hello holdtime
```

The holdtime should always be at least three times the hello timer. Also, if you decide to change the timers on a router, change them identically on all routers in the HSRP group.

Normally, after the active router fails and the standby becomes active, the original active router cannot immediately become active when it is restored. In other words, if a router is not already active, it cannot become active until the current active router fails—even if its priority is higher than the active router. An interesting case is when routers are just being powered up or added to a network. The first router to bring its interface up becomes the HSRP active router, even if it has the lowest priority of all.

You can configure a router to preempt or immediately take over the active role if its priority is the highest at any time. Use the following interface configuration command to allow preemption:

```
Switch(config-if)# standby group preempt [delay seconds]
```

By default, the router can preempt another immediately, without delay. You can use the **delay** keyword to force it to wait for *seconds* before becoming active. This is usually done if there are routing protocols that need time to converge.

HSRP can also use a simple cleartext authentication string as a means of preventing devices with a default configuration from participating. All routers in the group must have the same authentication string. Use the following interface configuration command to enable authentication:

```
Switch(config-if)# standby group authentication string
```

Conceding the Election

Consider an active router in an HSRP group—a group of clients send packets to it for forwarding, and it has one or more links to the rest of the world. If one of those links fails, the router remains active. If all of those links fail, the router still remains active. Sooner or later, the path to the rest of the world is either crippled or removed, and packets from the clients can no longer be forwarded.

HSRP has a mechanism to detect link failures and sway the election, giving another router an opportunity to take over the active role. When a specific interface is tracked, HSRP reduces the router's priority by a configurable amount as soon as the interface goes down. If more than one interface is tracked, the priority is reduced even more with each failed interface. To configure interface tracking, use the following interface configuration command:

```
Switch(config-if)# standby group track type mod/num decrementvalue
```

Keep in mind that the only way another router can take over the active role after interface tracking reduces the priority is if the following two conditions are met:

■ Another router now has a higher HSRP priority.

■ That same router is using **preempt** in its HSRP configuration.

Without preemption, the active role cannot be given to any other router.

HSRP Gateway Addressing

Each router in an HSRP group has its own unique IP address assigned to an interface. This address is used for all routing protocol and management traffic initiated by or destined to the router. In addition, each router has a common gateway IP address, the *virtual router* address, that is kept alive by HSRP. This address is also referred to as the *HSRP address* or the *standby address*. Clients can point to that virtual router address as their default gateway, knowing that a router always keeps that address active. Keep in mind that the actual interface address and the virtual (standby) address must be configured to be in the same IP subnet.

You can assign the HSRP address with the following interface command:

```
Switch(config-if)# standby group ip ip-address [secondary]
```

When HSRP is used on an interface that has secondary IP addresses, you can add the **secondary** keyword so that HSRP can provide a redundant secondary gateway address.

Naturally, each router keeps a unique MAC address for its interface. This MAC address is always associated with the unique IP address configured on the interface. For the virtual router address, HSRP defines a special MAC address of the form 0000.0c07.ac*xx*, where *xx* represents the HSRP group number as a two-digit hex value. For example, HSRP Group 1 appears as 0000.0c07.ac01; HSRP Group 16 appears as 0000.0c07.ac10, and so on.

Figure 14-1 shows a simple network where two multilayer switches use HSRP Group 1 to provide the redundant gateway address 192.168.1.1. Catalyst A is the active router, with priority 200, and answers the ARP request for the gateway address. Because Catalyst B is in the standby state; it is never used for traffic sent to 192.168.1.1. Instead, only Catalyst A performs the gateway routing function, and only its uplink to the access layer is utilized.

Figure 14-1 *Typical HSRP Scenario with One HSRP Group*

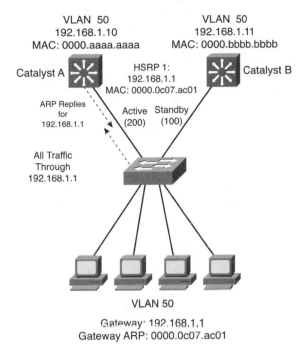

Load Balancing with HSRP

Consider a network where HSRP is used on two distribution switches to provide a redundant gateway address for access layer users. Only one of the two becomes the active HSRP router; the other remains in standby. All the users send their traffic to the active router, over the uplink to the active router. The standby router and its uplink essentially sit idle until a router failure occurs.

Load balancing traffic across two uplinks to two HSRP routers with a single HSRP group is not possible. Then, how is it possible to load balance with HSRP? The trick is to use two HSRP groups:

■   One group assigns an active router to one switch.

■   The other group assigns another active router to the other switch.

In this way, two different virtual router or gateway addresses can be used simultaneously. The rest of the trick is to make each switch function as the standby router for its partner's HSRP group. In other words, each router is active for one group and standby for the other group.

Figure 14-2 presents this scenario. Now, Catalyst A is not only the active router for HSRP Group 1 (192.168.1.1) but is also the standby router for HSRP Group 2 (192.168.1.2). Catalyst B is configured similarly, but with its roles reversed. The remaining step is to configure half of the client PCs with the HSRP Group 1 virtual router address and the other half with the Group 2 address. This makes load balancing possible and effective. Each half of the hosts uses one switch as their gateway over one uplink.

Figure 14-2 *Load Balancing with Two HSRP Groups*

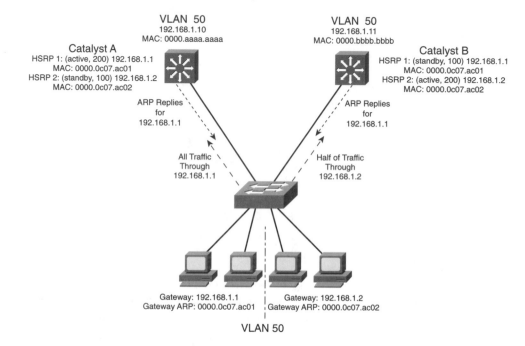

Virtual Router Redundancy Protocol (VRRP)

The Virtual Router Redundancy Protocol (VRRP) is a standards-based alternative to HSRP, defined in IETF standard RFC 2338. VRRP is so similar to HSRP, you only need to learn slightly different terminology and a couple of slight functional differences. After you understand HSRP operation and configuration, you will also understand VRRP. This section is kept brief, highlighting only the differences in the two protocols.

■   VRRP provides one redundant gateway address from a group of routers. The active router is called the *master router*, while all others are in the *backup state*. The master router is the one with the highest router priority in the VRRP group.

■   VRRP group numbers range from 0 to 255; router priorities range from 1 to 254 (254 is the highest; 100 is the default).

■ The virtual router MAC address is of the form 0000.5e00.01*xx*, where *xx* is a two-digit hex VRRP group number.

■ VRRP advertisements are sent at 1-second intervals. Backup routers can optionally learn the advertisement interval from the master router.

■ By default, all VRRP routers are configured to preempt the current master router, if their priorities are greater.

■ VRRP has no mechanism for tracking interfaces to allow more capable routers to take over the master role.

> **NOTE**   VRRP sends its advertisements to the multicast destination address 224.0.0.18 (VRRP), using IP protocol 112. VRRP was introduced in Cisco IOS Software Release 12.0(18)ST for routers. At press time, VRRP is available only for the Catalyst 6500 Supervisor 720 with Cisco IOS Software Release 12.2(14)SX.

To configure VRRP, use the following interface configuration commands documented in Table 14-2.

Table 14-2   *VRRP Configuration Commands*

Task	Command Syntax
Assign a VRRP router priority (default 100).	**vrrp** *group* **priority** *level*
Alter the advertisement timer (default 1 second).	**vrrp** *group* **timers advertise** [**msec**] *interval*
Learn the advertisement interval from the master router.	**vrrp** *group* **timers learn**
Disable preempting (default is to preempt).	**no vrrp** *group* **preempt**
Change the preempt delay (default 0 seconds).	**vrrp** *group* **preempt** [**delay** *seconds*]
Use authentication for advertisements.	**vrrp** *group* **authentication** *string*
Assign a virtual IP address.	**vrrp** *group* **ip** *ip-address* [**secondary**]

Gateway Load Balancing Protocol (GLBP)

You should now know how both HSRP and VRRP can be effective at providing a redundant gateway (virtual router) address. You can accomplish load balancing by configuring only multiple HSRP/VRRP groups to have multiple virtual router addresses. More manual configuration is needed so that the client machines are divided among the virtual routers. Each group of clients must point to the appropriate virtual router. This makes load balancing somewhat labor-intensive, having a more or less fixed, or static, behavior.

The Gateway Load Balancing Protocol (GLBP) is a Cisco-proprietary protocol designed to overcome the limitations of existing redundant router protocols. Some of the concepts are the same as HSRP/VRRP, but the terminology is different, and the behavior is much more dynamic and robust.

> **NOTE** GLBP was introduced in Cisco IOS Software Release 12.2(14)S for routers. At press time, GLBP is available only for the Catalyst 6500 Supervisor 720 with Cisco IOS Software Release 12.2(14)SX.

To provide a virtual router, multiple switches (routers) are assigned to a common GLBP group. Rather than having just one active router performing forwarding for the virtual router address, *all* routers in the group can participate and offer load balancing by forwarding a portion of the overall traffic.

The advantage is that none of the clients have to be pointed toward a specific gateway address—they can all have the same default gateway set to the virtual router IP address. The load balancing is provided completely through the use of virtual router MAC addresses in ARP replies returned to the clients. As a client sends an ARP request looking for the virtual router address, GLBP sends back an ARP reply with the virtual MAC address of a selected router in the group. The result is that all clients use the same gateway address but have differing MAC addresses for it.

Active Virtual Gateway

The trick behind this load balancing lies in the GLBP group. One router is elected the *active virtual gateway (AVG)*. This router has the highest priority value, or the highest IP address in the group, if there is no highest priority. The AVG answers all ARP requests for the virtual router address. Which MAC address it returns depends upon which load-balancing algorithm it is configured to use. In any event, the virtual MAC address supported by one of the routers in the group is returned.

The AVG also assigns the necessary virtual MAC addresses to each of the routers participating in the GLBP group. Up to four virtual MAC addresses can be used in any group. Each of these routers is referred to as an *active virtual forwarder (AVF)*, forwarding traffic received on its virtual MAC address. Other routers in the group serve as backup or secondary virtual forwarders, in case the AVF fails. The AVG also assigns secondary roles.

Assign the GLBP priority to a router with the following interface configuration command:

```
Switch(config-if)# glbp group priority level
```

GLBP group numbers range from 0 to 1023. The router priority can be 1 to 255 (255 is the highest priority), defaulting to 100.

As with HSRP, another router cannot take over an active role until the current active router fails. GLBP does allow a router to preempt and become the AVG if it has a higher priority than the current AVG. Use the following command to enable preempting and to set a time delay before preempting begins:

```
Switch(config-if)# glbp group preempt [delay minimum seconds]
```

Active Virtual Forwarder

GLBP uses a weighting function to determine which router becomes the AVF for a virtual MAC address in a group. Each router begins with a maximum weight value (1 to 254). As specific interfaces go down, the weight is decreased by a configured amount. GLBP uses thresholds to determine when a router can and cannot be the AVF. If the weight falls below the lower threshold, the router must give up its AVF role. When the weight rises above the upper threshold, the router can resume its AVF role.

By default, a router receives a maximum weight of 100. If you want to make a dynamic weighting adjustment, GLBP must know which interfaces to track and how to adjust the weight. You must first define an interface as a tracked object with the following global configuration command:

```
Switch(config)# track object-number interface type mod/num {line-protocol | ip routing}
```

The *object-number* is an arbitrary index (1 to 500) that is used for weight adjustment. The condition that triggers an adjustment can be **line-protocol** (the interface line protocol is up) or **ip routing** (IP routing is enabled, the interface has an IP address, and the interface is up).

Next, you must define the weighting thresholds for the interface with the following interface configuration command:

```
Switch(config-if)# glbp group weighting maximum [lower lower] [upper upper]
```

The maximum weight can range from 1 to 254 (default 100). The upper (default *maximum*) and lower (default 1) thresholds define when the router can and cannot be the AVF, respectively.

Finally, you must configure GLBP to know which objects to track so that the weighting can be adjusted with the following interface configuration command:

```
Switch(config-if)# glbp group weighting track object-number [decrement value]
```

When the tracked object fails, the weighting is decremented by *value* (1 to 254, default 10).

Likewise, a router that might serve as an AVF cannot preempt another when it has a higher weight value.

GLBP Load Balancing

The AVG establishes load balancing by handing out virtual router MAC addresses to clients in a deterministic fashion. Naturally, the AVG must first inform the AVFs in the group of the virtual MAC address that each should use. Up to four virtual MAC addresses, assigned in sequential order, can be used in a group.

You can use one of the following load-balancing methods in a GLBP group:

■ **Round robin**—Each new ARP request for the virtual router address receives the next available virtual MAC address in reply. Traffic load is distributed evenly across all routers participating as AVFs in the group, assuming each of the clients sends and receives the same amount of traffic. This is the default method used by GLBP.

■ **Weighted**—The GLBP group interface's weighting value determines the proportion of traffic that should be sent to that AVF. A higher weighting results in more frequent ARP replies containing the virtual MAC address of that router. If interface tracking is not configured, the maximum weighting value configured is used to set the relative proportions among AVFs.

■ **Host-dependent**—Each client that generates an ARP request for the virtual router address always receives the same virtual MAC address in reply. This method is used if the clients have a need for a consistent gateway MAC address. (Otherwise, a client could receive replies with different MAC addresses for the router over time, depending on the load-balancing method in use.)

On the AVG router (or its successors), use the following interface configuration command to define the method:

```
Switch(config-if)# glbp group load-balancing [round-robin | weighted | host-dependent]
```

Enabling GLBP

To enable GLBP, you must assign a virtual IP address to the group by using the following interface configuration command:

```
Switch(config-if)# glbp group ip [ip-address [secondary]]
```

If the *ip-address* is not given in the command, it is learned from another router in the group. However, if this router is to be the AVG, you must explicitly configure the IP address; otherwise, no other router knows what the value should be.

Figure 14-3 shows a typical network where three multilayer switches are participating in a common GLBP group. Catalyst A is elected the AVG, so it coordinates the entire GLBP process. The AVG answers all ARP requests for the virtual router 192.168.1.1. It has identified itself, Catalyst B, and Catalyst C as AVFs for the group.

Figure 14-3 *Multilayer Switches in a GLBP Group*

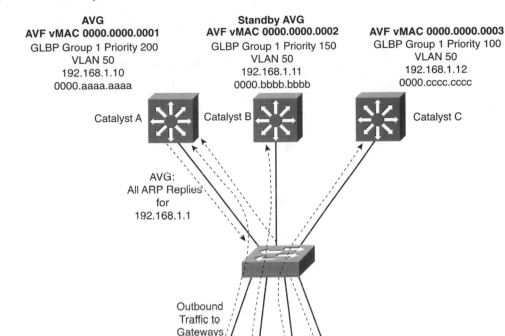

In this figure, round robin load balancing is being used. Each of the client PCs look for the virtual router address in turn, from left to right. Each time the AVG replies, the next sequential virtual MAC address is sent back to a client. After the fourth PC sends a request, all three virtual MAC addresses (and AVF routers) have been used, so the AVG cycles back to the first virtual MAC address.

Notice that only one GLBP group has been configured, and all clients know of only one gateway IP address — 192.168.1.1. However, all uplinks are being utilized, and all routers are proportionately forwarding traffic.

Redundancy is also inherent in the GLBP group—Catalyst A is the AVG, but the next-highest priority router can take over if the AVG fails. All routers have been given an AVF role for a unique virtual MAC address in the group. If one AVF fails, some clients remember the last known virtual MAC address that was handed out. Therefore, another of the routers also takes over the AVF role for the failed router, causing the virtual MAC address to remain alive at all times.

Figure 14-4 shows how these redundancy features react when the current active AVG fails. Catalyst A, prior to its failure, was the AVG because of its higher GLBP priority. After it failed, Catalyst B became the AVG, answering ARP requests with the appropriate virtual MAC address for gateway 192.168.1.1. Catalyst A had also been acting as an AVF, participating in the gateway load balancing. Catalyst B also picks up this responsibility, using its virtual MAC address 0000.0000.0002 as well as the one Catalyst A had been using, 000.0000.0001. Therefore, any hosts that know the gateway by any of its virtual MAC addresses can still reach a live gateway or AVF.

Figure 14-4 *How GLBP Reacts to a Component Failure*

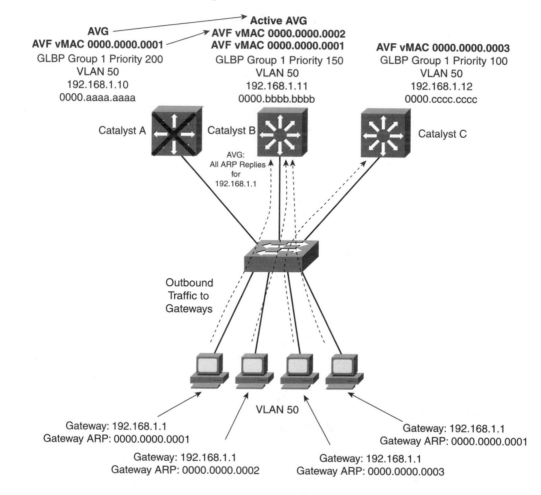

Server Load Balancing (SLB)

Each of the router redundancy protocols allows a router to mimic the identity of one or more others. This can also be handy to intelligently and transparently forward traffic to multiple destinations. In other words, one or more physical destinations can "hide" behind a single virtual IP address. You can configure the multilayer switch or router to decide which of the actual destinations services a request sent to the virtual address.

Server Load Balancing (SLB) is designed to provide a virtual server IP address to which clients can connect. The virtual server is, in fact, a group of real physical servers organized as a server farm. The client never knows exactly which real server it is connecting with—only the multilayer switch running SLB knows that for sure.

Figure 14-5 shows an example of SLB in a switched network. Two server farms, FARM1 and FARM2, are made up of logical groupings of real physical servers. Each real server has a unique IP address. SLB causes each server farm to appear as a single virtual server, VSERVER1 and VSERVER2, respectively. Client machines make connections to the virtual server addresses, 10.1.250.1 and 10.1.250.2, while SLB completes the connection to one of the real servers.

Figure 14-5   *Example of SLB Providing Virtual Servers*

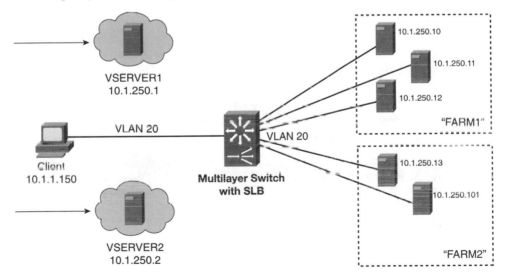

SLB controls how traffic is load balanced across the set of real servers. Load balancing can be configured as one of the following methods:

- **Weighted round-robin**—Each real server is assigned a weight that gives it the capability to handle connections, relative to the other servers. For a weight n, a server is assigned n new connections before SLB moves on to the next server.

- **Weighted least connections**—SLB assigns new connections to the real server with the least number of active connections. Each real server is assigned a weight m, where its capacity for active connections is m divided by the sum of all server weights. SLB assigns new connections to the real server with the number of active connections farthest below its capacity. New connections are rate-limited, allowing the number of connections to increase gradually to keep the server from becoming overloaded.

You can also assign connections so that they are "sticky"—the same client is connected to the last real server that it used.

By keeping the actual addresses of the real servers hidden from the outside world, an extra layer of security is possible. Also, because each virtual server is mapped to mutliple real servers, any of the real servers can be taken down for maintenance at any time.

SLB Configuration

SLB is configured in two basic stages. First, the server farms are defined and populated with real servers. Then, the virtual servers are defined and linked with the appropriate server farms.

> **TIP** SLB is a versatile and robust feature. As a result, many configuration commands can be used. The BCMSN course presents only the basic SLB operation. Therefore, this text covers just the commands needed to define server farms and virtual servers and bring them into service.
>
> If you plan on using SLB in your network, you would be wise to take advantage of the full set of its capabilities. Refer to the Cisco documentation or to the Cisco Press title, *Cisco Field Manual: Catalyst Switch Configuration,* for more details.

Server Farms

Configure each server farm by following this series of steps:

Step 1   Name the server farm:

```
Switch(config)# ip slb serverfarm serverfarm-name
```

The server farm is given a descriptive name, up to 15 characters.

Step 2   Choose a load-balancing method.

```
Switch(config-slb-sfarm)# predictor {roundrobin | leastconns}
```

Either weighted round-robin (the default) or weighted least connections can be used.

Step 3   Identify the real servers in the server farm:

```
Switch(config-slb-sfarm)# real ip-address
```

The server's actual IP address is given.

Step 4   Assign a weight for the relative server capacity:

```
Switch(config-slb-real)# weight weighting-value
```

The weighting value (1 to 255, default 8) indicates the server's capacity to accept new connections, relative to the other real servers in the server farm.

Step 5   Put the real server into service:

```
Switch(config-slb-real)# inservice
```

By default, SLB cannot use a real server until it is manually put into service. Later, the real server can be taken out of service for maintenance with the **no inservice** command. This removes it from use in the SLB server farm until it is returned to service again. (To take a real server out of service, first get into the real server configuration mode by using the commands from Steps 1 and 3.)

Virtual Servers

Configure each virtual server by the following series of steps:

Step 1   Name the virtual server:

```
Switch(config)# ip slb vserver virtual-server-name
```

The virtual server is given a descriptive name, up to 15 characters.

Step 2   Assign the virtual server to a server farm:

```
Switch(config-slb-vserver)# serverfarm serverfarm-name
```

SLB uses the virtual server as the front end for the server farm named. This server farm must already be configured, populated with one or more real servers.

Step 3   Assign an IP address to the virtual server:

```
Switch(config-slb-vserver)# virtual ip-address
```

Step 4   Control access to the virtual server:

```
Switch(config-slb-vserver)# client ip-address inverse-mask
```

By default, any client from any IP address can make connections to the virtual server. To limit the access, define only the IP subnet or address range (with subnet mask) that is allowed access. The *inverse-mask* here resembles that of an access list, where a 1-bit ignores and a 0-bit matches.

Step 5   Put the virtual server into service:

```
Switch(config-slb-vserver)# inservice
```

By default, SLB does not allow connections to be made to a virtual server until it is put into service. If a virtual server needs to be temporarily disabled for some reason, use the **no inservice** command.

Verifying Redundancy and Load Balancing

To verify the operation of the features discussed in this chapter, you can use the commands listed in Table 14-3. In particular, look for the active router, standby or backup routers, and load-balancing methods in use.

Table 14-3   *Redundancy and Load Balancing Verification Commands*

Task	Command Syntax
HSRP and VRRP	
Show HSRP status.	**show standby brief**
Show HSRP on an interface.	**show standby** *type mod/num*
Show VRRP status.	**show vrrp brief all**
Show VRRP on an interface.	**show vrrp interface** *type mod/num*
GLBP	
Show status of a GLBP group.	**show glbp** *group*
SLB	
Show server farms.	**show ip slb serverfarms**
Show real servers.	**show ip slb reals**
Show virtual servers.	**show ip slb vserver**
Show current SLB connections.	**show ip slb conns**

Foundation Summary

The Foundation Summary is a collection of information that provides a convenient review of many key concepts in this chapter. If you are already comfortable with the topics in this chapter, this summary can help you recall a few details. If you just read this chapter, this review should help solidify some key facts. If you are doing your final preparation before the exam, this information is a convenient way to review the day before the exam.

Table 14-4 *A Comparison of Router Redundancy Protocols*

	HSRP	VRRP	GLBP
Standard?	no; Cisco-proprietary, RFC 2281	yes; RFC 2338	no; Cisco-proprietary
Router roles	Active router, standby router	Master router, backup router	AVG, AVF
Load balancing	Only through multiple HSRP groups, different client gateways	Only through multiple VRRP groups, different client gateways	Inherent with one GLBP group; all clients use same gateway; several methods available
Interface tracking	yes	no	yes
Virtual router MAC address	0000.0c07.acxx	0000.5e00.01xx	assigned by AVG

Table 14-5 *HSRP Configuration Commands*

Task	Command Syntax
Set the HSRP priority.	**standby** *group* **priority** *priority*
Set the HSRP timers.	**standby** *group* **timers** *hello holdtime*
Allow router preemption.	**standby** *group* **preempt** [**delay** *seconds*]
Use group authentication.	**standby** *group* **authentication** *string*
Adjust priority by tracking an interface.	**standby** *group* **track** *type mod/num decrementvalue*
Assign the virtual router address.	**standby** *group* **ip** *ip-address* [**secondary**]

Table 14-6 *VRRP Configuration Commands*

Task	Command Syntax
Assign a VRRP router priority (default 100).	**vrrp** *group* **priority** *level*
Alter the advertisement timer (default 1 second).	**vrrp** *group* **timers advertise** [**msec**] *interval*
Learn the advertisement interval from the master router.	**vrrp** *group* **timers learn**
Disable preempting (default is to preempt).	**no vrrp** *group* **preempt**
Change the preempt delay (default 0 seconds).	**vrrp** *group* **preempt** [**delay** *seconds*]
Use authentication for advertisements.	**vrrp** *group* **authentication** *string*
Assign a virtual IP address.	**vrrp** *group* **ip** *ip-address* [**secondary**]

Table 14-7 *GLBP Configuration Commands*

Task	Command Syntax
Assign a GLBP priority.	**glbp** *group* **priority** *level*
Allow GLBP preemption.	**glbp** *group* **preempt** [**delay minimum** *seconds*]
Define an object to be tracked.	**track** *object-number* **interface** *type mod/num* {**line-protocol** | **ip routing**}
Define the weighting thresholds.	**glbp** *group* **weighting** *maximum* [**lower** *lower*] [**upper** *upper*]
Track an object.	**glbp** *group* **weighting track** *object-number* [**decrement** *value*]
Choose the load-balancing method.	**glbp** *group* **load-balancing** [**round-robin** | **weighted** | **host-dependent**]
Assign a virtual router address.	**glbp** *group* **ip** [*ip-address* [**secondary**]]

Table 14-8 *SLB Configuration Commands*

Task	Command Syntax
Name a server farm.	**ip slb serverfarm** *serverfarm-name*
Choose a load-balancing method.	**predictor** {**roundrobin** I **leastconns**}
Identify a real server.	**real** *ip-address*
Assign a relative weight to the real server.	**weight** *weighting-value*
Enable the server for use.	**inservice**
Name the virtual server.	**ip slb vserver** *virtual-server-name*
Link the virtual server to a server farm.	**serverfarm** *serverfarm-name*
Limit access to the virtual server.	**client** *ip-address network-mask*
Define the virtual server IP address.	**virtual** *ip-address*
Enable the virtual server for use.	**inservice**

Q&A

The questions and scenarios in this book are more difficult than what you should experience on the actual exam. The questions do not attempt to cover more breadth or depth than the exam; however, they are designed to make sure that you know the answer. Rather than allowing you to derive the answers from clues hidden inside the questions themselves, the questions challenge your understanding and recall of the subject. Hopefully, these questions will help limit the number of exam questions on which you narrow your choices to two options and then guess.

You can find the answers to these questions in Appendix A.

1. A multilayer switch has been configured with the command **standby 5 priority 120**. What router redundancy protocol is being used?

2. What feature can you use to prevent other routers from accidentally participating in an HSRP group?

3. What command can configure an HSRP group to use a virtual router address of 192.168.222.100?

4. The **show standby vlan 271** command produces the following output:

```
Vlan271 - Group 1
  Local state is Active, priority 210, may preempt
  Hellotime 3 holdtime 40 configured hellotime 3 sec holdtime 40 sec
  Next hello sent in 00:00:00.594
  Virtual IP address is 192.168.111.1 configured
    Secondary virtual IP address 10.1.111.1
    Secondary virtual IP address 172.21.111.1
  Active router is local
  Standby router is unknown expires in 00:00:37
  Standby virtual mac address is 0000.0c07.ac01
  2 state changes, last state change 5d17h
```

If the local router fails, which router takes over the active role for the virtual router address 192.168.111.1?

5. What is meant by preempting in HSRP?

6. What protocols discussed in this chapter support interface tracking?

7. The **show standby brief** command has been used to check the status of all HSRP groups on the local router. The output from this command is as follows:

```
Switch# show standby brief
                      P indicates configured to preempt.
                      |
Interface  Grp Prio P State   Active addr  Standby addr    Group addr
Vl100       1   210 P Active  local        192.168.75.2    192.168.75.1
Vl101       1   210 P Active  local        192.168.107.2   192.168.107.1
Vl102       1   210 P Active  local        192.168.71.2    192.168.71.1
```

Each interface is shown to have Group 1. Is this a problem?

8. How many HSRP groups are needed to load balance traffic over two routers?

9. What load-balancing methods can GLBP use?

10. What command can you use to see the status of the active and standby routers on the VLAN 171 interface?

11. How many GLBP groups are needed to load balance traffic over four routers?

12. When should you use SLB?

13. What command defines and names an SLB server farm?

14. A virtual server has just been defined with the following commands:

```
ip slb vserver CISCO
serverfarm CISCO-FARM
virtual 192.168.199.17
```

Can the virtual server be used immediately? If not, what additional command is needed?

This chapter covers the following topics that you need to master for the CCNP BCMSN exam:

- **Multicast Overview**—This section discusses multicast addressing and general multicast traffic forwarding.

- **Routing Multicast Traffic**—This section covers the protocols used by Layer 3 devices to maintain multicast groups and their members, and to constrain multicast forwarding.

- **Switching Multicast Traffic**—This section explains techniques that you can use to intelligently forward multicast traffic at Layer 2.

- **Verifying Multicast**—This section provides a brief summary of the commands that can verify the configuration and operation of multicast routing and switching.

CHAPTER 15

Multicast

Multicast traffic is typically sent by one source and received by a group of recipients, spread throughout a network and changing over time. Examples of multicast traffic include video streams for instruction or entertainment, certain audio conference calls, and one-to-many PC file imaging applications.

Because not everyone on a network wants to receive the traffic from a multicast source, switches and routers must have some means to forward traffic to exactly the destinations that want to receive it. This chapter covers IP multicast and the various protocols used to forward multicast packets.

"Do I Know This Already?" Quiz

The purpose of the "Do I Know This Already?" quiz is to help you decide what parts of this chapter to use. If you already intend to read the entire chapter, you do not necessarily need to answer these questions now.

The quiz, derived from the major sections in the "Foundation Topics" portion of the chapter, helps you determine how to spend your limited study time.

Table 15-1 outlines the major topics discussed in this chapter and the "Do I Know This Already?" quiz questions that correspond to those topics.

Table 15-1 *"Do I Know This Already?" Foundation Topics Section-to-Question Mapping*

Foundation Topics Section	Questions Covered in This Section
Multicast Overview	1–7
Routing Multicast Traffic	8–11
Switching Multicast Traffic	12

> **CAUTION** The goal of self-assessment is to gauge your mastery of the topics in this chapter. If you do not know the answer to a question or are only partially sure of the answer, you should mark this question wrong. Giving yourself credit for an answer you correctly guess skews your self-assessment results and might give you a false sense of security.

1. How many sources are typically present in a multicast group?

    a. 1

    b. 2

    c. As many as are registered with the router

    d. Cannot be determined

2. Which one of the following is a multicast address?

    a. 128.224.1.1

    b. 172.17.224.1

    c. 225.17.1.1

    d. 242.17.1.1

3. 224.1.2.3 corresponds to which of the following MAC addresses?

    a. 0102.0300.0000

    b. 0100.5e01.0203

    c. e000.0001.0203

    d. 1000.5e01.0203

4. How many unique multicast IP addresses can correspond to one multicast MAC address?

    a. 1

    b. 2

    c. 8

    d. 32

5. Which of the following is the test that is performed before a multicast packet can be forwarded?

   a. Shortest Path First

   b. Cyclic Redundancy Check

   c. Reverse Path Forwarding

   d. Multicast Route Verification

6. Which protocol registers hosts for multicast group membership?

   a. CGMP

   b. IGRP

   c. IGMP

   d. PIM

7. A host sends Internet Group Management Protocol (IGMP) packets to which of the following?

   a. The local switch

   b. The local router

   c. The multicast source

        of the multicast tree

     group has recipients on every subnet, which of the PIM modes should be used?

       ode

       node

       compress mode

       node

9. Which type of tree structure is built for sparse mode multicast routing?

   a. Spanning Tree

   b. Shared Tree

   c. Sparse Tree

   d. Simple Tree

10. What router maintains the RP-to-group correlation for Auto-RP in PIMv1?

    a. RP agent

    b. PIM root

    c. Mapping agent

    d. RP discovery server

11. What router advertises candidate RP routers in PIMv2?

    a. Auto-RP

    b. Mapping agent

    c. Bootstrap router

    d. PIM root

12. Which of the following methods requires a router to assist a Layer 2 switch in constraining multicast traffic?

    a. PIM

    b. IGMP

    c. CGMP

    d. IGMP snooping

You can find the answers to the "Do I Know This Already?" quiz in Appendix A, "Answers to Chapter 'Do I Know This Already?' Quizzes and Q&A Sections." The suggested choices for your next step are as follows:

- **10 or less overall score**—Read the entire chapter. This includes the "Foundation Topics," "Foundation Summary," and "Q&A" sections.

- **11 or 12 overall score**—If you want more review on these topics, skip to the "Foundation Summary" section and then go to the "Q&A" section at the end of the chapter. Otherwise, move to Chapter 16, "Quality of Service Overview."

Foundation Topics

Multicast Overview

In a network, three basic types of IP traffic traverse the routers and switches:

- **Unicast**—Packets that are sent from one source host address to a single destination host address. A router or Layer 3 switch forwards them by finding the destination IP address in its routing table. A Layer 2 switch relies only on the destination's MAC address.

- **Broadcast**—Packets that are sent from one source host address to a broadcast destination address. The destination can be all-hosts (255.255.255.255), a directed broadcast to a subnet (that is, 192.168.10.255), or some portion of a subnet. A router or Layer 3 switch will not forward these by default, unless some method of relaying has been configured. A Layer 2 switch floods the packet out all ports on the destination VLAN.

- **Multicast**—Packets that are sent from one source host address to a special group-based destination address. The destination represents only the hosts that are interested in receiving the packets, and no others. A router or Layer 3 switch does not forward these packets by default, unless some form of multicast routing is enabled. A Layer 2 switch cannot learn the location of the destination multicast address, the packets are flooded to all ports on the destination VLAN by default.

Two extremes are covered here—a unicast, which travels from host to host, and a broadcast, which travels from one host to everyone on a segment. Multicast falls somewhere in the middle, where the intention is to send packets from one host to only the users that want to receive them, namely those in the designated *multicast group*. Ideally, the recipients of multicast packets could be located anywhere, not just on the local segment.

Multicast traffic is generally unidirectional. Because many hosts are receiving the same data, it makes little sense to allow one of the hosts to send packets back toward the source over the multicast mechanism. Instead, a receiving host can send return traffic to the source as a unicast. Multicast traffic is also sent in a best-effort connectionless format. UDP (connectionless) is commonly used, whereas TCP (connection-oriented) is not.

Hosts that want to receive data from a multicast source can join or leave a multicast group dynamically. In addition, a host can decide to become a member of more than one multicast group at any time. The principle network task is then to figure out how to deliver multicast traffic to the group members without disturbing other uninterested hosts.

Multicast Addressing

Routers and switches must have a way to distinguish multicast traffic from unicasts or broadcasts. This is done through IP addressing, by reserving the Class D IP address range, 224.0.0.0 through 239.255.255.255, strictly for multicasting. Network devices can quickly pick out multicast IP addresses by looking at the four most-significant bits, which are always 1110.

How does a router or switch relate a multicast IP address with a MAC address? There is no Address Resolution Protocol (ARP) equivalent for multicast address mapping. Instead, a reserved Organizationally Unique Identifier (OUI) value is set aside so that multicast MAC addresses always begin with *0100.5e* (plus the next lower bit, which is zero). The lower 28 bits of the multicast IP address must also be mapped into the lower 23 bits of the MAC address by a simple algorithm.

Figure 15-1 shows the address mapping concept. Only the lower 23 bits of the address are copied from IP to MAC (or vice versa). The high-order prefix of both IP and MAC addresses are fixed, predictable values.

Figure 15-1 *Multicast IP-to-MAC Address Translation*

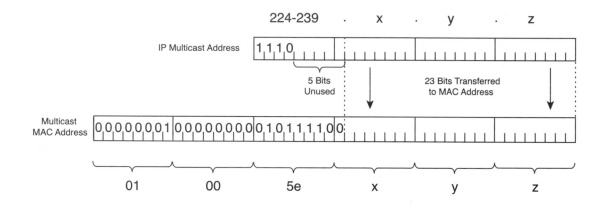

Notice, however, that 5 bits of the IP address are not transferred into the MAC address. This gives the possibility that the multicast MAC addresses are not entirely unique—there are 32 different multicast IP addresses that could all correspond to a single multicast MAC address.

Because of this ambiguity, a multicast host has a small problem when it receives an Ethernet frame destined for a multicast MAC address. That one MAC address could actually correspond to 32 different multicast IP addresses. Therefore, the host must receive and examine every frame that has the MAC address it is interested in—regardless to which of the 32 IP addresses the frame was originally destined. The host must examine the IP header inside each frame to verify that the more specific IP multicast address is a desired multicast group.

Some of the IP multicast address space has been reserved for a particular use:

- **Complete multicast space: 224.0.0.0 through 239.255.255.255**—The entire range of IP addresses that can be used for multicast purposes.

- **Link-local addresses (224.0.0.0 through 224.0.0.255)**—Used by network protocols only on the local network segment. Routers do not forward these packets.

    This space includes the *all-hosts* address 224.0.0.1, *all-routers* 224.0.0.2, *OSPF-routers* 224.0.0.5, and so on. These are also known as *fixed-group addresses* because they are well-known and predefined.

- **Administratively scoped addresses (239.0.0.0 through 239.255.255.255)**—Used in private multicast domains, much like the private IP address ranges from RFC 1918. These addresses are not routed between domains, so they can be reused.

- **Globally scoped addresses (224.0.1.0 through 238.255.255.255)**—Used by any entity; these addresses can be routed across an organization or the Internet, so they must be unique and globally significant. (Think of this range as neither local nor private; it is the rest of the multicast range.)

Routing Multicast Traffic

IP multicast traffic must be routed, just like any other Layer 3 packets. The difference is in knowing where to forward the packets. Unicast IP packets have only one destination interface (even if multiple paths exist), whereas multicast IP packets can have many destination interfaces, depending upon where the recipients are located.

Several multicast routing protocols are available. This text focuses only on Protocol Independent Multicast (PIM), as does the BCMSN course. Multicast routing as a whole is better covered in routing courses and textbooks. This section provides an overview of the PIM operation to provide a good understanding of the routing concepts. This is a necessary foundation for understanding multicast switching (Layer 2).

Regardless of the multicast routing protocol used, you must first enable multicast routing on the router or switch with the following global configuration command:

```
Switch(config)# ip multicast-routing
```

Multicast Trees

The routers (or multilayer switches) in a network must determine a forwarding path to get multicast packets from the source (sender) to each of the recipients. Think of the network as a tree structure. At the root of the tree is the source, blindly sending IP packets to a specific multicast address. Each router along the way sits at a branch or fork in the tree. If a router knows where all of the multicast group recipients are located, it also knows which branches of the tree to replicate the multicast packets onto. Some routers have no downstream recipients, so they do not forward the multicast traffic. Other routers have many downstream recipients.

This tree structure is somewhat similar to a Spanning Tree topology, as it has a root at one end and leaf nodes (the recipients) at the other end. The tree is also loop-free so that none of the multicast traffic gets fed back into the tree.

Reverse Path Forwarding

Routers usually have one test to perform on every multicast packet they receive. *Reverse Path Forwarding (RPF)* is a means to make sure packets are not being injected back into the tree at an unexpected location.

As a packet is received on a router interface, the source IP address is inspected. The idea is to verify that the packet arrived on the same interface where the source can be found. If this is true, the packet is actually proceeding out the branches of the tree, away from the source. If it is not true, someone else has injected the packet on an unexpected interface, headed back down the branches of the tree toward the source.

To perform the RPF test, the PIM router looks up the source address in its unicast routing table. If the next-hop interface used to reach the source address also matches the interface where the packet was received, the packet can be forwarded or replicated toward the multicast recipients. If not, the packet is quietly discarded.

IGMP

How does a router know of the recipients in a multicast group, much less of their locations? To receive multicast traffic from a source, both the source and every recipient must first join a common multicast group. This group is also known by its multicast IP address.

A host can join a multicast group by sending a request to its local router. This is done through the Internet Group Management Protocol (IGMP). IGMPv1 is defined in RFC 1112, and its successor, IGMPv2, in RFC 2236. When several hosts join a group by contacting their local routers, it is the multicast routing protocol (such as PIM) that "connects the dots" and forms the multicast tree between routers.

IGMPv1

To join a multicast group, a host can dynamically send a *Membership Report* IGMP message to its local router. This message tells the router what multicast address (group) the host is joining. The multicast address is used as the destination IP address, as well as the group address listed in the message.

Every 60 seconds, one router on each network segment queries all hosts to see if they are interested in receiving multicast traffic. This router is known as the *IGMPv1 Querier* and functions simply to invite hosts to join a group. Queries are sent to the 224.0.0.1 all-hosts multicast address for quick distribution. If a host is interested in joining a group, or if it wants to continue receiving a group that it has already joined, it must respond with a membership report.

Hosts can join multicast groups at any time. However, IGMPv1 does not have a mechanism to allow a host to leave a group if it is no longer interested in the group's content. Instead, routers age a multicast group out of an interface (network segment) if no membership reports are received for three consecutive query intervals. This means that, by default, multicast traffic is still sent onto a segment for up to 3 minutes after all the group members have stopped listening.

Notice that a router does not need to keep a complete host membership list for each multicast group that is active. Rather, it needs to only record which multicast groups are active on which interfaces.

IGMPv2

IGMP version 2 introduced several differences from the first version. Queries can be sent as *General Queries* to the all-hosts address (as in IGMPv1), as well as *Group-Specific Queries*, sent only to members of a specific group.

In addition, hosts are allowed to leave a group dynamically. When a host decides to leave a group it has joined, it sends a *Leave Group* message to the all-routers address (224.0.0.2). All routers on the local segment take note, and the Querier router decides to investigate further. It responds with a Group-Specific Query message, asking if anyone is still interested in receiving traffic for that group. Any other hosts must reply with a Membership Report. Otherwise, the Querier safely assumes that there is no need to continue forwarding the group traffic on that segment.

> **NOTE** If any IGMPv1 routers are on a segment, *all* routers on the segment must run IGMPv1. Otherwise, the IGMPv1 routers cannot understand the IGMPv2 messages.
>
> On interfaces where PIM is configured, IGMPv2 is enabled by default.

PIM

Protocol Independent Multicast (PIM) is a routing protocol that can be used for forwarding multicast traffic. PIM operates independent of any particular IP routing protocol. Therefore, PIM makes use of the IP unicast routing table and does not keep a separate multicast routing table. (The unicast routing table is itself routing protocol-independent because one or more routing protocols can be used to populate a single table.)

PIM can operate in two modes, depending on the density of the recipients in a multicast group. Cisco has developed a third hybrid mode, as well. The PIM modes are as follows:

- PIM Dense Mode
- PIM Sparse Mode
- PIM Sparse-Dense Mode

In addition, two versions of the PIM protocol can be used in a network: PIM version 1 and PIM version 2.

PIM Dense Mode

PIM routers can be configured for *Dense Mode* (also called PIM-DM) if it is safe to assume that a multicast group's recipients are located on every subnet. The multicast traffic's source becomes the root of the tree, and the multicast tree is known from the source to each of the recipients. This is also termed *(S,G)* multicast traffic, where the path between the source and group members is unique and well-defined.

The multicast tree is built by first allowing a flood of traffic from the source to every dense mode router in the network. The tree is grown from the top down. For a brief time, unnecessary traffic is allowed, much as a broadcast would do. However, as each router receives traffic for the group, it must decide whether it has active recipients wanting to receive the data. If so, the router can remain quiet and let the flow continue. If no hosts have registered for the multicast group with the router (via IGMP), the router sends a *Prune* message to its neighbor toward the source. That branch of the tree is then pruned off so that the unnecessary traffic does not continue.

Figure 15-2 shows dense mode's flood-then-prune operation. The tree is built by a wave of join requests moving through all dense mode multilayer switches. Then, the switches that have no interested hosts request to be pruned from the tree. The resulting tree and multicast flow is shown in Figure 15-4 in the section on PIM Sparse Mode.

PIM-DM routers become aware of their neighbors by exchanging hello messages. This neighbor information is used first to build the tree to all neighbors, and then to prune branches away.

If a multicast flow has begun, and the tree has been built and then pruned, the tree exists only where active group members are located. If a new host registers for the group, the branch of the network where it is located can be added or *grafted* back onto the tree.

To configure PIM Dense Mode on an interface, use the following interface configuration command:

```
Switch(config-if)# ip pim dense-mode
```

Figure 15-2 *PIM Dense Mode Constructs a Multicast Tree*

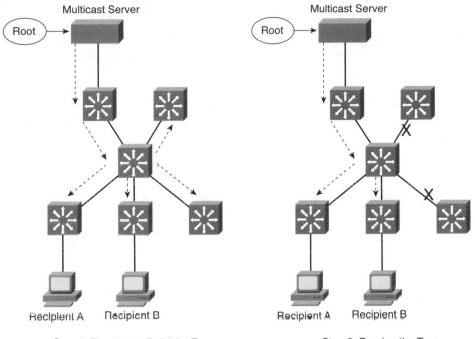

Step 1: Flooding to Build the Tree   Step 2: Pruning the Tree

PIM Sparse Mode

PIM Sparse Mode (also called PIM-SM) takes a different approach—the multicast tree isn't extended to a router unless a host there has already joined the group. The multicast tree is built by beginning with the group members at the end leaf nodes and extending back toward a central root point. The tree is built from the bottom up.

Sparse Mode also works on the idea of a shared tree structure, where the root is not necessarily the multicast source. Instead, the root is a PIM-SM router that is centrally located in the network. This root router is called the *Rendezvous Point (RP)*.

The tree from the RP to the group members is actually a subset of the tree that could be drawn from the source to the group members. If a multicast source anywhere in the network can register for group membership with the RP, the tree can be completed. Because of this, the Sparse Mode tree is called a shared tree. Sparse Mode multicast flows are described as *(*,G)* because the tree allows any source to send to a group.

As a recipient joins a multicast group (IGMP), the local router forwards the Membership Report toward the RP at the root of the tree. Each router along the way adds that branch to the shared tree. Pruning is performed only when a group member is removed from the group. This process is shown in Figure 15-3. Notice that it consists of only one step—only routers with active group members join the tree. The routers that did not join the group are not pruned because they never became a part of the tree.

Figure 15-4 illustrates the resulting tree structures for both PIM Dense and PIM Sparse Modes, along with the multicast data flow. Notice that both PIM modes have constructed identical tree structures, yielding the same multicast traffic flow patterns.

Figure 15-3 *PIM Sparse Mode Constructs a Multicast Tree*

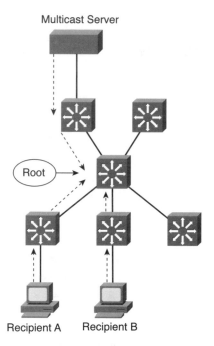

Step 1: Member join the group
to build a tree.

To configure PIM Sparse Mode on an interface, use the following interface configuration command:

```
Switch(config-if)# ip pim sparse-mode
```

Figure 15-4 *Identical Results from PIM Dense and Sparse Modes*

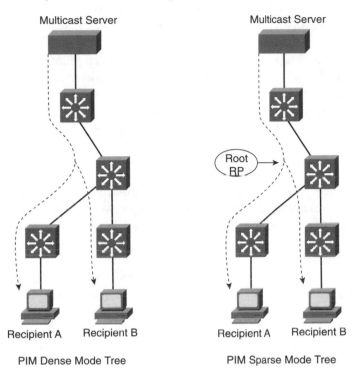

PIM Sparse-Dense Mode

PIM has the potential to support both Dense and Sparse Modes, because they exist on different multicast groups in a network. Cisco offers the hybrid *Sparse-Dense* Mode, allowing a PIM router to use Sparse or Dense Mode on a per group basis. If a group has an RP defined, Sparse Mode is used; otherwise, Dense Mode is used.

To configure PIM Sparse-Dense Mode on an interface, use the following interface configuration command:

```
Switch(config-if)# ip pim sparse-dense-mode
```

PIM Version 1

For routers using the first version of PIM, RPs can be configured manually or by the more dynamic *auto-RP* process. To manually identify an RP, use the following global configuration command:

```
Switch(config)# ip pim rp-address ip-address [access-list-number] [override]
```

You can limit the range of multicast groups supported by the RP by using an access list. The **override** keyword causes this RP to be preferred over any that is automatically determined. The RP must be defined on every router in the PIM domain, including the RP itself.

Cisco also provides a proprietary means to automatically inform PIM-SM routers of the appropriate RP for a group. This is known as *Auto-RP*. This is done by identifying a centrally located and well-connected router to function as the *mapping agent*. The mapping agent learns of all candidate RPs that are announced over the *Cisco-RP-Announce* multicast address 224.0.1.39. To define a router as a mapping agent, use the following global configuration command:

```
Switch(config)# ip pim send-rp-disovery scope ttl
```

The mapping agent sends RP-to-group mapping information to all PIM routers over the *Cisco-RP-Discovery* multicast address 224.0.1.40. The Time-To-Live (TTL) value is set in these messages to limit the scope of the mapping. This limits how many router hops away the information will still be valid.

You must then explicitly define each candidate RP router. Once a router knows it can be an RP, it begins sending announcements to the mapping agent. Configure a router as an RP with the following global configuration command:

```
Switch(config)# ip pim send-rp-announce type mod/num scope ttl group-list access-list-
number
```

The interface given corresponds to the advertised RP address. The announcement's scope is limited by the number of router hops (TTL). The router will also advertise itself as a candidate RP for the multicast groups permitted in the access list.

PIM Version 2

The second version of PIM also includes a dynamic RP-to-group mapping advertisement mechanism. This is known as the *boostrap router method*, and is standards-based.

PIMv2 is similar to the Cisco auto-RP method. First, a *bootstrap router (BSR)* is identified; this router learns about RP candidates for a group and advertises them to PIM routers. You need to configure only the BSR and candidate RPs; all other PIM routers learn of the appropriate RP from the BSR. Define a BSR using the following global configuration command:

```
Switch(config)# ip pim bsr-candidate type mod/num hash-mask-length [priority]
```

The interface used determines the BSR address. RP selection for a group is based on a hashing function. The length of the hash mask controls the number of consecutive multicast groups that hash to the same RP.

Next, you must identify each of the candidate RP routers. Configure each RP with the following global configuration command:

```
Switch(config)# ip pim rp-candidate type mod/num ttl group-list access-list-number
```

Finally, by default, the bootstrap messages permeate the entire PIM domain. You can limit the scope of the advertisements by defining PIMv2 border routers, which will not forward the bootstrap messages. Use the following global configuration command:

```
Switch(config)# ip pim border
```

Switching Multicast Traffic

Routers or multilayer switches can build multicast trees and set up forwarding in an efficient, intelligent manner. At Layer 2, however, a switch can examine only the Ethernet frame header to find the source and destination MAC addresses. These switches cannot enjoy the luxury of on-demand multicast forwarding at all; the best information they have is the destination multicast address, and that signifies only that the frame needs to be flooded out all ports on the VLAN.

Two methods have been developed to help switches make intelligent forwarding decisions for multicast traffic: IGMP snooping and CGMP. One method requires more sophisticated switching hardware, whereas the other method leans on a nearby router for assistance.

IGMP Snooping

In normal operation, a host desiring multicast group membership must contact a local router so that it gets added into the multicast tree. IGMP snooping allows a switch to cavesdrop on these IGMP membership reports, so that it can find out who is requesting which group.

Recall that to join a group, a host must send its IGMP membership report to the multicast address of the group itself. A Layer 2-only switch must listen to *every multicast frame* to find the IGMP information. Clearly, this becomes a burden to the switch CPU.

A multilayer or Layer 3 switch has a clear advantage—it can inherently pick out Layer 3 information within frames. This type of switch must listen only to *every IGMP packet*. When a membership report is overheard, the switch adds the multicast group's MAC address to its Content Addressable Memory (CAM) table (if it doesn't already exist), along with the source switch port where the IGMP packet was received. This links the group address with the host who requested membership.

As other hosts request membership to the group, the respective switch ports are added to the CAM table list for the group address. Now, when a frame destined for the multicast group arrives, it can be replicated out exactly the right ports to reach the recipients.

With IGMP snooping, there are two special cases of group membership in the CAM table:

■ All multicast routers known by the switch (dynamically learned) are also recorded for a group in the CAM table. Multicast frames must also be replicated toward any routers so that they can be routed elsewhere if needed.

■ The switch CPU itself is also a member of every multicast group so that it can watch IGMP messages come and go. Only IGMP traffic is processed; the CPU does not inspect other multicast frames.

IGMP snooping is enabled on all switch ports and VLAN interfaces, by default, on switch platforms that support it. This includes the Catalyst 2950, 3550, 4500, and 6500 families, as each has additional hardware to support Layer 3 functionality. To enable or disable IGMP snooping, use the following global configuration command:

```
Switch(config)# [no] ip igmp snooping
```

CGMP

When a Layer 2 switch cannot perform IGMP snooping itself, a nearby multicast router can assist. Cisco developed the proprietary Cisco Group Membership Protocol (CGMP) for this purpose.

A router or multilayer switch configured for multicast routing can also be configured for CGMP. As hosts send IGMP membership reports to join or leave multicast groups, the CGMP router relays this message to all interested switches. The CGMP messages are multicast over the well-known address *0100.0cdd.dddd*; by definition, this multicast group is flooded everywhere as a special case so that CGMP messages can be transported across non-CGMP switches.

The CGMP messages include the requesting host's MAC address, along with the MAC address of the multicast group it wants to join or leave. When a Layer 2 switch receives this CGMP information, it becomes a simple task to add the multicast group and associated hosts to its CAM table. In effect, the router has become a "hearing aid" for a switch that is IGMP snooping "hearing impaired."

By default, CGMP is disabled on all interfaces on multicast routers. To enable it, use the following interface configuration command:

```
Switch(config-if)# ip cgmp
```

Only the multicast router must be configured for CGMP. All IOS-based Layer 2 switches have CGMP enabled by default, so they will automatically process CGMP messages from routers.

> **NOTE** As a rule, IGMP snooping and CGMP are mutually exclusive—they cannot both be used simultaneously on a switch. For switches that have IGMP snooping capability, IGMP snooping is enabled by default. For switches that cannot do IGMP snooping, CGMP is enabled by default.
>
> If you are configuring IP multicast support in your network, be sure to identify any legacy Layer 2 switches that are capable only of flooding multicast traffic. Enable CGMP on these switches, and then enable CGMP on an upstream multicast router or multilayer switch. This way, your entire network will be able to intelligently constrain the flooding of multicast traffic.

Verifying Multicast Routing and Switching

To verify the operation of the features discussed in this chapter, you can use the commands listed in the sections that follow. In particular, look for the active router, standby or backup routers, and load-balancing methods in use.

Multicast Routing with PIM

Remember that PIM is based on the unicast routing table; no separate multicast routing table is kept. Table 15-2 lists those commands that you need to verify that the multicast routing with PIM operations is working as intended.

Table 15-2 *Commands for Verifying Multicast Routing with PIM*

Task	Command Syntax
Show valid routes.	**show ip route**
Show neighboring PIM routers.	**show ip pim neighbor**
Verify RPF information for a host address.	**show ip rpf** *ip address*
Show PIM RPs.	**show ip pim rp**
Show PIMv1 Auto-RP.	**show ip pim auto-rp**
Show PIM v2 BSRs.	**show ip pim bsr-router**

Multicast Switching

Table 15-3 lists those commands that you need to verify that IGMP snooping is configured and working as intended.

Table 15-3 *Commands for Verifying IGMP Operation*

Task	Command Syntax
List active IGMP groups and members.	**show ip igmp groups**
Show IGMP activity on an interface.	**show ip igmp interface** *type mod/num*
Show IGMP snooping activity.	**show ip igmp snooping**

You can also perform some multicast testing with multilayer switches. Choose a multicast group address that several switches can join. Configure a specific interface to join the group with the following interface configuration command:

```
Switch(config-if)# ip igmp join-group multicast-address
```

Then, you can use **show** commands to see information about the group and the IGMP membership. After several switches have joined the group, you can also issue a **ping** to the multicast group IP address. Every switch that has joined the group should answer with a reply.

What Would Happen Without a Multicast Router?

Suppose that a network is so small that a multicast router is not available. Instead, only one or more Layer 2 or Layer 3 switches are used. Can a multicast group be supported for users that want to view a streaming video from a server?

Multicast can always be supported, with or without a router. When a host sends an IGMP membership report to join a group, it does so blindly. After all, a host does not know about multicast routers at all—it just sends out a request to join and hopes that it will start receiving traffic destined for the multicast group address. Even if a multicast router is present, it doesn't send a reply to a host that has joined a group. A router only periodically sends out membership queries asking if hosts are still wanting to remain a member of the group.

In this small network, Layer 2 switches will simply flood the server's multicast traffic out all ports on the VLAN. No CGMP router is available to lend its intelligence. Layer 3 switches can use IGMP snooping, however, to constrain the multicast flooding. Although a router isn't present, the switch can still listen to the membership reports being sent to the nonexistent router.

Foundation Summary

The Foundation Summary is a collection of information that provides a convenient review of many key concepts in this chapter. If you are already comfortable with the topics in this chapter, this summary can help you recall a few details. If you just read this chapter, this review should help solidify some key facts. If you are doing your final preparation before the exam, this information is a convenient way to review the day before the exam.

- IP multicast addresses range from 224.0.0.0 to 239.255.255.255 (highest 4 bits are always 1110).

- Multicast MAC addresses always start with *0100.5e* (next bit is always 0). The lower 28 bits of the IP address are mapped over into the lower 23 bits of the MAC address.

- RPF decides whether a multicast packet can be forwarded—if it arrived on an interface where the source can be found, it is forwarded; if not, it is dropped.

- IGMP is the protocol used to join and leave (as well as to maintain) multicast groups.

- PIM is a multicast routing protocol used to build multicast tree topologies.

Table 15-4 *A Comparison of PIM Modes*

	Multicast Flows	Tree Construction	Tree Refinements
Dense Mode	(S,G)	Top-down; source is the root, recipients are leaf nodes	First flood, then prune
Sparse Mode	(*,G)	Bottom up; RP is the root, source can be anywhere, recipients are leaf nodes	Group extended from recipients toward RP; pruning only when member leaves group
Sparse-Dense Mode	(S,G) or (*,G)	Hybrid on a per-group basis	n/a

Table 15-5 *IP PIM Multicast Configuration Commands*

Task	Command Syntax
Enable multicast routing.	**ip multicast-routing**
Use PIM Dense Mode on an interface.	**ip pim dense-mode**
Use PIM Sparse Mode on an interface.	**ip pim sparse-mode**
Use PIM Sparse-Dense Mode.	**ip pim sparse-dense-mode**
Define a PIMv1 RP.	**ip pim rp-address** *ip-address* [*access-list-number*] [**override**]
Define a PIMv1 Auto-RP mapping agent.	**ip pim send-rp-discovery scope** *ttl*
Identify the PIMv1 Auto-RP RP routers.	**ip pim send-rp-announce** *type mod/num* **scope** *ttl* **group-list** *access-list-number*
Define a PIMv2 BSR.	**ip pim bsr-candidate** *type mod/num hash-mask-length* [*priority*]
Identify the PIMv2 candidate RP routers.	**ip pim rp-candidate** *type mod/num ttl* **group-list** *access-list-number*
Define a PIMv2 border router.	**ip pim border**

- IGMP snooping allows a switch to intercept IGMP messages to learn of group members and their port locations.

- CGMP allows a router to relay IGMP join and leave requests to Layer 2 switches. The switches then learn of group members and their port locations.

Q&A

The questions and scenarios in this book are more difficult than what you should experience on the actual exam. The questions do not attempt to cover more breadth or depth than the exam; however, they are designed to make sure that you know the answers. Rather than allowing you to derive the answers from clues hidden inside the questions themselves, the questions challenge your understanding and recall of the subject. Hopefully, these questions will help limit the number of exam questions on which you narrow your choices to two options and then guess.

The answers to these questions can be found in Appendix A.

1.   By default, what does a router or Layer 3 switch do with multicast packets?

2.   By default, what does a Layer 2 switch do with a multicast packet?

3.   What high-order bit combination signals that an IP address is used for multicast?

4.   If the IP-to-MAC multicast address mapping is somewhat ambiguous, how can a frame be forwarded to the correct destination group?

5.   What IP multicast address range is set aside for use only on the local network segment?

6.   For the RPF check, the source IP address is looked up in the unicast routing table. To forward the packet, what should the result of the test be?

7.   What important difference exists between IGMPv1 and IGMPv2?

8.   To join a multicast group, what type of message is sent? Where is this message sent?

9.   What is the purpose of the IGMP Querier?

10.   For PIM Dense Mode, how is the multicast tree built?

11.   Where is the root of the PIM Sparse Mode tree located?

12.   With PIM Sparse-Dense Mode, is the PIM mode determined per interface or per group?

13.   What routing table is used for PIM?

14.   What command is used to configure an interface for the hybrid PIM mode?

15.   When a switch performs IGMP snooping, what is it snooping for?

16.   What else does a Layer 2 switch need when it is configured for CGMP?

17.   When should IGMP snooping and CGMP be used together on a switch?

18.   At a trade show, several PCs and servers are connected to a single Layer 2 switch. The switch has CGMP enabled. When a server begins to send video data to a multicast address, what happens to that traffic?

PART IV: Campus Network Services

Chapter 16   Quality of Service Overview

Chapter 17   Diffserv QoS Configuration

Chapter 18   IP Telephony

Chapter 19   Securing Switch Access

Chapter 20   Securing with VLANs

This part of the book covers the following BCMSN exam topics:

- Describe the quality issues with voice traffic on a switched data network, including jitter and delay.

- Describe the QoS solutions that address voice-quality issues.

- Describe the features and operation of network analysis modules on Catalyst switches to improve network traffic management.

- Implement IP technology on a switched network with auxiliary VLANs.

- Configure QoS features on multilayer switched networks to provide optimal quality and bandwidth utilization for applications and data.

- Describe the general design models when implementing IP telephony in a switched network environment.

- Plan QoS implementation within a multilayer switched network.

This chapter covers the following topics that you need to master for the CCNP BCMSN exam:

- **DiffServ QoS**—This section discusses the Differentiated Services QoS model, where QoS is defined as a per-hop behavior. Each switch or router must be responsible for its part in the overall QoS strategy.

- **QoS Building Blocks**—This section explains each QoS feature or function that can be performed as part of the DiffServ model.

- **Switch Port Queues**—This section provides an overview of the queues that are available to a switch port.

CHAPTER 16

Quality of Service Overview

Traditionally, network congestion or the timely delivery of traffic has been handled by increasing link bandwidths and switching hardware. This does little to address how one type of traffic can be preferred or delivered ahead of another.

Quality of service (QoS) is the overall method used in a network to protect and prioritize time-critical or important traffic. QoS is composed of many smaller pieces, each interacting with the others. This chapter discusses the different QoS models, as well as each feature that you can utilize.

"Do I Know This Already?" Quiz

The purpose of the "Do I Know This Already?" quiz is to help you decide what parts of this chapter to use. If you already intend to read the entire chapter, you do not necessarily need to answer these questions now.

The quiz, derived from the major sections in the "Foundation Topics" portion of the chapter, helps you determine how to spend your limited study time.

Table 16-1 outlines the major topics discussed in this chapter and the "Do I Know This Already?" quiz questions that correspond to those topics.

Table 16-1 *"Do I Know This Already?" Foundation Topics Section-to-Question Mapping*

Foundation Topics Section	Questions Covered in This Section
DiffServ QoS	1–5
QoS Building Blocks	6–11
Switch Port Queues	12

CAUTION   The goal of self-assessment is to gauge your mastery of the topics in this chapter. If you do not know the answer to a question or are only partially sure of the answer, you should mark this question wrong. Giving yourself credit for an answer you correctly guess skews your self-assessment results and might give you a false sense of security.

1. Which of the following QoS models reserves bandwidth end-to-end?

    a. DiffServ

    b. IntServ

    c. Best Effort

    d. Cut-Through

2. Where is QoS implemented in the DiffServ model?

    a. On each client and server

    b. On each network device (per-hop)

    c. Everything between client and server (end-to-end)

    d. Only on routers

3. At what layer of the OSI model is class of service (CoS) used to pass QoS information?

    a. Layer 1

    b. Layer 2

    c. Layer 3

    d. Layer 7

4. What does the DSCP name "EF" mean?

    a. Extra Fast

    b. Enhanced Forwarding

    c. Expedited Forwarding

    d. Enhanced Field

5. In the DSCP codepoint name "AF31," what does the "3" digit represent?

    a. Per-hop behavior

    b. Class Selector

    c. Drop Precedence

    d. CoS

6. Which of the following terms is an element of DiffServ QoS that identifies traffic?

   a. Identification

   b. Marking

   c. Trust

   d. Classification

7. When a switch is configured at a trust boundary, which one of the following can be trusted?

   a. Source IP address

   b. CoS values

   c. QoS advertisements

   d. IP packet payload

8. What is the purpose of the marking process?

   a. To tag packets for CEF-based switching

   b. To add the ID of the switch that is marking

   c. To alter the DSCP value

   d. To flag packets that are used for QoS measurements

9. When would you use the scheduling process in a switch?

   a. To determine when to send a packet

   b. To determine when users can use the network

   c. To determine the order that packets are forwarded

   d. To determine when packets will be dropped

10. Which of the following methods unconditionally drops packets when a queue is full?

    a. WRR

    b. WRED

    c. Tail Drop

    d. Policing

11. How does WRED detect and avoid congestion?

    a. It signals the next-hop switch.

    b. It signals the sending host.

    c. It empties the queue before it gets full.

    d. It randomly drops packets.

12. A switch port has two standard queues, two WRED thresholds, and one strict priority queue. How can its queue type be written?

    a. 2s2t1p

    b. 1p2q2t

    c. 2q2t1p

    d. 2p2q1t

The answers to the "Do I Know This Already?" quiz are found in Appendix A, "Answers to Chapter 'Do I Know This Already?' Quizzes and Q&A Sections." The suggested choices for your next step are as follows:

- **10 or less overall score**—Read the entire chapter. This includes the "Foundation Topics," "Foundation Summary," and "Q&A" sections.

- **11 or 12 overall score**—If you want more review on these topics, skip to the "Foundation Summary" section and then go to the "Q&A" section at the end of the chapter. Otherwise, move to Chapter 17, "Diffserv QoS Configuration."

Foundation Topics

The Need for Quality of Service

The majority of this book has discussed how Layer 2 and Layer 3 Catalyst switches forward packets from one switch port to another. On the surface, it might seem that there is only one way to forward packets—just look up the next packet's destination in a Content Addressable Memory (CAM) or Cisco Express Forwarding (CEF) table and send it on its way. But that only addresses *if* the packet can be forwarded, not *how* it can be forwarded.

Different types of applications have different requirements for how their data should be sent end-to-end. For example, it might be acceptable to wait a short time for a web page to be displayed after a user requests it. That same user probably cannot tolerate the same delays in receiving packets that belong to a streaming video presentation or an audio telephone call. Any loss or delay in packet delivery could ruin the purpose of the application.

Three basic things can happen to packets as they are sent from one host to another across a network:

- **Delay**—As a packet is sent from one network device to another, its delivery is delayed by some amount of time. This can be caused by the time required to send the packet serially across a wire, the time required for a router or switch to perform table lookups or make decisions, the time required for the data to travel over a geographically long path, and so on. The total delay from start to finish is called the *latency*. This is most easily seen as the time from when a user presses a key until the time the character is echoed and displayed in a terminal session.

- **Jitter**—Some applications involve the delivery of a stream of related data. As these packets are delivered, variations can occur in the amount of delay so that they do not all arrive at predictable times. The variation in delay is called *jitter*. Audio streams are particularly succeptible to jitter; if the audio data is not played back at a constant rate, the resulting speech or music sounds choppy.

- **Loss**—In extreme cases, packets that enter a congested or error-prone part of the network will simply be dropped without delivery. Some amount of packet loss is acceptable and recoverable by a reliable, connection-oriented protocol such as TCP. Other protocols are not as tolerant, and dropped packets mean data is missing.

To address and alleviate these conditions, a network can employ Quality of Service (QoS) mechanisms.

Types of QoS

Three basic types of QoS can be used in a network:

- Best-effort delivery
- Integrated Services model
- Differentiated Services model

Keep in mind that QoS works toward making policies or promises to improve packet delivery from a sender to a receiver. The same QoS policies should be used on *every* network device that connects the sender to the receiver. QoS must be implemented end-to-end before it can be totally effective.

Best Effort Delivery

A network that simply forwards packets in the order they were received has no real QoS. Switches and routers then make their "best effort" to deliver packets as quickly as possible, with no regard to the type of traffic or the need for priority service.

To get an idea of how QoS operates in a network, consider a fire truck or an ambulance trying to quickly work its way through a crowded city. The lights are flashing and the siren is sounding to signal that this is a "priority" vehicle needing to get through ahead of everyone else. The priority vehicle does not need to obey normal traffic rules.

However, the best effort scenario says that the fire truck must stay within the normal flow of traffic. At an intersection, it must wait in the line or queue of traffic like any other vehicle—even if its lights and siren are on. It might arrive on time or too late to help, depending on the conditions along the road.

Integrated Services Model

One approach to QoS is the *Integrated Sevices (IntServ)* model. The basic idea is to prearrange a path for priority data along the complete path, from source to destination. Beginning with RFC 1633, the Resource Reservation Protocol (RSVP) was developed as the mechanism for scheduling and reserving adequate path bandwidth for an application.

The source application itself is involved by requesting QoS parameters through RSVP. Each network device along the way must check to see if it can support the request. After a complete path meeting the minimum requirements is made, the source is signaled with a confirmation. Then, the source application can begin using the path.

Applying the fire truck example to the IntServ model, a fire truck would radio ahead to the nearest intersection before it left the firehouse. Police stationed at each intersection would contact each other to announce the fire truck was coming, and to assess the traffic conditions. A special lane might be reserved by the police so that the fire truck could move at full speed toward the destination, regardless of what other traffic might be present.

Differentiated Services Model

As you might imagine, the IntServ model does not scale very well when many sources are trying to compete with each other to reserve end-to-end bandwidth. Another approach is the *Differentiated Services (DiffServ)* model, which permits each network device to handle packets on an individual basis. Each router or switch can be configured with QoS policies to follow, and forwarding decisions are made accordingly.

DiffServ requires no advance reservations; QoS is handled dynamically, in a distributed fashion. In other words, where IntServ applies QoS on a per-flow basis, DiffServ applies it on a per-hop basis. DiffServ also bases its QoS decisions on information contained in each packet header.

Continuing with the emergency vehicle analogy, here police are stationed at every intersection as before. However, none of them know a fire truck is coming until they see the lights or hear the siren. At each intersection, a decision is made as to how to handle the approaching fire truck. Other traffic can be held back, if needed, so that the fire truck can go right through.

The BCMSN course, as well as this text, focuses almost entirely on the DiffServ model. Many available tools exist for DiffServ use, which can cause some confusion about what each is used for and how each is configured. Try to see the bigger QoS picture and remember where each tool fits.

DiffServ QoS

DiffServ is a per-hop behavior, where each router or switch inspects each packet's header to decide how to go about forwarding that packet. All the information needed for this decision is carried along with each packet in the header. The packet itself has no idea how it will be handled; it merely presents some flags, or classifications and markings, and hopes that the switch will know what to do.

The necessary QoS policies are configured into the router or switch in the form of building blocks or tools. These building blocks are used internally to forward packets based on the combination of policies and QoS flags.

Layer 2 QoS Classification

Layer 2 frames themselves have no mechanism to indicate the priority or importance of their contents. One frame looks just as important as another. Therefore, a Layer 2 switch can only forward frames according to a best-effort delivery.

When frames are carried from switch to switch, however, an opportunity for classification occurs. Recall that a trunk is used to carry frames from multiple VLANs between switches. The trunk does this by encapsulating the frames and adding a tag indicating the source VLAN number. The encapsulation also includes a field that can mark the *class of service (CoS)* of each frame. This can be used at switch boundaries to make some QoS decisions. After a trunk is unencapsulated at the far-end switch, the CoS information is removed and lost.

The two trunk encapsulations handle CoS differently:

- **IEEE 802.1Q**—Each frame is tagged with a 12-bit VLAN ID and a User field. The User field contains three *802.1p priority bits* that indicate the frame CoS, a unitless value ranging from 0 (lowest-priority delivery) to 7 (highest-priority delivery). Frames from the native VLAN are not tagged at all (no VLAN ID or User field), so they receive a default CoS that is configured on the *receiving* switch.

- **Inter-Switch Link (ISL)**—Each frame is tagged with a 15-bit VLAN ID. In addition, next to the frame Type field is a 4-bit User field. The lower three bits of the User field are used as a CoS value. Although ISL is not standards-based, Catalyst switches make CoS seamless by copying the 802.1p CoS bits from an 802.1Q trunk into the User CoS bits of an ISL trunk. This allows CoS information to propagate along trunks of differing encapsulations.

Layer 3 QoS Classification with DSCP

From the beginning, IP packets have always had a *type of service (ToS)* byte that could be used to mark packets. This byte is divided into a 3-bit IP Precedence value and a 4-bit ToS value. This offered a rather limited mechanism for QoS because only the 3 bits of IP Precedence were used to describe the per-hop QoS behavior.

The DiffServ model keeps the existing IP ToS byte, but uses it in a more scalable fashion. This byte is also referred to as the *Differentiated Services (DS)* field, with a different format, as shown in Figure 16-1. The 6-bit DS value is known as the *Differentiated Service Code Point (DSCP)* and is the one value that is examined by any DiffServ network device.

Do not be confused by the dual QoS terminology—the ToS and DS bytes are one in the same, occupying the same location in the IP header. Only the names are different, along with the way the value is interpreted. In fact, the DSCP bits have been arranged to be backward-compatible with the IP precedence bits so that a non-DiffServ device can still interpret some QoS information.

Figure 16-1 *ToS and DSCP Byte Formats*

ToS Byte:	P2	P1	P0	T3	T2	T1	T0	Zero
DS Byte:	DS5	DS4	DS3	DS2	DS1	DS0	ECN1	ECN0
	(Class Selector)			(Drop Precedence)				

The DSCP value is broken up into a 3-bit Class Selector and a 3-bit Drop Precedence value. Refer to Table 16-2 to see how the IP Precedence, DSCP per-hop behavior, and DSCP codepoint name and numbers relate.

Table 16-2 *Mapping of IP Precedence and DSCP Fields*

IP Precedence (3 bits)			DSCP (6 bits)				
Name	**Value**	**Bits**	**Per-Hop Behavior**	**Class Selector**	**Drop Precedence**	**Codepoint Name**	**DSCP Bits (decimal)**
Routine	0	000	Default			Default	000 000 (0)
Priority	1	001	AF	1	1: Low	AF11	001 010 (10)
					2: Medium	AF12	001 100 (12)
					3: High	AF13	001 110 (14)
Immediate	2	010	AF	2	1: Low	AF21	010 010 (18)
					2: Medium	AF22	010 100 (20)
					3: High	AF23	010 110 (22)
Flash	3	011	AF	3	1: Low	AF31	011 010 (26)
					2: Medium	AF32	011 100 (28)
					3: High	AF33	011 110 (30)

continues

Table 16-2 *Mapping of IP Precedence and DSCP Fields (Continued)*

IP Precedence (3 bits)			DSCP (6 bits)				
Name	**Value**	**Bits**	**Per-Hop Behavior**	**Class Selector**	**Drop Precedence**	**Codepoint Name**	**DSCP Bits (decimal)**
Flash Override	4	100	AF	4	1: Low	AF41	100 010 (34)
					2: Medium	AF42	100 100 (36)
					3: High	AF43	100 110 (38)
Critical[1]	5	101	EF			EF	101 110 (46)[1]
Internetwork Control	6	110	—				(48-55)
Network Control	7	111	—				(56-63)

[1] IP Precedence value 5 (DSCP EF) corresponds to the range of DSCP bits 101000 through 101111, or 40-47. However, only the value 101110 or 46 is commonly used and is given the EF designation.

Class Selector

The three class selector bits (DS5 through DS3) coarsely classify packets into one of seven classes:

- Class 0, the default class, offers only best-effort forwarding.

- Classes 1 through 4 are called *Assured Forwarding (AF)* service levels. Higher AF class numbers indicate the presence of higher-priority traffic.

  Packets in the AF classes can be dropped, if necessary, with the lower-class numbers the most likely to be dropped. For example, packets with AF Class 4 will be delivered in preference to packets with AF Class 3.

- Class 5 is known as *Expedited Forwarding (EF)*, where those packets are given premium service. EF is the least likely to be dropped, so it is always reserved for time-critical data such as voice traffic.

- Classes 6 and 7 are called *Internetwork Control* and *Network Control*, respectively, and are set aside for network control traffic. Usually, routers and switches use these classes for things like Spanning Tree Protocol and routing protocols. This ensures timely delivery of the packets that keep the network stable and operational.

Drop Precedence

Each class represented in the DSCP also has three levels of *drop precedence*, contained in bits DS2 through DS0 (DS0 is always zero):

- Low (1)

- Medium (2)

- High (3)

Within a class, packets marked with a higher drop precedence have the potential for being dropped before those with a lower value. In other words, a lower drop precedence value gives better service. This gives finer granularity to the decision of what packets to drop when necessary.

> **NOTE**   The DSCP value can be given as a codepoint name, with the class selector providing the two letters and a number followed by the drop precedence number. For example, class AF Level 2 with drop precedence 1 (low) is written as *AF21*. The DSCP is commonly given as a decimal value. For AF21, the decimal value is 18. The relationship is confusing, and Table 16-2 should be a handy aid.
>
> You should try to remember a few codepoint names and numbers. Some common values are EF (46) and most of the classes with high drop precedences: AF41 (34), AF31 (26), AF21 (18), and AF11 (10). Naturally, the default DSCP has no name (0).

QoS Building Blocks

As a packet passes through a switch, many things can be examined or manipulated to alter its delivery in relation to other packets. QoS can then be thought of as a series of building blocks, where each represents a different operation on a packet.

Beyond that, the QoS building blocks can be identified in various internal locations within a Catalyst switch. To keep the QoS operations straight, always think of a packet traveling from the ingress port (where it arrives on a switch), through various internal queues and decisions, and to the egress port (where it exits the switch).

The QoS building blocks are discussed in the sections that follow. Refer to Figure 16-2 to see the packet flow path through a Catalyst switch, and where each QoS operation is performed. The path across the bottom of the figure shows how QoS parameters can be manipulated at each building block.

> **NOTE**   QoS within a Catalyst switch is based on the idea that each packet receives and carries an *internal DSCP* value with it while it moves through the switch. The internal DSCP is assigned according to how inbound QoS information is trusted, and can be manipulated or marked as a packet is forwarded.

Figure 16-2 *Catalyst Switch QoS Operations and Internal DSCP*

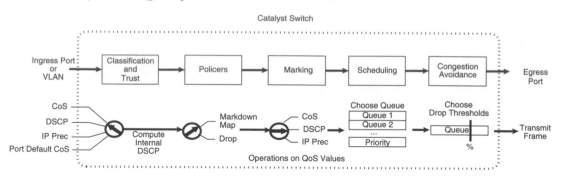

Ingress Queueing

As packets are received on a switch port, they are placed in an ingress queue. In the most basic form, packets are copied into an ingress queue in the order they are received. This queue gives some buffer space so that packets can be stored up during the time the switch is busy forwarding the previous packet.

Catalyst switches offer multiple ingress queues so that packets can be serviced differently—even as they arrive at a switch port. Most switches have two types of ingress queues: a *strict priority queue* and a *standard queue*. If QoS is enabled at all, some packets are automatically placed in the strict priority queue so that they can be serviced ahead of packets in the standard queue. Typically, packets that arrive on a trunk with a CoS value of 5 (usually the highest priority, used for voice traffic) are placed into the strict priority queue.

You can also tune the ingress queues according to their size ratio, how packets are scheduled for servicing, and so on.

> **TIP** The BCMSN course and this text do not cover ingress queueing strategies or configuration. This is because the most common QoS operations involve packet manipulation *after* the packet has been received. Be acquainted only with the fact that ingress queueing is always occurring in a Catalyst switch, and that it can be tuned.

Classification, Trust, and Marking

To manipulate packets according to QoS policies, a switch must somehow identify which level of service each packet should receive. This process is known as *classification*, where each packet is classified according to the type of traffic (UDP or TCP port number, for example), according to parameters matched by an access list, or something more complex, such as by stateful inspection of a traffic flow.

Recall that IP packets carry a ToS or DSCP value within their headers as they travel around a network. Frames on a trunk can also have CoS values associated with them. A switch can then decide whether to trust the ToS, DSCP, or CoS values already assigned to inbound packets. If it trusts any of these values, the values are carried over and used to make QoS decisions inside the switch.

If the QoS values are not trusted, they can be reassigned or overruled. This way, a switch can set the values to something known and trusted, and something that falls within the QoS policies that must be met. This prevents nonpriority users in the network from falsely setting the ToS or DSCP values of their packets to inflated levels so that they receive priority service.

Every switch must decide whether to trust incoming QoS values. Generally, an organization should be able to trust QoS parameters anywhere inside its own network. At the boundary with another organization or service provider, QoS should typically not be trusted. It is also prudent to trust only QoS values that have been assigned by the network devices themselves. Therefore, the QoS values produced by the end users should not be trusted until the network can verify or override them.

The perimeter formed by switches that do not trust incoming QoS is called the *trust boundary*. Usually, the trust boundary exists at the furthest reaches of the enterprise network (access layer switches and WAN or ISP demarcation points). After the trust boundary has been identified and the switches there are configured with untrusted ports, everything else inside the perimeter can be configured to blindly trust incoming QoS values.

Finally, you can configure switches to *mark* or alter the QoS values of packets when needed. For example, at a trust boundary, a switch can override all inbound packets to have a certain known and trusted DSCP value. Elsewhere, traffic belonging to a certain application (IP protocol, UDP or TCP port) can be marked with a specific DSCP value to differentiate it from other types of traffic.

Policers

After packets have been classified, you can configure a switch to limit the bandwidth that certain types of traffic can use. For example, peer-to-peer file sharing might be less desirable than the flow of data for a patient's MRI scans. The peer-to-peer traffic could be classified and then rate-limited to below a specific bandwidth.

Rate limiting is performed by traffic *policers*, which can determine if a classified type of traffic is being forwarded too often. If so, either those packets can be dropped to fall within the required bandwidth, or their DSCP values can be lowered to receive a lesser level of service.

Policers come in two varieties:

- **Microflow policers**—Keep track of the bandwidth used by very granular traffic flows, such as between a source and destination address, using specific source and destination port numbers.

- **Aggregate policers**—Monitor and control a cumulative flow that travels through one or more ingress ports or VLANs.

Traffic flows that fall within the policer limits are called *conforming* or *in-profile*. Flows that exceed the bandwidth limits are called *exceeding*, *violating*, or *out-of-profile*.

TIP   The BCMSN course and this text do not cover policers or their configuration. Be acquainted only with the basic knowledge that policers (both microflow and aggregate) are available in the QoS toolkit on Catalyst switches.

Scheduling

Packets that are ready for forwarding or delivery are placed into egress queues. The queues are then serviced according to a predefined configurable scheduling method. Scheduling is also called *egress queueing* or *congestion management* because it tends to deal with network congestion on an egress port after the congestion occurs.

Catalyst switches usually have multiple queues available to each egress switch port. One queue is reserved as a *strict priority queue* and is always serviced ahead of any other queue. The strict priority queue buffers time-critical packets, such as the voice stream in a voice over IP (VoIP) telephone call. The other egress queues are called *standard queues* and are serviced in a configurable priority—always below that of the strict priority queue.

Packets are assigned to the egress queues according to a mapping function, based on the CoS value. By default, packets with CoS 0 through 3 are assigned to the first standard queue, while CoS 4 through 7 go in the second standard queue.

Basically, congestion is managed in the way the queues are serviced. Catalyst switches use a technique called *Weighted Round Robin (WRR)*. The size of each queue is configured as a percentage of the total queue space. Then, each queue is given a weight so that one with a higher weight is serviced before a queue with a lower weight. Queues are serviced in a round-robin fashion, one after another. The only exception is the priority queue, which always gets serviced until it is empty.

Congestion Avoidance

Switch port queues function to provide space for packets waiting to be transmitted when the port cannot transmit them immediately. If a port becomes congested, the queue begins to fill. What happens when the congestion is severe enough that the queue fills to capacity? New packets to be forwarded cannot be stored in the queue and must be dropped.

Somehow, a switch must anticipate or avoid severe congestion in advance using one of the following available methods:

- Tail drop
- Weighted Random Early Detection

Tail Drop

Tail drop is used as a most basic and drastic means to avoid congestion in port queues. Packets are placed in a queue where the "head" end is closest to being transmitted, and the "tail" end is farthest back in the queue. After the queue fills to capacity, any new packets arriving at the queue are simply dropped at the tail end of the queue.

While tail drop is easy to implement and requires little sophistication, it can have bad effects on existing traffic flows. With a TCP connection, when a packet is dropped, the sender perceives that there is congestion and begins to back off its retransmission timer. The transmission rate is reduced exponentially until the sender receives an acknowledgment indicating that the congestion has improved. Rather than beginning to send at a rapid rate again, the sender must go into the slow-start state, where packets are sent incrementally faster.

The overall effect of tail dropping is that all active TCP connections go into congestion back-off and then slow-start. All the TCP connections do this simultaneously, producing a condition called *global synchronization*. Bandwidth utilization on the switch port oscillates between 100 percent and a low value, rather than smoothly transitioning as the congestion goes away.

Figure 16-3 illustrates tail drop where a switch port queue is experiencing temporary congestion so that no packets can be transmitted. As packets enter the queue on the left, the queue begins to fill. When the queue is full, newly arriving packets are simply dropped. This is the case for Packet E.

Figure 16-3 *Example of Tail Drop in a Switch Port Queue*

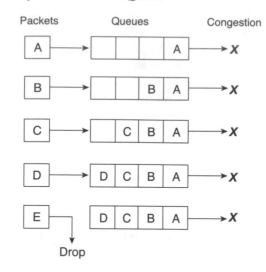

Weighted Random Early Detection

Weighted Random Early Detection (WRED) adds some intelligence to the tail drop congestion avoidance method. Rather than blindly dropping any packets that need to be added to a full queue, WRED attempts to randomly drop packets that are *already in the queue* so that the queue cannot become full.

Recall that each egress port has several assigned queues. Within each queue are several thresholds that WRED can use. Each threshold marks the queue level where WRED begins randomly dropping packets that have specific CoS values. For example, a queue might have threshold t1 at 50 percent for CoS values 0 and 1, and threshold t2 at 75 percent for CoS values 2 and 3. When the queue fills to 50 percent, WRED randomly drop packets with CoS 0 or 1 to reduce the queue size. If the queue fills to 75 percent, packets with CoS 2 or 3 randomly drop, but only after some CoS 0 or 1 packets are dropped first.

Figure 16-4 illustrates the WRED operation. A switch port queue has been configured with two WRED thresholds—t1 at 50 percent and t2 at 75 percent capacity. This port is undergoing congestion so that no packets can be transmitted. As packets arrive on the left, the queue begins to fill. For packets with CoS 0 or 1, WRED can randomly drop them from 0 percent up to the t1 threshold. This has happened to packet A (CoS 0). As packets D (CoS 2) and E (CoS 3) arrive, the same thing happens to packet B (CoS 0).

Figure 16-4 *Example of WRED in a Switch Port Queue*

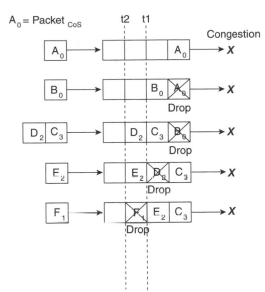

Packet D (CoS 2) has stayed below threshold t2. However, it too is subject to a random drop any-where from 0 percent to t2. When packet E (CoS 2) and F (CoS 1) arrive, packet F is positioned above threshold t1. Above this threshold, any packets with CoS 0 or 1 are unconditionally dropped—so it goes with packet F.

WRED keeps the queue size manageable, while still giving preference to packets with higher CoS values. You can configure this behavior differently, however. Any queue threshold can be mapped to any CoS value.

Switch Port Queues

At this point in the chapter, you should know that each switch port has multiple queues assigned to it—both priority and standard queues. The queue sizes are configurable, as well as the QoS values of the packets that are placed in them. For congestion avoidance, each queue has multiple thresholds that trigger various packet drop actions.

It is important to also understand queue terminology and how Cisco labels and differentiates the queues. Each queue is configured or referenced by its queue ID. The lowest-priority standard queue is always Queue 1. The next-higher priority standard queues follow, beginning with Queue 2. The strict priority queue always receives the highest queue ID number.

Each Catalyst switch port has a queue type notation associated with it. The type notation is of the form: *x***p***y***q***z***t**, where each letter indicates the following:

- **p**—The number of strict priority queues, given by *x*
- **q**—The number of standard queues, given by *y*
- **t**—The number of configurable WRED thresholds per standard queue, given by *z*

Therefore, a switch port of queue type **1p2q2t** has one strict priority queue, two standard queues, and two WRED thresholds per standard queue. (The priority queue never has a threshold because no packets are ever proactively dropped.) Here, the low-priority standard queue is called Queue 1, the next-higher standard queue is called Queue 2, and the strict priority queue is called queue 3. Figure 16-5 shows how this example's port queues are arranged and identified.

Figure 16-5 *Switch Port Queues and Their Type Notation*

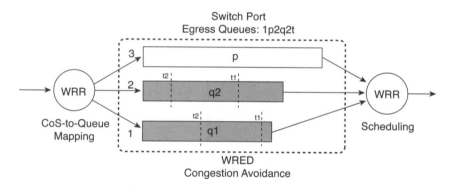

On a Catalyst 6500, you can see what type of transmit or egress queues are available on a port with the **show queueing interface** *type mod/num* command. This command output also shows how the queues are arranged by queue ID order. On all IOS-based Catalyst switches, you can use the **show interfaces** *type mod/num* **capabilities** command to display similar information. Example 16-1 shows sample output from these two commands on two different switches.

Example 16-1 *Determining the Transmit or Egress Queue Types Available on a Switch Port*

```
Switch-Cat6500# show queueing interface gigabitethernet 1/1
Interface GigabitEthernet1/1 queueing strategy:  Weighted Round-Robin
  Port QoS is enabled
  Port is untrusted
  Extend trust state: not trusted [COS = 0]
  Default COS is 0
```

Example 16-1 *Determining the Transmit or Egress Queue Types Available on a Switch Port*

```
Transmit queues [type = 1p2q2t]:
  Queue Id    Scheduling  Num of thresholds
  -----------------------------------------
     1           WRR low          2
     2           WRR high         2
     3           Priority         1
[more output deleted]


Switch-3550# show interface gigabitethernet 0/1 capabilities
GigabitEthernet0/1
  Model:                WS-C3550-48
  Type:                 unknown
  Speed:                1000
  Duplex:               full
  Trunk encap. type:    802.1Q,ISL
  Trunk mode:           on,off,desirable,nonegotiate
  Channel:              yes
  Broadcast suppression: percentage(0-100)
  Flowcontrol:          rx-(off,on,desired),tx-(off,on,desired)
  Fast Start:           yes
  QOS scheduling:       rx-(1q0t),tx-(4q2t),tx-(1p3q2t)
  CoS rewrite:          yes
  ToS rewrite:          yes
  UDLD:                 yes
  Inline power:         no
  SPAN:                 source/destination
  PortSecure:           yes
  Dot1x:                yes
Switch-3550#
```

Notice in the shaded Catalyst 3550 output that two different queueing schemes are reported for the GigabitEthernet port. The port itself has four queues, each with two thresholds. When the expedite or strict priority egress queue is disabled, all four queues are standard queues (4q2t); when it is enabled, one queue becomes the strict priority queue, leaving three other standard queues (1p3q2t).

Foundation Summary

The Foundation Summary is a collection of information that provides a convenient review of many key concepts in this chapter. If you are already comfortable with the topics in this chapter, this summary can help you recall a few details. If you just read this chapter, this review should help solidify some key facts. If you are doing your final preparation before the exam, this summarized information is a convenient way to review the day before the exam.

- Packet delivery can be affected by the following conditions:
  - Delay
  - Jitter
  - Loss

- QoS can be implemented as several models:
  - Best effort—Delivery occurs on a "first-come, first-served" basis with no special handling.
  - IntServ where the necessary bandwidth and handling is reserved from sender to receiver before the traffic flow can begin.
  - DiffServ where special handling of traffic is performed by each switch or router independently, on a per-hop basis. No reservations are necessary; each packet is examined and handled according to local QoS policies.

- QoS can be quantified by one of the following indicators:
  - **CoS**—A 3-bit value (0-7) that is carried along with packets in a trunk
  - **IP Precedence**—A 3-bit value (0-7) that is carried within each packet's IP header
  - **DSCP**—A 6-bit value (0-63) that is carried within each packet's IP header

- The DSCP codepoint is made up of the following two parts:
  - **Class Selector**—A 3-bit value that specifies a class of service
  - **Drop Precedence**—A 3-bit value that specifies how likely a packet is to be dropped (when necessary)

- DSCP codepoint names specify a per-hop behavior (AF or EF), along with the Class Selector (1-4 for AF) and Drop Precedence (1-3 for AF). Codepoint name EF is the best service available for user traffic and has no class or drop precedence notation, although it is actually Class 5.

- The following "building blocks" can perform QoS within a Catalyst switch:

  — **Ingress queueing**—Inbound packets are placed in specific ingress port queues and serviced accordingly.

  — **Classification**—Packets are identified or classified so that the proper QoS policies can be applied to them.

  — **Trust**—A switch can be configured to trust or not trust inbound QoS information from another source.

  — **Marking**—The QoS information of classified packets can be manipulated to obtain different, desired values.

  — **Policer**—The volume of classified traffic can be held within desired limits or can be dropped completely.

  — **Scheduling**—Packets are placed into specific egress queues based on QoS information. These queues are serviced accordingly. Weighted Round Robin (WRR) is normally used for queue scheduling.

  — **Congestion avoidance**—A port queue is protected from congestion proactively. This is normally done by Weighted Random Early Detection (WRED), where packets are randomly dropped to ease the demands for queue space.

- Switch port queues are described by a queue type notation: x**p**y**q**z**t**, where x is the number of **p** strict priority queues; y is the number of **q** standard queues; and z is the number of **t** WRED thresholds.

Q&A

The questions and scenarios in this book are more difficult than what you should experience on the actual exam. The questions do not attempt to cover more breadth or depth than the exam; however, they are designed to make sure that you know the answers. Rather than allowing you to derive the answers from clues hidden inside the questions themselves, the questions challenge your understanding and recall of the subject. Hopefully, these questions will help limit the number of exam questions on which you narrow your choices to two options and then guess.

The answers to these questions can be found in Appendix A.

1. What are some of the problems that QoS can help relieve?

2. Which protocol reserves network resources in the IntServ QoS model?

3. What protocol maintains the DiffServ QoS model?

4. What range of values can the CoS field contain?

5. How is the CoS information passed from LAN switch to LAN switch?

6. How is the IP Precedence field related to the DSCP field?

7. Put the following DSCP codepoints in order of increasing service quality:

    a. EF

    b. AF11

    c. AF23

    d. AF21

    e. Default

8. If a packet contains the DSCP codepoint name "AF31," what would the IP Precedence value be?

9. If a switch port is configured as "untrusted," what is the resulting CoS value of incoming packets?

10. Should there be a trust boundary at every switch, where each overwrites QoS information? Explain why or why not.

11. What method is used for scheduling in Catalyst switches?

12. Name one method that is used for congestion avoidance.

13. When are packets dropped from the strict priority queue on an interface?

14. What is the disadvantage of using the tail drop method to avoid congestion?

15. If WRED drops packets at random, is that bad?

16. A switch port has a queue type 1p1q4t. What does this mean?

17. If a switch port has a queue type 1p2q2t, what is the strict priority queue's queue number?

This chapter covers the following topics that you need to master for the CCNP BCMSN exam:

- **Applying QoS Trust**—This section discusses how the DiffServ per-hop behavior begins, by choosing whether to trust QoS information from other sources.

- **Defining a QoS Policy**—The DiffServ model is implemented through policies that can be defined and applied on a switch.

- **Tuning Egress Scheduling**—This section explains how you can configure a switch to correctly and efficiently buffer packets into queues before forwarding. Scheduling also involves the manner that packets are pulled from the queues as they are forwarded.

- **Using Congestion Avoidance**—This section discusses the configuration that allows a switch to avoid conditions that cause egress queues to fill and overflow.

- **Verifying and Troubleshooting QoS**—This section provides a brief summary of the commands that verify the configuration and operation of DiffServ QoS.

CHAPTER 17

DiffServ QoS Configuration

Chapter 16 covered the basic theory and functionality behind quality of service (QoS) operations on a Catalyst switch. This chapter extends the QoS topic by explaining how you can configure switches to implement DiffServ QoS. Remember that DiffServ is a per-hop behavior, so every switch along the traffic path must be configured to support equivalent QoS policies.

Catalyst switches have a rich, powerful QoS feature set. With power comes versatility, and with versatility comes many commands and confusion. This chapter presents the many QoS features and functions in a logical sequence. Some of the more esoteric features and commands have been omitted from this chapter because they are not covered in the BCMSN course and are too specific for the most common environments.

"Do I Know This Already?" Quiz

The purpose of the "Do I Know This Already?" quiz is to help you decide what parts of this chapter to use. If you already intend to read the entire chapter, you do not necessarily need to answer these questions now.

This 12-question quiz, derived from the major sections in the "Foundation Topics" portion of the chapter, helps you determine how to spend your limited study time.

Table 17-1 outlines the major topics discussed in this chapter and the "Do I Know This Already?" quiz questions that correspond to those topics.

Table 17-1 *"Do I Know This Already?" Foundation Topics Section-to-Question Mapping*

Foundation Topics Section	Questions Covered in This Section
Applying QoS Trust	1–2
Defining a QoS Policy	3–8
Tuning Egress Scheduling	9–10
Using Congestion Avoidance	11–12

> **CAUTION** The goal of self-assessment is to gauge your mastery of the topics in this chapter. If you do not know the answer to a question or are only partially sure of the answer, you should mark this question wrong. Giving yourself credit for an answer you correctly guess skews your self-assessment results and might give you a false sense of security.

1. By default, how does a switch port treat incoming QoS information?

   a. It is trusted.

   b. It is not trusted.

   c. It is just passed along with the packet.

   d. It is overridden according to the type of traffic.

2. What command can configure an interface to trust only the inbound DSCP information?

   a. **mls qos trust dscp**

   b. **no mls qos trust**

   c. **no mls qos untrusted dscp**

   d. **mls trust qos dscp**

3. Which of the following commands defines what traffic will be identified for a QoS policy?

   a. **service-policy**

   b. **policy-map**

   c. **class-map**

   d. **mls trust**

4. What classification method can match traffic flows that use dynamic UDP or TCP port numbers?

   a. Standard IP access list

   b. Extended IP access list

   c. Policer

   d. NBAR

5. Which configuration command can contain actions to take on classified traffic?

   a. **service-policy**

   b. **policy-map**

   c. **class-map**

   d. **mls trust**

6. Which one of the following is an action that cannot be taken on classified traffic?

   a. Mark with new QoS information.

   b. Trust inbound QoS information.

   c. Assign to an outbound interface.

   d. Police it to control the bandwidth used.

7. What command can apply a QoS policy to an interface?

   a. **access-group** *policy-name*

   b. **policy-group** *policy-name*

   c. **mls qos policy** *policy-name*

   d. **service-policy** *policy-name*

8. How many QoS policy maps can be applied to an interface?

   a. One, controlling both inbound and outbound traffic.

   b. Two; one in each inbound or outbound direction.

   c. As many as are configured

   d. None; policy maps cannot be applied to interfaces.

9. Which command configures WRR to service queue 2 16 times more than queue 1, for a 1p2q2t interface?

   a. **wrr-queue bandwidth 1 16**

   b. **wrr-queue bandwidth 16 255**

   c. A and B

   d. Neither A nor B

10. Which command configures WRR to service the strict-priority queue 64 times more than standard queue 1, for a 1p2q2t interface?

   a. **wrr-queue bandwidth 1 4 64**

   b. **wrr-queue bandwidth 2 8 128**

   c. **wrr-queue bandwidth 4 16 255**

   d. None of the above

11. Which command enables WRED on interface queue 2?

    a. **wred 2**

    b. **wrr-queue random-detect 2**

    c. **wred-queue random-detect 2**

    d. **wred-queue 2**

12. A switch port has a minimum WRED threshold configured at 25 percent. If the queue stays below 25 percent, what can happen to the queued packets?

    a. They can be dropped at random.

    b. They can never be dropped.

    c. They will always be dropped.

    d. The minimum threshold must always be at 0 percent.

The answers to the "Do I Know This Already?" quiz are found in Appendix A, "Answers to Chapter 'Do I Know This Already?' Quizzes and Q&A Sections." The suggested choices for your next step are as follows:

- **10 or less overall score**—Read the entire chapter. This includes the "Foundation Topics," "Foundation Summary," and "Q&A" sections.

- **11 or 12 overall score**—If you want more review on these topics, skip to the "Foundation Summary" section, and then go to the "Q&A" section at the end of the chapter. Otherwise, move to Chapter 18, "IP Telephony."

Foundation Topics

Before any QoS features can be configured and used on a Catalyst switch, QoS itself must be enabled. By default, QoS is disabled, so any of its features must be explicitly configured according to the unique policies needed.

Does this mean that the switch offers no QoS at all? Not really; having QoS disabled simply means that only "best effort" packet delivery is in use. For example, switch port queues use the tail-drop method during times of congestion. Although this might not be ideal, it does take care of the basic packet forwarding needs.

To enable QoS on a switch, use the following global configuration command:

Switch(config)# **mls qos**

Also, keep in mind that Catalyst switches implement the DiffServ per-hop behavior by basing QoS operations on an *internal Differentiated Services Code Point (DSCP)* value. Refer to Figure 17-1 to see how the internal DSCP is used as a packet moves through the switch at these locations:

1. Packets entering the switch are assigned an internal DSCP value that is derived only from the QoS parameter that is trusted on the inbound switch port. The trusted parameter is mapped into DSCP values.

2. As the packets are internally switched, each packet's internal DSCP value (as well as other QoS parameters) can be adjusted or acted upon.

3. As packets are queued at an engress port, the internal DSCP value is converted to a CoS (class of service) value, which is then used to determine the egress queueing or scheduling. The DSCP values are mapped into CoS values

Although the various QoS parameter maps add to the complexity of configuring QoS on a Catalyst switch, the maps are a simple concept to remember. They are explained in more detail at the appropriate points in this chapter.

Figure 17-1 *Mapping QoS Parameters to and from Internal DSCP Values*

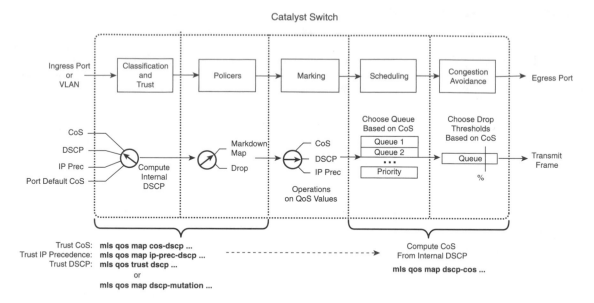

Applying QoS Trust

When inbound packets are accepted into a switch, the switch can be selective about which (if any) of each packet's QoS information will be trusted. If the packets originate from a trusted source, the QoS information can be safely trusted, too. Usually, it is a best practice to configure switches at the edge of a trusted QoS domain to verify or overwrite any QoS information that comes into the domain. This way, any other switch or router within the domain can blindly trust QoS information that is seen.

You can configure QoS trust in two ways:

■ Per-interface

■ As part of a QoS policy on specific types of traffic

The per-interface trust is described in the next section. Policy trust is described as part of the section, "Defining a QoS Policy."

Trust QoS on an Interface

On each interface where consistent QoS trust is to be defined, use the following interface configuration command:

```
Switch(config-if)# mls qos trust {cos | dscp | ip-precedence}
```

Here, one of the following values can be trusted and used internally as the switch makes forwarding decisions:

- The inbound CoS, which is taken from trunking tags
- DSCP, which is taken from the inbound IP packet headers
- IP Precedence, which is also taken from the inbound IP packet headers

Do Not Trust any QoS Information

If you choose to not trust any QoS information (the default condition), use the following interface configuration command:

```
Switch(config-if)# no mls qos trust
```

In this case, the inbound CoS and DSCP information are set to one of the following values:

- 0 (zero), which is the default
- The interface default CoS value, which is defined using the **mls qos cos** *cos-value* interface configuration command

Then, you can make further modifications to the QoS information as part of a QoS class-based policy.

Mapping Inbound QoS Information

Any inbound QoS information, whether trusted or a fixed CoS value (untrusted), must be mapped into internal DSCP values. Each packet receives this new DSCP value, which is used as the packet travels throughout the switch. A separate map can be configured for these inbound parameters:

- CoS—Each of the eight possible CoS values is mapped into an internal DSCP value.

  Table 17-2 provides the default mapping, with each DSCP value offering "best effort" delivery.

Table 17-2 *CoS-to-Internal DSCP Value Mapping*

CoS	0	1	2	3	4	5	6	7
DSCP	0 Default	8 AF10	16 AF20	24 AF30	32 AF40	40 EF	48 (Internet-work Control)	56 (Network Control)

To change the mapping, use the following global configuration command, where each of the *dscp* values is a number 0 to 63:

```
Switch(config)# mls qos map cos-dscp dscp1 ... dscp8
```

■ **IP Precedence**—Each of the eight possible IP Precedence values is mapped into an internal DSCP value.

Table 17-3 provides the default mapping, with each DSCP value offering "best effort" delivery.

Table 17-3 *IP Precedence-to-Internal DSCP Value Mapping*

IP Precedence	0	1	2	3	4	5	6	7
DSCP	0 Default	8 AF10	16 AF20	24 AF30	32 AF40	40 EF	48 (Internet-work Control)	56 (Network Control)

To change the mapping, use the following global configuration command, where each of the *dscp* values is a number from 0 to 63:

```
Switch(config)# mls qos map ip-prec-dscp dscp1 ... dscp8
```

■ **DSCP**—Inbound DSCP values can be mapped into different internal DSCP values using a DSCP mutation map. This can be handy when the switch is at the boundary between two QoS domains.

By default, no DSCP mutation occurs. If inbound DSCP information is trusted, it is used as-is for the internal DSCP.

To define a DSCP mutation map, first create a named map consisting of up to eight entries by repeating this global configuration command:

```
Switch(config)# mls qos map dscp-mutation dscp-mutation-name in-dscp to out-
dscp
```

Each of the *dscp* values is a number from 0 to 63. Then, apply the mutation map to a specific ingress interface with this interface configuration command:

```
Switch(config-if)# mls qos dscp-mutation dscp-mutation-name
```

NOTE The default mapping from CoS or IP Precedence to DSCP only uses DSCP values that indicate "best effort" delivery. That is fine for a default, but you should always alter the default mapping so that distinct drop precedences are used instead. For example, CoS 3 defaults to AF30 (the zero means "best effort"). It is better practice to map it to something like AF31 so that switches and routers along the way can attempt to drop other less-critical traffic in preference to this traffic.

For example, you can use a common CoS-to-DSCP mapping with the following command:

```
mls qos map cos-dscp 0 10 18 26 34 46 48 56
```

You can use Table 16-2 as a handy reference to convert between any QoS parameter or value.

Notice that the CoS values now map to these per-hop behaviors, each having a specific drop precedence: 0 (best effort), 10 (AF11), 18 (AF21), 26 (AF31), 34 (AF41), 46 (EF), 48 (Internetwork Control), and 56 (Network Control). Now, if other DSCP values occur within your network traffic, you know exactly how your mapped values will be handled in relation to the others. (DSCP values 48 and 56 do not usually have a class or drop precedence associated with them, because they are reserved for routing protocol and other maintenance protocol traffic.)

Defining a QoS Policy

QoS policies are easy to define and use, thanks to the Modular QoS CLI (MQC) feature. Policies are defined and used in this order:

1. One or more QoS *classes* are defined to classify (identify) specific traffic. Think of each class as a template that matches a particular kind of traffic flow.

2. One or more QoS *policies* are defined to reference or group multiple QoS classes as a single entity. The classes identify a group of different types of traffic. Each policy also contains actions that can mark, police, or shape traffic classifed by each class.

3. Each egress interface can be assigned one QoS policy in each direction. For example, one policy can be assigned for inbound traffic on the interface, while another policy can be assigned for outbound traffic. When assigned, the policy begins to classify and act on traffic passing through the interface.

These steps are described in more detail in the next several sections.

Defining a QoS Class to Classify Traffic

First, define the QoS class with this global configuration command:

```
Switch(config)# class-map class-name [match-all | match-any]
```

You can configure multiple conditions into the class map to match or classify different types of traffic. If the class should match against all the conditions (the default), use the **match-all** keyword. Otherwise, use the **match-any** keyword to allow any of the conditions to trigger a match.

You can classify packets with traditional access lists, matching against any parameter contained in the IP packet header. You can also use Network-Based Application Recognition (NBAR) to match against more complex or dynamic fields.

After you configure the final **match** command, use the **exit** command to leave the class map configuration mode.

Classifying Traffic with an Access List

You must define the IP access list separately, as a global configuration command and not part of the class map. After you configure the access list with the **access-list** *access-list-number* or the **ip access-list extended** command, you can reference the access list as a matching condition using the following class map configuration command:

```
Switch(config-cmap)# match access-group name access-list
```

Here, you can specify the access list by name or number.

> **NOTE** You can also easily match against CoS, IP Precedence, or DSCP values without defining a more complex access list. Do this with one of the following class map configuration commands, which match against up to eight values each:
>
> ```
> Switch(config-cmap)# match ip precedence ipprec1 [...ipprecN]
> Switch(config-cmap)# match ip dscp dscp1 [...dscpN]
> ```

Classifying Traffic with NBAR

NBAR offers a more complex inspection of IP packets. NBAR can recognize traffic from several applications, whether the UDP or TCP ports are statically or dynamically assigned. This allows the upper OSI layers to be inspected beyond simple port number matching. HTTP traffic can also be classified according to URL or host name.

To match a traffic flow with NBAR, use the following class map configuration command:

```
Switch(config-cmap)# match protocol protocol-name
```

The NBAR feature is periodically updated to support the recognition of newly developed applications. New protocol inspections can be added to an existing Cisco IOS Software version through the use of Packet Description Language Module (PDLM) files. This allows new additions to be added to the NBAR suite without having to upgrade the entire IOS image. You should review the most current information on Cisco.com to determine which protocols NBAR recognizes in your version of the IOS software.

> **NOTE** For more information about NBAR, refer to the article "Network-Based Application Recognition," which you can find at www.cisco.com/en/US/products/sw/iosswrel/ps1839/products_feature_guide09186a0080087cd0.html.
>
> The list of protocol names is rather lengthy. Do not worry about learning any of these; just be aware that there are many and expanding all the time. To give you an idea of the wide range of applications that NBAR recognizes, a sample listing of protocol name keywords can include the following:
>
> ■ Non-UDP/TCP protocols: **egp**, **eigrp**, **gre**, **icmp**, **ipinip**, **ipsec**

- Static UDP/TCP protocols: **bgp**, **cuseeme**, **dhcp**, **dns**, **finger**, **gopher**, **http**, **secure-http**, **imap**, **irc**, **kerberos**, **l2tp**, **ldap**, **pptp**, **sqlserver**, **netbios**, **nfs**, **nntp**, **notes**, **novadigm**, **ntp**, **pcanywhere**, **pop3**, **printer**, **rip**, **rsvp**, **secure-ftp**, **secure-imap**, **secure-irc**, **secure-ldap**, **smtp**, **snmp**, **secure-nntp**, **socks**, **secure-pop3**, **ssh**, **secure-telnet**, **syslog**, **telnet**, **xwindows**

- Stateful (dynamic) UDP/TCP protocols: **citrix**, **citrix app**, **ftp**, **exchange**, **fasttrack**, **gnutella**, **http**, **kazaa2**, **napster**, **netshow**, **rcmd**, **realaudio**, **rtp**, **sqlnet**, **streamwork**, **sunrpc**, **tftp**, **vdolive**

What Happens When NBAR Is Enabled?

As a bonus, think about what happens on a Catalyst switch when NBAR is enabled. Recall from Chapters 3 and 13 how a Layer 3 switch operates. Normally, Cisco Express Forwarding (CEF) is used to efficiently switch packets after the CEF and ternary content addressable memory (TCAM) tables are populated. Packets can be inspected with access lists by using the TCAM, with no performance penalty.

If NBAR is enabled on an interface, packets must also be inspected. For protocols that use a static port number, you can think of NBAR as using an access list for matching. Again, this might not impact switching performance if the TCAM is used. For other "stateful" protocols, involving dynamic port numbers or other information buried within the packet, NBAR must inspect beyond the IP header. In this case, neither access lists nor the TCAM can be used; instead, something must perform the inspection by brute force.

Therefore, when NBAR is configured on an interface, the switch CPU (the MSFC2, for example) must process *all* traffic passing in and out of that interface. Obviously, this is not as efficient as CEF-switching in hardware, so performance through the interface could suffer.

Defining a QoS Policy

First, define the QoS policy with the following global configuration command:

```
Switch(config)# policy-map policy-name
```

Class maps must then be identified so that traffic can be classified for the policy. You can use multiple commands to perform an action on the classified traffic. After the final policy map command is configured, use the **exit** command to leave the policy map configuration mode.

Identifying the QoS Class Maps

In the policy map, you must identify each class map that will be used as part of an overall QoS policy. Use the following policy map configuration command:

```
Switch(config-pmap)# class class-name
```

Marking QoS Information

After you use the class maps to correctly identify or classify the traffic, you can perform one of the following marking actions on that traffic:

- Mark the DSCP value.

      Switch(config-pmap)# `set ip dscp` `dscp-value`

  The DSCP value can be given as a decimal number (0 to 63) or as the name of a DSCP codepoint (**ef**, **af11**, or **af12**).

- Mark the IP Precedence value.

      Switch(config-pmap)# `set ip precedence` `ip-precedence-value`

  The IP Precedence value can be given as a decimal number (0 to 7).

Trusting QoS Information

In some cases, only certain QoS information contained in the classified traffic should be trusted. All other traffic is trusted according to other policies or conditions. Use the following policy map configuration command to establish policy-based trust:

      Switch(config-pmap)# `trust {cos | dscp | ip-precedence}`

For these packets, the specified QoS information will be accepted for use within the switch; however, this information can still be overwritten or manipulated as part of the QoS policy.

Policing Classified Traffic

Although QoS policing is not covered in the BCMSN course, it is mentioned here so that you have an understanding of its use within the QoS process.

A policer is defined according to the scope of the traffic it monitors, as well as to the action it takes upon that traffic flow. An aggregate policer monitors the cumulative amount of data produced by one or more individual flows between a source and destination. In a more granular case, a microflow policer monitors only a single flow between a source and a destination.

Policers use a token bucket algorithm, where the lengths of matching inbound frames are added to the bucket. Every 0.25 ms (or 1/4000 of a second), the maximum sustained *committed information rate (CIR)* targeted by the policer is subtracted from the bucket. Traffic can also burst over the CIR, up to the *normal burst rate*, for a short period of time. In addition, traffic that rises above the normal burst rate is measured against the *peak information rate (PIR)*. Traffic that stays within the policed limits (CIR and burst rates) is called *in-profile*, whereas excessive traffic is called *out-of-profile*.

Policers can take action on any traffic that stays under the CIR (*conform action*), rises above the burst rate (*exceed action*), and rises above the PIR (*violate action*). The action taken can be the following:

- Forward the traffic.
- Drop the traffic.
- Mark down the DSCP value of the traffic before forwarding.

To define a policer, use the following policy map configuration command:

```
police [aggregate name] [flow] bits-per-second normal-burst-bytes [extended-burst-
    bytes] [pir peak-rate-bps] [conform-action action] [exceed-action action] [violate-
    action action]
```

Here, an *action* can be one of the following:

- **drop**—Drop the packet.
- **set-dscp-transmit** [*new-dscp*]—Set the DSCP value in the packet.
- **set-prec-transmit** [*new-precedence*]—Set the IP Precedence value in the packet.
- **transmit**—Send the packet normally.

> **NOTE** A policer can also take other unique actions on matched traffic. For example, you can use a policer to identify and dispose of undesirable or unwanted traffic entering (or exiting) your network. A policer can drop packets that are classified by a class map. This is done by giving the policer bogus rates and making all actions (conform, exceed, and violate) set to **drop**.

Apply a QoS Policy to an Interface

After a QoS policy map has been defined, it can be applied to a physical interface on the switch. An interface can have only one active policy applied in each direction. This means that two policies can be applied to an interface:

- One for inbound traffic
- One for outbound traffic

Use the following interface configuration command to begin using a policy:

```
Switch(config-if)# service-policy [input | output] policy-name
```

Tuning Egress Scheduling

After you define and apply the QoS classes and policies, you can tune the scheduling process. Packet scheduling involves how the switch places each packet into an egress queue and how each queue is serviced. Catalyst switches support the Weighted Round Robin (WRR) scheduling algorithm.

Each queue associated with an interface is serviced according to its weight, relative to the other queues. Strict-priority queues do not have a weighting value; they are always serviced as long as they have packets waiting.

WRR looks at the weighting values to determine the ratio of how many packets to transmit from one queue versus another. Although the actual configuration command uses the keyword **bandwidth**, the values are actually relative weights used to form a ratio.

By default, interfaces with two standard queues are assigned weights 4 and 255, respectively. The second queue receives about 64 times the amount of data transmitted on its turn for every one unit of data from the first queue.

To change the weights of the queues, use the following interface configuration command:

```
Switch(config-if)# wrr-queue bandwidth weight1 weight2 [weight3] [weight4]
```

Weight values can range from 1 to 255. The number of *weight* parameters that you can set depends on the number of standard egress queues available on the interface. The number of standard queues varies between Catalyst platforms.

Using Congestion Avoidance

With egress queues, congestion avoidance is partnered with queue scheduling, so the two are indistinguishable. As a result, both features are configured with the WRR configuration commands beginning with **wrr-queue**.

Mapping Internal DSCP Values to CoS Values for Queueing

Recall that as packets travel within a switch, they each carry an internal DSCP value. That value is mapped from a trusted QoS information source when each packet enters the switch. After the switch determines which egress port each packet will use when exiting, some method must determine how the packet will be queued for transmission.

The internal DSCP values are mapped back into CoS values, which are then used for egress queueing and scheduling.

Table 17-4 provides the default DSCP-to-CoS mappings, with each range of DSCP values corresponding to a single CoS value.

Table 17-4   *Default DSCP-to-CoS Value Mappings*

DSCP	0-7	8-15	16-23	24-31	32-39	40-47	48-55	56-63
	Default	AF10-AF13	AF20-AF23	AF30-AF33	AF40-AF43	EF	Internetwork Control	Network Control
CoS	0	1	2	3	4	5	6	7

To change the mapping, repeat the following global configuration command as many times as necessary:

```
Switch(config)# mls qos map dscp-cos dscp-list to cos-value
```

Here, the *dscp-list* can be a single DSCP value (0 to 63), a hyphenated range of values, or multiple values and ranges separated by commas. The *cos-value* is a single CoS value (0 to 7).

Mapping Packets into Egress Queues

As packets are moved toward the egress ports, they must be sorted so that each is placed in the correct prioritized egress queue. Otherwise, all packets would be put in the same queue, with no preference to any flow or type of traffic.

WRR places packets into egress queues according to a mapping between the CoS value and the queue number. Packets can also be buffered in a queue that has a desired drop threshold. Drop thresholds are used during congestion avoidance, as discussed in the later section, "Setting WRED Thresholds."

To define the map that associates packet CoS values to specific egress queue drop thresholds, use the following interface configuration command:

```
Switch(config-if)# wrr-queue cos-map queue-id threshold-id cos-list
```

Packets with a CoS value specified in the *cos-list* will be placed in the queue ID given, with the threshold ID applied. By default, the CoS values are divided in half. CoS 0 and 1 go to queue 1 threshold 1, CoS 2 and 3 go to queue 1 threshold 2, CoS 4 goes to queue 2 threshold 1, and CoS 6 and 7 go to queue 2 threshold 2. CoS 5 always gets placed in the strict-priority queue, if one is available.

> **NOTE** Packets with CoS 5 are always placed in the strict-priority or egress expedite queue, *but that queue cannot be used until it is enabled.* Use the following interface configuration command to enable the strict-priority queue:
>
> ```
> Switch(config-if)# priority-queue out
> ```

Avoiding Congestion by Using Tail Drop

For standard tail-drop behavior, WRR must be disabled on an interface. After the egress queue fills, tail drop causes newly queued packets to be dropped instead. This occurs at the 100 percent mark of the queue. Normally, tail drop should not be used because it can adversely affect the network performance of TCP sessions.

> **NOTE** The strict-priority queue is never a candidate for WRR-based queue scheduling. In the event that the queue fills to capacity, new packets will be dropped, following standard tail-drop behavior.

To enable tail-drop operation for an egress queue, use the following interface configuration command:

```
Switch(config-if)# no wrr-queue random-detect queue-id
```

Avoiding Congestion by Using WRED

By default, each switch interface has WRED enabled. If tail drop is being used instead, WRED has been disabled. To revert back to WRED, it must be re-enabled. Note that WRED is used on a per-queue basis and that it must be enabled on each of the interface's queues individually. To enable WRED for a specific queue number, use this interface configuration command:

```
Switch(config-if)# wrr-queue random-detect queue-id
```

Setting WRED Thresholds

WRED keeps two thresholds per queue for most types of interfaces—a minimum threshold and a maximum threshold. If the queue level is below the minimum, WRED cannot drop any packets. While the level is between the minimum and maximum values, WRED is allowed to randomly drop packets at a rate proportional to the queue level. When the queue level rises above the maximum threshold, all new packets will be dropped. To set the WRED thresholds, use the following interface configuration command:

```
Switch(config-if)# wrr-queue random-detect {max-threshold | min-threshold} queue-id
    threshold-percent-1 ... threshold-percent-N
```

By default, queue 1 (the lowest-priority standard queue) has a minimum threshold of 0 and a maximum threshold of 40 percent. Queue 2 (the next-higher priority standard queue) has a minimum of 0 and a maximum of 100 percent.

The low-priority standard queue will always be susceptible to random drops (minimum is 0 percent). When the low-priority standard queue fills to 40 percent, all new packets will be dropped. The higher-priority queue is also susceptible to random drops (its minimum is also 0 percent); however, this queue's level must reach 100 percent before all packets are dropped.

> **NOTE** The strict-priority queue is never a candidate for WRED-based drops. Instead, all packets queued are guaranteed to be delivered. Only when the queue fills to capacity will new packets be dropped, following standard tail-drop behavior.

A QoS Configuration Example

QoS configuration within a single switch can be confusing and complex. To properly implement QoS policies in a common QoS domain (your entire network, for example), you must configure the QoS policies on each and every switch. This example is designed to help solidify the many topics presented in this chapter so that you can identify trust boundaries and configure QoS in a logical fashion.

Figure 17-2 shows a simple network consisting of two Catalyst multilayer switches. Catalyst A sits at the edge of the QoS domain, where this network joins another "public" network. Catalyst B, on the other hand, sits inside the QoS domain and interfaces to some end user devices. One port connects to a user PC and another port connects to a Cisco IP Phone. Another user PC connects to the IP Phone's data port.

Figure 17-2 *Network Diagram for the QoS Example*

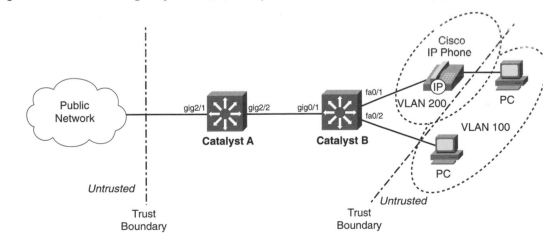

To configure QoS in this network, you must first define the QoS domain, where QoS information will be known and trusted. The edge of this domain lies at the points where QoS information is no longer trusted—at the *trust boundaries*. In Figure 17-2, a trust boundary exists where Catalyst A connects to the public network. Another trust boundary exists where Catalyst B meets the end users. The user PC should not be trusted because it might have applications that try to spoof or elevate the QoS information to bogus values in an effort to get better service. The IP Phone itself can be trusted because it is just another network device that can be configured and controlled. However, it lies at another trust boundary where another user PC connects. (The details of QoS trust with an IP Phone are discussed in Chapter 18 "IP Telephony.")

Configuring QoS Trust

First, you should configure Catalyst A for its trust boundary on interface GigabitEthernet 2/1. Any QoS information coming from the public network should be untrusted because you have no control over the values being sent or who is sending them. You can use the following configuration commands to accomplish this:

```
mls qos
interface gigabitethernet 2/1
    no mls qos trust
```

Notice that the first command enabled QoS on the switch. Do not forget this important first step. The interface is configured to consider all inbound QoS information as untrusted. As a result, any inbound CoS (assuming this interface is a trunk) and DSCP values are set to 0, the default.

Notice also that this interface configuration command is not necessary because all switch ports are configured as untrusted by default. This also means that all of Catalyst A's ports that are inside the QoS domain (the trusted side) will not trust QoS information that should be known and valid. Do not forget to configure the trusted ports—*every* switch port that connects to another switch inside your network. If you configure QoS consistently throughout your network, you can always trust the QoS information as it moves about.

For this network, inbound DSCP information will be used as the trusted quantity. This is possible because all the switches are multilayer switches and can understand and work with DSCP as an IP or Layer 3 quantity. Catalyst A's GigabitEthernet 2/2 interface is then configured as a trusted port with the following configuration commands:

```
interface gigabitethernet 2/2
    mls qos trust dscp
```

> **NOTE** Remember that only *inbound* QoS information can be trusted. Outbound QoS information is simply sent on to the next-hop switch or router where it will be evaluated against another trust relationship there. Any DSCP information that Catalyst A accepts from the internal network will also be forwarded out toward the public network on interface GigabitEthernet 2/1. Does the network on the other side of the QoS boundary have to accept or trust the QoS information you send? Only if it wants to. It is up to the network administrators on that end to decide what sort of trust relationship to configure on their switches.

Next, you must configure Catalyst B for its trust boundary. Interface GigabitEthernet 0/1 is on the inside or trusted side of the QoS domain. Therefore, DSCP information can be trusted:

```
mls qos
interface gigabitethernet 0/1
    mls qos trust dscp
```

Interface FastEthernet 0/2 connects to an end user's PC and should not trust any QoS information. The following configuration commands set the trust boundary and force any inbound CoS and DSCP values to 0 (by default):

```
interface fastethernet 0/2
    no mls qos trust
```

Interface FastEthernet 0/1 presents an interesting case. Here, a Cisco IP Phone is connected, transporting Voice over IP (VoIP) traffic, as well as normal data from the attached PC. As Chapter 18 discusses, a Catalyst switch can detect an IP Phone via Cisco Discovery Protocol (CDP) and can instruct the phone to extend a trust boundary to its auxiliary data port. The voice traffic from the phone should be implicitly trusted because the phone is both a Cisco device and a small switch that can be configured and controlled.

The PC connected to the phone, however, should normally be untrusted and have all inbound CoS values set to 0. This is mentioned here to show how trust boundaries also exist at any connected IP Phones. The following configuration commands for the phone trust boundary are fully explained in Chapter 18:

```
interface fastethernet 0/1
    switchport voice vlan 200
    switchport priority extend cos 0
```

Configuring a QoS Class to Classify Traffic

In this example, suppose you need to make sure some types of traffic receive premium service within your network. These types of traffic are classified at the QoS domain boundary, at Catalyst A. HTTP traffic from a server at 10.1.1.1 is considered to contain important, time-critical market data for your business. Any virtual private network (VPN) traffic using the IP Security (IPSec) protocol is also considered to carry encrypted data to and from your business partners and remote sites.

First, you must configure a class map to match the HTTP and IPSec traffic. Use an extended access list to identify TCP port 80 (HTTP), while using the NBAR feature to identify IPSec packets. Configure the class map on Catalyst A with the following commands:

```
ip access-list extended MarketWWW
    permit tcp host 10.1.1.1 any eq 80
class-map GoodTraffic match-any
    match access-group name MarketWWW
    match protocol ipsec
```

So far, the idea is to classify the time-critical, very important, or "good" traffic so that a QoS policy can guarantee better service. Sometimes, classifying nuisance or "bad" traffic so that it can be given a lower-level service migt also be necessary. In certain cases, you might choose to drop this type of traffic altogether. Lowering the level of service prevents undesirable traffic from using the network resources needed for more important traffic.

For this example, peer-to-peer file sharing traffic generated by the KaZaA version 2 applications is considered to be unrelated to your business. It is tolerated for the benefit of the employees, but it should receive only "best effort" service. Define a class map on Catalyst A to identify this type of traffic with the following commands:

```
class-map BadTraffic match-any
    match protocol kazaa2
```

Configuring a QoS Policy to Act on Classified Traffic

Now that class maps have been configured to classify or identify specific traffic, some action should be performed to adjust the QoS parameters. This makes up the actual QoS policy, which is defined as a policy map. First, traffic classified by the GoodTraffic class map is given a DSCP value of AF21 so that other switches know to provide good delivery service. Anything classifed by the BadTraffic class map is given a DSCP value of 0, where only "best effort" or default delivery service is requested.

After the policy map is configured, it is applied to an interface in the inbound direction. This classifies and marks traffic as it is received, at the QoS boundary. The policy map is configured on Catalyst A and applied with the following commands:

```
policy-map MyPolicy
    class GoodTraffic
        set ip dscp af21
    class BadTraffic
        set ip dscp 0
interface gigabitethernet 2/1
    service-policy MyPolicy in
```

Egress Queue Tuning

After packets have been classified and marked, you should also consider how the QoS information will be used to queue and schedule packet delivery. In this example, DSCP values AF21 (18) and 0 have been used to mark traffic. In addition, Voice over IP (VoIP) packets associated with the IP Phone on Catalyst B can be expected to have DSCP values AF31 (26) and EF (46). (Chapter 18 discusses this in more detail.) All other applications will have their packets marked to DSCP 0, as a result of the trust boundaries configured throughout the network.

At a minimum, you should look at how the known DSCP values will be mapped to CoS values as packets are sent to the egress queues. CoS is always used to decide how packets are queued and scheduled for transmission. In the default state, before any further configuration is done, the DSCP-to-CoS map looks like Table 17-5.

Table 17-5 *Default DSCP-to-CoS Value Mappings*

DSCP	0-7	8-15	16-23	24-31	32-39	40-47	48-55	56-63
	Default	AF10-AF13	AF20-AF23	AF30-AF33	AF40-AF43	EF	Internetwork Control	Network Control
CoS	0	1	2	3	4	5	6	7

GoodTraffic packets (DSCP 18) are mapped to CoS 2, BadTraffic packets (DSCP 0) are CoS 0, and VoIP packets (DSCP 26 and 46) become CoS 3 and 5, respectively.

After the CoS values are mapped, they are used to determine into which egress queue each packet will be placed. By default, all switch ports have WRED enabled. For an egress port with a 1p2q2t queueing strategy, the following scheduling occurs:

- CoS 0 and 1: Standard queue 1, threshold 1
- CoS 2 and 3: Standard queue 1, threshold 2
- CoS 4: Standard queue 2, threshold 1
- CoS 6 and 7: Standard queue 2, threshold 2
- CoS 5: Always sent to the strict-priority queue

Assume this is an acceptable scheduling configuration, as CoS 3 will be serviced before CoS 2, which will be serviced before CoS 0, and so on. CoS 5, used for the VoIP voice bearer packets, will always be sent to the strict-priority queue. That queue is, by definition, always serviced before any other queue. Indeed, that sounds reasonable for this example network. No other configuration should be necessary, right?

Actually, the default condition for every switch port is to disable the strict-priority or expedite egress queue. That is not what you need at all—the voice traffic having CoS 5 will be sent to a standard queue to contend with other less time-critical traffic. If you expect to use the strict-priority queues, do not forget to enable them. The example configuration concludes with the following configuration commands on Catalyst A:

```
interface range gigabitethernet 2/1 - 2
    priority-queue out
```

Catalyst B receives the following configuration commands:

```
interface gigabitethernet 0/1
    priority-queue out
interface range fastethernet 0/1 - 2
    priority-queue out
```

Verifying and Troubleshooting QoS

You can display information about many aspects of QoS on a Catalyst switch. Use the information in Table 17-6 to determine which command is useful for a particular situation.

Table 17-6 *Commands to Display Information About QoS on a Catalyst Switch*

Task	Command Syntax
Verify QoS trust settings on an interface.	**show mls qos interface** *type mod/num*
Verify egress queueing on an interface.	**show mls qos interface** *type mod/num* **queueing**
Verify QoS settings only on a Catalyst 6500 interface.	**show queueing interface** *type mod/num*
View all QoS parameter mappings.	**show mls qos maps**

The **show mls qos interface** command shows the following information about an interface:

- QoS trust (if any) configured on the interface
- Default CoS value (if any) used to override inbound CoS
- DSCP mutation map
- QoS trust extension to a connected Cisco IP Phone

Example 17-1 provides sample output from the **show mls qos interface** command.

Example 17-1   **show mls qos interface** *Command Output*

```
Switch# show mls qos interface gigabitethernet 0/1
GigabitEthernet0/1
trust state: trust cos
trust mode: trust cos
COS override: dis
default COS: 0
DSCP Mutation Map: Default DSCP Mutation Map
trust device: none
```

The **show mls qos interface queueing** command shows the following information about an interface:

- Current state of the strict-priority (expedite) queue
- WRR transmit queue weighting (bandwidth)
- Egress queue ratios (qid-weights)
- Egress queue scheduling (CoS-to-queue mapping)

Example 17-2 shows sample output from the **show mls qos interface queueing** command.

Example 17-2   **show mls qos interface queueing** *Command Output*

```
Switch# show mls qos interface gigabitethernet 0/1 queueing
GigabitEthernet0/1
Egress expedite queue: dis
wrr bandwidth weights:
qid-weights
 1 - 25
 2 - 25
 3 - 25
 4 - 25
Dscp-threshold map:
    d1 :  d2 0  1  2  3  4  5  6  7  8  9
    -------------------------------------
    0 :     01 01 01 01 01 01 01 01 01 01
    1 :     01 01 01 01 01 01 01 01 01 01
    2 :     01 01 01 01 01 01 01 01 01 01
    3 :     01 01 01 01 01 01 01 01 01 01
    4 :     01 01 01 01 01 01 01 01 01 01
    5 :     01 01 01 01 01 01 01 01 01 01
    6 :     01 01 01 01
```

continues

Example 17-2 **show mls qos interface queueing** *Command Output (Continued)*

```
Cos-queue map:
cos-qid
 0 - 1
 1 - 1
 2 - 2
 3 - 2
 4 - 3
 5 - 3
 6 - 4
 7 - 4
```

Notice from the shaded text that the strict-priority (expedite) queue is disabled. This is the default state for all interfaces, until the strict-priority queue is enabled with the **priority-queue out** interface configuration command. Example 17-3 provides the same output after the strict-priority queue has been enabled.

Example 17-3 **show mls qos interface queueing** *Command Output After Enabling the Strict-Priority Queue*

```
Switch# config term
Enter configuration commands, one per line.  End with CNTL/Z.
Switch(config)# interface gigabitethernet 0/1
Switch(config-if)# priority-queue out
Switch(config-if)#^Z
Switch#
Switch# show mls qos interface gigabitethernet 0/1 queueing
GigabitEthernet0/1
Egress expedite queue: ena
wrr bandwidth weights:
qid-weights
 1 - 25
 2 - 25
 3 - 25
 4 - 25     when expedite queue is disabled
Dscp-threshold map:
     d1 :  d2 0  1  2  3  4  5  6  7  8  9
     ---------------------------------------
      0 :    01 01 01 01 01 01 01 01 01 01
[other output deleted]
```

Foundation Summary

The Foundation Summary is a collection of information that provides a convenient review of many key concepts in this chapter. If you are already comfortable with the topics in this chapter, this summary can help you recall a few details. If you just read this chapter, this review should help solidify some key facts. If you are doing your final preparation before the exam, this summarized information is a convenient way to review the day before the exam.

You can configure a switch to trust the following inbound QoS parameters:

- CoS (from a trunk)
- DSCP (from IP headers)
- IP Precedence (from IP headers)

Table 17-7 *QoS Trust Configuration Commands*

Task	Command Syntax
Enable QoS on a switch.	**mls qos**
Choose inbound QoS info to trust on an interface.	**mls qos trust {cos | dscp | ip-precedence}**
Or none at all.	**no mls qos trust**

Remember the basic structure of modular QoS configuration:

1. Define a QoS class map to classify specific traffic for a policy; define as many class maps as necessary.

2. Define a QoS policy that uses class maps to identify traffic; the policy also contains actions with each class map that will be taken on classified traffic.

3. Apply the QoS policy to an interface. One policy can be applied to an inbound traffic flow and one to an outbound traffic flow.

Table 17-8 *QoS Class Configuration Commands*

Task	Command Syntax
Define a class map.	**class-map** *class-name* [**match-all** l **match-any**]
Classify with an access list.[1]	**match access-group name** *access-list*
Classify by IP Precedence.	**match ip precedence** *ipprec1* [*...ipprecN*]
Classify by DSCP.	**match ip dscp** *dscp1* [*...dscpN*]
Classify with NBAR.	**match protocol** *protocol-name*

[1] An access list (either numbered or named) must be configured separately, in global configuration mode.

Table 17-9 *QoS Policy Configuration Commands*

Task	Command Syntax
Define a policy map.	**policy-map** *policy-name*
Classify with a class map.	**class** *class-name*
Mark the DSCP value.	**set ip dscp** *dscp-value*
Mark the IP Precedence value.	**set ip precedence** *ip-precedence-value*
Trust inbound QoS information.	**trust** {**cos** l **dscp** l **ip-precedence**}
Police the classified flow.	**police ...**
Apply the policy map to an interface.	**service-policy** [**input** l **output**] *policy-name*

Table 17-10   *QoS Egress Queue Configuration Commands*

Task	Command Syntax
Set the WRR queue weighting.	**wrr-queue bandwidth** *weight1 weight2* [*weight3*]
Map packets into egress queues.	**wrr-queue cos-map** *queue-id threshold-id cos-list*
Use tail-drop queue management.	**no wrr-queue random-detect** *queue-id*
Use WRED.	**wrr-queue random-detect** *queue-id*
Set the WRED queue thresholds.	**wrr-queue random-detect** {**max-threshold**	**min-threshold**} *queue-id threshold-percent-1 ... threshold-percent-N*

Table 17-11   *Commands for Verifying QoS Operation*

Task	Command Syntax
Verify QoS trust settings on an interface.	**show mls qos interface** *type mod/num*
Verify egress queueing on an interface.	**show mls qos interface** *type mod/num* **queueing**
Verify QoS settings only on a Catalyst 6500 interface.	**show queueing interface** *type mod/num*
View all QoS parameter mappings.	**show mls qos maps**

Q&A

The questions and scenarios in this book are more difficult than what you should experience on the actual exam. The questions do not attempt to cover more breadth or depth than the exam; however, they are designed to make sure that you know the answers. Rather than allowing you to derive the answers from clues hidden inside the questions themselves, the questions challenge your understanding and recall of the subject. Hopefully, these questions will help limit the number of exam questions on which you narrow your choices to two options and then guess.

You can find the answers to these questions in Appendix A.

1. What two ways can QoS trust be configured on a switch?

2. If all QoS trust decisions will be applied as part of a QoS policy, what command should you use on an interface?

3. When a class map is configured, what types of commands must also be used?

4. Name two methods that you can use to identify or classify traffic.

5. What command can classify traffic with an extended IP access list?

6. What command can classify traffic with NBAR?

7. What does a policy map contain?

8. When a policy map is applied to an interface, does it control both inbound and outbound traffic?

9. What is the first command keyword used to configure WRED congestion avoidance?

10. What QoS information is used to map packets into the egress queues of a switch port?

11. What command can set the WRED thresholds of the strict-priority queue (1p2q2t) to 25 percent and 75 percent?

12. What command can display the QoS and queue information about a switch port?

This chapter covers the following topics that you need to master for the CCNP BCMSN exam:

- **Inline Power**—This section discusses how a Catalyst switch can provide power to operate a Cisco IP Phone.

- **Voice VLANs**—This section explains how voice traffic can be carried over the links between an IP Phone and a Catalyst switch.

- **Voice QoS**—This section provides an overview of the mechanisms that provide premium quality of service (QoS) for voice traffic.

- **Verifying IP Telephony**—This section provides a brief summary of the commands that can verify the configuration and operation of IP Telephony features.

CHAPTER 18

IP Telephony

Switched campus networks can carry packets that are related to telephone calls, as well as regular data. Voice over IP (VoIP), otherwise known as IP Telephony (IPT), uses IP Phones that are connected to switched Ethernet ports.

To properly and effectively carry the traffic for a successful phone call, a combination of many switching features must be used. For example, the Catalyst switches can provide power to IP Phones, form trunk links with IP Phones, and provide the proper level of QoS for voice packet delivery. This chapter covers all these topics as related to the Cisco IP Phone.

"Do I Know This Already?" Quiz

The purpose of the "Do I Know This Already?" quiz is to help you decide what parts of this chapter to use. If you already intend to read the entire chapter, you do not necessarily need to answer these questions now.

The quiz, derived from the major sections in the "Foundation Topics" portion of the chapter, helps you determine how to spend your limited study time.

Table 18-1 outlines the major topics discussed in this chapter and the "Do I Know This Already?" quiz questions that correspond to those topics.

Table 18-1 *"Do I Know This Already?" Foundation Topics Section-to-Question Mapping*

Foundation Topics Section	Questions Covered in This Section
Inline Power	1–2
Voice VLANs	3–7
Voice QoS	8–10
Verifying IP Telephony	11–12

> **CAUTION**   The goal of self-assessment is to gauge your mastery of the topics in this chapter. If you do not know the answer to a question or are only partially sure of the answer, you should mark this question wrong. Giving yourself credit for an answer you correctly guess skews your self-assessment results and might give you a false sense of security.

1.   For a Catalyst switch to offer inline power to a device, what must occur?

   a.   Nothing; inline power is always enabled on a port.

   b.   The switch must detect that the device needs inline power.

   c.   The device must send a CDP message asking for power.

   d.   The switch is configured to turn on inline power to the port.

2.   Which one of these commands can enable inline power to a switch interface?

   a.   **inline power enable**

   b.   **inline power on**

   c.   **power inline on**

   d.   **power inline auto**

3.   What does a Cisco IP Phone contain to allow it to pass both voice and data packets?

   a.   An internal Ethernet hub

   b.   An internal two-port switch

   c.   An internal three-port switch

   d.   An internal four-port switch

4.   How can voice traffic be kept separate from any other data traffic through an IP Phone?

   a.   Voice and data travel over separate links.

   b.   A special-case 802.1Q trunk is used to the switch.

   c.   Voice and data can't be separated; they must intermingle on the link.

   d.   Voice and data packets are both encapsulated over an ISL trunk.

5.   What command configures an IP Phone to use VLAN 9 for voice traffic?

   a.   **switchport voice vlan 9**

   b.   **switchport voice-vlan 9**

   c.   **switchport voice 9**

   d.   **switchport voip 9**

6. What is the default voice VLAN condition for a switch port?

    a. **switchport voice vlan 1**

    b. **switchport voice vlan dot1p**

    c. **switchport voice vlan untagged**

    d. **switchport voice vlan none**

7. If the switchport **voice vlan 50** command has been used, what VLAN numbers will the voice and PC data be carried over, respectively?

    a. VLAN 50, native VLAN

    b. VLAN 50, VLAN 1

    c. VLAN 1, VLAN 50

    d. native VLAN, VLAN 50

8. When a PC is connected to the PC switch port on an IP Phone, how is QoS trust handled?

    a. The IP Phone always trusts the class of service (CoS) information coming from the PC.

    b. The IP Phone never trusts the PC and always overwrites the CoS bits.

    c. QoS trust for the PC data is handled at the Catalyst switch port and not the IP Phone.

    d. The Catalyst switch instructs the IP Phone how to trust the PC QoS information.

9. An IP Phone should mark all incoming traffic from an attached PC to have CoS 1. Complete the following switch command to make that happen:

    ```
    switchport priority extend _____
    ```

    a. **untrusted**

    b. 1

    c. **cos 1**

    d. **overwrite 1**

10. Which switch port queue should voice bearer packets be placed in?

    a. Best effort queue

    b. Low-priority standard queue

    c. High-priority standard queue

    d. Strict-priority queue

11. What command can verify the inline power status of each switch port?

    a. **show inline power**

    b. **show power inline**

    c. **show interface**

    d. **show running-config**

12. What command can verify the voice VLAN used by a Cisco IP Phone?

    a. **show cdp neighbor**

    b. **show interface switchport**

    c. **show vlan**

    d. **show trunk**

The answers to the "Do I Know This Already?" quiz are found in Appendix A, "Answers to Chapter 'Do I Know This Already?' Quizzes and Q&A Sections." The suggested choices for your next step are as follows:

■ **10 or less overall score**—Read the entire chapter. This includes the "Foundation Topics," "Foundation Summary," and "Q&A" sections.

■ **11 or 12 overall score**—If you want more review on these topics, skip to the "Foundation Summary" section and then go to the "Q&A" section at the end of the chapter. Otherwise, move to Chapter 19, "Securing Switch Access."

Foundation Topics

IP Telephony Overview

IP Telephony here is focused on the addition of Cisco IP Phones to the switched campus network, centrally managed by Cisco CallManager servers.

Inline Power

A Cisco IP Phone is like any other node on the network—it must have power to operate. Power can come from two sources:

- An external AC adapter
- Inline power (DC) over the network data cable

The external AC adapter plugs into a normal AC wall outlet and provides 48V DC to the phone. These adapters, commonly called "wall warts," are handy if no other power source is available. However, if a power failure occurs to the room or outlet where the adapter is located, the IP Phone will fail.

A more elegant solution is available as *inline power*. Here, the same 48V DC supply is provided to an IP Phone over the same Category 5 cable that is used for Ethernet connectivity. The DC power's source is the Catalyst switch itself. No other power source is needed, unless an AC adapter is required as a redundant source.

Inline power has the benefit that it can be managed, monitored, and offered only to an IP phone. If a normal PC is plugged into the same switch port, power is not be offered to it. The Catalyst switch can also be connected to an uninterruptable power supply (UPS) so that it continues to receive and offer power even if the regular AC source fails. This allows an IP Phone to be available for use even across a power failure.

> **NOTE**   Inline power is also defined by the IEEE 802.3af standard, "DTE Power via MDI." At press time, this was still in draft form. After it becomes a standard, Cisco Catalyst switches will support it through Cisco IOS Software upgrades and updated hardware. For more information about 802.3af, refer to the article "IEEE P802.3af DTE Power via MDI Task Force" at www.ieee802.org/3/af/index.html.

How Inline Power Works

A Catalyst switch with inline power always keeps the power disabled when a switch port is down. When a switch port first comes up, the switch sends out a 340-kHz test tone on the transmit pair of the twisted-pair Ethernet cable. A tone is transmitted rather than DC power because the switch must first detect an inline power-capable device before offering it power. Otherwise, other types of devices could be damaged.

An IP Phone loops the transmit and receive pairs of its Ethernet connection, even while it is powered off. When it is connected to an inline power switch port, the switch can "hear" its test tone looped back. Then it safely assumes that a powered device is present, and power can be applied to it. Inline power is provided over pairs 2 and 3 (RJ-45 pins 1,2 and 3,6) at 48V DC.

Note that the switch power supply must be sized appropriately to offer continuous power to an IP Phone on every powered switch port. Inline power is available on the Catalyst 3550-24-PWR, Catalyst 4500, and Catalyst 6500 platforms.

A switch first offers a default power allocation to the powered device. On a Catalyst 3550-24-PWR, for example, an IP Phone first receives 15.0 watts (0.36 amps at 48V DC). Now, the device has a chance to power up and bring its Ethernet link up, too. The switch then attempts a Cisco Discovery Protocol (CDP) message exchange with the device. This allows it to learn that the device is a Cisco IP Phone, as well as to learn the phone's actual power requirements. The switch can then reduce the inline power to the amount requested by the phone.

To see this in operation, look at Example 18-1. Here, the power was reduced from 15,000 to 6300 milliwatts. This output was produced by the **debug ilpower controller** and **debug cdp packets** commands.

Example 18-1 *Displaying Inline Power Adjustment*

```
1d00h: ilpower_get_admin_state( Fa0/1 )
1d00h: ilpower_powerchange( Fa0/1 ) power: 15000
1d00h: ILP Power apply to ( Fa0/1 ) Okay
1d00h: ILP Power Accounting REQ_PWR ( Fa0/1 ) Okay
1d00h: ilpower_pd_statechange( Fa0/1 ) pd_class: 2
1d00h: ilpower_pd_power_statechange(Fa0/1) pd_power_state: 1
1d00h: %LINK-3-UPDOWN: Interface FastEthernet0/1, changed state to up
1d00h: %LINEPROTO-5-UPDOWN: Line protocol on Interface FastEthernet0/1, changed
state to up
1d00h: CDP-PA: version 2 packet sent out on FastEthernet0/1
1d00h: CDP-PA: Packet received from SEP003094C35E4D on interface FastEthernet0/1
1d00h: **Entry NOT found in cache**
1d00h: ILP CDP request received ( Fa0/1 ), processing...
1d00h: ilpower_powerchange( Fa0/1 ) power: 6300
1d00h: ilpower_pd_name_change_via_cdp ( Fa0/1 ) pd name: Cisco IP Phone 7960
```

Configuring Inline Power

Inline power configuration is simple. Each switch port can automatically detect the presence of an inline power-capable device before applying power, or the feature can be disabled to ensure that the port can never detect or offer inline power. By default, every switch port attempts to discover an inline-powered device. To change this behavior, use the following interface configuration command:

```
Switch(config-if)# power inline {auto | never}
```

Voice VLANs

A Cisco IP Phone provides a data connection for a user's PC, in addition to its own voice data stream. This allows a single Ethernet drop to be installed per user. The IP Phone can also control some aspects of how the packets (both voice and user data) are presented to the switch.

Most Cisco IP Phone models contain a three-port switch, connecting to the upstream switch, the user's PC, and the internal VoIP datastream, as illustrated in Figure 18-1. The voice and user PC ports always function as access-mode switch ports. The port that connects to the upstream switch, however, can operate as an 802.1Q trunk or as an access-mode (single VLAN) port.

Figure 18-1 *Basic Connections to a Cisco IP Phone*

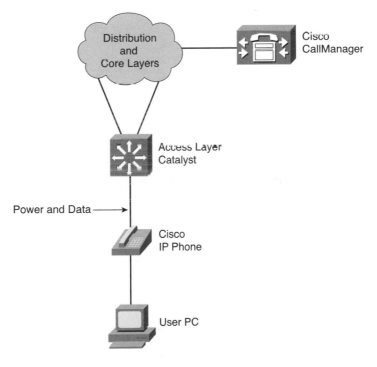

The link mode between the IP Phone and the switch is negotiated; you can configure the switch to instruct the phone to use a special-case 802.1Q trunk or a single VLAN access link. With a trunk, the voice traffic can be isolated from other user data, providing security and QoS capabilities. As an access link, both voice and data must be combined over the single VLAN. This simplifies other aspects of the switch configuration because a separate voice VLAN is not needed, but it could compromise the voice quality, depending on the PC application mix.

Voice VLAN Configuration

Although you can configure the IP Phone uplink as a trunk or nontrunk, the real consideration pertains to how the voice traffic will be encapsulated. The voice packets must be carried over a unique voice VLAN (known as the voice VLAN ID or *VVID*) or over the regular data VLAN (known as the native VLAN or the port VLAN ID, *PVID*). The QoS information from the voice packets must also be carried.

To configure the IP Phone uplink, just configure the switch port where it connects. The switch instructs the phone to follow the mode that is selected. In addition, the switch port does not need any special trunking configuration commands if a trunk is wanted. If an 802.1Q trunk is needed, a special-case trunk is negotiated by Dynamic Trunking Protocol (DTP) and CDP. Use the following interface configuration command to select the voice VLAN mode that will be used:

```
Switch(config-if)# switchport voice vlan {vlan-id | dot1p | untagged | none}
```

Figure 18-2 shows the four different voice VLAN configurations. Pay particular attention to the link between the IP Phone and the switch.

Table 18-2 documents the four different voice VLAN configurations.

Table 18-2 *Trunking Modes with a Cisco IP Phone*

Keyword	Representation in Figure 18-2	Native VLAN (untagged)	Voice VLAN	Voice QoS (CoS bits)
vlan-id	A	PC data	VLAN *vlan-id*	802.1p
dot1p	B	PC data	VLAN 0	802.1p
untagged	C	PC data / voice	N/A	N/A
none (default)	D	PC data / voice	N/A	N/A

Figure 18-2 *Trunking Modes for Voice VLANs with a Cisco IP Phone*

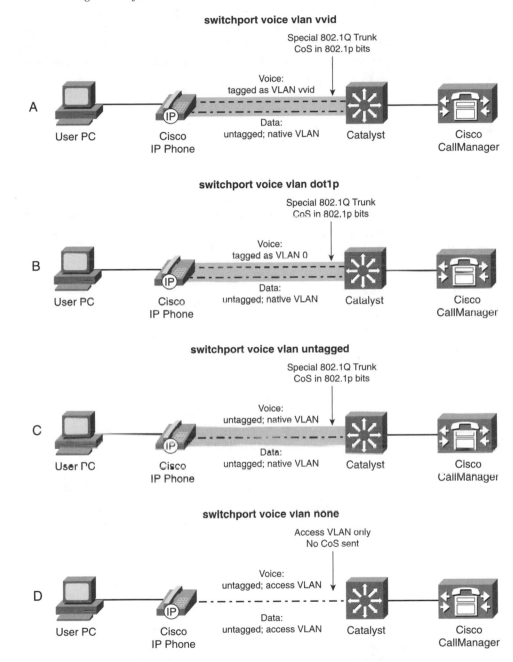

The default condition for every switch port is **none**, where a trunk is not used. All modes except for **none** use the special-case 802.1Q trunk. The only difference between the **dot1p** and **untagged** modes is the encapsulation of voice traffic. The **dot1p** mode puts the voice packets on VLAN 0, which requires a VLAN ID (not the native VLAN) but doesn't require a unique voice VLAN to be created. The **untagged** mode puts voice packets in the native VLAN, requiring neither a VLAN ID nor a unique voice VLAN.

The most versatile mode uses the *vlan-id*, as shown in case A in Figure 18-2. Here, voice and user data are carried over separate VLANs. VoIP packets in the voice VLAN also carry the CoS bits in the 802.1p trunk encapsulation field.

Be aware that the special-case 802.1Q trunk is always enabled—even if an IP Phone is not connected to that switch port. Because the user PC data is always carried over the native VLAN, it is always untagged. That also means that if a PC is connected to the switch port without the IP Phone, PC data continues to be carried over the untagged portion of the trunk. The PC has no idea that a trunk is in use; it just sends and receives frames normally.

> **NOTE** The trunk used between an IP Phone and a Catalyst switch port is dynamically created and can contain only two VLANs—a voice VLAN (tagged VVID) and the native VLAN (untagged). When the trunk is active, it is not shown in the trunking mode from any Cisco IOS Software **show** command.
>
> It does not matter which trunking mode (**auto**, **desirable**, **on**, or **off**) you configure on the switch port—the special trunk will be negotiated through DTP and CDP.
>
> Spanning Tree Protocol (STP) does run over the trunk, with two instances—one for the native VLAN and one for the voice VLAN. STP PortFast is also enabled automatically, so be careful that only a single host device is connected to the phone's PC port.

Voice QoS

The most important aspect of transporting voice traffic across a switched campus network is maintaining the proper QoS level. Voice packets must be delivered in the most timely fashion possible, with little jitter, little loss, and little delay. Remember, a user expects to receive a dial tone, a call to go through, and a good-quality audio connection with the far end when an IP Phone is used. Above that, any call that is made could be an emergency "911" call. It is then very important that QoS be properly implemented.

QoS Trust

Recall from Chapter 16, "Quality of Service Overview," that you must define a trust boundary for QoS information in a network. Inside this boundary, QoS information can be inherently trusted because every network device has similar QoS policies configured. QoS information coming from outside this boundary can be overwritten unconditionally or for specific conditions.

When a Cisco IP Phone is connected to a switch port, think of the phone as another switch (which it is). If you install the phone as a part of your network, you can probably trust the QoS information relayed by the phone.

However, remember that the phone also has two sources of data:

- **The VoIP packets native to the phone**—The phone can control precisely what QoS information is included in the voice packets because it produces those packets.
- **The user PC data switch port**—Packets from the PC data port are generated elsewhere, so the QoS information can not necessarily be trusted to be correct or fair.

A switch instructs an attached IP Phone through CDP messages as to how it should extend QoS trust to its own user data switch port. To configure the trust extension, use the following interface configuration command:

```
Switch(config-if)# switchport priority extend {cos value | trust}
```

Normally, the QoS information from a PC connected to an IP Phone should not be trusted. This is because the PC's applications might try to spoof CoS or Differentiated Services Code Point (DSCP) settings to gain premium network service. In this case, use the **cos** keyword so that the CoS bits are overwritten to *value* by the IP Phone as packets are forwarded to the switch. If CoS values from the PC cannot be trusted, they should be overwritten to a value of 0.

In some cases, the PC might be running trusted applications that are allowed to request specific QoS or levels of service. Here, the IP Phone can extend complete QoS trust to the PC, allowing the CoS bits to be forwarded through the phone unmodified. This is done with the **trust** keyword.

By default, a switch instructs an attached IP Phone to consider the PC port as untrusted. CoS values are overwritten to 0.

Voice Packet Classification

Cisco IP Phones use the following *Skinny* protocols (TCP ports 2000 through 2002) for call control information:

- **Skinny Client Control Protocol (SCCP)**—TCP port 2000
- **Skinny Station Protocol (SSP)**—TCP port 2001
- **Skinny Gateway Protocol (SGP)**—TCP port 2002

The Real-time Transport Protocol (RTP) carries all the voice-bearer traffic (the actual audio payload) using UDP ports negotiated by the call control protocols.

Switches needing to classify voice call control traffic used by Cisco IP Phones should match against the static TCP ports 2000 through 2002. This can be done with an IP access list and a **match access-group** command.

To classify the voice-bearer traffic, a switch must identify the RTP packets that are on negotiated UDP port numbers, which you can accomplish with the **match protocol rtp** Network-Based Application Recognition (NBAR) command.

A Cisco IP Phone marks its own QoS information, according to the following rules:

- SCCP voice control packets receive CoS 3, IP Precedence 3, and DSCP 26 (AF31).
- RTP voice bearer packets receive CoS 5, IP Precedence 5, and DSCP 46 (EF).
- PC data packets can be marked with a configurable CoS value or left unchanged.

Queuing for Voice Traffic

By default, most Catalyst switch ports are configured to have packets with specific CoS values placed in specific egress queues. For example, packets with CoS 3 are usually placed into the higher-threshold, lower-priority standard queue. Packets with CoS 5 are always placed into the strict-priority queue for premium service.

Notice that these two CoS values correspond to the values assigned to voice traffic by an IP Phone. Therefore, the default switch behavior gives the appropriate QoS to voice traffic—if each switch along the path has QoS properly enabled and configured.

Voice call control packets (Skinny protocol) are always marked with CoS 3 and are scheduled into the egress queues for better service than normal data (CoS 0, 1, or 2). Voice bearer packets (RTP) are always marked with CoS 5 and are always scheduled into the strict-priority queue. This ensures premium QoS treatment for the audio portion of a phone call.

Verifying Inline Power, Voice VLANs, and Voice QoS

Although you might encounter a wide variety of IP Telephony problems, this section details some of the more common issues to check, as covered in this chapter. For more thorough information about troubleshooting IP Telephony, consult the Cisco Press title, *Troubleshooting IP Telephony*.

Verifying Inline Power

You can verify the inline power status for a switch port with the following EXEC command:

```
Switch# show power inline [type mod/num]
```

Example 18-2 provides some sample output from this command.

Example 18-2 *Displaying Inline Power Status for a Switch Port*

```
Switch# show power inline
Interface  Admin  Oper      Power        Device
                            (Watts)
..........  .....  ..........  .......  ....................
Fa0/1      auto   on           6.3  Cisco IP Phone 7960
Fa0/2      auto   off            0  n/a
Fa0/3      auto   on           6.3  Cisco IP Phone 7960
```

> **CAUTION** A Catalyst switch waits for 4 seconds after inline power is applied to a port to see if an IP Phone does indeed come alive. If not, the power is removed from the port.
>
> Be careful if you plug an IP phone into a switch port, and then remove it and plug in a normal Ethernet device. The inline power could still be applied during the 4-second interval, damaging a nonpowered device. Wait 10 seconds after unplugging an IP Phone before plugging anything back into the same port.

Verifying Voice VLANs

Verifying the operation of the link between a switch port and an IP Phone is not easy. This is because the link can operate as a special-case, two-VLAN 802.1Q trunk, but the link never appears to be trunking according to any IOS **show** commands.

First, you should determine if the switch and IP Phone are actually communicating. Use the following EXEC command to see if the phone has advertised itself to the switch.

```
Switch# show cdp neighbors type mod/num detail
```

Next, verify the access VLAN being used on the switch port, along with the voice VLAN (if any). You can find these values with the following EXEC command:

```
Switch# show interface type mod/num switchport
```

Example 18-3 demonstrates some sample output from the **show cdp neighbors detail** and **show interface switchport** commands. Notice that the device is a Cisco IP Phone, a "native" trunk is being used, the native VLAN is 1, and the voice VLAN is 2.

Example 18-3 *Determining Switch/IP Phone Communication and Switch Port/Voice VLAN*

```
Switch# show cdp neighbors fast 0/1 detail
-------------------------
Device ID: SEP003094C35E4D
Entry address(es):
Platform: Cisco IP Phone 7960,  Capabilities: Host
Interface: FastEthernet0/1,  Port ID (outgoing port): Port 1
Holdtime : 144 sec


Version :
P00303020215


advertisement version: 2
Duplex: full
Power drawn: 6.300 Watts


Switch#
Switch# show interface fast 0/1 switchport
Name: Fa0/1
Switchport: Enabled
Administrative Mode: dynamic desirable
Operational Mode: static access
Administrative Trunking Encapsulation: negotiate
Operational Trunking Encapsulation: native
Negotiation of Trunking: On
Access Mode VLAN: 1 (default)
Trunking Native Mode VLAN: 1 (default)
Administrative private-vlan host-association: none
Administrative private-vlan mapping: none
Operational private-vlan: none
Trunking VLANs Enabled: ALL
Pruning VLANs Enabled: 2-1001
Protected: false
Unknown unicast blocked: disabled
Unknown multicast blocked: disabled
Voice VLAN: 2 (VLAN0002)
Appliance trust: none
Switch#
```

Verifying Voice QoS

A switch port can be configured with a QoS trust state with the connected device. If that device is an IP Phone, the switch can instruct the phone to extend QoS trust to an attached PC or not.

To verify how QoS trust has been extended to the IP Phone itself, use the following EXEC command:

```
Switch# show mls qos interface type mod/num
```

If the port is trusted, all traffic forwarded by the IP Phone is accepted with the QoS information left intact. If the port is not trusted, even the voice packets can have their QoS information overwritten by the switch. Example 18-4 demonstrates some sample output from the **show mls qos interface** command, where the switch port is trusting CoS information from the attached IP Phone.

Example 18-4 *Verifying QoS Trust to the IP Phone*

```
Switch# show mls qos interface fast 0/1
FastEthernet0/1
trust state: trust cos
trust mode: trust cos
COS override: dis
default COS: 0
DSCP Mutation Map: Default DSCP Mutation Map
trust device: none
```

Next, you can verify how the IP Phone has been instructed to treat incoming QoS information from its attached PC or other device. This is shown in the **trust device:** line in Example 18-4, where the device is the IP Phone's device. You can also use the following EXEC command:

```
Switch# show interface type mod/num switchport
```

Here, the device trust is called *appliance trust*, as shown in Example 18-5.

Example 18-5 *An Alternate Method for Verifying QoS Trust to an IP Phone*

```
Switch# show interface fast 0/1 switchport
Name: Fa0/1
Switchport: Enabled
[output deleted...]
Voice VLAN: 2 (VLAN0002)
Appliance trust: none
```

To see the queuing strategies for a switch port, use the following EXEC command:

```
Switch# show interface type mod/num capabilities
```

Example 18-6 shows some sample output from this command. Notice that this switch port has an egress queue type of 1p3q0t, hinting that there is one strict-priority queue (1p), three standard queues (3q), and no Weighted Random Early Detection (WRED) thresholds (0t).

Example 18-6 *Displaying Queuing Strategies for a Switch Port*

```
Switch# show int fas 0/1 cap
FastEthernet0/1
  Model:                 WS-C3550-24-PWR
  Type:                  10/100BaseTX
  Speed:                 10,100,auto
  Duplex:                half,full,auto
  Trunk encap. type:     802.1Q,ISL
  Trunk mode:            on,off,desirable,nonegotiate
  Channel:               yes
  Broadcast suppression: percentage(0-100)
  Flowcontrol:           rx-(off,on,desired),tx-(none)
  Fast Start:            yes
  QOS scheduling:        rx-(1q0t),tx-(4q0t),tx-(1p3q0t)
  CoS rewrite:           yes
  ToS rewrite:           yes
  UDLD:                  yes
  Inline power:          yes
  SPAN:                  source/destination
  PortSecure:            yes
  Dot1x:                 yes
Switch#
```

To verify how the CoS values map packets into the egress port queues, use one of the following EXEC commands:

```
Switch# show mls qos interface type mod/num queueing
Switch# show queueing interface type mod/num
```

The first command is used on a Catalyst 3550, while the second command is used on a Catalyst 6500.

Example 18-7 shows some sample output from the **show mls qos interface queueing** command. Notice that the strict-priority queue (also called the *expedite queue*) is enabled. Here, queues 1 through 3 are the standard queues, and queue 4 is the strict-priority queue. CoS value 3 (used for voice call control packets) is mapped into the medium-priority standard queue, while CoS 5 (used for voice bearer packets) goes into the highest-priority standard queue. Preferably, CoS 5 should be mapped to the strict-priority queue. The CoS-to-queue mapping can be reconfigured, if necessary.

Example 18-7 *Determining How CoS Values Map Packets to Egress Port Queues*

```
Switch# show mls qos interface fast 0/1 queueing
FastEthernet0/1
Egress expedite queue: ena
wrr bandwidth weights:
qid-weights
 1 - 25
 2 - 25
 3 - 25
 4 - 25     when expedite queue is disabled
Cos-queue map:
cos-qid
 0 - 1
 1 - 1
 2 - 2
 3 - 2
 4 - 3
 5 - 3
 6 - 4
 7 - 4
Switch#
```

Foundation Summary

The Foundation Summary is a collection of information that provides a convenient review of many key concepts in this chapter. If you are already comfortable with the topics in this chapter, this summary could help you recall a few details. If you just read this chapter, this review should help solidify some key facts. If you are doing your final preparation before the exam, this summarized information is a convenient way to review the day before the exam.

Table 18-3 *Commands for Configuring IP Telephony on a Catalyst Switch*

Task	Command Syntax
Set inline power behavior.	**power inline {auto	never}**
Define the trunking on a port to a Cisco IP Phone.	**switchport voice vlan {***vlan-id*	**dot1p	untagged	none}**
Define trust relationship of the IP Phone.	**switchport priority extend {cos** *value*	**trust}**

You can use the commands in Table 18-4 to verify or troubleshoot IP Telephony on a Catalyst switch.

Table 18-4 *Commands for Troubleshooting IP Telephony on a Catalyst Switch*

Task	Command Syntax
Show inline power status.	**show power inline** [*type mod/num*]
Verify the voice VLAN.	**show interface** *type mod/num* **switchport**
Show how QoS trust is extended to phone.	**show mls qos interface** *type mod/num*
Show queuing strategy of a port.	**show interface** *type mod/num* **capabilities**
See how CoS values are mapped into port queues.	**show mls qos interface** *type mod/num* **queueing**

Q&A

The questions and scenarios in this book are more difficult than what you should experience on the actual exam. The questions do not attempt to cover more breadth or depth than the exam; however, they are designed to make sure that you know the answers. Rather than allowing you to derive the answers from clues hidden inside the questions themselves, the questions challenge your understanding and recall of the subject. Hopefully, these questions will help limit the number of exam questions on which you narrow your choices to two options and then guess.

The answers to these questions can be found in Appendix A.

1. How does a Catalyst switch detect that a connected device is capable of using inline power?

2. What type of trunk can be used between a Catalyst switch port and a Cisco IP Phone?

3. When a trunk is used on an IP Phone, on which VLAN is the data from an attached PC carried?

4. What is the difference between the VVID and the PVID?

5. Can the CoS information from the voice traffic be passed when the **switchport voice vlan untagged** command is used? If so, how?

6. What is the advantage of using the **switchport voice vlan dot1p** command?

7. By default, does a Cisco IP Phone trust QoS information from an attached PC?

8. The command **switchport priority extend cos 5** is entered for a switch port. Is this a good decision? Why or why not?

9. How can a switch classify VoIP voice bearer packets that are carried by RTP?

10. The **show power inline** command is used to check the power status on each switch port. If the output is as shown here, what can you assume about interface fastethernet 0/1?

```
Interface  Admin  Oper        Power    Device
                              (Watts)
---------- -----  ----------  -------  --------------------
Fa0/1      auto   off              0   n/a
Fa0/2      auto   on             6.3   Cisco IP Phone 7960
```

11. What command can verify the QoS trust relationship between an IP Phone and its attached PC?

This chapter covers the following topics that you need to master for the CCNP BCMSN exam:

- **Switch Authentication, Authorization, and Accounting (AAA)**—This section discusses methods that you can use to control switch management access to users.

- **Port Security Using MAC Addresses**— This section explains how to configure switch ports to allow network access to only hosts with specific or learned MAC addresses.

- **Port-based Security Using IEEE 802.1x**— This section discusses a method you can use to require user authentication before network access is offered to a client host.

CHAPTER 19

Securing Switch Access

Traditionally, users have been able to connect a PC to a switched network and gain immediate access to enterprise resources. As networks grow and as more confidential data or restricted resources become available, it is important to limit the access that users receive.

Catalyst switches have a variety of methods that can secure or control user access. Users can be authenticated as they connect to or through a switch, and authorized to perform certain actions on a switch. User access can be recorded as switch accounting information. The physical switch port access can also be controlled based on the user's MAC address or authentication.

"Do I Know This Already?" Quiz

The purpose of the "Do I Know This Already?" quiz is to help you decide what parts of this chapter to use. If you already intend to read the entire chapter, you do not necessarily need to answer these questions now.

The quiz, derived from the major sections in the "Foundation Topics" portion of the chapter, helps you determine how to spend your limited study time.

Table 19-1 outlines the major topics discussed in this chapter and the "Do I Know This Already?" quiz questions that correspond to those topics.

Table 19-1 *"Do I Know This Already?" Foundation Topics Section-to-Question Mapping*

Foundation Topics Section	Questions Covered in This Section
Switch AAA	1–3
Port Security	4–7
Port-based Authentication	8–12

> **CAUTION** The goal of self-assessment is to gauge your mastery of the topics in this chapter. If you do not know the answer to a question or are only partially sure of the answer, you should mark this question wrong. Giving yourself credit for an answer you correctly guess skews your self-assessment results and might provide you with a false sense of security.

1. If the **username** command is used in a switch configuration, what method of authentication is implied?

   a. Remote

   b. Local

   c. RADIUS

   d. TACACS+

2. Which one of the following commands should be used to configure a vty line to use the "myservers" authentication method list?

   a. **line authentication myservers**

   b. **authentication myservers**

   c. **authentication method myservers**

   d. **login authentication myservers**

3. If a user needs to be in the privileged EXEC or enable mode, which part of AAA must succeed?

   a. Authentication

   b. Authorization

   c. Accounting

   d. Administration

4. Which switch feature can grant access through a port only if the host with MAC address 0005.0004.0003 is connected?

   a. SPAN

   b. MAC address ACL

   c. Port security

   d. Port-based authentication

5. Port security is being used to control access to a switch port. Which one of these commands will put the port into the errdisable state if an unauthorized station connects?

   a. **switchport port-security violation protect**

   b. **switchport port-security violation restrict**

   c. **switchport port-security violation errdisable**

   d. **switchport port-security violation shutdown**

6. If port security is left to its default configuration, how many different MAC addresses can be learned at one time on a switch port?

   a. 0

   b. 1

   c. 16

   d. 256

7. The following commands are configured on a Catalyst switch port. What happens when the host with MAC address 0001.0002.0003 tries to connect?

```
switchport port-security
switchport port-security maximum 3
switchport port-security mac-address 0002.0002.0002
switchport port-security violation shutdown
```

   a. The port shuts down.

   b. The host is allowed to connect.

   c. The host is denied a connection.

   d. The host can connect only when 0002.0002.0002 is not connected.

8. What protocol is used for port-based authentication?

   a. 802.1D

   b. 802.1Q

   c. 802.1x

   d. 802.1w

9. When 802.1x is used for a switch port, where must it be configured?

   a. Switch port and client PC

   b. Switch port only

   c. Client PC only

   d. Switch port and a RADIUS server

10. When port-based authentication is globally enabled, what is the default behavior for all switch ports?

    a. Authenticate users before enabling the port.

    b. Allow all connections without authentication.

    c. Do not allow any connections.

    d. There is no default behavior.

11. After port-based authentication is enabled, what method is available for a user to authenticate?

    a. Web browser

    b. Telnet session

    c. 802.1x client

    d. DHCP

12. The users in a department are using a variety of host platforms, some old and some new. All of them have been approved with a user ID in a RADIUS server database. Which one of these features should be used to restrict access to the switch ports in the building?

    a. AAA Authentication

    b. AAA Authorization

    c. Port security

    d. Port-based authentication

The answers to the "Do I Know This Already?" quiz are found in Appendix A, "Answers to Chapter 'Do I Know This Already?' Quizzes and Q&A Sections." The suggested choices for your next step are as follows:

- **10 or less overall score**—Read the entire chapter. This includes the "Foundation Topics," "Foundation Summary," and "Q&A" sections.

- **11 or 12 overall score**—If you want more review on these topics, skip to the "Foundation Summary" section and then go to the "Q&A" section at the end of the chapter. Otherwise, move to Chapter 20, "Securing with VLANs."

Foundation Topics

Switch AAA

You can manage user activity to and through a switch with authentication, authorization, and accounting (AAA) features. AAA uses standardized methods to challenge users for their credentials before access is allowed or authorized. Accounting protocols can also record user activity on a switch.

Authentication

Switch or network access can be granted only after a user's identity has been validated. User authentication is commonly used on switches and routers to limit Telnet access to the network administration staff. In this case, when someone uses Telnet to log on to a switch, that individual is first challenged with a username and password. The individual's credentials are then submitted to a device that can grant the user access.

User authentication can be handled by several methods:

- Usernames and passwords configured locally on the switch

- One or more external Remote Authentication Dial-In User Service (RADIUS) servers

- One or more external Terminal Access Controller Access Control System+ (TACACS+) servers

Any combination of these methods can be used. In fact, authentication must be defined by grouping the desired methods into a method list. The list contains the types or protocols that will be used, in the sequential order that they will be tried.

To use authentication on a Catalyst switch, you must configure several things in the following order:

Step 1   Enable AAA on the switch.

By default, AAA is disabled. Therefore, all user authentication is handled locally, by configured usernames and passwords. To enable AAA, use the following global configuration command:

```
Switch(config)# aaa new-model
```

The **new-model** refers to the use of method lists, where authentication methods and sources can be grouped or organized. The new model is much more scalable than the "old model," where the authentication source was explicitly configured.

Step 2   Define the source of authentication.

You can compare user credentials against locally configured usernames and passwords, or against a database managed by external RADIUS or TACACS+ servers.

Use locally configured usernames and passwords as a last resort, when no other authentication servers are reachable or in use on the network. To define a username, use the following global configuration command:

```
Switch(config)# username username password password
```

RADIUS or TACACS+ servers are defined in groups. First, define each server along with its secret shared password. This string is known only to the switch and the server and provides a key for encrypting the authentication session. Use one of the following global configuration commands:

```
Switch(config)# radius-server host {hostname | ip-address} [key string]
Switch(config)# tacacs-server host {hostname | ip-address} [key string]
```

Then, define a group name that will contain a list of servers, using the following global configuration command:

```
Switch(config)# aaa group server {radius | tacacs+} group-name
```

Define each server of the group type with the following server-group configuration command:

```
Switch(config)# server ip-address
```

You can define multiple RADIUS or TACACS+ servers by repeating these commands.

Step 3   Define a list of authentication methods to try.

You can list switch login authentication methods by giving the method a descriptive name or as the unnamed "default" method. List each method or protocol type in the order that it should be tried. If none of the servers for the first method respond, the switch tries the servers in the next method listed.

Use the following global configuration command to define a method list:

```
Switch(config)# aaa authentication login {default | list-name} method1
  [method2 ...]
```

Here, the methods refer to these values:

- **tacacs+**—Each of the TACACS+ servers configured on the switch will be tried, in the order that it was configured.

- **radius**—Each of the RADIUS servers configured on the switch will be tried, in the order that it was configured.

- **local**—The user's credentials will be compared against all of the **username** commands configured on the local switch.

- **line**—The line passwords authenticate any connected user. No usernames can be used.

> **NOTE** Be sure to add either the **local** or **line** method at the end of the list, as a last resort. This way, if all of the RADIUS or TACACS+ servers are unavailable or the switch is completely isolated from the rest of the network, a locally configured authentication method will still eventually be used. Otherwise, you will never be able to get into the switch.

Step 4   Apply a method list to a switch line.

First, select a line (console or vty for Telnet access) using the **line** *line* command. Then, trigger the user authentication on that line to use an AAA method list. Use the following line configuration command:

```
Switch(line)# login authentication {default | list-name}
```

You can use the default method list if only one list is sufficient for all circumstances on the switch. Otherwise, if you have configured named method lists, you can reference one of them here.

> **CAUTION**   After authentication is configured on a switch, it is a good idea to stay logged in on one session so that the authentication can be tested. If you exit the configuration session, you will not be able to log in again if the authentication is misconfigured. While you stay logged in on the original session, bring up a new Telnet session to the switch. If you can successfully authenticate, everything is properly configured.

Authorization

After a user is authenticated, the switch allows access to certain services or switch commands based on the user's privilege level. Authenticating puts the user at the EXEC level, by default. Certain commands, such as **show interface**, are available at the EXEC level. Other commands, such as **configure terminal**, are accessible only if the user is able to move into the privileged EXEC or "enable" mode.

Authorization provides a means to grant specific users the ability to perform certain tasks. Like authentication, authorization is performed by querying external RADIUS or TACACS+ servers. If the authorization server has an entry for a user and a service or command, the switch allows the user to perform that task.

You configure authorization by first defining any RADIUS or TACACS+ servers that will be used. These are normally defined as part of the authentication configuration and do not need to be redefined for authorization.

Next, define a method list of authorization methods that will be tried in sequence using the following global configuration command:

```
Switch(config)# aaa authorization {commands | config-commands | configuration | exec |
    network | reverse-access} {default | list-name} method1 [method2 ...]
```

Here, you specify the function or service needing authorization with one of the following values:

- **commands**—The server must return permission to use any switch command at any privilege level.

- **config-commands**—The server must return permission to use any switch configuration command.

- **configuration**—The server must return permission to enter the switch configuration mode.

- **exec**—The server must return permission for the user to run a switch EXEC session. The server can also return the privilege level for the user so that the user can immediately be put into the privileged EXEC ("enable") mode without having to type in the **enable** command.

- **network**—The server must return permission to use network-related services.

- **reverse-access**—The server must return permission for the user to access a reverse Telnet session on the switch.

You can identify the method with a descriptive name (*list-name*), if you are configuring more than one list. Otherwise, a single unnamed list is called the *default* list. Each authorization method is then listed in the order it will be tried. The methods can be any of the following values:

- **group** *group-name*—Requests are sent to the servers in a specific group.

- **group** {**radius** | **tacacs+**}—Requests are sent to all servers of this type.

- **if-authenticated**—Requests are granted if the user is already authenticated.

- **none**—No external authorization is used; every user is successfully authorized.

> **NOTE** Only TACACS+ servers can authorize users with permission to use specific commands. RADIUS servers offer more of an "all-or-nothing" approach.

Next, you can apply an authorization method list to a specific line on the switch. Users accessing the switch through that line will be subject to authorization. Use the following line configuration command:

```
Switch(config-line)# authorization {commands level | exec | reverse-access} {default |
    list-name}
```

If you do not use this command, the default group will be used for all lines.

Accounting

Catalyst switches also support the capability to use AAA for producing accounting information of user activity. RADIUS and TACACS+ servers can also collect this accounting information from switches, if wanted. Again, the RADIUS and TACACS+ servers must already be configured and grouped as part of the authentication configuration.

As usual, you must define a method list giving a sequence of accounting methods by using the following global configuration command:

```
Switch(config)# aaa accounting {system | exec | commands level} {default | list-name}
    {start-stop | stop-only | wait-start | none} method1 [method2 ...]
```

The function triggering the accounting can be one of the following:

■ **system**—Major switch events such as a reload will be recorded.

■ **exec**—User authentication into an EXEC session is recorded, along with information about the user's address and the time and duration of the session.

■ **commands** *level*—Information about any command running at a specific privilege level is recorded, along with the user that issued the command.

You can specify that certain types of accounting records be sent to the accounting server using the following keywords:

■ **start-stop**—Events are recorded when they start and stop.

■ **stop-only**—Events are recorded only when they stop.

■ **none**—No events are recorded.

Next, you can apply an accounting method list to a specific line on the switch. Users accessing the switch through that line will have their activity recorded. Use the following line configuration command to accomplish this:

```
Switch(config-line)# accounting {commands level | connection | exec} {default | list-name}
```

If you do not use this command, the default group will be used for all lines.

Port Security

In some environments, a network must be secured by controlling what stations can gain access to the network itself. Where user workstations are stationary, their MAC addresses can always be expected to connect to the same access layer switch ports. If stations are mobile, their MAC addresses can be dynamically learned or added to a list of addresses to expect on a switch port.

Catalyst switches offer the port security feature to control port access based on MAC addresses. To configure port security on an access layer switch port, begin by enabling it with the following interface configuration command:

```
Switch(config-if)# switchport port-security
```

Next, you must identify a set of allowed MAC addresses so that the port can grant them access. You can explicitly configure addresses or they can be dynamically learned from port traffic. On each interface that uses port security, specify the maximum number of MAC addresses that will be allowed access using the following interface configuration command:

```
Switch(config-if)# switchport port-security maximum max-addr
```

By default, only one MAC address will be allowed access on each switch port. You can set the maximum number of addresses in the range of 1 to 1024.

Each interface using port security dynamically learns MAC addresses by default. MAC addresses are learned as hosts transmit frames on an interface. The interface learns up to the maximum number of addresses allowed. Learned addresses can also be aged out of the table if those hosts are silent for a period of time. By default, no aging occurs.

You can also statically define one or more MAC addresses on an interface. Any of these addresses are allowed to access the network through the port. Use the following interface configuration command to define a static address:

```
Switch(config-if)# switchport port-security mac-address mac-addr
```

The MAC address is given in dotted-triplet format. If the number of static addresses configured is less than the maximum number of addresses secured on a port, the remaining addresses are dynamically learned. So, be sure to set the maximum number appropriately.

Finally, you must define how each interface using port security should react if a MAC address is in violation by using the following interface configuration command:

```
Switch(config-if)# switchport port-security violation {shutdown | restrict | protect}
```

A violation occurs if more than the maximum number of MAC addresses are learned, or if an unknown (not statically defined) MAC address attempts to transmit on the port. The switch port takes one of the following configured actions when a violation is detected:

- **shutdown**—The port is immediately put into the errdisable state, which effectively shuts it down. It must be re-enabled manually or through errdisable recovery to be used again.

- **restrict**—The port is allowed to stay up, but all packets from violating MAC addresses are dropped. The switch keeps a running count of the number of violating packets and can send an SNMP trap and a syslog message as an alert of the violation.

- **protect**—The port is allowed to stay up, as in the **restrict** mode. Although packets from violating addresses are dropped, no record of the violation is kept.

Port-Based Authentication

Catalyst switches can support port-based authentication, a combination of AAA authentication and port security. This feature is based on the IEEE 802.1x standard.

Basically, a switch port will not pass any traffic until a user has authenticated with the switch. If the authentication is successful, the user can use the port normally.

For port-based authentication, both the switch and the end –user's PC must support the 802.1x standard, using the Extensible Authentication Protocol over LANs (EAPOL). The 802.1x standard is a cooperative effort between the client and the switch offering network service. If the client PC is configured to use 802.1x but the switch does not support it, the PC abandons the protocol and communicates normally. However, if the switch is configured for 802.1x but the PC does not support it, the switch port remains in the unauthorized state so that it will not forward any traffic to the client PC.

> **NOTE** 802.1x EAPOL is a Layer 2 protocol. At the point where a switch detects the presence of a device on a port, the port remains in the unauthorized state. Therefore, the client PC cannot communicate with anything other than the switch by using EAPOL. If the PC does not already have an IP address, it cannot request one. The PC also has no knowledge of the switch or its IP address, so any means other than a Layer 2 protocol is not possible. This is why the PC must also have an 802.1x-capable application or client software.

An 802.1x switch port begins in the unauthorized state so that no data other than the 802.1x protocol itself is allowed through the port. Either the client or the switch can initiate an 802.1x session. The authorized state of the port ends when the user logs out, causing the 802.1x client to inform the switch to revert back to the unauthorized state. The switch can also time out the user's authorized session. In this event, the client must reauthenticate to continue using the switch port.

802.1x Configuration

Port-based authentication uses a variety of methods to authenticate potential clients. A method list is configured, defining the methods to be tried in sequence. Begin by configuring an 802.1x method list with the following global configuration command:

```
Switch(config)# aaa authentication dot1x {default | list-name} method1 [method2 ...]
```

Be sure that the **aaa new-model** command has already been configured. Here, a method is defined by one of the following keywords:

- **group** {*group-name* | **radius** | **tacacs+**}—Authentication servers are used to authenticate the user. These are configured as the group *group-name*. Otherwise, all the available RADIUS or TACACS+ servers are tried. These servers are configured exactly the same as the AAA feature.

- **enable**—The enable password authenticates the user.

- **line**—The line password authenticates the user. This applies only when 802.1x is being used on a switch line (console or vty).

- **local**—The locally defined usernames and passwords are used to authenticate the user.

- **none**—No authentication is performed.

If RADIUS or TACACS+ servers are used as a method, including one of the local methods at the end of the line is wise. This gives a predictable last-resort method if all of the authentication servers are unavailable. Otherwise, users or support staff could be locked out of the switch.

Next, enable the use of 802.1x on the switch with the following global configuration command:

```
Switch(config)# dot1x system-auth-control
```

You must configure each switch port that will use 802.1x. Use the following interface configuration command to set the authentication state:

```
Switch(config-if)# dot1x port-control {force-authorized | force-unauthorized | auto}
```

Here, the 802.1x state is one of the following:

- **force-authorized**—The port is forced to always authorize any connected client. No authentication is necessary. This is the default state for all switch ports when 802.1x is enabled.

- **force-unauthorized**—The port is forced to never authorize any connected client. As a result, the port cannot move to the authorized state to pass traffic to a connected client.

- **auto**—The port uses an 802.1x exchange to move from the unauthorized to the authorized state, if successful. This requires an 802.1x-capable application on the client PC.

It might be obvious that port-based authentication is tailored for controlling access to a single host PC that is connected to a switch port. However, it also supports cases where multiple hosts are attached to a single switch port through an Ethernet hub or another access layer switch.

If the switch should expect to find multiple hosts present on the switch port, use the following interface configuration command:

```
Switch(config-if)# dot1x multi-hosts
```

Foundation Summary

The Foundation Summary is a collection of tables that provides a convenient review of many key concepts in this chapter. If you are already comfortable with the topics in this chapter, this summary can help you recall a few details. If you just read this chapter, this review should help solidify some key facts. If you are doing your final preparation before the exam, these tables and figures are a convenient way to review the day before the exam.

Table 19-2 *AAA Configuration Commands*

Task	Command Syntax
Enable AAA on a switch.	**aaa new-model**
Use local authentication.	**username** *username* **password** *password*
Define individual authentication servers.	**radius-server host** {*hostname* | *ip-address*} [**key** *string*] **tacacs-server host** {*hostname* | *ip-address*} [**key** *string*]
Define a group of authentication servers.	**aaa group server** {**radius** | **tacacs+**} *group-name* **server** *ip-address*
Define a list of authentication methods to try.	**aaa authentication login** {**default** | *list-name*} *method1* [*method2 ...*]
Apply an authentication method list to a line.	**login authentication** {**default** | *list-name*}
Define a list of authorization methods to try.	**aaa authorization** {**commands** | **config-commands** | **configuration** | **exec** | **network** | **reverse-access**} {**default** | *list-name*} *method1* [*method2 ...*]
Apply an authorization method list to a line.	**authorization** {**commands** *level* | **exec** | **reverse-access**} {**default** | *list-name*}
Define a list of accounting methods to try.	**aaa accounting** {**system** | **exec** | **commands** *level*} {**default** | *list-name*} {**start-stop** | **stop-only** | **wait-start** | **none**} *method1* [*method2 ...*]
Apply an accounting method list to a line.	**accounting** {**commands** *level* | **connection** | **exec**} {**default** | *list-name*}

Table 19-3 *Port Security Configuration Commands*

Task	Command Syntax
Enable port security on an interface.	**switchport port-security**
Set the maximum number of learned addresses.	**switchport port-security maximum** *max-addr*
Define a static MAC address.	**switchport port-security mac-address** *mac-addr*
Define an action to take.	**switchport port-security violation** {**shutdown** | **restrict** | **protect**}

Table 19-4 *Port-based Authentication Configuration Commands*

Task	Command Syntax
Define a method list for 802.1x.	**aaa authentication dot1x** {**default** | *list-name*} *method1* [*method2* ...]
Globally enable 802.1x.	**dot1x system-auth-control**
Define the 802.1x behavior on a port.	**dot1x port-control** {**force-authorized** | **force-unauthorized** | **auto**}
Support more than one host on a port.	**dot1x multi-hosts**

Q&A

The questions and scenarios in this book are more difficult than what you should experience on the actual exam. The questions do not attempt to cover more breadth or depth than the exam; however, they are designed to make sure that you know the answers. Rather than allowing you to derive the answers from clues hidden inside the questions themselves, the questions challenge your understanding and recall of the subject. Hopefully, these questions will help limit the number of exam questions on which you narrow your choices to two options and then guess.

The answers to these questions can be found in Appendix A.

1. What does the acronym "AAA" stand for?

2. What external methods of authentication does a Catalyst switch support?

3. A RADIUS server is located at IP address 192.168.199.10. What command configures a Catalyst switch to find the server?

4. A Catalyst switch should be configured to authenticate users against RADIUS servers first, followed by TACACS+ servers. What command can define the authentication methods? Make sure users can still authenticate if none of the servers are available.

5. What is the purpose of authorization? What happens if authorization is not used?

6. Is it possible to use different methods to authorize users to run switch commands instead of making configuration changes?

7. When might the command **switchport port-security maximum 2** be used?

8. After port-based authentication is configured and enabled, can any host connect as long as the user can authenticate?

9. When the 802.1x **force-authorized** keyword is used, how does the switch react to users attempting to connect?

10. Can more than one host be authenticated on a single switch port with port-based authentication?

This chapter covers the following topics that you need to master for the CCNP BCMSN exam:

- **VLAN Access Lists**—This section discusses how traffic can be controlled within a VLAN. You can use VLAN access control lists (ACLs) to filter packets even as they are bridged or switched.

- **Private VLANs**—This section explains the mechanisms that you can use to provide isolation within a single VLAN. Private VLANs have a unidirectional nature; several of them can be isolated, yet share a common subnet and gateway.

- **Switch Port Monitoring**—This section presents the Catalyst features that allow traffic on switch ports or VLANs to be monitored on a different switch port.

CHAPTER 20

Securing with VLANs

Traditionally, traffic has been filtered only at router boundaries, where packets are naturally inspected before forwarding. This is true within Catalyst switches because access lists can be applied as a part of mutlilayer switching. Catalysts can also filter packets even if they stay within the same VLAN; and VLAN access control lists, or VACLs, provide this capabiltiy.

Catalyst switches also have the capability to logically divide a single VLAN into multiple partitions. Each partition can be isolated from others, with all of them sharing a common IP subnet and a common gateway address. Private VLANs make it possible to offer up a single VLAN to many disparate customers or organizations without any interaction between them.

Finally, switch ports must be monitored at times for troubleshooting purposes. Catalyst switches can mirror switch ports or VLANs onto other ports so that a network analysis device can capture or "listen in" on interesting traffic within the switch. The Switch Port Analysis (SPAN) feature can mirror ports on the same switch or across a switched network to a remote switch.

"Do I Know This Already?" Quiz

The purpose of the "Do I Know This Already?" quiz is to help you decide what parts of this chapter to use. If you already intend to read the entire chapter, you do not necessarily need to answer these questions now.

The quiz, derived from the major sections in the "Foundation Topics" portion of the chapter, helps you determine how to spend your limited study time.

Table 20-1 outlines the major topics discussed in this chapter and the "Do I Know This Already?" quiz questions that correspond to those topics.

Table 20-1 *"Do I Know This Already?" Foundation Topics Section-to-Question Mapping*

Foundation Topics Section	Questions Covered in This Section
VLAN ACLs	1–4
Private VLANs	5–8
Monitoring Switch Ports	9–12

> **CAUTION** The goal of self-assessment is to gauge your mastery of the topics in this chapter. If you do not know the answer to a question or are only partially sure of the answer, you should mark this question wrong. Giving yourself credit for an answer you correctly guess skews your self-assessment results and might give you a false sense of security.

1. Which one of the following can filter packets even if they are not routed to another Layer 3 interface?

   a. IP extended access lists

   b. MAC address access lists

   c. VLAN access lists

   d. Port-based access lists

2. In what part of a Catalyst switch are VLAN ACLs implemented?

   a. NVRAM

   b. CAM

   c. RAM

   d. TCAM

3. Which of the following commands can implement a VLAN ACL called "test?"

   a. **access-list vlan test**

   b. **vacl test**

   c. **switchport vacl test**

   d. **vlan access-map test**

4. After a VACL is configured, where is it applied?

   a. Globally on a VLAN

   b. On the VLAN interface

   c. In the VLAN configuration

   d. On all ports or interfaces mapped to a VLAN

5. Which of the following private VLANs is the most restrictive?

   a. Community VLAN

   b. Isolated VLAN

   c. Restricted VLAN

   d. Promiscuous VLAN

6. The **vlan 100** command has just been entered. What is the next command needed to configure VLAN 100 as a secondary isolated VLAN?

    a. **private-vlan isolated**

    b. **private-vlan isolated 100**

    c. **pvlan secondary isolated**

    d. No further configuration is necessary.

7. What type of port configuration should you use for private VLAN interfaces on a router?

    a. Host

    b. Gateway

    c. Promiscuous

    d. Transparent

8. Promiscuous ports must be _____ to primary and secondary VLANs, and host ports must be _____.

    a. mapped, associated

    b. mapped, mapped

    c. associated, mapped

    d. associated, associated

9. Which of the following allows a port to be mirrored to another port on the same switch?

    a. VSPAN

    b. RSPAN

    c. SPAN

    d. CSPAN

10. What must be used to connect switches used for RSPAN?

    a. An 802.1Q trunk

    b. Access-mode switch ports (single VLAN)

    c. A private VLAN over a trunk

    d. An RSPAN VLAN over a trunk

11. What is the most important difference between an RSPAN VLAN and a regular VLAN?

    a. The RSPAN VLAN disables MAC address learning.

    b. The RSPAN VLAN uses static MAC address definitions.

    c. The RSPAN VLAN has the RSPAN source and destination MAC addresses defined in the CAM table.

    d. The RSPAN VLAN cannot be carried over a trunk link.

12. To configure an RSPAN session's source switch, what is used for the session destination?

    a. The switch port leading to the destination switch

    b. The RSPAN VLAN

    c. The final destination switch port

    d. The next-hop router

The answers to the "Do I Know This Already?" quiz are found in Appendix A, "Answers to Chapter 'Do I Know This Already?' Quizzes and Q&A Sections." The suggested choices for your next step are as follows:

- **10 or less overall score**—Read the entire chapter. This includes the "Foundation Topics," "Foundation Summary," and "Q&A" sections.

- **11 or 12 overall score**—If you want more review on these topics, skip to the "Foundation Summary" section and then go to the "Q&A" section at the end of the chapter. Otherwise, move to Chapter 21, "Scenarios for Final Preparation."

Foundation Topics

VLAN Access Lists

Access lists can manage or control traffic as it passes through a switch. When normal access lists are configured on a Catalyst switch, they filter traffic through the use of the Ternary Content Addressable Memory (TCAM). Recall from Chapter 3, "Switch Operation," that access lists (also known as router access lists or RACLs) are merged or compiled into the TCAM. Each ACL is applied to an interface according to the direction of traffic—inbound or outbound. Packets can then be filtered in hardware with no switching performance penalty. However, only packets that pass *between* VLANs can be filtered this way.

Packets that stay in the same VLAN do not ever cross a VLAN or interface boundary and do not necessarily have a direction in relation to an interface. These packets might also be non-IP, non-IPX, or completely bridged; therefore, they never pass through the multilayer switching mechanism. VLAN access lists (VACLs) are filters that can directly affect how packets are handled *within* a VLAN.

VACLs are somewhat different from RACLs or traditional access control lists. Although they too are merged into the TCAM, they can permit, deny, or redirect packets as they are matched. VACLs are also configured in a route map fashion, with a series of matching conditions and actions to take.

VACL Configuration

VACLs are configured as a VLAN access map, in much the same format as a route map. A VLAN access map consists of one or more statements, each having a common map name. First, you define the VACL with the following global configuration command:

```
Switch(config)# vlan access-map map-name [sequence-number]
```

Access map statements are evaluated in sequence, according to the *sequence-number*. Each statement can contain one or more matching conditions, followed by an action.

Next, define the matching conditions that identify the traffic to be filtered. Matching is performed by access lists (IP, IPX, or MAC address ACLs), which you must configure independently. Configure a matching condition with the following access map configuration command:

```
Switch(config-access-map)# match {ip address {acl-number | acl-name}} | {ipx address
   {acl-number | acl-name}} | {mac address acl-name}
```

You can repeat this command to define several matching conditions; the first match encountered triggers an action to take. Define the action with the following access map configuration command:

```
Switch(config-access-map)# action {drop | forward [capture] | redirect interface type
    mod/num}
```

A VACL can either **drop** a matching packet, **forward** it, or **redirect** it to another interface. The TCAM performs the entire VACL match and action, as packets are switched or bridged within a VLAN, or routed into or out of a VLAN.

Finally, you must apply the VACL to a VLAN interface using the following global configuration command:

```
Switch(config)# vlan filter map-name vlan-list vlan-list
```

Notice that the VACL is applied globally to one or more VLANs listed and not to a VLAN interface (SVI). Recall that VLANs can be present in a switch as explicit interfaces or as inherent Layer 2 entities. The VLAN interface is the point where packets enter or leave a VLAN, so it does not make sense to apply a VACL there. Instead, the VACL needs to function *within* the VLAN itself, where there is no inbound or outbound direction.

For example, suppose you find a need to filter traffic within VLAN 99 so that host 192.168.99.17 is not allowed to contact any other host on its local subnet. An access list **local-17** is created to identify traffic between this host and anything else on its local subnet. Then, a VLAN access map is defined: If the IP address is permitted by the **local-17** access list, the packet is dropped; otherwise, it is forwarded. Example 20-1 shows the commands necessary for this example.

Example 20-1   *Filtering Traffic Within the Local Subnet*

```
Switch(config)# ip access-list extended local-17
Switch(config-acl)# permit ip host 192.168.99.17 192.168.99.0 0.0.0.255
Swtich(config-acl)# exit
Switch(config)# vlan access-map block-17 10
Switch(config-access-map)# match ip address local-17
Switch(config-access-map)# action drop
Switch(config-access-map)# vlan access-map block-17 20
Switch(config-access-map)# action forward
Switch(config-access-map)# exit
Switch(config)# vlan filter block-17 vlan-list 99
```

Private VLANs

Normally, traffic is allowed to move unrestricted within a VLAN. Packets sent from one host to another are normally heard only by the destination host, thanks to the nature of Layer 2 switching.

However, if one host broadcasts a packet, all hosts on the VLAN must listen. You can use a VACL to filter packets between a source and destination in a VLAN if both connect to the local switch.

Sometimes, it would be nice to have the ability to segment traffic within a single VLAN, without having to use multiple VLANs and a router. For example, in a single-VLAN server farm, all servers should be able to communicate with the router or gateway, but the servers should not have to listen to each other's broadcast traffic. Taking this a step further, suppose each server belongs to a separate organization. Now each server should be isolated from the others but still be able to reach the gateway to find clients not on the local network.

Another application is a service provider network. Here, the provider might want to use a single VLAN to connect to several customer networks. Each customer needs to be able to contact the provider's gateway on the VLAN. Clearly, the customer sites do not need to interact with each other.

Private VLANs (PVLANs) solve this problem on Catalyst switches. In a nutshell, a normal, or *primary,* VLAN can be logically associated with special unidirectional, or *secondary,* VLANs. Hosts associated with a secondary VLAN can communicate with ports on the primary VLAN (a router, for example), but not with another secondary VLAN. A secondary VLAN is configured as one of the following types:

- **Isolated**—Any switch ports associated with an isolated VLAN can reach the primary VLAN but not any other secondary VLAN. In addition, hosts associated with the same isolated VLAN cannot reach each other. They are, in effect, isolated from everything except the primary VLAN.

- **Community**—Any switch ports associated with a common community VLAN can communicate with each other and with the primary VLAN but not with any other secondary VLAN. This provides the basis for server farms and workgroups within an organization, while giving isolation between organizations.

All secondary VLANs must be associated with one primary VLAN to set up the unidirectional relationship. Private VLANs are configured using special cases of regular VLANs. However, VLAN Trunking Protocol (VTP) does not pass any information about the private VLAN configuration. Each of the private VLANs must be configured locally on each switch that interconnects them.

You must configure each switch port that uses a private VLAN with a VLAN association. You must also define the port with one of the following modes:

- **Promiscuous**—The switch port connects to a router, firewall, or other common gateway device. This port can communicate with anything else connected to the primary or any secondary VLAN. In other words, the port is in promiscuous mode, where the rules of private VLANs are ignored.

■ **Host**—The switch port connects to a regular host that resides on an isolated or community VLAN. The port communicates only with a promiscuous port or ports on the same community VLAN.

Figure 20-1 shows the basic private VLAN operation. Some host PCs connect to a secondary community VLAN. The two community VLANs associate with a primary VLAN, where the router connects. The router connects to a promiscuous port on the primary VLAN. A single host PC connects to a secondary isolated VLAN, so it can communicate only with the router's promiscuous port.

Figure 20-1 *Private VLAN Functionality Within a Switch*

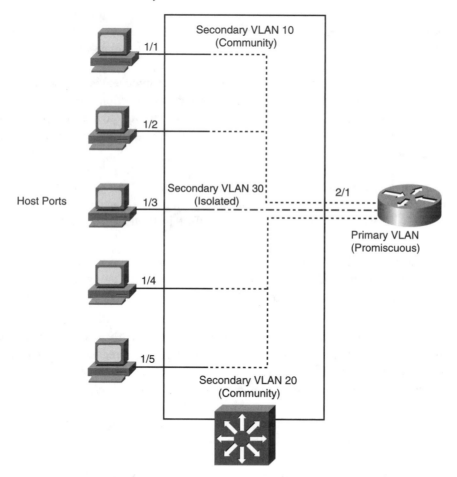

Private VLAN Configuration

Defining a private VLAN involves several configuration steps. These steps are described in the sections that follow so you can use them.

Configure the Private VLANs

To configure a private VLAN, begin by defining any secondary VLANs that are needed for isolation using the following configuration commands:

```
Switch(config)# vlan vlan-id
Switch(config-vlan)# private-vlan {isolated | community}
```

The secondary VLAN can be an isolated VLAN (no connectivity between isolated ports) or a community VLAN (connectivity between member ports).

Now, define the primary VLAN that will provide the underlying private VLAN connectivity using the following configuration commands:

```
Switch(config)# vlan vlan-id
Switch(config-vlan)# private-vlan primary
Switch(config-vlan)# private-vlan association {secondary-vlan-list | add secondary-vlan-
    list | remove secondary vlan-list}
```

Be sure to associate the primary VLAN with all of its component secondary VLANs using the **association** keyword. If the primary VLAN has already been configured, you can add (**add**) or remove (**remove**) secondary VLAN associations individually.

These VLAN configuration commands set up only the mechanisms for unidirectional connectivity from the secondary VLANs to the primary VLAN. You must also associate the individual switch ports with their respective private VLANs.

Associate Ports with Private VLANs

First, define the function of the port that will participate on a private VLAN using the following configuration command:

```
Switch(config-if)# switchport mode private-vlan {host | promiscuous}
```

If the host connected to this port is a router, firewall, or common gateway for the VLAN, use the **promiscuous** keyword. This allows the host to reach all other promiscuous, isolated, or community ports associated with the primary VLAN. Otherwise, any isolated or community port must receive the **host** keyword.

For a nonpromiscuous port (using the **switchport mode private-vlan host** command), you must associate the switch port with the appropriate primary and secondary VLANs. Remember, only the private VLANs themselves have been configured until now. The switch port must know how to interact with the various VLANs using the following interface configuration command:

```
Switch(config-if)# switchport private-vlan host-association primary-vlan-id secondary-
    vlan-id
```

> **NOTE** Configuring a static access VLAN on a switch port when the port is associated with private VLANs is not necessary. Instead, the port takes on membership in the primary and secondary VLANs simultaneously. This does not mean that the port has a fully functional assignment to multiple VLANs. Instead, it takes on only the unidirectional behavior between the secondary and primary VLANs.

For a promiscuous port (using the **switchport mode private-vlan promiscuous** command), you must map the port to primary and secondary VLANs. Notice that promiscuous mode ports, or ports that can communicate with any other private VLAN device, are mapped, while other secondary VLAN ports are associated. One (promiscuous mode port) exhibits bidirectional behavior, while the other (secondary VLAN ports) exhibits unidirectional or logical behavior.

Use the following interface configuration command to map promiscuous mode ports to primary and secondary VLANs:

```
Switch(config-if)# switchport private-vlan mapping {primary-vlan-id} {secondary-
    vlan-list} | {add secondary-vlan-list} | {remove secondary-vlan-list}
```

As an example, assume the switch in Figure 20-1 is configured as in Example 20-2. Host PCs on ports FastEthernet 1/1 and 1/2 are in community VLAN 10, hosts on ports FastEthernet 1/4 and 1/5 are in community VLAN 20, and the host on port FastEthernet 1/3 is in isolated VLAN 30. The router on port FastEthernet 2/1 is in promiscuous mode on primary VLAN 100. Each VLAN is assigned a role, and the primary VLAN is associated with its secondary VLANs. Then, each interface is associated with a primary and secondary VLAN (if a host is attached) or mapped to the primary and secondary VLANs (if a promiscuous host is attached).

Example 20-2 *Configuring Ports with Private VLANs*

```
Switch(config)# vlan 10
Switch(config-vlan)# private-vlan community
Switch(config)# vlan 20
Switch(config-vlan)# private-vlan community
Switch(config)# vlan 30
Switch(config-vlan)# private-vlan isolated
Switch(config)# vlan 100
Switch(config-vlan)# private-vlan primary
Switch(config-vlan)# private-vlan association 10,20,30
```

Example 20-2 *Configuring Ports with Private VLANs (Continued)*

```
Switch(config-vlan)# exit
Switch(config)# interface range fastethernet 1/1 - 1/2
Switch(config-if)# switchport private-vlan host-association 100 10
Switch(config)# interface range fastethernet 1/4 - 1/5
Switch(config-if)# switchport private-vlan host-association 100 20
Switch(config)# interface fastethernet 1/3
Switch(config-if)# switchport private-vlan host-association 100 30

Switch(config)# interface fastethernet 2/1
Switch(config-if)# switchport mode private-vlan promiscuous
Switch(config-if)# switchport private-vlan mapping 100 10,20,30
```

Associate Secondary VLANs to a Primary VLAN SVI

On switched virtual interfaces (SVIs), or VLAN interfaces configured with Layer 3 addresses, you must configure some additional private VLAN mapping. Consider the SVI for the primary VLAN, VLAN 100, that has an IP address and participates in routing traffic. Secondary VLANs 40 (an isolated VLAN) and 50 (a community VLAN) are associated at Layer 2 with primary VLAN 100 using the configuration in Example 20-3.

Example 20-3 *Associating Secondary VLANs to a Primary VLAN*

```
vlan 40
    private-vlan isolated
vlan 50
    private-vlan community
vlan 200
    private-vlan primary
    private-vlan association 40,50
interface vlan 200
    ip address 192.168.199.1 255.255.255.0
```

Primary VLAN 200 can forward traffic at Layer 3, but the secondary VLAN associations with it are only good at Layer 2. To allow Layer 3 traffic switching coming from the secondary VLANs as well, you must add a private VLAN mapping to the primary VLAN (SVI) interface, using the following interface configuration command:

```
Switch(config-if)# private-vlan mapping {secondary-vlan-list | add secondary-vlan-list |
    remove secondary-vlan-list}
```

The primary VLAN SVI function is extended to the secondary VLANs, instead of requiring SVIs for each of them. If some mapping has already been configured for the primary VLAN SVI, you can add (**add**) or remove (**remove**) secondary VLAN mappings individually.

For the example, you would map the private VLAN with the following command:

```
interface vlan 200
      private-vlan mapping 40,50
```

Switch Port Monitoring

Suppose a problem exists on your switched network and you want to use a network analyzer to gather data. Of interest is a conversation between two hosts connected to the switch, one on interface FastEthernet 1/1 and the other on FastEthernet 4/7. Both ports are assigned to VLAN 100. If you connect your analyzer to another port on VLAN 100, what will your packet capture show?

Recall that, by definition, switches learn where MAC addresses are located and forward packets directly to those ports. The only time a packet is flooded to ports other than the specific destination is when the destination MAC address has not already been located or when the packet is destined for a broadcast or multicast address. Therefore, your packet capture shows only the broadcast and multicast packets that were flooded to the analyzer's port. None of the interesting conversation will be overheard.

Catalyst switches can use the *Switched Port Analyzer (SPAN)* feature to mirror traffic from one source switch port or VLAN to a destination port. This allows a monitoring device, such as a network analyzer, to be attached to the destination port for capturing traffic.

When packets arrive on the source port or VLAN, they are specially marked so that they can be copied to the SPAN destination port as well as the true destination port. In this way, the packet capture receives an exact copy of the packets that are being forwarded from the source.

SPAN is available in several different forms:

■ **Local SPAN**—Both the SPAN source and destination are located on the local switch. The source is one or more switch ports.

■ **VLAN-based SPAN (VSPAN)**—A variation of local SPAN where the source is a VLAN rather than a physical port.

■ **Remote SPAN (RSPAN)**—The SPAN source and destination are located on different switches. Mirrored traffic is copied over a special-purpose VLAN across trunks between switches from the source to the destination.

The sections that follow describe each of these SPAN forms in more detail.

Local SPAN and VSPAN

The SPAN source can be identified as one or more physical switch ports, a trunk, or a VLAN. Packets that are being forwarded from the destination are also copied into the destination port's queue. Because the packets are merely copied, neither the original data nor its being forwarded is affected. Figure 20-2 demonstrates two cases where a network analyzer on the SPAN destination port is receiving frames that SPAN has copied from the source port. Here, SPAN session A monitors all communication on VLAN 100. SPAN session B uses a normal access mode source port to monitor communication between a server and its client PCs.

Figure 20-2 *Basic Local SPAN and VSPAN Operation*

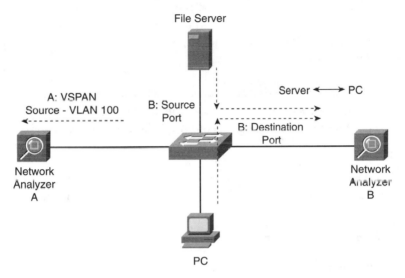

What happens if a speed mismatch occurs between the SPAN source and destination ports? This could easily happen if the source is a VLAN with many hosts, or if the source is a GigabitEthernet port and the destination is a FastEthernet port.

Packets are copied only into the destination port's egress queue. If the destination port becomes congested, the SPAN packets are dropped from the queue and are not seen at the destination port. Therefore, if the bandwidth of source traffic exceeds the destination port speed, some packets might not be seen at the destination port. Then, traffic from the SPAN source is not affected by any congestion at the SPAN destination.

Local SPAN and VSPAN Configuration

You can configure one or more simultaneous SPAN sessions on a Catalyst switch. These sessions are completely independent because no interaction occurs between the packet mirroring of each.

To configure a SPAN session, start by defining the source of the SPAN session data, using the following global configuration command:

```
Switch(config)# monitor session session source {interface type mod/num | vlan vlan-id}
   [rx | tx   | both]
```

SPAN sessions must be uniquely numbered using the *session* parameter. The maximum number of supported sessions varies among Catalyst platforms. For example, a Catalyst 3550 can support two sessions, whereas a Catalyst 6500 can support up to 64. If multiple sources are needed, you can repeat this command. The SPAN source can be a physical switch interface or a Layer 2 VLAN (not a logical VLAN interface or SVI).

Traffic can be selected for mirroring based on the direction it is traveling through the SPAN source. For example, you can select only traffic received on the source (**rx**), only traffic transmitted from the source (**tx**), or traffic in both directions (**both**). By default, both directions are used.

Next, identify the SPAN destination. You must assign the SPAN source and destination ports to the same VLAN within the switch; otherwise, the switch cannot copy frames from one VLAN to another. Use the following global configuration command to identify the SPAN destination:

```
Switch(config)# monitor session session destination {{interface type mod/num} | {vlan
   vlan-id} |   {analysis-module slot-number} | {data-port port-number}}
```

The session number here must match the one configured for the SPAN source. You can define only one destination port for each SPAN session. In addition, SPAN sessions cannot share a destination port. The destination can be a physical interface, a Layer 2 VLAN (not a VLAN SVI interface), or a Network Analysis Module (NAM, Catalyst 6500 only).

You can narrow down the data copied over from the source, if necessary. If the source is a trunk port, you can mirror only traffic from specific VLANs on the trunk with the following global configuration command:

```
Switch(config)# monitor session session-number filter vlan vlan-range
```

Also, if using a VACL, you can identify and mark interesting traffic for SPAN capture. In this case, use the **capture** keyword in the VACL action statement.

You can delete a SPAN session after the packet analysis is complete. SPAN sessions are numbered, so you can delete them by referencing the number. Use the following global configuration command to delete one or more sessions:

```
Switch(config)# no monitor session {{range session-range} | local | all | session}
```

Session numbers can be given as an individual *session*, a range of sessions, all **local** SPAN sessions, or **all** sessions (local or remote). To see the list of currently active SPAN sessions, use the **show monitor** EXEC command, as shown in Example 20-4. Here, two SPAN sessions are in use on a Catalyst 3550.

Example 20-4 *Displaying the Currently Active SPAN Sessions*

```
Switch# show monitor
Session 1
---------
 Type         : Local Session
Source Ports:
    RX Only:       None
    TX Only:       None
    Both:          Fa0/7
Source VLANs:
    RX Only:       None
    TX Only:       None
    Both:          None
Source RSPAN VLAN: None
Destination Ports: Fa0/47
    Encapsulation: Native
           Ingress: Disabled
Reflector Port:    None
Filter VLANs:      None
Dest RSPAN VLAN:   None

Session 2
---------
 Type         : Local Session
Source Ports:
    RX Only:       None
    TX Only:       None
    Both:          Gi0/1
Source VLANs:
    RX Only:       None
    TX Only:       None
    Both:          None
```

continues

Example 20-4 *Displaying the Currently Active SPAN Sessions (Continued)*

```
Source RSPAN VLAN: None
Destination Ports: Gi0/2
    Encapsulation: Native
          Ingress: Disabled
Reflector Port:    None
Filter VLANs:      None
Dest RSPAN VLAN:   None
```

CAUTION After you finish using a SPAN session, you should always disable or delete it. Otherwise, someone might try to connect to the port that is configured as the SPAN destination at some later date. You could spend a good bit of time troubleshooting that user's connectivity problem only to find that you left a SPAN session active!

NOTE When Local SPAN or VSPAN is enabled, the Spanning Tree Protocol (STP) is disabled on the destination port. This allows STP BPDUs to be captured and monitored but also allows the possibility for a bridging loop to form. Never connect a SPAN session's destination port back into an active network. If the monitored packets need to be sent toward another switch, use RSPAN instead.

Remote SPAN

In a large switched network or one that is geographically separated, it might not always be convenient to take a network analysis to the switch where a SPAN source is located. To make SPAN more extensible, Cisco developed the Remote SPAN (RSPAN) feature. With RSPAN, the source and destination can be located on different switches in different locations.

The RSPAN source is identified on one switch, just as with local SPAN. The RSPAN destination is identified on its local switch. Then, RSPAN can carry only the mirrored data over a special-purpose VLAN across trunk links and intermediate switches. As long as every switch along the way is RSPAN-capable, the source can be located at the far-end switch, while the network analyzer is conveniently located at the switch nearest you.

Figure 20-3 shows an example network using RSPAN where the packets from the file server (source port) on one switch are copied and transported over the RSPAN VLAN on trunk links. At the destination switch, packets are pulled off the RSPAN VLAN and copied to the network analyzer (destination port). The file server and network analyzer are stationed in geographically separate locations.

Figure 20-3 *Example of Remote SPAN Operation*

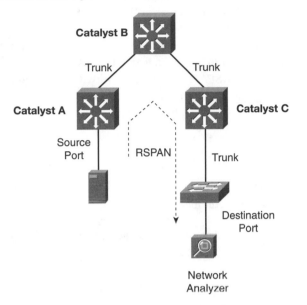

The RSPAN VLAN has some important differences from a regular VLAN. First, MAC address learning is disabled on the RSPAN VLAN. This is to prevent intermediate switches that transport the RSPAN VLAN from trying to forward the mirrored packets to their real destination MAC addresses. After all, the purpose of SPAN or RSPAN is to simply mirror or copy interesting frames—not forward them normally.

An RSPAN-capable switch also floods the RSPAN packets out all of its ports belonging to the RSPAN VLAN in an effort to send them toward the RSPAN destination. Intermediate switches have no knowledge of the RSPAN source or destination; rather, they know only of the RSPAN VLAN itself.

Remote SPAN Configuration

RSPAN configuration begins with the definition of the special-purpose RSPAN VLAN. If you configure the RSPAN VLAN on a VTP server, VTP correctly propagates it to other intermediate switches. If not using VTP, be sure to configure this VLAN for RSPAN explicitly on each intermediate switch. Otherwise, the RSPAN packets will not be delivered correctly.

In addition, if VTP pruning is in use, the RSPAN VLAN will be pruned from unnecessary trunks, limiting the traffic impact in unrelated areas of the network.

Create and maintain one or more RSPAN VLANs for the special monitoring purpose only. Set aside one RSPAN VLAN for each RSPAN session that will be used. Don't allow any normal hosts to join an RSPAN VLAN. Define an RSPAN VLAN on each switch between the source and destination with the following configuration commands:

```
Switch(config)# vlan vlan-id
Switch(config-vlan)# remote-span
```

Next, you must identify the RSPAN source *and* destination on the two switches where the source and destination are connected. At the source switch, identify the source and destination with the following global configuration commands:

```
Switch(config)# monitor session session source {interface type mod/num | vlan vlan-id}
  [rx | tx  | both]
Switch(config)# monitor session session destination remote vlan rspan-vlan-id
```

Here, the source is either a physical switch interface or a Layer 2 VLAN (not a VLAN SVI interface). Notice that the command syntax is identical to the Local SPAN **source** command. The RSPAN destination is simply the RSPAN VLAN. This allows the mirrored packets to be copied into the special VLAN and sent on their way toward the final RSPAN destination.

At the destination switch, you must again identify the RSPAN source and destination by using the following global configuration commands:

```
Switch(config)# monitor session session source remote vlan rspan-vlan-id
Switch(config)# monitor session session destination {interface type | vlan vlan-id}
```

Here, the roles are reversed. RSPAN packets are pulled from the RSPAN VLAN and placed onto the destination, which is either a physical switch interface or a Layer 2 VLAN.

NOTE Be aware that RSPAN traffic can increase the traffic load on a trunk, even though RSPAN is restricted to one special VLAN within the trunk. If the additional load is significant, the normal production and the monitored traffic contend with each other for available bandwidth. As a result, both types of traffic could suffer.

Also, RSPAN must allow the STP to run on the RSPAN VLAN to prevent bridging loops from forming. As a result, STP BPDUs are normally sent and received on the VLAN. You cannot monitor BPDUs with RSPAN.

In Example 20-5, RSPAN is configured on all three switches shown in Figure 20-3. The source is connected to Catalyst A port FastEthernet 1/1. The destination is a network analyzer connected to port FastEthernet 4/48 on Catalyst C. Catayst B simply passes the RSPAN session traffic over VLAN 999, transported by trunk links.

Example 20-5 *Configuring RSPAN on the Catalyst Switches in Figure 20-3*

```
Catalyst A
vlan 999
     remote-span
monitor session 1 source interface fastethernet 1/1 both
monitor session 1 destination remote vlan 999

Catalyst B
vlan 999
     remote-span

Catalyst C
vlan 999
     remote-span
monitor session 1 source remote vlan 999
monitor session 1 destination interface fastethernet 4/48
```

Foundation Summary

The Foundation Summary is a collection of information that provides a convenient review of many key concepts in this chapter. If you are already comfortable with the topics in this chapter, this summary can help you recall a few details. If you just read this chapter, this review should help solidify some key facts. If you are doing your final preparation before the exam, this information will hopefully be a convenient way to review the day before the exam.

- VLAN Access Lists (VACLs) can control packets that are bridged, switched, or routed. VACLs are effective on packets that stay *within* a single VLAN.

Table 20-2 *VLAN ACL Configuration Commands*

Task	Command Syntax
Define a VACL.	**vlan access-map** *map-name* [*sequence-number*]
Define a matching condition.	**match** {**ip address** {*acl-number* | *acl-name*}} | {**ipx address** {*acl-number* | *acl-name*} | {**mac address** *acl-name*}}
Define an action.	**action** {**drop** | **forward** [**capture**] | **redirect** *interface type mod/num*}
Apply the VACL to VLANs.	**vlan filter** *map-name* **vlan-list** *vlan-list*

- Private VLANs provide special unidirectional relationships between entities on a single VLAN.
- Private VLANs are implemented as *primary* and *secondary* VLANs.
- Primary VLANs allow hosts to communicate with any other type of private (secondary) VLAN.
- Secondary VLANs allow hosts to communicate with ports on a primary VLAN but not with other secondary VLANs.
- Secondary VLANs are categorized as follows:

  — **Isolated VLAN**—Hosts can communicate only with the primary VLAN not any other isolated port or secondary VLAN.

  — **Community VLAN**—Hosts can communicate with the primary VLAN and other hosts in the community VLAN but not with any other isolated or community VLAN.

- Secondary VLANs must be associated with one primary VLAN.

- You can configure switch ports using private VLANs as follows:

  — **Promiscuous**—Usually connects to a router, firewall, or gateway device; this type of port can communicate with any other type of private VLAN.

  — **Host**—Usually connects to regular hosts; this type of port can communicate with a promiscuous port or ports on the same community VLAN.

Table 20-3 *Private VLAN Configuration Commands*

Task	Command Syntax
Define a secondary VLAN.	**vlan** *vlan-id* **private-vlan** {**isolated** | **community**}
Define a primary VLAN; associate it with secondary VLANs.	**vlan** *vlan-id* **private-vlan primary** **private-vlan association** {*secondary-vlan-list* | **add** *secondary-vlan-list* | **remove** *secondary-vlan-list*}
Associate ports with private VLANs.	**switchport mode private-vlan** {**host** | **promiscuous**}
Associate nonpromiscuous ports with private VLANs.	**switchport private-vlan host-association** *primary-vlan-id secondary-vlan-id*
Associate promiscuous ports with private VLANs.	**switchport private-vlan mapping** {*primary-vlan-id*} {*secondary-vlan-list*} | {**add** *secondary-vlan-list*} | {**remove** *secondary-vlan-list*}
Associate secondary VLANs with a Primary VLAN Layer 3 SVI.	**private-vlan mapping** {*secondary-vlan-list* | **add** *secondary-vlan-list* | **remove** *secondary-vlan-list*}

- Switch port monitoring can monitor or capture interesting traffic on a Catalyst switch.

- Local SPAN copies frames from a source to a destination port on the local switch.

- VLAN SPAN (VSPAN) copies frames from a source VLAN to a destination port on the local switch.

- Remote SPAN (RSPAN) copies frames from a source on one switch to a destination on another switch. Frames are carried over a special RSPAN VLAN across intermediate switches and trunks.

Table 20-4 *Local or VLAN SPAN Commands*

Task	Command Syntax
Identify a SPAN session source.	**monitor session** *session* **source** {**interface** *type* I **vlan** *vlan-id*} [**rx** I **tx** I **both**]
Identify a SPAN session destination.	**monitor session** *session* **destination** {{**interface** *type mod/num*} I {**vlan** *vlan-id*} I {**analysis-module** *slot-number*} I {**data-port** *port-number*}}
Filter VLANs from a SPAN source trunk.	**monitor session** *session-number* **filter vlan** *vlan-range*
Remove a SPAN session.	**no monitor session** {{**range** *session-range*} I **local** I **all** I *session*}

Table 20-5 *RSPAN Commands*

Task	Command Syntax
Define an RSPAN VLAN for transport (all switches from source to destination).	**vlan** *vlan-id* **remote-span**
Source switch: identify the RSPAN source and destination.	**monitor session** *session* **source** {**interface** *type mod/num* I **vlan** *vlan-id*} [**rx** I **tx** I **both**] **monitor session** *session* **destination remote vlan** *rspan-vlan-id*
Destination switch: identify the RSPAN source and destination.	**monitor session** *session* **source remote vlan** *rspan-vlan-id* **monitor session** *session* **destination** {**interface** *type mod/num* I **vlan** *vlan-id*}

Q&A

The questions and scenarios in this book are more difficult than what you should experience on the actual exam. The questions do not attempt to cover more breadth or depth than the exam; however, they are designed to make sure that you know the answers. Rather than allowing you to derive the answers from clues hidden inside the questions themselves, the questions challenge your understanding and recall of the subject. Hopefully, these questions will help limit the number of exam questions on which you narrow your choices to two options and then guess.

You can find the answers to these questions in Appendix A.

1. When a VACL is implemented on a switch, how is the switching speed affected?

2. What actions can be taken on packets matching a VACL?

3. After a VACL is applied using the **vlan filter** command, how is the traffic direction (inbound or outbound) specified?

4. A secondary community VLAN is associated with a primary VLAN on a switch. Can hosts assigned to the community VLAN communicate with each other?

5. A secondary isolated VLAN is associated with a primary VLAN on a switch. Can hosts assigned to the isolated VLAN communicate with each other?

6. What command is needed to configure a promiscuous VLAN?

7. A router is identifed as the central gatewawy for a private VLAN. What command is needed to configure the switch port where a router is connected?

8. How many actual VLANs must be configured to implement a common router with two community VLANs?

9. How is switching performance affected when several SPAN sessions are enabled?

10. What command can specify the source of a SPAN session as VLAN 100?

11. When a SPAN session is enabled, what direction of traffic flow (relative to the source port) is mirrored for analysis?

12. What two things can identify more granular traffic to be mirrored to a SPAN destination?

13. Three switches are connected in series with trunk links. The RSPAN source is on the first switch and the destination is on the third. How does the intermediate (second) switch learn about the RSPAN's source and destination locations?

14. What must be configured on all switches connecting an RSPAN source and destination? What commands can be used?

15. One of the advantages of RSPAN is that mirrored traffic can be isolated in the RSPAN VLAN on a trunk. If a GigabitEthernet port is to be monitored on one switch, which is better to use as a transport for the RSPAN VLAN: a GigabitEthernet trunk already carrying user traffic in other VLANs, or an isolated GigabitEthernet trunk link set aside for RSPAN?

PART V: Scenarios for Final Preparation

Chapter 21   Scenarios for Final Preparation

The chapter in this part of the book emphasizes an overall understanding of switching concepts, configuration commands, and network operation. Although the CCNP BCMSN exam might not contain scenarios of this type, you can better prepare by thinking about the "bigger picture" of a network and how you can apply each switching topic.

Scenarios for Final Preparation

This chapter presents scenarios that you can use to review most of the concepts contained in this book. The scenarios are designed to assist you in final preparation for the BCMSN exam. Case studies are presented with network diagrams and questions covering many switching topics.

This chapter emphasizes an overall understanding of switching concepts, configuration commands, and network operation. Although the Cisco BCMSN exam might not contain scenarios of this type, you can become better prepared by thinking about the "bigger picture" of a network and how you can apply each switching topic.

Scenario 1: Trunking and DTP

This scenario is built around a network of switches connected by trunking links. You need to think about how DTP operates and how trunks are negotiated (or not) between switches. Consider the network shown in Figure 21-1 and answer the questions that follow. Assume that all switches shown support DTP.

Figure 21-1 *Diagram for Scenario 1*

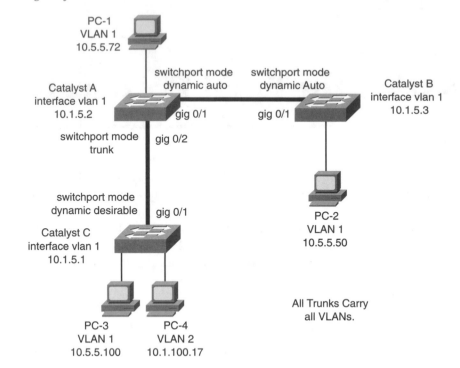

1.   What is the mode of the link between Catalyst A and Catalyst B?

2.   Suppose the network administrator types these commands for interface GigabitEthernet 0/1 on Catalyst B:

     ```
     switchport mode trunk
     switchport nonegotiate
     ```

     What will the link mode be now?

3.   Catalyst B has been given the command **no switchport nonegotiate** for interface GigabitEthernet 0/1. What is the link mode now?

4.   What is the mode of the link between Catalyst A and Catalyst C?

5.   Assume that all links between Catalyst switches are in trunking mode, transporting VLANs 1 through 1005. Can PC-2 ping PC-4?

6.   Suppose PC-1 begins to generate a broadcast storm. Where would the effects of this storm be experienced in this network? Consider both devices and links. Will PC-4 receive the broadcasts?

Scenario 2: VLANs, Trunking, and VTP

This scenario is designed to stir your thinking about VLAN and trunking connectivity. You also need to examine switch configurations and apply them to a network diagram. See the diagram shown in Figure 21-2 and answer the questions that follow. Portions of the configurations of the three Catalyst switches are shown above them.

Figure 21-2 *Diagram for Scenario 2*

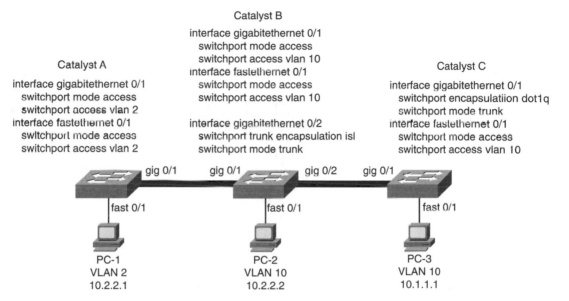

Catalyst B
```
interface gigabitethernet 0/1
  switchport mode access
  switchport access vlan 10
interface fastethernet 0/1
  switchport mode access
  switchport access vlan 10
```

Catalyst A
```
interface gigabitethernet 0/1
  switchport mode access
  switchport access vlan 2
interface fastethernet 0/1
  switchport mode access
  switchport access vlan 2
```

Catalyst C
```
interface gigabitethernet 0/1
  switchport encapsulatiion dot1q
  switchport mode trunk
interface fastethernet 0/1
  switchport mode access
  switchport access vlan 10
```

```
interface gigabitethernet 0/2
  switchport trunk encapsulation isl
  switchport mode trunk
```

gig 0/1   gig 0/1   gig 0/2   gig 0/1

fast 0/1   fast 0/1   fast 0/1

PC-1
VLAN 2
10.2.2.1

PC-2
VLAN 10
10.2.2.2

PC-3
VLAN 10
10.1.1.1

1. PC-1 and PC-2 are both configured with IP addresses on the same subnet. Notice that each PC connects to a different VLAN number. Given the switch configurations shown, can PC-1 ping PC-2?

2. PC-2 and PC-3 are assigned to the same IP subnet and the same VLAN. Can PC-2 and PC-3 ping each other?

3. Will the trunk link between Catalyst B and C come up successfully?

4. Suppose the trunk between Catalyst B and C is configured properly. Where will VLAN1 be pruned? Why?

5. Suppose Catalyst A is a VTP server, Catalyst C is a VTP client, and Catalyst B is configured for VTP transparent mode. All switches are in the "Bermuda" management domain. If VLAN14 is created on Catalyst A, which switches will also create VLAN 14 using VTP?

6. If VLAN 15 is created on Catalyst B, what other switches will also create VLAN 15 via VTP?

7. If VLAN 16 is created on Catalyst C, what will happen?

Scenario 3: Traditional STP

This scenario exercises your ability to think through the Spanning Tree Protocol operation. You are presented with a simple network of two switches. This keeps the STP complexity to a minimum while forcing you to think through the STP convergence process on a live network. Given the network diagram shown in Figure 21-3, complete the following exercises.

Figure 21-3 *Network Diagram for Scenario 3*

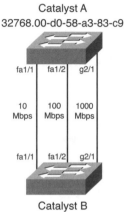

1. Manually compute the Spanning Tree topology. Note which switch is the Root Bridge, which ports are Root Ports and Designated Ports, and which ports are in the Blocking state.

2. If the 100-Mbps link (port FastEthernet 1/2) is disconnected, what happens with the STP?

3. If the 1000-Mbps link (port GigabitEthernet 2/1) is disconnected, how much time will elapse before the two switches can communicate again? (Assume both switches use the default STP timer values and no additional features for faster convergence.)

4. Assume that for some reason the physical 1000-Mbps link (port GigabitEthernet 2/1) stays up and active, but BPDUs are not allowed to pass (that is, an access list filter is blocking BPDUs). What happens and when?

Scenario 4: Advanced STP

A small network consists of two core switches, Catalyst C1 and C2, and an access switch, A1, as shown in Figure 21-4. Advanced Spanning Tree Protocol features will improve the convergence times and reduce the number of STP instances. Answer these questions.

Figure 21-4 *Network Diagram for Scenario 4*

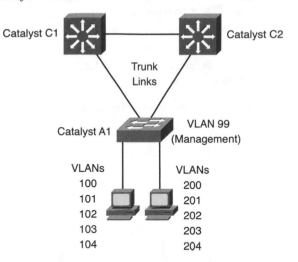

1. To prevent the possibility of a unidirectional link occurring on switch A1's uplinks, what switch feature can be used? What commands are necessary to enable this feature? Assume that the links should be disabled if a unidirectional condition is found. Which switches need to be configured this way?

2. For the links between switch A1 and the user PCs, what command is needed to configure these as RSTP edge ports?

3. Suppose MST is to be configured to reduce the number of STP instances, because 12 unique VLANs are being used across the network. How many MST instances are needed for the three switches shown in figure 21-4, assuming that traffic should be load-balanced across the two uplinks of switch A1?

4. What commands are needed to configure switch C1 for MST?

5. Now, make sure that C1 is configured as the Root Bridge for one MST instance. What commands are needed?

Scenario 5: Router Redundancy with HSRP and GLBP

This scenario covers two methods by which you can configure multilayer switches to provide redundant router or gateway functionality: HSRP and GLBP.

1. A network consists of two VLANs: 101 and 102. Suppose the PCs in VLAN 101 (192.168.101.0/24) use address 192.168.101.1 as their default gateway. The PCs in VLAN 102 (192.168.102.0/24) use 192.168.102.1. What commands are necessary to configure HSRP on a Catalyst switch so that it becomes the active router for VLAN 101 and the standby router for VLAN 102? If a failed router interface is restored, control should be passed back to it from the HSRP standby router. (You can use IP addresses 192.168.101.2 and 192.168.102.2, if needed.)

2. GLBP is to be used in the network shown in Figure 21-5. Answer the following questions about this network.

Figure 21-5 *Network Diagram for Scenario 5*

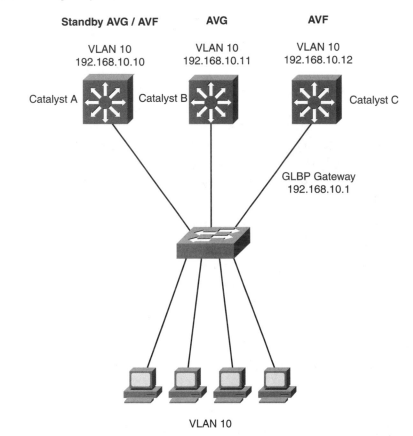

a. What command should you use to make Catalyst B become the active virtual gateway (AVG) for GLBP group 10?

b. The virtual gateway address is 192.168.10.1. Which switches should be configured for this, and with what command?

c. Give the command needed on the AVG to implement round-robin load-balancing, evenly distributing the virtual gateway MAC addresses across the set of AVFs.

d. Each of the AVF switches must be configured to become members of GLBP group 10. How can this be accomplished?

Scenario 6: Multicast

This scenario tests your knowledge of various multicast switching features. Think about how multicast traffic traverses a network, as well as how switches can be configured to participate in building multicast topologies. Then, consider how you can configure the switches to limit the forwarding of unnecessary multicast traffic.

1. Under what conditions is IGMP snooping more suitable than CGMP for handling multicast traffic?

2. Figure 21-6 shows a network diagram. Assume that all switches use the default multicast configurations. Where in the network will multicast traffic originating from PC-1 on Catalyst A (VLAN 101) be seen?

Figure 21-6 *Network Diagram for Scenario 6*

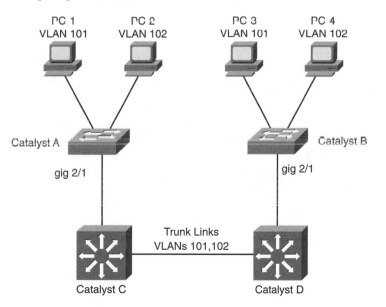

3. What configuration is needed on Catalysts C and D to limit multicast traffic to only those ports that explicitly join multicast groups, using CGMP with PIM dense mode? Assume this is needed on both VLANs 101 and 102. What configuration is needed on Catalysts A and B, which are not capable of IGMP snooping.

Scenario 7: QoS in a Switched Network

This scenario uses a simple two-switch network to reinforce the concepts needed to properly implement QoS. Think about QoS trust within this network, and how the switches can use QoS information to provide appropriate delivery of data and voice applications. Use Figure 21-7 as a reference for the following questions.

Figure 21-7 *Network Diagram for Scenario 7*

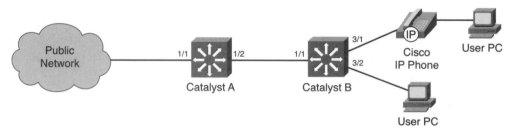

1. Where should a QoS trust boundary be implemented? In other words, which switches should trust incoming QoS information and which ones should not?

2. If Catalyst A port 1/1 is to have inbound QoS untrusted, what commands should you use?

3. Suppose two mission-critical applications are running on the "public" network. One is a streaming video application that uses UDP port 5000. The other is Citrix. What commands could you use on Catalyst A to configure a QoS class map that will classify this traffic specifically?

4. What other commands are necessary to use the class map from Question 3 in a complete QoS policy? Classified traffic should receive a DSCP codepoint AF31 (26). The policy will be applied to Catalyst A interface Gigabit 1/1.

5. After the DSCP has been marked to AF31, are additional commands needed to mark the IP Precedence value to 3?

6. On Catalyst B, configure interface FastEthernet 3/1 to inform the IP Phone to use VLAN 17 for voice traffic. Also, add a configuration command to ensure that no QoS trust is extended to the IP Phone's PC data port.

7. When voice traffic enters switch Catalyst B from the IP Phone on interface FastEthernet 3/1, it will be forwarded out Catalyst B's interface GigabitEthernet 1/1. What egress queue will the voice traffic be placed in on that interface? (Assume the interface is queue type 1p2q2t.)

Scenario 8: Securing Access and Managing Traffic in a Switched Network

This scenario is designed to stir your thinking about how to control access to switched networks, how to control traffic within a VLAN, and how to monitor traffic.

1. Network administrators want to have tight control over hosts moving around within their network. A Catalyst 3550 needs to have port-level security enabled on all 48 FastEthernet access layer ports. Only one host should be connected per port, so the default behavior of shutting the port down is acceptable. What commands are necessary to do this?

2. Port-level security is desired on a Catalyst 3550 interface FastEthernet 0/18, where 24 users are connected via an Ethernet hub. Rather than have the switch port shut down upon a security violation, network administrators want only the hosts in violation to be rejected. What command can accomplish this?

3. Configure a VLAN access control list that can perform packet filtering within a VLAN. Users in the 192.168.191.0 255.255.255.0 network should be allowed to use only HTTP (www) traffic to the web server 192.168.191.199/24, on VLAN 180. How can you configure the VACL to accomplish this?

4. Assume that a server is connected to interface GigabitEthernet 3/3 on a Catalyst 6500. What command can be used to monitor traffic transmitted and received on the server port with a network analyzer connected to interface GigabitEthernet 5/8 on the same switch?

5. Suppose that the only network analyzer available has a 10/100 Ethernet NIC. It is connected to Catalyst 6500 interface FastEthernet 2/1, to monitor the server on GigabitEthernet 3/3. Explain any problems you might encounter with this setup.

Scenario Answers

Scenario 1 Answers

1. The link is still an access link, with no trunking established, because both switches are set to *auto* mode. The switches are each passively waiting for the other to initiate trunking.

2. Trunking is still not established. Catalyst A is waiting to be asked to trunk, and Catalyst B is set to *nonegotiate*. Catalyst B will never try to negotiate trunking because its DTP packets have been silenced.

3. Trunking has finally been established. Both switches A and B will use DTP, and B will effectively ask A to bring up a trunk link.

4. Trunking. Catalyst A expects trunking on the link, while Catalyst C actively tries to negotiate trunking.

5. No. The two PC devices are connected to different VLANs. Without a router or Layer 3 device connecting the VLANs, no traffic will cross between them.

6. All hosts on VLAN 1 (PC-1, PC-2, and PC-3) will experience the broadcast storm. All trunk links between switches will transport the broadcast frames. In addition, all switch supervisor CPUs will receive and process the broadcasts because each switch has an IP address for management assigned to VLAN 1. (For this reason, it is recommended to reserve VLAN 1 for control protocol traffic only. User-generated broadcasts can overload the switch supervisor to the extent that it can no longer keep track of its control or "overhead" protocols such as VTP, CDP, and so forth. Instead, all user traffic should be kept off VLAN 1.)

Scenario 2 Answers

1. Yes. PC-1 and PC-2 are connected to access VLAN switch ports, VLAN 2 and VLAN 10 respectively. Normally, if these were assigned to different VLANs, they could not ping each other unless a Layer 3 device were present to route between the Layer 2 VLANs. In this case, however, the link between Catalyst A and B is the key. On one switch, the link is an access VLAN port on VLAN 2, and on the other end, an access VLAN port on VLAN 10. These are physically connected together, and each switch has no knowledge of what VLAN the other has assigned to the link. Therefore, data can pass across the link freely, connecting the two VLANs.

2. No. Again, the key is the link between Catalyst B and C. Catalyst B has the link configured as an ISL trunk, while Catalyst C has it configured as an 802.1Q trunk. Because the trunk encapsulations are different, no data will pass between them.

3. Yes, the trunk link on each switch will come up successfully, even though the trunk will not work end-to-end due to the encapsulation mismatch. This is because DTP packets will be exchanged, but both ends of the link are configured to trunk unconditionally.

    (As a side note, DTP and CDP packets will be exchanged between the switches. Both of these protocols are sent over VLAN 1. Because the trunk encapsulation is different on each end of the link, each switch will tag VLAN 1 differently. Therefore, VLAN 1 will not be contiguous across the link, and these protocols will not pass successfully.)

4. VLAN 1 will not be pruned at all. Although VLAN 1 is present on all switches, it is not pruned because VLAN 1 is ineligible for pruning by definition. Remember that VLAN 1 is usually used for management traffic and should be kept intact so that no switches become isolated.

5. Only Catalyst C creates VLAN 14 in response to VTP advertisements. Catalyst B in transparent mode relays only the VTP information, without interpreting the information.

6. Only Catalyst B creates VLAN 15. Because it is in transparent mode, no VLAN activity will be advertised to other neighboring switches. However, Catalyst B is allowed to create, delete, and rename VLANs freely. These VLANs are significant only to the local switch.

7. Catalyst C will not allow any VLANs to be created, unless they are learned from a VTP server in the "bermuda" domain. Because it is in VTP client mode, no VLAN changes can be performed from the console.

Scenario 3 Answers

1. The Spanning Tree topology should look like the diagram in Figure 21-8. Catalyst A is the Root Bridge, and only the 1000-Mbps link is Forwarding. The Root Ports (RP) and Designated Ports (DP) are labeled on the diagram.

Figure 21-8 *Resulting Spanning Tree Topology for Scenario 3*

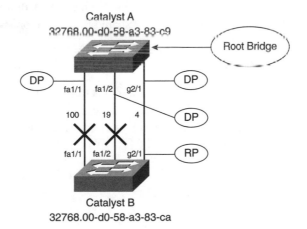

2. Because the 100-Mbps link is in the Blocking state on Catalyst B, no major change in the topology occurs. Effectively, this link was already "disconnected." However, after the physical link status goes down, both Catalyst A and Catalyst B sense the change and begin sending TCN BPDUs to notify each other of the topology change. Because Catalyst A is the Root Bridge, it acknowledges the TCN to Catalyst B. Both switches age out their MAC address tables in Forward Delay seconds.

3. Disconnecting the 1000-Mbps link causes Catalyst B to immediately find another Root Port. Ports 1/1 and 1/2 go into the Listening state, waiting to receive BPDUs. Port 1/2, with a cost of 19, become the next Root Port, as soon as Catalyst B computes the Root Path Cost (0+19) for it. Port 1/2 stays in the Listening state for Forward Delay (15 seconds), and then in the Learning state for Forward Delay (15 seconds). Port 1/2 moves into the Forwarding state, restoring connectivity in 30 seconds. (If PAgP is operating on the port, an additional delay of 20 seconds occurs.)

4. Because the 1000-Mbps link's status stays up, neither Catalyst detects a link failure. Therefore, no immediate attempt to find another Root Port occurs. Instead, Catalyst B will not receive BPDUs from Catalyst A over link GigabitEthernet 2/1 because they are being filtered out. After the MaxAge Timer expires (20 seconds), Catalyst B ages out the stored BPDU for Catalyst A on port GigabitEthernet 2/1. Catalyst B moves ports FastEthernet 1/1 and 1/2 into the Listening state to determine a new Root Port. As in Step 3, port FastEthernet 1/2 becomes the Root Port with a lower Root Path Cost than port FastEthernet 1/1. The port moves through the Listening (15 seconds) and Learning (15 seconds) states and into the Forwarding state. The total time that has elapsed before connectivity restores is 20 + 15 + 15 = 50 seconds. (Again, if PAgP is active on the port, an additional 20 seconds can be added to the delay.)

Scenario 4 Answers

1. The Unidirectional Link Detection (UDLD) feature can be used. You can use the **udld aggressive** global configuration command to enable UDLD on all fiber-optic ports. UDLD must be enabled on *both ends* of a link, so it should be enabled on switches A1, as well as C1 and C2.

2. The **spanning-tree portfast** interface configuration command defines an edge port.

3. A minimum of two MST instances are needed so that traffic can be load-balanced. One instance can support VLANs 100 through 104, while the other can support VLANs 200 through 204. To load-balance, traffic from one instance must be carried over one uplink, while the other instance is carried over the second uplink.

4.   You can use these configuration commands:

```
spanning-tree mode mst
spanning-tree mst configuration
    name NorthWestDivision
    revision 1
    instance 1 vlan 100,101,102,103,104,99
    instance 2 vlan 200,201,202,203,204
exit
```

Notice that VLAN 99, used for switch management traffic, is also mapped to an MST instance. It is sometimes easy to forget about nonuser or nonaccess VLANs.

5.   This command makes C1 become the MST Root Bridge for instance 1:

```
spanning-tree mst 1 root primary
```

This causes the uplink from C1 to A1 to be used for instance 1, by keeping it in the Forwarding state. Switch C2 should also be configured as the Root for MST instance 2 so that the other uplink can be used for those VLANs.

Scenario 5 Answers

1.   You can configure HSRP load-balancing with the following Catalyst configuration commands:

```
interface vlan 101
    ip address 192.168.101.2 255.255.255.0
    standby 101 priority 110
    standby 101 preempt
    standby 101 ip 192.168.101.1
interface vlan 102
    ip address 192.168.102.2 255.255.255.0
    standby 102 priority 100
    standby 102 preempt
    standby 102 ip 192.168.102.1
```

The default gateway address that is shared between the switches is configured as 192.168.101.1 for VLAN 101 and 192.168.102.1 for VLAN 102. In VLAN 101, the virtual interface has an IP address of 192.168.101.2. Two HSRP groups are defined, one for each VLAN. Interface VLAN 101 will be the active router for VLAN 101, due to its higher priority of 110 (over a default of 100 on the other Catalyst). If control is passed to the standby router, this router can assume control again through the use of the **preempt** command. For VLAN 102, the roles are reversed. This router becomes the standby router in Group 102, with its lower priority of 100. (The other switch will be configured with priority 110 for VLAN 102 to take the active router role.)

2. The four-part answers to Question 2 are as follows:

   a. By default, all switches have a GLBP priority of 100. Catalyst B's priority can be raised with the **glbp 10 priority 200** command.

   b. Only the AVG switch, Catalyst B, needs to be configured with the gateway address. It will inform all other members of the group. You should use the **glbp 10 ip 192.168.10.1** command.

   c. Glbp 10 load-balancing round-robin.

   d. Each AVF switch should receive the **glbp 10 ip** interface configuration command. No IP address is needed here because the virtual gateway address is learned from the group's AVG.

Scenario 6 Answers

1. With IGMP snooping, a switch can listen to IGMP activity for itself. Although this does burden the switch supervisor with examining IGMP reports from multicast group members, the learning process does not require a router or multilayer switch. However, if a switch does not have hardware capable of IGMP snooping natively, CGMP and help from an external router are required.

2. By default, a switch must forward broadcast and multicast frames out all available ports on a VLAN. The multicast traffic will be seen on all VLAN 101 ports on Catalyst A. In addition, Catalyst C and Catalyst D bridges the multicast traffic over the trunk links between them. Finally, all VLAN 101 ports on Catalyst B also forwards the multicasts.

3. In this network, CGMP configuration is needed on both types of switches, whether IGMP snooping can be used or not. You can use the following commands on one of the multilayer switches:

```
ip multicast-routing
interface vlan 101
   ip pim dense-mode
   ip cgmp
interface vlan 102
   ip pim dense-mode
   ip cgmp
```

On Catalyst A and B, only the following global configuration command **cgmp** is needed.

Scenario 7 Answers

1. The QoS domain should consist of the two Catalyst switches, A and B. QoS trust will be extended to the IP Phone connected to Catalyst B. QoS information should be trusted on the ports connecting switches A and B, along with the IP Phone port on switch B. QoS information

should not be trusted on Catalyst A port 1/1 (the public network), Catalyst B port 3/2 (PC), or the IP Phone's PC port. At these locations, incoming QoS information will be overwritten to known and trusted values.

2. You can use the following commands:

    ```
    mls qos
    interface gigabitethernet 1/1
        no mls trust
        mls qos cos 0
    ```

    Here, QoS must first be enabled. Then, the interface is configured to have no trust. The overriding CoS value on the untrusted interface is set to 0, although this is already the default value.

3. The following commands can classify the traffic according to UDP port 5000 and Citrix. For Citrix, NBAR is used to match against the specific protocol definition for Citrix:

    ```
    ip access-list extended apps
        permit udp any any eq 5000
    class-map importantapp match-any
        match access-group name apps
        match protocol citrix
    ```

4. The following commands can define and apply the QoS policy:

    ```
    policy-map apps-policy
        class importantapp
        set ip dscp 26
    interface gigabitethernet 1/1
        service-policy input apps-policy
    ```

5. No additional commands are needed, although it could be set with the **set ip precedence 3** policy map command. This is because the IP Precedence field is actually the DSCP Class Selector field (the codepoint name's first digit). In this case, the Class Selector for AF31 is 3. If you set one, the other is inherently set, too.

6. The following commands define VLAN 17 as the voice VLAN (VVID) and the IP Phone's data port as untrusted:

    ```
    interface fastethernet 3/1
        switchport voice vlan 17
        switchport priority extend cos 0
    ```

7. For the Skinny protocol, the voice bearer traffic (CoS 5, using RTP) will be placed in the strict priority egress queue on the interface. This is the queue referenced by the "1p" label and is queue number 3. Call control traffic (CoS 3) will be placed in a high-priority standard queue, referenced by the "q" label.

Scenario 8 Answers

1. On a Catalyst 3550, you can use the following commands:

```
interface range fastethernet 0/1 - 48
    switchport port-security
```

2. On a Catalyst 3550, you can use the following commands:

```
interface fastethernet 0/18
    switchport port-security
    switchport port-security maximum 24
    switchport port-security violation restrict
```

The first command line enables port-level security on the switch port. The second line configures port security to learn up to 24 MAC addresses dynamically on that port. The last line configures the switch to restrict any MAC addresses found to be in violation (any additional addresses learned beyond the 24). The port stays up, allowing the other users to communicate.

3. You can use the following commands:

```
access-list 101 permit tcp 192.168.191.0 0.0.0.255 host 192.168.191.199 eq
www
vlan access-map myfilter
    match ip address 101
    action forward
    match
    action drop
vlan filter myfilter vlan-list 180
```

The first line configures an access list that will be used only to match against traffic being forwarded on a VLAN. The **permit** keyword only causes matching traffic to be eligible for an action by the VACL—it does not cause the matching traffic to be forwarded or not. The VACL is configured to first match traffic with access list 101; this traffic is forwarded as normal. Then, a simple **match** statement is given so that all other traffic is matched; this remaining traffic is dropped so that it does not reach its destination. The VACL is then applied to VLAN 180.

4. The following commands can configure a local SPAN session on the Catalyst 6500:

```
monitor session 1 source interface gigabitethernet 3/3 both
monitor session 1 destination interface gigabitethernet 5/8
```

5. The only potential problem is with the mismatch in connection speeds. The server has a GigabitEthernet connection, while the analyzer is limited by its FastEthernet connection. If the server has a low utilization on its connection, the network analysis might turn out fine. Otherwise, if the server's connection is using most of the available 1000 Mbps of bandwidth, the analyzer misses a large portion of the mirrored packets.

The server and its connection will not suffer from the speed mismatch. The Catalyst switch continues to forward packets to and from the server as if no port mirroring was occurring. It is only when the packets are being copied over to the monitor port queue that they can potentially be dropped.

PART VI: Appendix

Appendix A   Answers to Chapter "Do I Know This Already?" Quizzes and Q&A Sections

Each chapter begins with a "Do I Know This Already?" quiz that helps you determine the amount of time you need to spend studying that chapter. In addition, each chapter ends with a "Q&A" section that provides mostly open-ended, rather than multiple-choice, questions as found on the exams. This helps you focus more on understanding the subject matter than on memorizing details. This appendix enables you to verify your answers for both; use it as a study sheet when your exam looms closer.

Answers to Chapter "Do I Know This Already?" Quizzes and Q&A Sections

Chapter 1

"Do I Know This Already?"

1. c
2. e
3. d
4. d
5. a
6. c
7. b
8. c
9. c
10. d
11. a

    The Catalyst 2950 is not the best choice for the distribution layer because it doesn't support Layer 3 functionality.

12. a

Q&A

1. For each layer of the OSI model, match the forwarding criteria used by a switch:

_C_ Layer 1	A. IP address
_D_ Layer 2	B. UDP/TCP port
_A_ Layer 3	C. None
_B_ Layer 4	D. MAC address

2. What is multilayer switching (MLS)?

MLS forwards traffic using information from Layer 2, Layer 3, and Layer 4—all in hardware at wire speed.

3. Fill in the blanks in the following statement:

In the 20/80 rule of networking, 20 percent of the traffic on a segment usually stays **local** while 80 percent **travels across the network**.

4. What is a collision domain, and where does it exist in a switched LAN?

A collision domain is a network segment where shared media access is supported. Devices on the shared media must compete for access when transmitting data. In a switched network, the collision domain is restricted to a single switch port and does not extend across the switch.

5. What is a broadcast domain, and where does it exist in a switched LAN?

A broadcast domain is the extent of a network where broadcast frames propagate. Basically, a broadcast domain covers an area where Layer 2 devices are located and terminates at the boundary of a Layer 3 device. In a switched network, the broadcast domain extends to all switch ports assigned to a common VLAN. This is because a switch forwards broadcasts out all available ports in a VLAN.

6. What is a VLAN, and why is it used?

A VLAN (virtual LAN) is a group of switch ports that communicate as if they were attached to a single shared-media LAN segment. VLANs can extend across buildings or backbones, as long as the VLAN is connected end-to-end through trunking or physical connections. A VLAN is a broadcast domain. VLANs segment networks for ease of management and better performance.

7. At what OSI Layer(s) do devices in the distribution layer usually operate?

Layers 2, 3, and 4

8. What is network segmentation? When is it necessary, and how is it done in a campus network design?

Segmentation is the process of dividing a LAN into smaller, discrete collision domains. If a large percentage of collisions is observed on a LAN, segmentation is appropriate. In a campus network design, segmentation occurs at each switch port. A similar form of segmentation involves reducing the size of broadcast domains. Placing Layer 3 devices in the distribution and core layers terminates the broadcast domains at those layer boundaries.

9. Is it possible to use Layer 2 switches in the distribution layer, rather than Layer 3 switches? If so, what are the limitations?

    It is generally best practice to use Layer 3 or multilayer switches in the distribution layer, as outlined in this chapter. However, in some environments, this might not be possible due to cost or implementation logistics. Layer 2 switches will work fine in the distribution layer but will not provide a VLAN or broadcast domain boundary in that layer. As a result, broadcasts will propagate on into the core layer, using unnecessary bandwidth.

10. Which of the following Cisco switch products should be used in a campus network's distribution layer? (Check all that apply.)

    a. Catalyst 2950

    b. Catalyst 3550 (SMI)

    c. Catalyst 3550 (EMI)

    d. Catalyst 4000/4500

    e. Catalyst 6500

    Answer: c, d, e

11. When might you select a Catalyst 4000 to use in a wiring closet? What attributes make it a good choice?

    A Catalyst 4000 might be a good choice for an access layer switch if a high port density exists in that location. A single switch could be used, whereas multiple Catalyst 2950 or 3550 switches would be needed to equal the same port density. This would allow a small number of high-speed uplinks to be used into the distribution layer. With multiple smaller switches, you would either require a number of uplinks, or the access layer switches would have to be daisy-chained or "stacked." Note that a single Catalyst 4000 does introduce a single point of failure into the network; if that unit failed, many users would lose network service. In that case, a Catalyst 4500, with its redundant features, would make a good choice.

12. Which Cisco switch family has the most scalable performance?

    The Catalyst 6500's large chassis and variety of modules makes it possible to support a high density of connections and increase switching capacity with new MLS hardware.

Chapter 2

"Do I Know This Already?"

1. c

2. c, d, e

3. a, b

4. a, c

5. c

6. d

7. a, c

8. c, d, e

9. b

10. b, c

11. c, d

12. a, b, c

Q&A

1. Where is the most appropriate place to connect a block of enterprise (internal) servers? Why?

You should connect a block of enterprise servers into the core, just as you would switch blocks. The server farm building block should have a layer of access and distribution switches, just as in any switch block. This maximizes connectivity from the servers to all other devices in the network. In effect, all users will see the same number of switch "hops" to access a server. Connecting into the core also provides maximum scalability because you can add more server blocks in the future.

2. How can you provide redundancy at the switch and core block layers? (Consider physical means, as well as functional methods using protocols, algorithms, and so on.)

In a switch block, you can provide redundancy through two distribution switches. Each access switch can be linked to both distribution switches for fault tolerance. The Layer 3 distribution layer allows both uplinks to be used at the same time, with little or no failover time required. In the core layer, a dual core can be used with two core switches. Each distribution switch has dual uplinks, with one link to each core switch. Here, the redundant links can stay active for load sharing and redundancy, thanks to the Layer 3 routing protocols running in the distribution and core layers.

3. What factors should you consider when sizing a switch block?

Consider traffic types, flows, and patterns, as well as the size and number of common workgroups. Additionally, the Layer 3 switching capacity in the distribution layer should be sized according to the amount of traffic crossing from one VLAN to another.

4. What are the signs of an oversized switch block?

The distribution switches begin to become bottlenecks in handling the interVLAN traffic volume. Access list processing in the distribution layer can also become a rate-limiting factor. Broadcast and multicast traffic forwarding can slow down the Layer 2 and Layer 3 switches in the block.

5. What are the attributes and issues of having a collapsed core block?

Attributes: Cost savings (no separate high-end core switches) and design simplicity.

Issues: Scalability becomes limited.

6. How many switches are sufficient in a core block design?

Two switches are usually sufficient in a core block, offering load sharing and redundancy. However, you can add more core switches as the size of the network and core traffic flow dictates.

7. What building blocks are used to build a scalable campus network?

The *switch block* is the template used to group access layer switches and their respective distribution layer switches. Switch blocks are then connected into the *core block* to build a scalable network. Depending on the other resources that are present in a campus network, other building blocks can include a *server farm block*, *network management block*, and *enterprise edge block*. The *service provider edge block* exists outside the campus network, although, it does interface with the enterprise edge block.

8. What are two types of core, or backbone, designs?

Collapsed core and dual core.

9. Why should links and services provided to remote sites be grouped in a distinct building block?

Remote sites and roaming VPN users should be considered corporate users, as if they were connected directly inside the enterprise network. These users should enjoy the same efficient access to any enterprise resource that internal users have. Additionally, VPN tunnels should terminate in a secure area of the enterprise network.

Connections into the Internet (through service providers) are just the inverse—users from all parts of the enterprise will need equal and efficient access to resources located out on the Internet. Therefore, a separate building block connected into the core is justified.

10. Why should network management applications and servers be placed in a distinct building block?

Network management applications must be able to poll, query, or access devices anywhere in the campus network. Moving these resources into a distinct building block provides redundant and efficient access into the network core so that all devices can be managed with equal access.

Chapter 3

"Do I Know This Already?"

1. b

2. b

3. b

4. c

5. c

6. b

7. c

8. d

9. b

10. c

11. d

12. b

Q&A

1. By default, how long are CAM table entries kept before they are aged out?

300 seconds

2. A TCAM lookup involves which values?

    Mask

    Value

    Result

3. How many table lookups are required to find a MAC address in the CAM table?

    1

4. How many table lookups are required to match a packet against an access list that has been compiled into 10 TCAM entries?

    1

5. How many value patterns can a TCAM store for each mask?

    8

6. Can all packets be switched in hardware by a multilayer switch?

    No; some must be flagged for process switching by the switch CPU.

7. Multilayer switches must rewrite which portions of an Ethernet frame?

    Source and destination MAC addresses

    IP time-to-live

    Checksums

8. If a station only receives Ethernet frames and doesn't transmit anything, how will a switch learn of its location?

    You must configure a static CAM entry with the station's MAC address and the switch port where it is located. Otherwise, the switch must flood each and every frame destined for that host out every switch port in an effort to find it.

9. What is a TCAM's main purpose?

    To process access lists as a single table lookup

10. Why do the TCAM mask and pattern fields consist of so many bits?

So that a combination of several address fields in a frame can be inspected at once

11. In a multilayer switch with a TCAM, a longer access list (more ACEs or statements) takes longer to process for each frame. True or false?

Answer: False

12. A multilayer switch receives a packet with a certain destination IP address. Suppose the switch has that IP address in its Layer 3 forwarding table, but no corresponding Layer 2 address. What happens to the packet next?

The switch CPU sends an ARP request.

13. If a multilayer switch can't support a protocol with CEF, it relies on fallback bridging. Can the switch still route that traffic?

No. That traffic is transparently bridged. An external multilayer switch or router is required to take the bridged packets and route them.

14. To configure a static CAM table entry, the **mac address-table static** *mac-address* command is used. Which two other parameters must also be given?

vlan *vlan-id*

interface *type mod/num*

15. As a network administrator, what aspects of a switch TCAM should you be concerned with?

The size of the TCAM resources

16. What portion of the TCAM is used to evaluate port number comparisons in an access list?

LOU

17. Someone has asked you where the host with MAC address 00-10-20-30-40-50 is located. Assuming you already know the switch it is connected to, what command can you use to find it?

show mac address-table dynamic address 0010.2030.4050

18. Complete this command to display the size of the CAM table: **show mac** _____.

show mac address-table count

19. What protocol is used to advertise CAM table entries among neighboring switches?

None; the entries are not advertised.

20. Suppose a host uses one MAC address to send frames and another to receive them. In other words, one address will always be the source address sent in frames, and the other is only used as a destination address in incoming frames. Is it possible for that host to communicate with others through a Layer 2 switch? If so, how?

Yes, but not very efficiently. The Layer 2 switch will learn one of the host's MAC addresses as the host sends frames. That address will be seen as the source address on frames arriving at the switch. However, because the second MAC address is never used to send frames, the switch will never be able to learn of its existence. When frames are sent to the host using that second MAC address, the switch is forced to flood the frames out all relevant switch ports. The host receives those frames only because it is connected to a port where the frames were flooded. All other hosts on the same VLAN also receive the flooded frames, even though they have no interest in that traffic.

Chapter 4

"Do I Know This Already?"

1. b

2. b

3. b

4. c

5. d

6. c

7. b

8. c

9. d

10. a

The **erase flash:** command erases all files contained in the Flash file system. This means that all Cisco IOS Software images that were present in Flash will now be erased. Therefore, the switch will not have an IOS image file to use when it reloads. The next logical step would be to copy another IOS image file into the Flash memory.

11. d

12. d

Q&A

1. When Cisco IOS Software is used on a Catalyst switch, the switch must perform routing. True or false?

Answer: False

2. What is the major difference between the IOS and CatOS command sets?

Cisco IOS Software uses the familiar router configuration commands and a hierarchy of configuration modes. CatOS uses "set" commands with no explicit configuration mode. Also, IOS configuration commands are not automatically saved across a power failure, whereas CatOS commands are. Cisco IOS Software also offers the ability to switch packets at Layer 3, whereas CatOS was never extended beyond Layer 2.

3. What switch command will enter privileged EXEC or "enable" mode on a Catalyst 4500?

enable

4. Match these default command line prompts with their respective modes:

a. Switch#   **d** Normal user EXEC mode

b. Switch(config)   **a** Privileged EXEC or enable

c. Switch(config-if)#   **b** Global configuration

d. Switch>   **c** Interface configuration

5. With the command line prompt **testlab#**, what command has been used to customize the prompt?

hostname testlab

6. The following commands have just been entered, assuming interface VLAN 10 did not previously exist:

```
interface vlan 10
ip address 192.168.199.10 255.255.255.0
no shutdown
```

Suddenly, the power cord is pulled out of the switch. What will happen when the power is restored?

Not only will interface VLAN 10 have no IP address, but also there won't even be an interface VLAN 10. Those commands were entered into the running-config configuration file, so they were not permanently applied. When the power is restored, the contents of the startup-config will be read and executed. Because the running-config was not saved, the VLAN 10 commands will no longer exist.

7. Can you configure an enable secret password (**enable secret** *password*) for the switch console and a different enable secret for Telnet access?

No, only one global enable secret password is allowed, and it applies to all lines on the switch.

8. When you configure an IP address and subnet mask on a Layer 2 switch for management purposes, which VLAN are you required to use?

   a. VLAN 1

   b. VLAN 0

   c. VLAN 1001

   d. Any VLAN that is appropriate

   e. You can't assign an IP address to a VLAN

   Answer: d

9. What commands will allow Telnet and ping access to a switch management interface at 192.168.200.10, subnet mask 255.255.255.0, on VLAN 5? A router is available at address 192.168.200.1.

   Answer:
   ```
   interface vlan 5
   ip address 192.168.200.10 255.255.255.0
   ip default-gateway 192.168.200.1
   no shutdown

   interface vlan 5
   ip address 192.168.200.10 255.255.255.0
   ip default-gateway 192.168.200.1
   ```

10. CDP advertisements occur every _____ seconds.

    Answer: 60

11. When a Cisco Catalyst switch receives a CDP multicast frame, it relays it to neighboring switches. True or false?

Answer: False

12. Eight access layer switches connect to a central distribution layer switch using Gigabit Ethernet connections. Each connection is assigned to VLAN 1 so that no link is in trunking mode. On one of the access switches, how many neighboring switches will be shown by the **show cdp neighbor gigabit 0/1**?

Only one neighboring switch will be shown—the single distribution layer switch that is directly connected. CDP messages are not forwarded; rather, they are received and processed only by the neighboring switch. Because all eight access switches are connected by another switch, CDP messages don't pass between them.

13. Which IOS image file is more recent—c3550-i5q3l2-mz.121-12c.EA1.bin or c3550-i9q3l2-mz.121-11c.EA1.bin?

c3550-i5q3l2-mz.121-12c.EA1.bin

14. A new switch has just been configured with 100 command lines from the console. You realize the need to save the new configuration and type **copy start run**. Where will your configuration be stored?

Unfortunately, the configuration you made might be lost or drastically changed. The startup-config file will be copied into, or overlaid onto, the running-config. Any commands that are different in the startup-config will overwrite the commands you entered in the running-config. Because this is a new switch containing only the default commands, you could end up effectively overwriting your changes with the default values that the switch had when it powered up for the first time. The correct command should have been **copy run start**.

15. What command can you use to see what Cisco IOS Software version is currently running on a switch?

show version

16. Complete this command so that the output is displayed starting with the configuration for interface VLAN 100:

show run _____

show run | begin Vlan100

17. The **debug spanning-tree all** command has been given from the EXEC mode command line. What commands can you use to stop or disable the debugging output?

    no debug all

    no debug spanning-tree all

    undebug all

18. What command can you use to verify CDP configuration on switch port GigabitEthernet 3/1?

    show cdp interface gigabit 3/1

Chapter 5

"Do I Know This Already?"

1. c
2. b
3. a
4. b
5. d
6. d
7. b
8. b
9. c
10. c
11. c
12. d
13. e

Q&A

1. Put the following Ethernet standards in order of increasing bandwidth:

    a. 802.3z

    b. 802.3ae

    c. 802.3

    d. 802.3u

    Answer: c, d, a, b

2. What benefits does switched Ethernet have over shared Ethernet?

    Switched Ethernet ports receive dedicated bandwidth, have a reduced collision domain, and show increased performance due to segmentation or fewer users per port.

3. When a 10/100 Ethernet link is autonegotiating, which will be chosen if both stations can support the same capabilities—10BASE-T full duplex, 100BASE-TX half duplex, or 100BASE-TX full duplex?

    100BASE-TX full duplex will be chosen because it has the highest autonegotiation priority and is common to both end stations.

4. How many pairs of copper wires does a 1000BASET connection need?

    Four pairs

5. A switch port is being configured as shown here. What command is needed next to set the port to full-duplex mode?

    ```
    Switch(config)# interface fastethernet 0/13
    Switch(config-if)#
    ```

    Enter the command **duplex full** at the prompt.

6. If a full-duplex Gigabit Ethernet connection offers 2 Gbps throughput, can a single host send data at 2 Gbps?

    No, a full-duplex Gigabit Ethernet connection allows only 1 Gbps simultaneously in each direction across the link.

7. Which GBIC would you use for a connection over multimode fiber (MMF)?

    You could use either a 1000BASE-SX or a 1000BASE-LX/LH.

8. When might Long Reach Ethernet be a good candidate for a connection?

In a multitenant building, such as an office or apartment building, where existing Category 1, 2, or 3 wiring is already present for telephone services.

9. A Category 5 cable having only pins 1,2 and 3,6 has been installed and used for a Fast Ethernet link. Can this same cable be used for a migration to Gigabit Ethernet using 1000BASE-T GBICs, assuming the length is less than 100 meters?

No. 1000BASE-T requires all four pairs of wires to be present.

10. A Catalyst 3550 switch port has been configured for 100 Mbps full-duplex mode, but a link cannot be established. What are some commands that you could use to investigate and correct the problem?

To see the current state of one or more ports, you could use the show interface command. This would show the ports' speed and duplex modes, as well as whether a link has been established. One reason the link is not established could be that the port is shut down or disabled. To enable the port, use the **no shutdown** interface configuration command. Because the port has been set to 100 Mbps full-duplex mode, it is possible that the end station can support only 10 Mbps at half duplex. Therefore, set the port for autonegotiate mode with the **speed auto** and **duplex auto** commands. Otherwise, you could set the port to a fixed speed and mode that would match the end station.

11. 10Gigabit Ethernet is backward-compatible with other forms of Ethernet at Layer __**2**__ but not at Layer __**1**__ .

12. What types of Ethernet are commonly used to connect geographically separate locations?

Metro Ethernet, transported over facilities contracted from a service provider

13. What form of Metro Ethernet allows several enterprise VLANs to be transported between locations—TLS or DVS?

Directed VLAN Service (DVS)

14. What one switch command will select Fast Ethernet interfaces 4/1 through 48 for a common configuration?

interface range fastethernet 4/1 - 48

(Don't forget spaces around the dash.)

15. What is a GBIC's purpose?

A GBIC is used as a modular media-independent connection for Gigabit Ethernet. A switch with a GBIC port will accept GBIC modules that support various network media types. Changing network media cabling requires only a low-cost GBIC module change.

16. Suppose you need to apply several different common configurations to Fast Ethernet interfaces 3/1 through 12, 3/34, 3/48, and 5/14 through 48. What commands are needed to create an interface macro to accomplish this, and what command would apply the macro?

define interface-range mymacro fastethernet 3/1 – 12, fastethernet 3/34 – 48 , fastethernet 5/14 – 48

interface range macro mymacro

17. If a switch port is configured with the **speed 100** and **duplex full** commands, what will happen if the PC connected to it is set for autonegotiated speed and duplex? Now reverse the roles (the switch will autonegotiate, but the PC won't). What will happen?

When the PC attempts to autonegotiate the link settings, it will detect the switch port's speed of 100 Mbps. However, the duplex cannot be detected without a two-way information exchange, so the PC will probably fall back to half duplex. The results are similar when the roles are reversed, as the switch will decide on 100 Mbps half duplex. In either case, a duplex mismatch will occur.

18. By default, what will a switch do if one of its ports has a serious error condition, and how can you tell when this has happened?

By default, every possible error condition is detected on every port. If any one of these conditions occurs, the port will be automatically shut down in the errdisable state. The **show interface status err-disabled** command shows a brief summary of all ports in the errdisable state.

19. What port speeds can you assign to a UTP Gigabit Ethernet switch port? Consider both 1000BASE-T GBIC and native RJ-45 copper switch module ports.

A 1000BASE-T GBIC is fixed at 1 Gbps, whereas switch modules with UTP Gigabit Ethernet ports can be 10 Mbps, 100 Mbps, or 1000 Mbps.

20. What command can you use to make sure that no switch ports are automatically shut down in an errdisable state for any reason?

Use the **no errdisable detect cause all** interface configuration command. Remember that all causes are enabled by default, so you must disable all causes first.

21. Suppose you commonly find that switch ports are being shut down in errdisable due to users making their connections go up and down too often. Thinking this might be due to odd PC behavior, you would like to visit each user to troubleshoot the problem. However, this is a minor error and you don't want to inconvenience the end users too much. What commands can you use to have the switch automatically reenable the ports after 10 minutes? Make sure a flapping link will be automatically recovered in this time frame.

errdisable recovery interval 600

errdisable recovery cause link-flap

22. Look at the following **show interface** output. Does the high number of collisions indicate a problem? Why or why not?

```
FastEthernet0/6 is up, line protocol is up
  Hardware is Fast Ethernet, address is 000a.f4d2.5506 (bia 000a.f4d2.5506)
  Description: kelly-107-1d1,pc
  MTU 1500 bytes, BW 10000 Kbit, DLY 1000 usec,
     reliability 255/255, txload 1/255, rxload 1/255
  Encapsulation ARPA, loopback not set
  Keepalive set (10 sec)
  Half-duplex, 10Mb/s
  input flow-control is off, output flow-control is off
  ARP type: ARPA, ARP Timeout 04:00:00
  Last input never, output 00:00:00, output hang never
  Last clearing of "show interface" counters never
  Input queue: 0/75/0/0 (size/max/drops/flushes); Total output drops: 0
  Queueing strategy: fifo
  Output queue :0/40 (size/max)
  5 minute input rate 0 bits/sec, 0 packets/sec
  5 minute output rate 0 bits/sec, 0 packets/sec
     1321140 packets input, 227738894 bytes, 0 no buffer
     Received 13786 broadcasts, 0 runts, 0 giants, 0 throttles
     1 input errors, 1 CRC, 0 frame, 0 overrun, 0 ignored
     0 watchdog, 42 multicast, 0 pause input
     0 input packets with dribble condition detected
     87798820 packets output, 2662785561 bytes, 1316 underruns
     6 output errors, 406870 collisions, 3 interface resets
     0 babbles, 0 late collision, 19458 deferred
     0 lost carrier, 0 no carrier, 0 PAUSE output
     1316 output buffer failures, 0 output buffers swapped out
```

Yes, this would probably be normal, considering that the interface is set for 10-Mbps half duplex. Collisions are to be expected on a link with shared bandwidth; in this case, the link is part of a collision domain. If the link were showing full duplex at any speed, collisions should never be detected.

Chapter 6

"Do I Know This Already?"

1. c

2. b

3. b

4. b

5. b

6. c

7. d

8. c

9. b

10. a

11. c

12. a

Q&A

1. What is a VLAN? When is it used?

   A VLAN is a group of devices on the same broadcast domain, such as a logical subnet or segment. VLANs can span switch ports, switches within a switch block, or closets and buildings. VLANs group users and devices into common workgroups across geographical areas. VLANs help provide segmentation, security, and problem isolation.

2. When a VLAN is configured on a Catalyst switch port, in how much of the campus network will the VLAN number be unique and significant?

   The VLAN number will be significant in the local switch. If trunking is enabled, the VLAN number will be significant across the entire trunking domain. In other words, the VLAN will be transported to every switch that has a trunk link supporting that VLAN.

3. Name two types of VLANs in terms of spanning areas of the campus network.

   Local VLAN

   End-to-end VLAN

4. What switch commands configure Fast Ethernet port 4/11 for VLAN 2?

interface fastethernet 4/11

switchport mode access

switchport access vlan 2

5. Generally speaking, what must be configured (both switch and end user device) for a port-based VLAN?

The switch port

6. What is the default VLAN on all ports of a Catalyst switch?

VLAN 1

7. What is a trunk link?

A trunk link is a connection between two switches that transports traffic from multiple VLANs. Each frame is identified with its source VLAN during its trip across the trunk link.

8. What methods of Ethernet VLAN frame identification can be used on a Catalyst switch trunk?

802.1Q

ISL

9. What is the difference between the two trunking methods? How many bytes are added to trunked frames for VLAN identification in each method?

ISL uses encapsulation and adds a 26-byte header and a 4-byte trailer. 802.1Q adds a 4-byte tag field within existing frames, without encapsulation.

10. What is the purpose of Dynamic Trunking Protocol (DTP)?

DTP allows negotiation of a common trunking method between endpoints of a trunk link.

11. What commands are needed to configure a Catalyst switch trunk port Gigabit 3/1 to transport only VLANs 100, 200 through 205, and 300 using IEEE 802.1Q? (Assume that trunking is enabled and active on the port already. Also, assume the **interface gigabit 3/1** command has already been entered.)

switchport trunk allowed vlan 100, 200-205, 300

12. Two neighboring switch trunk ports are set to the *auto* mode with *ISL* trunking encapsulation mode. What will the resulting trunk mode become?

Trunking will not be established at all. Both switches are in the passive *auto* state and are waiting to be asked to start the trunking mode. The link will remain an access link on both switches.

13. Complete this command to configure the switch port to use DTP to actively ask the other end to become a trunk:

switchport mode _____

switchport mode dynamic desirable

14. Which command can set the native VLAN of a trunk port to VLAN 100 after the interface has been selected?

switchport trunk native vlan 100

15. What command can configure a trunk port to stop sending and receiving DTP packets completely?

switchport nonegotiate

16. What command can be used on a Catalyst switch to verify exactly what VLANs will be transported over trunk link gigabitethernet 4/4?

show interface gigabitethernet 4/4 switchport

-OR-

show interface gigabitethernet 4/4 trunk

17. Suppose a switch port is configured with the following commands. A PC with a nontrunking NIC card is then connected to that port. What, if any, traffic will the PC successfully send and receive?

```
interface fastethernet 0/12
switchport trunk encapsulation dot1q
switchport trunk native vlan 10
switchport trunk allowed vlan 1-1005
switchport mode trunk
```

The PC expects only a single network connection, using a single VLAN. In other words, the PC can't participate in any form of trunking. Only untagged or unencapsulated frames will be understood. Recall that an 802.1Q trunk's native VLAN is the only VLAN that has untagged frames. Therefore, the PC will be able to exchange frames only on VLAN 10, the native VLAN.

18. What type of switch port must a customer present to a service provider if an IEEE 802.1Q tunnel is desired?

    802.1Q trunk

19. What type of switch port must a service provider present to a customer if an IEEE 802.1Q tunnel is desired?

    802.1Q tunnel

20. What command is needed to form a Layer 2 protocol tunnel for CDP traffic?

    l2protocol-tunnel cdp

Chapter 7

"Do I Know This Already?"

1. c
2. a
3. c
4. b
5. b
6. b, c
7. a
8. c
9. c
10. b
11. d
12. b

Q&A

1. True or false: You can use VTP domains to separate broadcast domains.

   Answer: False. Broadcast domains can be separated only with VLANs because a VLAN defines a broadcast domain's boundaries. A VTP domain is a different concept; it defines the management domain where a set of switches can exchange information about VLAN configuration.

2. What VTP modes can a Catalyst switch be configured for? Can VLANs be created in each of the modes?

   Server, *client*, and *transparent* modes. VLANs can be created in server mode. VLANs cannot be created in client mode. In transparent mode, VLANs can be created, but only on the local switch; they are not advertised to other switches.

3. How many VTP management domains can a Catalyst switch participate in? How many VTP servers can a management domain have?

   A switch can be a member of only one VTP management domain. A domain must have at least one server for VLAN changes to be propagated throughout the domain. There can be more than one server for redundancy.

4. What conditions must exist for two Catalyst switches to be in the same VTP management domain?

   Both switches must have the same VTP domain name defined and enabled; both switches must be adjacent on a trunk link; and trunking must be enabled and active between them.

   Two switches can also operate in the same VTP domain if one of them is new and has the default NULL domain name. That switch will listen and pick up the first VTP domain name it hears in VTP advertisements.

5. On a VTP server switch, identify what you can do to reset the VTP configuration revision number to 0.

   Set the VTP domain name to a bogus value and change it back.

   Configure the switch for VTP transparent mode and then configure the switch back to server mode.

6. How can you clear the configuration revision number on a VTP client?

You can't. The VTP client bases all VLAN and VTP information on advertisements from a VTP server. Therefore, the configuration revision number on the client comes directly from the same number on the server.

7. Complete this command to make all VLANs other than 30 and 100 eligible for pruning on the trunk interface:

   switchport trunk pruning vlan _____

   switchport trunk pruning vlan except 30,100

8. Which VLAN numbers are never eligible for VTP pruning? Why?

   VLAN numbers 1 and 1001 to 1005. VLAN 1 is reserved as a VLAN for control protocol traffic, while VLANs 1002 to 1005 are reserved as the default FDDI and Token Ring function VLANs.

9. What does the acronym VTP stand for?

   VLAN Trunking Protocol

10. What VTP domain name is defined on a new switch with no configuration?

    A NULL or empty string. The switch defaults to server mode and will learn a VTP domain name from the first VTP server heard on a trunk link. Otherwise, you must manually configure the domain name.

11. In a network of switches, VTP domain Engineering has been configured with VLANs 1, 10 through 30, and 100. The VTP configuration revision number is currently at 23. Suppose a new switch is connected to the network, and it has the following configuration: VTP domain Engineering, VTP server mode, only VLANs 1 and 2 are defined, and the configuration revision number is 30.

    What will happen when the switch is connected to the network?

    Because the new switch has a higher configuration revision number, the other switches in the VTP domain Engineering will learn all of its VLAN and VTP configuration information. The new switch has two VLANs configured on itself—VLAN 1 and 2. The other switches will assume they should delete all VLANs except for VLAN 1, and VLAN 2 will be created. Obviously, this will cause a major outage on the network because active VLANs 10 through 30 and 100 will be deleted and will go inactive. A network administrator will have to manually restore the configurations of those VLANs.

12. A VTP client switch has VLANs 1, 2, 3, 10, and 30 configured as part of a VTP domain; however, the switch has users connected only to access switch ports defined on VLANs 3 and 30. If VTP pruning is enabled and all VLANs are eligible, which VLANs will be pruned on the upstream switch?

   2, 10

13. The VTP domain Area3 consists of one server and several clients. The server's VTP configuration revision number is at 11. A new switch is added to the network. It has VTP domain name Area5, and a configuration revision number of 10. What will happen when the new switch is added to the network? What happens when the VTP domain name is changed to Area3 on the new switch?

   Domain Area5 will experience no change when the switch is added. The two domains, Area3 and Area5, will coexist on the same network with different sets of clients. The configuration revision numbers on both servers will stay unchanged.

   When the domain is changed to Area3, that domain will then have two VTP servers. The switch that has the newly configured domain name has a lower configuration revision number, so it will learn all VTP information from the existing server. The new switch's revision number will become 11, and its list of defined VLANs will change to match the existing server.

14. What command will show information about the VTP configuration on a Catalyst 3550?

   show vtp status

Chapter 8

"Do I Know This Already?"

1. e

   A maximum of 8 ports can be bundled, offering 8 × 200 Mbps (full-duplex), or 1600 Mbps.

2. c

3. c

4. d

5. c

6. c

7. a

8. d

9. b

10. c

11. c

12. c

13. c

Q&A

1. What are some benefits of an EtherChannel?

    Increased bandwidth

    Link redundancy

2. How many links can be aggregated into an EtherChannel?

    2 to 8

3. Traffic between two hosts will be distributed across all links in an EtherChannel. True or false?

    Answer: False

4. Which methods can you use to distribute traffic in an EtherChannel?

    MAC address

    IP address

    Layer 4 port

5. How does an EtherChannel distribute broadcasts and multicasts?

    Broadcasts and multicasts are distributed across the links within an EtherChannel, just like any other traffic. The broadcast or multicast addresses are used in the hash or load-balancing algorithm to determine the link index.

6. When load balancing, what hashing functions choose a link for a frame?

    If the hashing function is based on a single address (MAC, IP, or port), the low-order bits of that address are used as a link index. If two addresses or port numbers are used, the exclusive-OR (XOR) of those two values is used to derive the low-order bits that form a link index.

7. What protocols can negotiate an EtherChannel between two switches?

    PAgP

    LACP

8. Suppose a switch at one end of an EtherChannel is configured to use source MAC addresses for load balancing. The switch on the other end is configured to use both source and destination IP addresses. What will happen?

    The EtherChannel will successfully transport traffic between the two switches. However, the traffic load will not be distributed evenly or symmetrically across the links in the channel.

9. Two switches have a 4-port EtherChannel between them. Both switches are load balancing using source and destination IP addresses. If a packet has source address 192.168.15.10 and destination address 192.168.100.31, what is the EtherChannel link index?

    The link index is computed by an XOR of the source and destination IP addresses. Because this is a 4-port link, only the two low-order bits are needed. 10 XOR 31 can be computed by using binary values: 00001010 XOR 00011111 = 00010101. The lowest two bits (01) give a link index of 1.

10. What does the acronym PAgP stand for?

    Port Aggregation Protocol

11. Two switches should be configured to negotiate an EtherChannel. If one switch is using PAgP "auto" mode, what should the other switch use?

    PAgP "desirable" mode

12. What is the LACP system priority value used for?

    The switch with the lowest system ID (system priority + MAC address) is allowed to make decisions regarding which ports will actively participate in an EtherChannel and which ones will be held in a standby state.

13. Complete the following command to put an interface into EtherChannel group 3, and to use PAgP to ask the far-end switch to participate in the EtherChannel. This switch port should also require PAgP packets back from the far-end switch.

    Switch(config-if)# channel-group _____

    channel-group 3 mode desirable non-silent

14. What interface configuration command is needed to select LACP as the EtherChannel negotiation protocol?

channel-protocol lacp

15. What command could you use to see the status of every port in an EtherChannel?

show etherchannel summary

16. What command could you use to verify the hashing algorithm used for EtherChannel load balancing?

show etherchannel load-balance

17. Suppose a switch is used in a small data center where one server offers an IP-based application to many clients throughout the campus. An EtherChannel connects the data center switch to a Layer 3 core switch, which routes traffic to all clients. What EtherChannel load-balancing method might be most appropriate at the data center switch?

   a. Source MAC address

   b. Source IP address

   c. Destination MAC address

   d. Destination IP address

   e. Source and destination MAC address

   f. Source and destination IP address

Answer: d. Remember that the EtherChannel will only load balance outbound traffic, or that from the server toward the clients. Here are brief explanations of each of the choices to help clarify the answer.

a. Source MAC address—Not very useful. Because the source MAC address (the server) will always be the same. One link in the channel would always be selected.

b. Source IP address—Not very useful. Again, the source IP address (the server) is constant.

c. Destination MAC address—Not very useful. Because a Layer 3 switch is positioned in the core layer, it will always appear as the destination MAC address for all client destinations.

d. Destination IP address—This is the best choice because the destination IP addresses of the clients are diverse and not modified along the path.

e. Source and destination MAC address—Not very useful. Because the destination MAC address will always be the Layer 3 switch, only one link will be used.

f. Source and destination IP address—This would make a good choice, although the combination of addresses doesn't add anything. The source IP address (the server) will always be constant. Therefore, source XOR destination will always yield something similar to the destination address itself.

18. Suppose a mainframe is connected to a switch that has an EtherChannel uplink to a campus network. The EtherChannel has been configured with the **port-channel load-balance src-dst-ip** command. Most of the mainframe traffic is SNA (non-IP). What will happen to the SNA frames when they are switched? Would it be better to reconfigure the channel with **port-channel load-balance src-dst-mac**?

The SNA frames are non-IP, so only MAC addresses are relevant. The switch has been configured to load balance according to the XOR of the source and destination IP addresses. Obviously, the SNA frames will have neither of these values present. The switch will realize this and fall back to the "lower" method of src-dst-mac (XOR of the source and destination MAC addresses) for each SNA frame. No configuration changes are necessary for this to occur.

There really isn't a good reason to reconfigure for src-dst-mac because the switch is able to forward the SNA frames already. However, if it were reconfigured, any IP packets would be encapsulated in Ethernet frames, providing MAC addresses within the frames.

19. What attributes of a set of switch ports must match to form an EtherChannel?

Port speed

Port duplex

Trunking mode

Trunking encapsulation

Access or native VLAN

20. What happens if one port of an EtherChannel is unplugged or goes dead? What happens when that port is reconnected?

Traffic on the disconnected port will be moved to the next available link in the EtherChannel bundle. When the port is reconnected, traffic will not automatically move back to the bundle's original port. Rather, new traffic will be learned and applied to the restored link.

Chapter 9

"Do I Know This Already?"

1. c
2. c
3. b
4. b
5. c
6. c
7. a
8. b
9. d
10. b
11. b
12. c

Q&A

1. What is a bridging loop? Why is it bad?

   A bridging loop is a path through a bridged or switched network that provides connectivity in an endless loop. Unknown unicast, broadcast, or multicast frames introduced into the loop are propagated by each switch, causing the frames to circulate around and around the loop. Network bandwidth and CPU resources can be completely absorbed by the increasing amount of broadcast traffic. Breaking the loop connectivity can end Bridging loops.

2. Put the following STP port states in chronological order:

   a. Learning

   b. Forwarding

   c. Listening

   d. Blocking

   Answer: d, c, a, b

3. Choose two types of STP messages used to communicate between bridges:

   a. Advertisement BPDU

   b. Configuration BPDU

   c. ACK BPDU

   d. TCN BPDU

Answer: b, d

4. What criteria are used to select the following?

   a. Root Bridge

   b. Root Port

   c. Designated Port

   d. Redundant (or secondary) Root Bridges

Answers:

a. Lowest Bridge ID (Bridge priority, MAC address)

b. Lowest Root Path Cost

c. Lowest Root Path Cost on a shared segment

d. Next-to-lowest Bridge ID

If a tie occurs, these parameters are used to decide:

1. Lowest Bridge ID

2. Lowest Root Path Cost

3. Lowest Sender Bridge ID

4. Lowest Sender Port ID

5. Which of the following switches will become the Root Bridge, given the information in the table below? Which switch will become the secondary Root Bridge if the Root Bridge fails?

Switch Name	Bridge Priority	MAC Address	Port Costs
Catalyst A	32,768	00-d0-10-34-26-a0	All are 19
Catalyst B	32,768	00-d0-10-34-24-a0	All are 4
Catalyst C	32,767	00-d0-10-34-27-a0	All are 19
Catalyst D	32,769	00-d0-10-34-24-a1	All are 19

Catalyst C will become the primary Root because of its lower Bridge Priority value. (Bridge Priority has a greater weight on the election than a lower MAC address.) The secondary Root will be Catalyst B; both A and B have the next-lowest Bridge Priorities, but B also has a lower MAC address.

6. What conditions cause an STP topology change? What effect does this have on STP and the network?

A topology change occurs when a port moves to the Forwarding state, or from Forwarding or Learning to the Blocking state. During a topology change, addresses are aged out in Forward Delay seconds, whereas active stations are not aged out of the bridging table. The STP is not recomputed; TCN BPDUs are sent throughout the network, notifying other switches of the topology change. Only the port where the topology change is occurring is affected, by moving through the STP states.

7. A Root Bridge has been elected in a switched network. Suppose a new switch is installed with a lower Bridge ID than the existing Root Bridge. What will happen?

The new switch will begin life by advertising itself as the Root Bridge, thinking it is the only bridge on the network. Because it has a lower Bridge ID than the current Root, it will win the election after the BPDUs converge and all switches have a knowledge of the new, better choice.

8. Suppose a switch receives Configuration BPDUs on two of its ports. Both ports are assigned to the same VLAN. Each of the BPDUs announces Catalyst A as the Root Bridge. Can the switch use both of these ports as Root Ports? Why?

The STP doesn't allow more than one Root Port per switch (bridge). Because of this, both ports cannot become Root Ports. Only the port with the lowest Root Path Cost (or one of the successive STP tie-breaker decisions) will become the Root Port.

9. How is the Root Path Cost calculated for a switch port?

The Root Path cost is a cumulative value that is incremented as Configuration BPDUs are passed from switch to switch. A switch adds its local port's Port Cost to the current Root Path Cost value as a BPDU is received.

10. What conditions can cause ports on a network's Root Bridge to move into the Blocking state? (Assume that all switch connections are to other switches. No crossover cables are used to connect two ports together on the same switch.)

   By definition, all ports on the Root Bridge are Designated Ports because they are in the closest possible location to the Root Bridge. Therefore, those ports can never be put into the Blocking state. The only exception to this is if two of the Root Bridge switch's ports are connected together—a situation that could, but *shouldn't* ever, occur.

11. What parameters can be tuned to influence the selection of a port as a Root or Designated Port?

   Port Cost

12. After a bridging loop forms, how can you stop the endless flow of traffic?

   Turn the switch off or unplug a cable on a port that is part of the loop.

   Turning the switch off is obviously a drastic measure but does help to clear the loop. Any method might be used, as long as the loop is manually broken or disconnected. In some cases, the traffic volume caused by the loop can overwhelm the switch CPU. If that happens, you won't be able to connect to the switch CLI to shut down an interface or reload the switch.

13. In a BPDU, when can the Root Bridge ID have the same value as the Sender Bridge ID?

   When the switch that is sending the BPDU is also the Root Bridge.

14. Which of these is true about the Root Path Cost?

   a. It is a value sent by the Root Bridge that cannot be changed along the way.

   b. It is incremented as a switch receives a BPDU.

   c. It is incremented as a switch sends a BPDU.

   d. It is incremented by the Path Cost of a port.

   Answer: B, D

15. Suppose two switches are connected by a common link. Each must decide which one will have the Designated Port on the link. Which switch will take on this role, if these STP advertisements occur?

   - The link is on switch A's port number 12 and on switch B's port number 5.
   - Switch A has a Bridge ID of 32,768:0000.1111.2222, and switch B has 8192:0000.5555.6666.
   - Switch A advertises a Root Path Cost of 8, while B advertises 12.

   Switch A will have the Designated Port. The STP tie-breaking sequence must be used for the decision. The first relevant decision is that of the lowest Root Path Cost, advertised by switch A. If both switches advertised an identical Root Path Cost, the lowest Sender Bridge ID (that of switch B) would be used.

16. Using the default STP timers, how long does it take for a port to move from the Blocking state to the Forwarding state?

   30 seconds

17. If the Root Bridge sets the Topology Change flag in the BPDU, what must the other switches in the network do?

   Shorten their bridge table aging times

18. Over what VLAN(s) does the CST form of STP run?

   a. VLAN 1

   b. All active VLANs

   c. All VLANs (active or inactive)

   d. The native VLAN

   Answer: d

19. What is the major difference between PVST and PVST+?

   PVST+ interoperates with CST and PVST.

20. Two switches are connected by a common active link. When might neither switch have a Designated Port on the link?

    a. When neither has a better Root Path Cost.

    b. When the switches are actually the primary and secondary Root Bridges.

    c. When one switch has its port in the Blocking state.

    d. Never; this can't happen.

    Answer: d

Chapter 10

"Do I Know This Already?"

1. c

2. c

3. d

4. c

5. c

6. c

7. b

8. d

9. c

10. a

11. a

12. d

Q&A

1. What commands can configure a Catalyst 4500 switch as the Root Bridge on VLAN 10, assuming that the other switches are using the default STP values?

    spanning-tree vlan 10 root primary

2. Using your Root Bridge answer from Question 1, what commands can configure a Catalyst 3550 switch as a secondary or backup Root Bridge on VLAN 10?

    spanning-tree vlan 10 root secondary

3. Which of the following switches will become the Root Bridge, given the information in the following table? Which switch will become the secondary Root Bridge if the Root Bridge fails?

Switch Name	Bridge Priority	MAC Address	Port Costs
Catalyst A	32,768	00-d0-10-34-26-a0	All are 19
Catalyst B	32,768	00-d0-10-34-24-a0	All are 4
Catalyst C	32,767	00-d0-10-34-27-a0	All are 19
Catalyst D	32,769	00-d0-10-34-24-a1	All are 19

The Root Bridge will be Catalyst C because its Bridge Priority has the lowest value. The Bridge Priority is more significant because it is stored in the upper bits of the Bridge ID field. If Catalyst C fails in its duty as Root Bridge, Catalyst B will take over as the secondary Root Bridge. Because Catalyst B has the default Bridge Priority (32,768), along with another switch, the lowest MAC address will be the deciding factor.

Questions 4 through 7 are based on a network that contains two switches, Catalyst A and B. Their Bridge Priorities and MAC addresses are 32,768:0000.aaaa.aaaa and 32,768:0000.bbbb.bbbb, respectively.

4. Which switch will become the Root Bridge?

    Catalyst A; the Bridge Priorities are equal, so the lowest MAC address is the deciding factor.

5. If switch B's Bridge Priority is changed to 10,000, which one will be Root?

    Catalyst B will become the new Root Bridge because its new priority is the lowest.

6. If switch B's Bridge Priority is changed to 32,769, which one will be Root?

    Catalyst A will become the Root again because B's priority is slightly higher.

7. If switch C is introduced with 40000:0000.0000.cccc, which will be the secondary Root?

   Catalyst B was previously the secondary root, with the second-highest Bridge Priority. It will remain the secondary root because Catalyst C has a higher Bridge Priority.

8. Suppose a switch is configured with the **spanning-tree vlan 10 root primary** command. Then another switch is connected to the network. The new switch has a Bridge Priority of 8192. Which one of the following will happen?

   a. When the new switch advertises itself, the original Root Bridge will detect it and lower its Bridge Priority to 4096 less than the new switch.

   b. The new switch will become and stay the Root Bridge (Bridge Priority 8192).

   c. No change; both switches keep their current Bridge Priorities.

   d. The new switch will detect that a Root Bridge already exists and raise its own Bridge Priority to 32,768.

   Answer: b

9. Three switches in a network have the following Bridge Priorities: 32,768, 16,384, and 8192. If a fourth switch is configured with **spanning-tree vlan 1 root secondary**, what is the Bridge Priority of the switches that will become the primary and secondary Root Bridge?

   Primary root: 8192, Secondary root: 16,384

   (The switch configured with the **root secondary** keywords can't detect any other potential secondary Roots, so it can only set its priority to 28,672.)

10. What STP timer values can be automatically modified by setting the network diameter?

    Hello timer

    Forward Delay timer

    Max age timer

11. Which STP timer determines how long a port stays in the Listening state? What is its default value?

    The Forward Delay timer; default 15 seconds

12. What is the purpose of the Max Age timer?

    It sets the length of time received BPDUs are held if a neighboring switch is not heard from on a nondesignated port. After the Max Age timer expires, the BPDU for the neighbor is flushed and that port enters the Listening state, eventually becoming the new Designated Port on the segment.

13. Three switches are connected to each other, forming a triangle shape. STP prevents a loop from forming. What is the most accurate value that could be used for the network diameter?

Answer: 3

14. Which of the following will not benefit from STP UplinkFast?

   a. An access layer switch with one uplink port

   b. An access layer switch with two uplink ports

   c. An access layer switch with three uplink ports

   d. An access layer switch with four uplink ports

Answer: a

15. What command can enable the STP PortFast feature on a switch? What configuration mode must you enter first?

spanning-tree portfast, in the interface configuration mode

16. What happens if the STP Hello Time is decreased to 1 second in an effort to speed up STP convergence? What happens if the Hello Time is increased to 10 seconds?

Setting the Hello Timer to 1 second doubles the amount of Configuration BPDUs that a switch sends, as compared to the default 2 second timer. While this does share BPDU information more often, it doesn't help the long convergence delay when a port comes up. The significant delays come from the Forward Delay timer, which is used to move a port through the Listening and Learning states. By default, this process takes 30 seconds and is unaffected by the Hello Timer.

17. What switch command can safely adjust the STP timers on the Root Bridge in VLAN 7? Assume that the network consists of Catalyst A, B, and C, all connected to each other in a triangle fashion.

Because the three switches form a triangle loop, one link will eventually be placed in the Blocking state. Therefore, the maximum distance across the network is 3 switch hops. This value can be used to define the network diameter to safely adjust the STP timers for faster convergence:

spanning-tree vlan 7 root primary diameter 3

For questions 18 and 19, refer to the following output:

```
Switch# show spanning-tree vlan 50 brief
VLAN50
  Spanning tree enabled protocol ieee
  Root ID    Priority    8000
             Address     00d0.0457.3831
             Cost        12
             Port        49 (GigabitEthernet0/1)
             Hello Time   2 sec  Max Age 20 sec  Forward Delay 15 sec

  Bridge ID  Priority    32818  (priority 32768 sys-id-ext 50)
             Address     0009.b7ee.9800
             Hello Time   2 sec  Max Age 20 sec  Forward Delay 15 sec
             Aging Time 300

Interface                                  Designated
Name             Port ID Prio  Cost Sts    Cost Bridge ID            Port ID
---------------- ------- ---- ------ ---    ---- -------------------- -------
FastEthernet0/1  128.1    128     19 FWD    12 32818 0009.b7ee.9800 128.1
FastEthernet0/2  128.2    128     19 FWD    12 32818 0009.b7ee.9800 128.2
FastEthernet0/4  128.4    128    100 FWD    12 32818 0009.b7ee.9800 128.4
FastEthernet0/7  128.7    128     19 FWD    12 32818 0009.b7ee.9800 128.7
FastEthernet0/8  128.8    128     19 FWD    12 32818 0009.b7ee.9800 128.8
FastEthernet0/9  128.9    128     19 FWD    12 32818 0009.b7ee.9800 128.9
FastEthernet0/10 128.10   128     19 FWD    12 32818 0009.b7ee.9800 128.10
FastEthernet0/11 128.11   128     19 FWD    12 32818 0009.b7ee.9800 128.11
FastEthernet0/12 128.12   128     19 FWD    12 32818 0009.b7ee.9800 128.12
FastEthernet0/17 128.13   128     19 FWD    12 32818 0009.b7ee.9800 128.13
FastEthernet0/20 128.16   128     19 FWD    12 32818 0009.b7ee.9800 128.16
FastEthernet0/21 128.17   128     19 FWD    12 32818 0009.b7ee.9800 128.17
FastEthernet0/23 128.19   128     19 FWD    12 32818 0009.b7ee.9800 128.19
FastEthernet0/24 128.20   128     19 FWD    12 32818 0009.b7ee.9800 128.20
```

18. What is the Bridge ID for the current Root Bridge? Is the switch that produced this output the actual Root Bridge?

The Root Bridge ID is 8000:00d0.0457.3831. The local switch is not the Root Bridge, as its Bridge ID (32818:0009.b7ee.9800) is different from the Root.

19. What is the Path Cost of interface FastEthernet 0/4, and why is it different from the others?

The Path Cost is 100. This is because that interface is currently operating at 10Mbps (STP cost 100), whereas the others are operating at 100Mbps (STP cost 19).

20. Why does the column marked "Designated Bridge ID" have the same value for every switch port?

Each of the switch ports shown has won the election to become the Designated Port for its local segment. Each Designated Port must identify its own Bridge ID, which is 32818:0009.b7ee.9800. Naturally, the Bridge ID is the same for all ports on VLAN 50.

21. Suppose you need to troubleshoot your Spanning Tree topology and operation. What commands and information can you use on a switch to find information about the current STP topology in VLAN 39?

The **show spanning-tree vlan 39 root** command will display the current Root Bridge and the Root Port for VLAN 39. The **show spanning-tree vlan 39 brief** command will show a listing of every switch port on VLAN 39, along with its Path Cost and STP state. The Designated Bridge ID is also shown on every switch port segment. For a quick summary of the total number of ports participating in each active VLAN, use the **show spanning-tree summary** command.

Chapter 11

"Do I Know This Already?"

1. b

2. c

3. c

4. b

5. b

6. d

7. a

8. b

9. b

10. c

11. c

12. c

Q&A

1. Why would a unidirectional link be bad?

Switches must exchange BPDUs in both directions across a link. If one side of the link is disrupted, and the switches think the link is still operational, one of the switches will not receive BPDUs. If that switch had its end of the link in the blocking state to prevent a bridging loop, the absence of BPDUs will cause it to promote the link toward the forwarding state. At that point, the loop will form.

2. What condition must be met to keep a switch port in the blocking state?

   A constant flow of BPDUs. Without them, the switch thinks there is no need to block the port any longer.

3. If a switch port is shown to be in the root-inconsistent state, what has happened on it?

   Root guard has detected someone advertising a BPDU that is superior to the current Root Bridge.

4. When root guard has been triggered on a switch port, what must be done to enable the port for use again?

   Root guard will automatically allow the port to be moved through the STP states as soon as the superior BPDUs are no longer received.

5. When BPDU guard is enabled on a switch port, what state will the port be put in if a BPDU is received on it?

   errdisable

6. When BPDU guard has been triggered on a switch port, what must be done to enable the port for use again?

   If the errdisable timeout feature has been enabled, the switch will automatically put the switch port back into service after a set amount of time. Otherwise, the port will remain disabled until you manually enable it again.

7. What can happen if BPDUs are delayed or "skewed" as they pass along from switch to switch?

   A blocking link can be moved to forwarding, creating a bridging loop, if BPDUs are delayed or dropped.

8. What action does BPDU skew detection take when late BPDUs are detected?

   None, other than generating a syslog message to alert someone of the skewed condition.

9. When loop guard is enabled on a switch port, what state will the port be put in if BPDUs are noted to be missing?

   loop-inconsistent

10. Can STP loop guard be enabled on all switch ports?

    Yes; only the non-designated ports will be affected by loop guard.

11. When UDLD is enabled on a switch port, what else must be done to detect a unidirectional link on the port?

    Enable UDLD on the far-end switch on the same link.

12. What is the difference between the UDLD normal and aggressive modes?

    Normal mode detects a unidirectional link condition and reports it. Aggressive mode detects the condition, reports it, and moves the port to the errdisable state so that it can't be used.

13. What command enables UDLD aggressive mode on a switch interface?

    udld aggressive

14. If two switches enable UDLD on the ports that have a common link, do their UDLD message times have to agree?

    No. The UDLD messages are just echoed back, so the message times are only locally significant.

15. UDLD should be used on switch ports with what type of media?

    Fiber-optic media

16. Can UDLD be used on all switch ports without causing problems?

    Yes, although it is needed only on all fiber-based ports. The device on the far end of the port connection must also support UDLD so that UDLD messages can be echoed back to the switch.

17. Complete the following command to display all ports that are disabled due to STP protection features: **show spanning-tree** _____

    show spanning-tree inconsistentports

Chapter 12

"Do I Know This Already?"

1. d

2. c

3. a

4. c

5. a

6. b

7. c

8. d

9. c

10. d

11. b

12. c

Q&A

1. What is synchronization in RSTP?

   As RSTP works to converge a switched network, each switch effectively isolates itself from the next layer of neighbors until an agreement can be reached about who will have the designated port on each segment.

2. What is an Alternate Port?

   A port with an alternate path to the Root. The path is less desirable than the one through the Root Port but is flagged for immediate use if the Root Port path should fail.

3. What is the difference between an Alternate Port and a Backup Port?

   An Alternate Port connects to a different segment than the Root Port to provide an alternate path to the Root. A Backup Port connects to the same segment as another port on the local switch to provide another path out of the switch, but not necessarily another path back to the Root.

4. Can a switch port be a Designated Port and be in the Discarding state?

Yes; RSTP removes the linkage between a port's role and its state. In 802.1D, a Designated Port must be forwarding, but RSTP doesn't make the same requirement.

5. Which of the following ports can participate in RSTP synchronization?

a. Root Port

b. Designated Port

c. Edge Port

d. Nonedge Port

e. Point-to-point Port

Answer: a, b, d, e

6. What two messages must be exchanged during RSTP synchronization?

Proposal and Agreement

7. After an agreement message is received from a neighboring switch, how much time elapses before the port can begin forwarding? (Consider any timers that must expire or other conditions that must be met.)

The port will be moved to the Forwarding state immediately after the agreement message is received. With RSTP, no other conditions are necessary because two switches have completed a quick handshake by exchanging proposal and agreement messages.

8. After a switch receives news of a topology change, how long does it wait to flush entries out of its CAM table?

The switch flushes entries immediately, rather than employing the timer reduction that 802.1D uses.

9. What command configures a port as an RSTP edge port?

spanning-tree portfast

10. Suppose interface FastEthernet 0/1 is in half-duplex mode, but you want it to be considered a point-to-point link for RSTP. What command will accomplish this?

spanning-tree link-type point-to-point

11. Put the following in order of the number of supported STP instances, from lowest to highest:

    a. MST

    b. PVST+

    c. CST

    d. 802.1D

Answer; d, c, a, b (d and c both have a single instance.)

12. What three parameters must be configured to uniquely define an MST region?

The region name, configuration revision number, and the instance-to-VLAN mappings

13. What parameter does a switch examine to see if its neighbors have the same VLAN to MST instance mappings? How is that information passed among switches?

The VLAN-to-instance mapping is kept in a table of 4096 entries. This information is passed along in the MST BPDUs. Rather than passing the entire table, switches include only a digest of their current table contents.

14. Which MST instance in a region corresponds to the CST of 802.1Q?

The Internal Spanning Tree (IST) instance

15. Which MST instance is the IST?

IST is Instance 0. Instances 1 through 15 are available for other use.

16. When an MST region meets a PVST+ domain, how is each MST instance propagated into PVST+?

The BPDUs from each instance are replicated and sent into all the appropriate VLANs in the PVST+ switch.

17. Is it wise to assign VLANs to MST Instance 0? Why or why not?

No. By default, all VLANs are mapped to Instance 0, the IST. You should select the number of instances needed and map all active VLANs to them. Otherwise, you can't have full control over the topologies independent of IST and CST.

18. The commands have just been entered to define an MST region on a switch. You are still at the MST configuration prompt. What command must you enter to commit the MST changes on the switch?

exit (When the MST configuration mode is exited, the changes are committed immediately.)

19. Which of the following methods can you use to assign or propagate MST configuration information to other switches?

   a. Manual configuration

   b. CDP

   c. VTP

   d. MSTP

   Answer: a

20. A switch can interact with both 802.1D and RSTP. Can it run both PVST+ and MST simultaneously?

   No. A switch can run either PVST+ or MST. If a switch is running MST, it can interact and interoperate with PVST+, 802.1D, and RSTP.

Chapter 13

"Do I Know This Already?"

1. d

2. a

3. a

4. b

5. c

6. c

7. c

8. d

9. c

10. c

11. d

12. c

Q&A

1. What might you need to implement interVLAN routing?

   One or more Layer 3 interfaces

   One or more SVIs

   Static routes

   A dynamic routing protocol

2. Can interVLAN routing be performed over a single trunk link?

   Yes; packets can be forwarded between the VLANs carried over the trunk.

3. To configure an SVI, what commands are needed?

   (First, make sure the VLAN is defined on the switch.)

   interface vlan vlan-id

   ip address ip-address mask

   no shutdown

4. What command can verify the VLAN assignments on a Layer 2 port?

   show interface *type mod/num* **switchport**

   -OR-

   show interface status

5. A switch has the following interface configurations in its running configuration:

   ```
   interface fastethernet 0/1
   switchport access vlan 5
   interface vlan 5
   ip address 192.168.10.1 255.255.255.0
   no shutdown
   ```

   What is necessary for packets to get from the FastEthernet interface to the VLAN 5 SVI?

   Nothing; both are assigned to VLAN 5, so normal Layer 2 transparent bridging will take care of all forwarding between the two.

6. What is the source of FIB information?

    The routing table, as computed by the Layer 3 engine portion of a switch.

7. How often is the FIB updated?

    As needed; it is downloaded or updated dynamically by the Layer 3 engine whenever the routing topology changes or an ARP entry changes.

8. What is meant by the term "CEF punt?"

    A packet can't be forwarded or switched by CEF directly because it needs further processing. The packet is "punted" to the Layer 3 engine, effectively bypassing CEF for a more involved resolution.

9. What happens to the FIB when distributed CEF (dCEF) is used?

    It is simply replicated to each of the independent CEF engines. The FIB itself remains intact, so that each engine receives a duplicate copy.

10. What happens during a "CEF glean" process?

    The MAC address (ARP reply) for a next-hop FIB entry is not yet known. The Layer 3 engine must generate an ARP request and wait for a reply before CEF forwarding can continue to that destination.

11. What does a multilayer switch do to the IP TTL value just before a packet is forwarded?

    The TTL is decremented by one, as if a router had forwarded the packet.

12. What is fallback bridging?

    On switch platforms that cannot multilayer switch (route) all routable protocols, those protocols can be transparently bridged between VLANs instead.

13. Is it possible for an SVI to go down? If so, what are the reasons?

    Yes; the SVI can be administratively shut down with the **shutdown** command, as with any other interface. Also, if the VLAN associated with the SVI is not defined or active, the SVI will appear to be down.

Chapter 14

"Do I Know This Already?"

1. d
2. d
3. c
4. b
5. b
6. b
7. c
8. c
9. c
10. b
11. b
12. c

Q&A

1. A multilayer switch has been configured with the command **standby 5 priority 120**. What router redundancy protocol is being used?

   HSRP

2. What feature can you use to prevent other routers from accidentally participating in an HSRP group?

   HSRP authentication

3. What command can configure an HSRP group to use a virtual router address of 192.168.222.100?

   standby 1 ip 192.168.222.100

4. The **show standby vlan 271** command produces the following output:

```
Vlan271 - Group 1
  Local state is Active, priority 210, may preempt
  Hellotime 3 holdtime 40 configured hellotime 3 sec holdtime 40 sec
  Next hello sent in 00:00:00.594
  Virtual IP address is 192.168.111.1 configured
    Secondary virtual IP address 10.1.111.1
    Secondary virtual IP address 172.21.111.1
  Active router is local
  Standby router is unknown expires in 00:00:37
  Standby virtual mac address is 0000.0c07.ac01
  2 state changes, last state change 5d17h
```

If the local router fails, which router will take over the active role for the virtual router address 192.168.111.1?

None. There is no known standby router, so it has also failed.

5. What is meant by preempting in HSRP?

Normally, if the active router (highest priority) fails, another router takes over its active role. The original active router is not allowed to resume the active role when it is restored until the new active router fails. Pre-empting allows a higher-priority router to take over the active role immediately or after a configurable delay.

6. What protocols discussed in this chapter support interface tracking?

HSRP

GLBP

7. The **show standby brief** command has been used to check the status of all HSRP groups on the local router. The output from this command is as follows:

```
Switch# show standby brief
                     P indicates configured to preempt.
                     |
   Interface   Grp Prio P State   Active addr   Standby addr    Group addr
   Vl100       1   210  P Active  local         192.168.75.2    192.168.75.1
   Vl101       1   210  P Active  local         192.168.107.2   192.168.107.1
   Vl102       1   210  P Active  local         192.168.71.2    192.168.71.1
```

Each interface is shown to have Group 1. Is this a problem?

No, as long as there is no bridging between VLANs. The HSRP group number can be repeated because each group is isolated on its own VLAN.

8. How many HSRP groups are needed to load balance traffic over two routers?

   Two

9. What load-balancing methods can GLBP use?

   Round robin, weighted, host dependent

10. What command can you use to see the status of the active and standby routers on the VLAN 171 interface?

    show standby vlan 171

11. How many GLBP groups are needed to load balance traffic over four routers?

    One

12. When should you use SLB?

    When load balancing is needed for clients to access a server farm.

13. What command defines and names an SLB server farm?

    ip slb serverfarm serverfarm-name

14. A virtual server has just been defined with the following commands:

    ```
    ip slb vserver CISCO
    serverfarm CISCO-FARM
    virtual 192.168.199.17
    ```

    Can the virtual server be used immediately? If not, what additional command is needed?

    inservice

Chapter 15

"Do I Know This Already?"

1. a

2. c

3. b

4. d

5. c

6. c

7. b

8. a

9. b

10. c

11. c

12. c

Q&A

1. By default, what does a router or Layer 3 switch do with multicast packets?

It drops them because multicast routing is not enabled by default.

2. By default, what does a Layer 2 switch do with a multicast packet?

It floods the packet out all ports on the source VLAN, as if it were a broadcast packet.

3. What high-order bit combination signals that an IP address is used for multicast?

1110

4. If the IP-to-MAC multicast address mapping is somewhat ambiguous, how can a frame be forwarded to the correct destination group?

The IP header must be examined in addition to the multicast MAC destination address.

5. What IP multicast address range is set aside for use only on the local network segment?

224.0.0.0 – 224.0.0.255

6. For the RPF check, the source IP address is looked up in the unicast routing table. To forward the packet, what should the result of the test be?

The unicast route to the source must be out the interface where the packet arrived.

7. What important difference exists between IGMPv1 and IGMPv2?

Hosts can request to leave a multicast group immediately with IGMPv2. IGMPv1 doesn't have any mechanism for leaving a group, other than an aging-out process.

8. To join a multicast group, what type of message is sent? Where is this message sent?

   An IGMP Membership Report is sent. The IGMP message is with a destination address of the multicast group itself so that the nearest multicast router will receive it.

9. What is the purpose of the IGMP Querier?

   It is a router that periodically asks all hosts if any of them want to join the multicast group. Interested hosts must respond with a Membership Report.

10. For PIM Dense Mode, how is the multicast tree built?

    The source is the root of the tree, and all Dense Mode routers are included by default. After all of these have joined the group, a pruning phase occurs so that routers with no member hosts are pruned off the tree.

11. Where is the root of the PIM Sparse Mode tree located?

    At a Rendezvous Point (RP) router

12. With PIM Sparse-Dense Mode, is the PIM mode determined per interface or per group?

    Per group. If the group has an RP, Sparse Mode is used; otherwise, Dense Mode is used.

13. What routing table is used for PIM?

    The unicast routing table is used. PIM does not build or maintain its own multicast routing table.

14. What command is used to configure an interface for the hybrid PIM mode?

    ip pim sparse-dense-mode

15. When a switch performs IGMP snooping, what is it snooping for?

    It listens to all IGMP membership reports so that it can learn the location of hosts joining and leaving multicast groups.

16. What else does a Layer 2 switch need when it is configured for CGMP?

    A multicast router. The router relays group join and leave requests as CGMP packets that the switch can use.

17. When should IGMP snooping and CGMP be used together on a switch?

    Never; they are mutually exclusive features.

18. At a trade show, several PCs and servers are connected to a single Layer 2 switch. The switch has CGMP enabled. When a server begins to send video data to a multicast address, what will happen to that traffic?

    Even though CGMP is enabled, no multicast router is available to assist the switch with its multicast forwarding decisions. Therefore, the video packets will be flooded out all switch ports on the server's VLAN.

Chapter 16

"Do I Know This Already?"

1. b
2. b
3. b
4. c
5. b
6. d
7. b
8. c
9. c
10. c
11. d
12. b

Q&A

1. What are some of the problems that QoS can help relieve?

   Packet delay, packet loss, jitter

2. Which protocol is used to reserve network resources in the IntServ QoS model?

   RSVP

3. What protocol is used to maintain the DiffServ QoS model?

None; DiffServ is defined as a per-hop behavior, so no communication is needed between networking devices.

4. What range of values can the CoS field contain?

0 through 7 because CoS is three bits in length.

5. How is the CoS information passed from LAN switch to LAN switch?

Only across trunking links, where the CoS is contained in the trunk encapsulation.

6. How is the IP Precedence field related to the DSCP field?

They are both located in the same byte of the IP header. The three IP Precedence bits are actually the same as the first 3 bits of the DSCP (the Class Selector). However, the DSCP contains three additional bits for greater flexibility.

7. Put the following DSCP codepoints in order of increasing service quality:

  a. EF

  b. AF11

  c. AF23

  d. AF21

  e. Default

Answer: e, b, c, d, a

8. If a packet contains the DSCP codepoint name "AF31," what would the IP Precedence value be?

3; the Class Selector bits ("3" in the codepoint name) are the same as the IP Precedence bits.

9. If a switch port is configured as "untrusted," what is the resulting CoS value of incoming packets?

Each packet's CoS is overwritten with the default CoS value of the switch port itself. In the default case, the port's CoS is zero.

10. Should there be a trust boundary at every switch, where each overwrites QoS information? Explain why or why not.

No, although it is possible to do that. Instead, it is a best practice to define a trust boundary or domain for the bulk of the enterprise network where QoS information is known, predictable, or comes from a reliable source. Every switch at the QoS domain edge or the trust boundary should be configured to examine inbound QoS information and overwrite the values, if necessary.

11. What method is used for scheduling in Catalyst switches?

Weighted Round Robin (WRR)

12. Name one method that is used for congestion avoidance.

Tail drop or Weighted Random Early Detection (WRED)

13. When are packets dropped from the strict priority queue on an interface?

Packets are never dropped from the priority queue by WRED. The only condition that causes packets to be dropped is when the priority queue is full. In that case, packets are dropped by the tail drop method.

14. What is the disadvantage of using the tail drop method to avoid congestion?

Tail drop waits until the queue is full before dropping the latest arriving packets. This tends to avoid congestion after congestion occurs. The main disadvantage is with TCP connections, which begin to back off and enter the slow-start state once tail drop begins. All active TCP connections will do this simultaneously, synchronized with each other. This causes a widespread throughput issue and makes the overall network utilization oscillate.

15. If WRED drops packets at random, isn't that bad?

Not necessarily. Packets are randomly dropped only if the queue fills above a threshold. Then, drops are more probable the farther the queue fills above that threshold. Dropped packets are retransmitted as part of the connection protocol, so the effect is seen on only a few connections rather than on all connections with tail drop.

16. A switch port has a queue type 1p1q4t. What does this mean?

The port has one strict-priority queue (1p), one standard queue (1q), and four WRED thresholds per standard queue (4t).

17. If a switch port has a queue type 1p2q2t, what is the strict priority queue's queue number?

The strict-priority queue is queue 3. (The low-priority standard queue is 1, the high-priority standard queue is 2.)

Chapter 17

"Do I Know This Already?"

1. b

2. a

3. c

4. d

5. b

6. c

7. d

8. b

9. c

10. d

WRR always services the strict-priority queue before any other; therefore, there is no way to configure any other behavior.

11. b

12. b

Q&A

1. What two ways can QoS trust be configured on a switch?

Per-interface and per-policy

2. If all QoS trust decisions will be applied as part of a QoS policy, what command should you use on an interface?

no mls qos trust; All trust must be disabled on the interface because the policy will enable any specific trust conditions that are configured.

3. When a class map is configured, what types of commands must also be used?

   match commands, to match specific types of traffic

4. Name two methods that you can use to identify or classify traffic.

   Matching can be based on traffic that is permitted by an access list and on protocols identified by NBAR.

5. What command can classify traffic with an extended IP access list?

   match access-group name *access-list*

6. What command can classify traffic with NBAR?

   match protocol *protocol-name*

7. What does a policy map contain?

   It contains references to class maps that identify types of traffic and actions to take as a result of each class map.

8. When a policy map is applied to an interface, does it control both inbound and outbound traffic?

   The policy map must be applied in one direction only, each time it is configured on the interface. It can control only inbound or outbound traffic, unless it is applied twice to the interface—once in each direction.

9. What is the first command keyword used to configure WRED congestion avoidance?

   wrr-queue; This seems surprising because wrr-queue is also used to configure scheduling. However, Catalyst switches use the same components to schedule and perform WRED because both involve egress queue operations.

10. What QoS information is used to map packets into the egress queues of a switch port?

    CoS, through the use of a CoS-to-queue mapping function

11. What command can set the WRED thresholds of the strict-priority queue (1p2q2t) to 25 percent and 75 percent?

    None; WRED can't perform any operations on the strict-priority queue. Because of this, no packets can ever be randomly dropped.

12. What command can display the QoS and queue information about a switch port?

show queueing interface

Chapter 18

"Do I Know This Already?"

1. b
2. d
3. c
4. b
5. a
6. d
7. a
8. d
9. c
10. d
11. b
12. b

Q&A

1. How does a Catalyst switch detect that a connected device is capable of using inline power?

The device must first loop the Ethernet connection's transmit and receive pairs. The switch can then hear its own test tone, confirming that the device does indeed need inline power. After the power is enabled on the port, the switch and the device can exchange CDP messages so that the amount of power can be adjusted.

2. What type of trunk can be used between a Catalyst switch port and a Cisco IP Phone?

A special-case 802.1Q trunk with only two VLANs

3. When a trunk is used on an IP Phone, on which VLAN is the data from an attached PC carried?

PC data is always carried over the native (untagged) VLAN in the trunk. Voice packets can be carried over the native VLAN, too, or over a unique voice VLAN.

4. What is the difference between the VVID and the PVID?

VVID refers to the Voice VLAN ID, whereas PVID refers to the Port VLAN ID.

5. Can the CoS information from the voice traffic be passed when the **switchport voice vlan untagged** command is used? If so, how?

Yes, CoS information is passed within the 802.1p portion of the 802.1Q trunk encapsulation.

6. What is the advantage of using the **switchport voice vlan dot1p** command?

Voice traffic is carried over VLAN 0 on the IP Phone trunk, so a unique voice VLAN is not necessary. This can be an advantage when a new VLAN can't be added to a network or switch. CoS information is still carried over the trunk in the 802.1p field.

7. By default, does a Cisco IP Phone trust QoS information from an attached PC?

No. The phone will overwrite all QoS information (both CoS and DSCP) to 0, considering the PC an untrusted source.

8. The command **switchport priority extend cos 5** is entered for a switch port. Is this a good decision? Why or why not?

Probably not. After that is done, all packets from an attached PC will be marked with CoS 5 the same value the phone gives to its voice bearer packets. Any upstream switches will be unable to distinguish the two types of traffic just by examining the CoS value.

9. How can a switch classify VoIP voice bearer packets that are carried by RTP?

RTP uses negotiated UDP port numbers, so access lists can't be used. Instead, NBAR is able to classify the traffic by a stateful inspection. The **match protocol rtp** command can be used for this.

10. The **show power inline** command is used to check the power status on each switch port. If the output is as shown below, what can you assume about interface fastethernet 0/1?

```
Interface  Admin   Oper        Power    Device
                                (Watts)
---------- -----  ----------  -------  --------------------
Fa0/1      auto   off              0   n/a
Fa0/2      auto   on             6.3   Cisco IP Phone 7960
```

Interface fastethernet 0/1 shows an operational inline power state of "off," with 0 watts of power. This could mean that nothing is plugged into that switch port. It could also mean that an IP Phone is connected to the port but the port has inline power set to the "off" state.

11. What command can verify the QoS trust relationship between an IP Phone and its attached PC?

    show mls qos interface

    -OR-

    show interface switchport

Chapter 19

"Do I Know This Already?"

1. b

2. d

3. b

4. c

5. d

6. b

7. b

    The trick is in the "maximum 3" keywords. This sets the maximum number of addresses that can be learned on a port. If only one static address is configured, two more addresses can be learned dynamically.

8. c

9. a

10. b

11. c

12. c

    Because of the variety of user host platforms, port-based authentication (802.1x) cannot be used. The problem also states that the goal is to restrict access to physical switch ports, so AAA is of no benefit. Port security can do the job by restricting access according to the end users' MAC addresses.

Q&A

1. What does the acronym "AAA" stand for?

    Authentication, authorization, and accounting

2. What external methods of authentication does a Catalyst switch support?

RADIUS and TACACS+

3. A RADIUS server is located at IP address 192.168.199.10. What command can be used to configure a Catalyst switch to find the server?

radius-server host 192.168.199.10

4. A Catalyst switch should be configured to authenticate users against RADIUS servers first, followed by TACACS+ servers. What command can define the authentication methods? Make sure users can still authenticate if none of the servers are available.

aaa authentication login default radius tacacs+ local

5. What is the purpose of authorization? What happens if authorization is not used?

It allows an external server to decide if the authenticated user can gain access to specific resources or switch commands. If it is not used, the default behavior is that all users must authenticate as they move to the appropriate privilege level to run switch commands.

6. Is it possible to use different methods to authorize users to run switch commands instead of making configuration changes?

Yes; The **aaa authorization** command separates these functions so that each can have its own method list.

7. When might the command **switchport port-security maximum 2** be used?

The **switchport port-security maximum 2** command might be used if it is too much trouble to manually configure MAC addresses into the port security feature. Up to two MAC addresses would then be dynamically learned. The network administrator might also want to control what is connected to that switch port. If another switch or a hub were connected, the total number of active stations could easily rise above two.

8. After port-based authentication is configured and enabled, can any host connect as long as the user can authenticate?

No, only hosts that have 802.1x-capable applications can communicate with the switch port to properly authenticate at all.

9. When the 802.1x **force-authorized** keyword is used, how does the switch react to users attempting to connect?

The switch always authorizes any connecting user, without any authentication.

10. Can more than one host be authenticated on a single switch port with port-based authentication?

Yes, if the **dot1x multi-hosts** command is configured on the switch port interface.

Chapter 20

"Do I Know This Already?"

1. c

2. d

3. d

4. a

5. b

6. a

7. c

8. a

9. c

10. d

11. a

12. b

Q&A

1. When a VACL is implemented on a switch, how is the switching speed affected?

It isn't; VACLs are implemented in hardware, so packets can be inspected as they are being switched with no performance penalty.

2. What actions can be taken on packets matching a VACL?

Packets can be forwarded, dropped, marked for capture, or redirected to a different Layer 2 switch port.

3. After a VACL is applied using the **vlan filter** command, how is the traffic direction (inbound or outbound) specified?

It isn't; VACLs operate on packets as they are being forwarded within a VLAN. Therefore, there is no concept of direction within the VLAN. A direction can't be specified.

4. A secondary community VLAN is associated with a primary VLAN on a switch. Can hosts assigned to the community VLAN communicate with each other?

    Yes, they can. However, they can't communicate with any other community or isolated VLAN.

5. A secondary isolated VLAN is associated with a primary VLAN on a switch. Can hosts assigned to the isolated VLAN communicate with each other?

    No, hosts on an isolated VLAN can't even communicate among themselves. They can reach only the promiscuous host on the primary VLAN.

6. What command is needed to configure a promiscuous VLAN?

    This isn't possible. The primary VLAN can communicate with all the secondary VLANs that are associated with it. The only promiscuous objects that can be configured are promiscuous hosts, located on the primary VLAN.

7. A router is identifed as the central gatewawy for a private VLAN. What command is needed to configure the switch port where a router is connected?

    switchport mode private-vlan promiscuous

8. How many actual VLANs must be configured to implement a common router with two community VLANs?

    Three VLANs must be used: one for the primary VLAN where the router is connected and two more for the secondary community VLANs. The primary VLAN will be logically associated with the two community VLANs, but all three must be configured.

9. How is switching performance affected when several SPAN sessions are enabled?

    Switching performance is not affected. Packets are simply marked and copied into another switch port's queue during a SPAN session. The original traffic is still forwarded without being modified or affected.

10. What command can specify the source of a SPAN session as VLAN 100?

    monitor session 1 source vlan 100

11. When a SPAN session is enabled, what direction of traffic flow (relative to the source port) is mirrored for analysis?

    By default, traffic in both directions is mirrored.

12. What two things can identify more granular traffic to be mirrored to a SPAN destination?

    A VLAN ACL (VACL) can match and mark packets for capture. A SPAN VLAN filter can also identify specific VLANs to mirror, if the source is a trunk port.

13. Three switches are connected in series with trunk links. The RSPAN source is on the first switch and the destination is on the third. How does the intermediate (second) switch learn about the RSPAN's source and destination locations?

    It doesn't. The intermediate switch has no knowledge that RSPAN is being used. The only configuration needed is to define the RSPAN VLAN and to allow that VLAN on the trunk links. Beyond that, the intermediate switch can flood only the RSPAN packets to all ports carrying the RSPAN VLAN.

14. What must be configured on all switches connecting an RSPAN source and destination? What commands can be used?

    The special-purpose RSPAN VLAN must be configured. Define the VLAN number and then use the **remote-span** command.

15. One of the advantages of RSPAN is that mirrored traffic can be isolated in the RSPAN VLAN on a trunk. If a GigabitEthernet port is to be monitored on one switch, which is better to use as a transport for the RSPAN VLAN: a GigabitEthernet trunk already carrying user traffic in other VLANs, or an isolated GigabitEthernet trunk link set aside for RSPAN?

    The existing trunk will work fine because the RSPAN traffic will be isolated in its own VLAN. However, you must be careful not to place an excessive load on that trunk link. RSPAN traffic can easily add to the bandwidth burden on a link, considering that the source here is also a GigabitEthernet port. In this case, it might be better to transport the RSPAN mirrored traffic over its own trunk link, if one is available and cost-effective.

Index

Symbols

(*,G) multicast flows, 363
(S,G) multicast traffic, 362

Numerics

10 Mbps Ethernet, 112–113
10GbE, 118–119
80/20 rule, 18
802.1Q
  tunneling, 153–155
    configuring, 155
802.1x
  configuring, 461–463

A

AAA
  accounting
    enabling on Catalyst switches, 459
  authentication
    enabling on Catalyst switches, 455–457
  authorization
    enabling on Catalyst switches, 457–458
access layer, 20
  switches, 23
access layer switches, 22–23
accounting
  enabling on Catalyst switches, 459
aCEF (Accelerated CEF), 315
ACLs, 65
  See also VACLs
addressing
  multicast, 358

  OUI values, 358
  reserved addresses, 358
adjacency tables, 315–316
advertisements
  VTP, 172–173
    subset advertisements, 174
    summary advertisements, 173
aggregate policers, 390
aggressive mode (UDLD), 272
application-specific integrated circuits (ASICs), 10
applying
  trusts to QoS, 406
  VACLs to VLAN interfaces, 474
ARP throttling, 316
ASICs (application-specific), 10
assigning
  IP address to management VLAN, 90–91
authentication
  enabling on Catalyst switches, 455–457
  port-based
    configuring, 461–463
authorization
  enabling on Catalyst switches, 457–458
auto-RP process, 365
AVF (active virtual forwarder), 339
AVG (active virtual gateway), 338

B

baby giant frames, 149
BackboneFast, 254–255
best effort QoS, 382
Blocking state (STP), 225
blocks
  core, 42, 44

BßU
skew detection, 270
BPDU Guard, 268–269
BPDUs
BPDU Guard, 268–269
Configuration BPDUs, 217–218
convergence, 285–286
protecting agains sudden loss, 269
Root Guard, 267–268
RSTP, 285
TCN BPDUs, 228
Bridge IDs, 219
bridging
transparent
redundancy, 215
versus Ethernet switches, 213–214
bridging loops, 216
preventing with STP, 217
broadcast traffic, 357
building access switches, 20
building block model
enterprise edge block, 47
network managment block, 46–47
server farm blocks, 46
server provider edge block, 47
building blocks (QoS)
ingress queueing, 388
bundled ports (EtherChannel), 194
bundleds
distributed EtherChannel traffic, 194–195
bundles (EtherChannel)
troubleshooting, 200–203

C

CAM (Content Addressable Memory), 65
CAM tables, 70
troubleshooting, 76

campus networks, 25, 28
building blocks
enterprise edge block, 47
network management block, 46–47
server farm blocks, 46
server provider edge block, 47
LAN segmentation model, 14–15, 17
models, 12
modular design
core blocks, 41–45
switch blocks, 38–41
modular designs, 37
network traffic models, 17–18
predictable network model, 19
shared network model, 13–14
campus-wide VLANs
deploying, 145
Catalyst switches, 24–26
CDP, 91
file management, 92
configuration files, 93–94
image files, 92–93
moving files, 94–95
port security, 460–461
product summary, 25–26, 29
remote access, 90–91
SPAN, 480
local SPAN, 481, 483–484
RSPAN, 484–486
VSPAN, 481, 483–484
CatOS, 87
host name
changing, 88
passwords, 89
recovering, 90
troubleshooting, 96–98

cd flash command, 95
CDP
  viewing neighboring device information, 98
CDP (Cisco Discovery Protocol)
  inter-switch communication, 91
CEF, 312
  adjacency table, 315–316
  configuring, 316
  fallback bridging, 317
  FIB, 314–315
  packet rewrites, 316
  process switching, 69
  verifying, 319, 321
CEF (Cisco Express Forwarding), 67
CGMP (Cisco Group Membership Protocol), 368–369
Cisco IOS Software, 87
  running configuration, 89
Cisco IP Phones
  inline power, 435–436
    configuring, 437
    verifying, 443
  trunking modes, 438
class maps
  defining as QoS policy, 411
classification (packets), 388
client mode (VTP), 172
  configuring, 176
collapsed core blocks, 42–43
collision domain, 13
collisions
  preventing, 15
commands
  cd flash, 95
  copy flash, 95
  debug commands
    troubleshooting CatOS, 97–98
  delete flash, 95
  dir, 95
  erase flash, 95
  format flash, 95
  show commands
    troubleshooting CatOS, 96–97
  show etherchannel port-channel, 196
  show vtp status, 178
community VLANs, 475
comparing
  Ethernet switches and transparent bridges, 213–214

configuration
  dual core blocks, 44
  hierarchical network design, 25, 28
  modular network designs, 37
Configuration BPDUs, 217–218
configuration files
  manipulating, 95
  moving, 94–95
  switches, 93–94
configuring
  802.1Q tunneling, 155
  accounting on Catalyst switches, 459
  authentication on Catalyst switches, 455–457
  authorization on Catalyst switches, 457–458
  CEF, 316
  EtherChannel, 198
    LACP, 199–200
    load balancing, 195–197
    PAgP, 199
  inline power on Cisco IP Phones, 437
  interVLAN routing, 310
    Layer 2 mode, 310
    Layer 3 mode, 311
    SVI ports, 312
  Layer 2 protocol tunnels, 156
  local SPAN, 481–482, 484
  MST, 295–296
  PIM-DM, 362
  PIM-SM, 364
  port security on Catalyst switches, 460–461
  PVLANs, 477, 479
    associating secondary VLANs to primary VLANs, 479
    mapping promiscuous mode ports, 478
  QoS
    trust, 441
  RSPAN, 484–486
  RSTP, 290
  SLB, 344–345
  static VLANs, 143
  STP
    Root Bridges, 246–248
    timers, 250–251
    UDLD, 273
  switch ports, 123–124
    port mode, 125
    speed, 124
  VACLs, 473–474

VLAN trunks, 150–152
voice VLANs, 438, 440
VSPAN, 482–484
VTP
    client mode, 176
    management domains, 175
    pruning, 182
    server mode, 176
    transparent mode, 176
    version, 177–178
WRED
    thresholds, 416–417
congestion
    relieving, 13
congestion avoidance, 391
    mapping internal DSCP values to CoS
        values, 414–415
    mapping packets to egress queues, 415–416
    tail drop, 391, 416
    WRED, 392–393, 416
        thresholds, configuring, 416–417
connecting switch block devices, 121
    Gigabit Ethernet port cables, 121–122
connectivity, 21
    core blocks, 42, 44
    switch ports
        troubleshooting, 126–127
console ports
    connecting switch block devices, 120
convergence
    controlling on STP, 252
        with BackboneFast, 254–255
        with PortFast, 252
        with UplinkFast, 253–254
    STP timers, 227
convergences
    RSTP, 285–286
    TCN BPDUs, 228
copy flash command, 95
copying
    Catalyst switch files, 94–95
core blocks, 41–42, 44
    collapsed core, 42–43
    dual core, 43–45
core layer, 21
core layer switches, 24
CoS (class of service), 384
    mapping to internal DSCP values, 407

criteria for process switching, 69
CST (Common Spanning Tree), 229
customizing
    STP
        Port ID, 250
        Root Path Cost, 248–249
        timers, 250–251

D

DC inline power for Cisco IP Phones, 435–436
    configuring, 437
    verifying, 443
dCEF (Distributed CEF), 315
debug commands
    troubleshooting CatOS, 97–98
decision processes of packets in multilayer
  switches, 67, 69
defining
    QoS policies, 409
        class maps, 411
        marking, 412
        policing, 412–413
        traffic classification, 409–410
        trusted information, 412
    VACL matching conditions, 473–474
Delay, 381
delete flash command, 95
deleting SPAN sessions, 483
demand-based switching, 66
Dense Mode (PIM), 362
deploying
    VLANs, 144
        end-to-end, 145
        local, 145
design, 42
Designated Ports
    election procedure, 223–224
designing
    hierarchical networks
        access layer, 20
        core layer, 21
        distribution layer, 21
designing campus networks
    building block model
        enterprise edge block, 47
        network management block, 46–47

server farm block, 46
server provider edge block, 47
predictable network model, 19
designing hierarchical networks
devices, 21–22
access layer switches, 22–23
core layer switches, 24
distribution layer switches, 23–24
detecting
switch port error conditions, 125
devices
distribution layers, 21
hierarchical network design, 21–22, 25, 28
access layer switches, 22–23
core layer switches, 24
distribution layer switches, 23–24
Layer 2 switching, 10
Layer 3 routing, 10
Layer 3 switching, 11
Layer 4 switching, 12
MLS (multilayer switching), 12
DiffServ
example QoS configuration, 417–422
mapping CoS values to internal DSCP
values, 407
mapping IP Precedence values to internal
DSCP values, 408
marking, 389
packet classification, 388
packet scheduling, 390
policers, 389
policies
defining, 409–413
trust boundaries, 389
DiffServ QoS model, 383
congestion avoidance, 391
tail drops, 391
WRED, 392–393
Layer 2 classification, 384
Layer 3 classification, 384–385
class selector bits, 386
drop precedence, 386–387
dir command, 95
Disabled state (STP), 225
displaying
CDP information, 98
STP information, 255
VTP status, 178

distribution, 22, 24
distribution layer, 21
collapsed core bl, 42
distribution layer switches, 23–24
DSCP
internal DSCP value, 387
Layer 3 QoS classification, 384–385
class selector bits, 386
drop precedence, 386–387
DTP (Dynamic Trunking Protocol), 150
dual core blocks, 43–45
dual-homing, 46
dynamic VLANs, 144

E

**EAPOL (Extensible Authentication Protocol
over LANs)**
configuring, 461–463
edge ports (RSTP), 286
EF (Expedited Forwarding), 386
egress queueing, 390
example configuration, 421–422
mapping packet to egress queues, 415–416
election process of Designated Ports, 223–224
election process of HSRP routers, 332–333
election process of Root Bridges, 218–219
election process of Root Ports, 220–222
enable mode (CatOS), 88
enabling
GLBP, 340
QoS, 405
tail drop operation, 416
VTP pruning, 182
WRED, 416
end-to-end VLANs
deploying, 145
enterprise composite network model, 37
enterprise edge block, 47
EoMPLS (Ethernet over MPLS), 153, 157–158
erase flash command, 95
EtherChannel, 193
bundled ports, 194
configuring, 198
LACP, 198
configuring, 199–200

load balancing
  configuring, 195–197
PAgP, 197–198
  configuring, 199
traffic distribution, 194–195
troubleshooting, 200–203
XOR operation, 194
Ethernet
10 Gigabit Ethernet, 118–119
10 Mbps Ethernet, 112–113
Fast Ethernet, 114
  full-duplex, 115–116
Gigabit Ethernet, 117–118
LRE, 113–114
metro Ethernet, 119
switch block connections, 121
  Gigabit Ethernet port cables, 121–122
example of TCAM tables, 73
example QoS configuration, 417–418
egress queueing, 421–422
traffic classification, 419–420
trust, 418–419

F

fallback bridging, 69, 317
verifying configuration, 321
Fast Ethernet, 114
full-duplex, 115–116
FDDI (Fiber Distributed Data Interface), 10
FIB (Forwarding Information Base), 67, 314–315
Fiber Distributed Data Interface (FDDI), 10
fields
of Configuration BPDUs, 218
file management
on switches, 92
  configuration files, 93–94
  image files, 92–93
  moving files, 94–95
Flash file systems, 92
flooding
VTP pruning, 180, 182
format flash command, 95
forward, 11
Forward Delay timer (STP), 227, 251

forwarding
frames
  Layer 2 switching, 10
  Layer 3 switching, 11
packets
  Layer 3 routing, 10
  Layer 4 switching, 12
forwarding frames
decision processes, 63, 66
forwarding packets
MLS decision processes, 67, 69
Forwarding state (STP), 225
frames
BPDUs
  TCN BPDUs, 228
forwarding through Layer switches, 63, 66
Layer 2 PDUs, 155
Layer 2 switching, 10
Layer 3 switching, 11
multicast, 14
tagging, 146
  IEEE 802.1Q, 148–149
  internal tagging, 149
  ISL, 148
unknown unicast, 214
frames BPDUs
Configuration BPDUs, 217–218
full-duplex Fast Ethernet, 115–116
functionality
switching, 9–12

G

gateway addresses
redundancy, 331
  GLBP, 337–340
  HSRP, 332–336
  VRRP, 336–337
GBIC (Gigabit Interface Converter), 118
GBICs
Gigabit Ethernet media, 122
General Queries (IGMPv2), 361
Get Nearest Server (GNS), 13
Gigabit Ethernet, 117–118
port cables, 121–122

GLBP
AVF, 339
AVG, 338
enabling, 340
load balancing, 340
GLBP (Gateway Load Balancing Protocol), 337–338
global synchronization, 391
GNS (Get Nearest Server), 13
Group-Specific Queries (IGMPv2), 361

H

hardware-based bridging, 10
Hello Timer (STP), 227, 251
hierarchical network design, 19
access layer, 20
core layer, 21
devices, 21–22, 25, 28
access layer switches, 22–23
core layer switches, 24
distribution layer switches, 23–24
distribution layer, 21
higher, 24
host mode (switch ports), 475
host names
changing, 88
HSRP
gateway addressing, 334
load balancing, 335–336
router election process, 332–333
HSRP (Hot Standby Router Protocol), 332

I

identifying
VLAN frames, 146
IEEE 802.1Q, 148–149
ISL, 148
identifying switch ports, 124
IEEE 802.1D
See STP (Spanning Tree Protocol)
IEEE 802.1Q, 148–149, 384
tunneling, 153–155
configuring, 155
IEEE 802.1x
configuring, 461–463
IEEE 802.3
See Ethernet

IGMP, 360
IGMP snooping, 367–368
image files
switches, 92
naming conventions, 93
indirect failures on STP, 251
individual, 39
ingress queueing, 388
inline power for Cisco IP Phones, 435–436
configuring, 437
verifying, 443
interface configuration mode (CatOS), 88
internal DSCP, 387
internal tagging, 149
inter-switch communication
with CDP, 91
interVLAN routing
configuring, 310
interfaces, 310
Layer 2 mode
configuring, 310
Layer 3 mode
configuring, 311
SVI ports
configuring, 312
verifying, 318
IntServ QoS model, 382–383
IP multicast, 357
addressing, 358
reserved addresses, 358
IGMP, 360
multicast trees, 359
PIM, 361
Dense Mode, 362
Sparse Mode, 363
Sparse-Dense Mode, 365
verifying multicast routing, 369
Version 1, 366
Version 2, 367
RPF, 360
switching
CGMP, 368–369
IGMP snooping, 367–368
verifying multicast switching, 369
IP Precedence
mapping to internal DSCP values, 408
IP Telephony
Cisco IP Phones
inline power, 435–437

trunking modes, 438
verifying inline power, 443
QoS, 440
queuing mechanisms, 442
trust, configuring, 441
verifying, 444–447
voice packet classification, 442
voice VLANs, 437
configuring, 438, 440
verifying, 443–444
ISL (Inter-Switch Link), 148, 384
isolated VLANs, 475
IST (Internal Spanning Tree), 293
IST instances (MST), 293–294

J–L

jitter, 381

LACP (Link Aggregation Control Protocol), 198
configuring, 199–200
LAN segmentation model, 14–15, 17
LANs
campus network models, 12
shared network model, 13–14
Ethernet, 112–113
10 Gigabit Ethernet, 118–119
Fast Ethernet, 114–116
Gigabit Ethernet, 117–118
LRE, 113–114
metro Ethernet, 119
latency, 381
Layer 2 protocol tunnels, 155–156
configuring, 156
Layer 2 QoS classification, 384
Layer 2 switching, 10, 61
CAM table
troubleshooting, 75–76
CAM tables, 70
frame processing, 63, 66
TCAM table, 71
example, 73
port operation, 74
structure, 71–72
troubleshooting, 76
transparent bridging, 61, 63

Layer 3 QoS classification, 384–385
class selector bits, 386
drop precedence, 386–387
Layer 3 routing, 10
Layer 3 switching, 11
Layer 4 switching, 12
layers, 9–12
access
switches, 23
distribution, 21
Learning state (STP), 225
Leave Group messages (IGMPv2), 361
links
EtherChannel, 193
Listening state (STP), 225
load balancing
GLBP, 337–338, 340
AVF, 339
AVG, 338
SLB, 343
configuring, 344–345
verifying configuration, 346
with HSRP, 335–336
local SPAN
configuring, 481–482, 484
local VLANs
deploying, 145
location of Root Bridge
selecting, 243–244, 246
login passwords
user EXEC mode
configuring, 89
loop avoidance
STP
BPDU Guard, 268–269
BPDU skew detection, 270
loop guard, 271
protecting against sudden BPDU loss, 269
Root Guard, 267–268
troubleshooting, 273
UDLD, 271–273
loop guard, 271
loss, 381
LRE (Long Reach Ethernet), 113–114

M

management domains
  configuring, 175
  viewing status, 178
  VTP, 171
  VTP advertisement process, 172–173
    subset advertisements, 174
    summary advertisements, 173
management VLAN
  assigning IP address, 90–91
manipulating
  switch configuration files, 95
mapping
  CoS values to internal DSCP values, 407
  IP Precedence values to internal DSCP
    values, 408
**mapping internal DSCP values to CoS values,
  414–415**
mapping packets to egress queues, 415–416
**mapping promiscuous mode ports to VLANs,
  478**
marking
  defining as QoS policy, 412
marking packets, 389
matching conditions for VACLs
  defining, 473–474
MaxAge Timer (STP), 227, 251
Membership Report messages, 360
messages
  BPDU skew detection, 270
  IGMP Membership Report, 360
metro Ethernet, 119
microflow policers, 390
MLS
  CAM table, 70
    troubleshooting, 75–76
  CEF, 312
    adjacency table, 315–316
    configuring, 316
    fallback bridging, 317
    FIB, 314–315
    packet rewrites, 316
    verifying, 319, 321

interVLAN routing
    configuring, 310–312
    interfaces, 310
    verifying, 318
  TCAM table, 71
    example, 73
    port operation, 74
    structure, 71–72
    troubleshooting, 76
MLS, *See* **multilayer switching (MLS)**
models
  campus networks, 12
modifying STP timers, 250–251
modular network design, 37
  core blocks, 41–42
    collapsed core, 42–43
    dual core, 43–45
  switch blocks, 38–39
    sizing, 39–41
monitoring switch ports with SPAN, 480
  local SPAN, 481–482, 484
  RSPAN, 484–486
  VSPAN, 482–484
moving
  Catalyst switch files, 94–95
MPLS
  EoMPLS tunnels, 157–158
MSFC (Multilayer Switch Feature Card), 24
MST (Multiple Spanning Tree), 291–292
  configuring, 295–296
  IST instances, 293–294
  MST instances, 294–295
  regions, 292–293
MST instances (MST), 294–295
multicast, 357
  PIM, 361
    Dense Mode, 362
    Sparse Mode, 363
    Sparse-Dense Mode, 365
    verifying multicast routing, 369
    Version 1, 366
    Version 2, 367
  routing
    IGMP, 360
    multicast trees, 359
    RPF, 360

switching
> CGMP, *368–369*
> IGMP snooping, *367–368*
> verifying multicast switching, 369

multicast addressing, 358
> OUI values, 358
> reserved addresses, 358

multicast frames, 14

multicast groups, 357

multicast traffic, 14

multicast trees, 359

Multilayer Switch Feature Card (MSFC), 24

multilayer switching (MLS), 12, 66
> redundancy
> > SLB, *343–345*
> router redundancy, 331
> > GLBP, *337–340*
> > HSRP, *332–336*
> > VRRP, *336–337*
> > packet processing, *67*
> > packet processing exceptions, *69*

N

naming conventions
> of switch image files, 93

NBAR (Network-Based Application Recognition), 410

negotiation protocols (EtherChannel)
> LACP, 198
> PAgP, 197–198

nested IEEE 802.1Q trunks, 153

NetFlow LAN switching, 66

NetFlow switching, 313

network management block, 46–47

network traffic models, 17–18

networks, 24
> campus
> > models, *12*
> > modular designs, *37*
> distribution layer, 21
> swtiching functionality, 9–12

Normal mode (UDLD), 272

NVRAM
> startup configuration, 89

O–P

operating systems, 87–88
> CatOS
> > troubleshooting, *96–98*

OUI (Organizationally Unique Identifier) values, 358

packet filtering
> VACLs
> > configuring, *473–474*

packet forwarding, 331

packet rewrites, 316

packets
> classification, 388
> congestion avoidance, 391
> > tail drops, *391*
> > WRED, *392–393*
> ingress queueing, 388
> Layer 3 routing, 10
> Layer 4 switching, 12
> mapping to egress queues, 415–416
> processing through multilayer switches, 67, 69
> queuing, 442
> scheduling, 390

PAgP (Port Aggregation Protocol), 197–198
> configuring, 199

passwords
> CatOS, 89
> > recovering, *90*

Path Cost, 220–221

PDU (protocol data unit), 9, 155

permitting
> untrusted information on QoS, 407

PIM (Protocol Independent Multicast), 361
> Dense Mode, 362
> > configuring, *362*
> Sparse Mode, 363
> Sparse-Dense Mode, 365
> verifying multicast routing
> > verifying
> > > PIM multicast routing, 369
> Version 1, 366
> Version 2, 367

PMD (Physical Media Dependent) interfaces, 118

point-to-point ports (RSTP), 286

policers, 389

policing
defining as QoS policy, 412–413

port compatibility errors (EtherChannel)
troubleshooting, 202

Port ID (STP)
tuning, 250

port mode
configuring, 125

port operation of TCAM tables, 74

port security, 460–461

port speed
configuring, 124

port states
RSTP, 284
STP, 225–226

port-based authentication
configuring, 461–463

port-based membership
static VLANs, 142

PortFast, 252

predictable network model, 19

preparing for exam
multicast, 503
QoS in a switched network, 504–505
scenarios, 497
advanced STP, 500–501
router redundancy with HSRP and
GLBP, 501
traditional STP, 500
trunking and DTP, 497
VLANs, trunking, and VTP, 499
securing access and managing traffic in as
switched network, 505

preventing
collisions, 15

preventing routing loops
with RSTP
BPDUs, 285
configuring, 290
convergence, 285–286
port behavior, 283–284
port states, 284
synchronization, 287
topology changes, 288–289

preventing routing loops with STP
redundant link convergence, 252
BackboneFast, 254–255
PortFast, 252
UplinkFast, 253
Root Bridges
configuring, 246–248
placement, 243–244, 246
STP timers, modifying, 250–251
tuning Port ID, 250
tuning Root Path Cost, 248–249

primary VLANs, 475

privileged EXEC mode (CatOS), 88

process switching, 69

promiscuous mode (switch ports), 475
mapping to VLANs, 478

protecting against sudden BPDU loss, 269

protocol data unit (PDU), 9

pruning (VTP), 179–180
enabling, 182

PVLANs (private VLANs), 474–475
associating secondary VLANs to primary
VLANs, 479
configuring, 477–479

PVST (Per-VLAN STP), 229

PVST+ (Per-VLAN Spanning Tree Plus), 230

Q

Q-in-Q tunnels, 153

QoS, 440
best effort, 382
congestion avoidance, 391
mapping internal DSCP values to CoS
values, 414–415
mapping packets to egress queues,
415–416
tail drop, 391, 416
WRED, 392–393, 416–417
CoS
mapping to internal DSCP values, 407
DiffServ, 383
Layer 2 classification, 384
Layer 3 classification, 384–387

egress queueing
    example configuration, 421–422
egress scheduling
    tuning, 414
enabling, 405
example configuration, 417–418
ingress queueing, 388
IntServ, 382–383
IP Precedence
    mapping to internal DSCP values, 408
marking, 389
packet classification, 388
packet scheduling, 390
policers, 389
policies
    defining, 409–413
queuing mechanisms, 442
switch port queues, 393–395
traffic classification
    example configuration, 419–420
troubleshooting, 422–424
trust
    configuring, 441
    example configuration, 418–419
trust boundaries, 389
trusts
    applying, 406
untrusted information
    permitting, 407
verifying, 444–447
verifying operation, 422, 424
voice packet classification, 442
queueing
    ingress, 388
    switch port queues, 393–395
queuing, 442
    egress scheduling, 414

R

recovering
    passwords
        on CatOS switches, 90
recovering from switch port error conditions, 126

redundancy
    gateway addresses, 331
    of EtherChannel, 193
    of gateway addresses
        GLBP, 337–340
        HSRP, 332–336
        VRRP, 336–337
    SLB, 343
        configuring, 344–345
    verifying configuration, 346
redundant link convergence (STP), 252
    BackboneFast, 254–255
    PortFast, 252
    UplinkFast, 253–254
regions
    MST, 292–293
relieving network congestion, 13
remote access, 90–91
reserved IP multicast addresses, 358
restricting switch access
    accounting, 459
    authentication, 455–457
    authorization, 457–458
Root Bridge
    configuring, 246–248
    election procedure, 218–219
    placement of, 243–244, 246
Root Guard, 267–268
Root Path Cost (STP), 220
    tie conditions, 223
    tuning, 248–249
root ports (RSTP), 286
    election procedure, 220–222
route cache switching, 313
router redundancy
    verifying configuration, 346
routing
    IP multicast
        IGMP, 360
        RPF, 360
    Layer 3, 10
    multicast
        multicast trees, 359
    See also interVLAN routing

routing loops

preventing with STP

modifying STP timers, 250–251

redundant link convergence, 252–255

Root Bridge configuration, 246–248

Root Bridge placement, 243–244, 246

tuning Port ID, 250

tuning Root Path Cost, 248–249

RP (Rendezvous Point), 363

auto-RP process, 365

RPF, 360

RSPAN

configuring, 484–486

RSTP

BPDUs, 285

configuring, 290

convergence, 285–286

port behavior, 283–284

port states, 284

synchronization, 287

topology changes, 288–289

rules

80/20, 18

S

SAP (Service Advertisement Protocol), 13

scaling

Layer 2 switching, 10

scenarios, 497

advanced STP, 500–501

multicast, 503

QoS in a switched network, 504–505

router redundancy with HSRP and GLBP, 501

securing access and managing traffic in as switched network, 505

traditional STP, 500

trunking and DTP, 497

VLANs, trunking, and VTP, 499

scheduling

egress scheduling

tuning, 414

scheduling packets, 390

secondary VLANs, 475

associating to a primary VLANs, 479

security

CatOS

passwords, 89–90

segmentation, 11

selecting

Designated Ports (STP), 223–224

Root Ports (STP), 220–222

server farm blocks, 46

server mode (VTP), 171

configuring, 176

server provider edge block, 47

Service Advertisement Protocol (SAP), 13

shared network model, 13–14

show commands

troubleshooting CatOS, 96–97

show etherchannel port-channel command, 196

show vtp status command, 178

sizing

dual core blocks, 45

sizing switch blocks, 39–41

SLB (Server Load Balancing), 343

configuring, 344–345

SPAN (Switched Port Analyzer), 480

deleting sessions, 483

local SPAN, 481–482, 484

RSPAN, 484–486

VSPAN, 482–484

Spanning-Tree Protocol, 39

Sparse Mode (PIM), 363

Sparse-Dense Mode (PIM), 365

startup configuration, 89

static VLANs, 142

configuring, 143

store-and-forward switching, 61

STP (Spanning Tree Protocol)

Blocking state, 225

BPDU Guard, 268–269

BPDUs

Configuration BPDUs, 217–218

protecting against sudden loss, 269

skew detection, 270

TCN BPDUs, 228

bridging loop prevention, 217

CST, 229

Designated Ports
    election procedure, 223–224
Disabled state, 225
displaying information, 255
Forwarding state, 225
Learning state, 225
Listening state, 225
loop guard, 271
MST, 291–292
    configuring, 295–296
    IST instances, 293–294
    MST instances, 294–295
    regions, 292–293
Path Cost, 221
Port ID
    tuning, 250
PVST, 229
PVST+, 230
redundant link convergence, 252
    BackboneFast, 254 255
    PortFast, 252
    UplinkFast, 253
Root Bridge
    configuring, 246–248
    election procedure, 218–219
    placement, 243–244, 246
Root Guard, 267–268
Root Path Cost
    tuning, 248–249
Root Ports
    election procedure, 220–222
timers, 227
    modifying, 250–251
troubleshooting, 255, 273
UDLD, 271–273
structure of TCAM tables, 71–72
subset advertisements, 174
summary advertisements, 173
superior BPDUs, 268
support, 39
SVI ports
configuring, 312
SVIs (switched virtual interfaces), 479
switch, 41
switch block connections
console port, 120
Ethernet port cables, 121
Gigabit Ethernet port cables, 121–122

switch blocks, 38–39
sizing, 39–41
switch port aggregation
EtherChannel, 193
switch port queues, 393–395
switch ports
configuring, 123
connectivity
    troubleshooting, 126–127
error conditions, detecting, 125
error conditions, recovering from, 126
identifying, 124
port mode
    configuring, 125
SPAN, 480
    local SPAN, 481–482, 484
    RSPAN, 484–486
    VSPAN, 482–484
speed
    configuring, 124
switches
access layer, 22–23
Catalyst, 25
CatOS
    passwords, 89–90
CDP
    viewing information, 98
core layer, 24
distribution layer, 23–24
file management, 92
    configuration files, 93–94
    image files, 92–93
    moving files, 94–95
host names
    changing, 88
inter-switch communication, 91
operating systems, 87–88
port security, 460–461
remote access, 90–91
switching
CAM, 70
CAM table
    troubleshooting, 75–76
frame processing, 63, 66
functionality, 9–12
Layer 2, 10
Layer 3, 11
Layer 4, 12

MLS (multilayer switching), 12, 66
packet processing, 67, 69
multicast traffic
CGMP, 368–369
IGMP snooping, 367–368
store-and-forward, 61
TCAM tables, 71
example, 73
port operations, 74
structure, 71–72
troubleshooting, 76
transparent bridging, 61, 63
trunks
VTP, 171–174
synchronization
RSTP, 287
synchronization problem (VTP), 173

T

tagging, 146
IEEE 802.1Q, 148–149
ISL, 148
tail drops, 391
enabling, 416
TCAM (Ternary Content Addressable Memory), 65, 473
TCAM tables, 71
example of, 73
port operations, 74
structure of, 71–72
troubleshooting, 76
TCN BPDUs, 228
Telnet
remote access, 90–91
these, 23
throttling adjacencies, 316
tie conditions of Root Path Cost, 223
timers (STP), 227
modifying, 250–251
topology changes
detecting with RSTP, 288–289
ToS (type of service), 384
traffic
core blocks, 42, 44
flooding
VTP pruning, 180, 182
mulitcast, 14

traffic classification
defining as QoS policy, 409–410
example configuration, 419–420
transparent bridges
redundancy, 215
versus Ethernet switches, 213–214
transparent bridging, 61, 63
transparent mode (VTP), 172
configuring, 176
transported, 17
troubleshooting
CAM tables, 75–76
CatOS
debug commands, 97–98
show commands, 96–97
EtherChannel, 200–203
QoS, 422–424
QoS operation, 422, 424
STP, 255, 273
switch port error conditions, 125–126
switch ports
connectivity, 126–127
TCAM tables, 76
trunks, 159, 161
VLANs, 159, 161
VTP, 183
trunking
VTP
advertisements, 172–173
client mode, 172
configuring client mode, 176
configuring management domains, 175
configuring server mode, 176
configuring transparent mode, 176
configuring version, 177–178
management domains, 171
pruning, 179–180, 182
server mode, 171
subset advertisements, 174
summary advertisements, 173
transparent mode, 172
troubleshooting, 183
viewing status, 178
trunks, 146
configuring, 150–152
DTP, 150
troubleshooting, 159, 161

trust boundaries, 389
trusts
> applying to QoS, 406
> defining as QoS policy, 412

tuning
> egress scheduling, 414

tunneling
> 802.1Q, 153–155
>> *configuring, 155*
> EoMPLS, 157–158
> Layer 2 protocol tunneling, 155–156
>> *configuring, 156*

U

UDLD (unidirectional link detection), 271–273
unicast traffic, 357
unknown unicast flooding, 63
unknown unicast frames, 179, 214
unnecessary, 14
untrusted information
> permitting on interfaces, 407

UplinkFast, 253–254
used, 13
user authentication
> enabling on Catalyst switches, 455–457

user EXEC mode, 88
> login passwords
>> *configuring, 89*

V

VACLs
> configuring, 473–474
> matching conditions
>> *defining, 473–474*

verifying
> fallback bridging, 321
> inline power for Cisco IP Phones, 443
> MLS
>> *CEF, 319, 321*
>> *interVLAN routing, 318*
> multicast switching, 369
> QoS, 444–447
> QoS operation, 422, 424
> redundancy, 346
> voice VLANs, 443–444

viewing
> CDP information, 98
> STP information, 255
> VTP status, 178

virtual, 15
VLANs, 141
> deploying, 144
> dynamic VLANs, 144
> end-to-end
>> *deploying, 145*
> interVLAN routing
>> *configuring, 310–312*
>> *interfaces, 310*
>> *verifying, 318*
> local
>> *deploying, 145*
> management VLAN
>> *IP address assignment, 90–91*
> MST, 291–292
>> *configuring, 295–296*
>> *IST instances, 293–294*
>> *MST instances, 294–295*
>> *regions, 292–293*
> PVLANs
>> *associating secondary VLANs to primary VLANs, 479*
>> *configuring, 477–479*
> PVST, 229
> SPAN, 480
>> *deleting sessions, 483*
>> *local SPAN, 481–482, 484*
>> *RSPAN, 484–486*
>> *VSPAN, 482–484*
> static VLANs, 142
>> *configuring, 143*
> tagging, 146
>> *IEEE 802.1Q, 148–149*
>> *ISL, 148*
> troubleshooting, 159, 161
> trunks, 146
>> *configuring, 150–152*
>> *DTP, 150*
> tunneling
>> *802.1Q, 153–155*
>> *EoMPLS, 157–158*
>> *Layer 2, 155–156*
> voice VLANs, 437
>> *configuring, 438, 440*
>> *verifying, 443–444*
> See also VACLs
> *See also PVLANs, 474–475*

voice VLANs, 437
  configuring, 438, 440
  verifying, 443–444
VoIP
  Cisco IP Phones
    inline power, 435–437
    verifying inline power, 443
  QoS, 440
    queuing mechanisms, 442
    trust, configuring, 441
    verifying, 444–447
    voice packet classification, 442
  voice VLANs, 437
    configuring, 438, 440
    verifying, 443–444
VRRP (Virtual Router Redundancy Protocol), 336–337
VSPAN
  configuring, 482–484
VTP
  advertisements, 172–173
    subset advertisements, 174
    summary advertisements, 173
  client mode, 172
    configuring, 176
  management domains, 171
    configuring, 175
    viewing status, 178
  pruning, 179–180, 182
  server mode, 171
    configuring, 176
  transparent mode, 172
    configuring, 176
  troubleshooting, 183
  version
    configuring, 177–178

VTP synchronization problem, 173

W–X

workgroups, 18
WRED, 392–393
  enabling, 416
  thresholds
    configuring, 416–417
WRR (Weighted Round Robin) queueing
  WRR, 390
XDI
  See CatOS
XOR (exclusive-OR) operation, 194

Switching

Cisco LAN Switching
ISBN: 1-57870-094-9

CCIE Professional Development: Cisco LAN Switching is essential for preparation for the CCIE Routing and Switching exam track. As well as CCIE preparation, this comprehensive volume provides readers with an in-depth analysis of Cisco LAN Switching technologies, architectures and deployments. *CCIE Professional Development: Cisco LAN Switching* discusses product operational details, hardware options, configuration fundamentals, spanning tree, source-route bridging, multilayer switching, and other technology areas related to the Catalyst series switches. The book presents these issues at advanced levels, providing overviews of both LAN technologies and Cisco switching hardware, and covering Catalyst network design essentials not found anywhere else. CCIE candidates will gain exam preparation through the following book elements: chapter-opening overviews of objectives; scenarios that highlight real-world issues; configuration examples and case studies that help readers put the solutions presented to use; and review questions and exercises.

Cisco Field Manual: Catalyst Switch Configuration
ISBN: 1-58705-043-9

This field reference provides novice to experienced network engineers with an aid to configuring Cisco Catalyst switches during hands-on installation or troubleshooting sessions. Cisco offers two distinct operating systems in the Catalyst switch product line (the Catalyst OS COS and the traditional IOS). This book is based on the most current versions, with both COS and IOS commands appearing side-by-side throughout. *Cisco Field Manual: Catalyst Switch Configuration* is organized by like features, with sections marked by shaded tabs for quick reference. Information on each feature is presented in a concise format. This book begins with a review of how switching, then includes a comprehensive guide to configuration starting with basic design, and moves on to discuss Layer 2 and 3 configuration. Coverage then is provided on fundamental switching topics, like VLANs, multi-layer switching, multicast, accelerated server load balancing, access control, switch management, quality of service (QoS), and switching in a voice network.

Learning is serious buisiness. **Invest wisely.**

Switching

Cisco Catalyst QoS: Quality of Service in Campus Networks

ISBN: 1-58705-120-6

Cisco Catalyst QoS is the first book to concentrate exclusively on the application of QoS in the campus environment. This practical guide provides you with insight into the operation of QoS on the most popular and widely deployed LAN devices: the Cisco Catalyst family of switches. Leveraging the authors' extensive expertise at Cisco in the support of Cisco Catalyst switches and QoS deployment, the book presents QoS from the campus LAN perspective. It explains why QoS is essential in this environment in order to achieve a more deterministic behavior for traffic when implementing voice, video, or other delay-sensitive applications. Through architectural overviews, configuration examples, real-world deployment case studies, and summaries of common pitfalls, you will understand how QoS operates, the different components involved in making QoS possible, and how QoS can be implemented on the various Cisco Catalyst platforms to enable truly successful end-to-end QoS applications.

CCNP

CCNP Flash Cards and Exam Practice Pack
ISBN: 1-58720-091-0

Available October 2003

Prepare for all four NEW CCNP exams with over 2,200 flash cards, practice test questions and quick reference sheets

- Check topic comprehension with over 1200 Flash Cards in physical cards that are also downloadable to PC, Palm OS, and Pocket PC.

- Practice for exams with an electronic testing engine with over 800 questions covering all four exams

- Review exam topics with Quick Reference cards organized by exam

- Build confidence with tools from the only Cisco authorized publisher

*The CCNP Flash Card Practice Pack (CCNP Self-Study)*provides final-stage preparation tools for all of the new CCNP exams that are due to be released by Cisco Systems in June 2003. These exams, 642-801 BSCI, 642-811 BCMSN, 642-821 BCRAN, and 642-831 CIT, have all been re-written with new topical coverage updated to teach networking professionals all they need to know to manage their networks. All of the elements of this title have been created to provide comprehensive coverage of all the new topics in all four of the exams.

CCNP Certification Library, Third Edition
ISBN: 1-58720-104-6

Available December 2003

Cisco CCNP Certification Library, Third Edition, is a comprehensive review and practice package for the four Cisco Certified Network Professional (CCNP) exams: BSCI (642-801), BCMSN (642-811), BCRAN (642-821), and CIT (642-821). The four books contained in this value-priced package, *CCNP BSCI Exam Certification Guide, CCNP BCMSN Exam Certification Guide, CCNP BCRAN Exam Certification Guide,* and *CCNP CIT Exam Certification Guide,* present complete reviews and ample opportunity to test your knowledge of all the topics found on the new CCNP exams.

Learning is serious buisiness.   **Invest wisely.**

Cisco Press

Learning is serious business.

Invest wisely.

Switching

CCNP Practical Studies: Switching

ISBN: 1-58720-060-0

Available October 2003

CCNP Practical Studies: Switching provides networkers and CCNP candidates with an in-depth, hands-on experience in configuring Cisco Catalyst switches. This practical guide shows intermediate level networkers how to apply the theoretical knowledge they have gained through CCNP Coursework and exam preparation in a lab setting. Configuration labs performed within this book will cover all technologies tested upon in Switching exam #640-604, as well as a number of real world scenarios that will test the users overall understanding of multilayer switching. In addition to applicable labs this book also provides some general information on various switching technologies as well as tips, tricks, shortcuts, and caveats for deploying Cisco switching gear in production environments. Part of the Practical Studies series from the Cisco Press, this book provides self-study based hands-on experience. As such, it can be used in conjunction with other Cisco Press titles as well as being an excellent companion to instructor led training from a Cisco Learning Partner. This book is intended for CCNP candidates who are working on the BCMSN courseware and wish to evaluate their knowledge level or supplement existing material. A secondary audience for this book will be those who are implementing Cisco switched solutions and need configuration examples and/or a practical guide.

Learning is serious buisiness.   **Invest wisely.**

Cisco Press Security

CCNP BSCI Exam Certification Guide

ISBN: 1-58720-085-6

Available December 2003

CCNP BSCI Exam Certification Guide (CCNP Self-Study) is a revised edition of the all-time best-selling CCNP BSCI/CCNP Routing title ever! With updated technology and testing content, this book provides exceptional tutorial learning and exam preparation on advanced routing techniques and practices. It matches all the objectives of the new 642-801 BSCI exam launched in April! Written in smaller, easier to absorb chapters, this book breaks down larger concepts into manageable blocks of learning. This, combined with other new learning elements and a complete re-writing of the material, make it even easier to comprehend and retain the large amount of learning required for this essential building block of learning for a networker. As part of the CCNP, CCDP, and CCIP certifications, routing is an important building block that all networking professionals must master. This book teaches and prepares candidates for this challenging professional-level exam with chapter quizzes, foundation reviews, in-depth topical learning materials, real-world case studies, and, of course, the 200-plus question electronic testing engine on the CD-ROM included in the back of the book. This testing engine even includes simulation-based questions, just like on the actual exam. New coverage includes more on IS-IS (Intermediate System to Intermediate System), NAT (Network Address Translation), and a solid introduction to IPv6.

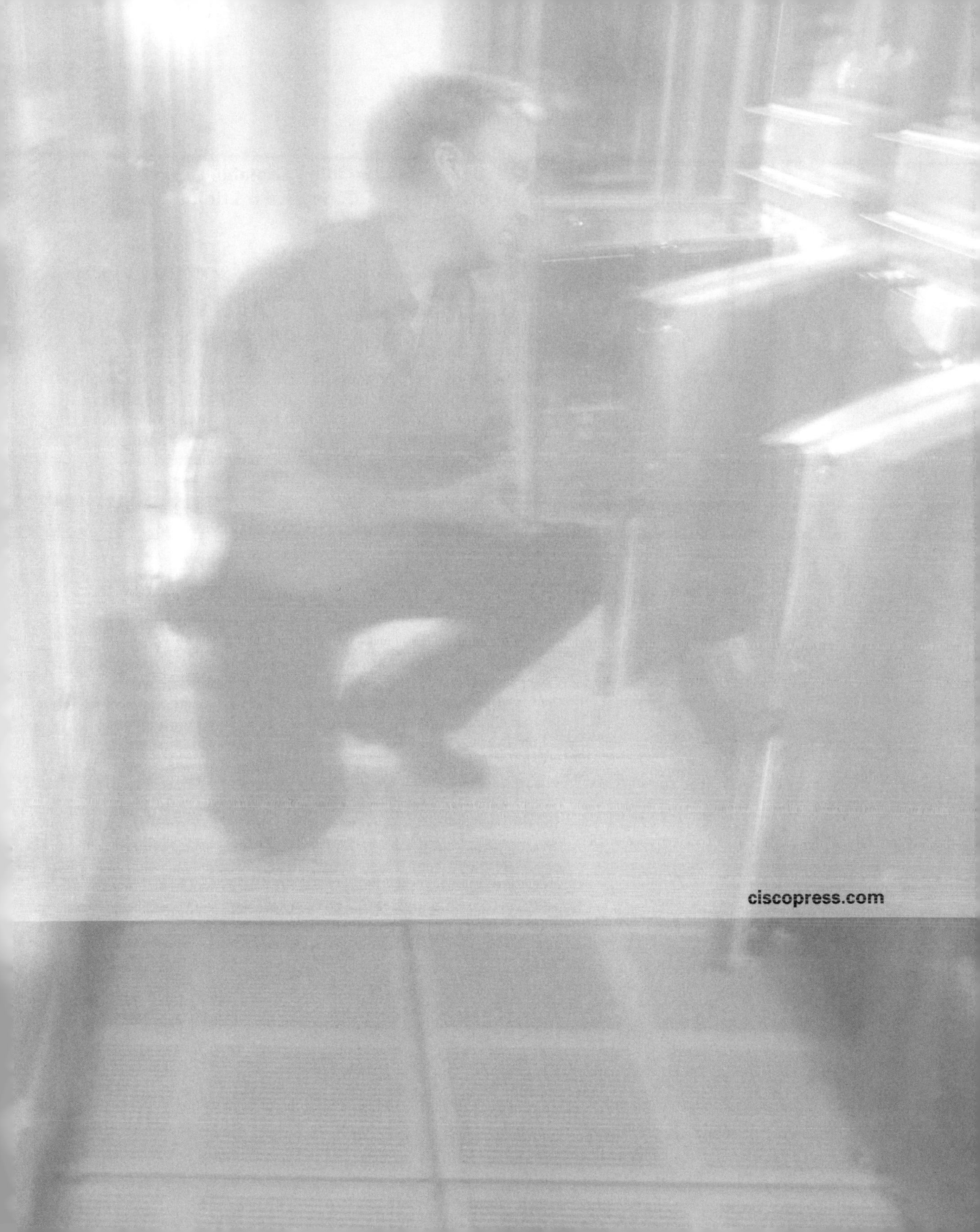
ciscopress.com

Cisco Press Security

CCNP Self-Study: Building Scalable Cisco Internetworks (BSCI), Second Edition
ISBN: 1-58705-146-X

Available April 2004

As part of the Cisco Press Self-Study series, *CCNP Self-Study: Building Scalable Cisco Internetworks (BSCI)*, Second Edition provides early and comprehensive foundation learning for the CCNP BSCI exam. This revision to the popular first edition is fully updated to include complete coverage of all important routing topics, including advanced IP addressing, routing principles, manipulating routing updates, and EIGRP, OSPF, IS-IS, and BGP configuration. In addition to the coverage of exam topics, supplemental appendices include helpful job aids, password recovery advice, and router command summaries.

CCNP Practical Studies: Routing
ISBN: 1-58720-054-6

Built upon the concepts central to the Routing portion of the CCNP certification, this practical guide shows beginning to advanced networkers how to apply the theoretical knowledge they have gained through CCNP coursework and exam preparation. The scenarios guide users through labs that can be practiced on remote-accessible networking labs, networking simulation programs or practice labs made of actual equipment. Each chapter addresses a section of the CCNP-Routing exam. For those lacking lab equipment, the book highlights the steps needed to accomplish various crucial tasks, providing the reader with concrete examples for the challenges faced in real-world configuration. In structure, this book closely follows the Building Scalable Cisco Networks course, to capitalize on existing successful topic structure and to leverage its usefulness as a supplement to a course or self-study regimen. A comprehensive reference guide that directs readers where they can purchase new and used Cisco® equipment for use in these labs is included

ciscopress.com

Learning is serious buisiness.   **Invest wisely.**

CCNP BCRAN

CCNP BCRAN Exam Certification Guide
ISBN: 1-58720-084-8

Available January 2004

- Learn the remote access design and management topics for the NEW Cisco CCNP 642-821 BCRAN exam with the only official preparation book.

- Practice with over 200 test questions including simulation based questions on the enclosed CD-ROM.

- Prepare for the CCNP and CCDP BCRAN exam with proven learning tools from the number 1 selling Exam Certification Guide Series from Cisco Press. *CCNP BCRAN Exam Certification Guide*, Second Edition is a comprehensive study tool for preparing for the new CCNP 642-821 BCRAN exam, due to be released in June 2003. This book is the second edition of the best-selling preparation title for the CCNP BCRAN exam from Cisco Press, also authored by Morgan and Dennis. Comprehensive coverage of all exam topics ensures readers will arrive at a complete understanding of what they need to master to succeed on the exam. This book follows a logical organization of the CCNP Remote Access exam objectives, and is written in a modular, small-chapter format to break down the elements to be learned into easier to absorb parts. It also contains the other valuable learning elements of an Exam Certification Guide from Cisco Press that ensure concept comprehension and retention. These include pre- and post-chapter quizzes, foundational review sections, scenario-based exercises and a CD-ROM testing engine with over 200 questions including simulation-based questions like on the actual exam. In addition to technologies like ISDN, DDR (Dial-on-Demand Routing), Frame Relay, NAT (Network Address Translation), AAA (Authentication, Authorization, Accounting) and other related technologies covered in the first edition, this edition will also contain an introduction to QoS (Quality of Service), VPN (Virtual Private Networks), VPDN (Virtual Private Dial-up Networks), and DSL (Digital Subscriber Line) technologies.

CCNP Self-Study: Building Cisco Remote Access Networks

ISBN: 1-58705-148-6

Available February 2004

As part of the Cisco Press Self-Study series, *CCNP Self-Study: Building Cisco Remote Access Networks (BCRAN)* provides early and comprehensive foundation learning for the CCNP BCRAN exam. This revision to the popular first edition is fully updated to include complete coverage of all important remote access topics, including WAN technologies/components; scalable access control with AAA; modem connections, configuration, and support; PPP configuration and network access control with PAP and CHAP; enhancing remote connectivity with ISDN and DDR; DDR interface optimization; establishing dedicated Frame Relay connections and controlling traffic flow; configuring dial backup and routing with the load backup feature; managing network performance with queuing and compression; scaling IP addresses with NAT; using cable and DSL broadband to access central sites; and using VPNs to secure remote access connections.

CCNP Practical Studies: Remote Access

ISBN: 1-58720-073-2

Available December 2003

Gain hands-on experience of CCNP Remote Access topics with lab scenarios for the new 642-821 BCRAN exam

- Prepare for the CCNP 642-821 BCRAN exam and gain a better, practical understanding of exam concepts

- Experience how remote access concepts work in a real network with practice labs that walk you through their implementation

- Review set-up guides that show you how to prepare a lab for study

- Ready yourself for the new simulation-based questions on the CCNP exams

CCNP CIT

CCNP CIT Exam Certification Guide
ISBN: 1-58720-081-3

Available November 2003

CCNP CIT Exam Certification Guide, Second Edition is a comprehensive study tool for preparing for the new CCNP 642-831 CIT exam. This book is the second edition of the best-selling preparation title for the CCNP CIT exam from Cisco Press, also authored by Amir Ranjbar. Comprehensive coverage of all exam topics ensures readers will arrive at a complete understanding of what they need to master to succeed on the exam. This book follows a logical organization of the CCNP CIT exam objectives, and is written in a modular, small-chapter format to break down the elements to be learned into easier to absorb parts. It also contains the other valuable learning elements of an Exam Certification Guide from Cisco Press that ensure concept comprehension and retention. These include pre- and post-chapter quizzes, foundational review sections, scenario-based exercises and a CD-ROM testing engine with over 200 questions including simulation-based questions like on the actual exam. The organization of this edition has been radically altered to align with the new CIT objectives that focus on troubleshooting methodologies to resolve problems at the Physical, Data Link, Network, Transport, and Application layers of the OSI Model.

CCNP Practical Studies: Troubleshooting
ISBN: 1-58720-057-0

CCNP Practical Studies: Troubleshooting prepares readers for the CCNP Troubleshooting exam and real-world application of LAN and WAN technologies through a series of lab scenarios. A guide to gaining hands-on experience, this title can serve as a valuable self-study element in a CCNP candidate's preparation. Each chapter includes a review of the applicable technology along with one or more real-world trouble tickets that are delivered through screen shots of relevant troubleshooting commands. Screen shots emphasize important concepts and trouble spots. Chapters suggest additional references such as utilities, web sites, and/or supplemental reading. All of the topics in the CCNP Support exam are covered in this book. Each chapter addresses a section of the CCNP Support exam, including IP, IPX, Ethernet, Frame Relay, ISDN, Dial, Cat, and vLANs. For those lacking the lab equipment to practice on, this title highlights the steps needed to accomplish various crucial tasks, providing concrete examples for the challenges faced in real-world configuration.